VOLUME 60

SCREEN WORLD™

The Films of 2008

BARRY MONUSH

JOHN WILLIS, EDITOR EMERITUS

APPLAUSE
THEATRE & CINEMA BOOKS

An Imprint of Hal Leonard Corporation • New York

SCREEN WORLD
Volume 60
Copyright © 2009 by Barry Monush

Published in 2009 by Applause Theatre & Cinema Books
An Imprint of Hal Leonard Corporation
7777 West Bluemound Road
Milwaukee, WI 53213

Trade Book Division Editorial Offices
19 West 21st Street, New York, NY 10010

Printed in the United States of America
Book design by Tony Meisel

ISBN 978-1-4234-7370-1
ISSN 1545–9020

www.applausepub.com

To **ANGELA LANSBURY,** who continues to be one of the most exciting, versatile, and brilliant of all actresses, still a viable presence in the industry more than 65 years after her debut, outlasting and surpassing so many of her peers by virtue of her exceptional talents.

Films: 1944: *Gaslight* (Academy Award nomination); **1945:** *National Velvet; The Picture of Dorian Gray* (Academy Award nomination); **1946:** *The Harvey Girls; The Hoodlum Saint; Till the Clouds Roll By;* **1947:** *The Private Affairs of Bel Ami; If Winter Comes;* **1948:** *Tenth Avenue Angel; State of the Union; The Three Musketeers;* **1949:** *The Red Danube; Samson and Delilah;* **1951:** *Kind Lady;* **1952:** *Mutiny;* **1953:** *Remains to Be Seen;* **1954:** *A Life at Stake/Key Man;* **1955:** *The Purple Mask; A Lawless Street;* **1956:** *The Court Jester; Please Murder Me;* **1958:** *The Long, Hot Summer; The Reluctant Debutante;* **1960:** *Season of Passion/Summer of the Seventeenth Doll; The Dark at the Top of the Stairs; A Breath of Scandal;* **1961:** *Blue Hawaii;* **1962:** *The Four Horsemen of the Apocalypse* (voice); *All Fall Down; The Manchurian Candidate* (Academy Award nomination); **1963:** *In the Cool of the Day;* **1964:** *The World of Henry Orient; Dear Heart;* **1965:** *The Greatest Story Ever Told; The Amorous Adventures of Moll Flanders; Harlow;* **1966:** *Mister Buddwing;* **1970:** *Something for Everyone;* **1971:** *Bedknobs and Broomsticks;* **1978:** *Death on the Nile;* **1980:** *The Lady Vanishes; The Mirror Crack'd;* **1982:** *The Last Unicorn* (voice); **1983:** *The Pirates of Penzance;* **1985:** *The Company of Wolves;* **1991:** *Beauty and the Beast* (voice); **1997:** *Anastasia* (voice); **2000:** *Fantasia 2000;* **2006:** *Nanny McPhee;* **2009:** *The Boys: The Sherman Brothers' Story.*

CONTENTS

PREFACE

Milk is Good for You

Judging from the robust box office returns, Hollywood did not fail to provide audiences with what *some* of them were looking for in 2008, which was pretty much what those same folks have been looking for since the new millennium: animation, comic books, sequels, remakes, adaptations of familiar properties, comedies, and some horror thrown in for good (or bad, depending on your point of view) measure. It is doubtful, however, that, as the years go by, much enduring affection will be held for many of the titles that filled the higher slots on the box office list, as it seems to be the function of too many movies these days to serve as nothing more than cotton candy, providing something colorful to fill you up for an evening, only to leave you wanting more when you come to the realization that substance has its virtues too.

There were gems to be had throughout the year, however, even if you had to go looking for them, which seems to be the norm these days, judging from the modern era's undependable and haphazard motion picture distribution patterns. You either catch certain titles during their limited runs in the major markets or you don't catch them on movie screens at all. It makes for a lot of repetition of the same titles on the majority of theatre marquees, leaving only the most avid of movie followers aware of the existence of some worthy product. But on to more encouraging thoughts …

That one of the five contenders for the Motion Picture Academy's 2008 Best Picture spot, *Milk*, dealt passionately with America's first openly gay politician, Harvey Milk, showed an appreciation of quality and an acknowledgment on Hollywood's part of important themes. Well-deserved Oscars went to Sean Penn for his striking performance in the leading role and for Dustin Lance Black's incisive screenplay about the necessity of human rights for *everyone* in a country built on the concepts of freedom and equality. The U.S. box office intake of $31 million could be looked upon as a testament to moviegoers' growing tolerance and understanding of a heretofore risky topic. However, the $100 million-plus difference between its grosses and those of another not-so-sure thing, the year's Best Picture Oscar Winner, *Slumdog Millionaire*, which looked at one young man's rise from poverty to success in India, might lead one to think that there is still an unfortunate resistance in certain territories in accepting gay themes. The majority of filmgoers preferred to patronize movies that featured superheroes, failing to consider the fact that there were few characters quite as genuinely heroic as Harvey Milk.

No matter, some of the quality presentations out there were appreciated, if not in massive numbers. Director Ron Howard gave us an adaptation of one of Broadway's more fascinating recent dramas, *Frost/Nixon* that not only preserved the exceptional work of Frank Langella and Michael Sheen, but showed once again that theater *can* be transferred quite marvelously into film. This was also the case with *Doubt*, which the playwright himself, John Patrick Shanley, brought to the screen, yielding no less than four Academy Award-nominated performances, including Meryl Streep, breaking her own record by bringing her Oscars nods up to 15. And speaking of performances, there were few as talked about as the mesmerizing, Academy Award-winning one the late Heath Ledger gave as the gleefully psychopathic Joker in the year's phenomenally popular top grosser (by a landslide), *The Dark Knight*, which also managed to be thought-provoking while

pleasing the genre fans. One of our finest current actresses, Kate Winslet, finally received her due from the Academy, who had two memorable performances to choose from, in *The Reader* and *Revolutionary Road*, the latter featuring another superb turn from another of our best actors on the scene, Leonardo DiCaprio.

Pixar yet again proved to be the surest bet in town by releasing another winner, *WALL*E*; musicals remained a viable option with the success of *Mamma Mia!*; and there was still the possibility of a best selling novel becoming a smash hit film, which happened with the vampire love story *Twilight*, though it helps to have a readership that doesn't find it odd to go to the movies.

Other highlights of the year included Woody Allen's most wholly satisfying feature in some time, *Vicky Cristina Barcelona*; Oliver Stone's *W.*, a reminder that twice electing someone this unqualified for public office was one of America's more catastrophic recent mistakes; *Rachel Getting Married*, which found a fine ensemble and director Jonthan Demme working at the top of their game; two terrific examples of how "indies" can reach mainstream audiences by concentrating on characterization and superior writing, *The Visitor* and *Frozen River*, both of which had their leads recognized by the Oscar committee; *Gran Torino*, in which 78-year-old Clint Eastwood proved yet again that there are few stars who can gauge what their audiences want so astutely; an engrossing recreation of one of history's most unfortunate failed missions, *Valkyrie*; a rare example of a revival of a television series clicking on screen, *Sex and the City*; two documentaries of value that managed to play *outside* the major markets, the Oscar-winning *Man on Wire* and Bill Maher's devastatingly perceptive *Religulous*; the intriguingly weird *Synecdoche, New York*, which really made you think about mortality, provided you had the patience to pay attention and figure it all out; yet another worthwhile examination of the contemporary military situation that audiences didn't bother to see, *Stop-Loss*; the cheeky, smartly written *In Bruges*, which managed to combine laughs and gunplay successfully; *Charlie Bartlett*, which provided a prime showcase for one of our most appealing young actors, Anton Yelchin; and the "comeback" story of the year, *The Wrestler*, which not only gave us the best Mickey Rourke has to offer, but was compact filmmaking at its most compelling.

Kudos too for Sally Hawkins being able to avoid crossing the line into irritation with her relentlessly up-beat characterization in *Happy-Go-Lucky*; the stunning visual blend of reality and special effects, used for the purpose of storytelling, in *The Curious Case of Benjamin Button*; *Nick & Norah's Infinite Playlist*, for aiming for a teen audience without falling back on simple-mindedness; *Marley & Me* for being something more than just the obvious doggie flick it looked like on the surface; *Ghost Town* for making good use of the pricelessly funny but hard-to-cast Ricky Gervais; *Elegy* for being the one film of several Ben Kingsley features from the year to actually make full use of his talents; France's *The Class*, for being one of the very best examples of the always interesting genre of the classroom drama; and the British *Boy A* for being a haunting examination of a difficult topic and unfortunately proving yet again that some of the very best movies out there often receive barely a nod to their very existence from either the critics or the public. But these and others *not* breaking attendance records will live on; mark my words.

– Barry Monush

ACKNOWLEDGMENTS

Anthology Film Archives, Balcony Releasing The Cinema Guild, Cinema Libre, Columbia Pictures, Scott Denny, DreamWorks, Brian Durnin, Emerging Pictures, Film Forum, First Independent, First Look, First Run Features, Focus Features, Fox Searchlight, Freestyle Releasing, Jason Hadzinikolov, Ben Hodges, IFC Films, International Film Circuit, Tim Johnson, Marybeth Keating, Kino International, Koch Lorber Films, Lionsgate, Tom Lynch, MGM, Magnolia Films, Anthony Meisel, Miramax Films, Daniel Munro, Music Box Films, New Line Cinema, New Yorker Films, Oscilloscope, Overture Films, Palm Pictures, Paramount Pictures, Paramount Vantage, Picture This!, Picturehouse, Regent/here!, Roadside Attractions, Rogue Pictures, Greg Rossi, Screen Gems, Seventh Art Releasing, Samuel Goldwyn Films, James Sheridan, Sony Pictures Classics, Strand Releasing, Summit Entertainment, ThinkFilm, TriStar, Truly Indie, Twentieth Century Fox, United Artists, Universal Pictures, Walt Disney Pictures, Warner Bros., The Weinstein Company

Tina Fey, Sigourney Weaver, Amy Poehler in Baby Mama © *Universal Studios*

John Malkovich in Burn after
Reading © *Focus Features*

Colm Feore, Angelina Jolie in Changeling *© Universal Studios*

Esmeralda Quertani, Rachel Regulier in The Class *© Sony Pictures Classics*

Michael Stahl-David, Jessica Lucas in Cloverfield
© *Paramount Pictures*

Tilda Swinton in The Curious Case of Benjamin Button
© *Paramount Pictures*

Jet Li, Jackie Chan in The Forbidden
Kingdom © *Lionsgate/Weinstein Co.*

Heath Ledger, Christian Bale in The Dark Knight *© Warner Bros.*

Brendan Gleeson, Colin Farrell in In Bruges *© Focus Features*

Emile Hirsch in Speed Racer *© Warner Bros.*

Jamie Bell, Daniel Craig in Defiance *© Paramount Vantage*

Frank Langella, Penny Moore in Frost/Nixon *© Universal Studios*

Tunde Adebimpe, Rosemarie DeWitt in Rachel Getting Married *© Sony Pictures Classics*

Below: *Tristan Wilds, Dakota Fanning in* The Secret Life of Bees *© Fox Searchlight*

Shia LaBeouf, Michelle Monaghan in Eagle Eye © *DreamWorks*

Channing Tatum in Stop-Loss © *Paramount Pictures*

Freddie Highmore, Sarah Bolger, Freddie Highmore in The Spiderwick Chronicles © *Paramount Pictures*

Clint Eastwood in Gran Torino © *Warner Bros.*

Daniel Craig, Olga Kurylenko in Quantum of Solace © *Columbia/MGM*

Zac Efron in High School Musical 3: Senior Year © *Walt Disney Pictures*

Jason Segel, Jonah Hill in Forgetting Sarah Marshall © *Universal Studios*

Sarah Jessica Parker in Sex and the City © *New Line Cinema*

Natalie Portman in The Other Boleyn Girl © *Columbia Pictures*

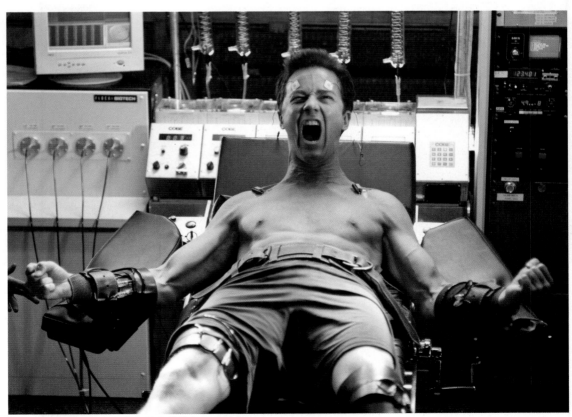

Edward Norton in The Incredible Hulk © *Universal Studios*

WALL•E in WALL•E © *Walt Disney Pictures*

Joseph Cross, Sean Penn, Diego Luna, Lucas Grabeel in Milk © *Focus Features* ·

John Hurt, Karen Allen, Harrison Ford, Shia LaBeouf, Ray Winstone in Indiana Jones and the Kingdom of the Crystal Skull © *Paramount Pictures*

Josh Brolin in W. © Lionsgate

Tom Cruise in Valkyrie © United Artists

DOMESTIC FILMS A

2008 Releases / January 1–December 31

ONE MISSED CALL

(WARNER BROS.) Producers, Broderick Johnson, Andrew A. Kosove, Scott Kroopf, Jennie Lew Tugend, Lauren C. Weissman; Executive Producers, Shinya Egawa, Timothy M. Bourne, Martin Schuerman, Josef Lautenschlager, Andreas Theismeyer; Director, Eric Valette; Screenplay, Andrew Klavan; Based upon the novel *Chakushin Ari* by Yasushi Akimoto; Photography, Glen MacPherson; Designer, Laurence Bennett; Costumes, Sandra Hernandez; Music, Johnny Klimek, Reinhold Heil; Editor, Steve Mirkovich; an Alcon Entertainment and Kadukawa Pictures presentation in association with Equity Pictures Medienfonds GmbH & Co. KG IV, of an Intermedia Films production; U.S.-German-Japanese-British; Dolby; Color; Rated PG-13; 86 minutes; Release date: January 4, 2008

Cast

Beth Raymond	**Shannyn Sossamon**
Jack Andrews	**Edward Burns**
Taylor Anthony	**Ana Claudia Talancón**
Ted Summers	**Ray Wise**
Leann Cole	**Azura Skye**
Brian Sousa	**Johnny Lewis**
Ray Purvis	**Jason Beghe**
Mickey Lee	**Margaret Cho**

Meagan Good (Shelley Baum), Rhoda Griffis (Marie Layton), Dawn Dininger (Monster Marie), Ariel Winter (Ellie Layton), Sarah Kubik (Monster Ellie), Raegan Lamb (Laurel Layton), Karen Beyer (Mrs. Ford), Alan Locke (Child Beth), Dave Spector (Gary), Mary Lynn Owen (Dr. Julie Cohn), Roy McCrerey (Dr. Painter), Lauren Peyton (Reception Nurse), Greg Corbett (John), Donna Biscoe (Coroner), Edith Ivey (Old Lady), Wilbur Fitzgerald (Lieutenant), Bart Hansard (Howie), Randy McDowell (Boost Mobile Clerk), Geoff McKnight (Fire Captain), Katie Kneeland (Maddie), Bob Seel (Taxi Driver), Jason Horgan (Dr. Ken Brown), Rona Nix (Production Assistant), Kaira Whitehead (Jewel), Jeff Portell (Patrolman), Luke Williams (Ariste), Brian Beegle (Player Guy), Kendyl McCray (Freshman), Amber Wallace (Student #2)

Several college students begin to realize that they are next in line to be killed when each of them receives a final "phone call" from the previous victim.

Edward Burns, Shannyn Sossamon

Katt Williams, Ice Cube, Tracy Morgan © Screen Gems

FIRST SUNDAY

(SCREEN GEMS) Producers, David E. Talbert, David McIlvain, Tim Story, Ice Cube, Matt Alvarez; Executive Producers, Stacy Kolker Cramer, Neil Machlis, Ronald Muhammad, Julie Yorn; Director/Screenplay, David E. Talbert; Photography, Alan Caso; Designer, Dina Lipton; Costumes, Gersha Phillips; Editor, Jeffrey Wolf; Music, Stanley Clarke; Associate Producers, Trae Ireland, Jessica McCullagh; Casting, Kim Taylor-Coleman; a Screen Gems presentation of a Cube Vision, Story Company, Firm Films production; Dolby; Deluxe color; Rated PG-13; 98 minutes; Release date: January 11, 2008

Cast

Durell	**Ice Cube**
Rickey	**Katt Williams**
LeeJohn	**Tracy Morgan**
Sister Doris	**Loretta Devine**
Deacon	**Michael Beach**
Judge B. Bennet Galloway	**Keith David**
Omunique	**Regina Hall**
Tianna	**Malinda Williams**
Pastor Arthur Mitchell	**Chi McBride**

Clifton Powell (Officer Eddie King), Nicholas Turturro (Office D'Agostino), Olivia Cole (Momma T), Red Grant (Harold), C.J. Sanders (Durell, Jr.), Rickey Smiley (Bernice Jenkins), Arjay Smith (Preston), Kim Staunton (Public Defender), Sterling A. Ardrey (Timmy),Gerry Black (Mr. Wally), Byron Blu Mitchell, Joy Brunson, Bashirrah Creswell (Choir Members), P.J. Byrne (Assistant D.A.), Paul Campbell (Blahka), Melanie Comarcho (Waitress), Antwone Dickey (Pirate), Startletta DuPois (Grandmother), Roy Jackson (Boyfriend), Patricia Mikel (Sister Baker), Aya Nagaski (Massage Attendant), Reynaldo Rey (Soul Joe), Martell Robinson (Mordecai), Tiffany Pollard (Omunique's Client), Marietta Sirleaf (Roberta), Kurt Carr, Nathaniel Kearney, Jr., Timothy P. Mason, Sheryl Harper (Choir Band)

Badly in need of money, Durell and Rickey come up with a scheme to rob a downtrodden church.

Christine Baranski, Meryl Streep, Julie Walters in Mamma Mia! © *Universal Studios*

Jennifer Aniston, Owen Wilson in Marley & Me © *Twentieth Century Fox*

Mickey Rourke in The Wrestler © *Fox Searchlight*

Leonardo DiCaprio, Kate Winslet in Revolutionary Road © *Paramount Vantage/DreamWorks*

CLOVERFIELD

(PARAMOUNT) Producers, J.J. Abrams, Bryan Burk; Executive Producers, Guy Riedel, Sherryl Clark; Director, Matt Reeves; Screenplay, Drew Goddard; Photography, Michael Bonvillain; Editor, Kevin Stitt; Designer, Martin Whist; Costumes, Ellen Mirojnick; Visual Effects Supervisors, Kevin Blank, Michael Ellis, Eric Leven; Visual Effects, Double Negative, Tippett Studio; Special Effects Coordinator, David Waine; Creature Designer, Neville Page; Stunts, Rob King; Casting, Alyssa Weisberg; a Bad Robot production; Dolby; Deluxe color; Rated PG-13; 85 minutes; Release date: January 18, 2008

Cast

Marlena Diamond	**Lizzy Caplan**
Lily Ford	**Jessica Lucas**
Hud Platt	**T.J. Miller**
Rob Hawkins	**Michael Stahl-David**
Jason Hawkins	**Mike Vogel**
Beth McIntyre	**Odette Yustman**
Bodega Cashier	**Anjul Nigam**
Jenn	**Margot Farley**
Antonio	**Theo Rossi**
Charlie	**Brian Klugman**
Clark	**Kelvin Yu**
Heather	**Liza Lapira**
Lei	**Lili Mirojnick**
Travis	**Ben Feldman**

Elena Caruso, Vakisha Coleman, Will Greenberg, Rob Kerkovich, Ryan Key, Hisonni Johnson, Rasika Mathur, Baron Vaughn, Charlyne Yi (Party Goers), Roma Torre (Herself), Rick Overton (Frantic Man), Martin Cohen (Burly Guy), Jason Cerbone (Police Officer), Pavel Lychnikoff (Russian Man on Street), Billy Brown (Staff Sgt. Pryce), Scott Lawrence, Jeffrey De Serano (Soldiers), Tim Griffin (Command Center Officer), Chris Mulkey (Lt. Col. Graff), Susse Budde, Jason Lombard (Medics), Jamie Martz (Helicopter Pilot)

A monster's rampage through New York is captured on one terrified citizen's video camera.

Michael Stahl-David, Odette Yustman

Michael Stahl-David, Odette Yustman, Jessica Lucas, T.J. Miller

Lizzy Caplan, Michael Stahl-David

© Paramount Pictures

27 DRESSES

(20th Century Fox) Producers, Roger Birnbaum, Gary Barber, Jonathan Glickman; Executive Producers, Bobby Newmyer, Becki Cross Trujillo, Michael Mayer, Erin Stam; Director, Anne Fletcher; Screenplay, Aline Brosh McKenna; Photography, Peter James; Editor, Priscilla Nedd Friendly; Music, Randy Edelman; Music Supervisor, Buck Damon; Designer, Shepherd Frankel; Costumes, Catherine Marie Thomas; Casting, Cathy Sandrich Gelfond, Amanda Mackey; a Fox 2000 Pictures and Spyglass Entertainment presentation of a Birnbaum/Barber production; Dolby; Deluxe color; Rated PG-13; 107 minutes; Release date: January 18, 2008

Cast

Jane Nichols	**Katherine Heigl**
Kevin	**James Marsden**
Tess	**Malin Akerman**
Casey	**Judy Greer**
George	**Edward Burns**
Maureen	**Melora Hardin**
Hal	**Brian Kerwin**
Trent	**Maulik Pancholy**
Young Tess	**Charli Barcena**
Young Jane	**Peyton Roi List**
Cousin Lisa	**Jane Pfitsch**
Flower Girl	**Alexa Gerasimovich**
Gina	**Krysten Ritter**
Bride Suzanne	**Danielle Skraastad**

Jennifer Lim (Bridal Salesgirl), Brigitte Bourdeauy (Salesgirl Olga), Anne Fletcher (Rude Taxi Stealer), Marilyn L. Costello (Bride Suzanne Minister), Michael Ziegfeld (Taxi Driver Khaleel), Yetta Gottesman (Hip Bridesmaid), Erin Fogel (Shari Rabinowitz), Laksh Singh (Hindu Priest), Maulik Pancholy (Trent), Bryan Radtke (Florist Delivery Guy), David Castro (Pedro), Mia Barron (Yoga Instructor), Ronald Guttman (Antoine), Lyralen Kaye (Cousin Julie), Lynne Matthew (Animal Shelter Worker), Ron Simons (Boathouse Chef), Robert Clohessy (Dive Bartender), Michael Mosley (Bar Dude), Alyssa Bresnahan, Ellen H. Schwartz (Diner Waitresses), Thaddeus Daniels (Jane's Neighbor), Jennifer Bassey (Jane's Aunt), Josh Casaubon (Mill's Tavern Caterer), Michelle Glick, Alexa Havins (Boat Brides), Richard O'Rourke (Jane's Minister), Bern Cohen (Rabbi Cohen)

A perpetual bridesmaid, Jane Nichols, finds herself torn between her feelings for her boss, who seems oblivious to her interest, and a reporter who plans to marry Jane's self-absorbed sister Tess.

Katherine Heigl

Malin Akerman, Edward Burns © 20th Century Fox

Katherine Heigl, James Marsden

CASSANDRA'S DREAM

(WEINSTEIN CO.) Producers, Letty Aronson, Stephen Tenenbaum, Gareth Wiley; Executive Producers, Vincent Maraval, Brahim Chioua, Daniel Wuhrmann; Coproducers, Helen Robin, Nicky Kentish Barnes; Co-Executive Producers, Jack Rollins, Charles H. Joffe; Director/Screenplay, Woody Allen; Photography, Vilmos Zsigmond; Designer, Maria Djurkovic; Costumes, Jill Taylor; Editor, Alisa Lepselter; Music, Philip Glass; Casting, Juliet Taylor, Gail Stevens, Patricia DiCerto; a Virtual Films (U.S.)/Wild Bunch (France) presentation of an Iberville Prods. production for Wolverine Prods.; American-French; Dolby; Color; Rated PG-13; 108 minutes; Release date: January 18, 2008

Ewan McGregor, Colin Farrell

Cast

Ian Blaine	**Ewan McGregor**
Terry Blaine	**Colin Farrell**
Angela Stark	**Hayley Atwell**
Kate	**Sally Hawkins**
Uncle Howard	**Tom Wilkinson**
Mr. Blaine	**John Benfield**
Mrs. Blaine	**Clare Higgins**
Martin Burns	**Phil Davis**
Garage boss	**Jim Carter**
Angela's father	**David Horovitch**
Angela's mother	**Cate Fowler**
Nigel	**Tom Fisher**
Boat-Owner	**Peter-Hugo Daly**
Lucy	**Ashley Madekwe**
Jerry	**Andrew Howard**

Keith Smee (Terry's Track Mate), Stephen Noonan (Mel), Dan Carter (Fred), Richard Lintern (Director), Jennifer Ingram (Helen), Lee Whitlock (Mike), Michael Harm (Estate Agent), Hugh Rathboen, Allan Ramsey, Paul Davis, Terry Budin-Jones, Franck Viano, Tommy Mack (Poker Players), Milo Bodrociz (Milo), Emily Gilchrist (Emily), George Richmond (George), Phyllis Roberts (Voice of Burns' Mother), Tamzin Outhwaite (Burns' Date), Matt Barlock (Jaguar Owner), Paul Gardner (Bentley Salesman), Mark Umbers (Eisley), Maggie McCarthy (Servant), Richard Graham, Ross Boatman (Detectives)

Tom Wilkinson, Ewan McGregor, Colin Farrell © The Weinstein Co.

Ian and Terry's wealthy Uncle Howard agrees to help them settle debts, only under the condition that they eliminate a witness set to blow the whistle on Howard's shady financial history.

Ewan McGregor, Colin Farrell

Sally Hawkins, Ewan McGregor, Hayley Atwell, Colin Farrell

MAD MONEY

(OVERTURE FILMS) Producers, Jay Cohen, James Acheson, Frank De Martini, Michael P. Flannigan; Executive Producers, Robert Green, Wendy Kram, Avi Lerner, Boaz Davidson, Danny Dimbort, Trevor Short; Director, Callie Khouri; Screenplay, Glenn Gers; Photography, John Bailey; Editor, Wendy Greene Bricmont; Music, Marty Davich, James Newton Howard; Music Supervisors, Budd Carr, Nora Felder; Designer, Brent Thomas; Costumes, Susie DeSanto; Casting, Junie Lowry-Johnson; a Lightspeed Media, Swingin' Prods., Big City Pictures (U.S.)/Granada (U.K.) production, presented with Millennium Films; U.S.-British; Dolby; Super 35 Widescreen; Technicolor; Rated PG-13; 103 minutes; Release date: January 18, 2008

Cast

Bridget Cardigan	**Diane Keaton**
Nina Brewster	**Queen Latifah**
Jackie Truman	**Katie Holmes**
Don Cardigan	**Ted Danson**
Glover	**Stephen Root**
Bryce Arbogast	**Chris McDonald**
Bob Truman	**Adam Rothenberg**
Barry	**Roger Cross**
Older Jimmy	**Sterling Blackmon**
Older Dante	**Peyton "Alex" Smith**
Cops	**Charlie Caldwell, Richard F. Law**
Mindy Arbogast	**Meagen Fay**
Counselor	**Denise Lee**
Selina	**Sylvia Castro Galana**
Molly	**Morgana Shaw**
Agent Wayne	**Marc Macaulay**

Andrew Sensenig (Cart Guy), Finesse Mitchell (Shaun), Maliek Golden (Young Dante), Khari King (Young Jimmy), Mathew Greer (Junior), Jim Cramer (Himself), John McIntosh (Headmaster), Bill Jenkins (Jeweler), Michael P. Flannigan (Foreman), Drew Waters, Tron Kendrick (Fed Guys), Ginnie Randall (Ms. Cobb), Joe Nemmers (Det. Smith), Julius Washington (Det. Jones), J.C. MacKenzie (Richard Mandelbrot), Cliff Fleming (Helicopter Pilot), Jennifer Wilkerson (Hotel Clerk), Bryan McMahon (District Attorney), Richard Folmer (IRS Man), Duke W. Scott, Jr. (Det. Scott), Clay Chamberlin (Waiter), Bryan Massey (Det. Brinkley)

Hoping to pay some debts, three bank custodians decide to abscond with the money earmarked for shredding.

Queen Latifah, Diane Keaton, Katie Holmes © Overture Films

Jess Weixler

John Hensley © The Weinstein Co./Lionsgate

TEETH

(ROADSIDE ATTRACTIONS) Producers, Joyce Pierpoline, Mitchell Lichtenstein; Director/Screenplay, Mitchell Lichtenstein; Photography, Wolfgang Held; Designer, Paul Avery; Costumes, Rita Ryack; Editor, Joe Landauer; Music, Robert Miller; Music Supervisor, Beth Amy Rosenblatt; Prosthetic Effects Supervisor, Doug Field; Visual Effects, TexFX; Line Producer, Rick Chaplin; Associate Producer, Richard Lormand; Casting, Billy Hopkins, Suzanne Crowley, Kerry Barden, Paul Schnee; Dolby; Technicolor; Rated R; 94 minutes; Release date: January 18, 2008

Cast

Dawn	**Jess Weixler**
Brad	**John Hensley**
Dr. Godfrey	**Josh Pais**
Tobey	**Hale Appleman**
Kim	**Vivienne Benesch**
Bill	**Lenny Von Dohlen**

Nicole Swahn (Melanie), Julia Garro (Gwen), Adam Wagner (Phil), Ashley Springer (Ryan), Hunter Ulvog (Little Brad), Ava Ryen Plumb (Little Dawn), Trent Moore (Mr. Vincent), Mike Yager (Elliot), Nathan Parsons (Soda Spritzer), Paul Galvan (Taunting Boy), Kasey Kitzmiller (Taunting Girl), Taylor Sheppard (Mr. Griffith), Denia Ridley (Biology Teacher), Kiri Weatherby (Curious Student), Michael Swanner (Police Detective), Tom Byrne (Surgeon), Andra Millian (O.R. Nurse), Frank Curcio (Coroner), Lana Dieterich (Admitting Nurse), Doyle Carter (Old Man)

A virginal high school girl, hell bent on practicing abstinence, develops a set of razor sharp teeth in her vagina to punish all men who dare to enter.

Bono © National Geographic Cinema Ventures

The Edge, Larry Mullen Jr., Bono

U2 3D

(NATIONAL GEOGRAPHIC CINEMA VENTURES) Producers, Jon Shapiro, Peter Shapiro, John Modell, Catherine Owens; Executive Producers, David Modell, Sandy Climan, Michael Peyser; Directors, Catherine Owens, Mark Pellington; Photography, Peter Anderson, Tom Krueger; Music Producer, Carl Glanville; Music Coproducer, Robbie Adams; Editor, Olivier Wicki; Stereo; Color; 3-D HD; Rated G; 85 minutes; Release date: January 23, 2008. Documentary capturing U2 during their Vertigo tour of 2005-2006

With
Bono, Adam Clayton, Larry Mullen, Jr., The Edge (U2)

UNTRACEABLE

(SCREEN GEMS) Producers, Steven Pearl, Andy Cohen, Tom Rosenberg, Gary Lucchesi, Hawk Koch; Executive Producers, Richard Wright, Eric Reid, James McQuaide, Harley Tannenbaum; Director, Gregory Hoblit; Screenplay, Robert Fyvolent, Mark R. Brinker, Allison Burnett; Story, Robert Fyvolent, Mark R. Brinker; Photography, Anastas Michols; Designer, Paul Eads; Costumes, Elisabetta Beraldo; Music, Christopher Young; Editors, David Rosenbloom; Casting, Deborah Aquila, Tricia Wood, Jennifer Smith; a Lakeshore Entertainment production in association with Cohen/Pearl Prods.; Dolby; Deluxe color; Rated R; 100 minutes; Release date: January 25, 2008

Cast

Jennifer Marsh	**Diane Lane**
Det. Eric Box	**Billy Burke**
Griffin Dowd	**Colin Hanks**
Owen Riley	**Joseph Cross**
Stella Marsh	**Mary Beth Hurt**
Richard Brooks	**Peter Lewis**
Tom Wilks	**Tyrone Giordano**
Annie Haskins	**Perla Haney-Jardine**
Herbert Miller	**Tim De Zarn**
David Williams	**Chris Cousins**
Arthur James Elmer	**Jesse Tyler Ferguson**
Mrs. Miller	**Brynn Baron**
Richard Weymouth	**John Breen**
Trey Resom – Spoiled Preppie	**Dan Callahan**
Melanie	**Erin Carufel**

Trina Adams, Ryan Deal, West A. Helfrich (Cops), Marilyn Deutsch, Jim Hyde (National Newscasters), Gray Eubank (Ray), Pete Ferryman, Kerry Tomlinson (Daytime Newscasters), David Freitas, Kimberly Maus (Five O'Clock Newscasters), Zack Hoffman (Chief of Police Michael Bagley), Sarah Brillhart, Diana Brillhart (Daughters of Mrs. Miller), Ryan Hopkins (Acne-Faced Kid), Len Huynh (Tom Park – Asian Man), Dax Jordan (Scotty Hillman), Daniel Liu (Det. Tom Moy), Kirk Mouser (FBI Agent Carter Thompson), Betty Moyer (Assistant), David Wilson, Katie O'Grady (Portland Reporters), Jamal Qutub (Young Stoner), Mike Smith, Todd Robinson (SWAT Team)

FBI agent Jennifer Marsh must track down a psychopath who is slowly kililng his victims on the Internet, utilizing the vast public interest in his crimes to help expedite the torturing process.

Diane Lane, Billy Burke © Screen Gems

RAMBO

(LIONSGATE) Producers, Avi Lerner, Kevin King-Templeton, John Thompson; Executive Producers, Jon Feltheimer, Peter Block, Harvey Weinstein, Bob Weinstein, Danny Dimbort, Boaz Davidson, Trevor Short, Andreas Thiesmeyer, Florian Lechner, Randall Emmett, George Furla; Coproducers, Josef Lautenschlager, Joachim Sturmes; Director, Sylvester Stallone; Screenplay, Art Monterastelli, Sylvester Stallone, based on the character created by David Morrell; Photography, Glen MacPherson; Editor, Sean Albertson; Music, Brian Tyler; Music Supervisor, Ashley Miller; Designer, Franco-Giacomo Carbone; Costumes, Lizz Wolf; Visual Effects Supervisor, Wes Caefer; Special Effects Supervisors, Alex Gunn, Rangsun Rangsimaporn (Thailand); Line Producers, Matt O'Toole, Russ Markowitz; Associate Producer, Christopher Petzel; Casting, Sheila Jaffe; a Nu Image production for Equity Pictures Medienfonds GMBH & Co. presented in association with Millennium Films; Dolby; Deluxe color; Rated R; 91 minutes; Release date: January 25, 2008

Sylvester Stallone

Cast

John Rambo	**Sylvester Stallone**
Sarah	**Julie Benz**
Michael Burnett	**Paul Schulze**
School Boy	**Matthew Marsden**
Lewis	**Graham McTavish**
En-Joo	**Tim Kang**
Diaz	**Rey Gallegos**
Reese	**Jake La Botz**
Tint	**Maung Maung Khin**
Arthur Marsh	**Ken Howard**

Cameron Pearson, Thomas Peterson, Tony Skarberg, James Wearing Smith (Missionaries), Shaliew Manrungbun, Kasikorn Niyompattana (Snake Hunters), Supakorn Kitsuwon (Myint), Aung Aay Noi (Lt. Aye), Aung Theng (Pirate Leader), Pornpop Kampusiri (Snake Village Owner), Wasawat Panyarat (Snake Village MC), Kammul Kawtep (Snake Village Young Charmer), Sornram Patchimtasanakarn (Tha), Noa Jei, Kjan Saen (Karen Interpreters), Aun Lung Su, Pan Dokngam, Han Pik (Burmese Hut Guards), Tip Tiya, Nee Lungjai (Burmese Gate Guards), Yupin Mu Pae (Begging Mother), Moan Adisak (Burmese Morning Guard), Somsak Wongsa, Surachai Muangdee (Burmese Dancers), Mana Sen-Mi (Burmese Patrol Boat Captain), Toole Khan Kham (Burmese Sergeant), Saiwan Lungta (Burmese Trooper – Lt. Aye's Hut), Warcharentr Sedtho (Burmese Young Boy), Rapimpa Dibu (Young Naked Girl), May Kung (Pirate Bar Hooker)

Having reluctantly agreed to escort a group of missionaries into the Burmese jungle, John Rambo must rescue them after they are captured by the enemy. Previous entries starring Sylvester Stallone were *First Blood* (Orion, 1982), *Rambo: First Blood Part II* (1985), and *Rambo III* (TriStar, 1988).

Julie Benz, Matthew Marsden

Left: *Rey Gallegos, Jake La Botz, Sylvester Stallone, Graham McTavis*
© *Lionsgate*

HANNAH MONTANA & MILEY CYRUS: BEST OF BOTH WORLDS CONCERT

(WALT DISNEY PICTURES) Producer, Art Repola; Executive Producers, Doug Merrifield, Vince Pace; Director, Bruce Hendricks; Hannah Montana character based on the series created by Michael Poryes, Rich Correll, Barry O'Brien; Photography, Mitch Amundsen; Costumes, Dahlia Foroutan; Editor, Michael Tronick; Stage Director, Kenny Ortega; Stereographer, Vince Pace; Associate Producer, Paul Lamori; Distributed by Buena Vista; Dolby; Color; 3-D HD; Rated G; 74 minutes; Release date: February 1, 2008. Miley Cyrus in concert as the character of Hannah Montana

With

Miley Stewart/Hannah Montana **Miley Cyrus**
Paul Becker, Billy Ray Cyrus, Teresa Espinoza, Joe Jonas, Nick Jonas, Paul Kevin Jonas, Marshall Lake, Kenny Ortega.

Miley Cyrus © Walt Disney Pictures

Jessica Alba, Parker Posey © Lionsgate/Paramount Vantage

THE EYE

(LIONSGATE/PARAMOUNT VANTAGE) Producers, Paula Wagner, Don Granger, Michelle Manning; Executive Producers, Mike Elliott, Peter Chan, Roy Lee, Doug Davison, Michael Paseornek, Peter Block, Tom Ortenberg, Darren Miller; Line Producer, Jack Murray; Directors, David Moreau, Xavier Palud; Screenplay, Sebastian Gutierrez; Based on the Chinese-language motion picture *Gin Gwai/Jian Gui* by Jo Jo Yuet-chun Hui, Oxide Pang, Danny Pang; Photography, Jeffrey Jury; Designer, James Spencer; Costumes, Michael Dennison; Music, Marco Beltrami; Music Supervisor, Jay Faires; Editor, Patrick Lussier; Casting, Nancy Nayor Battino, Kelly Martin Wagner; a C/W Prods. in association with Vertigo Entertainment; Dolby; Panavision; Technicolor; Rated PG-13; 97 minutes; February 1, 2008

Cast

Sydney Wells	**Jessica Alba**
Dr. Paul Faulkner	**Alessandro Nivola**
Helen Wells	**Parker Posey**
Simon McCullough	**Rade Serbedzija**
Ana Christina Martinez	**Fernanda Romero**
Rosa Martinez	**Rachel Ticotin**
Dr. Haskins	**Obba Babatunde**
Miguel	**Danny Mora**
Alicia	**Chloë Grace Moretz**

Brett A. Haworth (Shadowman), Kevin K (Tomi Cheung), Tamlyn Tomita (Mrs. Cheung), Esodie Geiger (Nurse), Karen Austin (Mrs. Hillman), Ryan J. Pezdirc (Nurse Room Attendant), James Salas (Jim), Brett Omara (Brett), Landall Goolsby (Alex), Sarah E. Baker (Cousin Sarah), Laura Slowinski (Cynthia), Richard Redlefsen (Richard), Amanda Shamis (Amanda), Kisha Sierra (Kisha), Mark Bankins (Peekaboo), David Milchard, Kimani Ray Smith (Café Waiters), Heather Doerksen (Sickly Woman), Peter King (Burned Hallway Man), Tegan Moss (Teeange Girl), Kam Hing Chau (Kam Lam Yuen Cook), Jasmin Dring (Kam Lam Yuen Waitress), James Spencer (Elevator Ghost), Ingrid M. Nelson (Children's Nurse), Daniel Romero (Village Kid), Zak Santiago (Emilio), Juan Carlos Cantu (Factory Foreman), Mike Elliott (Driver at Border), Mia Stallard (Little Girl), Jane E. Goold (Little Girl's Mother), Tone Forrest (Bus Driver), Danielle Lozeau (Teenage Girl on Bus)

Following a successful double corneal transplant to restore her sight, concert violinist Sydney Wells finds herself haunted by bizarre and frightening images. Remake of the 2002 Chinese film, *Gin gwai.*

FOOL'S GOLD

(WARNER BROS.) Producers, Donald De Line, Bernie Goldmann, Jon Klane; Executive Producers, Wink Mordaunt, Jim Dyer; Coproducer, Stephen Jones; Director, Andy Tennant; Screenplay, Andy Tennant, John Claflin, Daniel Zelman; Story, John Clafin, Daniel Zelman; Photography, Don Burgess; Editors, Troy Takaki, Tracey Wadmore-Smith; Music, George Fenton; Music Supervisor, Julianne Jordan; Designer, Charles Wood; Costumes, Ngila Dickson; Visual Effects Supervisor, Chris Godfrey; Casting, Juel Bestrop, Seth Yanklewitz; a De Line Pictures/Bernie Goldmann production; Dolby; Panavision; Technicolor; Rated PG-13; 112 minutes; Release date: February 8, 2008

Cast

Ben "Finn" Finnegan	**Matthew McConaughey**
Tess Finnegan	**Kate Hudson**
Nigel Honeycutt	**Donald Sutherland**
Gemma Honeycutt	**Alexis Dziena**
Alfonz	**Ewen Bremner**
Moe Fitch	**Ray Winstone**
Bigg Bunny	**Kevin Hart**
Cordell	**Malcolm-Jamal Warner**
Curtis	**Brian Hooks**
Cyrus	**David Roberts**
Eddie	**Michael Mulheren**
Gary	**Adam LeFevre**
Stefan	**Rohan Nichol**
Andras	**Roger Sciberras**

Elizabeth Connolly (Precious Gem Crew Nurse), Ali Ammouchi, Tom O'Sullivan, Edwina Ritchard (Precious Gem Crew Members), Duncan Young (Jim), Luke Pegler (Young), Xavier Fernandez (Petruchio), A. Ramel El, Nicholas Cooper, Andrew Allen, Glenn Suter (Moe's Divers), Peter Whitford (Judge), Laurence Coy (Finn's Attorney), Linda Cropper (Tess' Attorney), Clementine Heath, Ashley Cheadle (Co-Ed Girls), Jason Dundas, Todd Lasance (Frat Boys), Ray Bull (Vicar), Valentino del Toro (Barman, Key West), Frank Turner, Bill Watson (Old Men), Henry Browne, Jr. (Bartender Topsail Cay)

Ben Finnegan persuades his estranged wife Tess' wealthy boss to help finance a treasure hunt off the Florida coast, where Ben is certain a Spanish galleon loaded with gold lies.

Ewen Bremner, Malcolm Jamal-Warner, Matthew McConaughey, Brian Hooks

Ewen Bremner, Donald Sutherland, Adam LeFevre

Alexis Dziena, Kate Hudson, Matthew McConaughey © Warner Bros.

Martin Lawrence, Mo'Nique
© Universal Studios

WELCOME HOME, ROSCOE JENKINS

(UNIVERSAL) Producers, Scott Stuber, Mary Parent, Charles Castaldi; Executive Producers, Malcolm D. Lee, Timothy M. Bourne, Gary Barber, Roger Birnbaum; Director/Screenplay, Malcolm D. Lee; Photography, Greg Gardiner; Designer, William Elliott; Costumes, Danielle Hollowell; Music, David Newman; Music Supervisor, Bonnie Greenberg; Editors, George Bowers, Paul Millspaugh; Casting, Aisha Coley; a Spyglass Entertainment presentation of a Stuber-Parent production; Dolby; Technicolor; Rated PG-13; 114 minutes; Release date: February 8, 2008

Cast

Roscoe Jenkins (RJ)	**Martin Lawrence**
Papa Jenkins	**James Earl Jones**
Mamma Jenkins	**Margaret Avery**
Bianca Kittles	**Joy Bryant**
Clyde	**Cedric the Entertainer**
Lucinda	**Nicole Ari Parker**
Otis Jenkins	**Michael Clarke Duncan**
Reggie	**Mike Epps**
Betty	**Mo'Nique**
Jamaal	**Damani Roberts**
Amy	**Brooke Lyons**
Ruthie	**Liz Mikel**
Ms. Pearl	**Carol Sutton**
Ms. Addy	**Deeta West**
Marty	**Louis C.K.**
Junior	**Brandin Jenkins**
Callie	**Krystal Marea Braud**

Reginald Davis, Jr. (Young RJ), Gus Hoffman (Young Clyde), Ara Grigsby (Young Betty), Samantha Smith (Young Lucinda), Erin Cummings (Sally), Affion Crockett (Dayquan), Amber Duke (Racquel), Angie Fox (Flight Attendant), Robin McGee (Airline Employee), Taylor Polidore (Homely Girl), Werner Richmond (Family Pastor), Rich Medina (DJ)

Noted television host Roscoe Jenkins reluctantly returns home for a family gathering, despite his wishes to leave his past behind him.

STEP UP 2 THE STREETS

(TOUCHSTONE) Producers, Patrick Wachsberger, Erik Feig, Adam Shankman, Jennifer Gibgot; Executive Producers, Bob Hayward, David Nicksay, Anne Fletcher, Meredith Milton; Director, Jon M. Chu; Screenplay, Toni Ann Johnson, Karen Barna; Based on characters created by Duane Adler; Photography, Max Malkin; Designer, Devorah Herbert; Costumes, Luca Mosca; Music, Aaron Zigman; Music Supervisor, Buck Damon; Editors, Andrew Marcus, Nicholas Erasmus; Choreographers, Jamal Sims, Nadine "Hi Hat" Ruffin, Dave Scott; Casting, Joanna Colbert, Richard Mento, Terri Taylor; a Summit Entertainment production in association with Offspring Entertainment; Dolby; Super 35 Widescreen; Deluxe color; Rated PG-13; 98 minutes; Release date: February 14, 2008

Cast

Andie	**Briana Evigan**
Chase	**Robert Hoffman**
Moose	**Adam G. Sevani**
Sophie	**Cassie Ventura**
Missy	**Danielle Polanco**
Hair	**Christopher Scott**

Mari Koda (Jenny Kido), Janelle Cambridge (Fly), Luis Rosado (Monster), Harry Shum, Jr. (Cable), Lajon Dantzler (Smiles), Telisha Shaw (Felicia), Black Thomas (Tuck), Kejamel "K-Mel" Howell (K-Mel), Jeff "Rapid" Ogle (Rapid), Donnie "Crumbs" Counts (Crumbs), Ebone Johnson (EBZ), Rynan "Rainen" Paguio (Kid Rainen), James "Cricket" Colter (Cricket), Alison Faulk (Alstar), Shorty Welch (Shorty), Troy Kirby (Troy), Jeffrey "Machine" McCann (Machine), Sonja Sohn (Sarah), Channing Tatum (Tyler Gage), Boogie (DJ Sand), Amar Merritt (Charlie), Diasha Graf, Jimmie Jelani Manners, Shane Rutkowski, Laura Edwards, Samantha Zweben, Patrick Brennan (Blake's Class Dancers), Marian Licha (Mrs. Serrano), Sarah Rivera-Scott (Aunt Maria), Luis Salgado (Alejandro), Katie Corrado (Assistant), E. Dawn Samuel, Ava Lenet (Admissions Panel), Amanda Cieri (MSA Auditionee), Hi-Hat (Businesswoman on Subway), Herbert Matz (Older Man on Subway), Howard Chu, Ruth Chu, Lawrence Chu, Jess Braden Chu (Subway Family), Gavin Danger Russell (Subway Baby), Delia Goncalves (News Reporter), Jamal Sims (Bartender), Katie Berenson, Olivia Cipolla, Megan Kain, Kelly Lafarga, Carly Lang, Michaela Sprague (Goth Crew), Flo Master, Jesus Maldonado, Dondraico Johnson, Rhapsody James, Sharya Howell, Brandy Lamkin, Binkie, Chris Gatdula, Jeff Nguyen, Philippe Tayag (West Coast Rider), Gary Kendell (Jabbawockeez Crew), Kate Lacey (Administrator), BettyAnn Leeseberg-Lange (Vocal Coach), Dave Scott (Car Stereo Guy), Julie "Jules" Urich (B Girl), Nancy Thornton (Ensemble Dancer), Chase Benz (Club Dancer)

Rebellious newcomer Andie arrives at the Maryland School of the Arts, where ambitious Chase hopes to form a crew to compete in a Baltimore street dance battle.

Right: *Telisha Shaw, Black Thomas, Briana Evigan © Touchstone*

DEFINITELY, MAYBE

(UNIVERSAL) Producers, Tim Bevan, Eric Fellner; Executive Producers, Liza Chasin, Bobby Cohen; Co-Executive Producer, Kerry Orent; Director/Screenplay, Adam Brooks; Photography, Florian Ballhaus; Designer, Stephanie Carroll; Costumes, Gary Jones; Music, Clint Mansell; Music Supervisor, Nick Angel; Song: "I've Got a Crush on You" by George and Ira Gershwin/performed by Rachel Weisz; Editor, Peter Teschner; Casting, Laura Rosenthal, Ali Farrell; a Working Title production, presented in association with Studio Canal; Dolby; Super 35 Widescreen; Color; Rated PG-13; 112 minutes; Release date: February 14, 2008

Cast

Will Hayes	**Ryan Reynolds**
April	**Isla Fisher**
Russell McCormack	**Derek Luke**
Maya Hayes	**Abigail Breslin**
Emily (Sarah)	**Elizabeth Banks**
Summer Hartley (Natasha)	**Rachel Weisz**
Hampton Roth	**Kevin Kline**
Charlie	**Daniel Eric Gold**
Gareth	**Adam Ferrara**
Kelly	**Lian Balaban**
Anne	**Annie Parisse**
Arthur Robredo	**Nestor Serrano**
Simon	**Kevin Corrigan**
Rafael	**Jaime Tirelli**

An Nguyen (Ad Exec), Matthew Mason (Headphone Guy), Ricky Jay Ordon (Visitor from Planet Ordon), Sakina Jaffrey (School Mom), Bob Wiltfong (School Dad), Ryder Chasin (Boy with Book), Fiona Lane (Angry Girl), Dana Eskelson (Angry Girl's Mom), Blake Benitez, Paulina Gerzon, Victoria Goldsmith, Ashtyn Greenstein, Dylan Hartigan, Paul Mott, Alexander Pickett, Marquis Rodriguez, Ryann Shane, Anabel Sosa (School Kids), Geraldine Bartlett, James Biberi, Mercedes Herrero, Sarah Hudnut (School Parents), Xaiex Arriaga (Luis the Doorman), Keith Patterson (Madison Party Friend), Melisa McGregor (Bartender), Gerard Bianco, Melissa Rocco (High School Volunteers), Steven Richardson (Pollster), Joshua Caras (1994 Intern), Orlagh Cassidy (Nurse), Max Pomeranc (Robredo Campaign Worker), Robert Klein (Himself), Matt Flanders (Ring Salesman), Caryn Osofsky (Café Gitane Night Waitress), Emily Wickersham (1998 Intern), Adam Brooks, Kerri Kwinter (Bookstore Owners), Alexie Gilmore (Olivia), Marc Bonan (Kevin), Amy Safrankiova (Café Gitane Day Waitress), Dale Leigh (Bill Clinton), Lauren Norman (Cocktail Server), Lief Riddell (Cab Driver)

Having filed for divorce, Will Hayes is persuaded by his young daughter to tell him the true story of how her parents met, with the names of the women in his life changed to keep her guessing as to the outcome.

Abigail Breslin, Ryan Reynolds

Ryan Reynolds, Rachel Weisz

Ryan Reynolds, Isla Fisher

Elizabeth Banks, Ryan Reynolds © Universal Studios

THE SPIDERWICK CHRONICLES

(PARAMOUNT) Producers, Mark Canton, Larry Franco, Ellen Goldsmith-Vein, Karey Kirkpatrick; Executive Producers, Julia Pistor, Tony DiTerlizzi, Holly Black; Co-Producrs, Tom Peitzman, Steve Barnett, Julie Kane-Ritsch, Josette Perrotta; Director, Mark Waters; Screenplay, Karey Kirkpatrick, David Berenbaum, John Sayles; Based on the books by Tony DiTerlizzi, Holly Black; Photography, Caleb Deschanel; Designer, James Bissell; Costumes, Joanna Johnston; Music, James Horner; Editor, Michael Kahn; Visual Effects Supervisors, Tim Alexander, Pablo Helman; Animation Supervisor, Tim Harrington; Visual Effects and Animation, Industrial Light & Magic; Visual Effects, Tippett Studio; Creature Supervisor, Phil Tippett; Stunts, Dave McKeown; Associate Producer, Cheryl A. Tkach; Casting, Marci Liroff; a Nickelodeon Movies presentation of a Kennedy/Marshall and a Mark Canton production; Dolby; Super 35 Widescreen; Deluxe color; Rated PG; 97 minutes; Release date: February 14, 2008

Thimbletack © Paramount Pictures

Cast

Jared Grace/Simon Grace	**Freddie Highmore**
Mallory Grace	**Sarah Bolger**
Mulgarath	**Nick Nolte**
Helen Grace	**Mary-Louise Parker**
Aunt Lucinda Spiderwick	**Joan Plowright**
Arthur Spiderwick	**David Strathairn**
Voice of Hogsqueal	**Seth Rogen**
Young Lucinda	**Jordy Benattar**
Voice of Thimbletack	**Martin Short**
Richard Grace	**Andrew McCarthy**
Helen's Co-Worker	**Tod Fennell**
Nurse	**Mariah Inger**
Tow Truck Driver	**Jeremy Lavalley**
Mrs. Spiderwick	**Lise Durocher-Viens**

In his family's new house, young Jared Grace discovers that the place is surrounded by raging goblins under the orders of the wicked, shape-shifting Mulgarath, who hopes to obtain a mysterious book left behind by Jared's great-great-uncle, the eccentric Arthur Spiderwick.

Hogsqueal, Freddie Highmore

Freddie Highmore, David Strathairn

Freddie Highmore, Sarah Bolger, Freddie Highmore

JUMPER

(20TH CENTURY FOX) Producers, Arnon Milchan, Lucas Foster, Jay Sanders, Simon Kinberg; Executive Producers, Stacy Maes, Kim Winther, Vince Gerardis, Ralph M. Vicinanza; Coproducer, Joe Hartwick, Jr.; Director, Doug Liman; Screenplay, David S. Goyer, Jim Uhls, Simon Kinberg, based on the novel by Steven Gould; Photography, Barry Peterson; Designer, Oliver Scholl; Costumes, Magali Guidasci; Editors, Saar Klein, Don Zimmerman, Dean Zimmerman; Music, John Powell; Visual Effects Supervisors, Joel Hynek, Kevin Elam; Special Effects Supervisor, Yves Debono; Associate Producer, Simon Crane; Casting, Joseph Middleton; a New Regency/Hypnotic production, made in association with Dune Entertainment, presented in association with Regency Enterprises; Dolby; Panavision; Deluxe color; Rated PG-13; 88 minutes; Release date: February 14, 2008

Jamie Bell, Hayden Christensen

Cast

David Rice	**Hayden Christensen**
Griffin	**Jamie Bell**
Roland	**Samuel L. Jackson**
Millie Harris	**Rachel Bilson**
Mary Rice	**Diane Lane**
William Rice	**Michael Rooker**
Young Millie	**AnnaSophia Robb**
Young David	**Max Thierot**
Young Mark	**Jesse James**
Mr. Bowker	**Tom Hulce**
Sophie	**Kristen Stewart**
Mark Kobold	**Teddy Dunn**
Ellen	**Barbara Garrick**

Michael Winther (Day Bank Manager), Massimiliano Pazzaglia (Italian Desk Cop), Shawn Roberts (English Bartender), Nathalie Cox (English Beauty), Meredith Henderson (Fiona), Damir Andrei (Psychologist), Tony Nappo (NYPD Detective), George King (Owner of Millie's Old House), Clark Beasley, Jr. (Bank Guard), Simona Lisi (Italian Woman), Matteo Carlomagno (Italian Detective), Fabrizio Bucci, Giorgio Santangelo (Italian Police Officers), Marcello Santoni, Franco Salvatore Di Stefano (Italian Cabbies), Brad Borbridge (Coffee Shop Manager), Angelo Lopez (Doorman), Roberto Antonelli (Bellhop), Veronica Visentin (Italian Ticket Agent), Christian Pikes (Toby), George Ghali (Landlord), Ryny Gyto Ouk (Jungle Jumper), Frantisek Jicha, Robin Zenker (Kids in Detroit Airport), Masahiro Kishibata (Angry Japanese Chef), Sumiko Yamada (Japanese Chef's Wife), Tamaki Mihara (Japanese Chef's Daughter), Mansaku Ikeuchi (Japanese Scientist), Rolando Alvarez Giacoman (Mexican Truck Driver), Adam Chuckryk (London Pub Patron), Jordan Gatto, Nicholas Kusiba, Ariel Lukane, Vanessa Reid, Stephen Chandler Whitehead (Hoolihan's Bar Patrons), Mahmud Watts, Braden Munafo, Tamara Buchwald, Maia Smith (Surfers), Valentino Visentini (Police Officer), John Baker (Lamplighter Clerk), Josie Lau (Hospital Aid)

A young man who possesses the power to leap instantly from one location to another becomes the target of "paladins," who hope to eliminate all such "jumpers" whom they feel are an abomination of nature.

Hayden Christensen, Rachel Bilson

Left: *Samuel L. Jackson © 20th Century Fox*

CHARLIE BARTLETT

(MGM) Producers, Jay Roach, Sidney Kimmel, David Permut, Barron Kidd; Executive Producers, Trish Hofmann, Bruce Toll, William Horberg, Jennifer Perini; Coproducers, Steve Longi, Gustin Nash; Director, Jon Poll; Screenplay, Gustin Nash; Photography, Paul Sarossy; Designer, Tamara Deverell; Costumes, Luis Sequeira; Music, Christophe Beck; Music Supervisors, Dave Jordan, Jojo Villanueva; Editor, Alan Baumgarten; Casting, Robin D. Cook (Canadian), David Rubin, Richard Hicks; a Sidney Kimmel Entertainment presentation of an Everyman Pictures, Texon Entertainment, Permut Presentations production; Dolby; Color; Rated R; 97 minutes; Release date: February 22, 2008

Cast

Charlie Bartlett	**Anton Yelchin**
Principal Gardne	**Robert Downey, Jr.**
Marilyn Bartlett	**Hope Davis**
Susan Gardner	**Kat Dennings**
Murphy Bivens	**Tyler Hilton**
Kip Crombwell	**Mark Rendall**
Len Arbuckle	**Dylan Taylor**
Whitney Drummond	**Megan Park**
Dustin Lauderbach	**Jake Epstein**
Jordan Sunder	**Jonathan Malen**
Superintendent Sedgwick	**Derek McGrath**
Dr. Stan Weathers	**Stephen Young**
Henry Freemont	**Ishan Dave**
Officer Hansen	**Dave Brown**
Thomas	**Erick Fink**
Dean West	**Noam Jenkins**
Kelly	**Lauren Collins**
Daisy	**Annick Obonsawin**

Sarah Gadon (Priscilla), Aubrey Graham (A/V Jones), Michael D'Ascenzo (Scott), Dwane McLean (Bus Driver), Quancetia Hamilton (Mrs. Alberton), Richard Alan Campbell (Dr. Sam Costell), Kim Roberts (Dr. Linda Jenkins), David Fraser (Dr. Jacob Kaufmann), Marvin Karon (Dr. P. Sarossy), Brendan Murray (Dorm Head), Abigail Bernardez, Laura Jeanes, Annamaria Janice McAndrew (Cheerleaders), Amelia Tenttave, Annabelle Singson (Len's Girlfriends), Julia Cohen (Receptionist), Abby Zotz (Kip's Mom), Maddy Wilde, Airick Woodhead, Dorian Wolf, Daniel Woodhead (Spiral Beach)

Transferring to a new high school, quirky Charlie Bartlett manages to win over his skeptical peers by holding impromptu therapy sessions for his troubled classmates in the boys' bathroom.

Anton Yelchin, Robert Downey Jr. © MGM

Anton Yelchin, Kat Dennings

Hope Davis, Anton Yelchin

Anton Yelchin

BE KIND REWIND

(NEW LINE CINEMA) Producers, Michel Gondry, Julie Fong, Georges Bermann; Executive Producers, Toby Emmerich, Guy Stodel; Coproducer, Ann Ruark; Director/Screenplay, Michel Gondry;_Photography, Ellen Kuras; Editor, Jeff Buchanan; Music, Jean-Michel Bernard; Music Supervisor, Linda Cohen; Designer, Dan Leigh; Costumes, Rahel Afiley, Kishu Chand; Visual Effects Supervisor, Fabrice Lagayette; Visual Effects, BUF; Stunts, Stephen Pope; Associate Producer, Raffi Adlan; Casting, Jeanne McCarthy; a Partizan Films production. presented in association with Partizan Films; Dolby; J-D-C Widescreen; Deluxe color; Rated PG-13; 101 minutes; Release date: February 22, 2008

Jack Black, Melonie Diaz

Melonie Diaz, Jack Black, Mos Def © New Line Cinema

Jack Black, Danny Glover, Mos Def

Mos Def, Jack Black

Cast

Jerry	**Jack Black**
Mike	**Mos Def**
Elroy Fletcher	**Danny Glover**
Miss Falewicz	**Mia Farrow**
Alma	**Melonie Diaz**
Craig	**Chandler Parker**
Wilson	**Irv Gooch**
Manny	**Arjay Smith**
Q	**Quinton Aaron**
Randy	**Gio Perez**
Andrea	**Basia Rosas**
Carl	**Tomasz Soltys**
Ms. Lawson	**Sigourney Weaver**

Marcus Carl Franklin, Blake Hightower, Amir Ali Said (Kids), David Slotkoff (Jack), Frank Heins (Patrick), Heather Lawless (Sherry), Karolina Wydra (Gabrielle Bochenski), Harvey Hogan, Ted McElwee, Walter Helbig (Video Store Customers), Victor Dickerson, David M. Sheppard, Marc Alan Austen (Men in Video Store), Paul Barman (Young Man Watching TV), Karen Spitzer (Young Woman Watching TV), Allie Woods, Jr. (Doctor Bent), McKinley Page (Brother McDuff), Francisco Fabian (Simon from the Copy Shop), Kishu Chand (Alma's Sister), Ann Longo (Miss Falewicz's Friend), Parrie Hodges (Fats' Mom), August Darnell (West Coast Video Employee – Passaic), Jon Glaser (West Coast Video Employee – NYC), P.J. Byrne (Mr. Baker), Marceline Hugot (City Hall Employee), John Tormey (Demolition Chief), FranK Girardeau (Officer Gary), Matt Walsh (Officer Julian), Paul Dinello (Mr. Rooney)

When, through a freak occurrence, Jerry accidentally erases all the tapes in Mr. Fletcher's video store, he and head clerk Mike come up with the bizarre solution of filming their own versions of famous movies to compensate for the loss.

VANTAGE POINT

(COLUMBIA) Producer, Neal H. Moritz; Executive Producers, Callum Greene, Tania Landau, Lynwood Spinks; Coproducer, Ricardo Del Rio Galnares; Director, Pete Travis; Screenplay, Barry L. Levy; Photography, Amir Mokri; Designer, Brigitte Broch; Costumes, Luca Mosca; Music, Atli Orvarsson; Editor, Stuart Baird; Visual Effects Supervisor, Paddy Eason; Visual Effects, Rainmaker Animation and Visual Effects; Stunts, Spirao Razatos, Julian Bucio Mortemayor, Phil Culotta; Casting, Sarah Halley Finn, Randi Hiller; an Original Film production, presented in association with Relativity Media; Dolby; Panavision: Deluxe color; Rated PG-13; 89 minutes; Release date: February 22, 2008

Forest Whitaker, Dennis Quaid, Matthew Fox

Cast

Thomas Barnes	**Dennis Quaid**
Kent Taylor	**Matthew Fox**
Howard Lewis	**Forest Whitaker**
Phil McCullough	**Bruce McGill**
Javier	**Edgar Ramirez**
Suarez	**Saïd Taghmaoui**
Veronica	**Ayelet Zurer**
Angie Jones	**Zoe Saldana**
Rex Brooks	**Sigourney Weaver**
President Ashton	**William Hurt**
Ted Heinkin	**James LeGros**
Enrique	**Eduardo Noriega**
Holden	**Richard T. Jones**
Ron Matthews	**Holt McCallany**
Kevin Cross	**Leonardo Nam**
Marie	**Dolores Heredia**
Anna	**Alicia Jaziz Zapien**

Justin Sundquist (Parsons), Sean O'Bryan (Cavic), José Carlos Rodriguez (Mayor De Soto), Rodrigo Cachero (Luis), Guillermo Iván (Felipe), Xavier Massimi (Miguel), Shelby Fenner (Grace Riggs), Ari Brickman (Secret Service Agent), Brian McGovern (Mark Reinhart), Lisa Owen (American Woman), Rocío Verdejo (Paulina), Marisa Rubio (Police Woman)

The shocking assassination of the U.S. president in Mexico City is observed from multiple points of view by those witnessing the event, each story unlocking a different clue as to what really happened.

Saïd Taghmaoui

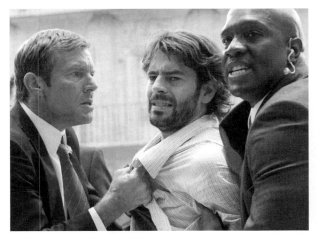

Dennis Quaid, Eduardo Noriega, Richard T. Jones © Columbia Pictures

Dennis Quaid, Leonardo Nam, Sigourney Weaver

BONNEVILLE

(SENART FILMS) Producers, Robert May, John Kilker; Executive Producers, Bob Brown, R. Michael Bergeron; Director, Christopher N. Rowley; Screenplay, Daniel D. Davis; Story, Christopher N. Rowley, Daniel D. Davis; Photography, Jeffrey L. Kimball; Editor, Anita Brandt Burgoyne; Music, Shie Rozow; Music Supervisor, Matt Kierscht; Designer, Christopher R. DeMuri; Costumes, Sue Gandy; Associate Producer, Lauren Timmons; Casting, Avy Kaufman;.a SenArt Films production in association with Drop of Water Prods.; Dolby; Panavision; Color; Rated PG; 102 minutes; Release date: February 29, 2008

Cast

Arvilla Holden	**Jessica Lange**
Margene Cunningham	**Kathy Bates**
Carol Brimm	**Joan Allen**
Francine Holden Packard	**Christine Baranski**
Bo	**Victor Rasuk**
Bill Packard	**Tom Amandes**
Arlo Brimm	**Tom Wopat**
Emmett L. Johnson	**Tom Skerritt**

Robert Conder (Taxi Driver), Jayson Creek (Maitre d'), Arabella Field (Motorcycle Cop), Kari Hawker (Newlywed), Kristen Marie Hullinger (Student), Ivey Lloyd Mitchell (Evelyn), Bruce Newbold (Bishop Paul Evans), Steve O'Neill (Doctor), Laura Park (Riva Fox), Jodi Russell (Alison)

Widowed Arvilla Holden and her friends Carol and Margene journey from Idaho to California in Arvilla's 1966 Bonneville convertible, the three women questioning their lives as Arvilla decides what to do with her late husband's ashes.

Joan Allen, Kathy Bates

Jessica Lange © Senart Films

Rennie Davis, Lee Weiner, Leonard Weinglass, Abbie Hoffman, William Kunstler, Thomas Hayden, Bobby Seale, John Froines, David Dellinger, Jerry Rubin © Roadside Attractions

CHICAGO 10

(ROADSIDE) Producers, Brett Morgen, Graydon Carter; Executive Producers, Wililam Pohlad, Laura Bickford, Jeff Skoll, Diane Weyermann, Peter Schlessel, Ricky Strauss; Director/Screenplay, Brett Morgen; Editor, Stuart Levy; Music, Jeff Danna; Animation, Curious Pictures; Additional Animation, Asterisk, Yowza Animation; Animation Production Designer/Digital Camera, Todd Winter; Casting, Billy Hopkins, Suzanne Crowley, Kerry Barden, Paul Schnee; a River Road Entertainment and Participant Prods. presentation in association with Consolidated Documentaries and Public Road Prods.; Dolby; Color/Black and white; HD; Rated R; 103 minutes; Release date: February 28, 2008.

Voice cast

Abbie Hoffman/Allen Ginsberg	**Hank Azaria**
David Dellinger/David Stahl	**Dylan Baker**
Thomas Foran	**Nick Nolte**
Jerry Rubin	**Mark Ruffalo**
Judge Julius Hoffman	**Roy Scheider**
William Kunstler	**Liev Schreiber**
Bobby Seale	**Jeffrey Wright**
Rennie Davis/Richard Schultz	**James Urbaniak**
Tom Hayden/Unidentified Yippie	**Reg Rogers**

Chuck Montgomery (Lee Weiner), Leonard Weinglass (Himself), Ebon Moss-Bachrach (Paul Krassner), Debra Eisenstadt (Mary Ellen Dahl/Waitress), Lloyd Floyd (Robert Pierson/Arthur Aznavoorian/Police Officer), Dave Boat (Norman Mailer/Marshal #1), Catherine Curtin (Barbara Callender), Roger L. Jacks (Marshal #2/Reporter #4/Reporter #6), Ted Marcoux (Robert Murray), Chris Murney (Meany/Oklepek #1/Reporter #1), Phillip Piro (Oklepek #2), Jay Potter (Reporter #3/Repoert #5), John Rubano (Weaver), Amy Ryan (Anita Hoffman)

A combination of archival footage and motion capture animation tells of the protestors who were arrested and tried for disrupting the Chicago Democratic Convention in 1968.

PENELOPE

(SUMMIT ENTERTAINMENT) Producers, Reese Witherspoon, Scott Steindorff, Jennifer Simpson; Executive Producers, Dylan Russell, Michael Roban, Chris Curling, Robin Greenspun, Andrew Molasky, Christian Arnold-Beutel; Coproducers, Leslie Caveny, Phil Robertson; Director, Mark Palansky; Screenplay, Leslie Caveny; Photography, Michel Amathieu; Designer, Amanda McArthur; Costumes, Jill Taylor; Music, Joby Talbot; Editor, Jon Gregory; Prosthetics Supervisor, Scott Stoddard; Visual Effects Supervisor, Jody Johnson; Line Producer, Paul Ritchie; Casting, Susie Figgis; a Stone Village Pictures presentation of a Type A Films and Tatira Active Film production in association with Grosvenor Park Media; American-British; Dolby; Super 35 Widescreen; Color; Rated PG; 103 minutes; Release date: February 29, 2008

James McAvoy

Christina Ricci
© Summit Entertainment

Peter Dinklage

Cast

Penelope Wilhern	Christian Ricci
Max Campion (Johnny)	James McAvoy
Franklin Wilhern	Richard E. Grant
Jessica Wilhern	Catherine O'Hara
Lemon	Peter Dinklage
Annie	Reese Witherspoon
Edward Vanderman, Jr.	Simon Woods
Wanda	Ronni Ancona
Shane	Jason Thornton
Ralph Wilhern	Nicholas Prideaux
Jake/Witch	Michael Feast
Leonard Wilhern	Paul Herbert
Doctor	Simon Chandler
Young Penelope	Andi-Marie Townsend
Station Cop	John Voce
Larry	Burn Gorman
Floorman in Card Club	Andrew Bailey
Max Campion	Nick Frost
Old Lady Card Player	Eve Pearce
Mr. Mosley	Rob Rouse

Rubria Negrao (Hotel Desk Clerk), Ross Boatman (Cheery Dealer), Nigel Havers (Mr. Vanderman), Richard James (New card Dealer), Lenny Henry (Krull), Tallulah Evans (Little Girl at Photobooth), Pam Philips (Old Lady at Photobooth), Richard Leaf (Jack the Bartender), RussellBrand (Sam the Jazz Club Owner), Martin McDougall (Dr. Stone), James Howard, Shaun Parkes (Reporters Outside Hospital), Scott MarshalL (Reporter in Mr. Vanderman's Office), Christina Greatrex (Mrs. Vanderman), Cornelius Booth, Colin Marsh (Pub Patrons), Tom Barker (Boy Pupil on Hillside), Todd Boyce (Preacher), Amaka Oditah, Preston Nyman, Rosie Stewart, Katie Hughes, Francesca Edgerton, Abigail Chan, Phoebe Llewellyn (Pupils)

Born with the snout of a pig, Penelope Wilhern is kept in seclusion by her humiliated parents, until they decide to entice a worthy suitor to marry the girl and hopefully remove the curse that has caused her deformity.

Reese Witherspoon

SEMI-PRO

(NEW LINE CINEMA) Producer, Jimmy Miller; Executive Producers, Lauren Shuler Donner, Michael Aguilar, Toby Emmerich, Cale Boyter, Kent Alterman, David Householter; Coproducer, Josh Church; Director, Kent Alterman; Screenplay, Scot Armstrong; Photography, Shane Hurlbut; Designer, Clayton Hartley; Costumes, Susan Matheson; Music, Theodore Shapiro; Editors, Debra Neil-Fisher, Peter Teschner; Visual Effects Sueprvisor, Dave Johnson; Stunts, Brian Machleit; Casting, Allison Jones; a Mosaic Media Group production; Dolby; Super 35 Widescreen; Deluxe color; Rated R; 91 minutes; Release date: February 29, 2008

Cast

Jackie Moon	**Will Ferrell**
Ed Monix	**Woody Harrelson**
Clarence "Coffee" Black	**Andre Benjamin**
Lynn	**Maura Tierney**
Dick Pepperfield	**Andrew Daly**
Lou Redwood	**Will Arnett**
Bobby Dee	**Andy Richter**
Commissioner	**David Koechner**
Kyle	**Rob Corddry**
Father Pat the Ref	**Matt Walsh**
Dukes	**Jackie Earle Haley**
Bee Bee Ellis	**DeRay Davis**
Twiggy Munson	**Josh Braaten**
Scootise Double Day	**Jay Phillips**
Vakidis	**Peter Cornell**
Petrelli	**Pat Kilbrane**
Jackie's Mom	**Patti LaBelle**
Cornelius Banks	**Tim Meadows**

Jason Sudeikis (Nacho Fan), Kristen Wiig (Bear Handler), Ellia English (Ms. Quincy), Ian Roberts (Spurs Coach), Phil Hendrie (Nets Coach), Ed Helms (Turtleneck), Brian Huskey (White Pants), Charlyne Yi (Wheelchair Jody), Rashid Byrd, Terrell Byrd, Tyus Tillman, Michael Westphal (Tropics Players), Collette Wolfe (Melinda), MaShae Alderman, Briana Barran, karen Berg, Charlie Gelbart, Leigha Kingsley, Kristin Pitts, Jenica Robinson, Erinn Selkis, Sandy Sunshine (Ball Girls), Steve Seagren, Gil Glasgow (Losing Owners), Noel Conlon (Man Being Hugged), Scot Armstrong (Cameraman), Steve Bannos (Cop at Jail), Anthony Rasheed Burrell, Dante Henderson, Dan Domenech (Dancers), Kate Luyben (Staci Moon)

Realizing his ABA team faces possible extinction, singer-turned-basketball player Jackie Moon hires fading NBA vet Ed Monix to whip his fellow players into shape.

Andre Benjamin

Jackie Earle Haley

Maura Tierney

Will Ferrell, Woody Harrelson, Matt Walsh © New Line Cinema

Gabe Nevins, Lauren McKinney

Gabe Nevins

Gabe Nevins

PARANOID PARK

(IFC FILMS) Producers, Neil Kopp, David Cress; Director/Screenplay/Editor, Gus Van Sant; Based on the novel by Blake Nelson; Photography, Christopher Doyle, Rain Kathy Li; Art Director, John Pearson-Denning; Costumes, Chapin Simpson; Casting, Lana Veenker; an MK2 and Meno Film Company production of a Marin Karmitz, Nathanael Karmitz presentation; U.S.-French; Dolby; FotoKem color; Rated R; 84 minutes; Release date: March 7, 2008

Cast

Alex	**Gabe Nevins**
Jennifer	**Taylor Momsen**
Jared	**Jake Miller**
Det. Richard Lu	**Dan Liu**
Macy	**Lauren McKinney**
Christian	**Winfield Jackson**
Paul	**Joe Schweitzer**
Alex's Mom	**Grace Carter**
Scratch	**Scott Green**
Security Guard	**John Michael Burrowes**
Alex's Dad	**Jay "Smay" Williamson**
Henry	**Dillon Hines**
Paisley	**Emma Nevins**
Jolt	**Brad Peterson**
Rachel	**Emily Galash**
Cal	**Oliver Garnier**

Eric Anderson, Jeremy Anderson (Other Kids), Esther Vaca (Elizabeth Goulet), Susan Ploetz (Ms. Adams), Addison Owen (Another Kid #1), Andres Alcala (Officer #1), Jordy Weimer (Elizabeth's Friend), M. Blash (Teacher), Nick Culbertson (Class Kid), Mubarak Ra'oof (Another Kid #2), Ben Burrowes (Burger Restaurant Employee), Richard Miller (Detective #2), Danny Minnick, Francisco Pedrasa (Skateboarders)

Aimless teenager Alex is tormented by an unfortunate incident that took place on the night he chose to go skateboarding at Portland's Paranoid Park hangout.

Gabe Nevins © IFC Films

MARRIED LIFE

(SONY CLASSICS) Producers, Sidney Kimmel, Jawal Nga, Steve Golin, Ira Sachs; Executive Producers, William Horberg, David Nicksay, Geoff Stier, Adam Shulman, Matt Littin, Alix Madigan-Yorkin, Bruce Toll; Director, Ira Sachs; Screenplay, Ira Sachs, Oren Moverman; Based on the novel *Five Roundabouts to Heaven* by John Bingham; Photography, Peter Deming; Designer, Hugo Luczyc-Wyhowski; Costumes, Michael Dennison; Music, Dickon Hinchcliffe; Editor, Alfonso Goncalves; Casting, Avy Kaufman; Canadian Casting, Coreen Mayrs, Heike Brandstatter; a Sidney Kimmel Entertainment presentation of an Anonymous Content/Firm Films production; Dolby; Deluxe color; Rated PG-13; 90 minutes; Release date: March 7, 2008

Cast
Richard Langley	**Pierce Brosnan**
Harry Allen	**Chris Cooper**
Pat Allen	**Patricia Clarkson**
Kay Nesbitt	**Rachel McAdams**
John O'Brien	**David Wenham**
Tom	**David Richmond-Peck**
Becky	**Erin Boyes**
Well-Tailored Man	**Malcolm Boddington**
Photo Store Clerk	**Rebecca Codling**
Nurse	**Pauline Crawford**
Ticket Taker	**Dolores Drake**
Operator	**Carrie Fleming**
Dr. Anderson	**Terence Kelly**
Miss Jones	**Annabel Hershaw**
Coat Check Girl	**Maria Marlow**
Policemen	**Ty Olsson, Sean Tyson**

Sheila Paterson (Mrs. Walsh), Timothy Webber (Alvin Walters), Anna Williams (O'Brien's Girlfriend), Kathleen Duborg, Dale Floyd, Fred Keating, Suzanne Ristic, Alex Stevens (Charade Players)

Wanting to settle down with his younger lover Kay and certain that his own marriage has run its course, Harry Allen decides the only way out is to murder his wife.

Pierce Brosnan, Rachel McAdams © Sony Classics

Raven-Symoné, Martin Lawrence, Donny Osmond, Molly Ephraim © Walt Disney Pictures

COLLEGE ROAD TRIP

(WALT DISNEY PICTURES) Producers, Andrew Gunn, Ann Marie Sanderlin, Anthony Katagas, Raven-Symoné, Michael Green; Director, Roger Kumble; Screenplay, Emi Mochizuki, Carrie Evans, Cinco Paul, Ken Daurio; Photography, Theo van de Sande; Designer, Ben Barraud; Costumes, Francine Jamison-Tanchuck; Music, Edward Shearmur; Music Supervisor, Lisa Brown; Casting, Marcia Ross, Gail Goldberg, Jennifer Euston; a Gunnfilms production; Distributed by Buena Vista; Dolby; Super 35 Widescreen; Deluxe color; Rated G; 83 minutes; Release date: March 7, 2008

Cast
James Porter	**Martin Lawrence**
Melanie Porter	**Raven-Symoné**
Doug	**Donny Osmond**
Nancy	**Brenda Song**
Trey	**Eshaya Draper**
Michelle	**Kym E. Whitley**
Grandma Porter	**Arnetia Walker**

Margo Harshman (Katie), Molly Ephraim (Wendy), Adam LeFevre (Judge), Eugene Jones (Hunter), Lucas Grabeel (Scooter), Matthew Schlein (Jury Foreman), Will Sasso (Deputy O'Mally), Geneva Carr (Mrs. O'Mally), Na'Kia Bell Smith (Young Melanie), Josh Meyers (Stuart), Lonny Ross (Student Guide), Kristian Kordula (Nick), Nicholas Leiter (Security Guard), Jessica St. Clair (Ms. Prince), Meghan Rafferty (Mrs. Jones), Jason Kolotouros (Mr. Jones), Lauren Sanchez (News Anchor), Joseph Gannascoli (Mr. Arcara), Tara Copeland (Lily), Chad Hessler (Ted), Thomas R. Pollieri (Room Service Waiter), Frank Ferrara, Jr. (Rocco), Chris Gombos (Mr. Arcara's Buddy), Ashley Clayton (Wedding Guest), Tatsuo Ichikawa (Japanese Man), Takeo Lee Wong (Mr. Matsouka), Joey Chanlin, Hanna Lee Sakakibara, Erika Sato, Frank Kamai, Al Twanmo, Sumie Maeda, Ron Nakahara (Japanese Singers), Mink Chu, Valerie Ho, Christopher Mai, Mary Lnn Tiep, Stephanie Vovou, Rieko Yamanaka, Yasu Suzuki (Japanese Dancers), Mike Hodge (Harold), Peggy Pope, Joan Shepard (Old Women), Bert Michael, Carlo Delorenzo (Cha-Cha Dancers), Douglas Torres (Angry Neighbor), Tiffany Green (Chris, Sorority Sister), Kelly Coffield Park (House Mother), Brianna Shea Russo (Ally), Jon Daly (Campus Security), Marc Goldsmith (Airline Employee), Michael Landes (Donny), Jack Chouchanian (Phil), Lonnie Lamont (Band Leader), Amy Hohn (Receptionist), Jennifer Gantwerker (College Interview Applicant), Molly O'Keefe (Resident Assistance), Julia Frisoli (Doug's Wife), Benjamin Patterson (Tracy), Edward James Hyland (General O'Keefe)

Worried about losing his teenage daughter when she goes off to college, police chief James Porter insists on escorting her on a road trip to check out potential universities.

SNOW ANGELS

(WARNER INDEPENDENT PICTURES) Producers, Dan Lindau, Paul Miller, Lisa Muskat, Cami Taylor; Executive Producer, Jeanne Donovan-Fisher; Coproducer, Derrick Tseng; Director/Screenplay, David Gordon Green; Based on the novel by Stewart O'Nan; Photography, Tim Orr; Designer, Richard Wright; Costumes, Kate Rose; Music, David Wingo, Jeff McIlwain; Editor, William Anderson; Casting, Billy Hopkins, Suzanen Crowley, Kerry Barden, Paul Schnee; a Crossroads Films production, presentation in association with Crossroads Films and True Love Prods.; Dolby; Super 35 Widescreen; Color; Rated R; 106 minutes; Release date: March 7, 2008

Kate Beckinsale, Nicky Katt

Cast

Annie	**Kate Beckinsale**
Glenn	**Sam Rockwell**
Arthur Parkinson	**Michael Angarano**
Louise Parkinson	**Jeannetta Arnette**
Don	**Griffin Dunne**
Nate Petite	**Nicky Katt**
Band Leader	**Tom Noonan**
Barb	**Amy Sedaris**
Lila Raybern	**Olivia Thirlby**
May Van Dorn	**Deborah Allen**
Mr. Eisenstat	**Peter Blais**
Frank Marchand	**Brian Downey**
Olive	**Carroll Godsman**

Chase Duffy, Brian Heighton (Troopers), Gracie Hudson (Tara), Martha Irving (Policewoman), Lita Llewellyn (Tricia Farr), Slavko Negulic (Oskar), Leah Ostry (Lily Raeburn), Connor Paolo (Warren Hardesky), David Pezzaniti (Anonymous Football Player #1), Hugh Thompson (Inspector Burns), Angela Vermeir (Marcia Dolan)

The sound of a gunshot causes sixteen-year-old Arthur Parkinson to think back on how his co-worker Annie's alcoholic ex-husband caused all manner of grief in his efforts to make contact with the couple's four-year-old daughter.

Michael Angarano, Olivia Thirlby © Warner Independent Pictures

Sam Rockwell, Kate Beckinsale

10,000 B.C.

(WARNER BROS.) Producers, Michael Wimer, Roland Emmerich, Mark Gordon; Executive Producers, Harald Kloser, Sarah Bradshaw, Tom Karnowski, Thomas Tull, William Fay, Scott Mednick; Coproducers, Ossie von Richthofen, Aaron Boyd; Director, Roland Emmerich; Screenplay, Roland Emmerich, Harald Kloser; Photography, Ueli Steiger; Designer, Jean-Vincent Puzos; Costumes, Odile Dicks-Mireaux, Renee April; Editor, Alexander Berner; Music, Harald Kloser, Thomas Wander; Visual Effects Supervisors, Karen Goulekas, Jim Mitchell; Visual Effects, Double Negative, The Moving Picture Co., Machine; Special Effects Supervisor, Dominic Tuohy; Hair and Makeup Designer, Thomas Nellen; Stunts, Franklin Henson; Casting, Leo Davis, Lissy Holm, Mali Finn; a Centropolis production, presented in association with Legendary Pictures; Dolby; Arri Widescreen; Technicolor; Rated PG-13; 109 minutes; Release date: March 7, 2008

Camilla Belle

Cast

D'Leh	**Steven Strait**
Evolet	**Camilla Belle**
Tic'Tic	**Cliff Curtis**
Nakudu	**Joel Virgel**
Warlord	**Affif Ben Badra**
Ka'Ren	**Mo Zinal**
Baku	**Nathanael Baring**
Old Mother	**Mona Hammond**
One-Eye	**Marco Khan**
Moha	**Reece Ritchie**
Lu'kibu	**Joel Fry**
Narrator	**Omar Sharif**
D'Leh's Father	**Kristian Beazley**
Tudu	**Junior Oliphant**
Baku's Mother	**Louise Tu'u**
Young D'Leh	**Jacob Renton**
Young Evolet	**Grayson Hunt Urwin**
High Priest	**Farouk Valley-Omar**
Quina	**Boubacar Badaine**
Chief of Guards	**Joe Vaz**

Charles Baloyi (Gatto), Tim Barlow (Pyramid God), Gabriel Malema (Kawu), Mark Simmons (Sono), Hannah Westbury (Cala), Antonio Fisher, Asteven Afrikaner (Young Priests), David Dennis, Antonio Caprari (Slave Guards), Matthew Navin (Young Ka'ren), Nimiah Rodgers (Young Moha), Kolby Pistak (Young Lu'Kibu), Ben Hart, Ben Coyle-Larner, Joshua Peters (Young Hunters), Heberth Somaeb (River Tribe Chief), Sadrag Nakale (Old Hunter), Mykhail Cohen, Janine Manuel, Kabelo Murray (Young Children)

Steven Strait, Cliff Curtis © Warner Bros.

When marauding horsemen kidnap his lover Evolet and several other villagers, D'Leh gathers some hunters from his small mountain tribe in hopes of rescuing them.

Steven Strait

Steven Strait

Brady Corbet, Tim Roth

Michael Pitt

Naomi Watts, Michael Pitt, Brady Corbet

FUNNY GAMES

(WARNER INDEPENDENT) Producers, Chris Coen, Hamish McAlpine; Executive Producers, Hengameh Panahi, Douglas Steiner, Carol Siller, Naomi Watts; Coproducers, Jonathan Schwartz, Rene Bastian, Linda Moran, Andro Steinborn, Christian Baute, Adam Brightman; Director/Screenplay, Michael Haneke; Based on his 1997 film of the same name; Photography, Darius Khondji; Designer, Kevin Thompson; Costumes, David C. Robinson; Music, Handel, Mascagni, Mozart; Editor, Monika Willi; Casting, Johanna Ray; a Celluloid Dreams (France)/Warner Independent Pictures (US) presentation of a Halcyon Pictures, Tartan Films (UK)/Celluloid Dreams (France)/X Filme Intl. (Germany)/Lucky Red (Italy) production; American-French-German-Italian; Dolby; Color; Rated R; 112 minutes; Release date: March 14, 2008

Cast

Anna Farber	**Naomi Watts**
George Farber	**Tim Roth**
Paul	**Michael Pitt**
Peter	**Brady Corbet**
Georgie Farber	**Devon Gearhart**
Fred Thompson	**Boyd Gaines**
Besty Thompson	**Siobhan Fallon**
Robert	**Robert LuPone**
Betsy's Sister-in-Law	**Susanne C. Hanke**
Eva	**Linda Moran**

A couple and their young son are terrorized in their home by a pair of deadly intruders who assure their captives that they will die by morning. Remake of the 1997 Austrian film that was released in the U.S. by Attitude Films in 1998.

Devon Gearhart © Warner Independent Pictures

Horton, Rudy, Kangaroo © 20th Century Fox

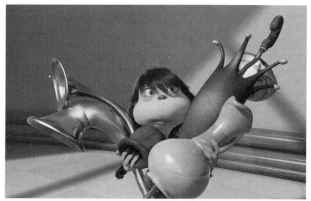

JoJo

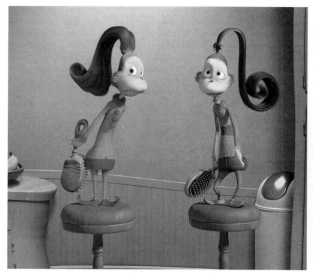

Mayor's Daughters

DR. SEUSS' HORTON HEARS A WHO!

(20TH CENTURY FOX) Producers, Bob Gordon, Bruce Anderson; Executive Producers, Audrey Geisel, Chris Wedge, Chris Meledandri; Directors, Jimmy Hayward, Steve Martino; Screenplay, Cinco Paul, Ken Daurio; Based on the story by Dr. Seuss; Music, John Powell; Editor, Tim Nordquist; Senior Supervising Animator, Mike Thurmeier; Head of Story, Ricardo Curtis; Modeling Supervisor, David Mei; Effects Supervisor, Kirk Garfield; Animation Supervisors, James Bresnahan, Galen Tan Chu, Aaron Hartline; Casting, Christian Kaplan; a 20th Century Fox Animation presentation of a Blue Sky Studios production; Dolby; Deluxe color; Rated G; 88 minutes; Release date: March 14, 2008

Voice cast

Horton	**Jim Carrey**
Mayor of Whoville	**Steve Carell**
Kangaroo	**Carol Burnett**
Vlad	**Will Arnett**
Morton	**Seth Rogen**
Councilman/Yummo Wickersham	**Dan Fogler**
Dr. Mary Lou Larue	**Isla Fisher**
Tommy	**Jonah Hill**
Sally O'Malley	**Amy Poehler**
Mrs. Quilligan	**Jaime Pressly**
Narrator	**Charles Osgood**
Rudy	**Josh Flitter**
Miss Yelp	**Niecy Nash**
JoJo	**Jesse McCartney**
Hedy/Hooly/Additional Voices	**Shelby Adamowsky**
Old Time Who/Additional Voices	**Jack Angel**
Helen	**Caitlin Rose Anderson**
Heather	**Emily Anderson**

Jan Rabson (Town Crier/Additional Voices), John Cygan (Who/Additional Voices), Jess Harnell (Another Who/Additional Voices), Debi Derryberry (Who Mom/Additional Voices), Samantha Drok (Hildy/Holly), Karen Disher (Who Kid), Marshall Efron, Tim Nordquist (Wickersham Guards), Bill Farmer (Willie Bear/Additional Voices), Jason Fricchione (Joe), Heather Goldenhersh (Who Girl/Additional Voices), Selena Gomez (Helga), Jimmy Hayward (Obnoxious Who), Joey King (Katie), Christina Martino (Heidi/Haley), Ellie Martino (Hanna/Additional Voices), Laraine Newman (Glummox Mom/Additional Voices), Colleen O'Shaughnessey (Angela/Additional Voices), Laura Ortiz (Jessica), Joe Pasquale (The Dentist), Isabella Acres, Mona Marshall, Connor Anderson, Mickie McGowan, Bob Bergen, Madison Pettis, Madison Davenport, Grace Rolek, Jennessa Rose, Teresa Ganzel, Ariel Winter, Danny Mann (Additional Voices)

A kindly elephant tries to prove that he has made contact with a world of tiny creatures, located on a sprig of clover.

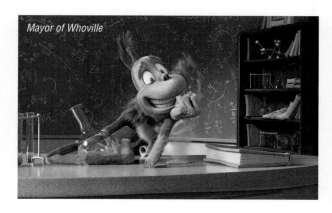

Mayor of Whoville

NEVER BACK DOWN

(SUMMIT ENTERTAINMENT) Producers, Craig Baumgarten, David Zelon; Coproducer, Bill Bannerman; Director, Jeff Wadlow; Screenplay, Chris Hauty; Photography, Lukas Ettlin; Designer, Ira Random; Costumes, Judy Ruskin Howell; Music, Michael Wandmacher; Music Supervisor, Julianne Jordan; Editors, Victor DuBois, Debra Weinfeld; Casting, Sarah Halley Finn, Randi Hiller; a Mandalay Independent Pictures and BMP, Inc. production; Dolby; Super 35 Widescreen; Deluxe color; Rated PG-13; 113 minutes; Release date: March 14, 2008

Cast
Jake Tyler	**Sean Faris**
Baja Miller	**Amber Heard**
Ryan McCarthy	**Cam Gigandet**
Max Cooperman	**Evan Peters**
Margot Tyler	**Leslie Hope**
Jean Roqua	**Djimon Hounsou**
Charlie Tyler	**Wyatt Smith**

Affion Crockett (Beatdown DJ Swagga), Neil Brown, Jr. (Aaron), Lauren Leech (Jenny), Tilky Jones (Eric), Steven Crowley (Ben Costigan), Tom Nowicki (Mr. Lloyd), David Zelon (Ryan's Dad), Chris Lindsay (Beat Down Referee), Kyle Sabihy (Jake's Teammate), Patrick Knutsson (Vocabulary Guy), Cameron Francis (ER Doctor), Jeremy Palkowetz (Running Back), Antony Matos, Daniel Hernandez, Justin A. Williams (Yellow Hummer Crew), Jon McIntosh (Beat Down Computer Kid), Chele André (Max's Girl), David J. Perez (Miles Dupree), Jocelyn Binder, Deon Stein (Hot Tub Chicks), Steve Zurk (Jake's Dad), Devin Higgins, Jennifer L. Miller, Delphine French, Joe Williams (Mansion Fighters), Angel Hernandez (African American Fighter), Rachael Thompson (Ex-Girlfriend Mansion Fighter), Ryan Frank Rayonec (Ex-Boyfriend Mansion Fighter), Ryan Watson (Mintz), Joop Katana (Camin), Frank Santore III (Taylor), Joseph Cortez (Lopez), Craig Raboteau (Nyah), Daniel Lovette (Himoff), Tony Fuh (Stackwell), Jonathan Eusebio (Dak Ho), Peter Allende (Villa), Remington Reed (Kline), Joshua Mueller (Last Year's Opponent)

Following a beating from the local bully, new kid in town Jake Tyler hooks up with a fight club to learn martial arts and extract his revenge.

Sean Faris, Amber Heard © Summit Entertainment

Alex Frost, David Dorfman, Josh Peck © Paramount Pictures

DRILLBIT TAYLOR

(PARAMOUNT) Producers, Judd Apatow, Susan Arnold, Donna Arkoff Roth; Executive Producer, Richard Vane; Coproducer, Kristofor Brown; Director, Steven Brill; Screenplay, Kristofor Brown, Seth Rogen; Story, Edmond Dantes, Kristofor Brown, Seth Rogen; Photography, Fred Murphy; Designer, Jackson DeGovia; Costumes, Karen Patch; Music, Christophe Beck; Music Supervisors, Manish Raval, Tom Wolfe; Editor, Thomas J. Nordberg; Casting, Juel Bestrop, Seth Yanklewitz; an Apatow/Roth/Arnold production; Dolby; Panavision; Deluxe color; Rated PG-13; 102 minutes; Release date: March 21, 2008

Cast
Drillbit Taylor	**Owen Wilson**
Lisa	**Leslie Mann**
Wade	**Nate Hartley**
Ryan	**Troy Gentile**
Emmit	**David Dorfman**
Filkins	**Alex Frost**
Ronnie	**Josh Peck**
Don	**Danny McBride**

Andrew Caldwell (Filkins' Buddy), Valerie Tian (Brooke), Lisa Ann Walter (Dolores), Ian Roberts (Jim), Beth Littleford (Barbara), Casey Boersma (Chuck), Dylan Boersma (Nick), David Koechner (Frightened Dad), Matt Walsh (Not for Pot Driver), Janet Varney (Attractive Woman Driver), Lisa Lampanelli (Ronnie's Mom), Bill O'Neill (Dean), Shaun Weiss (Bus Driver), Jordan Valley (Cute Girl on Stairs), Dana Nicole Silver (Hallway Girl), Vincent Malouf (Another Kid), Stacy Arnell (Police Officer on Bluff), David Bowe (Teacher), Tichina Arnold (Photography Teacher), Cedric Yarbrough (Bernie), Robert Musgrave (Stump), Joe Wilson (Homeless Man), Jeff Kahn (Café Manager), Adam Ho (Hendrix Kid), Stephen Root (Principal Doppler), Lauren Glenn, Leslie Ann Lizarde (Bikini Girls), Rance Howard (Older Man), Steve Bannos (Coffee Computer Guy), Da'Vone McDonald (Country Bodyguard), Amir Perets (Mossad Bodyguard), Roger Fan (Bodyguard with Knives), Cristos (Tattooed Bodyguard), Adam Baldwin (Disgruntled Bodyguard), Chuck Liddell (Himself), Robert "Bonecrusher" Mukes (Bodyguard), Frank Whaley (Jittery Bodyguard), Erik Stabenau (Coffee Bean Customer), Aisleagh Jackson (Barrista), Ellen Schwartz (Susan), Matt Besser (Pawn Shop Owner), Kevin Hart (Pawn Shop Employee), Matthew Cardarople (7-11 Clerk), Sarah Loew (Johnny Rockets Waitress), James Newmeyer (Sir James), Mary Pat Gleason (Mrs. Farber), Mary Brill (School Secretary), Jake Monkarsh (Mordor Castle Kid), Krista Norwood, Alejandra Jordan (Cute Girls), Cathy Immordino (Angry Locker Girl), Blaise Garza (High School Romeo), Julia Roth (High School Juliet), Eric Rosen (Drama Teacher), Michael Yama (Asian Heritage Speaker), Josh Greenberg (Kid Doing Lice Check), Vincent Laresca (Fence), John Kirk (Emmit's Dad), Hynden Walch (Emmit's Mom), Christian Pierce (7-11 Kid with Candy), Katharine Gill (Hot Girl), Jareb Dauplaise (Jareb), Max Van Ville (Kid with a Drink), Eddy Martin, Roshon Fegan, Kyle Kaplan, Jack Salvatore, Jr. (Random Kids), Barry Sigismondi (Police Officer at Party), Jerry Minor (Arresting Police Officer), Alex Donnelley (Filkins' Mom), Steven M. Gagnon (Filkins' Dad), Steven Brill (Doctor)

A trio of bullied high school boys enlists a homeless army vet to act as their bodyguard against their tormentors.

David Mann, Tamela Mann © Lionsgate

Tyler Perry's MEET THE BROWNS

(LIONSGATE) Producers, Tyler Perry, Reuben Cannon; Executive Producer, Michael Paseornek; Coproducers, Roger M. Bobb, Joseph P. Genier; Director/Screenplay, Tyler Perry; Based on his play; Photography, Sandi Sissel; Designer, Ina Mayhew; Costumes, Keith G. Lewis; Music, Aaron Zigman; Editor, Maysie Hoy; Stunts, Gus Williams, Lonnie R. Smith, Jr., Todd Perry; Casting, Kim Williams, Alpha Tyler; a Reuben Cannon Prods., Lionsgate production, presented with Tyler Perry Studios; Dolby; Technicolor; Rated PG-13; 101 minutes; Release date: March 21, 2008

Cast

Brenda	**Angela Bassett**
Harry	**Rick Fox**
Sarah	**Margaret Avery**
L.B.	**Frankie Faison**
Vera	**Jenifer Lewis**
Michael	**Lance Gross**
Cheryl	**Sofia Vergara**
Will	**Lamman Rucker**
Cora Brown	**Tamela Mann**
Leroy Brown	**David Mann**
Mildred	**Irma P. Hall**
Joe/Madea	**Tyler Perry**
Tosha	**Chloe Bailey**
Lena	**Mariana Tolbert**
Calvin	**Kristopher Lofton**
Michael Sr.	**Phillip Edward Van Lear**

LaVan Davis (Bus Driver), Olumiji Olawumi (Gang Memebr #1), Tory O. Davis (Man), Mark Russell Gray (Officer), LaNisa Renee Frederick (Bus Passenger), Jonathan Slocumb (Pastor), Robert C. Goodwin (Postman), Keith Kupferer (Supervisor), Jacquelnie Williams (Worker), Phil Ridarelli (Power Company Worker), David Kronawitter (News Reporter), Roy McCrerey (NBA Coach), Shawn Shepard (Doctor), Tom Clark, Tasia Grant (Press Members), Michael Cole (Richard), Adrienne Reynolds (Waitress), Penny Slusher, Mia Butler (Women), Wes Kennemore (Carnival Worker)

Having lost her factory job and facing an uncertain future, Brenda decides to attend the funeral of the father she never knew, discovering that her status as his illegitimate daughter is greeted in varying ways by his relatives.

Right: *Christopher McDonald, Drake Bell*

SUPERHERO MOVIE

(MGM) Producers, Robert K. Weiss, David Zucker, Craig Mazin; Executive Producers, Bob Weinstein, Harvey Weinstein, Matthew Stein; Coproducers, David Siegel, Scott Tomlinson; Director/Screenplay, Craig Mazin; Photography, Thomas E. Ackerman; Designer, Bob Ziembicki; Costumes, Carol Ramsey; Music, James L. Venable; Editors, Craig Herring, Daniel A. Schalk, Andrew S. Eisen; Special Effects, Alison O'Brien; Casting, Mary Vernieu, Venus Kanani; a Dimension Films production; Dolby; Color; Rated PG-13; 86 minutes; Release date: March 28, 2008

Cast

Rick Riker (Dragonfly)	**Drake Bell**
Jill Johnson	**Sara Paxton**
Lou Landers (Hourglass)	**Christopher McDonald**
Uncle Albert Adams	**Leslie Nielsen**
Trey	**Kevin Hart**
Aunt Lucille Adams	**Marion Ross**
Lance Landers	**Ryan Hansen**
The Chief of Police	**Keith David**

Brent Spiner (Dr. Strom), Robert Joy (Dr. Stephen Hawking), Jeffrey Tambor (Dr. Whitby), Robert Hays (Blaine Riker), Nicole Sullivan (Julia Riker), Sam Cohen (Young Rick), Tracy Morgan (Professor Xavier), Regina Hall (Mrs. Xavier), Marisa Lauren (Storm), Craig Bierko (Wolverine), Richard Tillman (Leg-Shaving Wolverine), Simon Rex (The Human Torch), Dan Castellaneta (Carlson), Atom Gorelick (Stretchy Boy), Alison Woods (Stretchy Girl), Eric Artell (Sneezo), Sean Simms (Barry Bonds), Pamela Anderson (Invisible Girl), Miles Fisher (Tom Cruise), Brian Carpenter (Matthews), Vincent Larusso (Bank Robber), Michael Papajohn ("Gimme your wallet"), Anan Osceola ("Dr. Hawking … I am such a fan"), Rod McLachlan (Actual Editor), John Getz (Lunatic Editor), Charlene Tilton (Jill's Mother), Jenica Bergere ("Mr. Landers!"), Byme Offutt (Reporter Ed), Vic Polizos (Undertaker), Daryl J. Johnson ("Well, an old guy did get shot over there"), Kent Shocknek (News Anchor), Amanda Carlin (Principal), Clay Greenbush (Dead Blonde Woman's Husband), Kurt Fuller (Bank Loan Officer), Seth McCook (Paperclip Guy), Craig Mazin ("O.K., I come back"), Jonathan Chase, Kourtney Kaas (Onlookers), Karlton Johnson (Truck Driver), Charles Woods Gray ("Thanks for the loan, Mr. Thompson"), Wendy Walsh (Live Reporter), Ian Patrick Williams (King of Sweden), Elisabeth Noone ("Take me …"), Aki Aleong (Dalai Lama), Howard Mungo (Nelson Mandela), David McKnight (Bishop Tutu), Freddie Pierce (Tony Bennett), Steve Monroe (Nerdy Dragonfly), Jeremiah Hu (Asian Hourglass), Matt Champagne ("Excuse me, there's a line!"), Susan Breslau (Mourner), Nick Kiriazis (Police Officer), Aubrie Lemon (Dead Blonde Woman), Ajay Mehta (Convenience Store Owner), Cameron Ali Sims (Xavier's Son), Kimberly Jones (Xavier's Daughter), Jordan Rubin (Toilet Paper Hand Man)

A bite from a dragonfly turns mild-mannered high school Rick Riker into a crime fighting superhero in this parody of the genre.

Drake Bell, Sara Paxton © MGM/Weinstein Co.

STOP-LOSS

(PARAMOUNT) Producers, Kimberly Peirce, Mary Roybal, Scott Rudin, Gregory Goodman; Director, Kimberly Peirce; Screenplay, Mark Richard, Kimberly Peirce; Photography, Chris Menges; Designer, David Wasco; Costumes, Marlene Stewart; Music, John Powell; Music Supervisors, Randall Poster, Jim Dunbar; Visual Effects Supervisor, Thad Beier; Second Unit Director/Stunts, Doug Coleman; Casting, Avy Kaufman; an MTV Films presentation of a Scott Rudin production; Dolby; Color; Rated R; 112 minutes; Release date: March 28, 2008

Abbie Cornish, Channing Tatum

Cast

Brandon King	**Ryan Phillippe**
Michele	**Abbie Cornish**
Steve Shriver	**Channing Tatum**
Tommy Burgess	**Joseph Gordon-Levitt**
Roy King	**Ciarán Hinds**
Lt. Col. Boot Miller	**Timothy Olyphant**
Rico Rodriguez	**Victor Rasuk**
Isaac "Eyeball" Butler	**Rob Brown**
Jeanie	**Mamie Gummer**
Senator Orton Worrell	**Josef Sommer**
Ida King	**Linda Emond**
Shorty	**Alex Frost**
Al "Preacher" Colson	**Terry Quay**
Harvey	**Matthew Scott Wilcox**
Curtis	**Connett M. Brewer**
Mrs. Butler	**Chandra Washington**
Theresa Rodriguez	**Cora Cardona**

Isreal Saldivar (Augustin), David Kroll (Pastor), Marie Mizener (Karen), Kasey Stevens (Sharon), Ricky Calmbach (Himself), Lee Stringer (Dennis), J.D. Evermore (Rainey), Cory Hart (Cowboy), Devin Moss (CIF Clerk), Roger Edwards (Clerk), Ric Maddox (Lieutenant One), Richard Dillard (Sheriff Boudreaux), David Precopia (Police Officer), James Dever (Capt. Dever), Mark Richard (Pastor Colson), Laurie Metcalf (Mrs. Colson), Steven Strait (Michael Colson), Jeff Gibbs (Receptionist), Tory Kittles (Josh), Margo Martindale (Voice of the Senator's Secretary), Ben Taylor (Bartender), Cameron Clapp, Clifton "Troy" Robinson (Vets), Peter Gerety (Carlson), Weston Scott Higgins (NCOIC of Pallbearers), Tim Minder (Honor Guard NCOIC), Victor García, Jr. (Grave Digger), Robert Farrior (Capt. Greg MacDonald)

Having proudly served his country in Iraq and figuring that his tour of duty is at an end, Brandon King is dismayed to learn that he has been ordered to report back to combat.

Ryan Phillippe

Joseph Gordon-Levitt, Mamie Gummer
© Paramount Pictures

Right: *Linda Emond, Ryan Phillippe, Ciarán Hinds*

(clockwise from top) Jim Sturgess, Jacob Pitts, Kevin Spacey, Liza Lapira, Aaron Yoo, Kate Bosworth

Kevin Spacey, Jim Sturgess

Laurence Fishburne, Spencer Garrett, Jack McGee
© *Columbia Pictures*

21

(COLUMBIA) Producers, Michael De Luca, Dana Brunetti, Kevin Spacey; Executive Producers, William S. Beasley, Brett Ratner, Ryan Kavanaugh; Director, Robert Luketic; Screenplay, Peter Steinfeld, Allan Loeb; Based on the book *Bringing Down the House* by Ben Mezrich; Photography, Russell Carpenter; Designer, Missy Stewart; Costumes, Luca Mosca; Music, David Sardy; Editor, Elliott Graham; Visual Effects Supervisor, Gray Marshall; Casting, Francine Maisler, Lauren Gray; a Trigger Street/Michael De Luca production, presented in association with Relativity Media; Dolby; HD Widescreen; Deluxe Color; Rated PG-13; 124 minutes; Release date: March 28, 2008

Cast

Ben Campbell	**Jim Sturgess**
Mickey Rosa	**Kevin Spacey**
Jill Taylor	**Kate Bosworth**
Choi	**Aaron Yoo**
Kianna	**Liza Lapira**
Jimmy Fisher	**Jacob Pitts**
Cole Williams	**Laurence Fishburne**
Terry	**Jack McGee**
Miles Connoly	**Josh Gad**
Cam	**Sam Golzari**
Ellen Campbell	**Helen Carey**
Bob Phillips	**Jack Gilpin**

Donna Lows, Butch Williams (Planet Hollywood Dealers), Jeffrey Ma (Jeff, Planet Hollywood Dealer), Frank Patton (Planet Hollywood Floor Manager), Steven Richard Vezina, Chaska T. Werner, Kyle D. Morris (Red Rock Dealers), Ernell Manabat (Red Rock Doorman), Frank DeAngelo (Red Rock Host), Marcus Weiss (Red Rock Valet), Anthony DiMaria (Hard Rock Doorman), Christopher Holley (Philosophical Gambler), Scott Beringer (Big Shot), Terasa Livingstone (Russian's Girlfriend), Jeff Dashnaw (Russian Mafioso), Colin Angle (Professor Hanes), Supriya Chakrabarti (Professor), Bradley Thoennes (Warren), Alice Lo (Chinese Woman #2), Sally Livingstone (Chemistry Review Girl), Henry Houh (Chinatown Dealer), Frank Chen (Chinatown Host), Spencer Garrett (Stemple), Celeste Oliva (Airport Screener), Tom McGowan (Husband), Ruby Hondros (Wife), Christian Mello, Gregory Seymore (Drunk Dudes)

Badly in need of money to ensure that he gets into Harvard Medical School, MIT student Ben Campbell agrees to become part of Professor Rosa's team of card counters, thereby allowing him to win big money in Las Vegas.

Kate Bosworth, Jim Sturgess

LEATHERHEADS

(UNIVERSAL) Producers, Grant Heslov, Casey Silver; Executive Producers, Barbara A. Hall, Jeffrey Silver, Bobby Newmyer, Sydney Pollack; Director, George Clooney; Screenplay, Duncan Brantley, Rick Reilly; Photography, Newton Thomas Sigel; Designer, Jim Bissell; Costumes, Louise Frogley; Music, Randy Newman; Editor, Stephen Mirrione; Casting, Ellen Chenoweth; a Smokehouse Pictures/Casey Silver production; Dolby; Technicolor; Rated PG-13; 113 minutes; Release date: April 4, 2008

Cast

Dodge Connolly	**George Clooney**
Lexie Littleton	**Renée Zellweger**
Carter Rutherford	**John Krasinski**
CC Frazier	**Jonathan Pryce**
Harvey	**Jack Thompson**
Commissioner Harkin	**Peter Gerety**
Coach Ferguson	**Wayne Duvall**
Suds	**Stephen Root**
Big Gus	**Keith Loneker**
Bakes	**Malcolm Goodwin**
Hardleg	**Tommy Hinkley**
Curly	**Matt Bushnell**
Ralph	**Tim Griffin**
Zoom	**Nick Paonessa**
Stump	**Robert Baker**
Bug	**Nick Bourdages**

David DeVries, Rick Forrester, Craig Harper (Princeton Reporters), Lance Barber (Toledo Referee), Jason Drago (Toledo Player), Bill Roberson (Mr. Dunn), Hi Bedford-Roberson (Mrs. Dunn), Mark Teich (Joe), Christian Stolte (Pete), Max Casella (Mack Steiner), Windy Wenderlich (Conductor), Marian Seldes (Clerk), Thomas Murphy (Cook), J.D. Cullum (Leonard), Randy H. Farmer (Foreman), George Nannarello, Dave Hager, Danny Vinson (Duluth Reporters), Tom Glynn (Newspaper Man), Mike O'Malley (Mickey), Dylan Kussman (Soldier Frank), Ryan Shively (Corporal Jack), Kyle Nudo (German Soldier), Tom Huff (Writer/Photographer), Heather Goldenhersh (Belinda, Flapper), Michael Scott (Athletic Trainer), J. Todd Anderson (Man in Pool), Ron Clinton Smith (Bouncer), Ledisi Young (Blues Singer), Christian Scott (Horn Player), Marcus Gilmore (Drummer), Mert Hatfield (Mayor), David Bryant (Piano), Luques Curtis (Bass), Dan John Miller (Desk Clerk), Scott Reynolds (Police Sergeant), John Vance (Suicidal Man), John "Spud" McConnell (Bullhorn Fireman), Rob Gorman, Ted Huckabee (Speakeasy Soldiers), Jeremy Ratchford (Eddie), Randy Newman (Piano Player), Sharlene Thomas (Secretary), Grant Heslov (Saul Keller), Craig A. Meyer (Chicago Reporter), Blake Clark (Chicago Referee), Patt Noday (Chicago Radio Announcer), David Pasquesi, Nick Toth (Voiceover Announcers)

Hoping to bring wider attention and legitimacy to football, Dodge Connolly secures the services of college player and wartime hero Carter "The Bullet' Rutherford.

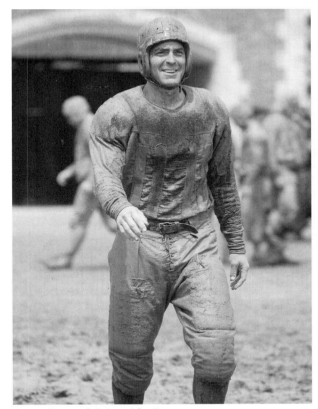

George Clooney © Universal Studios

George Clooney, John Krasinski, Renée Zellweger

Left: *Grant Heslov, Patt Noday*

SHINE A LIGHT

(PARAMOUNT CLASSICS) Producers, Michael Cohl, Zane Weiner, Steve Bing, Victoria Pearman; Executive Producers, Mick Jagger, Keith Richards, Charlie Watts, Ronnie Wood; Coproducers, Joseph Reidy, Emma Tillinger; Co-Executive Producer, Jane Rose; Director, Martin Scorsese; Photography, Robert Richardson; Camera in Hand, Albert Maysles; Editor, David Tedeschi; Concert Lighting Design, Patrick Woodroffe; Presented in association with Concert Prods. Intl. and Shangri-La Entertainment; Dolby; Deluxe color; Rated PG-13; 122 minutes; Release date: April 4, 2008. The Rolling Stones in concert at New York's Beacon Theater in the fall of 2006.

With

Mick Jagger, Keith Richards, Charlie Watts, Ronnie Wood, Christina Aguilera, Buddy Guy, Jack White III, Bill Clinton, Martin Scorsese, Darryl Jones, Chuck Leavell, Bobby Keys, Bernard Fowler, Lisa Fischer, Blondie Chaplin, Tim Ries, Kent Smith, Michael Davis, Albert Maysles, Byrdie Bell, Igor Cherkassky, Hilary Rodham Clinton, Aleksander Kwasniewski, Kimberly Magness, Rebecca Merle, Bob Richardson

Buddy Guy, Keith Richards, Charlie Watts © Paramount Vantage

Ronnie Wood, Charlie Watts, Mick Jagger, Keith Richards

Christina Aguilera, Mick Jagger

Mick Jagger, Ronnie Wood, Keith Richards, Charlie Watts

Abigail Breslin © 20th Century Fox

Jodie Foster

Gerard Butler

NIM'S ISLAND

(20th CENTURY FOX) Producer, Paula Mazur; Executive Producer, Stephen Jones; Directors, Mark Levin, Jennifer Flackett; Screenplay, Mark Levin, Jennifer Flackett, Paula Mazur, Joseph Kwong; Based on the novel by Wendy Orr; Photography, Stuart Dryburgh; Designer, Barry Robison; Costumes, Jeffrey Kurland; Music, Patrick Doyle; Editor, Stuart Levy; a Walden Media presentation of a Paula Mazur production; American-Australian; Dolby; Super 35 Widescreen; Color; Rated PG; 96 minutes; Release date: April 4, 2008

Cast

Nim Rusoe	**Abigail Breslin**
Alexandra Rover	**Jodie Foster**
Jack Rusoe/Alex Rover	**Gerard Butler**
Captain	**Michael Carman**
Purser	**Mark Brady**
First Mate	**Anthony Simcoe**
Ensign	**Christopher Baker**
Edmund's Father	**Peter Callan**
Edmund's Mother	**Rhonda Doyle**
Edmund	**Maddison Joyce**
Old Fisherman	**Russell Butler**
Cruise Director	**Colin Gibson**

Bryan Proberts, Andrew Nason (Australian Tourists), Dorothy Thorsen (Blue-haired Woman), Penny Everingham (Older Woman Tourist), Tony Bellette (Older Man Tourist), Jeff Dornan (Taxi Driver), Jay Laga'aia (Helicopter Pilot), Marea Lambert Barker (Flight Attendant), Nami Itonaga (Airport Gate Attendant), John Walton (Evil Captor), Jon-Claire Lee (Business Passenger), Steve Daddow (Rarotongan Taxi Driver), Craig Marriott (Pharmacy Deliver Guy), Matthew Little, Cheryl Craig (TSA Guards), Tania Pari (Street Vendor), Phoenix Leong (Goat Boy), Ashley Londno (Buffy Colt), Shannon van der Drift (Nim's Mother)

Hoping to rescue her dad, young Nim Rusoe reaches out to her idol, author Alexandra Rover, unaware that the creator of the fictional hero Alex Rover is, in fact, an agoraphobic and the antithesis of her fictional protagonist.

Gerard Butler, Jodie Foster

Dora Morrow © Fox Searchlight

YOUNG @ HEART

(FOX SEARCHLIGHT) Producer/Music Video Director, Sally George; Executive Producer, Hannah Beckerman; Director, Stephen Walker; Photography, Edward Marritz; Music Video Camera, Simon Poulter; Editor, Chris King; a Walker George Films presentation, in association with Channel Four; American-British; Color; Rated PG; 110 minutes; Release date: April 9, 2008. Documentary on members of the Young @ Heart Chorus, a group of senior citizens who give public performances singing rock songs.

With

Jim Armenti, William E. Arnold, Jr., Joe Benoit, Helen Boston, Louise Canady, Bob Cilman, Elaine Fligman, Jena Florio, Len Fontaine, Stan Goldman, Eileen Hall, Jeanne Hatch, Christopher Haynes, Frederick Alexander Johnson, Donald Jones, Fred Knittle, Norma Landry, John Larareo, Patricia Larese, Miriam Leader, Patricia Linderme, Brock Lynch, Steve Martin, Joseph Mitchell, Dora B. Morrow, Gloria Parker, Liria Petrides, Ed Rehor, Bob Salvini, Steven M. Sanderson, Jack Schnepp, Janice St. Laurence, Ed Wise.

The Young © Heart Chorus

DARK MATTER

(AMERICAN STERLING/FIRST INDEPENDENT PICTURES) Produces, Janet Yang, Mary Salter, Andrea Miller; Executive Producers, Kirk D'Amico, Linda Chiu; Director, Chen Shi-Zheng; Screenplay, Billy Shebar; Story, Chen Shi-Zheng; Billy Shebar; Photography, Oliver Bokelberg; Designer, Dina Golmdna; Costumes, Elizabeth Caitlin Ward; Music, Van Dyke Parks; Music Supervisor, Hal Willner; Editors, Michael Berenbaum, Pam Wise; Casting, Ellen Parks; Presented in association with Saltmill LLC; Dolby; Color; Sony HD Cam; Rated R; 86 minutes; Release date: April 11, 2008

Cast

Liu Xing	**Liu Ye**
Jacob Reiser	**Aidan Quinn**
Joanna Silver	**Meryl Streep**
Mama	**Chi Peng**
Baba	**Wang Yonggui**
Laurence Feng	**Lloyd Suh**
Zhang Ming	**Tsao Lei**
Wang Ying	**Shan Jing**

He Yu (Old Wu), Li Bo (Little Square), Sina Amedson (Salim), Erick Avari (Prof. Gazda), Blair Brown (Hildy), Rob Campbell (Rob Campbell), Joe Grifasi (Prof. Colby), Bill Irwin (Hal Silver), Zhang Hui (Monkey King), Boris McGiver (Reverend Hollings), Qian Yi (Cindy Feng), Johnny Rothman (Rene), Jodi Russell (Claire Reiser), Taylor Schilling (Jackie), Hong Ying (Laundry Worker), Zeng Hui (Neighbor Girl)

An ambitious Chinese student attending an American University finds himself slowly unraveling from the pressure of trying to strive for perfection while working for a professor who becomes increasingly competitive over the brilliant young man's capabilities.

Meryl Streep, Liu Ye

Liu Ye, Aidan Quinn © First Independent Pictures

PROM NIGHT

(SCREEN GEMS) Producers, Neal H. Moritz, Toby Jaffe; Executive Producers, Glenn S. Gainor, Marc Forby, J.S. Cardone, Bruce Mellon, William Tyrer, Chris J. Ball; Director, Nelson McCormick; Screenplay, J.S. Cardone; Photography, Checco Varese; Desigern, Jon Gary Steele; Costumes, Lyn Elizabeth Paolo; Music, Paul Haslinger; Music Supervisors, Greg Danylyshyn, Gerry Cueller; Editor, Jason Ballantine; Stunts, Lance Gilbert; Casting, Lindsey Hayes Kroeger, David H. Rapaport; an Original Film/Newmarket Films production in association with Alliance Films; Dolby; Super Widescreen; Color; Rated PG-13; 88 minutes; Release date: April 11, 2008

Cast

Donna Keppel	**Brittany Snow**
Bobby	**Scott Porter**
Claire	**Jessica Stroup**
Lisa Hines	**Dana Davis**
Ronnie Heflin	**Collins Pennie**
Michael	**Kelly Blatz**
Det. Nash	**James Ransome**
Richard Fenton	**Johnathon Schaech**
Det. Winn	**Idris Elba**

Brianne Davis (Crissy Lynn), Kellan Lutz (Rick Leland), Mary Mara (Ms. Waters), Ming Wen (Dr. Elisha Crowe), Jessalyn Gilsig (Aunt Karen Turner), Linden Ashby (Uncle Jack Turner), Jana Kramer (April), Rachel Specter (Taylor), Valeri Ross (Mrs. Hines), Jennie Lee Vaughn-Campbell (Donna's Stylist), Jay Phillips (DJ Tyler), Kevin Gould (Prom Photographer), Tom Tarantini (Inmate), Charles Hirsch (Clerk), Brian Oblak, David Kaufman, Ross Patridge (Businessmen), Jacqueline Herrera (Maid), Hugh Scott (New Clerk), Nicholas James (Denny Harper), Joshua Leonard (Bellhop), Andrew Fiscella, David Lowe, Shawn Driscoll (Officers), Marcuis Harris, Troy Blendell, Gina St. John (Reporters), Craig Susser (Officer Hicks), Nick DeMoura, Morgan Nagatani, Zena Foster, Alex Welch, Katie Orr, Anthony Clark, Allison Kyler, Johnny Erasme, Anthony Rue, Jen Talarico (Dancers)

While attending her senior prom, Donna Keppel finds herself and her friends terrorized by the psychopath who murdered her family years ago. Remake of the 1980 AVCO Embassy film that starred Jamie Lee Curtis.

Collins Pennie, Dana Davis, Jessica Stroup, Kelly Blatz, Scott Porter, Brittany Snow © Screen Gems

Jena Malone, Laura Ramsey, Shawn Ashmore, Jonathan Tucker © DreamWorks

THE RUINS

(DREAMWORKS/PARAMOUNT) Producers, Stuart Cornfeld, Jeremy Kramer, Chris Bender; Executive Producers, Ben Stiller, Trish Hofmann, Gary Barber, Roger Birnbaum; Director, Carter Smith; Screenplay, Scott B. Smith, based on his novel; Photography, Darius Khondji; Designer, Grant Major; Costumes, Lizzy Gardiner; Music, Graeme Revell; Editor, Jeff Betancourt; Visual Effects Supervisor, Gregory L. McMurry; Casting, Denise Chamian; a Spyglass Entertainment presentation of a Red Hour production; Dolby; Panavision; Color; Rated R; 90 minutes; Release date: April 11, 2008

Cast

Jeff McIntire	**Jonathan Tucker**
Amy	**Jena Malone**
Eric	**Shawn Ashmore**
Stacy	**Laura Ramsey**
Mathias	**Joe Anderson**
Dimitri	**Dimitri Baveas**
Lead Mayan	**Sergio Calderon**

Jesse Ramirez (Mayan Bowman), Patricio Almeida Rodriguez (Taxi Driver), Mario Jurado (Mayan Archer), Luis Ramos, Walter Quispe (Mayan Riflemen), Pauline Whyman (Wailing Woman), Nathan Vega (Mayan Boy), Tanisha Marquez-Munduate (Mayan Girl), Chris Argirousis, Alexander Gregory (Greeks), Michelle Atkinson, Bar Paly (Archeologists), Jordan Patrick Smith (Heinrich), Jovina Riveros Padilla, Lucia Caballero (Mayan Women), Rufino Hernandez, Carlos Enrique Delgado, Mario Freire Rivera, Elmer Alaya, Jesus Tugumbango (Mayan Guards), Robert Munns (Groundskeeper)

While exploring an ancient Mayan ruin, a group of tourists find themselves being terrorized by a supernatural force for daring to invade this forbidden realm.

THE VISITOR

(OVERTURE FILMS) Producers, Mary Jane Skalski, Michael London; Executive Producers, Omar Amanat, Jeff Skoll, Ricky Strauss, Chris Salvaterra; Director/Screenplay, Tom McCarthy; Photography, Oliver Bokelberg; Designer, John Paino; Costumes, Melissa Toth; Music, Jan A.P. Kaczmarek; Music Supervisor, Mary Ramos; Editor, Tom McArdle; Casting, Kerry Barden, Billy Hopkins, Suzanne Smith; a Participant Prods., Groundswell Prods. presentation in association with Next Wednesday; Dolby; Color; Rated PG-13; 103 minutes; Release date: April 11, 2008

Cast

Walter Vale	**Richard Jenkins**
Tarek Khalil	**Haaz Sleiman**
Zainab	**Danai Gurira**
Mouna Khalil	**Hiam Abbass**
Barbara	**Marian Seldes**
Karen	**Maggie Moore**
Charles	**Michael Cumpsty**
Darin	**Bill McHenry**
Jacob	**Richard Kind**
Zev	**Tzahi Moskovitz**
Mr. Shah	**Amir Arison**
Martin Revere	**Neal Lerner**
Cops	**Ramon Fernandez, Frank Pando**
Omar	**Waleed Zuaiter**
Upper Eastside Woman	**Deborah Rush**
Student	**Ashley Springer**
Nasim	**Laith Nakli**

Jacqueline Brogan (Waitress), Walter T. Mudu (Ronald Cole), Yevgeniy Dekhtyar (Slavic Man), Earl Baker, Jr. (Lester James), Walter the Dog (Sprinkles the Dog)

Returning to his New York City apartment after an extended absence, widowed college professor Walter Vale is surprised to find two illegal immigrants living in his home.

This film received an Oscar nomination for Actor (Richard Jenkins).

Richard Jenkins, Haaz Sleiman © Overture Films

Danai Gurira, Richard Jenkins

Danai Gurira, Haaz Sleiman

Richard Jenkins, Hiam Abbass

STREET KINGS

(FOX SEARCHLIGHT) Producers, Erwin Stoff, Alexandra Milchan, Lucas Foster; Executive Producers, Arnon Milchan, Michele Weisler, Bob Yari; Director, David Ayer; Screenplay, James Ellroy, Kurt Wimmer, Jamie Moss; Story, James Ellroy; Photography, Gabriel Beristain; Designer, Alec Hammond; Costumes, Michele Michel; Music, Graeme Revell; Editor, Jeffrey Ford; a Regency Enterprises presentation of a 3 Arts Entertainment production; Dolby; Super 35 Widescreen; Color; Rated R; 109 minutes; Release date: April 11, 2008

Cast

Det. Tom Ludlow	**Keanu Reeves**
Capt. Jack Wander	**Forest Whitaker**
Coates	**Common**
Grace Garcia	**Martha Higareda**
Capt. James Biggs	**Hugh Laurie**
Det. Paul Diskant	**Chris Evans**
Scribble	**Cedric "The Entertainer" Kyles**
Sgt. Mike Clady	**Jay Mohr**
Det. Terrence Washington	**Terry Crews**
Linda Washington	**Naomie Harris**
Quicks	**Noel G.**
Boss Kim	**Kenneth Choi**
Fremont	**Cle Sloan**
Det. Cosmo Santos	**Amaury Nolasco**
Det. Dante Demille	**John Corbett**
Grill	**The Game**

Kevin Benton (Lt. Van Buren), Kate Clarke (Demille's Girlfriend), Daryl Gates (The Chief), Michael Monks (Pathologist), Angela Sun (Julie Fukashima), Patrick Gallagher (LAPD Captain), Kirstin Pierce (Clady's Wife), Walter Wong (Thug Kim), Clifton Powell (Sgt. Green), Emilio Rivera (OG Vato), Jernard Burks (Money Shirt), Garret T. Sato (Toilet Man), Victor E. Kobayashi (Towel Man), Kerry Ph Wnog (Union Market Clerk), Aaron Earl McPhersno, Paul Anthony Barreras (Union Market Cops), Michael D. Roberts (Older Black Man), Kami Jones (Black Woman), Carlos Amezcua (Co-Anchor), Joanne Chew, Kel Ann Hsieh (Park Twins), Amy Dudgeon (Assistant D.A.), Yonda Davis, Siobhan Parisi (Prostitutes), Dorian Logan (Beating Victim), Michaela Pereira (News Anchor), Genesis Codina (Little Mexican Girl), Jaime Fitzsimons (Senior Captain), Kenyon Gilbert (Gang Banger)

When Internal Affairs suspects Detective Tom Ludlow of having played a part in the death of his partner, Ludlow teams with Paul Diskant to track down those responsible.

Cedric the Entertainer

Amaury Nolasco, Keanu Reeves, John Corbett

Chris Evans, The Game, Keanu Reeves

Hugh Laurie, Forest Whitaker © Fox Searchlight

SMART PEOPLE

(MIRAMAX) Producers, Bridget Johnson, Michael Costigan, Michael London, Bruna Papandrea; Executive Producers, Omar Amanat, Steffen Aumuller, Marina Grasic, Jennifer Roth, Kenneth Orkin, Ed Rugoff, Said Boudarga; Coproducers\, Claus Clausen, Glenn Stewart, Deborah Aquila, John Woldenberg; Director, Noam Murro; Screenplay, Mark Jude Poirier; Photography, Toby Irwin; Designer, Patti Podesta; Costumes, Amy Westcott; Music, Nuno Bettencourt; Editors, Robert Frazen, Yana Gorskaya; Casting, Deborah Aquila, Tricia Wood, Jennifer Smith; a Corduroy Films, Table Top Films production, in association with QED Intl., presented with Groundswell Prods., in association with Sheherezade, Vistor Pictures; Dolby; Super 35 Widescreen; Color; Rated R; 95 minutes; Release date: April 11, 2008

Dennis Quaid, Sarah Jessica Parker

Cast

Lawrence Wetherhold	**Dennis Quaid**
Janet Hartigan	**Sarah Jessica Parker**
Chuck Wetherhold	**Thomas Haden Church**
Vanessa Wetherhold	**Ellen Page**
James Wetherhold	**Ashton Holmes**
Nancy	**Christine Lahti**
Missy Chin	**Camille Mana**
William	**David Denman**
Hadley	**Don Wadsworth**
Roth	**Robert Haley**
Curtis	**Patrick Sebes**
Rodney	**Kevin James Doyle**

Paul Huber (Ben Onufrey), Iva Jean Saraceni (Volunteer), Richard John Walters (Parking Lot Attendant), Scott A. Martin (Weller), Jane Mowder (Julia Knight), Adam Kroloff (Talbot), Patrick Jordan (Waiter), Amanda Jane Cooper (Brooke), Kiley Caughey (Linsey), Christy Harst (Waitress), Rick Warner (Bloomberg), Barret Hackney (Joseph), José A Rivas, Benjamin Jeran McGinn (Students)

Widowed and wearied English lit professor Lawrence Wetherhold finds his life turning around in unexpected ways when an accident brings him into contact with a doctor who had once been a student of his, and when his layabout brother moves in with Lawrence and his family.

Dennis Quaid, Ellen Page, Thomas Haden Church, Ashton Holmes

Ellen Page © Miramax

Thomas Haden Church, Dennis Quaid

Jack McBrayer, Paul Rudd, Jason Segel

FORGETTING SARAH MARSHALL

(UNIVERSAL) Producers, Judd Apatow, Shauna Robertson; Executive Producers, Richard Vane, Rodney Rothman; Director, Nicholas Stoller; Screenplay, Jason Segel; Photography, Russ T. Alsobrook; Designer, Jackson De Govia; Costumes, Leesa Evans; Music, Lyle Workman; Music Supervisor, Jonathan Karp; Editor, William Kerr; Casting, Jeanne McCarthy; an Apatow production; Dolby; Technicolor; Rated R; 112 minutes; Release date: April 18, 2008

Cast

Peter Bretter	**Jason Segel**
Sarah Marshall	**Kristen Bell**
Rachel Jansen	**Mila Kunis**
Aldous Snow	**Russell Brand**
Brian Bretter	**Bill Hader**
Liz Bretter	**Liz Cackowski**
Wyoma	**Maria Thayer**
Darald	**Jack McBrayer**
Kemo	**Taylor Wily**
Dwayne the Bartender	**Da'Vone McDonald**
Dr. Rosenbaum	**Steve Landesberg**
Matthew the Waiter	**Jonah Hill**
Chuck	**Paul Rudd**
Greg	**Kala Alexander**

Kalani Robb (Helpful Hawaiian Waiter), Francesca Delbanco (Hostess the Buffet), Branscombe Richmond (Keoki), Billy Bush (Himself), William Baldwin (Detective Hunter Rush), Jason Bateman (Animal Instincts Detective), Peter Gray Lewis (Suspect on Animal Instincts), Trula Marcus (Lawyer on Crime Scene), Kirk Fox (Mixer), June Raphael (Ann at the Bar), Ahna O'Reilly (Leslie), Tanisha Harper (Model), Carla Gallo (Gag Me Girl), Murray Miller (Photographer), Cynthia Lamontagne (Bartender), Maxwell Alexander (Big Dracula Head), Kris Fitzgerald (Man who Proposes), Brittany Ross (Screaming Girlfriend), Joe "Kaleo" Kelii (Singer in Band), Peter Salett (Keyboard Player), Gedde Watanabe (Hotel Manager), Allan Jeff Ho, Chaunnel Salmon (Bar Patrons), Mervyn Lilo (Fire Dancer), Phlip Matila (Luau Band Leader), Danielle Prem, Tehina-Mai K. Mataele, Agnes Matila (Hula Dancers), Genny Wilson, Scott Francis Russell (Engaged Couple)

Devastated after being dumped by his girlfriend, Sarah Marshall, Peter Bretter decides to take a Hawaiian vacation, ending up at the very same resort where Sarah is now vacationing with her new lover.

Kristen Bell, Russell Brand

Mila Kunis, Jason Segel

Jason Segel © Universal Studios

THE LIFE BEFORE HER EYES

(MAGNOLIA) formerly *In Bloom*; Producers, Vadim Perelman, Aimee Peyronnet, Anthony Katagas; Executive Producers, Todd Wagner, Mark Cuban, Marc Butan; Coproducers, Chase Bailey, Couper Samuleson, Mike Upton, Ian McGolin; Director, Vadim Perelman; Screenplay, Emil Stern; Based on the novel by Laura Kasischke; Photography, Pawel Edelman; Designer, Maia Javan; Costumes, Hala Bahmnet; Music, James Horner; Editor, David Baxter; a 2929 presentation; Dolby; Panavision; Color; Rated R; 90 minutes; Release date: April 18, 2008

Cast

Diana (Adult	**Uma Thurman**
Diana (Teen)	**Evan Rachel Wood**
Maureen	**Eva Amurri**
Emma	**Gabrielle Brenna**
Paul	**Brett Cullen**
Marcus	**Oscar Isaac**

Jack Gilpin (Mr. McCleod), Maggie Lacey (Adult Amanda), John Magaro (Michael Patrick), Lynn Cohen (Sister Beatrice), Nathalie Nicole Paulding (Teen Amanda), Molly Price (Diana's Mother), Oliver Solomon (Detective), Anna Renee Moore (Blonde Student), Isabel Keating (Maureen's Mother), Adam Chanler-Berat (Ryan), Tanner Max Cohen (Nate Witt), Aldous McDonough (Librarian), Sharon Washington (Nurse), Kia Jam (Doctor), J.T. Arbogast (Reporter), Jewel Donohue (Mother at Shooting), Shayna Levine (Teen Page), Anslem Richardson (Policeman), Evan Neumann (Boy Kicked in Groin), Reathel Bean (Dean), Tuck Milligan (Clinic Doctor), Jessica Carlson (Girl at Shooting), Molly Schreger, T.J. Linnard (Students)

The adult Diana continues to be tormented over the high school shooting that took the life of her best friend.

Evan Rachel Wood, Eva Amurri

Uma Thurman © Magnolia

Morgan Spurlock

WHERE IN THE WORLD IS OSAMA BIN LADEN?

(WEINSTEIN CO.) Producers, Jeremy Chilnick, Stacey Offman, Morgan Spurlock; Executive Producers, Adam Dell, Steven Dell, Vincent Maravel, Agnes Mentre, John Sloss; Coproducers, James Brabazon, Julie "Bob" Lombardi, Stuart Macphee; Director, Morgan Spurlock; Screenplay, Jeremy Chilnick, Morgan Spurlock; Photography, Daniel Marracicno; Music, Jon Spurney; Editors, Julie "Bob" Lombardi, Gavin Coleman; Presented in association with Wild Bunch, Non-Linear Films, Warrior Poets; Dolby; Color; HD; Rated PG-13; 93 minutes; Release date: April 18, 2008. Documentary in which filmmaker Morgan Spurlock wanders from one Muslim country to another, speculating on why the U.S. has not yet captured Taliban leader Osama bin Laden

With

Morgan Spurlock, Alexandra Jamieson.

Morgan Spurlock (right) © Weinstein Co.

Collin Chou © Lionsgate/Weinstein Co.

THE FORBIDDEN KINGDOM

(LIONSGATE/WEINSTEIN CO.) Producer, Casey Silver; Executive Producers, Ryan Kavanaugh, Woo-Ping Yuen, Jon Feltheimer, Raffaella De Laurentiis; Co-Executive Producers, Willie Chan, Solon So, Steve Chaseman, Jason C. Lin, David U. Lee; Director, Rob Minkoff; Screenplay, John Fusco; Photography, Peter Pau; Designer, Bill Brzeski; Costumes, Shirley Chan; Music, David Buckley; Editor, Eric Strand; Senior Visual Effects Supervisor, Ron Simonson; Visual Effects, Macrograph, Digital Tetra Footage; Line Producer, Hester Hargett-Aupetit; Action Choreographer, Woo-Ping Yuen; Casting, Poping Auyeung, Nancy Foy; a Casey Silver production, in association with Relativity Media, in co-production with Huyai Brothers Media Group; Dolby; Panavision; Color; Rated PG-13; 105 minutes; Release date: April 18, 2008

Cast

Old Hop/Lu Yan	**Jackie Chan**
The Monkey King/The Silent Monk	**Jet Li**
Jason Tripitikas	**Michael Angarano**
Jade Warlord	**Collin Chou**
Golden Sparrow/Chinatown Girl	**Liu Yifei**
Ni Chang	**Li Bing Bing**
Lupo	**Morgan Benoit**
Kam	**Alexis Bridges**
Southie Gir	**Juana Collignon**
Southie	**Jack Posobiec**
Young Southie	**Thomas McDonell**

Ma Gui Zhi (Old Woman), Shen Shou He (Farmer), Jian Bin (Young Village Man), Yang Shao Hua (Jade Soldier), Yuan Zeng Yu (Inn Keeper), Wang De Shun (Jade Emperor), Liu XiaoLi (Queen Mother), Dong Xiao Mei (Inn Keeper's Wife), Matthew Tang, Cheng Hong Jun, Alan Ng (Jade Officers), Michelle Du (Painted Girl), Yang Jun, Jeffrey Kung (Heralds), Crystal Kung (Slave Girl), Xu Wei Jia (Tracker), Huang Min Sheng, Li Rui, Zhang Fei Long, Luo Cheng, Zhou Xiao, Lin Hai Bin, Zhi Hui Jie (Cult Killers), Shi Xiao Ju (Golden Sparrow's Mother), Guo Meng (Young Golden Sparrow), Cui Wen Lu (Goat Herder), Li Xiao Yong, Zhang Zhen (Young Monks), Ye Xiao Keng (Abbot), Zhao Zi Wan (Medicine Monk), Matthew Grant (Paramedic)

Teenage Jason Tripitikas dreams that he has been entrusted to bring a magical golden staff to a forbidden kingdom to help free the enslaved Monkey King.

Jet Li, Michael Angarano, Jackie Chan

Jet Li, Jackie Chan, Michael Angarano, Liu Yifei

Li Bing Bing

Leelee Sobieski, Al Pacino © Sony Pictures Entertainment

88 MINUTES

(SONY PICTURES ENTERTAINMENT) Producers, Jon Avnet, Randall Emmett, Gary Scott Thompson, Avi Lerner; Executive Producers, Danny Dimbort, Trevor Short, Boaz Davidson, George Furla, Andreas Thiesmeyer, Josef Lautenschlager, Lawrence Bender, John Baldecchi; Coproducers, Michael Flannigan, John Thompson, Samuel Hadida, Marsha Oglesby, Jochen Kamlah, Gerd Koechlin, Manfred Heid; Director, Jon Avent; Screenplay, Gary Scott Thompson; Photography, Denis Lenoir; Designer, Tracey Gallacher; Costumes, Mary McLeod; Music, Edward Shearmur; Editor, Peter Berger; Stunts, Scott Ateah, Owen Walstom; Casting, Rick Pagano; a TriStar Pictures and Millennium Films presentation of a Randall Emmett-George Furla (U.S.) production for Equity Pictures Medienfonds and Nu Image Entertainment (Germany); U.S.-German; Dolby; Super 35 Widescreen; FotoKem color; Rated R; 107 minutes; Release date: April 18, 2008

Cast

Dr. Jack Gramm	**Al Pacino**
Kim Cummings	**Alicia Witt**
Lauren Douglas	**Leelee Sobieski**
Shelly Barnes	**Amy Brenneman**
Frank Parks	**William Forsythe**
Carol Johnson	**Deborah Kara Unger**
Mike Stempt	**Benjamin McKenzie**
Jon Forster	**Neal McDonough**

Leah Cairns (Sara Pollard), Stephen Moyer (Guy LaForge), Christopher Redman (Jeremy Guber), Brendan Fletcher (Johnny D'Franco), Michael Eklund (J.T. Rycker), Kristian Copeland (Dale Morris), Tammy Hui (Janie Cates), Vicky Huang (Joanie Cates), Victoria Tennant (Kate), Michal Yannai (Leeza Pearson), Paul Campbell (Albert Jackson), Brenda McDonald (Mrs. Lowinsky), Carrie Genzel (Stephanie Parkman), Kaj-Erik Eriksen (Matt Wilner), Heather Dawn (Heather), Julian D. Christopher (Special Agent Mactire), Tim Henry (Sean McBain), Mike Dopud (Detective), Brad Turner, Michael Adamthwaite (Firemen), Jean Montanti (Woman in Crowd), Timothy Paul Perez, Marcus Hondo (Cabbies)

On the day accused Seattle Slayer Jon Forster is scheduled to be executed, the forensic psychiatrist whose testimony was instrumental in putting him behind bars receives a mysterious phone call informing him that he will die in 88 minutes to pay for his role in Forster's fate.

DECEPTION

(20TH CENTURY FOX) Producers, Arnold Rifkin, John Palermo, High Jackman, Robbie Brenner, David Bushell, Christopher Roberts; Executive Producer, Marjorie Shik; Director, Marcel Langenegger; Screenplay, Mark Bomback; Photography, Dante Spinotti; Designer, Patrizia von Brandenstein; Costumes, Sue Gandy; Music, Ramin Djawadi; Editors, Christian Wagner, Douglas Crise; Associate Producers, Amanda Schweitzer, Philip Eisen; Casting, Bonnie Timmerman; a R///E production in association with Seed Prods.; Dolby; Panavision; Color; Rated R; 108 minutes; Release date: April 25, 2008

Cast

Wyatt Bose	**Hugh Jackman**
Jonathan McQuarry	**Ewan McGregor**
S	**Michelle Williams**
Detective Russo	**Lisa Gay Hamilton**
Tina	**Maggie Q**
Wall Street Analyst	**Natasha Henstridge**
Wall Street Belle	**Charlotte Rampling**

Lynn Cohen (Woman), Danny Burstein (Clute Controller), Malcolm Goodwin (Cabbie), Frank Girardeau (Mr. Lewman), Bill Camp (Clancey Controller), Bruce Altman, Andrew Ginsburg (Lawyers), Stephanie Roth Haberle (Assistant Controller), Christine Kan (Tennis Player #1), Dante Spinotti (Herr Kleiner/ Mr. Moretti), Karolina Muller (Waitress), Agnete Oernsholt (Woman at Waldorf Astoria), Melissa Rae Mahnon, Rachle Montez Collins, Holly Cruikshank (Velvet Rope Dancers), Deborah Yates (Tango Dancer), Zoe Perry, Aya Cash (Secretaries), Paz de la Huerta, Daisy Bates, Shannan Click, Jordan Testay, Rachael Taylor (List Members), Sally Leung Bayer (Old Woman), Kenneth G. Yong (Lotus Hotel Clerk), Paul Sparks (Det. Ed Burke), James Mazzola (Locksmith), Lisa Kron (Receptionist), Margaret Colin (Ms. Pomerantz), Peter Scanavino (Rhiga Desk Clerk), Frank Deal (Police Officer), Florenciz Lozano (Clancey Receptionist), Emelie Jeffries (Medical Examiner), Chandler Parker (Uniform Cop), Peter Jay Fernandez (Businessman on Airplane), Mercedes Herrero (Bank Greeter), Daniel Lugo (Mr. Ruiz), Javier Godino (Bank Manager), Brian Slaen (Younger Officer)

Mild-mannered accountant Jonathan McQuarry's developing friendship with the manipulative Wyatt Bose finds him involved with a mysterious nameless girl and more trouble than he could possibly have anticipated.

Michelle Williams, Hugh Jackman © 20th Century Fox

Tina Fey, Steve Martin

Tina Fey, Greg Kinnear

BABY MAMA

(UNIVERSAL) Producers, Lorne Michaels, John Goldwyn; Executive Producers, Jill Messic, Louise Rosner, Ryan Kavanaugh; Director/Screenplay, Michael McCullers; Photography, Daryn Okada; Designer, Jess Gonchor; Costumes, Renée Ehrlich Kalfus; Music, Jeff Richmond; Music Supervisors, Kathy Nelson, Erin David; Editor, Bruce Green; Casting, Avy Kaufman; a Michaels/Goldwyn production, presented in association with Relativity Media; Dolby; Technicolor; Rated PG-13; 99 minutes; Release date: April 25, 2008

Cast
Angie Ostrowski	**Amy Poehler**
Kate Holbrook	**Tina Fey**
Rob Ackerman	**Greg Kinnear**
Carl	**Dax Shepard**
Oscar Loomis	**Romany Malco**
Chaffee Bicknell	**Sigourney Weaver**
Barry	**Steve Martin**
Caroline	**Maura Tierney**
Dan	**Stephen Mailer**
Rose Holbrook	**Holland Taylor**
Judge	**James Rebhorn**
Dr. Manheim	**Denis O'Hare**

Kevin Collins (Architect, Rick), Will Forte (Scott), Fred Armisen (Stroller Salesman), John Hodgman (Fertility Specialist), Siobhan Fallon Hogan (Birthing Teacher), Tom McCarthy (Kate's Date), Jason Mantzoukas, Dave Finkel (Gay Couple), Brian Stack (Dave), Felicity Stiverson (Wiccan), Anne L. Nathan (Bookstore Clerk), Jay Phillips (Boo-Boo Buster), Kathy Searle (Cool Mom), Almeria Campbell (Maternity Nurse), Alice Kremelberg (Rob's Daughter), Catherine Rose (Caroline's 4-year-old), Ian Colletti (Caroline's 7-year-old), Eric Zuckerman, Frank Rodriguez, Diane Chen (Community Members), Andra Eggleston (Waitress), Andrew Hillmedo (Dante), Jon Glaser (Vegan Waiter), Erica Berg (Yoga Mom), Curt Carlson (Bailiff)

Determined to have a baby, Kate Holbrook reluctantly agrees to let lowbrow Angie Ostrowski carry the child as its surrogate mother.

Amy Poehler, Romany Malco © Universal Studios

HAROLD & KUMAR ESCAPE FROM GUANTANAMO BAY

(NEW LINE CINEMA) Producers, Greg Shapiro, Nathan Kahane; Executive Producers, Joe Drake, Carsten Lorenz, Toby Emmerich, Richard Brener; Coproducers, Nicole Brown, Kelli Konop, Michael Disco, Samuel J. Brown, Jon Hurwitz, Hayden Schlossberg; Directors/Screenplay, Jon Hurwitz, Hayden Schlossberg; Based on their characters; Photography, Daryn Okada; Designer, Tony Fanning; Costumes, Shawn Holly Cookson; Music, George S. Clinton; Music Supervisor, Season Kent; Editor, Jeff Freeman; Casting, Richard Hicks, David Rubin; a Kingsgate Films produciton, presented in association with Mandate Pictures; Dolby; Deluxe color; Rated R; 102 minutes; Release date: April 25, 2008

Cast

Harold Lee	**John Cho**
Kumar Patel	**Kal Penn**
Ron Fox	**Rob Corddry**
Deputy Frye	**Jack Conley**
Dr. Beecher	**Roger Bart**
Himself	**Neil Patrick Harris**
Vanessa	**Danneel Harris**
Colton	**Eric Winter**
Maria	**Paula Garcés**
Raymus	**Jon Reep**
Raylene	**Missi Pyle**
Cyrus	**Mark Munoz**
George W. Bush	**James Adomian**
Sally	**Beverly D'Angelo**

Echo Valley (Tits Hemingway), David Krumholtz (Goldstein), Eddie Kaye Thomas (Rosenberg), Ava Santana (Tammi), Chantel Silvain (Trisha), Courtney Shay Young (Sparkle), Crystal Mantecon (Venus), Katheryn Ryce (Agnes), Todd Voltz (Travis), Richard Christy (Kenny), Adam Herschman (Archie), Jackson Beals (Carter), Amir Talali (Raza), Kristen de Nes (Kim), Mark Turner (Joe), Randal Reeder (Big Bob), Ed Helms (Interpreter), Errol Stiahal (Dr. Patel), Clyde Kusatsu (Mr. Lee), Mary Deese (Mrs. Lee), Juli Erickson (Old White Woman), Kelvin Payton, Ron Fagan (Random Passengers), Frank Mondaruli (Head of Security), D'Anthony Palms (Light-Skinned Black Security), Lester "Rasta" Speight (Dr. Jonavon), Hugo Perez (Ramon), Colton Gramm (Groomsman #1), Patrick Michael Carney, Jason Konopisos (Goons), Chris Warner (State Trooper), Carsten Lorenz (Carsten), Angus Sutherland (Anton), Marisa Rodriquez, Claudia Pena (Jacuzzi Girls), Rob Andrist Plourde (Random Amsterdam Stoner)

En route to Amsterdam, Harold and Kumar find themselves mistaken for terrorists and shipped to the military prison at Guantanamo Bay. Sequel to the 2004 film *Harold & Kumar Go to White Castle* with Cho, Penn, and several others repeating their roles.

Mark Munoz, John Cho

Neil Patrick Harris, Kal Penn, John Cho © New Line Cinema

Roger Bart, Rob Corddry

Kal Penn, Danneel Harris

Colin Firth, Helen Hunt

Bette Midler

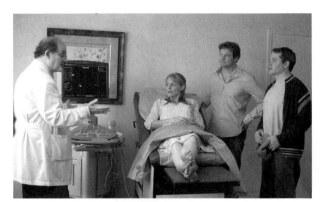

Salman Rushdie, Helen Hunt, Colin Firth, Matthew Broderick

THEN SHE FOUND ME

(THINKFILM) Producers, Pamela Koffler, Katie Roumel, Christine Vachon, Helen Hunt, Connie Tavel; Executive Producers, John Wells, Chip Signore, Louise Goodsill, Ralph Kamp, Victor Levin, Walter Josten, Jeff Geoffray, Howard Behar; Coproducer, Matthew Myers; Director, Helen Hunt; Screenplay, Alice Arlen, Victor Levin, Helen Hunt; Based on the novel by Elinor Lipman; Photography, Peter Donahue; Designer, Stephen Beatrice; Costumes, Donna Zakowska; Music, David Mansfield; Editor, Pam Wise; Casting, Bernie Telsey; a Killer Films production in association with Blue Rider Films and John Wells Prods.; Dolby; Color; Rated R; 100 minutes; Release date: April 25, 2008

Cast

April Epner	**Helen Hunt**
Frank	**Colin Firth**
Bernice Graves	**Bette Midler**
Ben	**Matthew Broderick**
Trudy	**Lynn Cohen**
Freddy	**Ben Shenkman**
Gianni	**David Callegati**
Alan	**John Benjamin Hickey**
Anne	**Stacie Linardos**
Jimmy Ray	**Tommy Nelson**
Dr. Masani	**Salman Rushdie**

Daisy Tahan (Daisy Tahan), Rabbi Kenneth Stern (Rabbi), Florence Annequin (Production Assistant), Cherise Boothe (Mother #1), Geneva Carr (Talk Show Guest), Chris Chalk (Orderly), Brother Douglas (Penthouse Benefit Guest), Audrey Elizabeth Fafard (Penthouse Host), Rachel Konstantin (April's Cousin), Andy Miller (Limo Driver), Jonathan Roumie (Partygoer), Maggie Siff (Girlfriend), Schuster Vance (Husband at PTA Meeting)

Thiry-nine-year-old school teacher April Epner faces a turning point in her life when her husband decides to end their marriage and a self-absorbed TV host shows up claiming to be April's biological mother.

Helen Hunt © ThinkFilm

IRON MAN

(PARAMOUNT) Producers, Avi Arada, Kevin Feige; Executive Producers, Louis D'Esposito, Peter Billingsley, Jon Favreau, Avi Arad, Stan Lee, David Maisel; Coproducer, Victoria Alonso; Director, Jon Favreau; Screenplay, Mark Fergus, Hawk Ostby, Art Marcum, Matt Holloway; Based on the Marvel comic book by Stan Lee, Don Heck, Larry Lieber, Jack Kirby; Photography, Matthew Libatique; Designer, J. Michael Riva; Costumes, Laura Jean Shannon; Music, Ramin Djawadi; Music Supervisor, Dave Jordan; Visual Effects Supervisor, John Nelson; ILM Visual Effects Supervisor, Ben Snow; Visual Effects and Animation, Industrial Light & Magic; Visual Effects, Pixel Liberation Front, The Orphanage; Stunts, Thomas Robinson Harper; Casting, Sarah Finn, Randi Hiller; a Marvel Entertainment presentation of a Marvel Studios production in association with Fairview Entertainment; Dolby; Panavision; Deluxe color; Rated PG-13; 126 minutes; Release date: May 2, 2008

Robert Downey, Jr., Jeff Bridges

Cast

Tony Stark (Iron Man)	**Robert Downey, Jr.**
Jim Rhodes	**Terrence Howard**
Obadiah Stane	**Jeff Bridges**
Pepper Potts	**Gwyneth Paltrow**
Christine Everhart	**Leslie Bibb**
Yinsen	**Shaun Toub**
Raza	**Faran Tahir**
Abu Bakaar	**Sayed Badreya**
General Gabriel	**Bill Smitrovich**
Agent Phil Coulson	**Clark Gregg**
Major Allen	**Tim Guinee**
Award Ceremony Narrator	**Will Lyman**
Voice of Jarvis	**Paul Bettany**
Jimmy	**Kevin Foster**
Pratt	**Garret Noel**
Ramirez	**Eileen Weisinger**
Ahmed	**Ahmed Ahmed**
Omar	**Fahim Fazli**
Howard Stark	**Gerard Sanders**
Hogan	**Jon Favreau**
Insurgents	**Marco Khan, Tom Morello**
Vipers	**Tim Rigby, Russell Richardson**
FBX Reporter	**Nazanin Boniadi**
Colonel Craig	**Thomas Craig Plumer**

Robert Downey, Jr., Leslie Bibb

Robert Downey, Jr., Terrence Howard

Robert Berkman (Dealer at Craps Table), Stacy Stas, Lauren Scyphers (Women at Craps Table), Dr. Frank Nyi (Engineer), Marvin Jordan (Air Force Officer), Jim Cramer, Stan Lee, Zorianna Kit (Themselves), Reid Harper, Summer Kylie Remington, Ava Rose Williams, Vladimir Kubr, Callie Marie Croughwell (Kids in SUV), Donna Evans Merlo (Woman in SUV), Javan Tahir (Gulmira Kid), Sahar Bibiyan (Gulmira Mom), Patrick O'Connell, Adam Harrington, Meera Simhan, Ben Newmark (Press Reporters), Ricki Noel Lander, Jeannine Kaspar, Sarah Cahill (Hot Stewardesses), Peter Billingsley (William), Justin Rex (Air Force Lieutenant), Lana Kinenar, Nicole Lindeblad, Masha Lund, Gabrielle Tuite (Stan's Girls), Tim Griffin, Joshua Harto, Micah Hauptman, James Bethea (CAOC Analysts), Daston Kalili, Ido Ezra (Screaming Insurgents), Samuel L. Jackson (Nick Fury).

Feeling guilty about building weapons of mass destruction, billionaire Tony Stark instead creates an armored suit that will enable him to battle the forces of evil.

This film received Oscar nominations for visual effects and sound editing.

Right: *Robert Downey, Jr., Shaun Toub*

Robert Downey, Jr. © Paramount Pictures

Gwyneth Paltrow

Gwyneth Paltrow

Robert Downey, Jr.

Robert Downey, Jr.

REDBELT

(SONY CLASSICS) Producer, Chrisann Verges; Director/Screenplay, David Mamet; Photography, Robert Elswit; Designer, David Wasco; Costumes, Debra McGuire; Music, Stephen Endelman; Editor, Barbara Tulliver; Fight Choreographer, Rico Chiapparelli; Casting, Sharon Bialy, Sherry Thomas; Dolby; Color; Rated R; 99 minutes; Release date: May 2, 2008

Cast

Mike Terry	**Chiwetel Ejiofor**
Laura Black	**Emily Mortimer**
Sondra Terry	**Alice Braga**
Chet Frank	**Tim Allen**
Jerry Weiss	**Joe Mantegna**
Bruno Silva	**Rodrigo Santoro**
Marty Brown	**Ricky Jay**
Joe Collins	**Max Martini**
Richard	**David Paymer**
Zena Frank	**Rebecca Pidgeon**

Matt Malloy (Lawyer), Matt Cable (Academy Fighter), Cathy Cahlin Ryan (Gini Collins), Jose Pablo Cantillo (Snowflake), Randy Couture (Dylan Flynn), Steve DeCastro (Knife Fighter on Set), Caroline de Souza Correa (Monica), Justin Fair (Non-Smoking Attendant), Vincent Guastaferro (Eddie Bialy), Damon Herriman (Official at Arena), Kei Hirayama (Japanese Interviewer), Enson Inoue (Taketa Morisaki), Jake Johnson (Guayabera Shirt Man), Allison Karman (Paralegal), John Machado (Ricardo Silva), Renato Magno (Romero), Ray Mancini (George), Marc Opitz (Reporter), James Ralph (Bartender), Galen Tong (Referee), Luciana Souza (Singer in Bar), Cyril Takayama (The Magician), Scott Barry (Billy the Bartender), Ricardo Wlike (Eduardo), Jack Wallace (Bar Patron), Dennis Keefer (Knife Fighter in Bar), Robert Reinis (Officer), Dominic Hoffman (Detective), Michael Kenner (Chauffeur), Mike Genovese (Desk Sergeant), Bob Jennings (Sammy), Jennifer Grey (Lucy Weiss), Linda Kimbrough (Murphy), Ed O'Neill (Hollywood Producer), Rico Chiapparelli (Sanchez), Martin Desideriom (Sanchez's Handler), Frank Trigg (Sanchez's Cornerman), Gilbert Gomez (Romero's Handler), Mike Goldberg, Jean Jacques Machado, Josh Rafferty, Scott Ferrall (Themselves), J.J. Johnston (Ring Announcer), Christina Grance (Ring Girl), Tony Mamet (Fight Commissioner), Simon Rhee, Troy Gilbert (Bruno's Henchmen), Dan Inosanto (The Professor), Gene Lebell (Old Stuntman), Lee Cohen, Mordecai Finley, Arvan Morgan, Peter Smith, Scott Voss (Undercard Fighters), Chris Lisciandro, Tino Struckmann, Adam Treanor, Clay Woods (Southside Jiu-Jitsu Academy Fighters)

Committed jiu-jitsu teacher Mike Terry finds himself involved with an unstable lawyer who has inadvertently fired a gun at his training school, as well as a movie star who enlists his services after Mike comes to his rescue in a bar fight.

Alice Braga, Rebecca Pidgeon, Tim Allen © Sony Pictures Classics

Chiwetel Ejiofor, John Machado

Rodrigo Santoro, Joe Mantegna

Emily Mortimer, Chiwetel Ejiofor

Patrick Dempsey, Sydney Pollack © Columbia Pictures

MADE OF HONOR

(COLUMBIA) Producer, Neal H. Moritz; Executive Producers, Callum Greene, Tania Landau, Amanda Lewis, Marty Adelstein, Aaron Kaplan, Sean Perrone, Ryan Kavanaugh; Director, Paul Weiland; Screenplay, Adam Sztykiel, Deborah Kaplan Harry Elfont; Story, Adam Sztykiel; Photography, Tony Pierce-Roberts; Designer, Kalina Ivanov; Costumes, Penny Rose; Music, Rupert Gregson-Williams; Music Supervisor, Nick Angel; Casting, Kim Davis Wagner, Justine Baddeley; an Original Film production, presented in association with Relativity Media; Dolby; Super 35 Widescreen; Deluxe color; Rated PG-13; 100 minutes; Release date: May 2, 2008

Cast

Tom	**Patrick Dempsey**
Hannah	**Michelle Monaghan**
Colin McMurray	**Kevin McKidd**
Felix	**Kadeem Hardison**
Dennis	**Chris Messina**
Gary	**Richmond Arquette**
Melissa	**Busy Philipps**

Whitney Cummings (Stephanie), Emily Nelson (Hilary), Kathleen Quinlan (Joan), Selma Stern (Grandma Pearl), Sydney Pollack (Thomas Sr.), James Sikking (Reverend Foote), Kevin Sussman (Tiny Shorts Guy), Beau Garrett (Gloria), Christine Barger (Psycho Blogger), Lilly McDowell (Lingerie Salesgirl), Kelly Carlson (Christie, Wife #6), Craig Susser (Christie's Lawyer), Corinne Reilly (Restaurant Hostess), Trip Davis (Waiter), Valerie Edmond (Cousin Kelly), Hannah Gordon (Colin's Mother), Cathleen McCarron (Cousin Cathy), Eoin McCarthy (Cousin Ewan), Clive Russell (Cousin Finlay), Myra McFadyen (Aunt Minna), Iain Agnew (Colin's Father), Mary Birdsong (Sharon at Bridal Shower), Elisabeth Hasselbeck (Herself), Grant Thomson (Huge Scottish Football Player), Te'onna Simone Tye (Felix's Daughter), Marty Ryan (Chaise Husband), Veronica Alicino (Long Island Wife), Sarah Mason (Sexy Blonde), Jaime Ray Newman (Ariel, Bakery Date), Ellie Knaus (Sick Monica), Annalaina Marks (Barbara, Antiques Date), Edith S. Wolfrey (Older Lady in Coffee Shop), James Earl Adair (Guy Selling Alligator Purse), Leah Elias (Flirting Brunette), Jeff Rudom (Large Burly Scotsman), Forbes KB (Man at Highland Games), Murray McArthur (Driver in Scotland), Rab Affleck (Sheep Herder), Finlay Welsh (Ferry Porter), Ron Donachie (Horse Owner), Jennifer De Minco (Woman in China Department), Christina Hogue (Beautiful Girl), Claire M. Fagin (Older Woman in Boat), Samuel L. Fagin (Older Man in Boat), Joe Weiland, Bella Weiland (Children in Scottish Church), Christopher Maggi (Flower Vendor), Brandon Saario (Paul)

Realizing that he is deeply in love with his best friend, Tom attempts to sabotage her upcoming wedding nuptials.

NOISE

(THINKFILM) Producers, Henry Bean, Susan Hoffman; Executive Producers, David Diamond, Paul de Souza; Coproducer, Tony Grazia; Director/Screenplay, Henry Bean; Photography, Andrij Parekh; Designer, Kelly McGehee; Costumes, Alex Alvarez; Music, Phillip Johnston; Editors, Lee Percy, Julie Carr; a Seven Arts, Fuller Films production; Dolby; Color; 35mm-to-DigitBeta; Not rated; 87 minutes; Release date: May 9, 2008

Cast

David Owen	**Tim Robbins**
Helen Owen	**Bridget Moynahan**
Mayor Schneer	**William Hurt**
Ekaterina Filippovna	**Margarita Levieva**
Chris Owen	**Gabrielle Brennan**
Gruska	**María Ballesteros**
Mayor's Chief of Staff	**William Baldwin**

Eric Lenox Abramas, Bradley Williams (Security Cops), Jessica Almasy (Crackpot Anarchist), Leora Barish (Tiny Juror), Michael J. Burg (Judson), Lou Carbonneau (Dante Moretti), Chuck Cooper (Judge Gibson), Catherine Curtin (Barbara), Maryam Myika Day (TV Reporter), Joel Diamond (Joel), Brother Eden Douglas (Chamber Music Guest), Ramon Fernandez (Arresting Officer), Steve Greenstein (Driver of Red Truck), Peggy Gormley (Small Claims Judge), Howard W. Gutman (David's Lawyer), Stephen Adly Guirgis (Anthony J. Corpitani), Viola Harris (Elderly Woman), Helen Hanft (Forceful Juror), Diane Hess (Mayor's Personal Assistant), Ryan Hilliard (Criminal Court Judge), Peter Hoffman (Judge Kornreich), Sara Jerez (Medical Trainee), Ed Jewett (Richie McIntyre), Ebony Jo Ann (City Clerk), Judah Lazarus (Manhole Cover Guy), Aaron Lohr, Craig Walker (Rowdy Drinkers), David Margulies (Heart Attack Man), Clark Middleton (Board of Elections Worker #1), Keir O'Donnell (Experienced Car Thief), Daniel Raymond (Glenn), Jackie Salit (Jackie), Vladimir Skomarovksy (Ekaterina's Uncle), D.J. Surgent (Mayor's Bodyguard), Francis Toumbakaris (Election Worker #2), Ivo Velon (Evan), Mark Elliott Wilson (Businessman with Lexus), James Yaegashi, Akira Yamaguchi (Japanese Businessmen)

New Yorker David Owen's contempt for car alarms escalates to such a degree that he becomes a one-man vigilante against excessive urban noise.

Tim Robbins © ThinkFilm

SPEED RACER

(WARNER BROS.) Producers, Joel Silver, Grant Hill, Andy Wachowski, Larry Wachowski; Executive Producers, David Lane Seltzer, Michael Lambert, Bruce Berman; Coproducers, Jessica Alan, Roberto Malerba, Henning Molfenter, Carl L. Woebcken; Director/Screenplay, The Wachowski Brothers; Based on the original animated series created by Tatsuo Yoshida and produced by Tasunoko Prods.; Photography, David Tattersall; Designer, Owen Paterson; Costumes, Kym Barrett; Music, Michael Giacchino; Editors, Zach Staenberg, Roger Barton; Visual Effects Supervisors, John Gaeta, Dan Glass; Visual Effects, Industrial Light & Magic, Digital Domain, Buf, Sony Pictures Imageworks, Evil Eye Pictures, Café FX, CIS-Hollywood, Rising Sun Pictures, Pixel Liberation Front, Starz Media/Film Roman, Pacific Title and Art Studio, Lola; Stunts, Chad Stahelski, David Leitch; Second Unit Director, James McTiegue; Casting, Lora Kennedy, Lucinda Syson; a Silver Pictures production in association with Anarchos Productions presented in association with Village Roadshow Pictures; Dolby; Widescreen; Technicolor; HD; Rated PG; 135 minutes; Release date: May 9, 2008

Cast

Speed Racer	**Emile Hirsch**
Trixie	**Christina Ricci**
Pops Racer	**John Goodman**
Mom Racer	**Susan Sarandon**
Racer X	**Matthew Fox**
E.P. Arnold Royalton	**Roger Allam**
Spritle Racer	**Paulie Litt**
Inspector Detector	**Benno Fürmann**
Mr. Musha	**Hiroyuki Sanada**
Taejo Togokahn	**Rain**
Ben Burns	**Richard Roundtree**
Sparky	**Kick Gurry**
Cruncher Block	**John Benfield**

Emile Hirsch, Christina Ricci

Matthew Fox

Christian Oliver (Snake Oiler), Moritz Bleibtreu (Grey Ghost), Ralph Herforth (Jake "Cannonball" Taylor), Ashley Walters (Prince Kabala), Scott Porter (Rex Racer), Nicholas Elia (Young Speed), Melissa Holroyd (Speed's Teacher), Ariel Winter (Young Trixie), Gian Ganziano (Everyman Announcer), Peter Fernandez (Local Announcer), Harvey Friedman (Harold Ledermann Announcer), Sadao Ueda (Japanese Announcer), Valery Tscheplanowa (Russian Announcer), Sami Loris (Italian Announcer), Olivier Marlo (French Announcer), Sean McDonagh (Celtic Announcer), Vinzez Kiefer (Crew Chief/Sempre Fi-Ber Driver), Mark Zak (Blackjack Benelli), Willy Kenzie (Chim Chim), Julia Joyce (Blonde Pack Leader), Clayton Nemrow (Race Announcer), Ricky Watson (Race Commentator), Brandon Robinson (Big Mouth), L. Trey Wilson (Press Man), Nayo K. Wallace (Minx), Lauren Blake (Flight Attendant), Cosma Shiva Hagen (Gennie), Waldemar Kobus (Vinny, Cruncher Thug), Max Hopp (Cruncher Thug), Julie T. Wallace (Truck Driver), Hiryuki Sanada (Mr. Musha), Matthias Redlhammer (Marvin the Cleaning Man), Eckehard Hoffmann (Joel Goldman), Stephen Marcus (Security Goon), Art LaFleur, Peter Navy Tuiasosopo (Fuji Announcers), Nna Yu (Horuko Togokahn), Paul Sirr (Dour Face), Ramon Tikaram (Casa Christo Announcer), Melvil Poupaud (Johnny "Goodboy" Jones), Kady Taylor (Queen of Casa Christo), Junior Sone Enang (Shark Driver), Jana Pallaske (Delila), Dari Maximova (Flying Fox), Werner Daehn (Sempre Fi-Ber Leader), Komi Togbonou (Thor-azine Leader), Leila Rozario (Hydro-cell Driver), Steven Wilson (C.I.B. Security Man), Karl Yune (Taejo Bodyguard), Togo Igawa (Mr. Togokahn), Jonathan Kinsler, Anatole Taubman (Fuji Reporters), Ben Miles (Cass Jones), Frank Witter (Security Official), Megan Gay (Senior Race Official), Corinne Orr (Grand Prix Announcer), Joe Mazza (Nitro), Joon Park (Yakuza Driver), Ludmilla Ismailow (Denise), Mlika Duno (Gearbox), Amira OSman (Count Down Tower Woman), Jens Neuhaus (German Announcer), Sesede Terziyan (Turkish Announcer), Ill-Young Kim (Korean Announcer), Yuriri Naka (Japanese Announcer), Óscar O. Sánchez (Spanish Announcer), Yu Fang (Chinese Announcer), Narges Rashidi (Persian Announcer), Andrés Cantor (Grand Prix Announcer), Luka Andres (Big Mouth), Alister Mazzotti (Pitter Pat), Alexander Yassin (Reporter, Grand Prix)

Haunted by the death of his brother in a racing accident, young Speed Racer is now given his chance to prove his worth on the track when tycoon Arnold Royalton invites him to join his team of drivers.

Roger Allam, Susan Sarandon, John Goodman

Emile Hirsch © Warner Bros.

Cameron Diaz, Ashton Kutcher

Rob Corddry, Ashton Kutcher © 20th Century Fox

WHAT HAPPENS IN VEGAS

(20TH CENTURY FOX) Producers, Michael Aguilar, Shawn Levy, Jimmy Miller; Executive Producers, Arnon Milchan, Joe Caracciolo, Jr., Dean Georgaris; Director, Tom Vaughan; Screenplay, Dana Fox; Photography, Matthew F. Leonetti; Designer, Stuart Wurtzel; Costumes, Renee Ehrlich Kalfus; Music, Christophe Beck; Music Supervisor, Deva Anderson; Editor, Matthew Friedman; Casting, Avy Kaufman; a Fox and Regency Enterprises presentation of a 21 Laps/Mosaic Media Group production; Dolby; Technicolor; Rated PG-13; 98 minutes; Release date: May 9, 2008

Cast

Joy McNally	**Cameron Diaz**
Jack Fuller	**Ashton Kutcher**
Steve "Hater" Hader	**Rob Corddry**
Tipper	**Lake Bell**
Mason	**Jason Sudeikis**
Jack Fuller, Sr.	**Treat Williams**
Mrs. Fuller	**Deirdre O'Connell**
Chong	**Michelle Krusiec**
Banger	**Dennis Farina**
Dave the Bear	**Zach Galifianakis**
Dr. Twitchell	**Queen Latifah**
Judge Whopper	**Dennis Miller**

Krysten Ritter (Kelly), Ricky Garcia (Fuller Closets Worker), Andrew Daly (Curtis), Benita Robledo (Maid), Amanda Setton, Toni Busker (Hot Women), Jessica McKee (Cute Girl), Ricardo Walker (Cop/Stripper), Valerie Orlik (Cop/Stripper), Ben Best (Cab Driver), Clem Cheung (Fruit Guy), Eric Zuckerman (Tour Guide), Caroline Willman (Sammy), Tommy McGoldrick (Uncle Pat), Billy Eichner (Band Leader), Heather Kristin (Band Singer), Brian M. Wixson (Band Member – Trumpet), Maddie Corman (Joy's Lawyer), Jerry V. Lindsay (Wedding Chapel Priest), Samantha Ridge (Tourist), Richard M. Schaeffer, Michael P. Molnar, John Eisenberg, Ciaran T. O'Kelly (NYMEX Traders), Jennifer Trier (Aunt Fuller), Michael Harkins, Patrick Knighton (Team Leaders), Adam Zuniga (Mr. Chong/Braniac), Aaron Nauta, Christopher Negrin (Hater's Friends), Brittany Dawn Beall, Ariel Shafir (Party Girls), Sheena Alonzo (Amanda Diamond), Bradley Morone (Club Manager), Cheryl Cosenza (Joy's 'Hot' Party Friend), Cassidy Gard, Meagan Gordon (Joy's Friends), Hector Lincoln (The DJ), Russ Spiegel (Ballroom Band Member)

After marrying in haste following a night of drunken revelry, Jack Fuller and Joy McNally plan to annul the nuptials until Jack wins a $3 million jackpot on a casino slot machine from Joy's quarter.

Ashton Kutcher, Cameron Diaz

THE CHRONICLES OF NARNIA: PRINCE CASPIAN

(WALT DISNEY PICTURES) Producers, Mark Johnson, Andrew Adamson, Philip Steuer; Executive Producer, Peggy Moore; Coproducer, Douglas Gresham; Director, Andrew Adamson; Screenplay, Andrew Adamson, Christopher Markus, Stephen McFeeley; Based on the book by C.S. Lewis; Photography, Karl Walter Lindenlaub; Designer, Roger Ford; Costumes, Isis Mussenden; Music, Harry Gregson-Williams; Editor, Sim Evan-Jones; Visual Effects Supervisors, Dean Wright, Wendy Rogers; Special Makeup & Creatures, Howard Berger, Gregory Nictoero; Stunt & Fight Coordinator, Allan Poppleton; a Walden Media presentation of a Mark Johnson/Silverbell Films production; Dolby; Technicolor; Rated PG; 150 minutes; Release date: May 16, 2008

Cast

Prince Caspian	**Ben Barnes**
Lucy Pevensie	**Georgie Henley**
Edmund Pevensie	**Skandar Keynes**
Peter Pevensie	**William Moseley**
Susan Pevensie	**Anna Popplewell**
Miraz	**Sergio Castellitto**
Trumpkin	**Peter Dinklage**
Nikabrik	**Warwick Davis**
Doctor Cornelius	**Vincent Grass**
General Glozelle	**Pierfrancesco Favino**
Glenstorm	**Cornell S. John**
Lord Sopespian	**Damian Alcazar**
Prunaprismia	**Alicia Borrachero**
The White Witch	**Tilda Swinton**
Voice of Aslan	**Liam Neeson**
Lord Scythely	**Simon Andreu**
Lord Donnon	**Pedja Bjelac**
Lord Gregoire	**David Bowles**
Lord Montoya	**Juan Diego Montoya Garcia**

Douglas Gresham (Telmarine Crier), Ash Jones (Geeky Boy), Klara Issova (Hag), Shane Rangi (Asterius/Wer-Wolf), Curtis Matthew (Faun), Mana Davis, Winham Hammond (Telmarine Soldiers in Boat), Hana Frejkova, Kristyna Madericova, Lucie Solarova, Karolína Matsoukova, Alina Phelan (Midwives), Joseph Moore, Isaac Bell (Boys), Lejla Abbasova, Ephraim Goldin, Yemi A.D., Carlos DaSilva (Glenstorm's Sons), Gomez Sandoval (Lightning Bolt Centaur), Jan Filipensky (Wimbleweather), David Mottil, Michaela Dvorska (Tyrus), John Bach, Jack Walley (British Homeguards), Marcus O'Donovan (Skeptical Telmarine), Adam Valdez (Telmarine Soldier Killed by Reepicheep); VOICES: Ken Stott (Trufflehunter), Harry Gregson-Williams (Pattertwig the Squirrel), Sim Evan-Jones (Peepiceek), David Walliams (Bulgy Bear), Eddie Izzard (Reepicheep)

The Pevensie children are summoned back to Narnia to help lead a battle to save the land from the tyrannical King Miraz. Second chapter in the chronicle, following *The Chronicles of Narnia: The Lion, the Witch and the Wardrobe* (Disney, 2005), with Keynes, Moseley, Popplewell, Henley, Swinton, and Neeson repeating their roles.

Ben Barnes, William Moseley, Skandar Keynes

Peter Dinklage, Warwick Davis

Sergio Castellitto

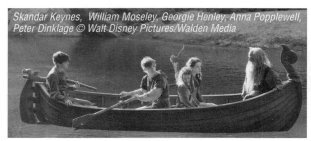

Skandar Keynes, William Moseley, Georgie Henley, Anna Popplewell, Peter Dinklage © Walt Disney Pictures/Walden Media

Georgie Henley, William Moseley, Ben Barnes, Anna Popplewell, Skandar Keynes

William Moseley

Ben Barnes

Pierfrancesco Favino, Sergio Castellitto, Damian Alcazar, David Bowler

Skandar Kenyes

Shia LaBeouf, Harrison Ford

Shia LaBeouf, Harrison Ford

Shia LaBeouf, Harrison Ford, Karen Allen © Paramount Pictures

Shia LaBeouf, Harrison Ford

Harrison Ford, Cate Blanchett

Shia LaBeouf, Harrison Ford, Karen Allen

Shia LaBeouf, Karen Allen

Ray Winstone, Harrison Ford

INDIANA JONES AND
THE KINGDOM OF THE CRYSTAL SKULL

(PARAMOUNT) Producer, Frank Marshall; Executive Producers, George Lucas, Kathleen Kennedy; Coproducer, Denis L. Stewart; Director, Steven Spielberg; Screenplay, David Koepp; Story, George Lucas, Jeff Nathanson; Based on characters created by George Lucas, Philip Kaufman; Photography, Janusz Kaminski; Designer, Guy Hendrix Dyas; Costumes, Mary Zophres; Music, John Williams; Editor, Michael Kahn; Visual Effects Supervisor, Pablo Helman; Visual Effect and Animation, Industrial Light & Magic; Stunts, Gary Powell; Casting, Deborah Zane; a Lucasfilms Ltd. Production; Dolby; Panavision; Deluxe color; Rated PG-13; 122 minutes; Release date: May 22, 2008

Cast

Indiana Jones	**Harrison Ford**
Irina Spalko	**Cate Blanchett**
Marion Ravenwood	**Karen Allen**
Mutt Williams	**Shia LaBeouf**
George "Mac" Michale	**Ray Winstone**
Professor Harold "Ox" Oxley	**John Hurt**
Dean Charles Stanforth	**Jim Broadbent**
Col. Dovchenko	**Igor Jijikine**
Russian Suits	**Dimitri Diatchenko, Ilia Volok**
Russian Soldiers	**Emmanuel Todorov, Pasha D. Lychnikoff, Andrew Divoff, Venya Manzyuk**
General Ross	**Alan Dale**
Taylor	**Joel Stoffer**
Smith	**Neil Flynn**
Minister	**VJ Foster**
Student in Library	**Chet Hanks**
Lettermen	**Brian Knutson, Dean L. Grimes**
Slugger	**Sasha Spielberg**
Diner Waitress	**Nicole Luther**
Malt Shop Teen	**Sophia Stewart**
College Brawlers	**Chris Todd, Dennis Nusbaum**
Teenage Boy	**T. Ryan Mooney**
Teenage Girls	**Audi Resendez, Helena Barrett**
Fast Speaking Inmate	**Carlos Linares**
Shouting Inmate	**Gustavo Hernandez**
Sanitarium Nun	**Maria Luisa Minelli**
Cemetery Warriors	**Nito Larioza, Ernie Reyes, Jr.**
Cave Warrior	**Jon Valera**
M.P. in Guard Hut	**Kevin Collins**
M.P. Sergeant	**Robert Baker**

College professor and part-time adventurer Indiana Jones journeys to Peru in an effort to locate the legendary Crystal Skull of Akator, all the while being pursued by Soviet officer Irina Spalko. Fourth film in the Paramount series starring Harrison Ford, following *Raiders of the Lost Ark* (1981), *Indiana Jones and the Temple of Doom* (1984), and *Indiana Jones and the Last Crusade* (1989); Karen Allen, who appeared in the first film, repeats her role here.

WAR, INC.

(FIRST LOOK) Producers, Les Weldon, Danny Lerner, John Cusack, Grace Loh; Executive Producers, Avi Lerner, Boaz Davidson, Danny Dimbort, Trevor Short; Coproducers, Doug Dearth, Katsu J.J. Yoshida; Director, Joshua Seftel; Screenplay, Mark Leyner, Jeremy Pikser, John Cusack; Photography, Zoran Popovic; Designer, Miljen "Kreka" Kljakovic; Costumes, Vicki Graef; Music, David Robbins; Editor, Michael Berenbaum; Casting, Victoria Thomas; a Millennium Films presentation of a New Crime production; Dolby; Color; Rated R; 106 minutes; Release date: May 23, 2008

Cast

Brand Hauser	**John Cusack**
Yonica Babyyeah	**Hilary Duff**
Natalie Hegalhuzen	**Marisa Tomei**
Marsha Dillon	**Joan Cusack**
Walken	**Ben Kingsley**
Mr. Vice President	**Dan Aykroyd**
Omar Sharif	**Lyubomir Neikov**

Serej Trifunovic (Ooq-Mi-Fay Taqnufmin), Ned Bellamy (Ooq-Yu-Fay Taqnufmini/Zuble), John McLaughlin (Himself), Montel Williams (GuideStar Voice), Nikolai Stanoev (Bhodi Bhufhang), George Zlatarev (Director), Bashar Rahal, Vesilav Pavlov, Zahari Baharov (Video Guys), Doug Dearth (Geoff), Ben Cross (Medusa Hair), Mark Roper (Choreographer), Andrei Slabakov (Cameraman), Joost Scholte (Cashier), Velizar Binev (German Businessman), Davorka Tovilo (German Woman), James Graves, Troy Rowland, Krasi Simeonov (Tamerlane Guards), Rachel O'Meara (Implanted Reporter), Nick Harvey (Interfaith Clergyman), Itai Djakov (Kid in Fallaf), Stanimir Stamatov (Posse Guy), Georgi Gatsov (Sound Man), Mark Johnson (Tamerlane Staple-Gun Guard), Zarko Peev (Thug), Shirly Brener (Hauser's Wife), Katerina Grableva (Hauser's Child), Sergio Buenrostro, Alex Brown (Tamerlane Airport Guards), Attia Hosni Attia (Arabic Waiter), Ivaio Kehajov (Dry Cleaning Soldier Posse), Teodor Tsolov (Cab Driver), William Cusack (Tamerlane Caffeinated Soldier)

Assigned by the former U.S. vice president to kill the oil minister of Turaqitan, hitman Brand Hauser goes undercover by pretending to be the chief organizer of a U.S. trade show.

John Cusack, Joan Cusack © First Look

Stephen Rea

Russell Hornsby, Mena Suvari © ThinkFilm

STUCK

(THINKFILM) Producers, Robert Katz, Jay Firestone, Ken Gord, Stuart Gordon; Executive Producers, Sam Grana, John F.S. Laing, Tim McGrath, Andrew Arno; Director/Story, Stuart Gordon; Screenplay, John Strysik; Photography, Denis Maloney; Designer, Craig Lathrop; Costumes, Carol Cutshall, Chris O'Neil; Music, Bobby Johnson; Editor, Andy Horvich; Special Effects Supervisor, Laird McMurray; a Regal Entertainment presentation of an Amicus Entertainment production, in association with Prodigy Pictures, Grana Prods.; American-Canadian; Dolby; Color; Rated R; 94 minutes; Release date: May 30, 2008

Cast

Brandi	**Mena Suvari**
Tom	**Stephen Rea**
Rashid	**Russell Hornsby**
Tanya	**Rukiya Bernard**

Jeffrey Combs (911 Operator), John Dartt (Cop), John Dunsworth (Cabbie), Mauricio Hoyos (Luis), Brian Johnson (Bouncer), Wally MacKinnon (Beat Cop), Patrick McKenna (Joe Lieber), Liam McNamara (Young Man), Marguerite McNeil (Mrs. Pashkewitz), Martin Moreno (Pedro), Buthivy Nou (Gloria), Carolyn Purdy-Gordon (Petersen), R.D. Reid (Manager), Lorena Rincon (Estela), Wayne Robson (Mr. Binckley), Sharlene Royer (Tiffany), Suzanne Short (Receptionist), Lionel Mark Smith (Sam)

Panicking after her car hits a stranger who ends up stuck in her windshield, irresponsible Brandi hides the vehicle in her garage while trying to decide what to do with the suffering man.

Liv Tyler, Laura Margolis © Rogue Pictures

Scott Speedman, Liv Tyler

Gemma Ward, Liv Tyler, Kip Weeks, Scott Speedman, Laura Margolis

THE STRANGERS

(ROGUE) Producers, Doug Davison, Roy Lee, Nathan Kahane; Executive Producers, Kelli Konop, Joe Drake, Sonny Mallhi, Trevor Macy, Marc D. Evans; Director/Screenplay, Bryan Bertino; Photography, Peter Sova; Designer, John D. Kretschmer; Costumes, Susan Kaufman; Music, Tomandandy; Music Supervisor, Sean Kent; Coproducer, Thomas J. Busch; Editor, Kevin Greutert; Casting, Lindsey Hayes Kroeger, David H. Rapaport; an Intrepid Pictures presentation of a Vertigo Entertainment/Mandate Pictures production; Dolby; Technicolor; Rated R; 85 minutes; Release date: May 30, 2008

Cast

Kristen McKay	**Liv Tyler**
James Hoyt	**Scott Speedman**
Dollface	**Gemma Ward**
The Man in the Mask	**Kip Weeks**
Pin-Up Girl	**Laura Margolis**
Mike	**Glenn Howerton**
Mormon Boy	**Alex Fisher, Peter Clayton-Luce**

A young couple, hoping to spend a romantic evening at his family's secluded vacation home, are terrorized by masked visitors.

Scott Speedman

SEX AND THE CITY

(NEW LINE CINEMA) Producers, Michael Patrick King, Sarah Jessica Parker, Darren Star, John Melfi; Executive Producers, Toby Emmerich, Richard Brener, Kathryn Busby, Jonathan Filley; Coproducer, Eric Cyphers; Director/Screenplay, Michael Patrick King; Based on characters from the book by Candace Bushnell and the TV series created by Darren Star; Photography, John Thomas; Designer, Jeremy Conway; Costumes, Patricia Field; Music, Aaron Zigman; Editor, Michael Berenbaum; Casting, Bernard Telsey; a Darren Star production, presented in association with Home Box Office; Dolby; Technicolor; Rated R; 145 minutes; Release date: May 30, 2008

Cast

Carrie Bradshaw	**Sarah Jessica Parker**
Samantha Jones	**Kim Cattrall**
Charlotte York	**Kristin Davis**
Miranda Hobbes	**Cynthia Nixon**
Mr. Big	**Chris Noth**
Enid Frick	**Candice Bergen**
Louise	**Jennifer Hudson**
Steve Brady	**David Eigenberg**
Harry Goldenblatt	**Evan Handler**
Jerry "Smith" Jerrod	**Jason Lewis**
Anthony Marentino	**Mario Cantone**
Magda	**Lynn Cohen**
Stanford Blatch	**Willie Garson**
Therapist	**Joanna Gleason**
Brady Hobbes	**Joseph Pupo**
Lily York Goldenblatt	**Alexandra Fong, Parker Fong**
Twenty-Something Girl Dreaming	**Kerry Bishé**
Twenty-Something Girls	**Polina Frantsena, Kate Rockwell, Amy Flanagan, Celina Carvajal**
Slapping Girl	**Amanda Setton**
Carol, Real Estate Agent	**Ching Valdes-Aran**
Building Agent	**Malcolm Gets**
Auctioneer	**Lorna Kelly**
Baby-Voiced Woman	**Daphne Rubin-Vega**
Vogue Fashion Photographer	**Patrick DeMarchelier**
Vogue Executive	**André Leon Talley**
Vogue Writer	**Plum Sykes**
Vogue Fashion Editor	**Lawren Howell**
Vogue Makeup Artist	**Gucci Westman**
Vogue Hairstylist	**Serge Normant**
Vogue Set Dresser	**Mary Howard**
Flower Delivery Guy	**Dave Bradford**
Dante	**Gilles Marini**

Chris Noth, Sarah Jessica Parker

Monica Mayhem, Michelle Minjung Kim, Aricka Evans, Roxy De Ville (Dante's Girls), Gilbert Cruz (Raoul), Damian Young (Karl), Ricky Aiello (Angry Driver), Rogelio Ramos (Paulo), Rene L. Moreno (Felix), Nati Cano's Mariachi Los Camperos (Themselves), Ricardo Molina (Resort Worker), Annaleigh Ashford (Spoiled Label Queen), Bridget Everett (Drunk Party Girl), Peter Kim (Business Guy), Gidget Gormley (Baby the Dog), Suzanne Cryer (Dog Rescue Woman), Josh Henry (Will), Henriette Mantel, Nancy Shayne (Activists), Kim Shaw (Valentine's Night Waitress), Van Hughes (Cater Waiter), Sara Gettelfinger (Flight Attendant), Bridget Regan (Hostess), Dreama Walker (Upper East Side Waitress), Ruby E. Crawford (Louise's Sister), Henry Strozier (Judge), Lisa Kron (Junior's Waitress), Lin-Manuel Miranda (Felix)

New York journalist Carrie Bradshaw prepares for her long=awaited nuptials to Mr. Big, while her three best friends cope with their own relationships. Based on the HBO series that ran from 1999 to 2004.

Jason Lewis, Kim Cattrall

Candice Bergen

Kristin Davis, Sarah Jessica Parker, Cynthia Nixon, Kim Cattrall
© New Line Cinema

Cynthia Nixon, David Eigenberg

Kristin Davis, Kim Cattrall, Cynthia Nixon

Cynthia Nixon, Kristin Davis, Sarah Jessica Parker, Kim Cattrall

Sarah Jessica Parker, Jennifer Hudson

YOU DON'T MESS WITH THE ZOHAN

(COLUMBIA) Producers, Adam Sandler, Jack Giaraputo; Executive Producers, Barry Bernardi, Robert Smigel; Coproducer, Kevin Grady; Director, Dennis Dugan; Screenplay, Adam Sandler, Robert Smigel, Judd Apatow; Photography, Michael Barrett; Designer, Perry Andelin Blake; Costumes, Ellen Lutter; Music, Rupert Gregson-Williams; Music Supervisors, Michael Dilbeck, Brooks Arthur; Editor, Tom Costain; Visual Effects Supervisor, Ryan Tudhope; Casting, Randi Hiller, Sarah Halley Finn; a Happy Madison production, presented in association with Relativity Media; Dolby; Panavision; Deluxe color; Rated PG-13; 113 minutes; Release date: June 6, 2008

Adam Sandler, Lainie Kazan

Cast

Zohan	**Adam Sandler**
Phantom	**John Turturro**
Dalia	**Emmanuelle Chriqui**
Michael	**Nick Swardson**
Gail	**Lainie Kazan**
Oori	**Ido Mosseri**
Salim	**Rob Schneider**
James	**Dave Matthews**
Walbridge	**Michael Buffer**

Charlotte Rae (Mrs. Greenhouse), Sayed Badreya (Hamdi), Daoud Heidami (Nasi), Kevin Nealon (Kevin), Robert Smigel (Yosi), Dina Doronne (Zohan's Mother), Shelley Berman (Zohan's Father), Chris Rock (Taxi Driver), Mariah Carey, John McEnroe, George Takei, Bruce Vilanch (Themselves), John Paul DeJoria (Paul Mitchell), Alec Mapa (Claude), Ahmed Ahmed (Waleed), Ben Wise (Yitzhak), John Farley (Tom), Joseph Marshak (Pinchas), Guri Weinberg (Aharon), Danny A. Abeckaser (Ze'ev), Ido Ezra (Hassan), Mousa Kraish (Bashir), Roni Levy (Ephraim), Reuven Bar-Yotam (Levi), Barry Livingston (Gray Kleibolt), Rick Gifford (Philip), Daniel Browning Smith (Real Estate Agent), Tyler Spindel (Doorman), Julia Wolov, Dana Min Goodman (Mariah's Assistants), Todd Holland (Fred), Kevin Grady (Coleman), Bobby Tisdale (Skizzy), Herzl Tobey (Commander), Ori Pfeffer (2nd Commander), Alex Luria (Koby), Guy Oseary (Avi), Yinon Sapir (Danny), Donna Feldman (Michal), Yamit Sol (Dorit), Naama Nativ (Sara), Dennis Dugan (Homeless Guy), Gerry Del Sol (Exploded Shop Owner), Shulie Cowen (Debbie), Maysoon Zayed (Nadira), Helen Siff (Mrs. Skitzer), Betty Murphy (Mrs. Haynes), Cynthia Frost (Mrs. Paulson), Anna Berger, Susan Grace, Bunny Levine, Norma Michaels, Marjorie Loomis, Carol Schlanger, Edith Wolfrey, Phoebe Dorin (Old Ladies in Salon), Lina So (Hip Salon Receptionist), Eloise DeJoria (Blonde at Salon), Vanessa Long (Catty Hairdresser), Donielle Artese (African American Salon Owner), Adria Tennor (Kids' Salon Owner), Blake Bertrand (Little Boy), Sid Ganis (Doctor), Laurie Meghan Phelps (Plus Size Girl at Disco), Kenneth Greenaway (DJ), Constance Barron, Kristen Lowman, Penelope Windust, Kathleen Noone (Women in Cab), Christopher Innvar (Angry Tall Driver), Ray Garvey (Truck Driver), Barbara Ann Davison (Dog Owner), Eric Lamonsoff (Hamdi's Passenger), Connor Wiles (Boy Customer),Jennifer De Minco (Arguing Customer), Nicole Bennett (Walbridge's Girlfriend), Edmund Lyndeck (Pharmacist), Lily Javaherpour (Inaz), Kristina Haddad (Hamdi's Wife), Larry Marko (Phantom's Trainer), Anne Marie Howard (Reporter), Veerta Motiani (Beach Girl), Billy Concha (Kayaker), Marco Kahn (Terrorist with Hand), Saman Sagheb, Latif Marotti, Christian Reeve (Disco Merchants),

Adam Sandler

Israeli agent Zohan fakes his own death so that he can move to America to pursue his true ambition of styling hair.

John Turturro, Adam Sandler, Emmanuelle Chriqui
© Columbia Pictures

Crane, Tigress, Monkey, Mantis, Viper

Po, Master Shifu

Tai Lung © DreamWorks

KUNG FU PANDA

(PARAMOUNT/DREAMWORKS) Producer, Melissa Cobb; Executive Producer, Bill Damaschke; Coproducers/Screenplay, Jonathan Aibel, Glenn Berger; Directors, John Stevenson, Mark Osborne; Story, Ethan Reiff, Cyrus Voris; Designer, Raymond Zibach; Art Director, Tang K. Heng; Music, Hans Zimmer, John Powell; Editor, Clare Knight; Visual Effects Supervisor, Markus Manninen; Head of Character Animation, Dan Wagner; Character TD Supervisor, Nathan Loofbourrow; Supervising Animator/Fight Choreographer, Rodolphe Guenoden; Casting, Leslee Fedlman; Dolby; Widescreen; Technicolor; Rated PG; 91 minutes; Release date: June 5, 2008

Voice cast

Po	**Jack Black**
Master Shifu	**Dustin Hoffman**
Tigress	**Angelina Jolie**
Tai Lung	**Ian McShane**
Monkey	**Jackie Chan**
Mantis	**Seth Rogen**
Viper	**Lucy Liu**
Crane	**David Cross**
Oogway	**Randall Duk Kim**
Mr. Ping	**James Hong**
Zeng	**Dan Fogler**
Commander Vachir	**Michael Clarke Duncan**

Wayne Knight (Gang Boss), Kyle Gass (KG Shaw), JR Reed (JR Shaw), Laura Kightlinger (Awed Ninja), Tanya Haden (Smitten Bunny), Stephen Kearin (Gong Pig/Grateful Bunny), Mark Osborne (Pig Patron), John Stevenson (Rhino Guard), Jeremy Shipp (Blind Gator), Melissa Cobb (Bunny Mom), Kent Osborne (Pig Fan), Emily Robison, Stephanie Harvey (Bunny Fans), Riley Osborne (Baby Tai Lung)

A bumbling Panda is shocked to learn that he is destined to be the Dragon Warrior, a martial arts virtuoso fated to save his community from evil.

This film received an Oscar nomination for animated feature.

Right: *Po, Master Shifu*

THE INCREDIBLE HULK

(UNIVERSAL) Producers, Avi Arad, Gale Anne Hurd, Kevin Feige; Executive Producers, Stan Lee, David Maisel, Jim Van Wyck; Director, Louis Leterrier; Screen Story/Screenplay, Zak Penn; Based on the Marvel comic book by Stan Lee and Jack Kirby; Photography, Peter Menzies, Jr.; Designer, Kirk M. Petruccelli; Music, Craig Armstrong; Music Supervisor, Dave Jordan; Editors, John Wright, Rick Shaine, Vincent Tabaillon; Associate Producer, Stephen Broussard; Visual Effects Supervisor, Kurt Williams; Casting, Laray Mayfield; a Marvel Entertainment presentation of a Marvel Studios production, a Valhalla Motion Pictures production; Dolby; Panavision; Technicolor; Rated PG-13; 112 minutes; Release date: June 13, 2008

Abomination, Hulk

Cast

Bruce Banner	**Edward Norton**
Betty Ross	**Liv Tyler**
Emil Blonsky	**Tim Roth**
General "Thunderbolt" Ross	**William Hurt**
Samuel Sterns	**Tim Blake Nelson**
Leonard	**Ty Burrell**
Major Kathleen Sparr	**Christina Cabot**
General Joe Geller	**Peter Menash**

Lou Ferrigno (Voice of the Hulk/Security Guard), Paul Soles (Stanley), Debora Nascimento (Martina),Greg Bryk, Chris Owens, Alan Vrkljan, Adrian Hein, John MacDonald (Commandos), Shaun McComb (Helicopter Soldier), Simon Wong (Grad Student), Pedro Salvin (Tough Guy Leader), Julio Cesar Torrest Dantas, Raimundo Camargo Nascimento, Nick Alachiotis (Tough Guys), Jason Burke (Communications Officer), Grant Nickalls (Helicopter Pilot), Joris Jarsky, Arnold Pinnock (Soldiers), Tig Fong, Jason Hunter (Cops), Maxwell McCabe-Lokos (Cab Driver), David Collins (Medical Technician), John Carvalho (Plant Manager), Robin Wilcock (Sniper), Imali Perera (Faculty Member), Wayne Robson (Boat Captain), Billy Parrott (Security Guard), Javier Lambert (Guatemalan Trucker), Martin Starr (Computer Nerd), Chris Ratz (Young Guy), Todd Hofley (Apache Helicopter Pilot), Fabio Dorea (Brazilian Liaison Officer), Joe La Loggia, Aaron Berg, David Miller, Tre Smith, Moses Nyarko (Soldiers), Tamsen McDonough (Colleague), Jim Annan (Intelligence Officer), Michael Kenneth Williams (Harlem Bystander), Roberto Bakker (Market Vendor), Ruru Sacha (Supply Driver), James Downing (Army Base Doctor), Rickson Gracie (Aikido Instructor), Stephen Gartner (Ross' Soldier), Nicholas Rose (McGee), Genelle Williams (Terrified Gal), P.J. Kerr (Wilson), Jee-Yun Lee (Reporter), Desmond Campbell (Gunner), Deshaun Clarke (Little Boy), Tony Nappo (Brave Cop), Russell Yuen (FBI Agent), Carlos A. Gonzalez, Anderson Paz (BOPE Officers), Yan Regis (Medic Soldier), Stephen Broussard (Handsome Soldier), Robert Morse (Command Van Soldier), Matt Purdy (Ross' Aide), Lenka Matuska (Medical Assistant), Scott Magee (Humvee Driver), Wes Berger (Sterns Lab Soldier), Avi Phillips (Student in Lab), Carla Nascimento (Large Woman), Krista Vendy (Bartender), Mila Stromboni (Hopscotch Girl), Stan Lee (Victim)

Edward Norton

As Bruce Banner hunts desperately for a cure for the gamma radiation that has poisoned his cells and turned him into the Hulk, General Ross hopes to track him down and exploit his powers.

Hulk, Tim Roth

Left: *Liv Tyler, William Hurt* © Universal Studios

Christopher Isherwood, Don Bachardy

Don Bachardy, Christopher Isherwood © Zeitgeist

A LOVE STORY ... CHRIS & DON

(ZEITGEIST) a.k.a. *Chris & Don: A Love Story*; Producers, Julia Scott, Tina Mascara, Guido Santi, James White; Executive Producers, James White, Andrew Herwitz; Directors/Editors, Guido Santi, Tina Mascara; Photography, Ralph Q. Smith; Designer, Francisco Stohr; Music, Miriam Cutler; Associate Producers, Signe Johnson, Martina Battisch; Character Animation, Katrina Swanger, Kristina Swanger; Photo Sequences, Rodney Ascher; Narrator of Isherwood's Diaries, Michael York; Stereo; Color; DV; Not rated; 90 minutes; Release date: June 13, 2008. Documentary on the successful relationship between author Christopher Isherwood and his younger partner, artist Don Bachardy.

With
Don Bachardy, Katherine Bucknell, Jim Berg, James P. White, Leslie Caron, Sara Hodson, John Boorman, Liza Minnelli

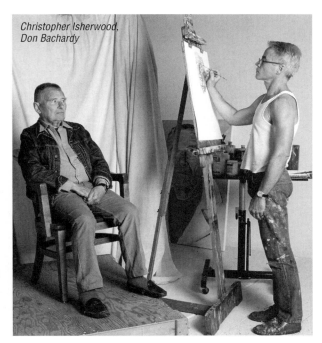

Christopher Isherwood, Don Bachardy

Right: *Don Bachardy, Christopher Isherwood*

THE HAPPENING

(20TH CENTURY FOX) Producers, M. Night Shyamalan, Sam Mercer, Barry Mendel; Executive Producers, Roger Birnbaum, Gary Barber, Ronnie Screwvala, Zarina Screwvala; Coproducers, Jose L. Rodriguez, Deven Khote; Director/Screenplay, M. Night Shyamalan; Photography, Tak Fujimoto; Designer, Jeannine Oppewall; Costumes, Betsy Heimann; Music, James Newton Howard; Editor, Conrad Buff; Visual Effects Supervisors, Ed Hirsh, David Ebner; Special Effects Makeup, Quantum creation FX; Casting, Douglas Aibel, Stephanie Holbrook; a Blinding Edge Pictures production, presented in association with UTV Motion Pictures and Spyglass Entertainment; Dolby; Deluxe color; Rated R; 89 minutes; Release date: June 13, 2008

Cast

Elliot Moore	**Mark Wahlberg**
Alma Moore	**Zooey Deschanel**
Julian	**John Leguizamo**
Mrs. Jones	**Betty Buckley**
Nursery Owner	**Frank Collison**
Jess	**Ashlyn Sanchez**

Spencer Breslin (Josh), Robert Bailey, Jr. (Jared), Jeremy Strong (Private Auster), Alan Ruck (Principal), Victoria Clark (Nursery Owner's Wife), M. Night Shyamalan (Voice of Joey), Alison Folland (Woman Reading on Bench with Hair Pin), Kristen Connolly (Woman Reading on Bench), Cornell Womack (Construction Foreman), Curtis McLarin (Construction Crew Member), Robert Lenzi (Jake), Derege Harding (Train Conductor), Kerry O'Malley (Woman on Cell Phone), Shayna Levine (Teenage Girl in Jeep), Stéphane Debac (French Bicyclist), Cyrille Thouvenin (French Bicyclist's Friend), Babita Hariani (Medical Correspondent), Alicia Taylor (U.S. Reporter), Edward James Hyland (Professor Kendall Wallace), Armand Schultz (Talk Show Host), Stephen Singer (Dr. Ross), Sophie Burke (Student Named Laura), Alex Van Kooy (Boy in Class), Charlie Saxton (Student Named Dylan), Kathy Hart (Vice Principal), Lisa Gunn (Teacher in Auditorium), Rick Foster (Railway Police Officer), Don Castro (Philadelphia Police Officer), Bill Chemerka (Taxi Driver), Jann Ellis (Older Woman with Dog), Whitney Sugarman, Mary Ellen Driscoll, Eoin O'Shea, Michael Quinlan, Lyman Chen (Passengers), Greg Wood (Passenger at Counter), Peter Appel (Diner Owner), Brian O'Halloran (Jeep Driver), Megan Mazaika, Richard Chew (Jeep Passengers), Keith E. Bullard (Man in Crowd at Crossroads), Joel de la Fuente (Realtor), Ashley Brimfield (Woman in Group), Mara Hobel (Woman with Hands Over Ears), James Breen (Farmhouse Voice), Carmen Bitoni (Mangled Construction Worker), Brian Anthony Wilson (Arguing Man in Crowd), Greg Smith Aldridge (Zoo Employee), Ukee Washington (Local News Anchor), John Ottavino (Network News Anchor), Sid Doherty (Radio News Anchor), Wes Heywood (Radio Voice), Nancy Sokerka (Radio Caller Fay), Julia Yorks (Young Woman Voice on Phone)

As an unexplainable force that causes its victims to commit acts of self-mutilation and suicide begins wiping out civilization, science teacher Elliott Moore and a small band of survivors try to escape its path.

Zooey Deschanel, Mark Wahlberg © 20th Century Fox

Justin Timberlake, Mike Myers © Paramount Pictures

THE LOVE GURU

(PARAMOUNT) Producers, Mike Myers, Michael de Luca; Executive Producers, Gary Barber, Roger Birnbaum, Donald J. Lee, Jr.; Coproducer, Josh Bratman; Director, Marco Schnabel; Screenplay, Mike Myers, Graham Gordy; Photography, Peter Deming; Designer, Charles Wood; Costumes, Karen Patch; Music, George S. Clinton; Music Supervisor, John Houlihan; Associate Producers, Graham Gordy, Sean Gannet; Casting, Kathleen Chopin; a Nomoneyfun Films/Michael de Luca production, presented in association with Spyglass Entertainment; Dolby; Panavision; Deluxe color; Rated PG-13; 87 minutes; Release date: June 20, 2008

Cast

Guru Pitka/Himself	**Mike Myers**
Jane Bullard	**Jessica Alba**
Jacques Grande	**Justin Timberlake**
Darren Roanoke	**Romany Malco**
Coach Punch Cherkov	**Verne Troyer**
Prudence Roanoke	**Meagan Good**

Omid Djalili (Guru Satchabigknoba), Manu Narayan (Rajneesh), John Oliver (Dick Pants), Stephen Colbert (Jay Kell), Jim Gaffigan (Trent Lueders), Ben Kingsley (Guru Tugginmypudha), Telma Hopkins (Lillian Roanoke), Jessica Simpson, Kanye West, Deepak Chopra, Rob Blake, Mariska Hargitay, Val Kilmer (Themselves), Daniel Tosh (Cowboy Hat), Rob Huebel (Frat Guy), Rob Gfroerer (Sickly Nerd), Rob Cohen (Nerd), Linda Kash (Reporter), Bob Bainborough (Assistant Coach), Gotham Chopra (Deepak, Early Twenties), Suresh John (Indian Man), Trevor Heins (Young Pitka), Jaan Padda (Young Deepak), Sean Cullen (Referee), Mike "Nug" Nahrgang (Angry Fan), Matt Baram (EMT #1), Boyd Banks (Medic #2), Samantha Bee (Cinnabon Cashier), Garry Robbins (Biker), Peter Schoelier (Uncle Jack), Ben Gans (Goal Post Judge), Taylor Flood, Alexia Filippeos (11-Year-Old Girls), Shakti Kupil (Sanjay), Graham Gordy (DJ), Michelle Marshall (Oprah Winfrey Voice Double)

Worried that their star player's depression over his marital woes will have its effect on the team, the Toronto Maple Leafs hire guru Pitka to help out.

Madison Davenport, Abigail Breslin, Brieanne Jansen © Picturehouse

Max Thieriot

Stanley Tucci, Joan Cusack

KIT KITTREDGE: AN AMERICAN GIRL

(PICTUREHOUSE) Producers, Elaine Goldsmith-Thomas, Lisa Gillan, Ellen L. Brothers, Julie Goldstein; Executive Producers, Julia Roberts, Marisa Yeres; Coproducers, Terry Gould, Jodi Goldberg; Director, Patricia Rozeman; Screenplay, Ann Peacock; Based on the Kit Kittredge stories by Valerie Tripp; Photography, David Boyd; Designer, Peter Cosco; Costumes, Trysha Bakker; Music, Joseph Vitarelli; Editor, Julie Rogers; Casting, Nancy Nayor; a Goldsmith-Thomas production, in association with Red Om Films; presented with New Line Cinema in association with HBO Films; Dolby; FotoKem color; Rated G; 100 minutes; Release date: June 20, 2008

Cast

Margaret "Kit" Kittredge	**Abigail Breslin**
Jack Kittredge	**Chris O'Donnell**
Margaret Kittredge	**Julia Ormond**
Miss Lucinda Bond	**Joan Cusack**
Ruthie Smithens	**Madison Davenport**
Louise Howard	**Glenne Headley**
Miss May Dooley	**Jane Krakowski**
Stirling Howard IV	**Zach Mills**
Mr. Pennington	**Colin Mochrie**
Mr. Gibson	**Wallace Shawn**
Will Shepherd	**Max Thieriot**
Jefferson Jasper Berk	**Stanley Tucci**
Willow Smith	**Countee Garby**
Freidreich	**Dylan Scott Smith**
Billy Peabody	**Douglas Nyback**

Dylan Roberts (Reporter), Martin Doyle (Teacher), Martin Roach (Hobo Doctor), Austin Macdonald (Roger), Brieanne Jansen (Frances Stone), Erin Hilgartner (Florence Stone), Peter MacNeill (Sheriff), Erin McMurtry, Joanna Swan (Garden Club Ladies), Eddie Huband (Blonde Bully), Frank McAnulty (Wallet Man), Anna Louise Richardson (Soup Kitchen Woman), David Talbot (Neighbor), Darryn Lucio (Deputy), John Healy (Mr. Stone), Colette Kendall (Mrs. Stone), Quincy Bullen (Newsboy), Elisabeth Perez, Jordan Rackley (Classmates), Eddie Graff (Sax-Playing Hobo)

Ten-year-old Kit Kittredge's seemingly idyllic world in 1934 Cincinnati comes crumbling apart when her family is affected by the Depression.

Abigail Breslin, Julia Ormond, Chris O'Donnell

GET SMART

(WARNER BROS.) Producers, Andrew Lazar, Charles Roven, Alex Gartner, Michael Ewing; Executive Producers, Peter Segal, Steve Carell, Brent O'Connor, Jimmy Miller, Dana Goldberg, Bruce Berman; Coproducer, Alan G. Glazer; Director, Peter Segal; Screenplay, Tom J. Astle, Matt Ember; Based on characters created by Mel Brooks and Buck Henry; Photography, Dean Semler; Designer, Wynn Thomas; Costumes, Deborah Scott; Music, Trevor Rabin; Editor, Richard Pearson; Visual Effects Supervisor, Joe Bauer; Choreographer, Jamal Sims; Casting, Roger Mussenden; a Mosaic Media Group/Mad Chance/Callahan Filmworks production, presented in association with Village Roadshow Pictures; Dolby; Technicolor; Rated PG-13; 110 minutes; Release date: June 20, 2008

Alan Arkin, Steve Carell

Cast

Maxwell Smart, Agent 86	**Steve Carell**
Agent 99	**Anne Hathaway**
Agent 23	**Dwayne Johnson**
The Chief	**Alan Arkin**
Siegfried	**Terence Stamp**
Agent 91	**Terry Crews**
Larabee	**David Koechner**
The President	**James Caan**
Agent 13	**Bill Murray**
Hymie	**Patrick Warburton**
Bruce	**Masi Oka**
Lloyd	**Nate Torrence**
Shtarker	**Ken Davitian**
Krstic	**David S. Lee**
Dalip	**Dalip Singh**
Vice President	**Geoff Pierson**
Judy	**Kelly Karbacz**
Russian Bad Guy	**Arthur Darbinyan**
Air Marshal	**Bill Romanowski**
Russian Guy in Bathroom	**Mark Ivanir**
Max's Dance Partner	**Lindsay Hollister**

Cedric Yarbrough, James Caan, Alan Arkin, Anne Hathaway, Dwayne Johnson

Dimitri Diatchenko (Russian Underling), Richard V. Licata (Russian Leader), Greg Joung Paik (North Korean General), Joey Yu (North Korean Soldier), Mike Akrawi, John Abiskaron (Arab Men), Kerry Lai Fatt (Tour Guide), David A. Parker (Agent 50), Bonnie Hellman (Karen), John Farley (Agent 38), Jonathan Loughran (Orange Team Guy), Felisha Terrell, Jeff Tanner (Control Assistants), Jasper Pendergrass (Budweiser Delivery Guy), Carl Crevier, David Schaap (Restaurant Agents), Peter Weireter, Thomas Garner, Danielle Bisutti (Airline Passengers), Jessica Barth (Flight Attendant), David Fabrizio (Pilot), John Eddins (Co-Pilot), Alex Kudrytsky (Russian Farmhand), Tatyana Kaboulova, Moshana Halbert (Pretty Women at Party), Sergey Priselkov (Russian Farmer), Jane Gilchrist (Bakery Counter Woman), Todd Sherry (KAOS Office Worker), Davud Aranovich (Russian Son), Ivy Bethune (Russian Mother), Larry Miller, Kevin Nealon (CIA Agents), Blake Clark (General), Cedric Yarbrough (Tate), James Moses Black (Control Prison Guard), Bernie Kopell (Opel Driver), Michael Peter Catanzarite, Tim DeKay (Secret Service Agents), Jerry Sherman (Conductor), Matthew Glave (Secret Service Agent Driver), Brad Grunberg (Golfer), Leonard Stern (Cesna Pilot), Sean Segal (Kid in Minivan), Karri Turner (Mom in Minivan), Stephen Dunham (Secret Service Commander), Oliver & Daisy (Fang), Ryan Seacrest (Himself)

Inept but intrepid Maxwell Smart finally gets his chance to prove his worth as an agent, when he is sent on a mission with Agent 99 to stop the nefarious Siegfried and KAOS from world domination. Based on the NBC/CBS series that ran from 1965-70 and starred Don Adams, Barbara Feldon, and Edward Platt.

Anne Hathaway, Steve Carell © Warner Bros.

Dwayne Johnson, Steve Carell

Nate Torrence, Masi Oka

Steve Carell

Steve Carell, Anne Hathaway

Terence Stamp, Ken Davitian

Anne Hathaway, Steve Carell

WANTED

(UNIVERSAL) Producers, Marc Platt, Jim Lemley, Jason Netter, Iain Smith; Executive Producers, Adam Siegel, Marc Silvestri, Roger Birnbaum, Gary Barber; Coproducers, Mark Millar, J. G. Jones, Chris Carlise; Director, Timur Bekmambetov; Screenplay, Michael Brandt, Derek Haas, Chris Morgan; Story, Michael Brandt, Derek Haas; Based on the series of comic books by Mark Millar and J.G. Jones; Photography, Mitchell Amundsen; Designer, John Myhre; Costumes, Varya Avdyushko; Music, Danny Elfman; Music Supervisor, Kathy Nelson; Editor, David Brenner; Stunts, Mic Rodgers, Nick Gillard, Martin Hub, Rick Lefevour; Fight Coordinator, C.C. Smiff; Visual Effects Supervisors, Stefen Fangmeier, Jon Farhat; Casting, Mindy Marin; Dolby; Panavision; Deluxe color; Rated R; 110 minutes; Release date: June 27, 2008

Cast
Wesley Gibson	**James McAvoy**
Sloan	**Morgan Freeman**
Fox	**Angelina Jolie**
Pekwarsky	**Terence Stamp**
Cross	**Thomas Kretschmann**
The Gunsmith	**Common**
Cathy	**Kristen Hager**
The Repairman	**Marc Warren**
Mr. X	**David Patrick O'Hara**
The Exterminator	**Konstantin Khabensky**
The Butcher	**Dato Bakhtadze**

Chris Pratt (Barry), Lorna Scott (Janice), Sophiya Haque (Puja), Brian Caspe (The Pharmacist), Mark O'Neal (Co-Worker), Bridget McManus (Check-Out Girl)

Mild-mannered Wesley Gibson is recruited by a secret organization to be a highly specialized trained assassin.

This film received Oscar nominations for sound mixing and sound editing.

James McAvoy, Common, Angelina Jolie

James McAvoy

Angelina Jolie © Universal Studios

Right: Thomas Kretschmann

Brittany Snow, Matthew Broderick © Magnolia

FINDING AMANDA

(MAGNOLIA) Producers, Wayne Rice, Richard Heller; Executive Producer, Leslie Tolan; Coproducer, Mark Benton Johnson; Director/Screenplay, Peter Tolan; Photography, Tom Houghton; Designer, Erich Schultz; Costumes, Alexis Scott; Music, Christopher Tyng; Editor, Paul Anderson; Casting, Monika Mikkelsen; a Capacity Pictures and Cloudland Films production; Dolby; Widescreen; Color; Rated R; 96 minutes; Release date: June 27, 2008

Cast

Taylor Mendon	**Matthew Broderick**
Amanda	**Brittany Snow**
Lorraine Mendon	**Maura Tierney**
Michael Henry	**Steve Coogan**
Greg	**Peter Facinelli**
Himself	**Ed Begley, Jr.**

Jenni Blong (Paula), Edward Carnevale (Beer Guy), Victoria De Mare (Hot Club Goer #1), Bill Fagerbakke (Larry), Patrick Fischler (Kevin), Jennifer Hall (Wendy), Brian Jones (Bellman), Signe Kiesel (Dealer), Colette Kilroy (Front Desk Woman), Bobby C. King (Casino Security Guard), J.P. Manoux (Tony), Allie McCulloch (Eve), Jack McGee (Guy in Racebook), Kate Micucci (Thin Girl), Katy Mixon (Girl #1), Brecken Palmer, Bridger Palmer (Larry's Twins), Michael Proctor (Hot Guy), Vitta Quinn (Vegas Hooker), Mike Rademaekers (Bearded Man), Mighty Rasta (BV), Jennifer Rau (Whisper), Daniel Roebuck (Link), Charley Rossman (Jerry, Security), LeeAnn Taylor (Cocktail Waitress), Atticus Todd (Gene), Tyler Tuione (TJ), Sam Vance (Bartender), Luke Van Pelt (Jack), Allan Wasserman (Psychiatrist)

TV producer Taylor Mendon, whose life has been unraveling because of his addiction to drinking and gambling, is sent to Las Vegas to retrieve his errant niece, who has become a hooker.

TRUMBO

(SAMUEL GOLDWYN) Producers, Will Battersby, Tory Tunnell, Alan Klingstein, David Viola; Executive Producer, Jim Kohlberg; Coproducer, Kurt Engfehr; Co-Executive Producers, Alan Hruska, Stelio Kitralakis; Director, Peter Askin; Screenplay, Christopher Trumbo, based on his play; Photography, Frank Prinzi, Jonathan Furmanski, Fred Murphy, Chris Norr; Designer, Stephanie Carroll; Costumes, Sarah Beers; Music, Robert Miller; Editor, Kurt Engfehr; Archival Supervisor, Ariana Garfinkel; Associate Producers, Ariana Garfinkel; Kirstin Kopp; a Safehouse Pictures/Filbert Steps Prods. presentation; Stereo; Color/black and white; DV; Rated PG-13; 96 minutes; Release date: June 27, 2008. Documentary on the effect the blacklist had on Hollywood screenwriter Dalton Trumbo; with Emanuel Azenberg, Walter Bernstein, Larry Ceplair, Kirk Douglas, Peter Hanson, Dustin Hoffman, Lew Irwin, Kate Lardner, Helen Manfull, Victor Navasky, Jean Rouverol, Christopher Trumbo, Mitzi Trumbo.

Trumbo's Letters Performed by:
Joan Allen, Brian Dennehy, Michael Douglas, Paul Giamatti, Nathan Lane, Josh Lucas, Liam Neeson, David Strathairn, Donald Sutherland.

Dalton Trumbo

Michael Douglas © Samuel Goldwyn

HANCOCK

(COLUMBIA) Producers, Akiva Goldsman, Michael Mann, Will Smith, James Lassiter; Executive Producers, Ian Bryce, Jonathan Mostow, Richard Saperstein; Coproducer, Allegra Clegg; Director, Peter Berg; Screenplay, Vy Vincent Ngo, Vince Gilligan; Photography, Tobias Schliessler; Designer, Neil Spisak; Costumes, Louise Mingenbach; Music, John Powell; Music Supervisor, George Drakoulias; Editors, Paul Rubell, Colby Parker, Jr.; Visual Effects Designer, John Dykstra; Special Effects Supervisor, John Frazier; Special Visual Effects and Animation, Sony Pictures Imageworks; Stunts, Simon Crane, Wade Eastwood; Casting, Francine Maisler; a Blue Light/Weed Road Pictures/Overbrook Entertainment production, presented in association with Relativity Media; Dolby; Panavision; Deluxe color; Rated PG-13; 92 minutes; Release date: July 2, 2008

Will Smith

Cast

John Hancock	**Will Smith**
Mary Embrey	**Charlize Theron**
Ray Embrey	**Jason Bateman**
Kenneth "Red" Parker, Jr.	**Eddie Marsan**
Jeremy	**Johnny Galecki**
Mike	**Thomas Lennon**
Aaron Embrey	**Jae Head**
Man Mountain	**David Mattey**
Matrix	**Maetrix Fitten**
Hottie	**Hayley Marie Norman**

Dorothy Cecchi (Woman in Dive Bar), Michelle Lemon (Girl at Bus Bench), Akiva Goldsman, Michael Mann, Brad Leland, Trieu Tran (Executives), Darrell Foster (Police Sergeant), Liz Wicker (Cop), Taylor Gilbert (Hostage), Caroll Tohme (Clapping Guy), Barbara Ali (Woman under Ray's Car), Ryan Radis, Elizabeth Dennehy, Darren Dowler (Rail Crossing Crowd), John Frazier (Train Engineer), Daeg Faerch (Michel), Matt King, Martin Magdaleno (Neighborhood Kids), Ronald W. Howard (Man on Street), Gregg Daniel (Police Chief), Nancy Grace (Herself), Atticus Shaffer (Boy at Bus Bench), Aaron Henderson, Huy Nguyen, Mary-Jessica Pitts, Kalee St. Clair (Ice Cream Truck Patrons), Donald Gibb, Ralph Richeson, Allan Havey, Tim Brennen, Anthony Ledesma, Steven Pierce, Dominic Prampin, Daniel Quinn, Mars Crain, Jack Axelrod, Eddie J. Fernandez, Martin Klebba (Convicts), Richard W. Gallegos, Marc Geschwind, Rob Maron (Angry Men), Aisha Jau (Sunglass Woman), Pritam Singh (Sikh), Cher Calvin, Shea Curry (Reporters), Bill McMullen (Valet), Antwoin Hagwood (Clapping Guy), Mike Epps (Criminal)

Will Smith, Charlize Theron © Columbia Pictures

After dissipated, sarcastic superhero John Hancock once again causes mayhem in his sloppy efforts to fight for justice, PR wiz Ray Embrey steps in to help change his soiled image.

Will Smith, Jason Bateman

Liz Wicker, Will Smith

Famke Janssen, Ben Kingsley

Mary-Kate Olsen, Ben Kingsley

Ben Kingsley, Josh Peck

THE WACKNESS

(SONY CLASSICS) Producers, Keith Calder, Felipe Marino, Joe Neurauter; Coproducer, Brian Udovich; Director/Screenplay, Jonathan Levine; Photography, Petra Korner; Designer, Annie Spitz; Costumes, Michael Clancy; Music, David Torn; Music Supervisor, Jim Black; Editor, Josh Noyes; Casting, Joanna Colbert, Richard Mento; an Occupant Films and SBK Pictures presentation; Dolby; Color; Rated R; 110 minutes; Release date: July 3, 2008

Cast

Dr. Squires	**Ben Kingsley**
Kristin Squires	**Famke Janssen**
Luke Shapiro	**Josh Peck**
Stephanie	**Olivia Thirlby**
Union	**Mary-Kate Olsen**
Eleanor	**Jane Adams**
Percy	**Method Man**
Justin	**Aaron Yoo**
Mrs. Shapiro	**Talia Balsam**
Mr. Shapiro	**David Wohl**
Grandpa Shapiro	**Bob Dishy**
Grandma Shapiro	**Joanna Merlin**

Shannon Briggs (Body Guard #1), Roy Milton Davis (Homeless Man), Alexander Flores (Kid in Bar), Ken Marks (Oliver), Kiah Fredricks (Police Officer #1), Robert Armstrong (Principal Edwards), Douglas J. Aguirre (Desk Officer in the Prison), Nicole Berger, Dawn Noel Pignuola, Natalie R. Ridley (Fly Girls), Charlene Biton (College Student), Jack Caruso (Arresting Police Officer), Peter Conboy (Man on Park Bench), Sean Dillon (Gruden), Nick Schutt (Albert)

A pot dealing teen hopes his life has found some meaning when he falls in love with the wizened stepdaughter of his therapist.

Olivia Thirlby, Josh Peck © Sony Classics

DIMINISHED CAPACITY

(IFC FIRST TAKE) Producers, Celine Rattray, Galt Niederhoffer, Daniel Taplin Lundberg; Executive Producers, Bill Benenson, Pamela Hirsch, Bruce Lunsford, Ed Hart, Eric Warren Goldman, Scott Hanson, John Allen; Coproducers, Hollise Gersh, Edward Gersh, Marilyn G. Haft, Sherwood Kiraly, John Gilroy, Joy Goodwin; Director, Terry Kinney; Screenplay, Sherwood Kiraly, based on his novel; Photography, Vanja Cernjul; Designer, Dan Davis; Costumes, Sarah Holden; Music, Robert Burger; Music Supervisor, Tracy McKnight; Editor, Tim Streeto; a Plum Pictures presentation, in association with Hart-Lunsford Films, Benedek Films and Steppenwolf Films; Dolby; Color; HD; Not rated; 87 minutes; Release date: July 4, 2008

Cast

Coope	**Matthew Broderick**
Uncle Rollie	**Alan Alda**
Charlotte	**Virginia Madsen**
Mad Dog McClure	**Dylan Baker**
Lee Vivyan	**Bobby Cannavale**
Stan	**Louis C.K.**
Dillon	**Jimmy Bennett**
Wendell Kendall	**Tom Aldredge**
Belle Tyke	**Lois Smith**
Donny Prine	**Jim True-Frost**

Carolyn Baeumler (Diane McClure), P.J. Brown (Reese), Brad Haugen, Joseph Kwasny, David Corbett (Chicago Cubs Security), Bhavana Kundanmal (Dr. Gupta), Mary Jo Mandula, Paul Mixon (Tribune Employees), Gentry Miller (Tribune Security Guard), Anthony Del Negro (Baseball Patron), Heidi Neurauter (Irene Sasso), Zsofia Otvos, Karla Strum (Riverwalk Girls), David Martin Rose (Frank "Wildfire" Schulte), Evan Shafran (Baseball Card Collector)

A Chicago journalist recovering from a recent head injury reluctantly journeys to the boondocks to take care of his increasingly erratic uncle Rollie, who holds a valuable baseball card in his possession.

Matthew Broderick, Alan Alda © IFC Films

Conchata Ferrell, Scott Prendergast

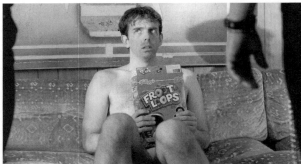

Scott Prendergast © Regent

KABLUEY

(REGENT) Producers, Jeff Balis, Rhodes Rader, Rick Rosenthal, Gary Dean Simpson, Douglas J. Sutherland; Executive Producers, Sarah Feinberg, Nancy Stephens; Coproducer, Ryan Peterson; Director/Screenplay, Scott Prendergast; Photography, Michael Lohmann; Designer, Walter Barnett; Costumes, Lisa Barnes; Music, Roddy Bottum; Editor, Lawrence Maddox; Casting, Anne McCarthy, Jay Scully; a West of Midnight presentation of a Whitewater Films production; Dolby; Color; Rated PG-13; 86 minutes; Release date: July 4, 2008

Cast

Leslie	**Lisa Kudrow**
Salman	**Scott Prendergast**
Suze	**Teri Garr**
Betty	**Christine Taylor**
Brad	**Jeffrey Dean Morgan**

Chris Parnell (Frank, the Grocery Store Manager), Conchata Ferrell (Kathleen), Angela Sarafyan (Ramona), Patricia Buckley (Elizabeth P.), Landon Henninger (Lincoln), Cameron Wofford (Cameron), Vivan Dugré (Missy Valdez St. Muffington), Elizabeth Hannah (Betsy the Copier), Sammy Harte (Party Girl), Matt Hensarling (Jared), Emily Kaye (Beth Sill), D'Anthony Palms (Harrison), Denman Powers (Grocery Store Employee), Step Rowe (Gina), Cassandra L. Small (Print Shop Manager), Phil Thoden (Noah), Cyrus Thompson (Kingston), Evie Thompson (Actress), Katherine Willis (Veronica Davis-Goldstein)

Socially inept Salman lands a job promoting home rentals in an oversized, oddball costume, bringing him into contact with Leslie, whose life is falling apart since her husband has left her to raise their two sons while he serves in Iraq.

Anita Briem, Brendan Fraser, Josh Hutcherson

Brendan Fraser, Josh Hutcherson, Anita Briem © New Line Cinema

Josh Hutcherson, Anita Briem, Brendan Fraser

JOURNEY TO THE CENTER OF THE EARTH 3D

(NEW LINE CINEMA) Producers, Charlotte Huggins, Beau Flynn; Executive Producers, Toby Emmerich, Brendan Fraser, Mark McNair, Tripp Vinson; Director, Eric Brevig; Screenplay, Michael Weiss, Jennifer Flackett, Mark Levin; Based on the novel by Jules Verne; Photography, Chuck Schuman; Designer, David Sandefur; Music, Andrew Lockington; Music Supervisor, Lindsay Fellows; Editors, Paul Martin Smith, Dirk Westervelt; Visual Effects Supervisor, Christopher Townsend; VFX Editor & 3D Consultant, Ed W. Marsh; Coproducers, Douglas Jones, Alex Schwartz, Mylan Stepanovich, Evan Turner, Cale Boyter, Michael Disco; Stunts, Marc Désourdy, Patrick Kerton; Casting, Elizabeth Rudolph; a Walden Media presentation; Dolby; Deluxe color; 3D; Rated PG; 93 minutes; Release date: July 11, 2008

Cast

Trevor Anderson	**Brendan Fraser**
Sean Anderson	**Josh Hutcherson**
Hannah Ásgeirsson	**Anita Briem**
Professor Alan Kitzens	**Seth Meyers**
Max Anderson	**Jean-Michel Paré**
Elizabeth	**Jane Wheeler**
Old Man	**Frank Fontaine**
Leonard	**Giancarlo Caltabiano**
Gum-Chewing Girl	**Kaniehtiio Horn**
Sigurbjörn Ásgeirsson	**Garth Gilker**

Using Jules Verne's classic novel as their guide, Trevor Anderson and his nephew Sean journey to Iceland in hopes of finding an entrance that will lead them to the center of the earth, and find out what happened to Sean's missing dad. Earlier film based on the novel was released in 1959 by 20th Century Fox and starred James Mason, Arlene Dahl, and Pat Boone.

Brendan Fraser

MEET DAVE

(20TH CENTURY FOX) Producers, Jon Berg, Todd Komarnicki, David T. Friendly; Executive Producers, Arnon Milchan, Thomas M. Hammel; Director, Brian Robbins; Screenplay, Rob Greenberg, Bill Corbett; Photography, Clark Mathis; Designer, Clay A. Griffith; Costumes, Ruth Carter; Music, John Debney; Editor, Ned Bastille; Visual Effects Supervisor, Mark Stetson; Visual Effects, Hydraulx, CIS-Hollywood; Stunts, Andy Gill; Casting, Joel Bastrop, Seth Yanklewitz; a Friendly Films/Guy Walks Into a Bar production, presented with Regency Enterprises; Dolby; Color; Rated PG; 90 minutes; Release date: July 11, 2008

Gabrielle Union, Eddie Murphy

Cast

Dave Ming Cheng/Captain	**Eddie Murphy**
Gina Morrison	**Elizabeth Banks**
No. 3	**Gabrielle Union**
Officer Dooley	**Scott Caan**
No. 2	**Ed Helms**
No. 17	**Kevin Hart**
Officer Knox	**Mike O'Malley**

Pat Kilbane (No. 4), Austyn Lind Myers (Josh Morrison), Judah Friedlander (Engineer), Marc Blucas (Mark Rhodes), Jim Turner (Doctor), Adam Tomei (No. 35), Brian Huskey (Lieutenant Right Arm), Shawn Christian (Lieutenant Left Arm), Jane Bradbury (No. 81), Brad Wilson (Lieutenant Right Leg), Miguel A. Nuñez (Burly Crew Member), John Gatins (Air Traffic Controller), Nick Berman (Young Bully), Smith Cho (Lieutenant Left Leg), Yung-I Chang (Apple Genius), David "Goldy" Goldsmith (Lieutenant Buttocks), Paul Scheer (Lieutenant Kneecap), James Michael Connor (Principal), Justin Robbins (What the Boy), Miles Robbins (Freckled Boy), Allisyn Ashley Arm (Nerdy Girl), Stephanie Venditto (MRI Technician), Richard Cerenzio (Announcer at Street Fair), Jane Altman (Old Woman), Philip Pavel (Old Navy Salesman), Yvette Nicole Brown (Old Navy Saleswoman), Charlie Guardino (Sgt. Vargas), Craig Gellis, Tim Sitarz (Robbers), Thomas Langston (Little Boy at Park), John Mainieri (Middle-Aged Man), Phyllis Kay (Middle-Aged Wife), Michael Izquierdo, Kristen Connolly (Make Out Couple), Monica Flores, Scott Levine, Boni Yanagisawa (Mouth Crew), Floud Levine (Old Man on Toilet), Richie Allan (Homeless Man), Alex Berg (Timid Crew Member), Brandon Molale (Security Guard), Phaedra Nielson (Waitress), Mel Cowan (Detective #1), Janine Edwards, Abbey Lerman (Apple Store Girls), Michael Winther (Tourist), Askao Takasue (Convenience Store Clerk), Makoto Tanaka, Mark Rangel (Engine Crew), Rashida Roy (No. 37), The Naked Cowboy (Himself), William Penick (Stockbroker), Paul Basile (Punk), Karen Berg (Right Arm Crew), Carol Commissiong (Police Officer #3), Peter Conboy (Tourist), Vince Cupone (Mac Genius), Michael Den Dekker (Construction Worker), Kimberly Dorsey (Stroller Mom in Liberty Park), Scott Forrester (No. 21), Jamel Gay (No. 7), Duncan Hale Murdoch (Gay Guy), Robert Jones (Crew Member), Hallie Lambert (No. 68), Mario Loya (Old Navy Customer), Orock Orock (No. 19), Madeleine Petrisi (Hot Dog Counter), Larry Purtell (Taxi Driver), Inbal Samuel (Nanny), Bill Sorice (Business Man), Sandy Sunshine (Milian Transformer–Upper Deck), Annette Nicole, Brandon Michael Vegas (Dancers), Village (NYPD Detective), Nick Wall (Carny), Christina Wun (Medical Facility Girl)

Scott Caan

A group of aliens create a human-sized vehicle in the image of their captain, Dave, in hopes of recovering a missing device that will help their planet but cause possible destruction to Earth.

Austyn Lind Myers, Eddie Murphy © 20th Century Fox

Doug Jones, Jeffrey Tambor

Doug Jones

Doug Jones, Selma Blair, Ron Perlman, John Alexander

Luke Goss, Ann Walton
© Universal Studios

HELLBOY II: THE GOLDEN ARMY

(UNIVERSAL) Producers, Lawrence Gordon, Mike Richardson, Lloyd Levin; Executive Producer, Chris Symes; Co-executive Producer, Mike Mignola; Director/Screenplay, Guillermo del Toro; Story, Guillermo del Toro, Mike Mignola; Based upon the Dark Horse Comic Book Created by Mike Mignola; Photography, Guillermo Navarro; Designer, Stephen Scott; Costumes, Sammy Sheldon; Music, Danny Elfman; Music Supervisor, Kathy Nelson; Editor, Bernat Vilaplana; Coproducer, John Swallow; Creature and Makeup Effects Designer, Mike Elizalde; Visual Effects Supervisor, Michael J. Wassel; Casting, Jeremy Zimmerman; Stunts, Bradley Allan; a Lawrence Gordon/Lloyd Levin production in association with Dark Horse Entertainment, presented in association with Relativity Media; Dolby; Deluxe color; Rated PG-13; 120 minutes; Release date: July 11, 2008

Cast

Hellboy	**Ron Perlman**
Liz Sherman	**Selma Blair**
Abe Sapien	**Doug Jones**
Johan Krauss	**John Alexander, James Dodd**
Voice of Johan	**Seth McFarlane**
Prince Nuada	**Luke Goss**
Princess Nuala	**Anna Walton**
Tom Manning	**Jeffrey Tambor**
Professor Broom	**John Hurt**

Brian Steele (Wink/Cronie/Space Shop Troll/Cathedral Head/Fragglewump), Andrew Hefler (Agent Flint), Ivan Kamaras (Agent Steel), Mike Kelly (Agent Marble), Jeremy Zimmermann (Auctioneer), Santiago Segura (Distinguished Buyer), Doug Jones (Chamberlain/Angel of Death), Roy Dotrice (King Balor), Aidan Cook (Two-Headed Shop Owner), Jeanne Mockford (Bag Lady), James Alexander (Bethmoora Goblin), Montse Ribe (Young Hellboy), Ferenc Elek (Fat Slob), Alex McSweeney, Justin Pierre (Policemen), Matthew O'Toole (Limb Vendor), Jaie Wilson (Cat Vendor), Kevin Hudson (Organ Grinder), Clive Llewellyn (Tadpole Vendor), Sándor Svigelj (Bagpipe Player), Brian Herring (Silkard/Fish Vendor), Pálma Pásztor (Mummy Vendor), Jimmy Kimmel (Himself), Tim Flavin, Belinda Henley, Blake Perlman, Matt Rippy (Newscasters), Judit Viktor (Lady with Dog), Szonja Oroszlán (Woman with Baby), Michael A. Mehlmann, Todd Williams (Auction Bidder Men), Beatrix Zentai (Auction Bidder Woman), Peter Horkay (Steward), Richard Rifkin (TV Pundit)

The Bureau for Paranormal Research and Defense summons Hellboy to put a stop to Prince Nuada's plan to unleash a long dormant army of killing machines upon the world. Sequel to the 2004 film *Hellboy* (Universal) with Perlman, Blair, Tambor and Hurt repeating their roles.

This film received an Oscar nomination for makeup.

MAMMA MIA!

(UNIVERSAL) Producers, Judy Craymer, Gary Goetzman; Executive Producers, Benny Andersson, Björn Ulvaeus, Rita Wilson, Tom Hanks, Mark Huffam; Director, Phyllida Lloyd; Screenplay, Catherine Johnson, based on her original musical book, originally conceived by Judy Craymer, based on the songs of ABBA; Photography, Haris Zambarloukos; Designer, Maria Djurkovic; Costumes, Ann Roth; Music and Lyrics, Benny Andersson, Björn Ulvaeus; Some Songs with Stig Anderson; Music Director, Martin Lowe; Musical Supervisor, Becky Bentham; Choreographer, Anthony Van Laast; Editor, Lesley Walker; Casting, Priscilla John, Ellen Lewis; a Playtone/Littlestar production, presented in association with Relativity Media; Dolby; Technicolor; Rated PG-13; 108 minutes; Release date: July 18, 2008

Christine Baranski, Meryl Streep, Julie Walters

Cast

Donna Sheridan	**Meryl Streep**
Sam Carmichael	**Pierce Brosnan**
Harry Bright	**Colin Firth**
Bill Anderson	**Stellan Skarsgård**
Rosie	**Julie Walters**
Sky	**Dominic Cooper**
Sophie Sheridan	**Amanda Seyfried**
Tanya	**Christine Baranski**
Ali	**Ashley Lilley**
Lisa	**Rachel McDowall**
Pepper	**Philip Michael**
Father Alex	**Niall Buggy**
Sam's PA	**Nancy Baldwin**
Harry's Housekeeper	**Heather Emmanuel**
Harry's Driver	**Colin Davis**
Stannos	**Ricardo Montez**
Arina	**Mia Soteriou**
Gregoris	**Enzo Squillino, Jr.**
Eddie	**Chris Jarvis**
Pano	**George Georgiou**
Dimitri	**Hemi Eroham**
Ione	**Maria Lopiano**
Petros	**Juan Pablo Di Pace**
Irini	**Norma Atallah**
Elena	**Myra McFadyen**
Ariana	**Leonie Hill**
Elpida	**Jane Foufas**

Meryl Streep, Amanda Seyfried © Universal Studios

Karl Bowe, Celestina Banjo, Emrhys Cooper, Maria DeSpina, Gareth Davis, Charlotte Habib, Gareth Derrick, Jennifer Leung, Kage Douglas, Lydia Louisa, Phillip Dzwonkiewicz, Kristina MacMillan, Tommy Franzen, Lauri Owen, Tom Goodall, Joanne Sandi, Aykut Hilmi, Christine Saunders, Jamie Hughes-Ward, Emma Slater, Taylor James, Helen Soraya, Jack Jefferson, Caterina Spano, Peter Le Brun, Michelle Theunissen, Sebastien Torkia, Kitty Whitelaw, Dylan Turner, Nikki Davis-Jones, Ed White, Michelle Trimboli, Sean Williams, Kirsty Mather, Lee Honey-Jones, Rebecca Lee, Gareth Chart, Clare Louise Connolly, Sonny Lee Hymas, Kirsty Swain, Tim Stanley, Lisa Reynolds, Sara West, Claire Fishenden (Stags & Hens)

On the eve of her wedding, Sophie summons three men from her mother's past, one of whom she is certain must be the father she has never known.

Christine Baranski, Meryl Streep, Julie Waters

Ashley Lilley, Amanda Seyfried, Rachel McDowall

Stellan Skarsgård, Pierce Brosnan, Colin Firth, Amanda Seyfried

Meryl Streep

Dominic Cooper

Pierce Brosnan, Meryl Streep

Julie Walters, Meryl Streep, Christine Baranski

THE DARK KNIGHT

(WARNER BROS.) Producers, Emma Thomas, Charles Roven, Christopher Nolan; Executive Producers, Benjamin Melniker, Michael E. Uslan, Kevin De La Noy, Thomas Tull; Director, Christopher Nolan; Screenplay, Jonathan Nolan, Christopher Nolan; Story, Christopher Nolan, David S. Goyer; Based upon characters appearing in comic books published by DC Comics: Batman created by Bob Kane; Photography, Wally Pfister; Designer, Nathan Crowley; Costumes, Lindy Hemming; Music, Hans Zimmer, James Newton Howard; Editor, Lee Smith; Visual Effects Supervisor, Nick Davis; Visual Effects, Double Negative, Framestore, Buf Compagnie, Cinesite; Stunts, Paul Jennings, Rick LeFevour, Tom Struthers; Casting, John Papsidera; a Syncopy production, presented in association with Legendary Pictures; Dolby; Panavision; Technicolor; Rated PG-13; 152 minutes; Release date: July 18, 2008

Cast

Bruce Wayne/Batman	**Christian Bale**
Alfred Pennyworth	**Michael Caine**
The Joker	**Heath Ledger**
Harvey Dent/Two-Face	**Aaron Eckhart**
Rachel Dawes	**Maggie Gyllenhaal**
Commissioner James Gordon	**Gary Oldman**
Lucius Fox	**Morgan Freeman**
Det. Anna Ramirez	**Monique Gabriela Curnen**
Det. Wuertz	**Ron Dean**
Scarecrow	**Cillian Murphy**
Lau	**Chin Han**
Mayor Anthony Garcia	**Nestor Carbonell**
Salvatore Maroni	**Eric Roberts**
The Chechen	**Ritchie Coster**
Mike Engel	**Anthony Michael Hall**
Det. Stephens	**Keith Szarabajka**
Commissioner Gillian B. Loeb	**Colin McFarlane**
Coleman Reese	**Joshua Harto**
Barbara Gordon	**Melinda McGraw**
James Gordon, Jr.	**Nathan Gamble**
Al Rossi	**Michael Vieau**

Michael Stoyanov (Dopey), William Smillie (Happy), Danny Goldring (Grumpy), Michael Jai White (Gambol), Matthew O'Neill (Chuckles), William Fitchner (Bank Manager), Olumiji Olwaumi (Drug Dealer), Gregory Beam (Drug Buyer), Erik Hellman (Junkie), Beatrice Rosen (Natascha), Vincenzo Nicoli (Crime Boss), Edison Chen (LSI VP), Nydia Rodriguez Terracina (Judge Surrillo), Andy Luther (Brian), James Farruggio, Tom McElroy (Men), Will Zahrn (Assistant DA), James Fierro (Thug at Party), Patrick Leahy (Unintimidated Gentleman at Party), Sam Derence, Jennifer Knox (Guests), Patrick Clear (Judge Freel), Sarah Jayne Dunn (Maroni's Mistress), Chucky Venn, Winston Ellis (Gambol's Bodyguards), David Dastmalchian (Joker's Thug), Sophia Hinshelwood, Thomas Gaitch (Reporters), Keith Kupferer (Heckler), Joseph Luis Caballero (Cop Heckler), Richard Dillane (Acting Commissioner), Daryl Satcher (Officer at Intersection), Chris Petschler (Convoy Leader), Aidan Feore (Fat Thug), Philip Bulcock (Det. Murphy), Paul Birchard (Cop with Fat Thug), Walter Lewis (Medic), Vincent Riotta (Cop at 250 52nd Street), Nancy Crane (Nurse), K. Todd Freeman (Polk), Matt Shallenberger (Officer Berg), Michael Andrew Gorman (Cop at Hospital), Lanny Lutz (Bartender), Peter Defaria (Civilian), Matt Rappy (First Mate), Andrew Bicknell (Prison Ferry Pilot), Ariyon Bakare (Guard Commander), Doug Ballard (Businessman), Helene Wilson (Mother), Tommy Campbell, Craig Heaney, Lorna Gayle, Lisa McAllister, Peter Brooke (Passengers), Joshua Rollins (SWAT Sniper), Dale Rivera (SWAT Leader), Matthew Leitch (Prisoner on Ferry), Tommy "Tiny" Lister (Tattooed Prisoner), William Armstrong (Evans), Adam Kalesperis (Honor Guard Man), Tristan Tait (Uniform Cop), Bronson Webb, David Ajala (Bounty Hunters), Gertrude Kyles (Fox's Secretary), Jonathan Ryland (Passenger Ferry Pilot), James Scales (Guardsman), Nigel Carrington (Warden), Ian Pirie (Corrections Officer), Lateef Lovejoy, Grahame Edwards, Roger Monk, Stephen Armourae, Martyn Cooper, Jay

Fuller, Robert Stoen (Prisoners), Ronan Summers (Prison Corrections Officer), Wai Wong (Hong Kong Detective), Michael Corey Foster (Honor Guard Leader), Hannah Gunn (Gordon's Daughter), Brandon Lambdin (Armored Car SWAT), Jeff Albertson (Gotham Police Officer), Tommy Bartlett (Salvatore Maroni's Defense Attorney), Nadia Cameron-Blakey (Cressida Spink), Jamie Cho (Lau's Bodyguard), Kelli Clevenger (Paramedic), Steven H. Hansen, Don Kress (Maroni Henchmen), Julie Theresa, Angelina Lyubomirova (Ballerinas), Sanjay Madhav (Senator), Teresa Mahoney-Bostridge (Refugee), Dean Mitchell (Firefighter), Kerri Parker (Maroni's Mistress), John Snowden (Detective), Chris Wilson (Gotham MCU Detective)

Gotham City's mysterious crimefighter Batman hopes crusading District Attorney Harvey Dent will successfully bring an end to crime, a plan that is thwarted by the psychopathic Joker, who is intent on exposing the caped crusader with a crimewave of terror. Second in the latest Batman Warner Bros. franchise following *Batman Begins* (2005), with Bale, Caine, Oldman, and Murphy repeating their roles.

2008 Academy Award winner for Best Supporting Actor (Heath Ledger) and Best Sound Editing.
This film received additional Oscar nominations for cinematography, art direction, visual effects, film editing, sound mixing, and makeup.

Christian Bale, Heath Ledger

Christian Bale, Morgan Freeman

Christian Bale

Christian Bale

Christian Bale

Nestor Carbonell, Gary Oldman © Warner Bros

Heath Ledger

Maggie Gyllenhaal, Aaron Eckhart

Michael Caine

Ham III

SPACE CHIMPS

(20TH CENTURY FOX) Producers, Barry Sonnenfeld, John H. Williams; Executive Producers, Jerry Davis, Louis Goodsill, John W. Hyde, Tom Jacomb, Ralph Kamp; Coproducer, Curtis Augspurger; Director/Story, Kirk DeMicco; Screenplay, Kirk DeMicco, Robert Moreland; Photography, Jericca Cleland; Art Director, Matthias Lechner; Editor, Debbie Berman; Music, Chris P. Bacon; Additional Music and Sound Design, Blue Man Group; Animation Director, Adam Wood; CG Supervisor, David Gutman; Casting, Matthew Jon Beck; a Starz Animation presentation, in association with Odyssey Entertainment, of a Vanguard Animation film; Dolby; Technicolor; Rated G; 81 minutes; Release date: July 18, 2008

Voice cast

Ham III	**Adam Samberg**
Luna	**Cheryl Hines**
Titan	**Patrick Warburton**
Zartog	**Jeff Daniels**
Dr. Jagu	**Omid Abtahi**
The Senator	**Stanley Tucci**
Dr. Poole	**Jane Lynch**
Comet	**Zack Shada**
Kilowatt	**Kristin Chenoweth**

Kenan Thompson (The Ringmaster), Carlos Alazraqui (Houston), Patrick Breen (Dr. Bob), Kath Soucie (Dr. Smothers), Wally Wingert (Splork/Infinity Probe/Pappy Ham), Jessica Gee (Ship Voice/Infinity Probe/Additional Voices), Tom Kenny (Newsreel), Jason Harris (Guard), Lloyd Jay Keiser (Cloud of Id), Tom Jacomb, Curtis Augspurger (Reporters), Jess Harnell, Ellie Harvie, Caitlin McKenna-Wilkinson (Additional Voices)

After decades of inactivity, three highly trained chimps are sent by NASA on an important mission to recover a valuable space probe that has crash landed on an alien planet.

Luna, Ham III © 20th Century Fox

BAGHEAD

(SONY CLASSICS) Producers, Jay Duplass, Mark Duplass, John Bryant; Coproducer, Jen Tracy Duplass; Directors/Screenplay, Jay Duplass, Mark Duplass; Photography, Jay Duplass; Music, J. Scott Howard; Editor, Jay Deuby; Special Effects, R. Zane Rutledge; a Duplass Brothers Movie; Dolby; Color; HD-to-35mm; Rated R; 88 minutes; Release date: July 25, 2008

Cast

Matt	**Ross Partridge**
Chad	**Steve Zissis**
Michelle	**Greta Gerwig**
Catherine	**Elise Muller**
Jett Garner	**Jett Garner**
"Priest," the Bouncer	**Anthony Cristo**

Stephanie Huettner (Girl in the Front Row), Jennifer Lafleur (Kristen Thompson), Cass Naumann (Cass), Amy Quick Parrish (Film Festival Attendee)

A quartet of aspiring actors spend a weekend in a cabin in the woods in hopes of writing a script, only to find themselves stalked by someone wearing a paper bag.

Baghead

Greta Gerwig, Steve Zissis, Ross Partridge, Elise Muller © Sony Classics

AMERICAN TEEN

(PARAMOUNT VANTAGE) Producers, Nanette Burstein, Jordan Roberts, Eli Gonda, Chris Huddleston; Executive Producers, Elisa Pugliese, Patrick Norris, Holly Thompson, Nancy Dubuc, Rob Sharenow; Coproducers, Ryan Harrington, Steve Rosenbaum; Director, Nanette Burstein; Photography, Laela Kilbourn, Wolfgang Held, Robert Hanna; Music, Michael Penn; Music Supervisor, Chris Douridas; Editors, Mary Mandhardt, Tom Haneke, Nanette Burstein; Casting, Tamra Barcinas; an A&E Indie Films presentation of a Firehouse Films and Quasiworld Entertainment production in association with 57th and Irving; Dolby; Color; HD Cam; Rated PG-13; 100 minutes; Release date: July 25, 2008. Documentary follows the lives of four high school seniors in middle-class Warsaw, Indiana.

With

Hannah Bailey, Colin Clemens, Megan Krizmanich, Jake Tusing, Geoff Haase, Mitch Reinholt, Ali Wikalinska.

Hannah Bailey © Paramount Vantage

Colin Clemens

Gillian Anderson, David Duchovny, Xzibit © 20th Century Fox

THE X FILES: I WANT TO BELIEVE

(20TH CENTURY FOX) Producers/Screenplay, Frank Spotnitz, Chris Carter; Executive Producer, Brent O'Connor; Director, Chris Carter; Based on the series created by Chris Carter; Photography, Bill Roe; Designer, Mark Freeborn; Costumes, Lisa Tomczeszyn; Music, Mark Snow; Editor, Richard A. Harris; Senior Visual Effects Supervisor, Mat Beck; Special Effects Makeup Effects Designer, William Terezakiks; Casting, Mindy Marin, Coreen Mayrs, Heike Brandstatter; a Ten Thirteen production; Dolby; Panavision; Deluxe color; Rated PG-13; 104 minutes; Release date: July 25, 2008

Cast

Fox Mulder	**David Duchovny**
Dana Scully	**Gillian Anderson**
ASAC Dakota Whitney	**Amanda Peet**
Father Joseph Crissman	**Billy Connolly**
Agent Mosley Drummy	**Alvin "Xzibit" Joiner**
Walter Skinner	**Mitch Pileggi**

Callum Keith Rennie (Janke Dacyshyn, 2nd Abductor), Adam Godley (Father Ybarra), Alex Diakun (Gaunt Man), Nicki Aycox (2nd Victim), Fagin Woodcock (Franz Tomczeszyn — 1st Abductor), Marco Niccoli (Christian Fearon), Carrie Ruscheinsky (Margaret Fearon), Spencer Maybee (Blair Fearon), Veronika Hadrava, Denis Krasnogolov (Assistants), Patrick Keating (Slight Man), Roger Horchow (Elderly Gent), Stephen E. Miller (Feed Store Proprietor), Xantha Radley (Monica Banna), Lorena Gale (On Screen Doctor), Donavon Stinson (Suited Man), Dion Johnstone (1st Cop), Sarah-Jane Redmond (Special Agent in Charge), Christina D'Alimonte (Doctor's Colleague), Vanesa Tomasino (Hallway Agent), Luvia Petersen (O.R. Nurse), Babz Chula (Surgeon), Marci T. House (Sheriff), J.P. Finn (Whispering Priest), Beth Siegler (Anesthesiologist), Stacee Copeland (Doctor), Tom Charron (Sheriff Horton), Brent C.S. O'Connor (Tow Truck Driver), Chris Carter (Man in Hospital Corridor)

Called back into service to investigate a missing person, agents Scully and Mulder are brought into contact with a fallen priest who may be experiencing psychic visions. Previous film in the series was *The X Files*, released by Fox in 1998 and also starring Duchovny and Anderson.

STEP BROTHERS

(COLUMBIA) Producers, Jimmy Miller, Judd Apatow; Executive Producers, Will Ferrell, Adam McKay, David Householter; Coproducer, Josh Church; Director, Adam McKay; Screenplay, Will Ferrell, Adam McKay; Photography, Oliver Wood; Designer, Clayton Hartley; Costumes, Susan Matheson; Music, Jon Brion; Editor, Brent White; Casting, Allison Jones; an Apatow Co./Mosaic Media Group/Gary Sanchez production, presented in association with Relativity Media; Dolby; Delux Color; Rated R; 95 minutes; Release date: July 25, 2008

Will Ferrell, John C. Reilly

Cast

Brennan Huff	**Will Ferrell**
Dale Doback	**John C. Reilly**
Nancy Huff	**Mary Steenburgen**
Dr. Robert Doback	**Richard Jenkins**
Derek Huff	**Adam Scott**
Alice Huff	**Kathryn Hahn**
TJ	**Jason Davis**
Blind Man	**Wayne Federman**
Wine Mix Heckler	**Kyle Felts**
Redheaded Kid	**Travis Flory**
1st Homebuyer Husband	**Chris Henchy**
9-year-Old Brennan	**Bryce Hurless**
Interviewer	**Brian Huskey**
Employment Agent	**Ken Jeong**
Rental Agent	**Paula Killen**
Student	**Breaunna Lake**

Phil LaMarr (2nd Homebuyer Husband), Logan Manus (Chris Gardoski), Lili McKay (7-Year-Old Girl), Seth Morris (Doctor), Erica Vittina Phillips (2nd Homebuyer Wife), Shira Piven (Nurse), Lurie Poston (Tommy Huff), Maria Quiban (TV Anchor), Rob Riggle (Randy), Ian Roberts (Therapist), Seth Rogen (Sporting Goods Manager), Horatio Sanz (Lead Singer), Andrea Savage (Denise), Dmitri Schuyler-Linch (6-Year-Old Derek), Laimarie Serrano (TJ's Wife), Jake Szymanski (Caterer), Gillian Vigman (HR Woman), Matt Walsh (Drunk Corporate Guy), Brent White (Therapy Patient), Elizabeth Yozamp (Tiffany Huff)

After Nancy Huff and Robert Doback fall in love and marry, their forty-year-old, wildly immature sons are forced to share their home together.

Will Ferrell, Mary Steenburgen, Richard Jenkins, John C. Reilly
© Columbia Pictures

John C. Reilly, Will Ferrell

John C. Reilly, Will Ferrell

Chau Sang Anthony Wong, Yeti © Universal Studios

Luke Ford, Maria Bello, Brendan Fraser

Jet Li

THE MUMMY: Tomb of the Dragon Emperor

(UNIVERSAL) Producers, Sean Daniel, James Jacks, Stephen Sommers, Bob Ducsay; Executive Producer, Chris Brigham; Director, Rob Cohen; Screenplay, Alfred Gough, Miles Millar; Photography, Simon Duggan; Designer, Nigel Phelps; Costumes, Sanja Milkovic Hays; Music, Randy Edelman; Editors, Joel Negron, Kelly Matsumoto; 2nd Unit Director/Supervising Stunt Coordinator, Vic Armstrong; Visual Effects Producers, Ginger Theisen, Garv Thorp; Special Effects Coordinator, Bruce Steinheimer; Casting, Ronna Kress; a Sommers Company/ Alphaville production, presented in association with Relativity Media; Dolby; Technicolor; Rated PG-13; 112 minutes; Release date: August 1, 2008

Cast

Rick O'Connell	**Brendan Fraser**
Emperor	**Jet Li**
Evelyn O'Connell	**Maria Bello**
Jonathan Carnahan	**John Hannah**
Zi Yuan	**Michelle Yeoh**
Alex O'Connell	**Luke Ford**
Lin	**Isabella Leong**
General Yang	**Chau Sang Anthony Wong**
Ming Guo	**Russell Wong**
Maguire	**Liam Cunningham**
Roger Wilson	**David Calder**
Choi	**Jessey Meng**
Li Zhou	**Liang Tian**
Chu Wah	**Albert Kwan**

Wu Jing, Wei Bingua, Guo Jing (Assassins), Alison Louder (Woman in Bookstore), Marcia Nasatir (Russian Princess), Emerald Starr (Man in Bar), Helen Feng (Nightclub Singer), Stella Maryna Troshyna (Brunette at Imhotep's), James Bradford (Butler Jameson), Daniel Giverin (Benjamin Fry), Ken C. Tran, Allan Chou, Fernando Fu-Nan Chien, Jeffrey Ong, Chris Mark, James Mark, Mike Ching, Darryl Quon, Alex Chiang, Paul Wu, Larry Lam, Brian Ho, Luu Vi-Hung, Huy-Phong Doan (Yang's Soldiers), Kyle Burnett Cashulin, Charles Esposito (Mad Dog's Pals), Mike Scherer, Scott Taylor (Yeti), Kham Tri Vixaysy, Don Lew (Chinese Diggers), Regis Attiow, Tony Wai, Wu Yungstun, Guangxu Xiang, Lam Cong-Quyen (Mystics)

Explorer Rick O'Connell tries to stop a resurrected Chinese Emperor, awakened from a 2,000 year-old curse, who is hell bent on controlling the world. Third in the Universal series starring Brendan Fraser, following *The Mummy* (1999) and *The Mummy Returns* (2001).

Michelle Yeoh, Russell Wong

FROZEN RIVER

(SONY CLASSICS) Producers, Heather Rae, Chip Hourihan; Executive Producers, Charles S. Cohen, Donald A. Harwood; Coproducer, Molly Conners; Co-executive Producer, Jay B. Itkowitz; Director/Screenplay, Courtney Hunt; Photography, Reed Dawson Morano; Designer, Inbal Weinberg; Costumes, Abby O'Sullivan; Music, Peter Golub, Shahzad Ali Ismaily; Editor, Kate Williams; a Harwood Hunt Prods./ Cohen Media Group presentation in association with OffHollywood Pictures; Color; DV; Rated R; 96 minutes; Release date: August 1, 2008

Cast

Ray Eddy	**Melissa Leo**
Lila	**Misty Upham**
Trooper Finnerty	**Michael O'Keefe**
Jacques Bruno	**Mark Boone Junior**
T.J.	**Charlie McDermott**
Ricky	**James Reilly**
Jimmy	**Dylan Carusona**
Guy Versailles	**Jay Klaitz**
Billy Three Rivers	**Michael Sky**
Bernie Littlewolf	**John Canoe**
Chen Li	**Nancy Wu**

Pun Bandhu (Chinese Man #1), Rajesh Bose (Pakistani Father), Joey Chanlin (Chinese Trafficker), Thahnhahténhtha Gilbert (Little Jake), Adam Lukens (Mitch), Betty Ouyang (Li Wei), Craig Shilowich (Matt), Gargi Shinde (Pakistani Mother) Facing never-ending financial hardships, single mother Ray Eddy agrees to make some needed cash by transporting illegal aliens across the U.S./Canadian border.

This film received Oscar nominations for actress (Melissa Leo) and original screenplay.

Charlie McDermott

Melissa Leo, Mark Boone Junior © Sony Classics

Misty Upham, Melissa Leo

Melissa Leo, Michael O'Keefe

Stanley Tucci, Kelsey Grammer

Paula Patton, Kevin Costner

Kevin Costner, Madeline Carroll © Touchstone

SWING VOTE

(TOUCHSTONE) Producers, Jim Wilson, Kevin Costner; Executive Producers, Robin Jonas, Ted Field, Terry Dougas, Paris Kasidokostas Latsis; Director, Joshua Michael Stern; Screenplay, Jason Richman; Joshua Michael Stern; Photography, Shane Hurlbut; Designer, Steve Saklad; Costumes, Lisa Jensen; Music, John Debney; Editor, Jeff McEvoy; Casting, Mary Vernieu, Venus Kanani; a Treehouse Films production, presented in association with Radar Pictures and 1821 Pictures; Dolby; Widescreen; Deluxe color; Rated PG-13; 119 minutes; Release date: August 1, 2008

Cast

Bud Johnson	**Kevin Costner**
Kate Madison	**Paula Patton**
President Andrew Boone	**Kelsey Grammer**
Donald Greenleaf	**Dennis Hopper**
Art Crumb	**Nathan Lane**
Martin Fox	**Stanley Tucci**
John Sweeney	**George Lopez**
Molly Johnson	**Madeline Carroll**
Walter	**Judge Reinhold**
Larissa Johnson	**Mare Winningham**

Mark Moses (Attorney General Wyatt), Nana Visitor (Galena Greenleaf), Willie Nelson, Richard Petty, Tony Blankley, Aaron Brown, Campbell Brown, Tucker Carlson, James Carville, Matt Frei, Mary Hart, Arianna Huffington, Larry King, Anne Kornblut, Bill Maher, Chris Matthews, Lawrence O'Donnell (Themselves), Floyd "Red Crow" Westerman (Chief Running Bear), Shawn Prince (Jed), Dale O'Malley (Hank), Mary Sue Evans (Mrs. Abernathy), Gary Farmer (Curly), Adam Taylor (Justice Brower), Bruce McIntosh (Father in Classroom), Tom Romero (Ad Exec), Forrest Fyre (Ted Dark), Ivan Brutsche (Carl), Sheila Ivy Traister, Jeremy Jojola, Suzanne Michaels (Vermont Reporters), Cynthia Ruffin, Jason Henning (Boone Staffers), Les Shapiro (Network Reporter), Cynthia Straus (Darlene), Charles Moore (UPS Delivery Man), Colin James (KNME Techie), Trista Callandar (Commercial Director), Richard M. Dereyes, Shaun Clark, Debra-Jayne Brown, Price Hall (Market Reporters), Olajida Kashu (Gay Doctor), Jessica Morin (Butch Gay Cop), Tim Janis (Gay Soldier), Scott Meyer, Brent Lambert (Gay Partners), Christopher Dempsey, David Meeker (Secret Service Agents), Janeal Arison (TV Producer), Madelin Whelpley, Ayssa Gutierrez, Amber Midthunder, Taylor Warden, Angelo Martinez, Isaiah Bergert (Students), Arron Shiver, Kate Schroeder, David Dalton, Heather Hitt (Greenleaf Aides), Pierre Barrera (Henry), Todd Lewis (ET Segment Producer), Dan Gerrity, Cris Ornelas, Esodi Geiger, Constance Hsu, Catalina Parish (Trailer Reporters), Joshua Michael Stern (Commercial Director), Tony Stern (Gospel Minister), Mara Holguin (Waitress), John J. Coinman, Blair Forward, Teddy Morgan, Larry Cobb, Charles Park Chisholm, Bobby Yang (Bud's Band), Burly Cain (Secret Service Agent), Dave Colon (News Reporter), Pamela Finley (First Lady Boone), David Giammarco (CJ), Chaz Grundy (Greenleaf Aide), Rachel Hroncich (Reporter), Bob Jesser (Softball), Chance Romero (Pizza Guy)

Ne'er-do-well Bud Johnson becomes an overnight celebrity when a technical mishap makes his vote the deciding one in a neck-and-neck presidential race.

Nathan Lane, Dennis Hopper

Seth Rogen,
James Franco
© Columbia Pictures

Craig Robinson, Danny McBride,
Kevin Corrigan

Seth Rogen,
James Franco,
Danny McBride

PINEAPPLE EXPRESS

(COLUMBIA) Producers, Judd Apatow, Shauna Robertson: Executive Producers, Seth Rogen, Evan Goldberg; Coproducer, Sara Weintraub; Director, David Gordon Green; Screenplay, Seth Rogen, Evan Goldberg; Story, Judd Apatow, Seth Rogen, Evan Goldberg; Photography, Tim Orr; Designer, Chris Spellman; Costumes, John Dunn; Music, Graeme Revell; Music Supervisor, Jonathan Karp; Editor, Craig Alpert; Stunts, Gary H. Hymes, Mike Smith; Casting, Billy Hopkins, Suzanne Crowley; an Apatow Co. Production, presented in association with Relativity Media; Dolby; Panavision; Deluxe color; Rated R; 112 minutes; Release date: August 6, 2008

Cast

Dale Denton	**Seth Rogen**
Saul Silver	**James Franco**
Ted Jones	**Gary Cole**
Carol	**Rosie Perez**
Red	**Danny McBride**
Budlofsky	**Kevin Corrigan**
Matheson	**Craig Robinson**
Angie Anderson	**Amber Heard**
Robert Anderson	**Ed Begley, Jr.**
Shannon Anderson	**Nora Dunn**
Bobby	**Bobby Lee**
General Brat	**James Remar**
School Guy #1	**Ricky Dôminguez**
Mr. Edwards	**Joe Lo Truglio**
Clark	**Arthur Napiontek**
Police Liaison Officer	**Cleo King**
Private Miller	**Bill Hader**

Jonathan Walker Spencer (Scientist), Dana Lee (Cheung), Bobby Lee (Bobby), Ken Jeong (Ken), David C. Cook (Chris Gebert), Howard S. Lefstein (Mark), Connie Sawyer (Faye Belogus), David McDivitt (Police Officer #1), Mae LaBorde (Mrs. Mendelson), Kendall Carly Browne (Old Woman), George Lew (Old Man), John Robert Tramutola (Walt), Adam Crosby (Ack), Andrew Heald (Blake), Jeanette Arnette (Sandra Danby), Carlos Aleman (Omar Leyva (Guys in car), Sam Carson (Xerox Secretary), Jack Kehler (Walter — Accountant), Robert Longstreet (Dr. Terrence), Peter Lewis (Peter, Thug #1), Steve Bannos (Jared, Thug #2), Eddie Rouse (Lance, Thug #5), Mark Whigham (Thug #3), Brian Scannell (Thug #4)

A stoner and his dealer find themselves in deep trouble after the former leaves behind a half-smoked joint at the scene of a murder.

Gary Cole, Rosie Perez

BOTTLE SHOCK

(FREESTYLE) Producers, J. Todd Harris, Marc Toberoff, Brenda Lhormer CQ, Marc Lhormer, Jody Slavin, Randall Miller; Executive Producers, Dan Schryer, Art Klein, Erik Cleage, Robert Blaizer, Diane Jacobs; Coproducer, Elaine Dysinger; Director, Randall Miller; Screenplay, Jody Slavin, Randall Miller, Ross Schwartz; Story, Ross Schwartz, Lannette Pabon, Jody Savin, Randall Miller; Photography, Michael J. Ozier; Designer, Craig Stearns; Costumes, Jillian Kreiner; Music, Mark Adler; Editors, Randall Miller, Dan O'Brien; Casting, Rick Pagano; an IPW presentation in association with Zin Haze Prods. of an Unclaimed Freight production; Dolby; Panavision; Color; Rated PG-13; 112 minutes; Release date: August 6, 2008

Dennis Farina, Chris Pine

Cast

Steven Spurrier	**Alan Rickman**
Bo Barrett	**Chris Pine**
Jim Barrett	**Bill Pullman**
Sam	**Rachael Taylor**
Gustavo Brambilia	**Freddy Rodriguez**
Maurice	**Dennis Farina**
Prof. Saunders	**Bradley Whitford**
Mr. Garcia	**Miguel Sandoval**
Joe	**Eliza Dushku**
Bill	**Joe Regalbuto**
Shenky	**Hal B. Klein**
Loan Officer	**Kirk Baily**
Pierre Tari	**Philippe Bergeron**

Frank Avila (Field Hand), Geoff Callan (Man #3), James Carraway (James, Vitner #3), Amiée Conn (Bo's Friend), Mark Famiglietti (Waiter), Marcia Firesten (Winery Owner), Jean-Pierre Gillain (Pierre Brejoux), Mary Pat Gleason (Marge), Leslie Goodman (Wine Tasting Spectator), Richard Gross (Lt. Randall), Arlo Hemphill (French Waiter), Matthew Kimbrough, Valerie Long (Vintners), Larry Kitagawa (Country Club Member), Krystal Landrum (TWA Ticket Agent), Al Liner (Hotel Clerk), Justin Malachi, Mario Vendetti (Valets), Kathy McGraw (Ms. Relyea), Randall Miller (Patron), Deborah O'Brien (TWA Attendant), Jeff Redlick (Pedestrian), Karl-Heinz Teuber (German Tourist), Scott Updegrave (Attorney)

The true story of how the wine industry was disrupted by a California winery's presence in a French tasting contest.

Bill Pullman, Chris Pine

Eliza Dushku, Freddy Rodriguez

Alan Rickman © Freestyle Releasing

THE SISTERHOOD OF THE TRAVELING PANTS 2

(WARNER BROS.) Producers, Debra Martin Chase, Denise Di Novi, Broderick Johnson, Kira Davis; Executive Producers, Andrew A. Kosove, Christine Sacani, Alison Greenspan, Leslie Morgenstein, Bob Levy; Coproducers, Steven P. Wegner, Yolanda T. Cochran, Gaylyn Fraiche; Director, Sanaa Hamri; Screenplay, Elizabeth Chandler; Based on the novels by Ann Brashares; Photography, Jim Denault; Designer, Gae Buckley; Costumes, Dona Granata; Music, Rachel Portman; Music Supervisor, Julia Michels; Editor, Melissa Kent; Casting, Laura Rosenthal; an Alcon Entertainment presentation, in association with Alloy Entertainment of a Di Novi Pictures/Debra Martin Chase production; Dolby; Technicolor; Rated PG-13; 111 minutes; Release date: August 6, 2008

Cast

Tibby Tomko-Rollins	**Amber Tamblyn**
Lena Kaligaris	**Alex Bledel**
Carmen Lowell	**America Ferrera**
Bridget Vreeland	**Blake Lively**
Julia	**Rachel Nichols**
Ian	**Tom Wisdom**
Carmen's Mom	**Rachel Ticotin**
Brian McBrian	**Leonardo Nam**

Michael Rady (Kostos), Shohreh Aghdashloo (Prof. Nasrin Mehani), Blythe Danner (Greta), Jesse Williams (Leo), Lucy Kate Hale (Effie Kaligaris), Maria Konstadarou (Yia Yia), Ernie Lively (Bridget's Father), Stevie Ray Dallimore (Nigel O'Bannon), Alison Folland (Stage Manager Margaret), Zacharoula Klimatsaki (Melia), Nastas Ippokratis (Priest), Panagiotis Pitsilos (Old Fisherman), Nathaniel Martello-White (Dig Site Student Ray), Emmanuel Leconte (Dig Site Student Miles), Stavros Parisis (Nasrin's Husband), Danae Sawa (Nasrin's Daughter), Maryanne Urbano (Art Teacher Annika), Paul Coughlan (Carmen's Stepdad), Rebekah Aramini (Lena's Mom), Cory Nichols (Nicky Rollins), Carly Rose Sonenclar (Kathryn Rollins), Erik Jensen (Video Store Manager Phi), Adrienne Bailon, Cannon Smith (Cute Video Couple), Dylan Sheridan, Lindsay Michelle Nader (Video Store Customers), Crystal McCrary Anthony (Mom with Screaming Kids), Nicole Patrick, Josh Barclay Caras, Jack Sneed (Apprentices), Kiely Williams (Yaffa Waitress), Max Woertendyke (Yale Stagehand), Victor Slezak (Doctor), Marceline Hugot (Nurse), Bill Corsair (Old Shepherd), Kyle MacLachlan (Theatre Workshop Director), Samantha Safdie (Teenager)

While Carmen attends theater camp, her best friends find themselves on various romantic adventures, Tibby ending up at a Manhattan summer school; Lena in an art class; and Bridget joining an archeological dig in Turkey. Sequel to the 2005 film.

Clockwise from top: *Alexis Bledel, Blake Lively, America Ferrera, Amber Tamblyn* © *Warner Bros.*

Brian Cox

Kyle Gallner, Noel Fisher © Magnolia

RED

(MAGNOLIA) Producers, Trygve Allister Diesen, Norman M. Dreyfus; Executive Producers, Bill Straus, Lawrence Mattis, Randy Ostrow; Coproducer/Screenplay, Stephen Susco; based on the novel by Jack Ketchum; Directors, Trygve Allister Diesen, Lucky McKee; Photography, Harald Gunnar Paalgard; Designers, Leslie Keel, Tiffany Zappulla; Costumes, Michelle Posch; Music, Soren Hylgaard; Editor, Jon Endre Mork; Casting, Shannon Makhanian; a Norman M. Dreyfus presentation in association with Billy Goat Pictures of a Tenk production; Dolby; Deluxe color; HD; Rated R; 95 minutes; Release date: August 8, 2008

Cast

Avery Ludlow	**Brian Cox**
Danny	**Noel Fisher**
Michael McCormack	**Tom Sizemore**
Harold	**Kyle Gallner**
Pete Doust	**Shiloh Fernandez**

Marcia Bennett (Emma Siddons), Lauren Birkell (Molly Flick), Keith Buterbaugh (Dean), Kim Dickens (Carrie Donnel), Robert Englund (Willie Doust), Ashley Laurence (Mrs. McCormack), John-Luke Montias (Cop), Katie Piel (Gloria), Amanda Plummer (Mrs. Doust), Richard Riehle (Sam Berry), Ivana Shein (Girlfriend), Greg Stuhr (Fire Marshal), Delaney Williams (Clarence)

When his beloved dog Red is senselessly killed, storekeeper Avery Ludlow becomes determined to find remorse in those responsible.

Ben Kingsley, Dennis Hopper

Ben Kingsley, Patricia Clarkson

Peter Sarsgaard

ELEGY

(SAMUEL GOLDWYN FILMS) Producers, Tom Rosenberg, Gary Lucchesi, Andre Lamal; Executive Producers, Richard Wright, Eric Reid, Terry A. McKay, Judd Malkin; Director/Music Supervisor, Isabel Coixet; Screenplay, Nicholas Meyer; Based on the novel *The Dying Animal* by Philip Roth; Photography, Jan Claude Larrieu; Designer, Claude Pare; Costumes, Katia Stano; Editor, Amy Duddleston; Casting, Heike Brandstatter, Coreen Mayrs; a Lakeshore Entertainment presentation and production; Dolby; Color; Video-to-35mm; Rated R; 111 minutes; Release date: August 8, 2008

Cast

Consuela Castillo	**Penélope Cruz**
David Kepesh	**Ben Kingsley**
George O'Hearn	**Dennis Hopper**
Carolyn	**Patricia Clarkson**
Kenneth Kepesh	**Peter Sarsgaard**
Amy O'Hearn	**Deborah Harry**
Himself	**Charlie Rose**
Beth	**Sonja Bennett**
Susan Reese	**Chelah Horsdal**
Kris Banjee	**Shaker Paleja**
Consuela's Brother	**Kris Pope**

Antonio Cupo (Consuela's Imagined Lover), Michelle Harrison (Student #1), Marci T. House (Nurse), Alessandro Juliani (Actor #3 in Play), Laura Mennell (Cute Girl)

Aging literary professor David Kepesh begins an affair with one of his recently graduated students, only to find it unexpectedly blossoming into an intense love of the sort he had never expected to experience.

Ben Kingsley, Penélope Cruz © Samuel Goldwyn Films

TROPIC THUNDER

(DREAMWORKS/PARAMOUNT) Producers, Stuart Cornfeld, Ben Stiller, Eric McLeod; Executive Producer, Justin Theroux; Coproducer, Brian Taylor; Director, Ben Stiller; Screenplay, Justin Theroux, Ben Stiller, Etan Cohen; Story, Ben Stiller, Justin Theroux; Photography, John Toll; Designer, Jeff Mann; Costumes, Marlene Stewart; Music, Theodore Shapiro; Music Supervisor, George Drakoulias; Editor, Greg Hayden; Visual Effects Supervisor, Michael Fink; Visual Effects, CIS Visual Effects Group, Hammerhead Prods., Pacific Title and Art Studio, Asylum, Digital Backlot; Stunts, Brad Martin; Casting, Kathy Driscoll, Francine Maisler; a Red Hour production; Dolby; Panavision; Deluxe color; Rated R; 106 minutes; Release date: August 13, 2008

Cast

Tugg Speedman	**Ben Stiller**
Jeff Portnoy	**Jack Black**
Kirk Lazarus	**Robert Downey, Jr.**
Four Leaf Tayback	**Nick Nolte**
Damien Cockburn	**Steve Coogan**
Kevin Sandusky	**Jay Baruchel**
Cody	**Danny McBride**
Alpa Chino	**Brandon T. Jackson**
Studio Executive Rob Slolom	**Bill Hader**
Tran	**Brandon Soo Hoo**
Byong	**Reggie Lee**
Tru	**Trieu Tran**
Rick Peck	**Matthew McConaughey**
Lee Grossman	**Tom Cruise**

Jeff Kahn (Snooty Waiter), Anthony Ruivivar (Platoon Sergeant Shot in Head), Eric Winzenried (Chopper Pilot), Valerie Azylynn (Damien's Assistant), Matt Levin (Cameraperson), David Pressman (First Assistant Director), Amy Stiller (Script Supervisor), Dempsey Silva (Special Effects Assistant), Jeff Weidemann, Nadine Ellis, Rachel Avery (Speedman Assistants), Darryl Farmer, Rod Tate (Alpa's Posse), Maria Menounos, Tyra Banks, Jon Voight, Jennifer Love Hewitt, Jason Bateman, Lance Bass, Alicia Silverstone, Kathy Hilton, Tobey Maguire (Themselves), Christine Taylor (Rebecca), Jel Galiza (Speedman's Chef), Andrea De Oliveira (Speedman's Trainer), Yvette Nicole Brown (Peck's Assistant), J. Thomas Chon, Jacob Chon (Half Squat), Mini Alden (Grossman's Secretary), Mike Hoagland (Grossman's Assistant), Miko Hughes (Radio DJ), Jillian Johnston (Four Leaf's Date), Kevin Pollak (Head Priest)

A group of pampered Hollywood actors, filming a dramatic war story in Southeast Asia, fail to realize that they are no longer simply acting but are under attack by a heroin kingpin and his rebel troops.

This film received an Oscar nomination for supporting actor (Robert Downey, Jr.).

Jay Baruchel, Robert Downey, Jr., Jack Black

Danny McBride, Nick Nolte

Steve Coogan, Robert Downey, Jr.

Ben Stiller, Robert Downey, Jr. © DreamWorks

Paula Patton, Kiefer Sutherland © 20th Century Fox

MIRRORS

(20ᵀᴴ CENTURY FOX) Producers, Alexandra Milchan, Marc Sternberg, Gregory Levasseur; Executive Producers, Marc S. Fischer, Kiefer Sutherland, Andrew Hong; Coproducer, Eun Young Kim; Director, Alexandre Aja; Screenplay, Alexandre Aja, Gregory Levasseur; Based on the motion picture *Into the Mirror* written by Kim Sung Ho; Photography, Maxime Alexandre; Designer, Joseph Nemec III; Costumes, Ellen Mirojnick, Michael Dennison; Music, Javier Navarette; Editor, Baxter; Visual Effects Supervisors, David Fogg, Jamison Scott Goei; Special Visual Effects and Digital Animation, Rez-Illusion Digital Visual Effects, Look Effects; Casting, Deborah Aquila, Tricia Wood, Jennifer Smith; a New Regency production, presented with Regency Enterprises; Dolby; Arri Widescreen; Deluxe color; Rated R; 111 minutes; Release date: August 15, 2008

Cast
Ben Carson	**Kiefer Sutherland**
Amy Carson	**Paula Patton**
Angela Carson	**Amy Smart**
Anna Esseker	**Mary Beth Peil**
Michael Carson	**Cameron Boyce**
Daisy Carson	**Eric Gluck**
Robert Esseker	**Julian Glover**
Lorenzo Sapelli	**John Shrapnel**

Jason Flemyng (Larry Byrne), Tim Ahern (Dr. Morris), Josh Cole (Gary Lewis), Ezra Buzzington (Terrence Berry), Doina Aida Stan (Rosa), Ioana Abur (Front Desk Sister), Darren Kent (Jimmy Esseker), Roz McCutcheon (Jimmy's Mother), Adina Rapiteanu (Young Anna), William Meredith (Young Doctor), Bart Sidles (Police Inspector), Cai Man, Jingdong Qin (Neighbors), Anca Damacus (Burning Woman), Tudor Stroescu (Delivery Man), Lilian Donici, Aurelia Radulescu, George Dumitrescu, Irina Saulescu, Valeriu Pavel (Mirror People)

A disgraced detective takes a job as a night watchman at a department store shuttered because of a fire and finds himself experiencing weirdly supernatural visions.

FLY ME TO THE MOON

(SUMMIT ENTERTAINMENT) Producers, Charlotte Clay Huggins, Caroline Van Iseghem, Gina Gallo, Mimi Maynard; Executive Producers, Eric Dillens, Domonic Paris, Ben Stassen; Director, Ben Stassen; Screenplay, Domonic Paris; Art Director, Jeremie Degruson; Music, Ramin Djawad; Animation Supervisor, Philippe Taillez; Visual Effects Supervisor, Jerome Escobar; Casting, Mimi Maynard, Gina Gallo; an nWave Pictures production, in association with Illuminata Pictures; Dolby; Color; 3-D; Rated G; 89 minutes; Release date: August 15, 2008

Voice cast
Nat	**Trevor Gagnon**
Nat's Mom	**Kelly Ripa**
IQ	**Philip Daniel Bolden**
Scooter	**David Gore**
Grandpa	**Christopher Lloyd**
Nadia	**Nicollette Sheridan**
Yegor	**Tim Curry**
Himself	**Buzz Aldrin**

Robert Patrick (Louie), Ed Begley, Jr. (Poopchev), Adrienne Barbeau (Scooter's Mom), Cam Clark (Ray), Grant George (Russian Fly), Steve Kramer (Leonide), Mimi Maynard (IQ's Mom), Scott Menville (Butch), Lorraine Nicholson (Katie), Sophie Simpson (Polly), Sandy Simpson (Neil Armstrong), Doug Stone (Russian Announcer), Jeffrey Braer (Horse Fly #2)

Three houseflies find themselves unexpectedly lending a hand when they end up aboard the historic Apollo 11 flight to the moon.

Neil Armstrong © Summit Entertainment

Scooter, Nat, IQ

STAR WARS: THE CLONE WARS

(WARNER BROS.) Producer, Catherine Winder; Executive Producer, George Lucas; Director, Dave Filoni; Screenplay, Henry Gilroy, Steven Melching, Scott Murphy; Animation Directors, Jesse Yeh, Kevin Jong; Music, Kevin Kiner; Editor, Jason W.A. Tucker; CG and Lighting Supervisor, Andrew Harris; Casting, Sue Blu; a Lucasfilm production from Lucasfilm Animation; Dolby; Panavision; Color; Rated PG; 98 minutes; Release date: August 15, 2008

Voice cast

Anakin Skywalker	**Matt Lanter**
Ahsoka Tano	**Ashley Eckstein**
Obi-Wan Kenobi/4-A7/	
Medical Droid	**James Arnold Taylor**
Clone Troopers/Captain Rex/	
Cody Dee	**Bradley Baker**
Yoda/Narrator/Admiral Yularen	**Tom Kane**
Asajj Ventress/Tee-C-Seventy	**Nika Futterman**
Chancellor Palpatine/Darth Sidious	**Ian Abercrombie**
General Loathsom/Ziro	
The Hutt/Kronos-327	**Corey Burton**
Padme Amidala	**Catherine Taber**
Battle Droids	**Matthew Wood**
Jabba the Hutt	**Kevin Michael Richardson**
Rotta the Huttlet	**David Acord**
Mace Windu	**Samuel L. Jackson**
C-3PO	**Anthony Daniels**
Count Dooku	**Christopher Lee**

Yoda © Warner Bros.

Clones

As Anakin Skywalker searches for the kidnapped son of Jabba the Hutt, the nefarious Count Dooku plots to have the young Jedi knight assassinated.

Left: *Ahsoka Tano, Anakin Skywalker*

Obi-Wan Kenobi

Steve Coogan, Elisabeth Shue, Amy Poehler © Focus Features

Natalie Amenula, Steve Coogan, Melonie Diaz, Arnie Pantoja

Steve Coogan, Skylar Astin

HAMLET 2

(FOCUS) Producers, Eric Eisner, Leonid Rozhetskin, Aaron Ryder; Executive Producers, Albert Berger, Ron Yerxa, Michael Flynn; Director, Andrew Fleming; Screenplay, Andrew Fleming, Pam Brady; Photography, Alexander Gruaynaki; Designer, Tony Fanning; Costumes, Jill Newell; Music, Ralph Sall; Editor, Jeff Freeman; Casting, Pam Dixon; an L+E Pictures production; Dolby; Color; HD; Rated R; 94 minutes; Release date: August 20, 2008

Cast

Dana Marschz	**Steve Coogan**
Brie Marschz	**Catherine Keener**
Octavio	**Joseph Julian Soria**
Rand Posin	**Skylar Astin**
Epiphany Sellars	**Phoebe Strole**
Ivonne	**Melonie Diaz**
Vitamin J	**Arnie Pantoja**
Chuy	**Michael Esparaz**
Yolanda	**Natalie Amenula**
Principal Rocker	**Marshall Bell**
Gary	**David Arquette**
Herself	**Elisabeth Shue**
Cricket Feldstein	**Amy Poehler**
Noah Sappaerstein	**Shea Pepe**

Marco Rodriguez (Mr. Marquez), Deborah Chavez (Mrs. Marquez), Kevin Wiggins, Johnnie Hector (Policemen), Nat Faxon (Glenn from Copy Shop), Steve Corona (Horace), Arron Shiver (Virgil), Josh Berry (Mr. Mann), Margarita Wilder (Julia De La Huerta), Evan Adrian (Danny the Waiter), J.D. Garfield (Man with Envelope), Mary Evans, Tomas Sanchez (Parents), Mike Hatfield (Man in Truck), John Hardman (Old Dude), Stephen Eiland (Scary Gang Banger), Cynthia Straus (Hysterical Woman), Will Gluck, Tom Romero (Men at Play), Jenny Gabrielle (Prayer Girl), Frank Bond (Ron from the *Times*), Todd Anderson (Redneck Parent), Daniel Quiñones (Giggles)

Threatened with the elimination of his department because of budget cuts, failed actor-turned-drama teacher Dana Marschz decides to risk it all by staging a self-penned sequel to *Hamlet.*

Catherine Keener, David Arquette

Kim Rivers Roberts, Scott Roberts

Scott Roberts (right) © Zeitgeist Films

TROUBLE THE WATER

(ZEITGEIST) Producers, Tia Lessin, Carl Deal; Executive Producers, Joslyn Barnes, Danny Glover, Todd Olson, David Alcaro; Coproducers, T. Woody Richman, Amir Bar-Lev; Directors, Tia Lessin, Carl Deal; Photography, P.J. Raval, Kimberly Roberts; Music, Davidge/Del Naja CQ (Robert del Naja and Neil Davidge); Music Supervisor, Barry Cole; Editor, T. Woody Richman; a Louverture Films presentation of an Elsewhere Films production; Dolby; Color; Not rated; 93 minutes; Release date: August 22, 2008
Documentary on the devastation left behind on New Orleans by Hurricane Katrina as seen from the perspective of one family who stayed at home during the storm.

With
Kimberly Roberts, Scott Roberts, Brian Nobles, Jerome Baham, Kendall "Wink" Rivers, Larry

This film received an Oscar nomination for documentary feature.

MOMMA'S MAN

(KINO) Producers, Alex Orlovsky, Hunter C. Gray; Executive Producers, Paul Mezey, Tyler Brodie; Director/Screenplay, Azazel Jacobs; Photography, Tobias Datum; Music, Mandy Hoffman; Editor, Darrin Navarro; an Artists Public Domain presentation; Color; Not rated; 99 minutes; Release date: August 22, 2008

Cast
Mikey	Matt Boren
Dad	Ken Jacobs
Mom	Flo Jacobs
Laura	Dana Varon
Tom	Richard Edson
Dante	Piero Arcilesi
Bridget	Eleanor Hutchins

Paying a visit to his aging parents in New York, Mikey decides to leave behind his life in Los Angeles and stay with them.

Matt Boren © Kino Intl.

Matt Boren, Flo Jacobs, Ken Jacobs

THE HOUSE BUNNY

(COLUMBIA) Producers, Adam Sandler, Jack Giarraputo, Allen Covert, Heather Parry; Executive Producers, Anna Faris, Kirsten Smith, Karen McCullah Lutz; Coproducers, Debra James, Jason Burns, Richard Rosenzweig; Director, Fred Wolf; Screenplay, Karen McCullah Lutz, Kirsten Smith; Photography, Shelly Johnson; Designer, Missy Stewart; Music, Waddy Wachtel; Music Supervisors, Michael Dilbeck, Brooks Arthur; Editor, Debra Chiate; Casting, Lisa London, Catherine Stroud; a Happy Madison production, in association with Alta Loma Entertainment, in association with Relativity Media; Dolby; Deluxe color; Rated PG-13; 98 minutes; Release date: August 22, 2008

Cast

Shelley Darlingson	**Anna Faris**
Oliver	**Colin Hanks**
Natalie	**Emma Stone**
Mona	**Kat Dennings**
Harmony	**Katharine McPhee**
Joanne	**Rumer Willis**
Lilly	**Kiely Williams**
Carrie Mae	**Dana Goodman**
Tanya	**Kimberly Makkouk**
Cassandra	**Monet Mazur**
Colby	**Tyson Ritter**
Himself	**Hugh M. Hefner**
Dean Simmons	**Christopher McDonald**
Mrs. Hagstrom	**Beverly D'Angelo**

Leslie Del Rosario (Sienna), Sarah Wright (Ashley), Rachel Specter (Courtney), Julia Lea Wolov (Sweet Prostitute), Owen Benjamin (Marvin), Holly Madison, Bridget Marquardt, Kendra Wilkinson, Sean Salisbury, Matt Leinart, Shaquille O'Neal (Themselves), Tyler Spindel (Steve), Sara Jean Underwood (Sara, Playmate), Lauren Michelle Hill (Lauren, Playmate), Hiromi Oshima (Hiromi, Playmate), Dan Patrick (Cop), Nick Swardson (Playboy Photographer), Jay Hayden (Kip), Matt Barr (Tyler), Christopher Titone (Guy at Bar), Michael Bernardi, Mike Falkow, Marlon Hunter (Karaoke Trio), Josh Richman, Tony Ervolina (Paramedics), Tanner Redman (Trent), Michelle Fields (Michelle), Nikki Deloach (Tall Blonde Girl), Linsey Godfrey (Short Burnette Girl), Alison Koellish (Medium Blonde Girl), Jackie Benoit (Fannie), Katheryn Cain, Amanda Columbus, Katheryne Ashley Cover, Danni Katz, Aya Nagasaki, Rachel Saydak, Ashley Schneider (Girls at Panhellenic), Jennifer Tisdale (Phi Iota Mu), Adam Shapiro (Mona's Interviewee), Angela V. Shelton (Mean Prostitute), Jonathan Loughran (Tall Prostitute), Kathleen Gati (Boutique Manager), Missy Stewart (Kappa Eta Sigma Housemother), Robert H. Harvey (Guy at Pool Table), Ryan Rottman (Calendar Buyer), Mitch Gibney (Post Office Clerk), Ben Lyons (Limbo Guy), Dale Thomas Krupla (Karaoke MC), Charles Robinson (Francis)

Booted out of the Playboy mansion for being too old, a guileless "bunny" finds herself taking charge of a sorority house of misfit girls.

Anna Faris
© Columbia Pictures

Colin Hanks, Anna Faris

Kat Dennings, Anna Faris, Katharine McPhee, Emma Stone, Rumer Willis

Tyson Ritter, Emma Stone, Anna Faris

DEATH RACE

(UNIVERSAL) Producers, Paula Wagner, Jeremy Bolt, Paul W. S. Anderson; Executive Producers, Roger Corman, Dennis E. Jones, Don Granger, Ryan Kavanaugh; Director/Screen Story and Screenplay, Paul W.S. Anderson; Based on the film *Death Race 2000* produced by Roger Corman; Photography, Scott Kevan; Designer, Paul Denham Austerberry; Costumes, Gregory Mah; Music, Paul Haslinger, Music Supervisor, Kathy Nelson; Editor, Niven Howie; Visual Effects Supervisor, Dennis Berardi; Stunts, Andy Gill, Dave McKeowen; Fight Coordinator, Phil Culotta; an Impact Pictures-C/W production in association with Roger Corman, Relativity Media; Dolby; Technicolor; Rated R; 98 minutes; Release date: August 22, 2008

Cast

Jensen Ames	**Jason Statham**
Hennessey	**Joan Allen**
Coach	**Ian McShane**
Machine Gun Joe	**Tyrese Gibson**
Case	**Natalie Martinez**
Pachenko	**Max Ryan**
Ulrich	**Jason Clarke**
Lists	**Fred Koehler**
Gunner	**Jacob Vargas**
Travis Colt	**Justin Mader**
Grimm	**Robert LaSardo**
14K	**Robin Shou**
Suzy	**Janaya Stephens**
Neo Nazi	**John Fallon**
Old Timer	**Bruce McFee**

Benz Antoine, Danny Blanco Hall, Christian Paul (Joe's Navigators), Marcello Bezina, Jere Gillis (Policemen), Cory Fantie (Disgusted Worker), Russell Ferrier (Angry Worker), Anna Marie Frances Lea (Nasty Teller), Dan Jeannotte (Hennessey Tech)

One time speedway champ Jensen Ames is sent to prison on trumped-up charges so that he can take the place of the recently deceased Frankenstein, a revered driver who has become the star attraction of *Death Race*, an extreme racing competition broadcast from the Terminal Island penal facility. Remake of the 1975 film *Death Race 2000*, which starred David Carradine, Simone Griffeth, and Sylvester Stallone.

Fred Koehler, Jason Statham, Ian McShane, Jacob Vargas

Tyrese Gibson

Jason Clarke, Jason Statham, Joan Allen

Jason Statham, Natalie Martinez © Universal Studios

Don Cheadle, Jeff Daniels

Don Cheadle, Saïd Taghmaoui

Mozhan Marno, Neal McDonough, Guy Pearce

TRAITOR

(OVERTURE) Producers, David Hoberman, Todd Lieberman, Don Cheadle, Jeffrey Silver; Executive Producers, Ashok Amritraj, Steve Martin, Arlene Gibbs, Kay Liberman; Coproducer, Richard Schlesinger; Director/Screenplay, Jeffrey Nachmanoff; Story, Steve Martin, Jeffrey Nachmanoff; Photography, J. Michael Muro; Designer, Laurence Bennett; Costumes, Gersha Phillips; Music, Mark Kilian; Editor, Billy Fox; Visual Effects, Intelligent Creatures, Ghost VFX; Stunts, Matt Birman, Philippe Guegan; Casting, Deborah Aquila, Tricia Wood, Kate Dowd; a Mandeville Films, Hyde Park Entertainment, Crescendo production; Dolby; Panavision; Technicolor; Rated PG-13; 113 minutes; Release date: August 27, 2008

Cast

Salim Horn	**Don Cheadle**
Roy Clayton	**Guy Pearce**
Omar	**Saïd Taghmaoui**
Max Archer	**Neal McDonough**
Fareed	**Ally Khan**
Chandra Dawkin	**Archie Panjabi**
Nathir	**Raad Rawi**
Bashir	**Hassam Ghancy**
Leyla	**Mozhan Marno**
Hamzi	**Adeel Akhtar**
Carter	**Jeff Daniels**
Dierdre Horn	**Lorena Gale**

Scali Delpeyrat (Inspector Gilles), Mehdi Ortelsberg (Ali), Aizoun Abdelkader (Ahmed), Mohamed Choubi (Security Force Captain), Farid Regragui (Wadi), Hamdane Habibe (Scarecrow), Youness Sardi, Joseph Beddelem, Alan Oumouzoune (Omar's Crew), Tom Barnett (Andrew Kelly), Simon Reynolds (Ted Blake), Matt Gordon (Simon), P. Rodney Barnes, Shahla Kareen, Ali Momen, Paulino Nunes (Suicide Bombers), Alexandra Castillo (Dark Haired Woman), Jeff Kassel (Software Company Manager), Mike McPhaden (Computer Tech), Dani Jazzar (Munir), Jonathan Lloyd Walker (Hayes), José Heuze (Alvarez), Scott Wickware (Dupree), Elias Zarou (Iqbal), Catherine Galloway (BBC Reporter), Myriam Blanckaert (Inspector Gilles' Deputy), Nick Alachiotis (Ship Crew Member), Alex Poch-Goldin (FBI Surveillance Agent), Natasha Roy (Translator #1), Yassine Mamadou (Samir, 10 Years Old), Omar Mamadou (Samir's Father), Mostafa Hniny (Fake Policeman), Michaël Troude (Spanish Patrolman), Rodriguez Gelos (Tour Group Employee Alfonso), Ron Bell (Bus Driver)

A bombing at the U.S. consulate in Nice leads FBI agent Roy Clayton to investigate African-born Muslim American Samir Horn's involvement in the event.

Guy Pearce, Don Cheadle © Overture Films

BANGKOK DANGEROUS

(LIONSGATE) Producers, Jason Shuman, William Sherak, Nicolas Cage, Norm Golightly; Executive Producers, Andrew Pfeffer, Derek Dauchy, Denis O'Sullivan, Ben Waisbren; Director, The Pang Brothers; Screenplay, Jason Richman; Based on the film *Bangkok Dangerous* by the Pang Brothers; Photography, Decha Srimantra; Designer, James Newport; Costumes, Surasak Warakijcharoen, Kristin Burke; Music, Brian Tyler; Editors, Mike Jackson, Curran Pang; Visual Effects Supervisor, Bruce Jones; Fight Choreographer, Dave Leitch; Casting, Tarinee Thaima; an IEG Virtual Studios presentation of a Saturn Films, Blue Star Entertainment production; Dolby; Color; Rated R; 98 minutes; Release date: September 5, 2008

Cast

Joe	**Nicolas Cage**
Kong	**Shahkrit Yamnar**
Fon	**Charlie Young**
Aom	**Panward Hemmanee**
Surat	**Nirattisai Kaljareuk**
Aran	**Dom Hetrakul**

Tuck Napaskorn (Kong's Brother), Steve Baldocchi (Michigan), Chris Heebink (USC), James With (Chicago), Peter Shadrin (Anton), Arthajid Puengvicha (Official), Duangjai Srisawang (Man in Arena), Veerasak Boonchard (Winai), Sakol Palvanichkul (Tuk Tuk Driver), Savaros Sriratum, Pornpat Tipthongkum (News Anchors), Thanrada Kao-Im (Waitress), Aratchporn Satead (Vendor Lady), Winai Thawattana (White Target), Gonthron Bossarakam (Man in Slum), Thanapon Parnjaroen (Bell Man), Jeremy Thana (Gangster #2), Allwarin Apirakyothin (Aom's Sister), Andrew Pfeffer (Caucasian Prisoner), Oliver Steel (European Crying Boy), Kitchanpon Apirakyothin (Fat Man), Chalita Chaisaeng, Chatchaya Watcharakitikorn, Arnunthaya Suksalak (Fat Man's Girls), Thanitar Jirapanid, Nareerat Jeanmahan (Girls with Target), Suwatjanee Suriyapas, Pariwut Pratchayanun (Last Target's Kids), Tuengtanpon Thongnawakun (Last Target's Wife), Keang Kunsri (Last Target Man), Chris Lowenstein, Oliver Ackerman, Russell Wald, Laura Herold, David L. Michaels, Ronald Anderson (Past Targets), Chollomark Chiengthong (Surat's Wife), Armondthap Limdusit (Target Man #1), Jirakit Suwannapab (Target #1's Driver), Chatchai Phuengparyun (Target Boat Driver #1), Arkrapong Pimpajak, Songsak Sampanpim (Target #1's Bodyguards), Duangrutai Suwannarat (Thai Garland Girl), Songpohl Dittasom (Waiter)

A hitman arrives in Bangkok to carry out four contracts he hopes will be his last.

Nicolas Cage © Lionsgate

Jimmy Tsai

PING PONG PLAYA

(IFC FILMS) Producers, Anne Clements, Joan Huang; Executive Producer, Jeffrey Gou; Director, Jessica Yu; Screenplay, Jessica Yu, Jimmy Tsai; Photography, Frank G. DeMarco; Designer, Denise Hudson; Costumes, Jessica Flaherty; Music, Jeff Beal; Music Supervisor, Shaun Young; Editor, Zene Baker; Casting, Jason L. Wood; a Cherry Sky Films presentation of a Joan Huang/Anne Clements production; Dolby; Color; Super 16mm-to-HD; Rated PG-13; 96 minutes; Release date: September 5, 2008

Cast

Christopher "C-dub" Wang	**Jimmy Tsai**
Felix	**Andrew Vo**
JP Money	**Khary Payton**
Mr. Wang	**Jim Lau**
Michael Wang	**Roger Fan**
D.B. Redd	**Shelley Malil**
Mrs. Wang	**Elizabeth Sung**
Prabakar	**Javin Reid**
Gerald	**Peter Paige**

Smith Cho (Jennifer), Scott Lowell (Tom), Adam Bobrow (Dan Furlie), Romeo Brown (Kevin), Martin Chow (Jerry Lin), Catherine Dao (Mrs. Sun), Cici Lau (Mrs. Chen), Esther Song (Miss Chinatown), Elan Tom (Wilson), Stephanie Weir (Cheryl Davis), Jordan Green, Alexander Agate (Loser Kids), Percival Arcibal (Teenage Ping Pong Player), William Behlendorf (Another Kid), Joey Brander, Jordan Walker Ross (Basketball Kids), Joseph Stephens, Jr. (Referee), Jason Stuart (Doctor)

Hoping to play professional basketball, "C-dub" Wang instead ends up having to defend his family's Golden Cock Ping Pong title.

Scott Lowell, Peter Paige © IFC Films

George Clooney, Frances McDormand © Focus Features

John Malkovich

BURN AFTER READING

(FOCUS) Producers, Joel Coen, Ethan Coen; Executive Producers, Tim Bevan, Eric Fellner, Robert Graf; Director/Screenplay, Joel Coen, Ethan Coen; Photography, Emmanuel Lubezki; Designer, Jess Gonchor; Costumes, Mary Zophres; Music, Carter Burwell; Editor, Roderick Jaynes; Casting, Ellen Chenoweth; a Working Title production, presented in association with Studio Canal and Relativity Media; Dolby; Deluxe color; Rated R; 95 minutes; Release date: September 12, 2008

Cast

Harry Pfarrer	**George Clooney**
Linda Litzke	**Frances McDormand**
Osbourne Cox	**John Malkovich**
Katie Cox	**Tilda Swinton**
Chad Feldheimer	**Brad Pitt**
Ted Treffon	**Richard Jenkins**
Sandy Pfarrer	**Elizabeth Marvel**
CIA Officer	**David Rasche**
CIA Superior	**J.K. Simmons**
Krapotkin	**Olek Krupa**
Alan	**Michael Countryman**
Cosmetic Surgeon	**Jeffrey DeMunn**
Divorce Lawyers	**Kevin Sussman, J.R. Horne**
Peck	**Hamilton Clancy**
Olson	**Armand Schultz**
Doug Magruder	**Pun Bandhu**

Karla Mosley (Party Guest #2), Richard Poe (Stretching Gym Patron), Carmen M. Herlihy (Prospective Gym Customer), Raul Aranas (Manolo), Judy Frank (Lawyer's Secretary), Sándor Técsy (Russian Embassy Escort), Yury Tsykun (Senior Russian Embassy Man), Brian O'Neill (Hal), Robert Prescott (Process Server), Matt Walton, Lori Hammel (Morning Show Hosts), Crystal Bock (PR Woman), Patrick Boll (Sandy's Man), Logan Kulick (Four-Year-Old Patient), Dermot Mulroney (Star of *Coming up Daisy*)

Kicked out of the CIA, analyst Osborn Cox sets out to write an explosive memoir, only to have the disk end up in the hands of some clueless fitness center employees.

George Clooney

Left: *Richard Jenkins, Brad Pitt, Frances McDormand*

RIGHTEOUS KILL

(OVERTURE) Producers, Rob Cowan, Avi Lerner, Randall Emmett, Jon Avnet, Lati Grobman, Alexandra Milchan, Daniel M. Rosenberg; Executive Producers, Danny Dimbort, Boaz Davidson, George Furla, Trevor Short; Coproducer, Marsha Oglesby; Director, Jon Avnet; Screenplay, Russell Gewirtz; Photography, Denis Lenoir; Designer, Tracey Gallacher; Costumes, Debra McGuire; Music, Edward Shearmur; Music Supervisor, Ashley Miller; Editor, Paul Hirsch; Visual Effects Supervisor, Vesselina Hary Georgieva; Stunts, Buddy Joe Hooker; Casting, Nancy Klopper; Presented in association with Millennium Films, in association with Emmett/Furla Films and Grosvenor Park Media; Dolby; Widescreen; Technicolor; Rated R; 100 minutes; Release date: September 12, 2008

Carla Gugino, Robert De Niro

Cast

Tom "Turk" Cowan	**Robert De Niro**
David "Rooster" Fisk	**Al Pacino**
Spider	**Curtis Jackson**
Karen Corelli	**Carla Gugino**
Det. Simon Perez	**John Leguizamo**
Det. Ted Riley	**Donnie Wahlberg**
Lt. Hingis	**Brian Dennehy**
Jessica	**Trilby Glover**
Gwen Davis	**Saidah Arrika**
Stein	**Alan Rosenberg**
Rogers	**Sterling K. Brown**
Dr. Prosky	**Barry Primus**
Natalya	**Shirly Brener**
Cheryl Brooks	**Melissa Leo**
Martin Baum	**Alan Blumenfeld**

Oleg Taktarov (Yevgeny Mugalat), Frank John Hughes (Charles Randall), Terry Serpico (Jonathan Van Luytens), Liza Colón-Zayas (Judge Angel Rodriguez), Malachy McCourt (Father Connell), Ajay Naidu (Dr. Chadrabar), Charles F. Krichman, Jr. (Umpire), Rob Dyrdek (Rambo), James Shanahan (ESU Officer), Fatso-Fasano (Stubby), Mia Barron (Jill Goldman), Andrew Blake (Officer Jones), Chris Centiempo (Joseph Cianci), Judy Del Guidice (Hostess), Bryan Chatlien (Ellis Lynde), Shalaya Patty Ford (Latasha), Shaun Kelvin (Cop #2), Merrit Wever (Rape Victim), Les Chantery (Lawyer #2), Katie Bukovsky (Coach), Tyrone Smith (Fly Ty), Jim Jones (Jim Jones), Darryl Pittman (39 D/R Period), Margaret Head (Hot Girl), Katarzyna Wolejnio (Dancer)

When various criminals who had eluded prosecution end up murdered, veteran detectives Rooster and Turk start to wonder if a cop is responsible for the executions.

Al Pacino, Brian Dennehy, Robert De Niro

Curtis Jackson
© Overture Films

Meg Ryan, Annette Bening © Picturehouse

Annette Bening, Jada Pinkett Smith, Debra Messing

Bette Midler

Cloris Leachman, Tilly Scott Pedersen

THE WOMEN

(PICTUREHOUSE) Producers, Victoria Pearman, Mick Jagger, Bill Johnson, Diane English; Executive Producers, Jim Seibel, Joel Shukovsky, Bobby Sheng, James W. Skotchdopole, Bob Berney, Carolyn Blackwood; Director/Screenplay, Diane English; Based on the play by Clare Boothe Luce and the 1939 motion picture screenplay by Anita Loos and Jane Murfin; Photography, Anastas Michos; Designer, Jane Musky; Costumes, John Dunn; Music, Mark Isham; Music Supervisor, Chris Douridas; Editor, Tia Nolan; Casting, Amanda Mackey, Cathy Sandrich Gelfond; a Jagged Films and Inferno production, with Shukovsky English Entertainment, presented in association with Inferno and Double Edge Entertainment; Dolby; Color; Rated PG-13; 114 minutes; Release date: September 12, 2008

Cast

Mary Haines	**Meg Ryan**
Sylvie Fowler	**Annette Bening**
Crystal Allen	**Eva Mendes**
Edie Cohen	**Debra Messing**
Alex Fisher	**Jada Pinkett Smith**
Leah Miller	**Bette Midler**
Catherine Frazier	**Candice Bergen**
Bailey Smith	**Carrie Fisher**
Maggie	**Cloris Leachman**
Tanya	**Debi Mazar**
Molly Haines	**India Ennenga**
Natasha	**Natasha Alam**
Pat	**Ana Gasteyer**
Barbara Delocorte	**Joanna Gleason**
Uta	**Tilly Scott Pedersen**

Lynn Whitfield (Glenda Hill), Jill Flint (Annie), Emily Seymour, Allison Seymour (April Cohen), Lauren Lefebvre, Lindsay Lefebvre (May Cohen), Isabella Pateledes, Olivia Panteledes (June Cohen), Madaliene Black, Meredith Black (January Cohen), Jana Robbins (Lingerie Saleswoman), Maya Ri Sanchez (Dora), Ruby Hondros (Jimmy Choo Wearer), NiCole Robinson (Makeover Lady), Danielle Perry (Salon Assistant), Lindsay Flathers (Taylor), Christy Scott Cashman (Jean), Celeste Oliva (Gilda), Denece Ryland (Cory), Allyssa Maurice (Sweet Woman), Jordan Schechter (Ashley), Marina Re (Helene), Stephanie Clayman (Admissions Nurse), Maria Elena Ramirez (OB-GYN Maria), Pamela Lambert (Scrub Nurse), Ellen Withrow (Nurse at Recovery Hotel)

Mary Haines' seemingly charmed life and stable marriage are placed in jeopardy when she is made privy to gossip about her husband's affair with perfume saleslady Crystal Allen. Remake of the 1939 film of the same name which starred Norma Shearer, Joan Crawford, and Rosalind Russell; which was, in turn, remade as *The Opposite Sex* (MGM, 1956), with June Allyson, Joan Collins, and Ann Miller.

TOWELHEAD

(WARNER INDEPENDENT) formerly *Nothing is Private*; Producers, Ted Hope, Steven Rales, Alan Ball; Executive Producers, Anne Carey, Scott Rudin, Peggy Rajski; Director/Screenplay, Alan Ball; Based on the novel by Alicia Erian; Photography, Newton Thomas Sigel; Designer, James Chinlund; Costumes, Danny Glicker; Casting, Wendy Goldstein; a This is That/Indian Paintbrush production in association with Your Face Goes Here Entertainment; Dolby; Panavision; Color; HD; Rated R; 121 minutes; Release date: September 12, 2008

Cast

Jasira Maroun	**Summer Bishil**
Travis Vuoso	**Aaron Eckhart**
Rifat Maroun	**Peter Macdissi**
Melina Hines	**Toni Collette**
Gail Monahan	**Maria Bello**
Thomas Bradley	**Eugene Jones**
Gil Hines	**Matt Letscher**
Evelyn Vuoso	**Carrie Preston**
Zack Vuoso	**Chase Ellison**
Denise	**Gemmenne de la Peña**
Thena Panos	**Lynn Collins**
Barry	**Chris Messina**
Mr. Joffrey	**Robert Baker**

Eamonn Roche (School Photographer), Irina Voronina ("Snow Queen" Centerfold), Cleo King (Sales Clerk), Michael McShae, D.C. Cody (Middle School Jerks), Soledad St. Hilaire (Janitor), Nathalie Walker ("Golf Girl" Centerfold), Kim Knight, LoriDawn Messuri (Topless Golfers), Lorna Scott (French Teacher), Shari Headley (Mrs. Bradley), Randy Goodwin (Mr. Bradley), Larry Cedar (Glamour Photographer), Virginia Louise Smith (Nurse), Lee von Ernst (OR-OB/GYN Nurse)

A thirteen-year-old girl, forced to live with her short-tempered Lebanese father, finds herself intrigued by an adult neighbor's budding sexual interest in her.

Peter Macdissi, Summer Bishil

Summer Bishil, Eugene Jones

Aaron Eckhart © Warner Independent

Toni Collette, Matt Letscher

Tyler Perry, Taraji P. Henson, Alfre Woodard

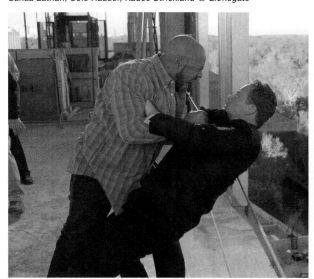

Sanaa Lathan, Cole Hauser, Kadee Strickland © Lionsgate

Rockmond Dunbar, Cole Hauser

Tyler Perry's THE FAMILY THAT PREYS

(LIONSGATE) Producers, Tyler Perry, Reuben Cannon; Executive Producer, Michael Paseornek; Coproducer, Roger M. Bobb, Joseph P. Genier; Director/Screenplay, Tyler Perry; Photography, Toyomichi Kurita; Designer, Ina Mayhew; Costumes, Keith G. Lewis; Music, Aaron Zigman; Music Supervisor, Joel C. High; Editor, Maysie Hoy; Casting, Alpha Tyler; a Tyler Perry Studios/Reuben Cannon Prods./Lionsgate production; Dolby; Technicolor; Rated PG-13; 111 minutes; Release date: September 12, 2008

Cast

Alice Pratt	**Alfre Woodard**
Andrea	**Sanaa Lathan**
Chris	**Rockmond Dunbar**
Jillian Cartwright	**Kadee Strickland**
William Cartwright	**Cole Hauser**
Pam	**Taraji P. Henson**
Abby	**Robin Givens**
Ben	**Tyler Perry**
Charlotte Cartwright	**Kathy Bates**
Nick	**Sebastian Siegel**
Christopher	**Santana Pruitt**
Robin	**Kaira Whitehead**

Ron Clinton Smith (Construction Foreman), Jeffrey Alan Chase (Austin), Johnell J. Easter (Customer), T. Alan Brown (Preacher), Mark Adam (Man on Street), Eric Goins (Man #2), Jeff Rose (Loan Officer), Michelle Keller (Teller), Andrew Hyatt Masset (Sam Walton), Jason MacDonald (Bartender), Todd Coley (Dancer), Crissy Collins (Church Soloist), Benjamin Brown (Abby's Husband)

Two widows, well-to-do Charlotte and her blue-collar friend Alice, embark on a cross-country trip while hoping to settle the problems of their offspring.

Kathy Bates

Billy Campbell, Téa Leoni, Jeff Hiller

Ricky Gervais, Michael-Leon Wooley, Kristen Wiig

Ricky Gervais © DreamWorks

GHOST TOWN

(DREAMWORKS/PARAMOUNT) Producer, Gavin Polone; Executive Producers, Roger Birnbaum, Gary Barber, Ezra Swerdlow; Director, David Koepp; Screenplay, David Koepp, John Kamps; Photography, Fred Murphy; Designer, Howard Cummings; Costumes, Sarah Edwards; Music, Geoff Zanelli; Editor, Sam Seig; Casting, Pat McCorkle, John Papsidera; a Spyglass Entertainment presentation of a Pariah production; Dolby; Color; Rated PG-13; 102 minutes; Release date: September 19, 2008

Cast
Bertram Pincus	**Ricky Gervais**
Frank Herlihy	**Greg Kinnear**
Gwen	**Téa Leoni**
Richard	**Billy Campbell**
Marjorie Pickthall	**Dana Ivey**
Dr. Prashar	**Aasif Mandvi**
Surgeon	**Kristen Wiig**
Ghost Dad	**Alan Ruck**
Hospital Lawyer	**Michael-Leon Wooley**
Naked Guy	**Jeff Hiller**
Young Husband	**Jordan Carlos**
Young Wife	**Dequina Moore**

Joe Badalucci, Brian Hutchison (Accident Bystanders), Tyre Simpson (Sneezy Cop), Julia K. Murney (Sneezy Lady), Claire Lautier (Upper East Side Lady), Bridget Moloney (Receptionist), Raymond Lee (Greenpeace Guy), Joey Mazzarino (Food Delivery Guy), Brad Oscar (Day Doorman), Kathleen Landis (Resident), Audrie Neenan (Admitting Nurse), Aaron Tveit (Anesthesiologist), Deborah S. Craig (Nurse), Betty Gilpin (WWII Nurse), Angelis Alexandris, Elaine Cusick (Elderly Couple), Kim Russell (Tennis Lady), Brian Tarantina (Ghost Cop), Darren Pettie, Jesse Means, Robert Kelly (Construction Worker Ghosts), Gabrielle Fink (Violin Student), Michael-Leon Wooley (Hospital Lawyer), Monte Bezell (Cab Driver), Sebastian Lacause (Bartender), Miles Grose (Night Doorman), Lou Sumrall (Harley Guy), Raymond McAnally, Amy Van Nostrand, Ira Hawkins, Danai Gurira (Assorted Ghosts), Richard O'Rourke (Man at Lecture), Brian d'Arcy James (Irish Eddie), Phoenix, Jazz (Leonard), Josh Clayton (Waiter), Lisa Datz, James Ludwig (Happy People at Bar), Melissa Thomas (Dr. Prashar's Patient), Shawn Hill (Bongo Player), Megan Byrne (Mrs. Pickthall's Daughter), José Ramón Rosario (Crane Operator), Jose Soto (Welder), Candace Thaxton (Harley Guy's Old Lady), Dylan Clark Marshall (Little Alex)

Following a near-death experience during an operation, nihilistic Manhattan dentist Bertram Pincus discovers, much to his horror, that he can see dead people who hope he can help them pass along messages to those they left behind and find closure.

Greg Kinnear, Ricky Gervais

LAKEVIEW TERRACE

(SCREEN GEMS) Producers, Will Smith, James Lassiter; Executive Producers, Joe Pichirallo, John Cameron, David Loughery, Jeffrey Graoup; Coproducer, Orin Woinsky; Director, Neil LaBute; Screenplay, David Loughery, Howard Korder; Story, David Loughery; Photography, Rogier Stoffers; Designer, Bruton Jones; Costumes, Lynette Meyer; Music, Mychael Danna, Jeff Danna; Editor, Joel Plotch; Visual Effects Supervisor, Rocco Passionino; Casting, Heidi Levitt; an Overbrook Entertainment production; Dolby; Deluxe color; Rated PG-13; 106 minutes; Release date: September 19, 2008

Cast

Abel Turner	**Samuel L. Jackson**
Chris Mattson	**Patrick Wilson**
Lisa Mattson	**Kerry Washington**
Harold Perreau	**Ron Glass**
Donnie Eaton	**Justin Chambers**
Javier Villareal	**Jay Hernandez**
Celia Turner	**Regine Nehy**
Marcus Turner	**Jaishon Fisher**
Captain Wentworth	**Robert Pine**
Clarence Darlington	**Keith Loneker**
Damon Richards	**Caleeb Pinkett**
Jung Lee Pak	**Robert Dahey**
Sang Hee Pak	**Ho-Jung**
Nadine	**Bitsie Tulloch**

Michael Sean Tighe (Manager), Valeri Ross (Old Woman), Darateena Dee Bryant (Woman), Dallas Raines (TV Weatherman), Dale Godboldo (Dale), Lynn Chen (Eden), Wiley Pickett, Vincent Laresca, Paul Terrell Clayton, Jeff Cockey (Officers), Wrenna Monet, Tabitha Taylor, Khira Thomas (Strippers), Cassius Willis (Officer Friendly), Vanessa Bell Calloway (Aunt Dorrie), Coca Brown (Bartender), Marc Chaiet (Neighbor), Zorianna Kit (TV Reporter), Hiep Le (Nurse), Ajay Mehta (Doctor), Sarah Lieving (Emergency Technician), Eva Larue (Lt. Morgada), Lonnie B. Moore, Jr. (Bachelor), Jamie Vandevert (Sheriff Deputy), Lisa Dewitt (Officer #4), Michael Landes (Lt. Bronson)

An interracial couple moves into what appears to be a peaceful and accommodating neighborhood only to find themselves being harassed by their next-door neighbor, an angry black police officer with a chip on his shoulder.

Patrick Wilson, Samuel L. Jackson

Samuel L. Jackson © Screen Gems

Patrick Wilson, Kerry Washington

Jay Hernandez

Viggo Mortensen, Ed Harris

Renée Zellweger, Ed Harris

APPALOOSA

(NEW LINE CINEMA) Producers, Ed Harris, Robert Knott, Ginger Sledge; Executive Producers, Michael London, Toby Emmerich, Sam Brown, Caldecott Chubb; Director, Ed Harris; Screenplay, Robert Knott, Ed Harris; Based on the novel by Robert B. Parker; Photography, Dean Semler; Designer, Waldemar Kalinowski; Costumes, David C. Robinson; Music, Jeff Beal; Editor, Kathryn Himoff; Casting, Nicole Abellera, Jeanne McCarthy; a Groundswell production, presented in association with AXon Films; Distributed by Warner Bros.; Dolby; Panavision; Deluxe color; Rated R; 115 minutes; Release date: September 19, 2008

Cast

Virgil Cole	**Ed Harris**
Everett Hitch	**Viggo Mortensen**
Allison French	**Renée Zellweger**
Randall Bragg	**Jeremy Irons**
Phil Olson	**Timothy Spall**
Ring Shelton	**Lance Henriksen**
Abner Raines	**Tom Bower**
Earl May	**James Gammon**
Katie	**Ariadna Gil**
Vince	**Timothy V. Murphy**
Joe Whitfield	**Gabriel Marantz**
Judge Elias Callison	**Bob Harris**
Marshall Jack Bell	**Bobby Jauregui**
Dean	**Luce Rains**
Chalk	**Jim Tarwater**

Boyd Kestner (Bronc), Benjamin Rosenshein (Town Boy), Cerris Morgan-Moyer (Tilda), Erik J. Bockheimer (Fat Wallis), Fred Hice, Neil Summers (Bragg's Men), Tim Carroll (Wagon Driver), Bounthanh Xaynhachack (Chin), Art Usher (Clerk), Clark Sanchez (Teamster), Cliff Gravel (Barber), Mike Watson (Night Rider), Rex Linn (Sheriff Clyde Stringer), Corby Griesenbeck (Charlie Tewksbury), Adam Nelson (Mackie Shelton), Daniel T. Parker (Mueller), Ed Pennybacker (Conductor), Alvin Lunak (Sharps), Martin Connelly (Apache Elder), Edmo (Young Brave), Argos MacCallum (Beauville Sheriff Russell), Cynthia Huerta (Mexican Woman)

Roving lawmen Virgil Cole and Everett Hitch agree to help the town of Appaloosa restore order and put a stop to gang leader Randall Bragg's efforts to control the territory.

Viggo Mortensen, Ed Harris © New Line Cinema

Jeremy Irons, Viggo Mortensen

HOUNDDOG

(EMPIRE) Producers, Deborah Kampmeier, Jen Gatien, Raye Dowell, Terry Leonard, Lawrence Robbins; Executive Producers, Robin Wright Penn, Scott Franklin, Henri Kessler, Rebecca Cleary, Stacey Bakula; Coproducerss, Kelly R. Tenney, Kathi Scharer, Gabrielle Berberich, Jim Czarnecki; Co-Executive Producers, Sam Froelich, Chris Hanley, Roberta Hanley, Michael Shane, Gary Smith; Director/Screenplay, Deborah Kampmeier; Photography, Ed Lachman, Jim Denault; Designer, Tim Grimes; Costumes, Leigh Leverett; Editor, Sabine Hoffman; Casting, Craig Fincannon, Lisa Mae Fincannon, Mary Vernieu; a Motion Picture Group production in association with full Moon Films and Deerjen Prods.; Dolby; Color; Rated R; 102 minutes; Release date: September 19, 2008

Cast

Llewellen	**Dakota Fanning**
Buddy	**Cody Hanford**
Granny	**Piper Laurie**
Daddy	**David Morse**
Charles	**Afemo Omilami**
Strange Lady	**Robin Wright Penn**
Grasshopper	**Isabelle Fuhrman**

Ron Prather (Truck Driver), Jill Scott (Big Mama Thornton), Oliver Clayton-Luce (Boy 3), Ryan Pelton (Elvis Presley), Christoph Sanders (Wooden's Boy), Frank Hoyt Taylor (Doctor), Jody Thompson (Preacher), Sean Andrew Wallace (Boy), William Smith Yelton (Wooden Boy Friend)

In a Southern backwoods town, twelve-year-old Llewellen finds herself growing up fast when she is forced to cope with her father's mental deterioration and her own traumatic sexual assault.

Robin Wright Penn, Dakota Fanning © Empire

Igor, King Malbert © MGM

Igor, Jaclyn

IGOR

(MGM) Producers, John D. Eraklis, Max Howard; Executive Producer, Jean-Luc De Fanti; Director, Tony Leondis; Screenplay, Chris McKenna; Art Director, Olivier Besson; Editor, Herve Schneid; Animation Supervisors, Christele Jolens, Yoshimichi Tamura; Animation, Sparx Animation Studios; Character Designer, Valerie Hadida; an Exodus Film Group production; Dolby; Color; Rated PG; 86 minutes; Release date: September 19, 2008

Voice cast

Igor	**John Cusack**
Scamper	**Steve Buscemi**
Dr. Glickenstein	**John Cleese**
Jaclyn	**Jennifer Coolidge**
Carl Cristall	**Arsenio Hall**
Brain	**Sean Hayes**
Dr. Schadenfreude	**Eddie Izzard**
King Malbert	**Jay Leno**
Eva	**Molly Shannon**
Schadenfreude's Igor	**Christian Slater**

Myleene Klass (Dr. Holzwurm), Robin Howard (Holzwurm's Igor), Matt McKenna (Dr. Herzschlag), Jesse Harnell (Announcer/Royal Guard #2), Zoë Bright (Blind Woman/Killiseum Fan #1), Sophia Eraklis (Blind Orphan #1), A. Cheron Hall, Alexander Leondis, Juliana Leondis, Michael Leondis, Nicole Leondis, Robin Tisserand (Blind Orphans), Paul C. Vogt (Buzz Offmann), Kay Cole (Grand Dame), James Lipton (Himself), Tayah Howard (Tatiana), Justin Eick (Royal Guard #1), John Eraklis, Max Howard, Tony Leondis, Chris McKenna (Killiseum Fans)

After his evil master perishes in a lab accident, an ambitious and misunderstood hunchbacked assistant seizes his chance to create his own monster and compete in the kingdom's annual science fair.

Faye Yu, Henry O

A THOUSAND YEARS OF GOOD PRAYERS

(MAGNOLIA) Producers, Yukie Kito, Rich Cowan, Wayne Wang; Executive Producers, Yasushi Kotani, Taizo Son; Director, Wayne Wang; Screenplay, Yiyun Lee, Based on her short story; Photography, Patrick Lindenhamier; Designer, Vincent de Felice; Music, Lesley Barber; Editor, Deirdre Slevin; Casting, Todd Thaler, Philip Huffman; an Entertainment Farm presentation of a Good Prayers production; Dolby; Color; HD Video; Not rated; 83 minutes; Release date: September 19, 2008

Cast
Mr. Shi	**Henry O**
Yilan	**Faye Yu**
Madam	**Vida Ghahremani**
Boris	**Pavel Lychnikoff**

Megan Albertus (Bikini Girl), Wes Deitrick (Antique Owner), Angela Dierdorff Petro (Maggie), Liz Mathews (Business Woman), Ryan Sanson (Plane Passenger), Tracy Schornick (Troy), Trent Sweeney (Boy), Patrick Treadway (Homeless Man), Lonny W. Waddle (City Bus Passenger), Jared Wagner (Airport Greeter)

American-resident and recent divorcee Yilan reluctantly pays host to her estranged, visiting Chinese father, whom she has not seen in twelve years.

Henry O, Vida Ghahremani © Magnolia Pictures

BATTLE IN SEATTLE

(REDWOOD PALMS) Producers, Kirk Shaw, Maxime Remillard, Mary Aloe, Stuart Townsend; Executive Producer, Julien Remillard; Coproducer, Lindsay MacAdam; Director/Screenplay, Stuart Townsend; Photography, Barry Ackroyd; Designer, Chris August; Costumes, Andrea Des Roches; Music, One Point Six; Editor, Fernando Villena; Casting, Randi Hiller, Sarah Finn; an Insight Film Studios, Remstar production, in association with Proud Mary Entertainment, Hyde Park Entertainment, 120dB Films and Grosvenor Park Media Ltd.; American-Canadian-German; Dolby; Color; Rated R; 98 minutes; Release date: September 19, 2008

Cast
Django	**André Benjamin**
Dale	**Woody Harrelson**
Jay	**Martin Henderson**
Mayor Tobin	**Ray Liotta**
Jean	**Connie Nielsen**
Lou	**Michelle Rodriguez**
Dr. Maric	**Rade Serbedzija**
Johnson	**Channing Tatum**
Ella	**Charlize Theron**

Ivana Milicevic (Carla), Joshua Jackson (Randall), Barbara Tyson (Anna), Tobias Mehler (Jonathan), Max Teichan (Man/Father), Richard Ian Cox (Mayor's Assistant), Richard Hendery (Santa), Ryan McDonald (Passerby), Deborah DeMille (Doctor), Alistair Abell (Eric), Kelly King, Peter Shinkoda, Alberto Valenzuela, Marsha Regis, Michael Agostini, Alberta Mayne, Gina Holden, Michael Taylor Donovan (Union Marshals), Tony Alcantar (Mark Harrington), Brett Dier, Paul Anthony (Protestors), Douglas Arthur (Smith), Daniel Bacon (Civilian), Lindsay Bourne (Dickson), Mark Brandon (News Anchor), Jennifer Carpenter (Sam), Louis Chirillo (Individual), Isaach De Bankolé (Abassi), Rik Deskin (Delegate), Debra Donohue (Shopper), Glenn Ennis, Ken Kirzinger (Officers), Austin Farwell (Officer D. Andrew), Mark Gibson (Squad Leader), Joel Ross, Tyler Hazelwood (Anarchists), Adrian Holmes (Journalist), Adrian Hough (Durell), Lear Howard (Hostess), Gary Hudson (Lieutenant), Dee Jay Jackson (Bus Driver), Christopher Jacot (Michael), Nels Lennarson (WTO Delegate), Matthew MacCaull (Drummer), Tzi Ma (Governor), Kelly-Ruth Mercier (Prison Guard), Dean Moen (Officer Jeremy), Linda Muir (Topless Woman #1), Yaroslav Poverlo (Lovitz), Arminder Randhawa (Mayor's Assistant), Chris Robson (Staff Member), Haskell Wexler (Wexler, Haskell)

An account of the protests and violence that erupted during the 1999 World Trade Organization ministerial conference in Seattle.

André Benjamin, Michelle Rodriguez © Redwood Palms

Richard Gere, Scott Glenn

Richard Gere, James Franco

Diane Lane, Christopher Meloni © Warner Bros.

Richard Gere, Diane Lane

NIGHTS IN RODANTHE

(WARNER BROS.) Producer, Denise Di Novi; Executive Producers, Doug Claybourne, Alison Greenspan, Dana Goldberg, Bruce Berman; Director, George C. Wolfe; Screenplay, Ann Peacock, John Romano; Based on the novel by Nicholas Sparks; Photography, Affonso Beato; Designer, Patrizia von Brandenstein; Costumes, Victoria Farrell; Music, Jeanine Tesori; Editor, Brian A. Kates; Visual Effects Supervisor, Eric Durst; Casting, Lynn Kressel; a Di Novi Pictures production, presented in association with Village Roadshow Pictures; Dolby; Panavision; Technicolor; Rated PG-13; 96 minutes; Release date: September 26, 2008.

Cast

Dr. Paul Flanner	**Richard Gere**
Adrienne Willis	**Diane Lane**
Jack Willis	**Christopher Meloni**
Jean	**Viola Davis**
Dot	**Becky Ann Baker**
Robert Torrelson	**Scott Glenn**
Jill Torrelson	**Linda Molloy**
Charlie Torrelson	**Pablo Schreiber**
Amanda Willis	**Mae Whitman**
Danny Willis	**Charlie Tahan**
Jenny	**Carolyn McCormick**
Old Gus	**Ted Manson**
Jean's Lover	**Ato Essandoh**
Mark Flanner	**James Franco**

Terri Denise Johnson (Medical Resident), Jessica Lucas (Admiring Nurse), Marisela Ramirez (Ecuadorian Patient), Kimberly Sauls (Pregnant Woman), Irene Ziegler (Real Estate Woman), Dihedry Aguilar (Bus Passenger), William D. Hooper (Fisherman), Hal Scarborough (Ferry Boat Captain), Candy Dennis, Gail Lane, Chookie Ramsey (Ferry Women)

Trying to come to terms with her disintegrating marriage, Adrienne Willis agrees to oversee her friend's beachfront inn, where she falls in love with its only guest, Paul Flanner, a doctor who is coping with his own problems.

MIRACLE AT ST. ANNA

(TOUCHSTONE) Producers, Roberto Cicutto, Luigi Musini, Spike Lee; Executive Producers, Marco Valerio Pugini, Jon Kilik; Director, Spike Lee; Screenplay, James McBride, based on his novel; Photography, Matthew Libatique; Designer, Tonino Ohori; Costumes, Carlo Poggioli; Music, Terence Blanchard; Editor, Barry Alexander Brown; Visual Effects Supervisor, Grady Cofer; Casting, Kim Taylor Coleman (U.S.), Beatrice Kruger (Europe); a 40 Acres and a Mule Filmworks production, presented in association with On My Own, Produzioni Cinematografiche and RAI Cinema; American-Italian; Dolby; Widescreen; Deluxe color; Rated R; 160 minutes; Release date: September 26, 2008

Matteo Sciabordi, Omar Benson Miller, Michael Ealy, Laz Alonso, Derek Luke

Cast

2nd Staff Sgt. Aubrey Stamps	**Derek Luke**
Sgt. Bishop Cummings	**Michael Ealy**
Cpl. Hector Negron	**Laz Alonso**
Pvt. 1st Class Sam Train	**Omar Benson Miller**
Peppi "The Great Butterfly" Grotta	**Perfrancesco Favino**
Renata	**Valentina Cerri**
Angelo Torancelli (The Boy)	**Matteo Sciabordi**
Tim Boyle	**Joseph Gordon-Levitt**
Det. Antonio "Tony" Ricci	**John Turturro**
Enrico	**John Leguizamo**
Zana Wilder	**Kerry Washington**
Col. Driscoll	**D.B. Sweeney**
Gen. Ned Almond	**Robert John Burke**

Omari Antonutti (Platoon Commander Huggs), Omero Antonutti (Ludovico), Sergio Albelli (Rodolfo), Lidia Biondi (Natalina), Matteo Romoli (Gianni), Massimo Sarchielli (Franco), Giselda Volodi (Iole), Giulia Weber (Ida), Max Malatesta (Maj. Gerhard Bergmann), Ralph Palka (Lt. Claussen), Massimo De Santis (Don Innocenzo Lazzeri), Livia Taruffi (Anna), Michele De Virgilio (Paolo), Michael K. Williams (Tucker, Scared Soldier), Laila Petrone (Pina), Luigi Lo Cascio (Angelo Torancelli, Adult), Alexandra Maria Lara (Axis Sally), Jan Pohl (Hans Brundt), Walton Goggins (Capt. Nokes), Tory Kittles (Lt. Birdsong), Stephen Monroe Taylor (Capt. Rudden), Andre Holland (Pvt. Needles), Christian Berkel (Capt. Eichholz), Waldemar Kobus (Col. Pflueger), Chiara Francini (Fabiola), Giovanni Zilgiotto (Italo), Federigo Ceci (Umberto), Agnese Nano (Paselli), Leonardo Borzonaca (Arturo), Malcolm Goodwin (Higgins), Sean Ryal (Pfc. Daniel Shaw), Bradley Williams (Trueheart Frazier), Rodney "Bear" Jackson (Ilion Hinson), Oliver Korittke (Fritz Bennecke), Kai Meyer (Karl Lessner), Alexander Beyer (Shell Shocked German Nazi Soldier), Usman Sharif (Radio Operator Hughes), Matteo Bonetti (Blind Accordion Player), Leland Gantt (Livingston), John Earl Jelks (Det. Dillard), Al Palagonia (Det. Haggerty), Curt Lowens (Dr. Everton Brooks), John Hawkes (Herb Redneck), Douglas M. Griffin (MP Freddy Naughton), Joe Chrest (MP Doyle Ellis), Peter Frechette (District Attorney), De'Adre Aziza (Bailiff), Limary Agosto (Sonia, Postal Worker), Lemon Anderson (Sixto, Postal Worker), Marcia Jean Kurtz (Post Officer Customer), Colman Domingo (West Indian Postal Customer), Peter Kubart (Judge Trinkoff), Rebecca Naomi Jones (Zana Wilder's Assistant), Michael Den Dekker (Legal Aid Attorney), Karyl Sloan (Herb's Wife), Robinson Wendt (Herb's Son), Kesia Elwin (Lourdes Negron), Hans Schoeber, Dieter Riesle, Eugene Brell, Lars Gerhard, Nicholas Thompson, Matthew Carroll (German POWs), Leonard Borzonasca (Arturo), Earl Kalon Jackson (American Buffalo Sniper), Timo Jacobs (Herman the Sniper), Yarc Lewinson, Shawn Luckey, Bryant Pearson (Buffalo Soldiers), Max H. Maxy (Court Officer), Dirk Sikorski (Wehrmachtsoldier Walters), Tom Sommerlatte (German NCO Möller), Adrian Zwicker (German NCO Schenck)

Michael Ealy, Valentina Cervi © Walt Disney Pictures

The shocking killing of a patron by a postal worker is traced back to an incident in World War II when a group of black soldiers were holed up in an Italian village awaiting the German enemy.

Pierfrancesco Favino, Sergio Albelli

Michael Chiklis, Rosario Dawson
© DreamWorks

EAGLE EYE

(DREAMWORKS/PARAMOUNT) Producers, Alex Kurtzman, Roberto Orci, Patrick Crowley; Executive Producers, Steven Spielberg, Edward McDonnell; Director, D.J. Caruso; Screenplay, John Glenn, Travis Adam Wright, Hillary Seitz, Dan McDermott; Story, Dan McDermott; Photography, Dariusz Wolski; Designer, Tom Sanders; Costumes, Marie-Sylvie Deveau; Music, Brian Tyler; Editor, Jim Page; Visual Effects Supervisor, Jim Rygiel; Special Effects Coordinator, Peter Chesney; Casting, Deborah Aquila, Tricia Wood; a Kurtzman/Orci production; Dolby; Deluxe color; Rated PG-13; 117 minutes; Release date: September 26, 2008

Cast

Jerry Shaw/Ethan Shaw	**Shia LaBeouf**
Rachel Holloman	**Michelle Monaghan**
Zoe Perez	**Rosario Dawson**
Defense Secretary Callister	**Michael Chiklis**
Major William Bowman	**Anthony Mackie**
Agent Toby Grant	**Ethan Embry**
Agent Thomas Morgan	**Billy Bob Thornton**
Ranim Khalid	**Anthony Azizi**

Cameron Boyce (Sam Holloman), Lynn Cohen (Mrs. Wierzbowski), Bill Smitrovich (Admiral Thompson), Charles Carroll (Mr. Miller), William Sadler (Jerry's Dad), Deborah Strang (Jerry's Mom), Dariush Kashani (Translator), Sean Kinney (JTAC Team Leader), Bob Morrisey (Director of Intelligence), J. Patrick McCormack (Pentagon General Council), Lorenzo Eduardo (Kwame), Madylin Sweeten (Becky), James Huang, Jorge-Luis Pallo (Intel Officers), Gerald Downey (Console Tech), Tony Flores (Team Leader), Donnie Jeffcoat (FBI Agent), Craig Harris (Man on Train), Jimmie L. Akins (Transit Cop on Train), Eric Christian Olsen (Craig), Marc Singer (Explosives Developer), Michael Maize (Master Sergeant), Eiko Nijo (Masako Tour Guide), Peter Gail (PFPA Officer), Brad Grunberg (Circuit City Salesperson), Cylk Cozart, Manny Perry (Sectran Couriers), James C. Gohrick (Agent in Alley), Josh Todd (Convenience Store Clerk), Colby French (Console Tech), Matt DeCaro (Stranger at Airport), Judith Moreland (Security Attendant at Airport), Rolando Molina (TSA Agent), Michael Kostroff (Jeweler), Nigel Gibbs (Callister Aide), Michael Daniel Cassady (White House Staffer), David Grant Wright, Stephen Simon (Secret Service Agents), Jarod Einsohn (Reaper Control Tech), David Heckel (Squadron Commander), Jamie Martz (Northcom Control Tech), Greg Collins (Two Star General), McKay Stewart (F-16 Pilot), Terry Walters (Woman in Prius), Katija Pevec (Teenage Page), Chase Penny, Dean Cudworth (Capitol Policemen), Madison Mason (President), Kevin Quinn (Pentagon Aide), Sebastian Tillinger (Pentagon Agent), Enver Gjokaj (Remote Pilot), Michael Potter (Doorkeeper), Webster Williams (Committee Head), Peggy Roeder, Gary Houston (Forensics Agents), Jonathan Chase (Suited Agent), Lindsay Corinn Luecht (Girl on Train), Nicol Paone, Brittany Ishibashi (Rachel's Friends), Stacey Scowley (Waitress), David Arakelyan (Ballochi Kid), Salah Salea (Funeral Chanter), Susan Armon (Woman in Ballochi Village), Fahim Fazli (Al Kohei), Elijah Moreland (Guard at Library of Congress), David Rowden (Sectran Truck Driver), Brenda Goodbread (Speaker of the House), Carolien A. Jenkins (Page), Roger Groh (Executive Aide to Callister), Leslie Stahl, Leyna Nguyen, Ralph Garman, Rick Chambers, Sharon Tay, Kent Shocknek (Newscasters), Brandon Caruso (Boy on Train)

Two strangers are thrown together by a mysterious phone caller who uses advanced technology to allow them to escape the FBI, assuring that they will help her carry out a dangerous operation.

Shia LaBeouf, Michelle Monaghan

Billy Bob Thornton, Ethan Embry

CHOKE

(FOX SEARCHLIGHT) Producers, Beau Flynn, Tripp Vinson, Johnathan Dorfman, Temple Fennell; Executive Producers, Mike S. Ryan, Derrick Tseng, Gary Ventimiglia, Mary Vernieu; Director/Screenplay, Clark Gregg; Based on the novel by Chuck Palahniuk; Photography, Tim Orr; Designer, Roshelle Berliner; Costumes, Catherine George; Music, Nathan Larson; Editor, Joe Klotz; Casting, Mary Vernieu; an ATO Pictures presentation of a Contrafilm/ATO production; Dolby; Color; HD Cam; Rated R; 92 minutes; Release date: September 26, 2008

Cast

Victor Mancini	**Sam Rockwell**
Ida Mancini	**Anjelica Huston**
Paige Marshall	**Kelly Macdonald**
Denny	**Brad William Henke**
Lord High Charlie	**Clark Gregg**
Ursula	**Bijou Phillips**
Beth (Cherry Daquiri)	**Gillian Jacobs**
Young Victor	**Jonah Bobo**
Nico	**Paz de la Huerta**
Eva Muller	**Viola Harris**
Phil	**Joel Grey**

Kathryn Alexander (Agnes, Mousy Girl), Teodorina Bello (Jamaican Lady), Kate Blumberg (Edwin's Wife), Willi Burke (Deranged Socialite), Heather Burns (Internet Date, Gwen), David Fonteno (Edwin), Matt Gerald (Det. Ryan), Michelle Hurst (Shapely Nurse), Jen Jones (Old Lady with Note), Jordan Lage, Solo Scott (Mob Members), Matt Malloy (Det. Foushee), Mary B. McCann (Det. Dorfman), Alice Barrett Mitchell (Lanky Woman on Airplane), David Shumbris, Marty Murphy (Troopers), Neil Pepe (Zoo Security Guard), Peggy Pope (Sister Angela), Denise Raimi (Pretty Foster Mom), Donald Rizzo (Guard Captain Norm), Judith Anna Roberts (Elegant Lady), Yolonda Ross (Cute Teacher), Mike S. Ryan (Lonnie), Suzanne Shepherd (Waitress), Sebastian Sozzi (Tito), Kate Udall (Tall Nurse), Melinda Wade (Mob Leader), Isiah Whitlock, Jr. (Det. Palmer)

A sex addict, leading a dead-end life as a historical interpreter at a New England theme park, finds himself attracted to a physician at the hospital where his mother is slowly losing her mind.

Gillian Jacobs, Sam Rockwell, Brad William Henke

Sam Rockwell, Anjelica Huston

Sam Rockwell, Kelly Macdonald

Brad William Henke, Sam Rockwell © Fox Searchlight

THE LUCKY ONES

(LIONSGATE/ROADSIDE ATTRACTIONS) Producers, Brian Koppelman, David Levien, Rick Schwartz, Neil Burger, Executive Producers, Bill Block, Paul Hanson, Elliot Ferwerda, Brian McCormack, Marina Grasic, Jan Korbelin; Coproducer, Glenn Stewart; Director, Neil Burger; Screenplay, Neil Burger, Dirk Wittenborn; Photography, Declan Quinn; Designer, Leslie Pope; Music, Rolfe Kent; Editor, Naomi Geraghty; Casting, Deborah Aquila, Claire Simon, Mary Tricia Wood; a QED Intl. presentation of a Koppelman & Levien and Overnight ans Block/Hanson production in association with Sherezade Films and Visitor Pictures; Dolby; Technicolor; Rated R; 113 minutes; Release date: September 26, 2008

Cast

Colee Dunn	**Rachel McAdams**
Frec Cheaver	**Tim Robbins**
TK Poole	**Michael Peña**
Pat Cheaver	**Molly Hagan**
Scott Cheaver	**Mark L. Young**

Howard Platt (Stan Tilson), Arden Myrin (Barbara Tilson), Coburn Goss (Peter Tilson), John Heard (Bob), Jennifer Joan Taylor (Bob's Wife), Katherine LaNasa (Janet), Leo Ford (Janet's Husband), Susan Yeagley (Kendra), Emily Swallow (Brandi), John Diehl (Tom Klinger), Annie Corley (Jeanie Klinger), Katie Korby (Shannon), Krik B.R. Woller (Army Psychologist), James Errico (Soldier in Hospital), Meredith Siemsen (Woman in Airport), Michael Aaron Linder (Guy on Cellphone), Jason Knowles (Reporter on TV), Vis Brown (Rental Car Agent), J.D. Mathein (Car Dealer), Kerry Bishé (College Girl), Brianne Carden (College Girl), Sarah Steele (Girl with Jacket), Glen Pruett (Carl), Karin McKie (Clinic Nurse), Anthony Lee Irons (Mechanic), Anne Jagues (Woman in Church), Spencer Garrett (Pastor Nolan), Scott Jaeck (Guitar Store Owner), Katherine Cuba (Bartender at Airport), John Hoogenakker (Army Recruiter), Michael Rizza (Croupier), Christian Stolte (Police Desk Sergeant), Kevin Michael Doyle, K. Todd Freeman (Detectives), Tim Gamble (Police Captain), Rachel Foszcz (Caterer)

Finding their individual flights cancelled, three soldiers, newly returned to the U.S. after a tour of duty in Iraq, agree to share a car together to travel cross country to the various destinations they each hope will bring them the peace of mind they seek.

Michael Peña, Rachel McAdams © Lionsgate

Kirk Cameron
© Samuel Goldwyn Films

FIREPROOF

(GOLDWYN/AFFIRM FILMS) Producers, Stephen Kendrick, Alex Kendrick, David Nixon; Executive Producers, Michael C. Catt, Jim McBride, Terry Hemmings; Director, Alex Kendrick; Screenplay, Alex Kendrick, Stephen Kendrick; Photography, Bob Scott; Designer, Sheila McBride; Music, Mark Willard; Editor, Bill Ebel; a Kendrick Brothers production, presented in associaiton with Samuel Goldwyn Films, Sherwood Pictures, Provident Films and Carmel Entertainment; Dolby; Color; Rated PG; 122 minutes; Release date: September 26, 2008

Cast

Caleb Holt	**Kirk Cameron**
Catherine Holt	**Erin Bethea**
Michael Simmons	**Ken Bevel**
John Holt	**Harris Malcom**
Eric Harmon	**Jason McLeod**

Stephen Dervan (Wayne Floyd), Eric Young (Terrell Sanders), Blake Bailey (Stephanie Mills), Anthony Brown (James Turner), Walter Burnett (Dr. Anderson), Bailey Cave (Ross Spencer), Janet Lee Dapper (ER Nurse), Allison Dawson (Mrs. Turner), Stephen Dervan (Wayne Floyd), Taylor Glow (Megan), Carla Hawkins (Tina Simmons), Sue Holt (Mrs. Campbell), Heidi Johnson (Dispatcher), Kelly Johnson (Bethany Wilson), Alex Kendrick (Pastor Strauss), Dot Majors (Erma Rudolph), Stephanie Makulinski (Robin Cates), Phyllis Malcom (Cheryl Holt), Amberly Marquard (Ashley Phillips), Jim McBride (Carl Hatcher), Tommy McBride (Kyle Joiner), Perry Revell (Gavin Keller), Faye Sharber (Anna Stone), Bill Stafford (Mr. Rudolph), Deena Taylor (Misty Harper), Melanie Tomlinson (Kelsey Jackson), Dwan Williams (Deidra Harris), Renata Williams (Latasha Brown), Ray Wood (Mr. Campbell)

In an effort to repair his floundering marriage, Caleb Holt agrees to commit to "The Love Dare," a forty-day program inspired by the teachings of the Bible.

RELIGULOUS

(LIONSGATE) Producers, Bill Maher, Palmer West, Jonah Smith; Executive Producer, Charlie Siskel; Director, Larry Charles; Photography, Anthony Hardwick; Editors, Jeffrey Werner, Jeff Groth, Christian Kinnard; Associate Producers, Alexandra Lambrinidis, Lisa Rudin; a Thousand Words/Bill Maher production; Dolby; Deluxe color; Rated R; 101 minutes; Release date: October 1, 2008. Documentary in which comedian/commentator Bill Maher questions the beliefs of various religious groups.

With

Bill Maher, Julie Maher, Kathie Maher, Andrew Newberg, John Westcott, Sen. Mark Pryor, Jose Luis de Jesus Miranda, Steve Berg, Ken Ham, Francis Collins, Jeremiah Cummings, Mohammad Hourani, Father Reginald Foster, Mohammed Junas Gatfar, Rabbi Dovid Weiss, Rabbi Schmuel Strauss, Dean Hamer, Rev. Terre van Beverren, Propa-Gandhi, Ray Suarez, Geert Wilders, Fatima Elatik, Father George Coyne, Tal Bachman, Bill Gardiner, Larry Charles.

Bill Maher

Bill Maher (right)

Bill Maher © Lionsgate

Bill Maher

JimMyron Ross © Strand Releasing

JimMyron Ross, Michael J. Smith, Sr.

JimMyron Ross, Tarra Riggs

Michael J. Smith, Sr.

BALLAST

(STRAND) Producers, Lance Hammer, Nina Parikh; Executive Producers, Andrew Adamson, John J. Hammer, Mark Johnson, Aimee Shieh; Director/Screenplay/Editor, Lance Hammer; Photography, Lol Crawley; Costumes, Caroline Eselin-Schaefer; Casting, Francine Thomas; an Alluvial Film Company presentation; Dolby; Widescreen; Technicolor; Not Rated; 96 minutes; Release date: October 1, 2008

Cast

Lawrence	**Michael J. Smith, Sr.**
James	**JimMyron Ross**
Marlee	**Tarra Riggs**
John	**Johnny Phail**

Ventress Bonner, Jimenz Alexander, Jean Paul Guillroy, Marcus Alexander, Marquice Alexander, Lawrence Jackson (Teens), Jeremy Jordan, Steve Cabell (Paramedics), Samuel Dobbins (Ambulance Driver), Neil Pettigrew (Dispatcher's Voice), Sanjib Shrestha (Dr. Shrestha), Carol Clark, Lee G. Beck, Michael Johnston, Valeace Bright (Nurses), Cassandra Campbell (Lab), Darla Johnson Lloyd (Respiratory), Lance Anderson (Radiology), Albert Jay Levy (Social Worker), Edward Whithead (Forensic Pathologist), Patricia Lee, Earl Ray (Marlee's Neighbors), Zachary Coleman (Attorney), Rafe D. Simpson (Simpson's Grocery clerk), Donald Johnson, Hurstine Watts (Lucky's 49 Customers), Fredrick Harris, Willie Nasno (Beer Delivery Men), Sam Watson, Mary Goodson (Lucky's 49 Suppliers, Voices), Anita R. Ballard (Elementary School Administrator)

Recovering from a suicide attempt after his twin brother has OD'd, Lawrence looks back on his relationship with single mother Marlee and her twelve-year-old son.

Anne Hathaway, Rosemarie DeWitt

Anne Hathaway, Tunde Adebimpe, Rosemarie DeWitt, Mather Zickel

Anne Hathaway

Jerome LePage, Debra Winger, Anne Hathaway

Mather Zickel, Anne Hathaway, Rosemarie DeWitt, Tunde Adebimpe

Anne Hathaway, Rosemarie DeWitt

Anisa George, Rosemarie DeWitt

Bill Irwin, Anna Deavere Smith

Debra Winger, Rosemarie DeWitt, Anne Hathaway © Sony Classics

RACHEL GETTING MARRIED

(SONY CLASSICS) Producers, Jonathan Demme, Neda Armian, Marc Platt; Executive Producers, Ilona Herzberg, Carol Cuddy; Coproducer, H.H. Cooper; Director, Jonathan Demme; Screenplay, Jenny Lumet; Photography, Declan Quinn; Designer, Ford Wheeler; Costumes, Susan Lyall; Music, Zafer Tawil, Donald Harrison, Jr.; Editor, Tim Squyres; Casting, Bernard Telsey; a Clinica Estetico production, in association with Marc Platt Prods.; Dolby; Color; HD; Rated R; 111 minutes; Release date: October 3, 2008

Cast

Kym	**Anne Hathaway**
Rachel	**Rosemarie DeWitt**
Kiernan	**Mather Zickel**
Paul	**Bill Irwin**
Carol	**Anna Deavere Smith**
Emma	**Anisa George**
Sidney	**Tunde Adebimpe**
Abby	**Debra Winger**
Andrew	**Jerome LePage**
Norman Sklear	**Beau Sia**
Dorian Lovejoy	**Dorian Missick**
Sidney's Sister	**Kyrah Julian**
Sidney's Mom	**Carol-Jean Lewis**
Sidney's Grandmother	**Herreast Harrison**
Sidney's Cousin	**Gonzales Joseph**
Ukranian Al	**Paul Lazar**
Themselves	**Donald Harrison, Jr., Fab 5 Freddy**
Judge Castle	**Robert Castle**
Nice Family Friend	**Christy Pusz**
Molly	**Molly Hickok**

Tareq Abboushi, Johnny Farraq, Gaida Hinnawi, Dimitrios Mikelis, Amir El Saffar (Musicians), Jimmy Joe Roche (Videographer), Maria Dizzia (Hip Young Guest), Josephine Demme (Neighborhood Girl), Marin Ireland (Angela Paylin), Elizabeth Hayes (Susanna), Cyro Baptista, Jose Muairicio De Faria, Lisette Santiago De Faria, Marcus Santos (Brazilian Drummers), Roslyn Ruff (Rosa, Staffer), Sebastian Stan (Walter, Patient), Pastor Mel Jones (Speaker at Meeting), Andrew Blake (Stylist), Dequina Moore (Rachel's Stylist), Joe Toutebon (Cop), Annaleigh Ashford (Counter Girl), Quincy Tyler Bernstine (Nurse), Van Hughes (Valet), Tamyra Gray (Sidney's Ex), Christian Scott (Christian), Paul Sparks (Paul), Michelle Federer (Michelle), Darrrell Larson (Darrell), Matt Stadelmann (Matthew), Floanne Ankah (Flo), Alix Derrick (Rachel's College Roommate), Victoria Haynes (Bridesmaid), Edie Hofstatter (Paramedic), Joey Perillo (Bob the Neighbor), Matt Rabinowitz (Matt R.), Jim Roche (Dr. Curve), Anita Sarko (Herself), Richard Shankman (Dog Walker)

Fresh from her latest stay in rehab, and having never emotionally recovered from her involvement in a tragic accident, Kym cautiously attends the wedding of her sister Rachel.

This film received an Oscar nomination for actress (Anne Hathaway).

NICK AND NORAH'S INFINITE PLAYLIST

(COLUMBIA) Producers, Kerry Kohansky, Chris Weitz, Paul Weitz, Andrew Miano; Executive Producers, Joe Drake, Nathan Kahane, Adam Brightman; Coproducers, Nicole Brown, Kelli Konop; Director, Peter Sollett; Screenplay, Lorene Scafaria; Based on the novel by Rachel Cohn and David Levithan; Photography, Tom Richmond; Designer, David Doernberg; Costumes, Sandra Hernandez; Music, Mark Mothersbaugh; Editor, Myron Kerstein; Casting, Joseph Middleton; a Mandate Pictures presentation of a Depth of Field production; Dolby; Deluxe color; Rated PG-13; 90 minutes; Release date: October 3, 2008

Jay Baruchel, Kat Dennings © Columbia Pictures

Cast

Nick	**Michael Cera**
Norah	**Kat Dennings**
Thom	**Aaron Yoo**
Dev	**Rafi Gavron**
Caroline	**Ari Graynor**
Tris	**Alexis Dziena**
Lethario	**Jonathan Bradford Wright**
Gary	**Zachary Booth**
Tal	**Jay Baruchel**
Randy (Are You Randy)	**Jeremy Haines**
Sammy (Are You Randy)	**Sammy Marc Rubin**
Korean Guy	**Glenn Kubota**
Ukranian Waitress	**Marika Daciuk**
Drunk Kid	**Marcel Simoneau**

Justin Rice, Christian Rudder, Giorgio Angelini, Darbie Nowatka, Cully Symington (Bishop Allen), Seth Meyers (Drunk Guy in Yugo), Lorene Scafaria (Drunk Girl in Yugo), Billy Griffith (Homeless Man), Ruth Maleczech (Homeless Caroline), Eddie Kaye Thomas (Jesus), Frankie Faison (Ticket Salesman), Marilyn McDonald (Janitor), John Cho (Hype Man), Kevin Corrigan (Man at Port Authority), John Cantwell, Nora Burns, Eric Bernat (Nellie Olesons), Tony Chem (Are You Randy Fan), Devendra Banhart (Customer in Deli), Simon Dasher, Philip E. Jones (Caroline's Admirers)

Michael Cera, Aaron Yoo, Kat Dennings, Jonathan Bradford Wright, Rafi Gavron

Having recently been dumped by their partners, Nick and Norah meet at a downtown rock club and spend the rest of the night in the city opening up to one another and ultimately falling in love.

Alexis Dziena

Michael Cera, Ari Graynor, Kat Dennings

Lauren Graham, Greg Kinnear, with kids

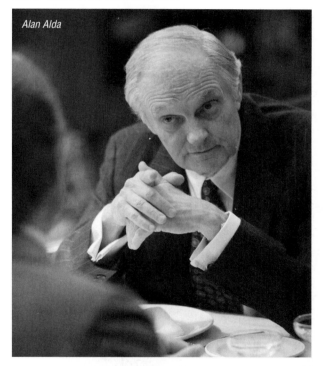

Alan Alda

FLASH OF GENIUS

(UNIVERSAL) Producers, Gary Barber, Roger Birnbaum, Michael Lieber; Executive Producers, Jonathan Glickman, J. Miles Dale, Thomas A. Bliss, Eric Newman; Director, Marc Abraham; Screenplay, Philip Railsback; Based on *The New Yorker* article "The Flash of Genius" by John Seabrook; Photography, Dante Spinotti; Designer, Hugo Luczyc-Wyhowski; Costumes, Luis Segueira; Music, Aaron Zigman; Music Supervisors, G. Marq Roswell, Adam Swart; Editor, Jill Savitt; Casting, Denise Chamian; a Spyglass Entertainment presentation of a Barber/Birnbaum production, a Strike Entertainment production; Dolby; Deluxe color; Rated PG-13; 119 minutes; Release date: October 3, 2008

Cast

Bob Kearns	**Greg Kinnear**
Phyllis Kearn	**Lauren Graham**
Gil Previck	**Dermot Mulroney**
Gregory Lawson	**Alan Alda**
Frank Sertin	**Daniel Roebuck**
Macklin Tyler	**Mitch Pileggi**
Ian Meillor	**Aaron Abrams**
Judge Franks	**Bill Smitrovich**
Pete	**Karl Pruner**
Scott	**Bill Lake**
Young Dennis	**Landon Morris**
Young Kathy	**Shae Norris**
Young Tim	**Steven Woodworth**
Young Maureen	**Victoria Learn**
Young Patrick	**Dylan Authors**

Jake Abel (Dennis, 21 Years), Tim Kelleher (Charlie Defao), Ronn Sarosiak (Reverend), Gavin & Ben Kuiack (Baby Bob, Jr.), Tom Rooney (Jerry Barnley), Kate Parker, Nicole Crozier (Waitresses), Andrew Gillies (Paul Previck), Duane Murray (Jim), Kate Greenhouse (Jean Previck), Philip Nessel (Club Member), Liam Titcomb (Joe Warwick), Sal Scozzari (Workman #1), Richard Blackburn (Executive One), Michael Spencer Davis (Real Estate Agent), Michael Rhoades (Salesman), Sergio Di Zio (Louis), Ashley Wright (Security Officer), Jonathan Whittaker (MC/Singer), Jared Durand (Student), London Angelis (Wade), Matthew Edison (Nerdy Student), Kristian Truelsen (Doctor), Simon Reynolds (Angry Driver), Denis Akiyama (Dr. Ito), Liam & Owen Wright (Toddler Bob, Jr.), Quancetia Hamilton (Case Worker), Tatiana Maslany (Older Kathy), Conor O'Farrell (Chris Finley), Isaac Lupien (Bob Jr.), Grant Boyle (Older Patrick), Ashton Doudelet (Older Tim), Josette Halpert (Older Maureen), Bruce Gooch (Jury Foreman), Chuck Shamata (Prof. Irwin)

The true story of how university professor and amateur inventor Robert Kearns challenged the Ford Motor Company in an effort to receive the credit he was due for developing the intermittent windshield wiper.

Greg Kinnear (right) © Universal Studios

Greg Kinnear, Dermot Mulrone

Piper Perabo, Chloe, Jamie Lee Curtis

Manuel, Chico © Walt Disney Pictures

BEVERLY HILLS CHIHUAHUA

(WALT DISNEY PICTURES) Producers, David Hoberman, Todd Lieberman, John Jacobs; Executive Producer, Steve Nicolaides; Coproducer, Ricardo Del Rio Galnares; Director, Raja Gosnell; Screenplay, Analisa LaBianoc, Jeff Hushell; Photography, Phil Meheux; Designer, Bill Boes; Costumes, Mariastela Fernandez; Music, Heitor Pereira; Music Supervisor, Buck Damon; Editor, Sabrina Plisco; Casting, Amanda Mackey, Cathy Sandrich Gelfond; a Mandeville Films/Smart Entertainment production; Dolby; Widescreen; Color; Rated PG; 91 minutes; Release date: October 3, 2008

Cast
Rachel Ashe Lynn	**Piper Perabo**
Sam Cortez	**Manolo Cardona**
Aunt Viv	**Jamie Lee Curtis**
Vasquez	**José Maria Yazpik**

Axel Alba (Pedro), Maury Sterling (Rafferty), Jesús Ochoa (Officer Ramirez), Eugenio Derbez (Store Owner), Omar Levya, Naomy Romo (Rangers), Ali Hillis (Angela), Marguerite Moreau (Blair), Nick Zano (Bryan), Carmen Vera (Inn Keeper Lady), Gina Gallego (Shelter Director), Hiram Vilchez (Desk Clerk), Alberto Reyes (Bellman), Enrique Chavero (Doorman, The Carthay), Andres Pardave (Doorman, Baja Sur Hotel), Juan Carlos Martín (Armand), Juan Antonio Saldaña (Conductor), Sal Lopez (Ring Announcer), Giovanna Acha (Museum Guide), Fernando Manzano (Desk Sergeant), Randall England (Butler), Claudia Cervantes, Lilly Lange (Chic Owners), Brandon Keener (Waiter), Jack Plotnick (Dog Nanny), Mary Paz Mata (Shaman Lady), Mayra Serbulo (Poor Woman), Montserrat de León (Baja Sur Desk Clerk), Bernice Romero (Lady), Antonio Infante, Tomihuatzi Xelhuantzin (Museum Security Guards), Erick Fernando Cañete (Little Boy), David Goldsmith (Limo Driver), Julie Claire (Claire), Holly Bonelli (Shop Girl)

Biminy, Sebastian, Delta, Chloe

Voice cast
Chloe	**Drew Barrymore**
Delgado	**Andy Garcia**
Papi	**George Lopez**
Manuel	**Cheech Marin**
Chico	**Paul Rodriguez**
Monte	**Plácido Domingo**
Diablo	**Edward James Olmos**
Delta	**Loretta Devine**
Chucho	**Luis Guzmán**

Eddie "Piolin" Sotelo (Rafa), Carlos Juvera (Tomás), Alex Mendoza (Frightened Terrier/Gang Leader Bull Dog), Lombardo Boyar (Praying Dog), Jon Molerio (Fight Mutt #1/Gang Dog #1), Margo Reymundo (Carthay Hotel Pekingese), Lisa Marie Quillinan (Carthay Hotel Poodle), Ed F. Martin (Coyote), Grey DeLisle (Mother Dog), Pascal Petardi (Train Dog), Michael Urie (Sebastian)

A pampered Beverly Hills Chihuahua ends up lost in Mexico after she is placed in the care of her owner's irresponsible niece.

José Maria Yazpik, Maury Sterling

Tim Robbins (right)

Martin Landau © 20th Century Fox

Harry Treadaway, Saoirse Ronan

Bill Murray

CITY OF EMBER

(20TH CENTURY FOX) Producers, Tom Hanks, Gary Goetzman, Steven Shareshian; Executive Producers, John D. Schofield, Diana Choi Sachs; Director, Gil Kenan; Screenplay, Caroline Thompson; Based on the book *The City of Ember* by Jeanne Duprau; Photography, Xavier Perez Grobet; Designer, Martin Laing; Costumes, Ruth Myers; Music, Andrew Lockington; Music Supervisor, Lindsay Fellows; Editors, Zach Staenberg, Adam P. Scott; Senior Visual Effects Supervisor, Eric Durst; Visual Effects Supervisors, Vincent Cirelli, Olivier Cauwet; Casting, Gail Stevens, David Rubin, Richard Hicks; a Walden Media presentation of a Playtone production; Dolby; Super 35 Widescreen; Deluxe color; Rated PG; 94 minutes; Release date: October 10, 2008

Cast

Lina Mayfleet	**Saoirse Ronan**
Donn Harrow	**Harry Treadaway**
Mayor Cole	**Bill Murray**
Sul	**Martin Landau**
Mrs. Murdo	**Mary Kay Place**
Barton Snode	**Toby Jones**
Clary	**Marianne Jean-Baptiste**
Looper	**Mackenzie Crook**
Loris Harrow	**Tim Robbins**
Poppy	**Amy Quinn, Catherine Quinn**
Granny	**Liz Smith**
Chief Builder	**David Ryall**

B.J. Hogg (Mayor's Guard), Lucinda Dryzek (Lizzie Bisco), Lara McIvor (Roner), Myles Thompson (Smat), Ian McElhinney (Builder #2), Eoin McAndrew, Rachel Morton, Conor MacNeil (Students), Lorraine Hilton (Miss Thorn), Liam Burke (Mr. Boaz), Simon Kunz (Captain Fleery), Frankie McCafferty (Arbin Swinn), Heathcoate Williams (Sadge Merrall), Maureen Dow (Mrs. Sample), Becky Stark (Song Master), Brid Ni Chionaola (Seely Schnap), Mark Mulholland (Portrait Painter), Valerie O'Connor (Person in Line), Ann Queensberry (Doctor Tower)

Two teenagers race against time when they come to the realization that their underground city is about to collapse around them, having been designated to function for a 200 year span that is coming to an end.

THE EXPRESS

(UNIVERSAL) Producer, John Davis; Executive Producers, Derek Dauchy, Arne L. Schmidt, Ryan Kavanaugh; Director, Gary Fleder; Screenplay, Charles Leavitt; Based on the book *Ernie Davis: The Elmira Express* by Robert Gallagher; Photography, Kramer Morgenthau; Designer, Nelson Coates; Costumes, Abigail Murray; Music, Mark Isham; Music Supervisors, Peter Afterman, Margaret Yen; Editors, William Steinkamp, Padraic McKinley; Coproducer, Adam Copland; Casting, Deborah Aquila, Tricia Wood, Jennifer Smith; a Davis Entertainment Company production in association with Relativity Media; Dolby; Super 35 Widescreen; Technicolor; Rated PG; 130 minutes; Release date: October 10, 2008

Dennis Quaid © Universal Studios

Cast

Ernie Davis	**Rob Brown**
Ben Schwartzwalder	**Dennis Quaid**
Jim Brown	**Darrin Dewitt Henson**
Jack Buckley	**Omar Benson Miller**
Will Davis, Jr.	**Nelsan Ellis**
Willie "Pops" Davis	**Charles S. Dutton**
Young Ernie	**Justin Martin**
Young Will	**Justin Jones**
Sarah Ward	**Nicole Beharie**
Marie Davis	**Aunjanue Ellis**
Elizabeth Davis	**Elizabeth Shivers**
Roy Simmons	**Clancy Brown**
Bill Bell	**Danny McCarthy**
Sister	**Regina Hoyles**
Lew Andreas	**Chelcie Ross**
Art Modell	**Saul Rubinek**

Rob Brown, Omar Benson Miller, Linara Washington, Nicole Beharie

Rob Brown, Charles S. Dutton

Craig Hawksley (George Marshall), Jeff Still (Al Malette), Geoff Stults (Bob Lundy), Derek Graf (Maury Youmans), Evan Jones (Roger "Hound Dog" Davis), Maximilian Osinski (Gerhard Schwedes), Enver Gjokaj (Dave Sarette), LaRoyce Hawkins (Art Baker), Lucas Ellman (Squirrel), Josh Odor (Darrell Royal), Matt Trissel (Clay Taylor), Chad L. Stevens (Peter Logan), Keir Thirus (Bob Ferguson), Chaz Black (Jimmy Saxton), Garth Gelker (Holy Cross Linebacker), David Darlow (Cotton Bowl Official), Michael Skewes (Cotton Bowl Referee), Gary Houston (Marty Harrigan), Ned Schmidtke (Bill Clark), Keith Kupferer (Small Fry Coach), Christopher Sullivan (Assistant All-Star Coach), Aaron Roman Weiner (Opposing Coach), Tim Grimm (W. Virginia Coach), Matthew Settle (President Kennedy), Stu Lisson (Man in a Suit), Lance Baker (Reporter), Christian Stolte (Dan Boyle), Mike Bradecich (Tom Martin), Chris Farrell (W. Virginia Sportswriter), Doug James (CBS Announcer), Ron Hawking (Syracuse Announcer), Linara Washington (Gloria Baker), Chadwick Boseman (Floyd Little), Kevin R. Kelly (Man in Dark Suit), Bruce Jarchow (Dr. Hewlett), Ridge Canipe (Gang Leader), Stephen Louis Grush, Louie Cesario (Gang Members), Paul Turner (Longhorn Scout), Rick Uecker (Middle-Aged Man), Kris Wolff (Groundskeeper), Jeffrey Zabrin (Small Fry QB), Darryl Warren (Heisman Official), Brian Mahoney (Buffalo Doctor), Philip Rayburn Smith (Business Lawyer), Laurie Larson (Proprietor), Will Zahrn (Doctor), Phillip Vanlear (NAACP Member), Michael Hargrove (Arthur), F. David Roth (Photographer), Richard Henzel (W. Virginia Booster), Howie Johnson, James Zoccoli (W. Virginia Hecklers), Eddie Bo Smith (Dallas Bellhop), Jeff Christian (Syracuse Trainer), Victor Cole (Hotel Worker), William Dick (Heisman Man in Suit), Sam Derence (Sports Reporter), Brian Boland (Cleveland Browns Asst. Coach), Walker Howard (Robert Field), Leonard House (Alan Touissant), Allan Graf (W. Virginia Referee), Kevin Stark, Kurt Naebig (Reporters, Team Bus), Ernest Perry, Jr. (Preacher), Ed Smaron (Play-by-Play Announcer), Dan Flannery (Hot Shot), Chet Coppock (PA Announcer), Robert Cullen (Petie), Guy Klinzing (Chancelor Tully), Barry Tolli (Elmira Free Academy Quarterback), Chris Cowan (Boston College Linebacker), Michael Malczyk (Penn State Linebacker), Torrey Vogel (Brokaw), Kenya Drew (Pretty Girl), John Anderson (Cotton Bowl Referee), Jeff Welsh (Texas Quarterback), Michael Ullrich (Franklin), Lonnie Brooks (Singer)

The true story of how football player Ernie Davis overcame racial barriers in the late 1950s and early 1960s as he became the first African-American to win the coveted Heisman Trophy.

Leonardo DiCaprio, Golshifteh Farahani

Russell Crowe, Leonardo DiCaprio

BODY OF LIES

(WARNER BROS.) Producers, Ridley Scott, Donald De Line; Executive Producers, Michael Costigan, Charles J.D. Schlissel; Director, Ridley Scott; Screenplay, William Monahan; Based on the novel by David Ignatius; Photography, Alexander Witt; Designer, Arthur Max; Costumes, Janty Yates; Music, Marc Streitenfeld; Editor, Pietro Scalia; Visual Effects Supervisor, Sheena Duggal; Stunts, G.A. Aguilar; Casting, Avy Kaufman, Jina Jay; a Scott Free/De Line production; Dolby; Arri Widescreen; Technicolor; Rated R; 129 minutes; Release date: October 10, 2008

Cast

Roger Ferris	**Leonardo DiCaprio**
Ed Hoffman	**Russell Crowe**
Hani Salaam	**Mark Strong**
Aisha	**Golshifteh Farahani**
Bassam	**Oscar Isaac**
Al-Saleem	**Alon Aboutboul**
Garland	**Simon McBurney**
Skip	**Vince Colosimo**
Omar Sadiki	**Ali Suliman**
Nizar	**Mehdi Nebbou**
Holiday	**Michael Gaston**
Mustafa Karami	**Kais Nashif**
Marwan	**Jameel Khoury**
Aisha's Sister Cala	**Lubna Azabal**

Ghali Benlafkih (Aisha's Nephew Rowley), Youssef Srondy (Aisha's Nephew Yousef), Ali Khalil (Zayed Ibishi), Giannina Facio (Hoffman's Wife), Chase Edmunds (Hoffman's Son Timmy), Morgan A. Vick (Hoffman's Daughter), Michael Stuhlbarg (Ferris' Attorney), Sherif Eltayeb (Executioner), David Ganly (Doctor at Qatar Military Base), Bijan Daneshmand (Amman Clinic Doctor), Houda Zbit (Hani's Wife), Omar Berdouni (Al-Saleem's Lieutenant), Richard De Mayo (Tony), Clara Khoury (Bassam's Wife), Abdu Rahim Kashmir (Safe House Jihadist), Sami Samir (Taxi Driver – Syrian Border), Xanthe Elbrick (Manchester News Reporter), Ali Alvi, Vedant Gokhale (Manchester Bombers), Ran Nikfam (Amsterdam Bomber), Albert Twanmo (Japanese Tourist Husband with Camera), Ellie K. Wang (Japanese Tourist Wife), Allen Lidkey (Medic in Helicopter), Drif Said (Turkish Engineer/Explosives Expert), Zakaria Atifi (Al-Masri), William Meredith (Soldier in Qatar), Howard W. Overshown, Kathy K. Brady, Quentin Mare, Matt Gulbranson (Predator Operators, Langley), Jill Wolsey (Soccer Mom), Annabelle Wallis (Hani's Girlfriend in Bar)

FBI agent Roger Ferris creates a fictitious rival terrorist organization in hopes that it will bring him into contact with the real Islamic mastermind behind several bombings.

Right: *Mark Strong, Leonardo DiCaprio*

QUARANTINE

(SCREEN GEMS) Producers, Doug Davison, Roy Lee, Sergio Aguero; Executive Producers, Glenn S. Gainor, Drew Dowdle, Julio Fernandez, Carlos Fernandez; Director, John Erick Dowdle; Screenplay, John Erick Dowdle, Drew Dowdle; Based on the film *REC* written by Jaume Balaguero, Luis A. Berdejo, Paco Plaza; Photography, Ken Seng; Designer, Jon Gary Steele; Costumes, Maya Lierberman; Editor, Elliot Greenberg; Casting, Lindsey Hayes Kroeger, David H. Rapaport; a Vertigo Entertainment/Andale Pictures and Filmax production; Dolby; Deluxe color; Rated R; 86 minutes; Release date: October 10, 2008

Elaine Kagan, Rade Serbedzija, Craig Susser

Cast

Angela Vidal	**Jennifer Carpenter**
Scott Percival	**Steve Harris**
Jake	**Jay Hernandez**
George Fletcher	**Johnathon Schaech**
Danny Wilensky	**Columbus Short**
James McCreedy	**Andrew Fiscella**
Yuri	**Rade Serbedzija**
Lawrence	**Greg Germann**
Bernard	**Bernard White**
Sadie	**Dania Ramirez**
Wanda Marimon	**Elaine Kagan**
Kathy	**Marin Hinkle**
Briana	**Joey King**
Nadif	**Jermaine Jackson**
Jwahir	**Sharon Ferguson**
Randy	**Denis O'Hare**

Stacy Chbosky (Elise Jackson), Jeannie Epper (Ms. Esponioza), Barry Sigismondi (Bob Orton), Ace Hatem (Wounded Woman), Christian Svensson, Scott Donovan (Armed Guards), Michael Potter (Chief of Police), Jane Park Smith (News Reporter), Craig Susser (Hazmat Doctor), Bert Jernigan (Hazmat Guard), Doug Jones (Thin Infected Man), John Meier (Repelling Guard #1), Shawn Driscoll, Bryan Ross (Firefighters), Benjamin Stockham (Infected Child), Michael Hyland (Video Guy), Ben Messmer (Griffin)

Columbus Short, Jay Hernandez

Tagging along on a 911 call a reporter and her cameraman find themselves quarantined inside an apartment building where a mysterious virus has turned some of the residents into flesh-eating killers.

Jennifer Carpenter

Dania Ramirez, Jennifer Carpenter © Screen Gems

Nelly Furtado, Mark Wahlberg © 20th Century Fox

MAX PAYNE

(20TH CENTURY FOX) Producers, Julie Yorn, Scott Faye, John Moore; Executive Producers, Rick Yorn, Karen Lauder, Tom Karnowski; Director, John Moore; Screenplay, Beau Thorne, based on the videogame published by Rockstar Games; Photography, Jonathan Sela; Designer, Daniel T. Dorrance; Costumes, George L. Little; Music, Marco Beltrami; Editor, Dan Zimmerman; Visual Effects Supervisor, Everett Burrell; Visual Effects, Spin VFX; Stunts, Jimmy N. Roberts III, John Stoneham, Jr.; Casting, Mindy Marin; a Firm Films/Depth Entertainment production; Dolby; Super 35 Widescreen; Deluxe color; Rated PG-13; 100 minutes; Release date: October 17, 2008

Cast

Max Payne	**Mark Wahlberg**
Mona Sax	**Mila Kunis**
BB Hensley	**Beau Bridges**
Jim Bravura	**Chris "Ludacris" Bridges**
Jason Colvin	**Chris O'Donnell**
Det. Alex Balder	**Donal Logue**
Jack Lupino	**Amaury Nolasco**
Nicole Horne	**Kate Burton**
Natasha Sax	**Olga Kurylenko**

Rothaford Gray (Joe Salle), Joel Gordon (Owen Green), Jamie Hector (Lincoln deNeuf), Andrew Friedman (Trevor Duncan), Marianthi Evans (Michelle Payne), Nelly Furtado (Christa Balder), Jay Hunter (Pawnshop Man), Maxwell McCabe-Lokos (Doug), Kerr Hewitt (Kid), Stephen R. Hart (Tattoo Artist Owner), Martin "Mako" Hindy (Demon), Herbert Johnson (Train Attendant), Philip Williams (Sgt. Adams), Warren Belle, Janice Nguyen (Detectives), Ted Atherton (Det. Shipman), Katie Odegaard (Jackie, Receptionist), Rico Simonini (Det. Sgt. Amerini), P.J. Lazic (Junkie), Brandon Carrera (Young Cop), Joshua Barilko (Ragna Rok Guard #1), Larry Wheatley (Bartender), Gouchy Boy (Doorman), Spike Adamson (Aesir Security Guard), Carlos Gonzalez-vlo (Man Who Gets Dosed with Drug), Lana Denis, Barrington Bignall, James Rogers, Christina Jocic, Noelle Gray, Candice Hotchkiss (Nude People Making Out), Genadijs Dolganovs (Enforcer), Dale Yim (Beat Cop), Tig Fong (Lead Aesir Security Guard), Siobhan Murphy (Receptionist #2), Sergei Nikolich (Anton), Kristina Falcomer (Girl at Party)

Determined to find out who was responsible for the murder of his family, cop Max Payne teams up with the sister of a slain model to investigate both crimes, leading them to the realization that a major pharmaceutical company is involved.

THE ELEPHANT KING

(UNISON FILMS) Producers, Tamar Sela, Tom Waller, Emanuel Michael; Executive Producers, Emanuel Michael, Alex Morcos, Thomas Werner; Coproducer, Cassandra Kulukundis; Director/Screenplay, Seth Grossman; Photography, Diego Quemada Diez; Designer, Lee Yaniv; Costumes, Karen Yan; Music, Adam Balazs; Editors, Saar Klein, Inbal B. Lessner, Lee Chatametikool; Casting, Cassandra Kulukundis; presented in association with De Warrenne Pictures; American-Thai; Dolby; Panavision; Technicolor; Rated R; 92 minutes; Release date: October 17, 2008

Cast

Diana Hunt	**Ellen Burstyn**
Oliver Hunt	**Tate Ellington**
Lek	**Florence Faivre**
Jake Hunt	**Jonno Roberts**
Bill Hunt	**Josef Sommer**

Debra Azar (Linda), Joe Cummings (Drug Dealer), Georgia Hatzis (Leah), Pawalit Mongkolpisit (Daeng), Michael Pand (Helmut), Porntip Papanai (No. 49)

A suicidal writer is asked by his mother to bring home his wastrel brother, who has taken up residence amid the bars and brothels of Thailand.

Ellen Burstyn, Jonno Roberts © Unison Films

Jonno Roberts, Tate Ellington

W.

(LIONSGATE) Producers, Bill Block, Moritz Borman, Eric Kopeloff, Paul Hanson; Executive Producers, Albert Yeung, Thomas Sterchi, Elliot Ferwerda, Johnny Hon, Teresa Cheung, Tom Ortenberg, Christopher Mapp, David Whealy, Matthew Street, Peter Graveds; Coproducers, Ethan Smith, Suzie Gilbert; Co-Executive Producers, Jon Kilik; Director, Oliver Stone; Screenplay, Stanley Weisler; Photography, Phedon Papamichael; Designer, Derek Hill; Costumes, Michael Dennison; Music, Paul Cantelon; Editor, Julie Monroe; Casting, Halley Finn; a Lionsgate, Omnilab Media, QED Intl. and Block/Hanson presentation in association with Emperor Motion Pictures, Millbrook Picture and Global Entertainment Group of a Moritz Borman/Ixtlan production; Dolby; Panavision; Deluxe color; Rated PG-13; 129 minutes; Release date: October 17, 2008

Cast

George W. Bush	**Josh Brolin**
Laura Bush	**Elizabeth Banks**
Barbara Bush	**Ellen Burstyn**
George H.W. Bush	**James Cromwell**
Dick Cheney	**Richard Dreyfuss**
Donald Rumsfeld	**Scott Glenn**
Karl Rove	**Toby Jones**
Rev. Earle Hudd	**Stacy Keach**
George Tenet	**Bruce McGill**
Condoleezza Rice	**Thandie Newton**
Colin Powell	**Jeffrey Wright**
Prime Minister Tony Blair	**Ioan Gruffudd**
Ari Fleischer	**Rob Corddry**
Paul Wolfowitz	**Dennis Boutsikaris**
Don Evans	**Noah Wyle**
Jeb Bush	**Jason Ritter**
Fraternity President	**Jesse Bradford**
Speechwriter #1	**Colin Hanks**
Fraternity Enforcer	**Wes Chatham**
Fraternity Pledges	**Sean Stone, Ben Mayer**
Oil Worker	**Juan Gabriel Pareja**
Oil Rig Driller	**Shea Lewis**
Oil Rig Foreman	**Randal Reeder**
Fran	**Marley Shelton**
1971 Houston Oilmen	**Litt Martin, James Ron Parker**
General Tommy Franks	**Michael Gaston**
Marvin Bush	**Keenan Harrison Brand**
Skeeter	**Bryan Massey**
Jim Sale	**Bill Jenkins**
Joe O'Neill	**Brent Sexton**

Jonathan Breck (Corn Dog), Jennifer Sipes (Suzie Evans), Jonna Juul-Hansen (Jan O'Neill), Paul Rae (Kent Hance), David Born (Texas Debate Moderator), John Buffalo Mailer (Speechwriter #2), James Martin Kelly (NSC Official), William Lanier (Resort Waiter), Gregory Alan-Williams (Evangelical Minister), Jon Davis (1988 Campaign Aide #1), Andrew Sensenig, Gabriela Ostos, Lisa Fairchild, Paul T. Taylor (Texas Reporters), Halley Rachel, Dottie McWhiney (Park Bench Voters), Ronan Summers (CIA Official), John Neisler (Cheney's Lawyer), Charles Fathy (Pres. Jacques Chirac, Voice), James A. Garrity, Anne Pressly (TV Commentators), Randall Newsome (Paul Bremer), Jewel Williams (Legless Soldier), Oscar Contreras (Burned Soldier), Tom Kemp (David Kay), Teresa Cheung ("Miss China"), Brad Sham (White House Reporter)

The true story of how, despite his total lack of qualification for the job, George W. Bush ended up as the 43rd President of the United States.

Josh Brolin, Elizabeth Banks

Josh Brolin, Stacy Keach

Josh Brolin, Noah Wylie © Lionsgate

Ellen Burstyn, James Cromwell

Thandie Newton

Josh Brolin, Toby Jones

Richard Dreyfuss, Josh Brolin, Toby Jones, Rob Corddry,
Thandie Newton

Jeffrey Wright, Toby Jones, Richard Dreyfuss, Josh Brolin

Richard Dreyfuss, Josh Brolin

THE SECRET LIFE OF BEES

(FOX SEARCHLIGHT) Producers, Lauren Shuler Donner, James Lassiter, Will Smith, Joe Pichirallo; Executive Producer, Jada Pinkett Smith; Coproducers, Ed Cathell III, Ewan Leslie; Director/Screenplay, Gina Prince-Bythewood; Based on the novel by Sue Monk Kidd; Photography, Rogier Stoffers; Designer, Warren Alan Young; Costumes, Sandra Hernandez; Music, Mark Isham; Music Supervisor, Linda Cohen; Editor, Terilyn A. Shropshire; Casting, Aisha Coley, Lisa Mae, Craig Fincannon, Mark Fincannon; an Overbrook Entertainment/Donners' Co. production; Dolby; J-D-C Scope; Deluxe color; Rated PG-13; 110 minutes; Release date: October 17, 2008

Nate Parker, Alicia Keys

Cast

Lily Owens	**Dakota Fanning**
August Boatwright	**Queen Latifah**
Rosaleen Daise	**Jennifer Hudson**
June Boatwright	**Alicia Keys**
May Boatwright	**Sophie Okonedo**
T. Ray Owens	**Paul Bettany**
Deborah Owens	**Hilarie Burton**
Zach Taylor	**Tristan Wilds**
Neil	**Nate Parker**
Greta	**Shondrella Avery**
Doll	**Renée Clark**
Violet	**Sharon Morris**
Cressie	**Nicky Buggs**

Jasmine Burke (Sugar Girl), Emma Sage Bowman, Emily Anlyn Lind, Addy Miller (Young Lily), Taylor Kowalski (Teenager), Bob Hungerford (Frank Posey), Richard Todd Sullivan (Mechanic), Chris Moore (Posey's Buddy), Bill Oberst, Jr. (Sheriff Gaston), Cullen Dean Moss (Young White Policeman), Walt Elder (Driver), Dan Beene (Mr. Kirven), Joe Chrest (Mr. Forrest), Robin Mullins (Miss Lacy), Tom Conder, Jay Pearson (White Men), Dan Cox (Sheriff Brooks), Quentin Kerr (Police Officer)

Escaping from her abusive father, young Lily Owens and the family housekeeper, Rosaleen, who has been subjected to racism following the signing of the Civil Rights Acts, are taken in by the Boatwright sisters, who offer them safety and a genuine sense of family on their honey farm.

Paul Bettany © Fox Searchlight

Queen Latifah, Sophie Okonedo, Jennifer Hudson, Alicia Keys, Dakota Fanning

Catherine Keener, Emily Alpern

WHAT JUST HAPPENED

(MAGNOLIA) Producers, Robert De Niro, Art Linson, Jane Rosenthal, Barry Levinson; Executive Producers, Todd Wagner, Mark Cuban, Eric Kopeloff; Director, Barry Levinson; Screenplay, Art Linson; Based on his book *What Just Happened: Bitter Hollywood Tales from the Front Line*; Photography, Stephane Fontaine; Designer, Stefania Cella; Costumes, Ann Roth; Music, Marco Zarvos; Editor, Hank Corwin; a 2929 Productions presentation of a Tribeca/Linson films production; Dolby; Panavision; Technicolor; Rated R; 104 minutes; Release date: October 17, 2008

Cast

Ben	**Robert De Niro**
Lou Tarnow	**Catherine Keener**
Himself	**Sean Penn**
Dick Bell	**John Turturro**
Jeremy Brunell	**Michael Wincott**
Kelly	**Robin Wright Penn**
Zoe	**Kristen Stewart**
Scott Solomon	**Stanley Tucci**
Himself	**Bruce Willis**
Pollster	**Jason Kravitz**
Johnny	**Mark Ivanir**
Jimmy	**Remy Selma**
Studio Marketing Guy	**Christopher Evan Welch**
Dawn	**Lily Rabe**

Sam Levinson (Carl), Logan Grove (Max), Alessandra Danielle (Sophie), Karina Buck (Verna), Peter Jacobson (Carl), Moon Bloodgood (Laura), Ari Barak (Aba Peterson), Paul Herman (Jerry), Jonathan C. Kaplan (Suit #1), Brandon Keener (Young Studio Executive), Terrance Yates (Dance Instructor), Ron Li-Paz (Rabbi), Jacques Maroun (French Taxi Driver), Dey Young (Ben's First Wife), Emily Alpern (Lou's Assistant), Marin Hinkle (*Vanity Fair* Coordinator), Paul Lieber (*Vanity Fair* Photographer), Lombardo Boyar (Guard at Studio Gate), Lindy Booth (Hostess), Kate Burton (Dr. Randall), William Ragsdale (Agent #1), Brent Rose (1st AD), Bess Rous (Actor's Assistant), Ayla Kell, Paydin Lopachin (Mary), Jean-Michel Richaud (Festival Host), Alex Norca (Guard at Cannes Airport), Cayleen Davies (Young Woman in Maserati), John Schiappa (*Fiercely* Villain), Annie Parisse (*Fiercely* Actress), Tienne Vu, Viginia Nguyen, Thao Le (Manicurists)

A beleaguered Hollywood producer must cope with a temperamental star who refuses to shave his beard for a role, and convince a director that he must re-shoot the ending of a film that has not tested well with audiences, all the while trying to engineer some sort of reconciliation with his ex-wife.

Kristen Stewart, Robert De Niro

Bruce Willis, Robert De Niro, John Turturro, Stanley Tucci
© Magnolia Pictures

CHANGELING

(UNIVERSAL) Producers, Clint Eastwood, Brian Grazer, Ron Howard, Robert Lorenz; Executive Producers, Tim Moore, Jim Whitaker; Director/Music, Clint Eastwood; Screenplay, J. Michael Straczynski; Photography, Tom Stern; Designer, James J. Murakami; Costumes, Deborah Hopper; Editors, Joel Cox, Gary D. Roach; Visual Effects Supervisor, Michael Owens; Casting, Ellen Chenoweth; an Imagine Entertainment presentation in association with Relativity Media of a Malpaso production; Dolby; Panavision; Technicolor; Rated R; 141 minutes; Release date: October 24, 2008

Cast

Christine Collins	**Angelina Jolie**
Rev. Gustav Briegleb	**John Malkovich**
Captain J.J. Jones	**Jeffrey Donovan**
Det. Lester Ybarra	**Michael Kelly**
Chief James E. Davis	**Colm Feore**
Gordon Northcott	**Jason Butler Harner**
Carol Dexter	**Amy Ryan**
Walter Collins	**Gattlin Griffith**
Arthur Hutchins	**Devon Conti**
Sanford Clark	**Eddie Alderson**
S.S. Hahn	**Geoff Pierson**
Dr. Jonathan Steele	**Denis O'Hare**

Michelle Gunn (Sandy), Frank Wood (Ben Harris), Jan Devereaux, Eric Grant, Antonia Bennett, Kerri Randles (Operators), Morgan Eastwood (Girl on Tricycle), Madison Hodges (Neighborhood Girl), Ric Sarabia (Man at Diner), J.P. Bumstead (Cook), Debra Christofferson (Police Matron at Train), Russell Edge, Stephen W. Alvarez (Reporters on Train), Peter Gerety (Dr. Earl W. Tarr), Pete Rockwell (Reporter at Precinct), John Harrington Bland (Dr. John Montgomery), Pamela Dunlap (Mrs. Fox), Roger Hewlett (Officer Morelli), Jim Cantafio (Desk Sergeant), Maria Rockwell (Police Matron at Precinct), Wendy Worthington (Reception Nurse), Riki Lindhome (Examination Nurse), Dawn Flood (Morning Nurse), Dale Dickey (Patient), Sterling Wolfe (Briegleb's Aide), Mike McCafferty (Ticket Vendor), David Goldman (Administrator), Anthony DeMarco, Joshua Moore, Joe Karpielian (Abducted Kids), Muriel Minot (Secretary), Kevin Glikmann (Orderly), Drew Richards (Holding Officer), Hope Shapiro (Medication Nurse), Caleb Campbell, Jeff Cockey (Backup Detectives), Zach Mills (News Vendor), Kelly Lynn Warren (Rachel Clark), Colby French (Bob Clark), Scott Leva, Rich King, Clint Ward (Mounties), Reed Birney (Mayor Cryer), Michael Dempsey (Man on Street), Peter Breitmayer (Chairman Thorpe), Phil Van Tee (Councilman), Jim Nieb (Reporter at Hearing), Lily Knight (Mrs. Leanne Clay), Jeffrey Hutchinson (Mr. Clay), Brian Prescott (Courtroom Bailiff), Ryan Cutrona (Judge), Mary Stein (Janet Hutchins), Gregg Binkley (Jury Foreman), William Charlton, Cooper Thorton (Prison Guards), E.J. Callahan (Warden), Asher Axe (David Clay), Devon Gearhart, Dalton Stumbo (Winslow Boys), Austin Mensch (Boy in Coop)

After reporting her young son missing, Christine Collins is dismayed to have a boy returned to her who is, in fact, not her child though the police insist otherwise.

This film received Oscar nominations for actress (Angelina Jolie), cinematography, and art direction.

Jeffrey Donovan, Angelina Jolie

Jason Butler Harner © Universal Studios

John Malkovich, Angelina Jolie, Geoff Pierson

Olesya Rulin, Vanessa Hudgens, KayCee Stroh, Monique Coleman, Britt Stewart

HIGH SCHOOL MUSICAL 3: SENIOR YEAR

(WALT DISNEY PICTURES) Producers, Bill Borden, Barry Rosenbush; Executive Producer/Director, Kenny Ortega; Coproducer, Don Schain; Screenplay, Peter Barsocchini, based on his characters; Photography, Daniel Aranyo; Designer, Mark Hofeling; Costumes, Caroline B. Marx; Music, David Lawrence; Editor, Don Brochu; Songs by various composers; Choreographers, Kenny Ortega, Charles Klapow, Bonnie Story; Casting, Jason La Padura, Natalie Hart; a Borden & Rosenbush Entertainment production; Dolby; Color; Rated G; 109 minutes; Release date: October 24, 2008

Cast

Troy Bolton	**Zac Efron**
Gabriella Montez	**Vanessa Hudgens**
Sharpay Evans	**Ashley Tisdale**
Ryan Evans	**Lucas Grabeel**
Chad Danforth	**Corbin Bleu**
Taylor McKessie	**Monique Coleman**
Coach Jack Bolton	**Bart Johnson**
Ms. Darbus	**Allyson Reed**
Kelsi Nielsen	**Olesya Rulin**
Zeke Baylor	**Chris Warren, Jr.**
Jason Cross	**Ryne Sanborn**
Martha Cox	**KayCee Stroh**
Jimmie Zara	**Matt Prokop**
Donny Dion	**Justin Martin**
Tiara Gold	**Jemma McKenzie-Brown**

Leslie Wing Pomeroy (Mrs. Bolton), Socorro Herrera (Mrs. Montez), David Reivers (Mr. Danforth), Yolanda Wood (Mrs. Danforth), Robert Curtis Brown (Mr. Evans), Jessica Tuck (Mrs. Evans), Joey Miyashima (Principal Matsui), Stan Ellsworth (Mr. Riley), Dave Fox (Coach Kellogg), Jeremy Banks (Stagehand), Tara Starling (Ms. Juilliard), Manly "Little Pickles" Ortega (Sharpay's Dog Boi), Bayli Baker, Tia Robinson (Principal Dancers), Ben Naccarato (Teacher)

As high school sweethearts Troy Bolton and Gabriella Montez face an uncertain future, because of their intention to head off to different colleges, drama teacher Ms. Darbus invites a recruiter from Juillard to watch this year's senior musical, in hopes that one student will be given a scholarship. The first theatrically released installment of the *High School Musical* franchise; the first two movies premiered on the Disney Channel, in 2006 and 2007, respectively.

Lucas Grabeel, Ashley Tisdale, Jemma McKenzie-Brown

Zac Efron, Corbin Bleu

Zac Efron, Vanessa Hudgens © Walt Disney Pictures

SYNECDOCHE, NEW YORK

(SONY CLASSICS) Producers, Anthony Bregman, Charlie Kaufman, Spike Jonze, Sidney Kimmel; Executive Producers, William Horberg, Bruce Toll, Ray Angelic; Director/Screenplay, Charlie Kaufman; Photography, Frederick Elmes; Designer, Mark Friedberg; Costumes, Melissa Toth; Music, Jon Brion; Editor, Robert Frazen; Visual Effects Supervisor, Mark Russell; Casting, Jeanne McCarthy; a Likley Story/Projective Testing Service/Russia, Inc. production; Dolby; Super 35 Widescreen; Color; Rated R; 124 minutes; Release date: October 24, 2008

Philip Seymour Hoffman, Samantha Morton

Cast

Caden Cotard	**Philip Seymour Hoffman**
Hazel	**Samantha Morton**
Claire Keen	**Michelle Williams**
Adele Lack	**Catherine Keener**
Tammy	**Emily Watson**
Ellen Bascomb/Millicent Weems	**Dianne Wiest**
Maria	**Jennifer Jason Leigh**
Madeleine Gravis	**Hope Davis**
Sammy Barnathan	**Tom Noonan**

Sadie Goldstein (Olive, 4 years old), Robin Weigert (Adult Olive), Daniel London (Tom), Robert Seay (David), Stephen Adly Guirgis (Davis), Frank Girardeau (Plumber), Paul Sparks (Derek), Jerry Adler (Caden's Father), Lynn Cohen (Caden's Mother), Dierdre O'Connell (Ellen's Mother), Daisy Tahan (Ariel), William Ryall (Jimmy), Christopher Evan Welch (Pastor), Timothy Doyle (Michael), Peter Friedman (Emergency Room Doctor), Charles Techman (Like Clockwork Patient), Josh Pais (Dr. Eisenberg, Ophthalmologist), Amy Wright (Burning House Realtor), Kat Peters (Ellen, 10 Years Old), John Rothman (Dentist), Amanda Fulks (Emergency Room Nurse), Frank Wood (Evaluative Services Doctor), Deanna Storey (Jazz Singer), Elizabeth Marvel (Warehouse Realtor), Laura Odeh (Toy Store Clerk), Mark Lotito (Minister), Erica Berg (German Woman), Raymond Angelic Sr. (German Doctor), Cliff Carpenter (Old Man), Amy Spanger (Soap Opera Nurse), Nick Wyman (Soap Actor Doctor), Portia (Therapy Patient Actress), Dan Ziskie (Leg Tremor Doctor), Chris McGinn (Lady at Caden's Mom's), Gerald Emerick (Man in Line), Alvin Epstein (Man with Nose Bleed), Rosemary Murphy (Frances), Tim Guinee (Needleman Actor), Kristen Bush (Actress Playing Claire), Greg McFadden (Actor Playing Needleman Actor), Barbara Haas (Warehouse Actress), Joe Lisi (Maurice), Alice Drummond (Actress Playing Frances), Michael Higgins (Actor Playing Man with Nose Bleed), Stanley Krajewski (Actor as Caden), Tom Greer (Medic), Michael Medeiros (Eric)

Philip Seymour Hoffman, Michelle Williams, Tom Noonan

As his relationships and his physical state begin to deteriorate, theater director Caden Cotard rents out a giant warehouse in which to stage his ultimate work, instructing his players to act out their mundane lives in an effort to change to course of his own, ultimately blurring the line between what is fake and what is real.

© Sony Classics

Emily Watson, Dianne Wiest

Carmen Ejogo, Edward Norton

Lake Bell, Colin Farrell

Jon Voight, Jennifer Ehle, Noah Emmerich © New Line Cinema

PRIDE AND GLORY

(NEW LINE CINEMA) Producer, Gregory O'Connor; Executive Producers, Toby Emmerich, Cale Boyter, Marcus Viscidi; Coproducer, Josh Fagin; Director, Gavin O'Connor; Screenplay, Joe Carnahan, Gavin O'Connor; Story, Gavin O'Connor, Gregory O'Connor, Robert Hopes; Photography, Declan Quinn; Designer, Dan Leigh; Costumes, Abigail Murray; Music, Mark Isham; Editors, Lisa Zeno Churgin, John Gilroy; Casting, Randi Hiller, Sarah Halley Finn; a Solaris Entertainment/O'Connor Brothers production; Distributed by Warner Bros.; Dolby; Deluxe color; Rated R; 129 minutes; Release date: October 24, 2008

Cast
Ray Tierney	**Edward Norton**
Jimmy Egan	**Colin Farrell**
Frances Tierney, Sr.	**Jon Voight**
Francis Tierney, Jr.	**Noah Emmerich**
Abby Tierney	**Jennifer Ehle**
Ruben Santiago	**John Ortiz**
Kenny Dugan	**Shea Whigham**
Eddie Carbone	**Frank Grillo**

Lake Bell (Megan Egan), Rick Gonzalez (Eladio Casado), Wayne Duvall (Bill Avery), Carmen Ejogo (Tasha), Ramon Rodriguez (Angel Tezo), Manny Perez (Coco Dominguez), Maximiliano Hernández (Carlos Bragon), Leslie Denniston (Maureen Tierney), Hannah Riggins (Caitlin Tierney), Carmen LoPorto (Francis Tierney), Lucy Grace Ellis (Bailey Tierney), Ryan Simpkins (Shannon Egan), Ty Simpkins (Matthew Egan), Flaco Navaja (Tookie Brackett), Raquel Jordan (Lisette Madera), José Ramón Rosario (Mayor Arthur Caffey), Christopher Michael Holley (Det. Miller), Jason Rodriguez (Corner Store Owner), Jessica Pimental (Angelique Domenguez), Popa Wu (Rev. Farraud), Nikkole Salter (Trish Mercer), David Pinon (Bodega Owner), Lissette Espaillat (Bodega Owner's Wife), Francisco Burgos (Bodega Boy), Sekhar Chandra (Dr. Khomar), Cuba Libre (Dominican Thug #1), Bill McHugh (Gabriel Lopez Chaplin), Robert P. Alongi (Capt. Lavier), Bo Eason (Investigator Lieberthal), Howard Overshown (Investigator Duerson), Peter Moog (NYPD Coach Kowalski), Edward Gardner (NYPD Offensive Coordinator), Kenneth Pepe (NYPD Defensive Coordinator), James Cavanagh Burke (Detroit Metro Coach), Richie Thorton (Detroit Metro Assistant Coach), John Comer (NYPD Football Player), Thomas Pilkington (Duty Captain Banks), Glenn E. Cunningham, Stephen A. DiShiavi, William McNelly (Detectives), Rick Tirelli (DEA Representative), Jamie McShane (Lt. Fricker), John Mariano (Task Force Lieutenant), Robert Hopes, Jim O'Neill (Task Force Detectives), Eddie Molina (Uniform Cop), Karl Bury (Patrol Sergeant), Sean Gavigan, Christina Cabot (Patrol Cops), Sal DiGiovani, Tom Pellegrino, Nancy McCabe, Bill McKinney, Joseph Roman, Kubrat Hristoff, William Geiger, Keith Fallon, Craig Garland, Steve Benvegn, Carl Bocker, Tim Byrne (Crime Scene Cops), Gerald M. Kline (Desk Lieutenant), William Clemente (Arresting Police Officer), Joe Blozis (Crime Scene Detective), Tom Nonnon (Chief), Scotty Dillin (Police Officer Dillin), Nicoye Banks (Lonnie Mercer), Denia Brache (Domengeuz Mother), Roz Abrams (TV News Anchor), Sandra Endo (News Anchor), Dick Brennan (News Reporter Dehaven), Dominic Carter (Reporter), Yanko Perez (EMT), Sujeilee Ramos (Girl in Bar), Michael Angelo Ortiz, Juan Lopez, Argelis Parra, Miguel Ventura, Billy Joe Marrero (Thug Kids), Sean Dougherty (Billy Cavanagh), Tammy Tunyavongs (Dugan's Wife), Jaime N. Garcia (Doctor), Pablo Gonzalez (Dominican Perp), Louise G. Colón (Woman on Stairs), Cecilia Riddett (Bragon Receptionist), Tony Rhune (Arvell "Amp" Poines), Andrew Rogers (Driver), Luis Da Silva, Jr. (Dominican Bodega Customer)

Following a drug bust in which four cops are killed, Detective Frances Tierney coaxes his son Ray into joining the task force investigating the case, only to have Ray discover that his brother-in-law is responsible.

Chace Crawford, Haley Bennett

Shanna Collins, Haley Bennett © Freestyle Releasing

THE HAUNTING OF MOLLY HARTLEY

(FREESTYLE) Producers, Jennifer Hilton, Mickey Liddell; Executive Producer, Stephen Kay; Coproducer, Jerry P. Jacobs; Director, Mickey Liddell; Screenplay, Rebecca Sonnenshine, John Travis; Photography, Sharone Meir; Designer, John Larena; Costumes, Anita Cabada; Music, James. T. Sale; Music Supervisor, Christopher Mollere; Editor, Zene Baker; Visual Effects Supervisor, Ken Johnson; Associate Producer, Todd J. Ulman; Casting, Joseph Middleton; a Liddell Entertainment production, Dolby; Color; Rated PG-13; 86 minutes; Release date: October 31, 2008

Cast

Molly Hartley	**Haley Bennett**
Robert Hartley	**Jake Weber**
Joseph Young	**Chace Crawford**
Leah	**Shannon Marie Woodward**
Alexis	**Shanna Collins**
Suzie	**AnnaLynne McCord**
Jane Hartley	**Marin Hinkle**

Nina Siemaszko (Dr. Emerson), Josh Stewart (Mr. Draper), Randy Wayne (Michael), Jamie McShane (Father), Ron Canada (Mr. Bennett), Kevin Cooney (Dr. Donaldson), Jessica Lowndes (Laurel), Ross Thomas (Jock), Charles Rahi Chun (Doctor), John Newton (Mr. Young)

Following a brutal attack on her by her own mother, Molly Hartley hopes to start life anew at the Huntington Academy but instead ends up reacting traumatically to her new surroundings.

SPLINTER

(MAGNET) Producers, Kai Barry, Ted Kroeber; Executive Producers, Chad Burris, Jamie Carmichael, Graham Begg, Todd Wagner, Mark Cuban; Coproducers, John Glosser, Iqbal Ahmed, Raj Patil; Director, Toby Wilkins; Screenplay, Ian Shorr, Kai Barry; Photography, Nelson Cragg; Designer, Jennifer Spence; Music, Elia Cmiral; Editor, David Michael Maurer; Creature Design/Special Makeup Effects, Quantum Creation FX; Special Makeup/Creature Effects Producer, Christian Beckman; Stunts, Jackson Burns; Casting, Lauren Bass, Chris Friedhofer; a ContentFilm Intl. and Magnet Releasing presentation in association with Indion Entertainment Group and Kish Prods.; Dolby; Deluxe color; Rated R; 82 minutes; Release date: October 31, 2008

Cast

Dennis Farrell	**Shea Whigham**
Seth Belzer	**Paulo Costanzo**
Polly Watt	**Jill Wagner**
Lacey Belisle	**Rachel Kerbs**
Blake Sherman, Jr.	**Charles Baker**
Sheriff Terri Frankel	**Laurel Whitsett**

Abducted while on a camp trip, Seth and Polly find themselves trapped inside a convenience store by a spiked creature bent on destruction.

Jill Wagner, Paolo Costanzo © Magnet

Jill Wagner, Shea Whigham

Seth Rogen, Elizabeth Banks

Seth Rogen, Elizabeh Banks © Weinstein Co.

ZACK AND MIRI MAKE A PORNO

(MGM/WEINSTEIN CO.) Producer, Scott Mosier; Executive Producers, Harvey Weinstein, Bob Weinstein, Carla Gardini; Director/Screenplay/Editor, Kevin Smith; Photography, Dave Klein; Designer, Robert Holtzman; Costumes, Salvador Perez; Music, James L. Venable; a View Askew production; Dolby; Technicolor; Rated R; 101 minutes; Release date: October 31, 2008

Cast

Zack Brown	**Seth Rogen**
Miri Linsky	**Elizabeth Banks**
Delaney	**Craig Robinson**
Lester	**Jason Mewes**
Deacon	**Jeff Anderson**
Bubbles	**Traci Lords**
Stacey	**Katie Morgan**
Barry	**Ricky Mabe**
Bobby Long	**Brandon Routh**
Mr. Surya	**Gerry Bednob**
Brandon	**Justin Long**
Customer	**Edward Janda**
Teens	**Nicholas Lombardi, Chris Milan**
Betsy	**Jennifer Schwalbach**

Kenny Holtz (Zack II), Anne Wade (Roxanne), Tom Savini (Jenkins), Tisha Campbell-Martin (Delaney's Wife), Jim Norton, Jean-Pierre Nutini, Alice G. Eisner, David Early, Matt Potter (Auditioners), Lena Cheney (Auditioning Girl), Marie Blanchard, Deanna Betros, Danielle Fortwangler, Katelyn Hoffman, Ashley Kunich (Strippers), Milos Milicevic (Construction Foreman), James W. Smith (Indecisive Customer), Lauren Anne Miller (Moaner and Groaner)

Desperately in need of money, platonic friends and roommates Zack Brown and Miri Linsky decide to make their own porno film.

Seth Rogen, Elizabeth Banks

ROLE MODELS

(UNIVERSAL) Producers, Mary Parent, Scott Stuber, Luke Greenfield; Executive Producers, Dan Kolsrud, Andrew Z. Davis, Matt Siegel, William Sherak, Jason Shuman; Director, David Wain; Screenplay, Paul Rudd, David Wain, Ken Marino, Timothy Dowling; Story, Timothy Dowling, William Blake Herron; Photography, Russ T. Alsobrook; Designer, Stephen Lineweaver; Costumes, Molly Maginnis; Music, Craig Wedren; Editor, Eric Kissack; Coproducer, Juan Castro; Casting, Lisa Beach, Sarah Katzman; a Stuber/Parent production, presented in association with Relativity Media; Dolby; Technicolor; Rated R; 101 minutes; Release date: November 7, 2008

Elizabeth Banks, Paul Rudd

Cast

Wheeler	**Seann William Scott**
Danny	**Paul Rudd**
Augie	**Christopher Mintz-Plasse**
Ronnie	**Bobb'e J. Thompson**
Beth	**Elizabeth Banks**
Sweeny	**Jane Lynch**
King Argotron	**Ken Jeong**
Jim Stansel	**Ken Marino**
Lynette	**Kerri Kenney-Silver**
Martin	**A.D. Miles**
Kuzzik	**Joe Lo Truglio**
Davith of Glencracken	**Matt Walsh**
Karen	**Nicole Randall Johnson**

Allie Stamler (Esplen), Carly Craig (Connie), Jessica Morris (Linda the Teacher), Vincent Martella (Artonius), Armen Weitzman (Party Dude), Jorma Taccone (Mitch from Graphics), Nate Hartley (Rule Master), David Wain (Chevron Blaine), Amanda Righetti (Isabel), Shane Arenal (Student in Hall), Tina Casciani (Gretchen), Nina Hellman (Barista), Louis CK (Security Guard), Zaid Farid (Tow Truck Driver), Hunter Brochu (Boy in Video), Zandy Hartig (Panda-Loving Big), Keegan-Michael Key (Duane), Emily Mostyn-Brown (Laire Singer), Joshua Patterson (Gleebo), Peter Salett (Ladislas of Leisure), Lorna Scott (Horse Scooter Woman), Caleb Collins (Little at Campfire), Nick Nervies (Ronnie's Friend JJ), Kurt Doss (Ronnie's Friend Kyle), Tajh Bellow (Ronnie's Friend Zak), Shawn Huang (Ronnie's Friend Little Jack), Seth Herzog (Bell-Ringing Winged Creature), Eva Card (Chocolate Strawberry Girl), James Henderson (Partygoer), Jenny Robertson (Elevator Mom), Jeanine Jackson (Burge Hole Waitress), Matt Ballard (Valconian Swordsman), Cody Lawrence (Skateboard Kid)

Christopher Mintz-Plasse, Paul Rudd

Arrested for causing a public disturbance, two highly unmotivated energy drink salesman end up spending 150 service hours as part of a mentorship program trying to help some troubled kids.

Jane Lynch, A.D. Miles © Universal Studios

Bobb'e J. Thompson, Nicole Randall Johnson, Seann William Scott

Gloria, Melman

King Julien, Maurice

Zuba, Alex's Mom, Alex

MADAGASCAR: ESCAPE 2 AFRICA

(PARAMOUNT/DREAMWORKS) Producers, Mirelle Soria, Mark Swift; Directors, Eric Darnell, Tom McGrath; Screenplay, Etan Cohen, Eric Darnell, Tom McGrath; Designer, Cronkhite-Shaindlin; Art Director, Shannon Jeffries; Senior Animation Supervisor, Denis Couchon; Head Character Animation, Rex Grignon; Head of Story, Robert Koo; Head of Layout, Nol Le Meyer; Head of Effects, Scott Peterson; Casting, Leslee Feldman; Kendala PDI/DreamWorks Animation production; Dolby; Color; Rated PG; 88 minutes; Release date: November 7, 2008

Voice cast

Alex	**Ben Stiller**
Marty/Zebras	**Chris Rock**
Melman	**David Schwimmer**
Gloria	**Jada Pinkett Smith**
King Julien	**Sacha Baron Cohen**
Maurice	**Cedric the Entertainer**
Mort	**Andy Richter**
Zuba	**Bernie Mac**
Makunga	**Alec Baldwin**
Alex's Mom	**Sherri Shepherd**
Moto Moto	**Will.I.Am**
Nana	**Elisa Gabrielli**

Tom McGrath (Skipper/Lemur #1), Chris Miller (Kowalski), Christopher Knights (Private), Conrad Vernon (Mason), Quinn Dempsey Stiller (Baby Alex), Fred Tatasciore (Teetsi/Poacher #1/Elephant), Eric Darnell (Joe the Witch Doctor/Poacher #2), Willow Smith (Baby Gloria), Thomas Stanley (Baby Marty), Zachary Gordon (Baby Melman), Meredith Vieira, Lesley Stahl, Al Roker (Newscasters), David Soren (Lemur #2), Phil LaMarr (Guide), Stephen Kearin (Stephen/Tourist with Video Camera/Rhino), Dan O'Connor (Tourist with University Shirt/Cape Buffalo), Edie Mirman (Telephone Recording), Stacy Ferguson (Hippo Girlfriend), Harland Williams (Additional Giraffe), Danny Jacobs (Tourist with New York T-Shirt), Bridget Hoffman (Tourist), Terrence Hardy, Jr. (Lion Cub), Conner Raynburn (Little Giraffe), Holly Dorff (Fish), David Smith (Bobby the Dik Dik), Lynnanne Zager (Lioness), Jackie Gonneau (Additional Dik Dik), John Bentley (Additional Voices), Kathryn Feller (Ostrich #1), Michele Specht (Nurse Sandy)

Hoping to fly back to New York, a group of misfit animals instead end up in the jungles of Africa, where Alex, a lion, is recognized as the long-missing son of the local pride's chief.

Below: *Kowalski, Rico, Skipper, Private* © *DreamWorks*

SOUL MEN

(MGM) Producers, David T. Friendly, Charles Castaldi, Steve Greener; Executive Producers, Harvey Weinstein, Bob Weinstein, Mark McNair; Director, Malcolm D. Lee; Screenplay, Robert Ramsey, Matthew Stone; Photography, Matt Leonetti; Designer, Richard Hoover; Costumes, Danielle Hollowell; Music, Stanley Clarke; Music Supervisor, Alex Steyermark; Editors, Paul Millspaugh, Bill Henry; Choreographer, Jamal Sims; Casting, Aisha Coley; a Dimension Films presentation of a Friendly Films production; Dolby; Technicolor; Rated R; 100 minutes; Release date: November 7, 2008

Bernie Mac, John Legend, Samuel L. Jackson

Cast

Louis Hinds	**Samuel L. Jackson**
Floyd Henderson	**Bernie Mac**
Cleo	**Sharon Leal**
Philip	**Adam Herschman**
Danny Epstein	**Sean Hayes**
Lester	**Affion Crockett**
Pay-Pay	**Fatso-Fasano**
Zig-Zag	**Jackie Long**
Duane Henderson	**Mike Epps**
Marcus Hooks	**John Legend**
Himself	**Isaac Hayes**
Full-Figured Neighbor	**Vanessa del Rio**
Floyd's Doctor	**P.J. Byrne**

Samuel L. Jackson, Sharon Leal, Bernie Mac

Ken Davitian (Ardesh Kezian), Jennifer Coolidge (Rosalle), Sara Erikson (Chastity), Soledad O'Brien, Willie Hall, Ben Cauley, Skip Pitts (Themselves), Randy Jackson (Narrator), Jackie Johnson (Weather Woman), Shane Sampson, Dylan Sampson (Henderson Twins), Bart Hansard (Flagstaff Lounge Manager), Michael Brouillet (Keyboard Player, Flagstaff), Sean Goulding (Trombone Player, Flagstaff), Ritchie Montgomery (Emmett the Drunk), Clay Yocum (Audience Member, Flagstaff), Juan Gabriel Pareja (Tow Truck Driver), Lara Grice (Peabody Desk Clerk), Paul T. Taylor (Peabody Hotel Manager), Monyetta Shaw (Odetta), Jody Thompson (Deputy), Maurice DuBois (Newscaster), Miko DeFoor (Apollo Stage Manager), Michael Showers (Detective in Charge), Millie Jackson (Claudette), Scott Bomar (Bassist), Archie "Hubie" Turner (Keyboard), Art Edmaiston (Baritone Saxophone), Marc Franklin (Trombone), Robin Moffett, Ketrick Robinson (Singers), Michael Franklin (Trumpet Player), Jovan "Jr." Taylor (Baritone Sax Player), Nathan Adams (Tenor Sax Player)

An invitation to sing at the Apollo Theater in New York, in tribute to the lead singer they once sang backup for, brings together long-estranged Louis Hinds and Floyd Henderson.

Bernie Mac, Samuel L. Jackson © MGM

Bernie Mac, Isaac Hayes, Samuel L. Jackson

Bolt, Penny © Walt Disney Studios

Pigeons, Bolt

Bolt, Penny

BOLT

(WALT DISNEY STUDIOS) Producers, Clark Spencer; Executive Producer, John Lasseter; Directors, Chris Williams, Byron Howard; Screenplay, Dan Fogelman, Chris Williams; Art Director, Paul Felix; Music, John Powell; Music Supervisor, Tom Macdougall; Director of Look and Lighting, Adolph Lusinsky; Visual Effects Supervisor, John Murrah; Head of Story, Nathan Greno; Technical Supervisor, Hank Driskill; CG Supervisor, Mark Empey; Animation Supervisor, Doug Bennett; Layout Supervisor, Terry Moews; Casting, Curtis A. Koller; Dolby; Deluxe color; 3-D; Rated PG; 96 minutes; Release date: November 21, 2008

Cast

Bolt	**John Travolta**
Penny	**Miley Cyrus**
Mittens	**Susie Essman**
Rhino	**Mark Walton**
Dr. Calico	**Malcolm McDowell**
The Director	**James Lipton**
The Agent	**Greg Germann**
Veteran Cat	**Diedrach Bader**
Blake	**Nick Swardson**
Tom	**J.P. Manoux**
Billy	**Dan Fogelman**
Mindy	**Kari Wahlgren**
Young Penny	**Chloe Moretz**

Randy Savage (Thug), Ronn Moss (Dr. Forrester), Gregy DeLisle (Penny's Mom), Sean Donnellan (Penny's TV Dad), Lino DiSalvo (Vinnie), Todd Cummings (Joey), Tim Mertens (Bobby), Kellie Hoover (Ester), Brian Stepanek (Martin), Jeff Bennett (Lloyd), Daran Norris (Louie), John Di Maggio (Saul), Jenny Lewis (Assistant Director), Stephen J. Anderson, June Christopher, Christin Ciaccio Briggs, David Cowgill, Terri Douglas, Jackie Gonneau, Forrest Iwaszewski, Nathan Greno, Holly Kane, Daniel Kaz, Phil LaMarr, Anne Lockhart, Dara McGarry, Scott Menville, Jonathan Nichols, Paul Pape, Lynwood Robinson, Karen Ann Ryan, Tara Strong, Pepper Sweeney, Joe Whyte, Chris Williams (Additional Voices)

Bolt, the dog star of a television action series who is unaware that his capabilities are enhanced by the trickery of the medium, must depend upon his natural skills when he accidentally ends up ends up on the streets of New York.

This film received an Oscar nomination for animated feature.

Rhino, Bolt

TWILIGHT

(SUMMIT ENTERTAINMENT) Producers, Greg Mooradian, Mark Morgan, Wyck Godfrey; Executive Producers, Karen Rosenfelt, Marty Bowen, Guy Oseary, Michele Imperator Stabile; Director, Catherine Hardwicke; Screenplay, Melissa Rosenberg; Based on the novel by Stephenie Meyer; Photography, Eliott Davis; Designer, Dan Bishop; Costumes, Wendy Chuck; Music, Carter Burwell; Editor, Nancy Richardson; Visual Effects Supervisors, Richard Kidd, Bill George, Jamison Scott Goei; Stunts, Andy Cheng; Casting, Tricia Wood, Deborah Aquila; a Temple Hill production, in association with Maverick Films/Imprint Entertainment; Dolby; Super 35 Widescreen; Deluxe color; Rated PG-13; 121 minutes; Release date: November 21, 2008

Cast

Bella Swan	**Kristen Stewart**
Edward Cullen	**Robert Pattinson**
Charlie Swan	**Billy Burke**
Alice Cullen	**Ashley Greene**
Rosalie Hale	**Nikki Reed**
Jasper Hale	**Jackson Rathbone**
Emmett Cullen	**Kellan Lutz**
Dr. Carlisle Cullen	**Peter Facinelli**
James	**Cam Gigandet**
Jacob Black	**Taylor Lautner**
Jessica Stanley	**Anna Kendrick**
Mike Newton	**Michael Welch**
Angela Weber	**Christian Serratos**
Billy Black	**Gil Birmingham**
Esme Cullen	**Elizabeth Reaser**
Laurent	**Edi Gathegi**
Victoria	**Rachelle Lefevre**
Renee Dwyer	**Sarah Clarke**
Waylon Forge	**Ned Bellamy**
Tyler Crowley	**Gregory Tyree Boyce**
Eric Yorkie	**Justin Chon**
Phil Dwyer	**Matt Bushell**
Mr. Molina	**Jose Zuniga**
Sam Uley	**Solomon Trimble**
Mine Security Guard	**Bryce Flint-Sommerville**
Young Bella	**Catherine Grimme**
Cora	**Ayanna Berkshire**
Waitress	**Katie Powers**
High School Administrator	**Trish Egan**
Woman in Diner	**Stephenie Meyer**
Frat Boys	**Alexander Mendeluk, Hunter Jackson, Gavin Bristol, Sean McGrath**

Relocating to Forks, Washington to live with her dad, Bella Swan finds herself drawn to a strange young man who happens to be part of a local sect of peaceful vampires.

Kristen Stewart, Robert Pattinson

Peter Facinelli, Edi Gathegi

Right: *Rachelle Lefevre*

Jackson Rathbone, Ashley Greene

Kristen Stewart, Billy Burke, Gil Birmingham, Taylor Lautner

Robert Pattinson © Summit Entertainment

Nikki Reed, Kellan Lutz

Cam Gigandet

WERE THE WORLD MINE

(SPEAK PRODS.) Producers, Tom Gustafson, Cory Krueckeberg, Peter Sterling; Director, Tom Gustafson; Screenplay, Tom Gustafson, Cory Krueckeberg; Photography, Kira Kelly; Designer, Cory Krueckeberg; Costumes, Elizabeth Powell Wislar; Original Songs, Jessica Fogle; Music, Tim Sandusky; Choreographer, Todd Underwood; Casting, TP&R Casting; a Speakproductions production, in association with the Group Entertainment; Color; Super 16-to-DV; Not rated; 96 minutes; Release date: November 21, 2008

Cast

Timothy	**Tanner Cohen**
Ms. Tebbit	**Wendy Robie**
Donna	**Judy McLane**
Frankie	**Zelda Williams**
Nora	**Jill Larson**
Max	**Ricky Goldman**
Jonathon	**Nathaniel David Becker**
Coach Driskill	**Christian Stolte**
Dr. Bellinger	**David Darlow**

Parker Croft (Cooper), Brad Bukauskas (Cole), Reid Dawson (Russ), Alexander Aguilar (Taylor), Yoni Solomon (Bradley), Colleen Skemp (Becky), Waymon Arnette (Henry), Sach Gray (Ian), Julia Black (Crystal), Peggy Roeder (Cole's Mother), Ora Jones (Mrs. Boyd), Annabel Armour (Phyllis), Ken Hasch, Adam Gauzza, Matthew McMunn, Walter Thon (Dancers), Michael Hargrove (Henry's Father), Martie Sanders (Academy Mother), Dev Kennedy (Angry Father), Charin Alvarez (Board Member), J.R. Rose (Mayor Robbins), Paul Lisnek (Newscaster)

After landing a part in his school's production of *A Midsummer Night's Dream*, a gay teen gets revenge on his tormentors when he concocts a love potion, inspired by the Shakespeare comedy, causing anyone sprayed with it to instantly fall in love with the first person they see.

Zelda Williams © Speak Prods

Tanner Cohen, Nathaniel David Becker

Nathaniel David Becker, Tanner Cohen

Nathaniel David Becker

Jon Favreau, Vince Vaughn

Vince Vaughn, Reese Witherspoon, Kristin Chenoweth, Mary Steenburgen

Vince Vaughn, Reese Witherspoon
© New Line Cinema

FOUR CHRISTMASES

(NEW LINE CINEMA) Producers, Roger Birnbaum, Gary Barber, Jonathan Glickman; Executive Producers, Toby Emmerich, Michael Disco, Richard Brener, Mark Kaufman, Guy Riedel, Peter Billingsley; Director, Seth Gordon; Screenplay, Matt R. Allen, Caleb Wilson, Jon Lucas, Scott Moore; Story, Matt R. Allen, Caleb Wilson; Photography, Jeffrey L. Kimball; Designer, Shepherd Frankel; Costumes, Sophie de Rakoff; Music, Alex Wurman; Additional Music, John O'Brien; Music Supervisor, Bob Bowen; Casting, Juel Bestrop, Seth Yanklewitz; a Birnbaum/Barber production, a Wild West Picture Show/Type A Films production, presented in association with Spyglass Entertainment; Dolby; Deluxe color; Rated PG-13; 88 minutes; Release date: November 26, 2008

Cast

Brad	**Vince Vaughn**
Kate	**Reese Witherspoon**
Howard	**Robert Duvall**
Paula	**Sissy Spacek**
Creighton	**Jon Voight**
Denver	**Jon Favreau**
Marilyn	**Mary Steenburgen**
Pastor Phil	**Dwight Yoakam**
Dallas	**Tim McGraw**
Courtney	**Kristin Chenoweth**
Susan	**Katy Mixon**
Aunt Donna	**Colleen Camp**

Jeanette Miller (Gram-Gram), Jack Donner (Grandpa), Steve Wiebe (Jim), Zak Boggan (Cody), Skyler Gisondo (Connor), True Bella (Kasi), Patrick Van Horn (Darryl), Marissa Tejada Benekos (News Reporter), Cedric Yarbrough (Stan), Brian Baumgartner (Eric), Peter Billingsley (Ticket Agent), Sterling Beaumon, T'y Brown, Ryder Bucaro, Callie Croughwell, Taylor Geare, Zachary Gordon, Reef Graham, Zai Moore, Destiny Petty, Diamond Petty, Bryce Robinson, Cort Rogers, Mackenzie Smith, Ava Rose Williams, Haidyn Winther (Kids in Jump-Jump), Stephanie Venditto (Angel), Creagen Dow (Sheep), Noah Munch, Matthew Glen Johnson (Screaming Kids), Bubba Dean Rambo (Elder Baritone Singer), Quinn Van Antwerp (Glee Club Alto Singer), Alison Martin, Daniel Hagen, Vernon Vaughn, Shea Gonzales, Ronald D. Brown, Jimmy Gonzales, Constance Maris, Tossaporn Banks (Church-Goers), Howard Leese, Richie Onori, Stu Simone, Stuart Smith, Sean McNabb (Band Members), Laura Johnson (Cheryl), Haley Hallak (Baby Clementine), JoAnn Jansen (Dance Instructor), David Aranovich, Steve Byrne, Irena A. Hoffman, Collette Wolfe (Dancers), Kayla Blake (Nurse), Lora McLaughlin (News Reporter)

Unable to leave San Francisco when their flight is grounded, Brad and Kate now feel obliged to visit each of their dysfunctional families on Christmas day.

Robert Duvall, Katy Mixon, Reese Witherspoon

MILK

(FOCUS) Producers, Dan Jinks, Bruce Cohen; Executive Producers, Michael London, Dustin Lance Black, Bruna Papandrea, Barbara A. Hall, William Horberg; Director, Gus Van Sant; Screenplay, Dustin Lance Black; Photography, Harris Savides; Designer, Bill Groom; Costumes, Danny Glicker; Music, Danny Elfman; Editor, Elliot Graham; Casting, Francine Maisler; a Focus Features presentation in association with Axon Films of a Groundswell production, a Jinks/Coen Company production; Dolby; Deluxe color; Rated R; 128 minutes; Release date: November 26, 2008

Cast

Harvey Milk	**Sean Penn**
Cleve Jones	**Emile Hirsch**
Dan White	**Josh Brolin**
Jack Lir	**Diego Luna**
Scott Smith	**James Franco**
Anne Kronenberg	**Alison Pill**
Mayor George Moscone	**Victor Garber**
John Briggs	**Denis O'Hare**
Dick Pabich	**Joseph Cross**
Rick Stokes	**Stephen Spinella**
Danny Nicoletta	**Lucas Grabeel**
Jim Rivaldo	**Brandon Boyce**
David Goodstein	**Zvi Howard Rosenman**
Michael Wong	**Kelvin Yu**
Art Agnos	**Jeff Koons**
Dennis Peron	**Ted Jan Roberts**
Denton Smith	**Robert Boyd Holbrook**
Themselves	**Frank Robinson, Allan Baird, Tom Ammiano**
Thelma	**Carol Ruth Silver**
Mary Ann White	**Hope Goblirsch**
McConnelly	**Steven Wiig**
Dianne Feinstein	**Ashlee Temple**
Carol Ruth Silver	**Wendy King**
Gordon Lau	**Kelvin Han Yee**
Phil Burton	**Robert Chimento**
Lily	**Ginabel Machado**
Young Teen	**Daniel Landroche**
Boy with Flier	**Trace Webb**
Morning Show Host	**Velina Brown**

Scott Patrick Green (House Boy), Mary Dilts (Channel 5 Reporter), Roman Alcides (City Hall Engineer), Robert George Nelson, Brian Danker (San Francisco Cops), Richard Gross (Riot Cop), Borzin Mottaghian (Briggs' Driver), Brian Yates Sharber (Gay Man), Camron Palmer (Medora Paine), Cully Fredricksen (Assistant Sheriff), Mark Martinez (Sylvester)Daniel Glicker (Customer), Catherine Cook (Opera Performer, Tosca), Joe Meyers (Opera Performer, Spoletta), Dominic Sahagun (Another Protester), William McElroy (Barber), Joey Hoeber (Union Man), Mark E. Stanger (Priest), Christopher Greene (Reporter), Jesse Caldwell (Chamber Clerk), Paul Arnold, Jack Dunston, Ron Gruetter, Awele Makeba, Tony Vella, William M. Verducci (Supervisors), Gilbert Baker, Shavi Blake, Brent Corrigan, Draco Dewar, Dave Franco, Alex Gonzalez, Olen Holm, Elias McConnell, Tom Randol (Telephone Tree), Lynn McRee (Moscone's Secretary), Cleve Jones (Don Amador), John Parson (Castro Man), Jay Kerzner (Speaker), Kristen Marie Holly (Anne's Friend), Sandi Ippolito (Relative), Roger Groh (Reporter), Maggie Weiland (Girl on Motorcycle), Dustin Lance Black (Castro Clone), Drew Kuhse (Pizza Delivery Man), Eric Cook (Robert Hillsborough)

The true story of how Harvey Milk became the first openly gay man elected to a major public office in the United States when he joined the San Francisco Board of Supervisors.

2008 Academy Award winner for Best Actor (Sean Penn) and Best Original Screenplay.

This film received additional Oscar nominations for picture, director, supporting actor (Josh Brolin), costume design, film editing, and original score.

Josh Brolin, Sean Penn

James Franco, Sean Penn

James Franco

Emile Hirsch

Sean Penn, Diego Luna

Sean Penn, Victor Garber

Alison Pill, Emile Hirsch

Sean Penn © Focus Features

FROST/NIXON

(UNIVERSAL) Producers, Brian Grazer, Ron Howard, Tim Bevan, Eric Fellner; Executive Producers, Peter Morgan, Matthew Byam Shaw, Karen Kehela Sherwood, David Bernardi, Debra Hayward, Liza Chasin, Todd Hallowell; Director, Ron Howard; Screenplay, Peter Morgan, based on his stage play; Photography, Salvatore Totino; Designer, Michael Corenblith; Costumes, Daniel Orlandi; Music, Hans Zimmer; Editors, Mike Hill, Dan Hanley; Casting, Jane Jenkins, Janet Hirshenson; an Imagine Entertainment/Working Title Films presentation in association with Studio Canal and Relativity Media of a Brian Grazer/Working Title production; Dolby; Clairmont Widescreen; Deluxe color; Rated R; 122 minutes; Release date: December 5, 2008

Frank Langella, Kevin Bacon

Cast

Richard Nixon	**Frank Langella**
David Frost	**Michael Sheen**
James Reston, Jr.	**Sam Rockwell**
Jack Brennan	**Kevin Bacon**
John Birt	**Matthew Macfadyen**
Bob Zelnick	**Oliver Platt**
Caroline Cushing	**Rebecca Hall**
Swifty Lazar	**Toby Jones**
Frank Gannon	**Andy Milder**
Diane Sawyer	**Kate Jennings Grant**
Ken Khachigian	**Gabriel Jarret**
Ray Price	**Jim Meskimen**
Pat Nixon	**Patty McCormack**
Interview Director	**Geoffrey Blake**
Lloyd Davis	**Clint Howard**
Ollie	**Rance Howard**
White House Director	**Gavin Grazer**
Frost Show Director	**Simon James**
Manolo Sanchez	**Eloy Casados**
Neil Diamond	**Jay White**
Sammy Cahn	**Will Albert**
Mary Minoff	**Keith MacKechnie**

Frank Langella, Patty McCormack

Penny Moore (Lady with Dachshund), Janneke Arent (Frost's Assistant), David Ross Paterson (Birt TV Show Presenter), Jennifer Hanley (Makeyp Woman), Robert Pastoriza, Louie Mejia (Interview Cameramen), Kevin Kearns (Fan at Airport), David Kelsey, James Ritz, Pete Rockwell (Smith House Reporters), Ned Vaughn (Secret Serviceman), Simone Kessell (Airport Check-In Woman), Ben Pauley (Australian Stage Manager), Noah Craft (Australian Stage Director), Taylor Singer (Stewardess), Kaine Bennett Charleston (Sydney Assistant Director), Gregory H. Alpert (White House Cinematographer), Kimberly Robin (Ma Maison Girl), Michelle Manhart (Disco Girl), Steve Kehela, Antony H. Acker (Premiere Reporters), John Kerry (Man at Disco), Jenn Gotzon (Tricia Nixon), Googy Gress, Marc McClure, Joe Spano (Network Executives)

Having landed an exclusive televised interview with former president Richard Nixon, talk show host David Frost realizes this is his chance to earn himself some credibility by getting the disgraced chief executive to open up about the Watergate scandal.

This film received Oscar nominations for picture, director, actor (Frank Langella), adapted screenplay, and film editing.

Michael Sheen, Rebecca Hall

Michael Sheen, Frank Langella

Frank Langella, Michael Sheen © Universal Studios

Gabriel Jarret, Jim Meskimen, Andy Milder, Kate Jennings Grant

Toby Jones, Michael Sheen, Frank Langella

Frank Langella, Sam Rockwell, Oliver Platt

Right: Michael Sheen, Matthew Macfadyen

CADILLAC RECORDS

(COLUMBIA) Producers, Andrew Lack, Sofia Sondervan; Executive Producers, Beyoncé Knowles, Marc Levin; Coproducer, Petra Hoebel; Director/Screenplay, Darnell Martin; Photography, Anastas Michos; Designer, Linda Burton; Costumes, Johnetta Boone; Music, Terence Blanchard; Music Supervisor, Amy Rosenblatt; Executive Music Producer, Marshall Chess; Editor, Peter C. Frank; Casting, Kimberly R. Hardin, Michelle D. Adams; a Sony Music Film and Parkwood Pictures presentation of a Sony Music Film production; Dolby; Super 35 Widescreen; Color; Rated R; 108 minutes; Release date: December 5, 2008

Beyoncé Knowles
© Columbia Pictures

Cast

Leonard Chess	**Adrien Brody**
Muddy Waters	**Jeffrey Wright**
Geneva Wade	**Gabrielle Union**
Little Walter	**Columbus Short**
Willie Dixon	**Cedric the Entertainer**
Revetta Chess	**Emmanuelle Chriqui**
Howlin' Wolf	**Eamonn Walker**
Chuck Berry	**Mos Def**
Etta Jame	**Beyoncé Knowles**
Lomax	**Tony Bentley**
Isabelle Allen	**Tammy Blanchard**
Alan Freed	**Eric Bogosian**
Phil Chess	**Shiloh Fernandez**
Shirley Feder	**Jill Flint**
Hubert Smulin	**Albert Jones**

Norman Reedus (Chess), Jake Robards (Robert), Jay O. Sanders (Mr. Feder), Tim Bellow (Man in the Caddy), Lawrence P. Beron (Overseer), Marc Bonan (Keith Richards), Wayne Cobham (Piano, Etta's Group), Ryan Curtis (Picnic Boyfriend), Veronika Dash (Blonde), Eshaya Draper (Charles Waters, 7 Years Old), John Farrer (Violinist, Etta's Group), Doug W. Goldman (Trumpet, Etta's Group), Gano Grills (Slick Pimp), Suzette Gunn (Minnie), Evan Hart (Young Lover), Osas Ighodaro (Vicky, Maid), Kevin Jackson (Mysterious Black Man), Rayan Lawrence (Harmonica Player), Clyna Layne (Juanita), Malikha Mallette (Little Walter's Girlfriend), Kevin Mambo (Jimmy Rogers), Anthony Del Negro (Bandstand Dancer), Natasha Ononogbo (Muddy's Girlfriend), Ginnie Randall (Muddy's Grandmother), Stephen Seidel (Officer Brown), Derrick Simmons (Dice Player), Valence Thomas (James Cotton), Dwan Dink Young (Drums, Etta's Group)

The true story of how Leonard Chess established Chess Records in Chicago and nurtured such important blues artists as Muddy Waters and Etta James.

Columbus Short,
Adrien Brody

Mos Def

Cedric the Entertainer, Adrien Brody, Jeffrey Wright

Alan Rickman, Mary Steenburgen, Shawn Hatosy

NOBEL SON

(FREESTYLE) Producers, Jody Savin, Randall Miller; Executive Producers, Art Klein, Tom Soulanille, Michael Ravine; Coproducers, Ronald Savin, J.P. O'Neill, Jane Baum, Henry Suarez, John Faiz Kayyem; Director/Editor, Randall Miller; Screenplay, Jody Savin, Randall Miller; Photography, Michael J. Ozier; Designer, Craig Stearns; Costumes, Kathryn Morrison; Music, Paul Oakenfold, Mark Adler; Casting, Rick Pagano; a Gimme Five Films/Prama Corp. presentation of an Unclaimed Freight production; Dolby; Color; Rated R; 110 minutes; Release date: December 5, 2008

Cast

Professor Eli Michaelson	**Alan Rickman**
Barkley Michaelson	**Bryan Greenberg**
Thaddeus James	**Shawn Hatosy**
Sarah Michaelson	**Mary Steenburgen**
Max Mariner	**Bill Pullman**
City Hall	**Eliza Dushku**
Gastner	**Danny DeVito**
Harvey Parrish	**Ted Danson**
Lasasso	**Ernie Hudson**

Tracey Walter (Simon Ahrens), Lindy Booth (Beth), Kevin West (Jaundice), Kirk Baily (Wil Cavalere), Dawn Balkin (Stewardess), Greg Collins (Foreman), Reid Collums (Delivery Guy), Tiffany Downey (Model), Bennett Dunn (Bartender), Mark Famiglietti (Officer Relyea), Mary Pat Gleason (Ruby), Brendon Graham (Soldier), Joyce Guy (Eileen Moses), Larry Hankin (Dr. Polaczek), Juliette Jeffers (Claire), Matthew Kimbrough (Deacon), Hal B. Klein (Tully's Guy), Joe Koons (Poet), Valerie Long (Excrement Woman), Wayne Lopez (Cabbie), Danika Osterman (Opera Singer), Dean Rader-Duval (Ernie), Johanna Torell (Analea), Matt Winston (Clifford), Avis Wrentmore (Model)

The son of egomaniacal Nobel Prize winning professor Eli Michaelson is kidnapped by a mechanical genius who claims to be his victim's illegitimate half-brother.

Bryan Greenberg, Eliza Dushku © Freestyle Releasing

WENDY AND LUCY

(OSCILLOSCOPE) Producers, Neil Kopp, Anish Savjani, Larry Fessenden; Executive Producers, Todd Haynes, Phil Morrison, Rajen Savjani, Joshua Blum; Director/Editor, Kelly Reichardt; Screenplay, Kelly Reichardt, Jon Raymond; Based on the story *Train Choir* by Jon Reymond; Photography, Sam Levy; a FilmScience, Glass Eye Pix production; FotoKem color; Not rated; 80 minutes; Release date: December 10, 2008

Cast

Wendy	**Michelle Williams**
Mechanic	**Will Patton**
Icky	**Will Oldham**
Andy	**John Robinson**
Security Guard	**Wally Dalton**
Man in Park	**Larry Fessenden**

Brenna Beardsley (Grocery Cashier), Ayanna Berkshire (Pound Employee), M. Blash (Dan's Voice), John Breen (Mr. Hunt), Michael Brophy (Grocery Store Stocker), Deneb Catalan (Jamie), Max Clement (Kid by Fire), Holly Cundiff (Security Guard's Woman), David Rives Curtright (Man Reading Book), Roger D. Faires (Recycler in Wheelchair), Skeeter Greene (Cop), George Haapala (Homeowner), Marilyn Faith Hickey (Police Administrator), Dave Hubner, David Koppell, Sid Shanley (Kids by Fire), Jeanine Jackson (Grocery Cashier), Winfield Jackson, Josh Larson, Connor O'Shea (Teenagers by Car), Boggs Johnson (Recycler), Lucy (Lucy the Dog), Deirdre O'Connell (Deb), Greg Schmitt (Garage Mechanic), Barry Seltzer (Market Shopper), Tanya Smith (Grocery Checker), Dan Wilson (Man on Bus), Michelle Worthey (Sadie), James Yu (Cab Driver)

Arrested for shoplifting while traveling through the Pacific Northwest, Wendy returns to the scene of the crime only to discover that her faithful dog Lucy is nowhere to be found.

Lucy, Michelle Williams © Oscilloscope

Kate Winslet © Weinstein Co.

David Kross, Kate Winslet

Below: *Ralph Fiennes*

Kate Winslet, David Kross

Kate Winslet, David Kross

THE READER

(WEINSTEIN CO.) Producers, Anthony Minghella, Sydney Pollack, Donna Gigliotti, Redmond Morris; Executive Producers, Bob Weinstein, Harvey Weinstein; Coproducers, Henning Molfenter, Christoph Fisser, Carl Woebcken; Co-executive Producer, Jason Blum; Director, Stephen Daldry; Screenplay, David Hare; Based on the novel *Der Vorleser* (*The Reader*) by Bernhard Schlink; Photography, Chris Menges, Roger Deakins; Designer, Brigitte Broch; Costumes, Ann Roth, Donna Maloney; Casting, Simone Baer, Jina Jay; a Mirage Enterprises (U.S.)/Neunte Babelsberg Film (Germany) production; American-German; Dolby; Technicolor; Rated R; 123 minutes; Release date: December 10, 2008

Cast

Hanna Schmitz	**Kate Winslet**
Michael Berg	**Ralph Fiennes**
Young Michael	**David Kross**
Rose Mather/Ilana Mather	**Lena Olin**
Professor Rohl	**Bruno Ganz**
Peter Berg	**Matthias Habich**
Carla Berg	**Susanne Lothar**
Marthe	**Karoline Herfurth**
Young Ilana	**Alexandra Maria Lara**
Dieter Spenz	**Volker Bruch**
Judge	**Burghart Klaussner**
Julia	**Hannah Herzsprung**
Sophie	**Vijessna Ferkic**
Ms. Brenner	**Linda Bassett**
Brigitte	**Jeanette Hain**
Emily Berg	**Alissa Wilms**
Thomas Berg	**Florian Bartholomäi**
Angela Berg	**Friederike Becht**
Doctor	**Frieder Venus**
Hanna's Neighbor	**Marie-Anne Fliegel**
Woodyard Worker	**Hendrik Arnst**
Teacher	**Rainer Sellien**
Sports Master	**Torsten Michaelis**
Holger	**Moritz Grove**
Stamp Dealer	**Joachim Tomaschewsky**

Barbara Philipp (Waitress), Hans Hohlbein (Clerk), Jürgen Tarrach (Gerhard Bade), Kirsten Block, Burghart Klaußner (Judges), Vanessa Berthold (Sophie's Friend), Benjamin Trinks (Holger's Friend), Fritz Roth (Tram Supervisor), Jacqueline Macaulay (Heidelberg Lecturer), Max Mauff (Rudolf), Ludwig Blochberger, Jonas Jägermeyr, Alexander Kasprik (Seminar Group Students), Sylvester Groth (Prosecuting Council), Fabian Busch (Hanna's Defense Council), Margarita Borich, Marie Gruber, Lena Lessing, Merelina Kendall, Hildegard Schroedter (Co-defendants), Martin Brambach, Michael Schenk (Remand Prison Guards), Ava Eusepi-Harris (Young Julia), Nadja Engel, Anne-Kathrin Gummich (Mail Room Guards), Carmen-Maja Antoni (Prison Librarian), Petra Hartung (Head Prison Guard), Beata Lehmann (Ms. Brenner's Secretary), Heike Hanold-Lynch (Prison Guard), Bettina Scheuritzel (Gate Guard), Robin Lyn Gooch (Ilana's Maid)

Michael Berg looks back upon the passionate affair he carried on with Hanna Schmitz, never realizing at the time that she withheld a shocking revelation about her past.

2008 Academy Award winner for Best Actress (Kate Winslet).

This film received additional Oscar nominations for picture, director, adapted screenplay, and cinematography.

Left: *Kate Winslet*

NOTHING LIKE THE HOLIDAYS

(OVERTURE) formerly *Humboldt Park*; Producers, Robert Teitel, George Tillman, Jr.; Executive Producers, Rene M. Rigal, Paul Kim, Reid Brody, Freddy Rodriguez; Coproducer, Thomas J. Busch; Director, Alfredo De Villa; Screenplay, Alison Swan, Rick Najera; Photography, Scott Kevant; Designer, Daniel B. Clancy; Costumes, Sue Kaufman; Music, Paul Oakenfold; Music Supervisors, Budd Carr, Nora Felder; Editors, Amy Duddleston, Paul Coniglio; Casting, Mary Vernieu; a State Street Pictures production; Dolby; Panavision; Technicolor; Rated PG-13; 98 minutes; Release date: December 12, 2008

Debra Messing, John Leguizamo, Elizabeth Peña, Alfred Molina, Freddy Rodriguez

Cast

Edy Rodriguez	**Alfred Molina**
Anna Rodriguez	**Elizabeth Peña**
Jesse Rodriguez	**Freddy Rodriguez**
Johnny	**Luis Guzman**
Ozzy	**Jay Hernandez**
Mauricio Rodriguez	**John Leguizamo**
Sarah Rodriguez	**Debra Messing**
Roxanna Rodriguez	**Vanessa Ferlito**
Marissa	**Melonie Diaz**
Hector	**Alexander Bautista**
Fernando	**Ramses Jimenez**
Alexis	**Manny Perez**
Tina	**Claudia Michelle Wallace**

Cheryl Hamada (Dr. Susan Lee), Manny Sosa (Father Torres), David Hernandez (Cheuy Flores), Sam Dyer (Customer), Nydia Rodriguez Terracina (Alexis' Mom), Ulises Acosta (Stock Boy), Gail Rastorfer (Stewardess), Ana María Alvarez (Gladys), Marica Wright (Patron), Jessica Zweig (Brunette), Jessica Camacho (Blonde), Eddie Martinez (Bartender, Julio's), Jaslene Gonzalez (Fine Girl), Mike Reyes (Party Goer), Brian Sills (Josh, Agent), Tanya Saracho (Sister Maria), Brandy McClendon (Woman with Babies), Llou Johnson (Van Driver), Patrick Zielinski (Snoring Guy), Cedric Young (Spencer), Gennae Bewernick (Hero Singer), Johnny "Kooklout" Starks (Alexis' Thug), Tony Castillo (Tony, Suitor)

Freddy Rodriguez, Vanessa Ferlito, Jay Hernandez, Melonie Diaz

The Rodriguez family gathers for Christmas in Chicago only to have their mother announce that she is planning on divorcing their father.

Freddy Rodriguez, John Leguizamo, Vanessa Ferlito

Right: *Luis Guzman* © *Overture Films*

Jennifer Connelly, Keanu Reeves

© *20th Century Fox*

THE DAY THE EARTH STOOD STILL

(20TH CENTURY FOX) Producers, Gregory Goodman, Paul Harris Boardman; Director, Scott Derrickson; Screenplay, David Scarpa; Based on the screenplay by Edmund H. North; Photography, David Tattersall; Designer, David Brisbin; Costumes, Tish Monaghan; Music, Tyler Bates; Editor, Wayne Wahrman; Visual Effects Supervisor, Jeffrey A. Okun; Visual Effects & Animation, WETA Digital; Special Makeup Effects and Practical Creature Effects, Mastersfx, Todd Masters; Stunts, J.J. Makaro, Steve Davison; Casting, Mindy Marin, Coreen Mayrs, Heike Brandstatter; a 3 Arts Entertainment production, presented in association with Dune Entertainment III; Dolby; Panavision; Deluxe color; Rated PG-13; 103 minutes; Release date: December 12, 2008

Cast

Klaatu	**Keanu Reeves**
Helen Benson	**Jennifer Connelly**
Regina Jackson	**Kathy Bates**
Jacob Benson	**Jaden Smith**
Professor Barnhardt	**John Cleese**
Michael Granier	**Jon Hamm**
John Driscoll	**Kyle Chandler**
Colonel	**Robert Knepper**
Mr. Wu	**James Hong**
Dr. Myron	**John Rothman**

Sunita Prasad (Rouhani), Juan Riedinger (William Kwan), Sam Gilroy (Tom), Tanya Champoux (Isabel), Rukiya Bernard (Student), Alisen Down (Laptop Woman), David Lewis (Plainsclothes Agent), Lloyd Adams (Agent Driver), Mousa Kraish (Yusef), J.C. MacKenzie (Grossman), Kurt Max Runte (Civil Engineer), Daniel Bacon (Winslow), Richard Keats, Bill Mondy, Judith Maxie (Helicopter Scientists), Reese Alexander (Sergeant), Serge Houde, Lorena Gale (Scientists), Stefanie Samuels (Guardswoman), Richard Tillman (Army Sergeant), Camille Atebe, Thomas Bradshaw, Terence Dament (NYPD), Patrick Sabongui, Jacob Blair, Shaine Jones, Jake McLaughlin (Soldiers), George Sharperson (Cop), Shaker Paleja, Doug Chapman, Marci T. House (Medics), Aaron Craven (Technician), Roger Cross (General Quinn), Heather Doerksen (Regina's Aide), Hiro Kanagawa (Dr. Ikegawa), Craig Stanghetta, Stefan Busse (Grey Men), Dean Redman (Military Policeman), David Richmond-Peck (Polygraph Operator), Andrew Wheeler (Guardsman), Darien Provost (Little Boy), Daniel St. Andrews, Brad Dryborough (Train Passengers), Ken Kirzinger (Arguing Evacuee), William "Big Sleeps" Stewart (Transit Cop), Blair Redford (Fighter Pilot #1), Daniel Wisler (Army Fighter Pilot #2), Mark Kogan (Air Traffic Controller), Brandon T. Jackson (Target Tech), Edward Fong (Wu's Grandson), Sandy Colton (Army Corps Engineer Captain), Ty Olsson II (Flash Chamber Colonel), Jay-Nicolas Hackleman (State Trooper), Dawn Chubai (News Anchor), Joshua Close (Flash Chamber Engineer), Leanne Adachi (Flash Chamber Tech), Geoff Meed (Field Commander Communications Officer), Michael Hogan (General), Ben Cotton (Truck Driver), Kevan Kase (Pickup Truck Driver), Jennifer Paterson (Girlfriend), Josue Aguirre (Humvee Soldier)

A sphere lands in Manhattan, from which emerges alien Klaatu, who has come to Earth to warn its leaders to do something about the sorry state of their planet. Remake of the 1951 Fox film which starred Michael Rennie and Patricia Neal.

Left: *David Richmond-Peck, Keanu Reeves*

GRAN TORINO

(WARNER BROS.) Producers, Clint Eastwood, Robert Lorenz, Bill Gerber; Executive Producers, Jenette Kahn, Adam Richman, Tim Moore, Bruce Berman; Director, Clint Eastwood; Screenplay, Nick Schenk; Story, Dave Johansson, Nick Schenk; Photography, Tom Stern; Designer, James J. Murakami; Costumes, Deborah Hopper; Music, Clint Eastwood, Michael Stevens; Editors, Joel Cox, Gary D. Roach; Casting, Ellen Chenoweth; a Double Nickel Entertainment, Malpaso production, presented in association with Village Roadshow Pictures; Dolby; Panavision; Technicolor; Rated R; 117 minutes; Release date: December 12, 2008

Clint Eastwood, Bee Vang, Brooke Chia Thao, Chee Thao, Ahney Her

Cast

Walt Kowalski	**Clint Eastwood**
Thao Vang Lor	**Bee Vang**
Sue Lor	**Ahney Her**
Father Janovich	**Christopher Carley**
Mitch Kowalski	**Brian Haley**
Karen Kowalski	**Geraldine Hughes**
Steve Kowalski	**Brian Howe**
Ashley Kowalski	**Dreama Walker**
Tim Kennedy	**William Hill**
Barber Martin	**John Carroll Lynch**
Vu	**Brooke Chia Thao**
Grandma	**Chee Thao**
Youa	**Choua Kue**
Trey	**Scott Eastwood**
Kor Khue	**Xia Soua Chang**
Smokie	**Sonny Vue**
Spider	**Doua Moua**
Bartender	**Greg Trzasakoma**
Al	**John Johns**
Darrell	**Davis Gloff**
Mel	**Tom Mahard**
Duke	**Cory Hardrict**
Monk	**Nana Gbweonyo**
Prez	**Arthur Cartwright**

Austin Douglas Smith (Daniel Kowalski), Conor Liam Callaghan (David Kowalski), Michael E. Kurowski (Josh Kowalski), Julia Ho (Dr. Chang), Maykao K. Lytongpao (Gee), Carlos Guadarrama (Head Latino), Andrew Tamez-Hull, Ramon Camacho, Antonio Mireles (Latino Gangbangers), Ian Vue Yang, Zoua Kue (Hmong Flower Women), Elvis Thao, Jerry Lee, Lee Mong Vang (Hmong Gangbangers), Tru Hang (Hmong Grandfather), Alice Lor (Hmong Granddaughter), Tony Pao Kue (Hmong Husband), Douacha Ly (Hmong Man), Parng D. Yarng (Hmong Neighbor), Nelly Yang Sao Yia (Hmong Wife), Marty Bufalini (Lawyer), My-Ishia Cason-Brown (Muslim Receptionist), Clint Ward (Officer), Stephen Kue (Officer Chang), Rochelle Winter (Waitress), Claudia Rodgers (White Woman Neighbor), Vincent Bonasso (Tailor)

Christopher Carley, Clint Eastwood

A bigoted, retired autoworker who refuses to budge from his rapidly changing Detroit neighborhood finds himself unexpectedly drawn into the lives of his Asian neighbors when they are threatened by a gang.

Right: Clint Eastwood © Warner Bros.

Bee Vang, Clint Eastwood

Bee Vang

Brooke Chia Thao, Bee Vang, Ahney Her, Clint Eastwood

Bee Vang, Jerry Lee, Elvis Thao, Sonny Vue, Doua Moua

Clint Eastwood

Amy Adams

Viola Davis

Philip Seymour Hoffman, Amy Adams

Meryl Streep

Meryl Streep, Philip Seymour Hoffman

DOUBT

(MIRAMAX) Producers, Scott Rudin, Mark Roybal; Executive Producer, Celia Costas; Director/ Screenplay, John Patrick Shanley, based on his play; Photography, Roger Deakins; Designer, David Gropman; Costumes, Ann Roth; Music, Howard Shore; Editor, Dylan Tichenor; Casting, Ellen Chenoweth; a Scott Rudin production; Dolby; Deluxe color; Rated PG-13; 104 minutes; Release date: December 12, 2008

Cast

Sister Aloysius Beauvier	**Meryl Streep**
Father Brendan Flynn	**Philip Seymour Hoffman**
Sister James	**Amy Adams**
Mrs. Miller	**Viola Davis**
Sister Veronica	**Alice Drummond**
Sister Raymond	**Audrie Neenan**
Mrs. Carson	**Susan Blommaert**
Christine Hurley	**Carrie Preston**
Warren Hurley	**John Costelloe**
Jimmy Hurley	**Lloyd Clay Brown**
Donald Miller	**Joseph Foster II**
William London	**Mike Roukis**
Zither Player	**Haklar Dezso**
Kevin	**Frank Shanley**
Organist	**Robert Ridgell**
Girl in Church	**Alannah Iacovano**
Ralph	**Frank Dolce**
Tommy Conroy	**Paulie Litt**
Raymond	**Matthew Marvin**
Sarah	**Molly Chiffer**
Alice	**Lydia Grace Jordan**
Mrs. Kean	**Suzanne Hevner**
Sister Teresa	**Helen Stenborg**
Monsignor Benedict	**Tom Toner**
Father Sherman	**Michael Puzzo**
Mrs. Shields	**Margery Beddow**
Mr. McGuinn	**Jack O'Connell**
Mrs. Deakins	**Marylouise Burke**

Valda Setterfield (Parishoner), Sarah Giovanniello, Katie Shelnitz, Aaron O'Neill, Thomas J. Meehan, Samantha Chadbourne, Christina Angelina Celone, Melissa Viezel, Emily Swimmer, Katelyn Snell, Shayne Fischman, Coby D. Moran (Choir Singers), Philip Post, Thomas J. Kennedy, Thomas. A. Varrone, Sabrina Costa, Samantha Buczek, Gabriella Renne DiMaria, Ariana Silvestro, Michele Ciago, Anna Lonczak, Brandy Panfili (Sister James' Students)

A nun and a priest clash at a Catholic school when she becomes certain that he has had inappropriate relations with a young boy.

This film received Oscar nominations for actress (Meryl Streep), supporting actor (Philip Seymour Hoffman), 2 for supporting actress (Amy Adams, Viola Davis), and adapted screenplay.

Philip Seymour Hoffman © Miramax Films

WHAT DOESN'T KILL YOU

(YARI FILM GROUP) Producers, Bob Yari, Marc Frydman, Rod Lurie; Executive Producers, William J. Immerman, Peter McIntosh; Director, Brian Goodman; Screenplay, Brian Goodman, Donnie Wahlberg, Paul T. Murray; Photography, Christopher Norr; Designer, Henry Dunn; Costumes, Roemehl Hawkins; Music, Alex Wurman; Editor, Robert Hoffman; Casting, Donna DeSeta, Angela Peri; a Yari Film Group presentation of a Bob Yari Prods./Battleplan production; Dolby; Color; Rated R; 100 minutes; Release date: December 12, 2008

Cast

Brian Reilly	**Mark Ruffalo**
Paulie McDougan	**Ethan Hawke**
Stacy Reilly	**Amanda Peet**
Sully	**Will Lyman**
Pat Kelly	**Brian Goodman**
Detective Moran	**Donnie Wahlberg**
Katie	**Angela Featherstone**

Eddie Lynch (Jackie), Brian S. Goodman (Jay), Michael Yebba (Roundman/Old Lady), Brian Connolly (Sean), Nathaniel Smyth (Mark, 5 Years Old), Oscar Wahlberg (Mark, 10 Years Old), Thomas Regan (Young Paulie), Jean-Pierre Serret (Young Brian), George Khoury (Delivery Man), Holly Karrol Clark (Kim, Waitress), Leif Riddell (Off-Duty Officer), Lenny Clarke (Hogie), Jay Giannone (Matt), Michael Balcanoff (Marius), Richard Lane, Jr. (Gunther, Poodle Napper), John Fiore (Creep, Murder Victim), Joseph Bavis (Polack), Katelyn Cahill (Young Stacy), Rick Skinner (Chappy), Dennis Lynch (Carpet Store Driver), Michael Testone (Anthony), T. Sean Ferguson (Alcoholic Speaker #1), Brienne De Beau (Lisa, Waitress), Richard Italiano (Tommy), Will Le Bow (Burt, Jeweler), Danny Naten (Callahan, Guard), Bo Cleary, Kevin McCormick, Dylan Kelley (Steroid Geeks), Lindsey McKeon (Nicole), Bates Wilder (Doctor), Jack Ordway (Ronnie Dents), Kelly Holleman (Kathleen, Nurse), Ryan Mahoney (Ray, Alcoholic Speaker), Kristen Mastroianni-Pascucci (Anchorwoman), Vic Clay (Robert Stavos, Child Molester), Tom Kemp (Captain Stover), Robert Kelly (Gas Man), Mark Goodman (City Worker), Steve Sweeney (Power Wash Jerry), Brian Scannell (Eddie), Thomas Olson (Richie the Slob), Mandy Olsen (Patty, Sidewalk Café Worker), Ally Flaherty (Café Patron), Christopher Connolly (Mo, Bartender)

A petty criminal barely making ends meet for his family begins to reassess his dead-end life when he ends up behind bars.

Mark Ruffalo, Nathaniel Smyth, Amanda Peet © Yari Film Group

Gabriel Mann, Bijou Phillips © Samuel Goldwyn Films

DARK STREETS

(GOLDWYN) Producers, Glenn M. Stewart, Claus Clausen, Andrea Balen, Corina Danckwerts; Executive Producer, Steffen Aumueller; Coproducer, Jeremy Alter; Director, Rachel Samuels; Screenplay, Wallace King; Based on the play *The City Club* by Glenn M. Stewart; Photography, Sharone Meir; Designer, Frank Bollinger; Costumes, Maria Schicker; Music, George Acogny; Songs, James Compton, Tim Langhorne Brown, Tony De Meur; Choreographer, Keith Young; Editors, Anne Goursaud, Michael J. Duthie; Casting, Johanna Ray; a Sherezade Films and Capture Film Intl. presentation; Dolby; Technicolor; Rated R; 83 minutes; Release date: December 12, 2008

Cast

Chaz Davenport	**Gabriel Mann**
Crystal	**Bijou Phillips**
Madelaine	**Izabella Miko**
Lieutenant	**Elias Koteas**
Pale Man	**Jarreth J. Merz**
Nathaniel	**Michael Fairman**

Toledo Diamond (Prince), Jordi Caballero (Slim), Tracy Phillips (Rose), Mike Muscat (Guard), Kimberly Sanders (Ballroom Dancer), David Aldridge (VIP Dinner Guest), Noel Arthur (EMT), Sybil Azur (Lilly), Luna Rocio Cantale (Cigarette Girl), Samuel Bliss Cooper (Deliver Man), Pat Crawford Brown (Delroes), Palmer Davis (Darlene), Keith Glover (Plant Guard), Diana Kyle (Woman in Feathered Cape), Sebastian Leger (Musician), Alexandra Mann (Lorna), Howard S. Miller (Frank), James Otis (Tommy), Matt O'Toole (Harry), Paul Palo (Drug Dealer), F. William Parker (Man in Overalls), Vanessa Peters (Woman at Table), Bashar Rahal (Bartender), Ken Rosier (Governor), Carolyn Seymour (Gloria), Chip Sickler (Man in Top Hat), Eve Sigall (Neighbor), John Solari (The Goon), Brian Toth (Transvestite), Alexi Wasser (Claudia), Keith Young (Choreographer), Marina Benedict, Gigi Chavoshi, Henriette Dyer, Sharon Ferguson, Sharon Ferrol-Young, Roosevelt Flenoury, Gigi Hunter, Michele Martinez, Jaayda McClanahan, Liz Ramos, Lauri Serene, Adriana Souza, Christie Stover, Emily Williams, Tara Wilson (Dancers)

A struggling New Orleans nightclub owner finds himself entangled in a web of corruption when he uncovers information that suggests his father might have been murdered.

Mickey Rourke © Fox Searchlight

Marisa Tomei, Mickey Rourke

Evan Rachel Wood, Mickey Rourke

THE WRESTLER

(FOX SEARCHLIGHT) Producers, Scott Franklin, Darren Aronofsky; Executive Producers, Vincent Maraval, Agnes Mentre, Jennifer Roth; Coproducer, Mark Heyman; Director, Darren Aronofsky; Screenplay, Robert Siegel; Photography, Maryse Alberti; Designer, Timothy Grimes; Costumes, Amy Westcott; Music, Clint Mansell; Music Supervisors, Jim Black, Gabe Hilfer; Casting, Mary Vernieu, Suzanne Smith-Crowley; a Wild Bunch (France) presentation of a Protozoa Pictures (U.S.) production; American-French; Dolby; Widescreen; Techincolor; Rated R; 109 minutes; Release date: December 17, 2008

Cast

Randy "The Ram" Robinson	**Mickey Rourke**
Cassidy (Pam)	**Marisa Tomei**
Stephanie Robinson	**Evan Rachel Wood**
Lenny	**Mark Margolis**
Wayne	**Todd Barry**
Nick Volpe	**Wass Stevens**
Scott Brumberg	**Judah Friedlander**
The Ayatollah	**Ernest Miller**
Necro Butcher	**Dylan Keith Summers**
Tommy Rotten	**Tommy Farra**
Lex Lethal	**Mike Miller**

Marcia Jean Kurtz (Admissions Desk Woman), John D'Leo (Adam), Ajay Naidu (Medic), Gregg Bello (JAPW Promoter Larry Cohen), Scott Siegel (Greg), Maurizio Ferrigno (Spotter), Donnetta Lavinia Grays (Jen), Andrea Langi (Alyssa), Armin Amiri (Dr. Moayedizadeh), Lynn Tovale Anoai (Pharmacist), Ryan Lynn (Strip Club Best Man), Michael Drayer (Strip Club Bachelor), Alyssa Bresnahan (Cheeques Bartender), Jeff Chena (Hotel Bartender), Vernon Campbell (Big Chris), Felice Choi (Beautician), Bernadette Penotti (Tanning Salon Owner), Johnny Valiant (The Legend Johnny Valiant), Ron Killings (Ron "The Truth" Killings), Giovanni Roselli (Romeo Roselli), Robert Siegel, Scott Franklin (Autograph Fans), Sylvia Kauders (Hudson Acres Lady at Deli Counter), Alissa Reisler (Young Housewife at Deli Counter), Willy Rosner (Touchdown Man at Deli Counter), Rebecca Darke (German Potato Salad Lady at Deli Counter), E.J. Carroll (Teamster at Deli Counter), Abraham Aronofsky (Annoyed Man at Deli Counter), Charlotte Aronofsky (Annoyed Woman at Deli Counter), T.J. Kedzierski (Jameson), Jen Cohn (Get a Room Lady), Maven Bentley (WXW Announcer), Douglas Crosby (WXW Referee), Larry Legend (CZW Announcer), Nick Papagiorgio (CZW Referee), Kevin Foote (ROH Announcer), Jon Trosky (ROH Referee), Andrew Anderson, Austin Aries, Blue Meanie, Nicky Benz, Brolly, Lamar Braxton Porter, Claudio Castagnoli, Cobian, Doc Daniels, Bobby Demsey, Billy Dream, Whacks, Rob Eckos, Nate Hatred, Havoc, DJ Hyde, Inferno, Joker, Judas, Kid U.S.A., La Smooth, Toa Maivia, Kevin Matthews, Devon Moore, Pete Nixon, Paul E. Normous, Papadon, Sabian, Jay Santana, Sugga, Larry Sweeney (Wrestlers), Robert Rosen (Voice of Ring Announcer), Elizabeth Wood (Melissa)

An aging wrestler, facing an uncertain future, tries to find solace in his relationship with a stripper and by reestablishing contact with his long-estranged daughter.

This film received Oscar nominations for actor (Mickey Rourke) and supporting actress (Marisa Tomei).

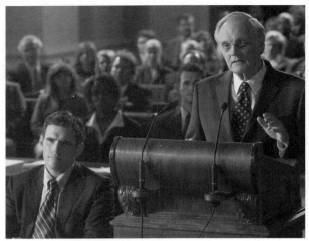

Matt Dillon, Alan Alda © Yari Film Group

NOTHING BUT THE TRUTH

(YARI FILM GROUP) Producers, Marc Frydman, Rod Lurie, Bob Yari; Executive Producers, Dennis Brown, David C. Glassner, William J. Immerman, James Spies; Director/ Screenplay, Rod Lurie; Photography, Alik Sakharov; Designer, Eloise Stammerjohn; Costumes, Lynn Falconer; Music, Larry Groupe; Music Supervisor, Kevin Edelman; Editor, Sarah Boyd; Casting, Mary Jo Slater; a Batteplan production; Dolby; Widescreen; Color; Rated R; 108 minutes; Release date: December 17, 2008

Cast

Rachel Armstrong	**Kate Beckinsale**
Patton Dubois	**Matt Dillon**
Bonnie Benjamin	**Angela Bassett**
Alan Burnside	**Alan Alda**
Erica Van Doren	**Vera Farmiga**
Ray Armstrong	**David Schwimmer**
Agent O'Hara	**Courtney B. Vance**
Avril Aaronson	**Noah Wyle**

Floyd Abrams (Judge Hall), Preston Bailey (Timmy Armstrong), Kristen Bough (Allison Van Doren), Julie Ann Emery (Agent Boyd), Robert Harvey (Warden), Michael O'Neill (CIA Director), Kristen Shaw (Angel Rabinowitz), Angelica Torn (Molly Meyers), Jamey Sheridan (Oscar Van Doren), Pamela Jones (Guard Washington), Jennifer McCoy (Jesse), David Bridgewater (Riggens), Jenny Odle Madden (Olivia), Rod Lurie (Larry), Janie Paris, Jim Palmer, Clay Chamberlin (Editors), Joseph Murphy (Bloomington), Ashley LeConte Campbell (Teacher), Scott Williamson (President Lyman), Dan Abrams (Himself), Elizabeth Anne Wilson (Producer), Jon Sparks (Rumpled Man), Erin Dangler (Gretchen Monroe), Randall Hartzog (Principal), Craig Wright (Guard), Phil Darius Wallace (FBI Agent Coddington), Kelly Holleman (Clerk, *Sun Times*), Allen Overton Battle III (Gentleman), Teri Itkin (Miss Potter), Angie Gilbert (Trustee), Antonio Morton (Deputy), Blake Brooks (Intern), CaroL Russell (Waitress), Verda Davenport Booher (Police Clerk), Robert P. Campbell (Polygraphist), Michael Detrio (David), Jeffrey W. Bailey (AUSA), Garnet Brooks (Secret Service Agent), William J. Immerman (Chief Justice), D'Army Bailey (Supreme Court Judge), Lowell Perry (Federal Marshal), Merle Dandrige (Celia)

After reporter Rachel Armstrong interviews a covert CIA agent who tells the truth behind an unjustified U.S. military attack on Venezuela, she is subpoenaed to reveal the source of her explosive story but refuses to divulge the information.

William Hurt © Arthur Cohn Prods.

THE YELLOW HANDKERCHIEF

(ARTHUR COHN PRODS.) Producer, Arthur Cohn; Executive Producer, Lillian Birnbaum; Line Producer, Rob Ortiz; Director, Udayan Prasad; Screenplay, Erin Dignam; Based on the story by Pete Hamill; Photography, Chris Menges; Designer, Monroe Kelly; Music, Eef Barzelay, Jack Livesay; Editor, Christopher Tellefsen; Casting, Sharon Howard-Field; Dolby; Color; Not rated; 102 minutes; Release date: December 17, 2008

Cast

Brett	**William Hurt**
May	**Maria Bello**
Martine	**Kristen Stewart**
Gordy	**Eddie Redmayne**

Kaori Momoi (Motel Owner), Emanuel K. Cohn (Doctor), Nurith Cohn, Holly O'Quinn (Nurses), Jetta Jones (Garage Owner), Veronica Russell (Pregnant Woman), Grover Coulson (Farnsworth), Lisha Brock (Waitress), Lucy Adiar Faust (Snotty Girl), John Gregory Willard (Blonde), Rebecca Newman (Ilene), Ross Britz (Friend), Marshall Cain, Shane Tingle (Ferry Drivers), Aimee Fortier (Teenage Mother), Ross Francis (Boyfriend), Douglass M. Griffin, Jeff Galpin (Policemen), Ashlynn Ross (Delivery Girl), Tanner Gill (Man in Rain), Eric Adams (Bank Accessor), Michael Kennedy (Tony Freckles), Paige Pareti (Girl in Video), Veronica Russell (Warden Genaro), Bello Nock (Bello), Victor Brunette (Chippy White), B. Martin Williams (Bob), Noelle Bercy (Dancer #1), Dawna Williams (Waitress)

After serving six years for manslaughter, Brett Hanson accepts a ride with a pair of troubled teens, while trying to decide if he should resume his life with the woman he left behind.

William Hurt, Kristen Stewart

YES MAN

(WARNER BROS.) Producers, Richard D. Zanuck, David Heyman; Executive Producers, Marty Ewing, Dana Goldberg, Bruce Berman; Coproducers, Katterli Frauenfelder, Tiffany Daniel; Director, Peyton Reed; Screenplay, Nicholas Stoller, Jarrad Paul, Andrew Mogel; Based on the book by Danny Wallace; Photography, Robert Yeoman; Designer, Andrew Laws; Costumes, Mark Bridges; Music, Lyle Workman; Editor, Craig Alpert; Casting, David Rubin, Richard Hicks; a Heyday Films/Zanuck Co. production, presented in association with Village Roadshow Pictures; Dolby; Panavision; Technicolor; Rated PG-13; 104 minutes; Release date: December 19, 2008

Cast

Carl Allen	**Jim Carrey**
Allison	**Zooey Deschanel**
Peter	**Bradley Cooper**
Nick	**John Michael Higgins**
Norman	**Rhys Darby**
Rooney	**Danny Masterson**
Tillie	**Fionnula Flanagan**
Terence Bundley	**Terence Stamp**
Lucy	**Sasha Alexander**
Stephanie	**Molly Sims**
Homeless Guy	**Brent Briscoe**
Wes	**Rocky Carroll**

John Cothran (Tweed), Spencer Garrett (Multack), Sean O'Bryan (Ted), Kai Lennox (Flyer Guy), Cecelia Antoinette (Bank Employee), Patrick Labyorteaux (Marv Winchell), Jamie Denbo (Marv's Wife), Shelby Zemanek (Sophie Winchell), Alfred De Contreras (Orange Seller), Peter Giles (Loan Applicant), Rebecca Corry, Whit Anderson, Pride Grinn, Kerry Hoyt (Yes Patrons), Anna Khaja (Faranoosh), Maile Flanagan (Janet), Roni Meron (Bigfoot Waitress), Heidi Herschbach (Daphne), Graham Shiels (Scary Boyfriend), Brandon Walter (Mormon), Emily Chen, Ashley Martinez (Buttercup Girls), Kenneth Searle (Flight Instructor), John H. Song (Korean Instructor), Lauren Kim (Korean Class Student), Mike Gomez (Father at Homeless Shelter), E.J. Callahan (Farmer), Kelly Harris, Becky Kupersmith, Julian Iva Meador (Munchausen by Proxy Band Members), Jarrad Paul (Reggie), Aaron Takahashi (Lee), Jon Baggio (Quidditch Player), Peter Spellos (Security Guard, Hollywood Bowl), Vivian Bang (Soo-Mi), William Will Simm (Chul-Soo), Jackie Harris (Bystander), Trent Minx (Guy in Crowd), Sally Stevens, Eric Bradley, Teri Koide, Guy Maeda, John Pagano (Singers), Lisa Long (Airline Representative), Mary-Pat Green (Tour Guide), Stephanie Hodge (Ticket Lady), Matt Miller (Corporate Exec), J.R. Nutt (Caddy), Kat Sawyer-Young (Woman in Gallery), Lance Wesley (Tow Truck Driver), Katsy Chappell (Nurse), Poetri (Security Guard at Hospital), Luis Guzmán (Jumper)

Realizing that his life is closing down because he is quick to turn down offers to do anything, bank loan officer Carl Allen decides to attend a self-help seminar where the participants are encouraged to say "yes" to everything that is proposed to them.

Zooey Deschanel, Jim Carrey © Warner Bros.

Jim Carrey, Rhys Darby

Jim Carrey, John Michael Higgins, Terence Stamp

Danny Masterson, Jim Carrey, Bradley Cooper

THE TALE OF DESPEREAUX

(UNIVERSAL) Producers, Gary Ross, Allison Thomas; Executive Producers, William Sargent, Ryan Kavanaugh, David Lipman, Robin Bissell; Directors, Sam Fell, Rob Stevenhagen; Screen Story, Will McRobb, Chris Viscardi; Based on the book by Kate DiCamillo; Coproducer, Tracy Shaw; Designer, Evgeni Tomov; Supervising Art Director, Olivier Adam; Animation Supervisor, Gabriele Zucchielli; Visual Effects Supervisor, Barry Armour; Photography, Brad Blackbourn; Editor, Mark Solomon; Music, William Ross; Casting, Debra Zane; a Larger Than Life production in association with Framestore Animation, presented in association with Relativity Media; Dolby; Technicolor; Rated G; 90 minutes; Release date: December 19, 2008

Despereaux, Andre

Voice cast

Despereaux	**Matthew Broderick**
Roscuro	**Dustin Hoffman**
Princess Pea	**Emma Thompson**
Miggery Sow	**Tracey Ullman**
Andre	**Kevin Kline**
Lester	**William H. Macy**
Boldo	**Stanley Tucci**
Botticelli	**Ciaran Hinds**
Gregory	**Robbie Coltrane**
Furlough	**Tony Hale**
Antoinette	**Frances Conroy**
Mayor	**Frank Langella**
Principal	**Richard Jenkins**
Hovis	**Christopher Lloyd**
Pietro	**Charles Shaughnessy**
Narrator	**Sigourney Weaver**

Patricia Cullen (Queen), Sam Fell (Ned/Smudge), Jane Karen (Louise), Bronson Pinchot (Town Crier), McNally Sagal (Teacher)

A tiny mouse, with oversized ears and an unconventional outlook on life, befriends a banished rat and ends up helping to save the Kingdom of Dor from doom.

Lester, Antoinette, Furlough, Doctor

Roscuro, Princess Pea

Despereaux

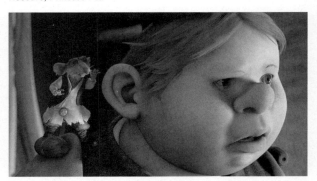

Roscuro, Miggery Sow © Universal Studios

Woody Harrelson, Will Smith

Will Smith

Will Smith, Rosario Dawson

SEVEN POUNDS

(COLUMBIA) Producers, Todd Black, James Lassiter, Jason Blumenthal, Steve Tisch, Will Smith; Executive Producers, David Crockett, David Bloomfield, Ken Stovitz, Domenico Procacci; Coproducers, Molly Allen, Chrissy Blumenthal; Director, Gabriele Muccino; Screenplay, Grant Nieporte; Photography, Philippe Le Sourd; Designer, J. Michael Riva; Costumes, Sharen Davis; Music, Angelo Milli; Editor, Hughes Winborne; Casting, Denise Chamian, Angela Demo; an Overbrook Entertainment production, an Escape Artists production, presented in association with Relativity Media; Dolby; Super 35 Widescreen; Deluxe color; Rated PG-13; 123 minutes; Release date: December 19, 2008

Cast

Ben Thomas	**Will Smith**
Emily Posa	**Rosario Dawson**
Ezra Turner	**Woody Harrelson**
Ben's Brother	**Michael Ealy**
Dan	**Barry Pepper**
Connie Tepos	**Elpidia Carrillo**
Sarah Jenson	**Robinne Lee**
Larry, Hotel Owner	**Joseph A. Nuñez**
George Ristuccia	**Bill Smitrovich**
Stewart Goodman	**Tim Kelleher**
Dr. Briar	**Gina Hecht**
George's Doctor	**Andy Milder**
Holly Apelgren	**Judyann Elder**
Susan	**Sarah Jane Morris**

Madison Pettis (Connie's Daughter), Ivan Angulo (Connie's Son), Octavia Spencer (Kate, Home Health Care Nurse), Cynthia Rube (Assisted Living Nurse), Jack Yang (Apogee Engineer), Quintin Kelley (Nicholas, Bald Boy), Louisa Kendrick (Dan's Wife), Fiona Hale (Inez), Amanda Carlin (Neighbor Lady), Connor Cruise (Young Ben), David Haines (Young Ben's Father), Casey Morris (911 Operator), Audrey Wasilewski, Sonya Eddy (Nurses), Charlene Amoia (Woman in Diner), Todd Cahoon (Man in Diner), Rich Hutchman, Michael Spellman (Elevator Doctors), Dale Raoul (St. Matthew's Volunteer), Steve Tom (Bone Marrow Doctor), Jora Senane, Robert Figueroa (Ben's OR Doctors), Kevin Cooney (Hospital Administrator), Nadia Shazana (Dialysis Nurse), Markus Flanagan (Neurosurgeon), Leif Rogers (ER Doctor), Gaspar Uriarte (Emily's OR Doctor), Nichole Ambriz (OR Nurse), Lee Von Ernst (EP Nurse)

IRS agent Ben Thomas sets out to help seven strangers in an effort to atone for a terrible occurrence for which he feels responsible.

Will Smith © Columbia Pictures

Owen Wilson, Jennifer Aniston, Marley

Owen Wilson, Marley

Ben Hyland, Owen Wilson, Marley, Eric Dane © 20th Century Fox

MARLEY & ME

(20TH CENTURY FOX) Producers, Karen Rosenfelt, Gil Netter; Executive Producers, Arnon Milchan, Joe Caracciolo, Jr.; Director, David Frankel; Screenplay, Scott Frank, Don Roos; Based on the book by John Grogan; Photography, Florian Ballhaus; Designer, Stuart Wurtzel; Costumes, Cindy Evans; Music, Theodor Shapiro; Music Supervisor, Julia Michaels; Editor, Mark Livolsi; Head Animal Trainer/Coordinator, Mark Forbes; Casting, Margery Simkin; a Fox 2000 Pictures and Regency Enterprises presentation of a Gil Netter/Sunswept Entertainment production; Dolby; Deluxe color; Rated PG; 115 minutes; Release date: December 25, 2008

Cast

John Grogan	Owen Wilson
Jenny Grogan	Jennifer Aniston
Sebastian	Eric Dane
Mrs. Kornblut	Kathleen Turner
Arnie Klein	Alan Arkin
Patrick (age 10)	Nathan Gamble
Lisa	Haley Bennett
Dr. Platt	Ann Dowd
Editor	Clarke Peters
Conor (age 8)	Finley Jacobsen
Colleen (age 5)	Lucy Merriam
Patrick (age 7)	Bryce Robinson
Conor (age 5)	Ben Hyland
Neighbor Mom (Nurse)	Sarah O'Kelly
Big Guy	Keith Hudson
Debby	Haley Hudson

Alec Mapa (Jorge), Sandy Martin (Lori), Joyce Van Patten (Mrs. Butterly), Zabryna Guevara (OB/GYN Nurse), Megan Mazaika (Secretary), Haley Higgins (Shannon), Ana Ayora (Viviana), Matthew J. Walters (Billy), Nicole Herold (Sunbather), Paul Tei (Dude), Natalie Miller (Realtor), Gaston Renaud (Metro Reporter), Angelina Assereto (Waitress), Emmett Robin (Boy), Lisa Varga (Still Photographer), Dylan Henry (Patrick, age 3), Stephen Lee Davis (Neighbor Steve), Michael Baskin (Party Guy Michael), Bradley Aldan Frishman (Patrick, age 20 months), Eric Conger (Newscaster)

John and Jenny Grogan's decision to bring a dog into their lives turns about to be both a blessing and test of love as Marley proves a rambunctious handful.

Owen Wilson, Marley, Jennifer Aniston

Liane Balaban, Dustin Hoffman

James Brolin, Kathy Baker, Dustin Hoffman

Emma Thompson, Eileen Atkins

Dustin Hoffman, Emma Thompson © Overture Films

LAST CHANCE HARVEY

(OVERTURE) Producers, Tim Perell, Nicola Usborne; Director/Screenplay, Joel Hopkins; Photography, John de Borman; Designer, Jon Henson; Costumes, Natalie Ward; Music, Dickon Hinchcliffe; Music Supervisor, Michael Hill; Line Producer, Guy Tannahill; Editor, Robin Sales; Casting, Laura Rosenthal, Ali Farrell, Elaine Grainger; a Process production; Dolby; Technicolor; Rated PG-13; 94 minutes; Release date: December 25, 2008

Cast

Harvey Shine	**Dustin Hoffman**
Kate Walker	**Emma Thompson**
Maggie	**Eileen Atkins**
Jean	**Kathy Baker**
Susan	**Liane Balaban**
Brian	**James Brolin**
Marvin	**Richard Schiff**
Johnnie	**Tim Howard**
Aggie	**Wendy Mae Brown**
Oonagh	**Bronagh Gallagher**
Matt	**Jeremy Sheffield**
Scott	**Daniel LaPaine**
Simon	**Patrick Baladi**
Josh Hillman	**Adam James**
Peter Turner	**Michael Landes**
Doctor Butler	**Jamie Sives**

Kate Harper (Jill), Angela Griffin (Melissa), Alex Avery (Andrew), Tim Ahern (Barry), Charlotte Lucas (Gwen), Nadia Cameron-Blakey (Attractive Woman), Lauren Dennington (Airline Stewardess), Figs Jackman (Barman), Adam Astill (Business Man), Rhydian Jones, Andrea Harris (Check-In Stewards), Vincent Brimble (Concierge), Paul Haley (Elderly Man), Gaia Wise, Amy Younger (Girls at Wedding), Leslie Randall (Mild Mannered Mike), Imogen Byron (Niece at Wedding), Ginny Holder (Nurse), Paschal Scott (Paddy the Postman), Robert Jezek (Polish Neighbor), Heather Bleasdale (Receptionist), Femi Oguns (Room Service Waiter), Noah Marullo (Silent Boy), Mark Kempner (Taxi Cab Driver), Nick Cavaliere (Waiter, Reception), Mickey Sumner (Friend of Bride), Kitty, Daisy & Lewis (Buskers)

In London to attend his daughter's wedding at which he feels like an outsider, Harvey Shine finds himself drawn to the equally lonely Kate Walker.

VALKYRIE

(MGM/UA) Producers, Bryan Singer, Christopher McQuarrie, Gilbert Adler; Executive Producers, Chris Lee, Ken Kamins, Daniel M. Snyder, Dwight C. Schar, Mark Shapiro; Coproducers, Nathan Alexander, Henning Molfenter, Carl Woebcken, Christoh Fisser; Director, Bryan Singer; Screenplay, Christopher McQuarrie, Nathan Alexander; Photography, Newton Thomas Sigel; Designers, Lilly Kilvert, Patrick Lumb; Costumes, Joanna Johnston; Music/Editor, John Ottman; Visual Effects Supervisor, Richard R. Hoover; Stunts, Greg Powell; Casting, Roger Mussenden; a Bad Hat Harry production; American-German; Dolby; Super 35 Widescreen; Color; Rated PG-13; 121 minutes; Release date: December 25, 2008

Tom Cruise, Kenneth Branagh

Cast

Colonel Claus von Stauffenberg	**Tom Cruise**
Major-General Henning von Tresckow	**Kenneth Branagh**
General Friedrich Olbricht	**Bill Nighy**
General Friedrich Fromm	**Tom Wilkinson**
Nina von Stauffenberg	**Carice van Houten**
Major Otto Ernst Remer	**Thomas Kretschmann**
Ludwig Beck	**Terence Stamp**
General Erich Fellgiebel	**Eddie Izzard**
Dr. Carl Goerdeler	**Kevin McNally**
Colonel Mertz von Quirnheim	**Christian Berkel**
Angry SS Officer	**Andy Gatjen**
Lieutenant Werner von Haeften	**Jamie Parker**
Adolf Hilter	**David Bamber**
Colonel Heinz Brandt	**Tom Hollander**
Erwin von Witzleben	**David Schofield**
Field Marshal Wilhelm Keitel	**Kenneth Cranham**
Margarethe von Oven	**Halina Reijn**
Major Ernst John von Freyend	**Werner Daehn**
Dr. Joseph Goebbels	**Harvey Friedman**
Lieutenant Herber	**Mathias Schweighöfer**
Police Chief Wolf-Heinrich von Helldorf	**Waldemar Kobus**
Second Lieutenant Hagen	**Florian Panzner**
Pompous General	**Ian McNeice**
Captain Haans	**Danny Webb**
Sergeant Helm	**Chris Larkin**
Lieutenant-General Adolf Heusinger	**Matthew Burton**
Treschkow's Aide	**Philipp von Schulthess**
Sergeant Kolbe	**Wotan Wilke Möhring**
Sergeant-Major Adam	**Christian Oliver**
Confident General – Desert	**Bernard Hill**
Young Lieutenant – Desert	**Julian Morris**
Dr. Roland Freisler	**Helmut Stauss**

Tim Williams (Doctor), Alexander Seidel, Timo Huber, Justus Kammerer, Annika & Marie Becker (Stauffenberg Children), Katharine Mehrling (Singer), Andy Gätjen (Angry SS Officer), Achim Buch (Soldier), Anton Algrang (Albert Speer), Matthias Freinhof (Reichsführer Heinrich Himmler), Gerhard Haase-Hindenberg (Reich Marshal Hermann Göring), Jon Collin Barclay (Second Lieutenant Kretz), Matthias Ziesing (Young Officer–Wolf's Lair), Tom Wlaschiha (Communications Officer), Carsten Voigt (Checkpoint Guard), Miles O'Shea (Sentry–OKH), Anna Holmes (Central Communications Operator), Michael Schumacher (Young Officer), Niklas Bardeli, Christoph Förster (Aides to Stauffenberg), Andre Schwedt (Keitel's Adjutant), Isabella Drischel (War Ministry Secretary), Max Urlacher (Officer), Justin Beard (Wolf's Lair Operator), Tilmann von Blomberg (Arresting Officer), Karsten Mielke (Remer's Driver)

Kenneth Branagh

The true story of how Colonel Claus von Stauffenberg and the German Resistance plotted to kill Adolf Hitler and hopefully restore honor to their country.

Tom Cruise, Carice van Houten

Tom Cruise

Eddie Izzard

Thomas Kretschmann

Tom Cruise, Bernard Hill © United Artists/MGM

Bill Nighy, Jamie Parker, Christian Berkel

Tom Wilkinson, Tom Cruise

THE CURIOUS CASE OF BENJAMIN BUTTON

(PARAMOUNT/WARNER BROS.) Producers, Kathleen Kennedy, Frank Marshall, Ceán Chaffin; Director, David Fincher; Screenplay, Eric Roth; Screen Story, Eric Roth, Robin Swicord; Based on the short story by F. Scott Fitzgerald; Photography, Claudio Miranda; Designer, Donald Graham Burt; Costumes, Jacqueline West; Music, Alexandre Desplat; Editors, Kirk Baxter, Angus Wall; Visual Effects Supervisor, Eric Barba; Visual Effects and Animation, Digital Domain; Visual Effects, Asylum, Lola Visual Effects, Matte World Digital, Hydraulx, Ollin Studio, Savage Visual Effects; Special Effects Coordinator, Burt Dalton; Special Makeup, Greg Cannom; Makeup Effects Supervisor, Brian Sipe; Casting, Laray Mayfield; a Kennedy/Marshall production; Dolby; Super 35 Widescreen; Deluxe color; HD; Rated PG-13; 167 minutes; Release date: December 25, 2008

Cast

Benjamin Button	**Brad Pitt**
Daisy	**Cate Blanchett**
Queenie	**Taraji P. Henson**
Caroline	**Julia Ormond**
Thomas Button	**Jason Flemyng**
Tizzy	**Mahershalalhashbaz Ali**
Captain Mike	**Jared Harris**
Monsieur Gateau	**Elias Koteas**
Grandma Fuller	**Phyllis Somerville**
Elizabeth Abbott	**Tilda Swinton**
Preacher	**Lance E. Nichols**
Ngunda Oti	**Rampai Mohadi**
Daisy, age 7	**Elle Fanning**
Daisy, age 10	**Madisen Beaty**
Dorothy Baker	**Faune A. Chambers**
Blanche Devereaux	**Donna DuPlantier**
Martin Gateau	**Jacob Wood**
Man at Train Station	**Earl Maddox**
Teddy Roosevelt	**Ed Metzger**
Priest Giving Last Rites	**Danny Vinson**
Doctor at Benjamin's Birth	**David Jensen**
Mrs. Hollister	**Fiona Hale**
Dr. Rose	**Patrick Thomas O'Brien**
General Winston	**Danny Nelson**
Mrs. Horton	**Marion Zinser**
Benjamin 1928-31	**Peter Donald Badalamenti II**
Sybil Wagner	**Paula Gray**
Filamena Gilea	**Troi Bechet**

Ted Manson (Mr. Daws), Clay Cullen (Young Mr. Daws), Edith Ivey (Mrs. Maple), Robert Towers (Benjamin 1932-34), Sonya Leslie-Shepherd (Daisy's Nurse), Yasmine Abriel (Prostitute with Benjamin), Tom Everett (Benjamin 1934-37), Don Creech (Prentiss Mayes), Joshua DesRoches (Rick Brody), Christopher Maxwell (Vic Brody), Richmond Arquette (Jon Grimm), Josh Curtis (Pleasant Curtis), Ilia Volok (Russian Interpreter), David Ross Paterson (Walter Abbott), Taren Cunningham (Young Elizabeth Abbott), Myrton Running Wolf (Dennis Smith), Stephen Monroe Taylor (Sailor), Devyn A. Tyler (Queenie's Daughter, age 14), Adrian Armas (David), Wilbur Fitzgerald (TV Reporter), Ashley Nolan (Doctor), Louis Herthum (Man at Caroline's Party), Katta Hules (Caroline – age 12), Rus Blackwell (Robert Williams), Joel Bissonnette (David Hernandez), Deneen Tyler (Queenie's Daughter – age 40), Spencer Daniels (Benjamin, age 12), Chandler Canterbury (Benjamin, age 8), Charles Henry Wyson (Benjamin, age 6), Jessica Cropper, Katherine Crockett (Featured Dancers)

As Daisy lays dying she tells her daughter the story of her relationship with Benjamin Button, who was born an old man and aged backwards.

2008 Academy Award winner for Best Art Direction, Best Visual Effects, and Best Makeup.

This film received additional Oscar nominations for picture, director, actor (Brad Pitt), supporting actress (Taraji P. Henson), adapted screenplay, cinematography, costume design, film editing, sound mixing, and original score.

Mahershalalhashbaz Ali

Brad Pitt, Cate Blanchett

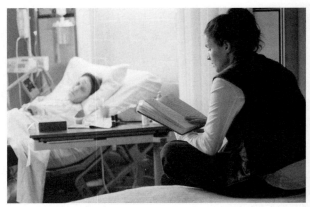

Cate Blanchett, Julia Ormond

Taraji P. Henson, Brad Pitt

Elle Fanning

Cate Blanchett, Joshua DesRoches

Cate Blanchett, Charles Henry Wyson

Brad Pitt © Paramount/Warner Bros.

BEDTIME STORIES

(WALT DISNEY PICTURES) Producers, Andrew Gunn, Adam Sandler, Jack Giarraputo; Executive Producers, Adam Shankman, Jennifer Gibgot, Ann Marie Sanderlin, Garrett Grant; Coproducer, Kevin Grady; Director, Adam Shankman; Screenplay, Matt Lopez, Tim Herlihy; Story, Matt Lopez; Photography, Michael Barrett; Designer, Linda DeScenna; Costumes, Rita Ryack; Music, Rupert Gregson-Williams; Music Supervisors, Michael Dilbeck, Brooks Arthur; Visual Effects Supervisor, John Andrew Berton, Jr.; Visual Effects, Cinesite Europe, Hydraulx; Casting, Roger Mussenden; a Happy Madison/Gunn Films/Offspring production; Dolby; Panavision; Deluxe color; Rated PG; 99 minutes; Release date: December 25, 2008

Guy Pearce,
Lucy Lawless

Cast

Skeeter Bronson	**Adam Sandler**
Jill	**Keri Russell**
Kendall	**Guy Pearce**
Mickey	**Russell Brand**
Barry Nottingham	**Richard Griffiths**
Violet Nottingham	**Teresa Palmer**
Aspen	**Lucy Lawless**
Wendy	**Courtney Cox**
Patrick	**Jonathan Morgan Heit**
Bobbi	**Laura Ann Kesling**
Marty Bronson	**Jonathan Pryce**
Engineer	**Nick Swardson**
Mrs. Dixon	**Kathryn Joosten**
Ferrari Guy	**Allen Covert**
Hot Girl	**Carmen Electra**

Adam Sandler, Keri Russell
© Walt Disney Pictures

Tim Herlihy (Young Barry), Thomas Hoffman (Young Skeeter), Abigail Leone Droeger (Young Wendy), Melany Mitchell (Young Mrs. Dixon), Andrew Collins (Young Mr. Dixon), Aisha Tyler (Donna Hynde), Julia Lea Wolov, Dana Min Goodman, Sarah Buxton, Catherine Kwong, Lindsey Alley (Hokey Pokey Women), Blake Clark, Bill Romanowski (Bikers), Paul Dooley (Hot Dog Vendor), Johntae Lipscomb, James Burdette Cowell (Birthday Party Kids), Mikey Post (Angry Dwarf), Sebastian Saraceno (Gremlin Driver), Seth Howard (Cubby the Home Depot Guy), Jackie Sandler (Lady Jacqueline), Sadie Sandler (Sweetest Medieval Girl of All Time), Valerie Gervickas (Teacher), Debbie Carrington (Booing Goblin), Billy Tyler (Big Hairy Guy on Beach), Lorna Scott (Secretary), Annalise Basso (Tricia Sparks), Shu Lan Tuan (Luau Waitress), Jonathan Loughran, Bob Harvey (Party Guests), Mike Andrella (Truck Drive), J.D. Donaruma (Nottingham Pool Waiter), Jon Schueler (Nobleman), Denverly Grant (Lady at Fountain), Claudius Falisimus (Pete Brown), Rodrick Hersh (Rabbi) A hotel handyman, asked to babysit his sister's kids, tells them bedtime stories, which begin to impact his real life.

Adam Sandler

Adam Sandler,
Teresa Palmer

Eric Balfour, Eva Mendes

Gabriel Macht, Dan Lauria

Scarlett Johansson, Samuel L. Jackson

THE SPIRIT

(LIONSGATE) Producers, Deborah Del Prete, Gigi Pritzker, Michael E. Uslan; Executive Producers, Michael Burns, Michael Paseornek; Coproducers, Linda McDonough, F.J. Desanto; Co-Executive Producers, Jeff Andrick; Line Producer, Alton Walpole; Director/ Screenplay, Frank Miller; Based on the comic book series created Will Eisner; Photography, Bill Pope; Art Director, Rosario Provenza; Costumes, Michael Dennison; Music, David Newman; Editor, Gregory Nussbaum; Senior Visual Effects Supervisor, Stu Maschwitz; Senior Visual Effects Producer, Nancy St. John; Casting, Tricia Wood, Jennifer Wood, Deborah Aquila; an OddLot Entertainment presentation; Dolby; Color; Rated PG-13; 108 minutes; Release date: December 25, 2008

Cast

The Spirit (Denny Colt)	**Gabriel Macht**
Sand Saref	**Eva Mendes**
Ellen Dolan	**Sarah Paulson**
Det. Dolan	**Dan Lauria**
Plaster of Paris	**Paz Vega**
Mahmoud	**Eric Balfour**
Lorelei Rox	**Jaime King**
Silken Floss	**Scarlett Johansson**
The Octopus	**Samuel L. Jackson**
Pathos, etc.	**Louis Lombardi**
Morgenstern	**Stana Katic**
Donenfeld	**Richard Portnow**
Young Spirit	**Johnny Simmons**

Kimberly Cox (Damsel in Distress), Larry Reinhardt-Meyer (Officer MacReady), Frank Miller (Liebowitz), Arthur the Cat (Himself), Brian Lucero, David B. Martin (Thugs), Daniel Hubbert (Medic), Seychelle Gabriel (Young Sand), Michael Milhoan (Uncle Pete), John Cade (Mafioso), David Weigand (Officer Saref), Chad Brummett, Meeghan Holaway (Reporters), Mark Delgallo (Seth), Aaron Toney (Handbag Thief), Dean Eldon Squibb (Handbag Man), Al Goto (Poker Player), Roman Tissera, Frank Bond, Hugh Elliot (Doormen), Robert Douglas Washington, Bill Pope, Paul Levitz, Emily Cheung, Keith Kuhl, Cayley Bell, Jasmine Mohamed (Onlookers), Benjamin Petry (Son), Marina Lyon (Young Mother), T. Jay O'Brien (Wino), Rio Alexander (Creep), Drew Pollock (Officer Klink)

Denny Colt, a murdered cop mysteriously reborn as The Spirit, continues to fight crime in Central City, battling the nefarious Octopus who hopes to get his hands on a precious treasure that has come into the possession of jewel thief Sand Saref.

Sarah Paulson © Lionsgate

Leonardo DiCaprio, Kate Winslet

Leonardo DiCaprio, Michael Shannon, Richard Easton, Kathy Bates, Kate Winslet

Kate Winslet, Leonardo DiCaprio

Leonardo DiCaprio, Kate Winslet

Leonardo DiCaprio © Paramount Vantage

Leonardo DiCaprio, Kate Winslet

Kathy Bates

David Harbour, Kathryn Hahn

Zoe Kazan

REVOLUTIONARY ROAD

(PARAMOUNT VANTAGE/DREAMWORKS) Producer, John N. Hart, Scott Rudin, Sam Mendes, Bobby Cohen; Executive Producers, Marion Rosenberg, David M. Thompson, Henry Fernaine; Coproducers, Ann Ruark, Gina Amoroso; Co-Executive Producers, Peter Kalmbach, Nina Wolarsky, Pippa Harris; Director, Sam Mendes; Screenplay, Justin Haythe; Based on the novel by Richard Yates; Photography, Roger Deakins; Designer, Kristi Zea; Costumes, Albert Wolsky; Music, Thomas Newman; Music Supervisor, Randall Poster; Editor, Tariq Anwar; Casting, Ellen Lewis, Debra Zane; an Evamere Entertainment, BBC Films, Neal Street production, in association with Goldcrest Pictures; American-British; Dolby; Arri Widescreen; Deluxe color; Rated R; 119 minutes; Release date: December 26, 2008

Cast

Frank Wheeler	**Leonardo DiCaprio**
April Wheeler	**Kate Winslet**
Helen Givings	**Kathy Bates**
John Givings	**Michael Shannon**
Milly Campbell	**Kathryn Hahn**
Shep Campbell	**David Harbour**
Jack Ordway	**Dylan Baker**
Howard Givings	**Richard Easton**
Maureen Grube	**Zoe Kazan**
Bart Pollock	**Jay O. Sanders**
Ed Small	**Max Casella**
Jennifer Wheeler	**Ryan Simpkins**
Michael Wheeler	**Ty Simpkins**
Woman in Audience	**Catherine Curtin**
Knox Elevator Operator	**Dan Da Silva**
Ted Bandy	**Keith Reddin**
Vince Lathrop	**Max Baker**
American Express Clerk	**Jon Sampson**
Knox Receptionist	**Christopher Fitzgerald**
Steve Kovac	**Duffy Jackson**
Mrs. Brace	**Kristen Connolly**
Mr. Brace	**Jon Behlmann**

Samantha Soule, Jonathan Roumie, Neal Bledsoe, Marin Ireland, Heidi Armbruster, Sam Rosen (Party Guests), Maria Rusolo, Gena Oppenheim, Kathryn Dunn, Joe Komara, Allison Twyford (Party Dancers), John Ottavino, Adam Mucci, Jo Twiss, Frank Girardeau (Other Actors in Play), Peter Barton, Kevin Barton, Evan Covey, Dylan Clark Marshall (Campbell Kids), Bethann Schebece, Kelsey Robinson, Jason Etter, Adair Moran, Tommaso Antico, Justin Misenhelder, Will Vought, Emaline Green, Isabella Zubor, Kal Thompson, Racheline Maltese, Lauren Hubbell (Vito's Log Cabin Dancers), Dan Zanes, Vince Giordano, Jon-Erik Kellso, Andrew Burton, Will Sanderson, Alex Hoffman (The Steve Kovac Band)

Frank and April marry and settled into 1955 suburbia only to conclude that they have put their future dreams on hold to live the lives everyone expects of them, a realization that takes its toll on their marriage.

This film received Oscar nominations for supporting actor (Michael Shannon), art direction, and costume design.

DEFIANCE

(PARAMOUNT VANTAGE) Producers, Edward Zwick, Pieter Jan Brugge; Executive Producer, Marshall Herskovitz; Coproducers, Clayton Frohman, Roland Tec; Director, Edward Zwick; Screenplay, Clayton Frohman, Edward Zwick; Based on the book *Defiance: The Bielski Partisans* by Nechama Tec; Photography, Eduardo Serra; Designer, Dan Weil; Costumes, Jenny Beavan; Music, James Newton Howard; Editor, Steven Rosenblum; Special Effects Coordinator, Neil Corbould; Stunts, Steve Griffin; Casting, Gail Steven, Victoria Thomas; a Grosvenor Park/Bedford Falls production; Dolby; Deluxe color; Rated R; 137 minutes; Release date: December 31, 2008

Cast

Tuvia Bielski	**Daniel Craig**
Zus Bielski	**Liev Schreiber**
Asael Bielski	**Jamie Bell**
Lilka Ticktin	**Alexa Davalos**
Shimon Haretz	**Allan Corduner**
Isaac Malbin	**Mark Feuerstein**
Ben Zion Gulkowitz	**Tomas Arana**
Tamara Skidelsky	**Jodhi May**
Riva Reich	**Kate Fahy**
Yitzchak Shulman	**Iddo Goldberg**
Bella	**Iben Hjejle**

Martin Hancock (Peretz Shorshaty), Ravil Isyanov (Viktor Panchenko), Jacek Koman (Konstanty "Koscik" Kozlowski), George McKay (Aron Bielski), Jonjo O'Neill (Lazar), Sam Spruell (Arkady Luczanski), Mia Wasikowska (Chaya Dziencielsky), Mark Margolis (Jewish Elder), Markus von Lingen (German SS Scout), Rolandas Boravskis (Gramov), Algirdas Dainavicius (Motl Luvzanski), Aurelija Prashuntaite (Rachel), Vidas Petkevicius (Avram Rubinski), Ina Frismanaite (Avram's Daughter), Ana Goldberg (Lila), Rimante Valiukaite (Miriam), Leonardas Pobedonoscevas (Jacov), Kristina Bertasiute (Dark Haired Beauty), Kristina Skokova (Red Haired Woman), Remigijus Bilinskas (Pinchas Zuckerman), Rimgaudas Karvelis (Oppenheim), Leonas Ciunis (Accountant), Janina Matiekonyte (Well-Dressed Woman), Aleksandr Zila (Chaya's Father), Iveta Nadzeikiene (Chaya's Mother), Clayton Frohman (Isadore Skidelsky), Marc Levy (Yechael Efrati), Zoe Rosenblum (Sarah Oppenheim), Sakalas Uzdavinys (Lova Volkin), Saulius Janaviciu (Israel Kotler), Leonidas Kotkias (Krensky), Dalia Micheleviciute (Rosa), Tadas Kavaliauskas (Levine), Matas Cancingeris (Little Boy), Diana Aneviciute-Valiusaitiene (Kosick's Wife), Sigitas Rackys (Belarussian Police Captain), Vaidas Kublinkas, Valentin Novopolskij (Police Captain's Sons), Ervinas Martynas Peteraitis (Kissely the Milkman), Dmitrij Denisiuk (Policeman), Antanas Surna (Orthodox Rabbi), Dalius Mertinas, Vaidotas Martinaitis (Belarussian Police Officers), Aldona Bendoriute, Edita Uzaite (Jewish Mothers Separated from Children), Darius Gumauskas, Irmantas Bacelis (Jewish Fathers being Beaten), Jordan Bielsky (Villager Getting Shot), Gediminas Girdvainis (Screaming Man), Stanislav Adamickij (German Captain), Klemens Becker (SS Captain), Jonas Tamulevigius (German Courier), Jaroslav Psenicka (German Officer in Car), Jolanta Dapkunaite (Woman in Car), Miroslav Lhotka (German Officer), Giacommo Strasser (German Private), Mac Steinmeier (German Sergeant), Dmitri Slepovitch, Arkjadij Gotesman, Borisas Kiezeneris, Raimondas Sviackevicius (Musicians)

The true story of how three Jewish brothers lead a small resistance group against the Nazis in Belorussia during World War II.

This film received an Oscar nomination for original score.

Liev Schreiber, Daniel Craig

Mia Wasikowska, Jamie Bell © Paramount Vantage

DOMESTIC FILMS B

2008 Releases / January 1–December 31

LIBERTY KID (Glass Eye Pix) Producers, Roger Kass, Mike Ryan, Larry Fessenden; Executive Producers, Claude Wasserstein, Andrea Van Beuren; Coproducer, Mike King; Director/Screenplay, Ilya Chaiken; Photography, Eliot Rockett; Designer, Jesse Cain; Editor, Chaiken, Dave Rock; Music, Jeff Grace; Music Supervisor, Alan Wilkis; Casting, Victoria Asness, Nate Williams; a Glass Eye Pix presentation in association with RingTheJing Entertainment, of a Glass Eye Pix production; Stereo; Color; HD; Not rated; 96 minutes; Release date: January 9, 2008. CAST: Al Thompson (Derrick), Kareem Saviñon (Tico), Raquel Jordan (Denice), Rosa Ramos (Awilda), Anny Mariano (Sister), Johnny Rivera (Nelson), Rayniel Rufino (Mike), Jarrett Alexander (Rahim), Plinio Villablanca (Tico's Father), Mimi Rodriguez, Yixi Villar (Dates), Marti J. Cooney, Jack Fitz (Tourists), Lila Blake-Palmer (Veronica), Jerry Gonzales (Liberty Island Manager), Joe Bataan (Bodega Man), Anubhav Jain (Arab Boy), Mike S. Ryan (Diner Manager), Kevin McKelvy (Sgt. Willis), Leonardo Paulino (Recruiter), Femi Percy (Dequan, age 3), Tobi Percy (Dequan, age 5), Ray Macmore, William Morgan, Jason J. Cruz (Drug Buyers), Alice Goguen (Clumsy Party Girl), Carlos Valdez (Santos), Andrew Hillmedo (Santos' Accomplice), Fly Williams (Milton), Ephraim Benton (Milton's Driver), R. Mike King (Warehouse Supervisor), Hamlet Saviñon (Sgt. Nunez), Jack Caruso (Warden), Teresa Yenque (Tico's Mother), Jessie Harris (V.A. Counselor), Jessica Perez (Jeanette), Kristen Myles (Destiny, age 5), Father Timothy Dore (Priest), Tom Greer (Battery Park Cop)

Al Thompson in Liberty Kid © *Glass Eye Pix*

THE BUSINESS OF BEING BORN (Red Envelope/Intl. Film Circuit) Producers, Abby Epstein, Amy Slotnick, Paulo Netto; Executive Producer, Ricki Lake; Director, Abby Epstein; Photography, Paulo Netto; Editor, Madeleine Gavin; Color; Not rated; 87 minutes; Release date: January 9, 2008. Documentary on the different choices women make in the way they deliver their babies, with Dr. Michel Odent, Susan Hodges, Dr. Jacques Moritz, Dr. Robbie Davis-Floyd, Carolyn Havens Nelmann, Elan Vital McAllister, Ina May Gaakin, Dr. Marsden Wagner, Louann Brizendine, Eugene Declerq, Tina Cassidy, Nadine Goodman, Anna Verwaal Doula, Ana Paula Markel, Cara Muhlhahn, Cathy Tanksley, Lesley Cragen, Patricia Burkhardt, Dr. Ronaldo Cortes, Dr. Michael Brodman, Dr. Abbe Wain, Paulo Netto, Carol Leonard, Sylvie Blaustein, Dr. Michael Silverstein, Dr. Eden Fromberg.

RUNNING WITH ARNOLD (Red Envelope Entertainment) Producers, Mike Gabrawy, Jennifer Hughes, Dan Cox; Executive Producers, Gregg Michael, Abrams Jeffrey Orenstein, Eric Gardner; Director/ Screenplay, Dan Cox; Photography, Josh Hartzog, Rick Benavides; Music, Clifford J. Tasner; Editors, Katina Zinner, Ron Frank, Rick Benavides; Narrator, Alec Baldwin; Color; Not rated; 72 minutes; Release date: January 11, 2008. Documentary on the career of actor-turned-governor Arnold Schwarzenegger.

The Business of Being Born © *Intl. Film Circuit*

THE PIRATES WHO DON'T DO ANYTHING (Universal) Producers, Paula Marcus, David Pitts, Phil Vischer, Mike Nawrocki; Executive Producers, Terry Pefanis, Mike Heap, Jane Smith; Director, Mike Nawrocki; Screenplay, Phil Vischer; Designer, Charles Vollmer; Music, Kurt Heinecke; Editor, John Wahba; Animation Production, Starz Animation; Casting, Sue Blu; a Big Idea production, an Entertainment Rights Group company presentation; Dolby; Color; Rated G; 85 minutes; Release date: January 10, 2008. VOICE CAST: Phil Vischer (George/Sedgewick/ Willory/Sir Frederick/Mr. Hibbing/Bob the Tomato/Pirate Spy/Pirate Philippe Pea), Mike Nawrocki (Elliot/Pirate Jean Claude Pea/Theater Foe/Pirate Spy Sidekick/Pirate with Dummy/Rock Monster Father), Cam Clarke (Robert the Terrible/The King), Laura Gerow (Eloise), Yuri Lowenthal (Alexander), Alan Lee (Blind Man/One-Eyed Louie), Cydney Trent (Bernadette), Keri Pisapia (Ellen), Megan Murphy (Madame Blueberry), Sondra Morton Chaffin (Caroline), Jim Poole (Pirate Scooter Carrot), Tim Hodge (Jolly Joe/King's Ship Officer), Drake Lyle (George, Jr./Rock Monster Boy), Ally Nawrocki (Lucy/Rock Monster Girl), Patrick Kramer (Collin), Sloan Yarborough (Photographer), Joe Spadaford (Jacob Lewis/Stubb Pirate Overboard/Stubb Pirate Coward), John Wahba (Pirate Guard/Pirate with Dummy Sidekick), Colleen Curtis (Theater Customer Woman), Brian Roberts (Steadfast Soldier/Theater Customer Man/Pirate Pilot)

Princess Eloise, Elliot, George, Willory, The Butler, Sedgewick in The Pirates Who Don't Do Anything © *Universal Studios*

LITTLE CHENIER (Radio London) Producers, Bethany Ashton Wolf, Ron West, Jace Johnson, Gavin Boyd; Executive Producer, William Doré; Director, Bethany Ashton Wolf; Screenplay, Bethany Ashton Wolf, Jace Johnson; Photography, Tanja Koop; Designer, C.J. Strawn; Music, Michael Picton; Editor, Brian Anton; Casting, Jeanie Bacharach; a Doré Productions in association with Sweet Jane Productions and Tagline Pictures presentation; Dolby; Color; Rated R; 120 minutes; Release date: January 18, 2008. CAST: Johnathon Schaech (Beauxregard "Beaux" Dupuis),

Frederick Koehler (Pemon Dupuis), Tamara Braun (Marie-Louise DeBauve), Jeremy Davidson (Carl Lebauve), Clifton Collins, Jr. (T-Boy Trahan), Chris Mulkey (Sheriff Kline Lebauve), Tommy Barnes (Zip), Marshall Bell (Tuck Dupuis), David Born (Oggie), Amy Brassette (Nadine), John Scott Desormeaux (The Town Priest), Fiona Dourif (Jo Jo), Tim Dugas (The Drummer), Jack Friedberg (Altar Boy), Carol Anne Gayle (Bessie Gautreaux), James Grant (Bearded Man), Jeremy Mallett, Beau Guidry (Teenage Boys), Peter Guillory (Sugarman), Abagail Heath-Richard (Ms. Thibodeaux), Isabella Hofmann (Gwenivere Lebauve), Alan Hunt (Mr. Guilmont), Jace Johnson (Chute), Mark Krasnoff (Jimmy), Jeff Leblanc (The Lead Guitarist), John Leger (The Accordion Player), Earl Maddox (Boot), Abe Manuel (The Fiddler), Robin McGee (Lamont), Juen McGehee (Widow Touchet), Michael McHale (Larry Eagle), Catherine Obre (Annabelle), Laurie O'Brien (Faye), Brett Rickaby (Jed), Jean Baptiste Saucier (Himself), Jessica Schatz (Radio DJ Voice), Pat Smith (The Guitar Player), Courtenay Taylor (Mercy), Claudia Troll (Miss Ebbie), Matt Troll (Miss Ebbie's Friend), Steve Uzell (The Man), James Vincent (The Bridge Controller), Greg Welsch (Mr. Peggy), Barbara Williams (Bernell)

DAY ZERO (First Look) Producer, Anthony Moody; Executive Producer/Screenplay, Rob Malkani; Line Producer, Daniel Sollinger; Director/Editor, Bryan Gunnar Cole; Photography, Matthew Clark; Designer, Laurie Krupp; Costumes, Andrea Huelse; Music, Erin O'Hara; Music Supervisor, Jim Black; Casting, Judy Henderson; a Glass Key presentation; Color; Rated R; 92 minutes; Release date: January 18, 2008. CAST: Elijah Wood (Aaron Feller), Jon Bernthal (James Dixon), Chris Klein (George Rifkin), Ginnifer Goodwin (Molly Rifkin), Elisabeth Moss (Patricia), Ally Sheedy (Dr. Reynolds), Sofia Vassilieva (Mara), John Rothman (Rifkin's Father), Daniel Orskes (Gus), Tinashe Kajese (Rifkin's Secretary), Bob Hogan (Senior Partner), Adam Le Fevre (Client), Amir Arison (Lawyer), Ian Kahn (Liberal Man at Party), Jordan Ruderman (Liberal Woman at Party), Annie Rohling (First Woman at Party), Clark Middleton (Porn Clerk), Charlene Biton (Peep Show Girl), Alexandra Rose Sullivan (Rifkin's Niece), Janelle Robinson (Bar Patron), Malachy Cleary (Oncologist), M.J. Di Benedetti (Prostitute), Jon David Casey (Pimp), Jamison Stern, Phil Burke (Gay Men), Malina Linkas (Lounge Woman), Beth Beyer (Taxi Customer), Michael Shapiro (Voice of News Announcer)

Elijah Wood in Day Zero © First Look

DOC (TVS/PBS) Producer/Director, Immy Humes; Associate Producers, Anne Lise Bruening, Hannah Ireland, Patricia Soledada, Llosa, Annie Vought; Photography, Antonio Ferrera, Roger Grange, Claudia Raschke; Drawings, Thomas Libetti; Editors, Doug Cheek, Mona Davis, Immy Humes; Consulting Editor, Susanne Rostock; Music, Zev Katz; Color; Not rated; 98 minutes; Release date: January

23, 2008. Documentary on author-activist-filmmaker and co-founder of *The Paris Review*, Harold Louis "Doc" Humes; with George Plimpton, Norman Mailer, Peter Matthiessen, William Styron, Paul Auster, Jonas Meekas, Timothy Leary.

MEET THE SPARTANS (20th Century Fox) Producers/Directors/Screenplay, Jason Friedberg, Aaron Seltzer; Executive Producer, Arnon Milchan; Coproducers, Mark McNair, Hal Olofsson; Photography, Shawn Maurer; Editor, Peck Prior; Music, Christopher Lennertz; Music Supervisors, Dave Jordan Jojo Villanueva; Designer, William Elliott; Art Director, Wm. Ladd Skinner; Costumes, Frank Helmer; Casting, Eyde Belsaco; a Regency Enterprises presentation of a New Regency/3 in the Box production; Dolby; Deluxe color; Rated PG-13; 83 minutes; Release date: January 25, 2008. CAST: Sean Maguire (Leonidas), Carmen Electra (Queen Margo), Ken Davitian (Xerxes), Kevin Sorbo (Captain), Diedrich Bader (Traitoro), Method Man (Persian Emissary), Jareb Dauplaise (Dilio), Travis Van Winkle (Sonio), Phil Morris (Messenger), Jim Piddock (Loyalist/Simon Cowell Look-a-Like), Nicole Parker (Paula Abdul Look-a-Like/Britney Spears Look-a-Like/Ellen DeGeneres Look-a-Like/Hunchback Paris), Ike Barinholtz (Dane Cook Look-a-Like/Bond Villain/Prophet), Crista Flanagan (Spartan Woman/Ugly Betty Look-a-Like), Hunter Clary (Leo, Jr.), Emily Watson (Lindsay Lohan Look-a-Like), Thomas McKenna (Tom Cruise Look-a-Like), Tiffany Haddish, Willie Macc, Kenny Yates (Urban Kids), John Di Domenico (Donald Trump Look-a-Like), Christopher Lett (Randy Look-a-Like), Jenny Costa (Tyra Banks Look-a-Like), Belinda Waymouth (Twiggy Look-a-Like), Jesse Lewis IV (Ms. Jay Look-a-Like), Zachary Dylan Smith (10-Year-Old Leonidas), Ryan Fraley (Brad Pitt Look-a-Like), Tiffany Claus (Angelina Jolie Look-a-Like), Nick Steele (K-Fed Look-a-Like), Jim Nieb (President Bush Look-a-Like), Dean Cochran (Rocky Balboa/Rambo), Nate Hadden (Ryan Seacrest Look-a-Like), Tony Yalda (Sanjaya Look-a-Like)

Carmen Electra, Sean Maguire, Kevin Sorbo in Meet the Spartans © Twentieth Century Fox

SHOOT DOWN (Rogues Harbor Studios) Producer, Douglas Iger; Director, Cristina Khuly; Photography, Claudia Raske-Robinson; Editor, Malcom Jamieson; Music, Ed Bilious; Color; HD; Not rated; 87 minutes; Release date: January 25, 2008. Documentary on two civilian planes that were shot down by Cuban military aircraft in February of 1996; with Maggie Alejandre Khuly, Richard Nuccio, Nancy Morales, Marlene Alejandre-Triana, Mario T. de la Pena, Jorge Lares, Arnaldo Iglesias, Gen. John J. Sheehan, Jeffrey Houlihan, Leonel Morejon Almagro, Ana Martinez, Sal Landau, William Leo Grande, Ronald Klineman

THE AIR I BREATHE (ThinkFilm) Producers, Emilio Diez Barroso, Darlene Caamano Loquet, Paul Schiff; Executive Producers, Tai Duncan, Christopher Pratt; Director, Jieho Lee; Screenplay, Jieho Lee, Bob DeRosa; Photography, Walt Lloyd; Editor, Robert Hoffman; Music, Marcello Zarvos; Designer, Bernardo Trujillo; Costumes, Michele Michel; Casting, Mary Vernieu; a NALA Films/Paul Schiff production; Dolby; Color; HD-to-35mm; Rated R; 97 minutes; Release date: January 25, 2008. CAST: Brendan Fraser (Pleasure), Sarah Michelle Gellar (Sorrow), Kevin Bacon (Love), Forest Whitaker (Happiness), Andy Garcia (Fingers), Julie Delpy (Gina), Emile Hirsch (Tony), Cecilia Suarez (Allison), Diana Garcia (Brunette), Evan Parke (Danny), Sherry Ham Bernard (Nurse), Clark Gregg (Henry), Andrew Deichaman (Pizza Delivery Guy), Jason Dolley (Young Pleasure), Alex Terminel (Markie), Eduardo Victoria, John Cho (Bankers), Norma Angelica (Clothing Shop Woman), Lenny Zundel (Shop Owner), Todd Stashwick (Frank), Jon Bernthal (Interviewer), Lisa Owen (Nurse #2), Taylor Nichols (Sorrow's Father), Victor Rivers (Finger's Bodyguard), Kelly Hu (Jiyoung), Josh Flaum (Wesley), Sasha Pieterse (Young Sorrow), Tomas Goros (Gangster), Will Maier (Mr. Park), Jake Koenig (Speedy Old Man), Sophie Gomez (Stewardess), Rodrigo Santacruz, Catherine Papile (Teenagers), Emilo Savinni (Tuddy), Claudia Cervantes (Redhead), George Belanger (Old Distinguished Man), Fervio Castillo (Young Love), Tania Himelfarb (Young Heidi)

Lior Liebling, Shawn in Praying with Lior © *First Run Features*

Calhoun), Blake Cark (Dick), Justin Long (Junior), Jeff Garlin (Ed Lawson), Ernest Borgnine (Milas), Jake Abel (Conservationist), Kevin Alejandro, Geno Kirkland (Hispanic Men), Rick Batalla (Johnny B), Terrence Beasor (Elderly Man) Richard Cassese (Richard), Alvarez Ricardez, Steven Arthur Chaves, Rene Marentes (Federales), Judith Drake (Elderly Woman), John Farley (Doctor), Ayda Field (Mountain Nurse), Oliver Hudson (TJ, Animal Handler), Sheila Lussier (Bill's Wife), David Mattey (Bigfoot), Jim Meskimen (Park Ranger Don), Mitsuyuki Oishi (Angry K-PIP Employee), Michelle Paniz (Girl with Magazine), Jennifer Perkins (Debbie), Emilio Rivera (Border Guard), Bryan Ross (Bryan), Mario Soto, Roberto "Sanz" Sanchez (Border Guards), Jason Sandler (Jason), Angela Shelton (Dental Receptionist), Meg Wolf (Judy, K-PIP Receptionist), Molly Wolf (Little Girl), Shawn Woodward (Shawn)

Brendan Fraser, Emile Hirsch in The Air I Breathe © *ThinkFilm*

PRAYING WITH LIOR (First Run Features) Producer, Ilana Trachtman; Coproducer, Roberta Morris Purdee; Director, Ilana Trachtman; Photography, Slawomir Grunberg, Ari Haberberg; Editor, Zelda Greenstein; Music, Andy Statman; a Ruby Pictures production; Color; DigiBeta; Not rated; 87 minutes; Release date: February 1, 2008. Documentary about Rabbi Mordecai Liebling and his family's dedication to helping his Down syndrome son, Lior.

STRANGE WILDERNESS (Paramount) Producer, Peter Gaulke; Executive Producers, Adam Sandler, Jack Giarraputo, Glenn S. Gainor, Bill Todman, Jr., Edward Milstein, Paul Schwake; Director, Fred Wolf; Screenplay, Peter Gaulke, Fred Wolf; Photography, David Hennings; Designer, Perry Andelin Blake; Costumes, Maya Lieberman; Music, Waddy Wachetl; Music Supervisors, Michael Dilbeck, Bryan Bonwell; a Level I Entertainment presentation of a Happy Madison production; Dolby; Color; Rated R; 85 minutes; Release date: February 1, 2008. CAST: Steve Zahn (Peter Gaulke), Allen Covert (Fred Wolf), Jonah Hill (Cooker), Kevin Heffernan (Whitaker), Ashley Scott (Cheryl), Peter Dante (Danny Guiterrez), Harry Hamlin (Sky Pierson), Robert Patrick (Gus Hayden), Joe Don Baker (Bill

Jonah Hill, Ernest Borgnine, Justin Long, Peter Dante, Steve Zahn, Allen Covert in Strange Wilderness © *Paramount Pictures*

TRE (Cinema Libre) Producer, Philippe Diaz; Executive Producers, Kimberly Debarros Connolly; Director, Eric Byler; Screenplay, Kimberly-Rose Wolter, Eric Byler; Photography, Rob Humphreys; Music, Michael Brook; Editor, Tom Moore; Color; Not rated; 88 minutes; Release date: February 1, 2008. CAST: Daniel Cariaga (Tre), Kimberly-Rose Wolter (Kakela), Erik McDowell (Gabriel), Alix Koromzay (Nina), Teddy Chen Culver (Lyle), Erik Hackett (Rick), Jackie O'Brian (Mom)

OVER HER DEAD BODY (New Line Cinema) Producers, Paul Brooks, Peter Safran; Executive Producers, Scott Niemeyer, Norm Waitt; Director/Screenplay, Jeff Lowell; Photography, John Bailey; Editor, Matthew Friedman; Music, David Kitay; Music Supervisor, Sarah Webster; Designer, Cory Lorenzen; Costumes, Tracy Tynan; Special Effects, Amalgamated Pixels; Casting, Eyde Belasco; a Gold Circle Films presentation of a Safran Co. production; Dolby; Panavision; Color; Rated PG-13; 95 minutes; Release date: February 1, 2008. CAST: Eva Longoria Parker (Kate), Paul Rudd (Henry), Lake Bell (Ashley), Jason Biggs (Dan), Lindsay Sloane (Chloe), Stephen Root (Sculptor), William Morgan Sheppard (Father Marks), Wendi McLendon-Covey (Lona), Ali Hillis (Karen), Deborah Theaker (Mary), Natalia Safran (Bride), Andy Kreiss (Groom), Ben Livingston (Minister), Jack Conley (Cab Driver), Kali Rocha (Angel), Colin Fickes (Don), Armen Weitzman (Tom), Bru Muller (Rude Customer), Richard Tillman (Gym Employee), Freddy Andreiuci (Hot Dog Vendor), Brooke Bloom (Margaret's Owner), Edith Fields (Mrs. Williams), Heather Mazur (Sue), Misha Collins (Brian), Patricia Belcher (Helen), Sam Pancake (Bill), Antonio Charity (Airport Guard), Jeff Lowell (Parrot)

Paul Rudd, Lake Bell in Over Her Dead Body *© New Line Cinema*

VINCE VAUGHN'S WILD WEST COMEDY SHOW: 30 DAYS & 30 NIGHTS–HOLLYWOOD TO THE HEARTLAND (Picturehouse) Producer, Vince Vaughn; Executive Producers, Peter Billingsley, Victoria Vaughn, John Isbell; Director, Ari Sandel; Editor, Dan Lebental, Jim Kelly; Music, John O'Brien; a Wild West Picture Show production; Dolby; Color; HD; Rated R; 100 minutes; Release date: February 8, 2008. Documentation of actor Vince Vaughn's 2005 touring comedy show, with Vince Vaughn, Ahmed Ahmed, John Caparulo, Bret Ernst, Sebastian Maniscalco, Peter Billingsley, Keir O'Donnell, Justin Long.

Justin Long, Vince Vaughn in Wild West Comedy Show *© Picturehouse*

THE HOTTIE & THE NOTTIE (Regent/here!) Producers, Victoria Nevinny, Neal Ramer, Myles Nestel, Hadeel Reda; Executive Producers, Paris Hilton, Hans G. Syz; Coproducers, Grace M. Lee, Josh Lekach, Roger Crotti, Craig Chapman; Director, Tom Putnam; Screenplay, Heidi Ferrer; Photography, Alex Vendler; Editors, Jeff Malmberg, James Miley; Music, David E. Russo; Music Supervisor, Chris Violette; Art Director, Helen Harwell; Costumes, Christopher Lawrence; Casting, Sunday Boling, Meg Morman; a Purple Pictures production; Dolby; Color; Rated PG-13; 91 minutes; Release date: February 8, 2008. CAST: Paris Hilton (Cristabelle Abbott), Joel David Moore (Nate Cooper), Christine Lakin (June Phigg), Johann Urb (Johann Wutrich), Adam Kulbersh (Cole Slawsen), Greg Wilson (Arno Blount), Marianne Muellerleile (Mrs. Blount), Samantha Bailey (Little Girl), Erin Cardillo (Yoga Instructor), Karley Scott Collins (Young Cristabelle), Alessandra Daniele (Young June), Walter Delmar (Geek), Kurt Doss (Young Arno), Kathryn Fiore (Jane), Marcus Lindsey (Evil Konieval), Alexandra Nowak (Yoga Patron), Gino Anthony Pesi (Cheesy Guy), Lorraine Smith (Herself), Jason Thornton (Barry Abbott)

Christine Lakin, Joel David Moore in The Hottie & the Nottie *© Regent Releasing*

MILITARY INTELLIGENCE AND YOU! (Anywhere Road) Producers, Greg Reeves, P. James Keitel, Dale Kutzera; Director/Screenplay, Dale Kutzera; Photography, Mark Parry; Editor, Joseph Butler; Associate Producers, Joseph Butler, Brian Kutzera, David Mickel; Casting, Janet Farris, Leanna Shelton; a Pax Americana Pictures production; Dolby; Black and white; Not rated; 78 minutes; Release date: February 8, 2008. CAST: Patrick Muldoon (Major Nick Reed), Elizabeth Ann Bennett (Lt. Monica Tasty), Mackenzie Astin (Major Mitch Dunning), John Rixey Moore (General Jake Tasker), Eric Jungmann (Corporal Skip Andrews)

SPIRAL (Anchor Bay) Producers, Cory Neal, Jeremy Danial Boreing; Executive Producers, Jim Sowell, Zachary Levi, Rachelle Ryan, Joel David Moore; Coproducers, David Muller, Kurt Schemper; Director, Adam Green, Joel David Moore; Screenplay, Jeremy Danial Boreing, Joel David Moore; Photography, Will Barratt; Editor, Cory Livingston; Music, Todd Caldwell, Michael "Fish" Herring; Designer, Travis Nicholas Zariwny; Art Director, Tyler B. Robinson; Costumes, Michelle Sandvig; Visual Effects Supervisor, Tyler A. Hawes; Special Effects Coordinator, Jerry Buxbaum; a Coattails Entertainment/ArieScope Picture; Color; HD DV; Rated PG-13; 90 minutes; Release date: February 8, 2008. CAST:

Joel David Moore (Mason), Zachary Levi (Berkeley), Amber Tamblyn (Amber), Tricia Helfer (Sasha), David Muller (Will), Annie Neal (Diana), Arlene Ancheta, Todd Chatalas, Matt Kimmel, Todd Robinson (Phone Bank Employees), Jeremy Danial Boreing (Concerned Employee), Ryan Chase (Chad), Amber Dahl (Miss Tennessee), Kristen Luman (Miss Idaho), Patrick Semmes (Ticket Vendor), Nick Sowell (Cashier), Rileah Vanderbilt (Girl on Bus), Lori Yohe (Valerie)

HOW TO ROB A BANK (IFC) Producers, Rick Lashbrook, Darby Parker, Arthur Sarkissian, Tim O'Hair; Executive Producers, Randolph De Lano, Tamara De Lano, Peter Sussman; Coproducer, Brent Morris; Director/Screenplay, Andrew Jenkins; Photography, Joseph Meade; Editor, M. Scott Smith; Music, Dider Lean Rachou; Designer, Max Biscoe; Costumes, Birgitte Mann; Casting, Anne McCarthy, Jay Scully; a Rick Lashbrook Films, Williamsburg Media Cult, Villa Entertainment Group production; Dolby; Panavision; FotoKem color; Not rated; 81 minutes; Release date: February 8, 2008. CAST: Nick Stahl (Jason "Jinx" Taylor), Erika Christensen (Jessica), Terry Crews (Officer Degepse), Leo Fitzpatrick, Nicolo Cole (Gunmen), Adriano Aragon (Officer Lindstrom), David Carradine (Nick), Renee Cohen, Silke Fernald, Sabrina Machado (Hostages), Britt Delano (Key Witness)

Erika Christensen, Nick Stahl in How to Rob a Bank © *IFC Films*

A WALK TO BEAUTIFUL (Engel Entertainment) Producers, Steven Engle, Mary Olive Smith, Amy Bucher; Executive Producer, Steven Engle; Coproducer, Allison Shigo; Director, Mary Olive Smith; Co-Director, Amy Bucher; Photography, Tony Hardmon, Smith; Editor, Andrew Ford; Music, David Schommer; Presented in association with Nova; Color; HD; Not rated; 85 minutes; Release date: February 8, 2008. Documentary on the women of Ethiopia suffering from obstetric fistulas and how their poor living conditions prove a hindrance to seeking medical assistance.

ME & YOU, US, FOREVER (Five & Two Pictures) Producer/Director/Screenplay, Dave Christiano; Photography, Philip Hurn; Designer, Stephanie King; Music, Jasper Randall; Editor, Shane McMullin; Casting, Marty Siu; Presented in association with Dave Christiano Films; Dolby; Color; Rated PG; 100 minutes; Release date: February 15, 2008. CAST: Michael Blain-Rozgay (Dave), Stacey J. Aswad (Carla), Hugh McLean (Paul), Jenna Bailey (Sue), Karla Droege (Nikki), Terry Loughlin (Group Leader), Sandi Fix (Mary), Kathryn Worsham (Mary, age 16), Kate Leahey (Amanda), Leanna Spear (Michelle), Genevieve Borden (Ashley), Jake Goodchild (Dave)

GEORGE A. ROMERO'S DIARY OF THE DEAD (Weinstein Co.) Producers, Peter Grunwald, Artur Spigel, Sam Englebardt, Ara Katz; Executive Producers, Dan Fireman, John Harrison, Steve Barnett; Director/Screenplay, George A. Romero;

Photography, Adam Swica; Editor, Michael Doherty; Music, Norman Orenstein; Designer, Rupert Lazarus; Costumes, Alex Kavanagh; Special Makeup Effects Producer, Greg Nicotero; Special Makeup Effects, Gaslight Studio; Visual Effects, Spin; an Artfire Films, Romero-Grunwald production; Dolby; Color; Rated R; 95 minutes; Release date: February 15, 2008. CAST: Michelle Morgan (Debra), Joshua Close (Jason), Shawn Roberts (Tony Ravello), Amy Lalonde (Tracy Thurman), Joe Dinicol (Eliot Stone), Scott Wentworth (Andrew Maxwell), Philip Riccio (Ridley Wilmott), Megan Park (Francine Shane), Chris Violette (Gordo Thorsen), Tatiana Maslany (Mary Dexter), Martin Roach (Stranger), Boyd Banks (White Man), George Buza (Tattooed Biker), Janet Lo (Asian Woman), Laura DeCarteret (Brie), Todd William Schroeder (Brody), Daniel Kash (Police Officer), Tino Monte (Newscaster), Alan Van Sprang (Colonel), Matt Birman (Zombie Trooper), Trish Adams (Dead Mrs. Moynahan), Nick Alachiotis (Fred), Alexandria DeFabiis (Zombie), Wes Craven, Stephen King, Simon Pegg, Quentin Tarantino, Guillermo del Toro (Voices of Newsreaders), George A. Romero (Police Chief)

Chris Viollette, Joe Dinicol in Diary of the Dead © *Weinstein Co.*

DOG DAYS OF SUMMER (Level Path Prods.) Producer/Director, Mark Freiburger; Executive Producer, Rick Eldridge; Co-Executive Producer, Michael E. Wekall; Screenplay, Travis Beacham, Christopher J. Waild; Story, Travis Beacham, Mark Freiburger, Christopher J. Waild; Photography, Rob C. Givens; Designer, Andrew Cappella; Music, Rob Pottorf; Editor, Jonathan Olive; a Tamiami Films production; Color; Not rated; 88 minutes; Release date: February 22, 2008. CAST: Will Patton (Eli Cottonmouth), Richard Herd (Frank Cooper), Devon Gearhart (Philip Walden), Colin Ford (Jackson Patch), R. Keith Harris (Pastor Salem), Gregory Alan Williams (Sheriff Lem Baker), Colin Key (Phil Walden), Wayne Crawford (Quincy Patch), Mark Joy (Chuck Walden), Megan Blake (May Walden), Richard Fullerton (The General), Patricia Herd (Marilyn Rockwell), Joe Inscoe (Doc Rockwell), Bonnie Johnson (Martha), Logan Fahey (Chip Robinson), George Lee (Register Clerk), John Becker (Rudd Bentley), Amanda Deibert (Linda), Paul Silver (Brock Walden), Jessica Webb (Camille)

COVER (American Cinema Intl.) Producers, Corey Redmond, Warren Kohler, Bill Duke; Executive Producers, Michael A. DiManno, R. Scott Reid; Coproducer, Bayard Johnson; Co-Executive Producers, Gus Blackmon, Ken Dixon, Sharon Pinkenson; Director, Bill Duke; Screenplay, Aaron Rahsaan Thomas, based on a screenplay by Aliya Jackson; Photography, Francis Kenny; Editor, Cari Coughlin; Music, Kurt Farquhar; Music Supervisors, Alison Ball, David Lombard; Designer, Jesse Rosenthal; Costumes, Tersa Binder-Westby; a Duke Media/Redmond Enterprises presentation in association with Redwood Palms Pictures; Color;

Will Patton in Dog Days of Summer © *Level Path Prods.*

HD; Rated PG-13; 98 minutes; Release date: February 22, 2008.CAST: Aunjanue Ellis (Valerie Maas), Razaaq Adoti (Dutch Maas), Leon (Ryan Chambers), Louis Gossett, Jr. (Detective Hicks), Paula Jai Parker (Monica Wilson), Richard Gant (Robert Maas), Mya Harrison (Cynda), Victoria Gabrielle Platt (Charlotte Chabers), Vivica A. Fox (Zahara Milton), Patti LaBelle (Mrs. Persons), Tomorrow Baldwin Montgomery (Nicole Maas), Sakinah Bingham (Jenny), Kenya Cagle (Damascene Pierre Paul (Police Officers), Ray Ford (Concierge), Christopher Michael Holley (DL Father), Ingrid Johnson (Valeri's Cellmate), Clayton Prince (Greg), Roger Guenveur Smith (Kevin Wilson), Ricky Staub (Bartender), Karen Vicks (Mrs. Dunn)

WITLESS PROTECTION (Lionsgate) Producers, J.P. Williams, Alan Blomquist; Executive Producers, Tom Ortenberg, Thomas Busch; Director/Screenplay, Charles Robert Carner; Story, Alan Blomquist, Charles Robert Carner; Photography, Michael Goi; Designer, Cabot McMullen; Costumes, Susan Kaufmann; Music, Eric Allaman; Editor, Marc Leif; Associate Producers, Maggie Houlehan, Jennifer Novak; Casting, Junie Lowry Johnson, Libby Goldstein, Deborah George, Sharon King; a Shaler Entertainment/Samwilla production, presented with Parallel Entertainment Pictures; Dolby; Color; Rated PG-13; 97 minutes; Release date: February 22, 2008. CAST: Larry the Cable Guy (Deputy

Joe Mantegna, Ivana Milicevic, Larry the Cable Guy in Witless Protection © *Lionsgate*

Larry Stalder), Ivana Milicevic (Madeleine), Yaphet Kotto (Alonzo Mosely), Peter Stormare (Arthur Grimsley), Eric Roberts (Wilfrod Duvall), Joe Mantegna (Dr. Rondog "Doc" Savage), Jenny McCarthy (Connie), Richard Bull (Sheriff Smoot), J. David Moeller (Elmer), Will Clinger (Bo), Omar Kent Dykes (Gus), Reno Collier (Tater), Dan Waller (Agent Orange), Rick Lefevour, Joe Caballero (MIB's), Sean Bridgers (Norm), Gerry Bednob (Omar), Claudia Michelle Wallace (TSA Woman), Emir Yonzon (TSA Supervisor), Gary Tippett (TSA Dog Handler), Jesse Dabson (TSA Expert), Jessica Orr (Vibiana), Kurt Naebig (Mark Bedell), Michael Carner (Young Boy), Gail Rastorfer (Morgana), Lynette Gaza (Lillian Grimoire)

THE SIGNAL (Magnolia) Producers, Alexander A. Motlagh, Jacob Gentry; Executive Producers, Hilton Garrett, Morris Ruskin; Coproducer, Lab 601; Directors/Screenplay/ Editors, David Bruckner, Jacob Gentry, Dan Bush; Photography, Chris Campbell; Music, Ben Lovett; Designer, Lisa Yeiser; Costumes, Caroline Deiter; Makeup, Gretchen Mathis; Special Effects Supervisor, Jason Price; Visual Effects, Itaki Design Studio; Stunts, Nils Onsager; Associate Producers, JD Taylor; a POPfilms and Shoreline Entertainment presentation of an Alexander A. Motlagh production; Lab 601 color; DV; Rated R; 101 minutes; Release date: February 22, 2008. CAST: AJ Bowen (Lewis Denton), Anessa Ramsey (Mya Denton), Justin Welborn (Ben), Scott Poythress (Clark), Sahr Nguajah (Rod), Cheri Christian (Anna), Matt Stenton (Jerry), Suehyla El-Attar (Janice), Christopher Thomas (Ken), Lindsey Garrett (Laura), Chad McKnight (Jim Parsons), Robin Acker, Jeff Adelman, Ben Bailey, Terril A. Closs, Tiffany Dennise, Alexis Hale, Quillian Hightower, Scott Hodges, Marirosa Hoffman, Robert Lane, Kasey Perdue, Bill Rampley. Melissa Randle, Peggy Randle, David Strickland, Patrick Thompson, Marcellus Thuman (Random Bodies), J. Howard Bach, Becky Ballard (Deranged People), Claire Bronson (Sightless Woman), David Bruckner, Dan Bush, Ryan Lewis (Screaming Men), Nikki Hansen (Deaf Woman), Edward Morgan (Arguing Man), Alexander Motlagh (Chainsaw Man), Kid Richmond (Man on Fire), Robert Sanders (Homeless Vet), Steve Warren (Pajama Man)

Cheri Christian, AJ Bowen, Scott Poythress in The Signal © *Magnolia Films*

CHOP SHOP (Koch Lorber) Producers, Lisa Muskat, Marc Turtletaub, Jeb Brody; Executive Producer, Peter Saraf; Coproducers, Pradip Ghosh, Bedford Tate Bentley III; Director/Editor, Ramin Bahrani; Screenplay, Bahareh Azimi, Ramin Bahrani; Photography, Michael Simmonds; Music, M.L.O.; Designer, Richard Wright; Costumes, Daphne Javitch; Line Producer, Kathryn Dean; a Big Beach production in association with Muskat Filmed Properties & Noruz Films; Dolby; DuArt color; Not rated; 85 minutes; Release date: February 27, 2008. CAST: Alejandro Polanco (Alejandro), Isamar Gonzales (Isamar), Rob Sowulski (Rob), Carlos Zapata (Carlos), Ahmad Razvi (Ahmad), Sherman Alpert (Truck "John"), Carlos Ayala (Carlos the Pigeon Worker), Nick Bentley (Broken Mirror Customer), Anthony Felton (Carlos's Uncle), Nick Jaspirizza (The "John"), Farooq "Duke" Muhammad (Duke), Michael "Gringo" Nieto (Construction Foreman), Evelisse "Lilah" Ortiz (Lilah), Laura Patalano (Laura), Manny Albos, Angelo Carillo, Tyrone Gray (Worker of Willet's Point), Pedro Altamirano, Raoul Chucaralao (Ahmad's Workers), Sneha Amin, Nicholas Corelisco, Shawn Leon Thomas III, Anna Torevski, Aben Garces Zavala, Killian Zavala (Amhad's Friends), Carla Cubit (Ahmad's Escort), Nicole Dangee (Woman with Baby), Jesus Manuel Gutierrez, Cesar Di Parra (Car Thieves), Nicholas Elliott (Subway Customer), Edwin Rojas, Roy Franisco Green, Billy Klatzis (Rob's Workers), Frank Lukacs (Parking Lot Cop), Damien Velez, William Anthony Morales (Lilah's Friends), Jimmy Peña, Roberto Ramirez (Cell Phone Customers)

THE UNFORESEEN (The Cinema Guild) Producers, Douglas Sewell, Jeff Sewell, Laura Dunn; Executive Producers, Terrence Malick, Robert Redford; Coproducer, Rose Hansen Smith; Director, Laura Dunn; Photography, Lee Daniel; Music, Arvo Part, Sigur Ros, Patty Griffin, Craig Ross; Editor, Emily Morris; Motion Graphics, Jeff Sewell; Associate Producers, Madeleine Akers, Carolyn Merriman; an Ojo Partners presentation of a Two Birds film; Color; HD vid/16mm; Not rated; 94 minutes; Release date: February 29, 2008. Documentary on how the overdevelopment of Austin, Texas has impacted the environment; with Gary Bradley, Henry Brooks, Dick Brown, Judah Folkman, William Greider, Marshall Kuykendall, Willie Nelson, Pedro Perez, Ronnie Perez, Robert Redford, Ann Richards; and the voice of Wendell Berry.

The Unforeseen © *The Cinema Guild*

A LAWYER WALKS INTO A BAR ... (Indican) Producer, Tasha Oldham, Eric Chaikin; Executive Producers, Brandon Camp, Mike Thompson, Jonathan Osborne; Director, Eric Chaikin; Photography, Stephanie Martin; Editor, Deborah Barkow; a Camel's Back Films presentation; Color; Not rated; 92 minutes; Release date: February 29, 2008. Documentary on the American legal system's obsession with lawsuits; with Donald Baumeister, Sam Garrett, Cassandra Hooks, Magda Madrigal, Megan Meadows, Tricia Zunker, Eddie Griffin, Michael Ian Black, Senator John Cornyn, Catherine Crier, Alan Dershowitz, Nancy Grace, Len Jacoby, Joseph D. Jamail, Vernon Jordan, W. Mark Lanier, Robert L. Shapiro, John Stossel, Scott Turow.

TRYING TO GET GOOD: THE JAZZ ODYSSEY OF JACK SHELDON (Bialystock & Bloom/February Films) Producer/Director/Screenplay, Doug McIntyre, Penny Peyser; Photography, John Gannon; Music, Jack Sheldon; Editor, Matt McUsic; Color; Not rated; 90 minutes; Release date: March 5, 2008. Documentary on trumpeter Jack Sheldon; with Jack Sheldon, Alan Bergman, Chris Botti, Billy Crystal, Dom DeLuise, Clint Eastwood, Dave Frishberg, Tery Gibbs, Merv Griffin, Johnny Mandel, Frank Marshall, Mark Rydell, Tierney Sutton, Joe Bagg, James A. Baker, Wayne Bergeron, Chuck Berghofer, Shelly Berg, Helen Borgers, Ray Brinker, William Claxton, Marty Harris, Bill Henderson, Christian Jacob, Tom Kubis, Bruce Lett, Leonard Maltin, Chuck McCann, Michael Melvoin, Ken Peplowski, Uan Rasey, Howard Rumsey, Jesse Sheldon, Ross Tompkins, David Tull

FROWNLAND (Frownland, Inc.) Producer, Marc Raybin; Director/Screenplay/Editor, Ronald Bronstein; Photography, Sean Price Williams; Music, Paul Grimstad; Dolby; Eastmancolor; Not rated; 106 minutes; Release date: March 7, 2008. CAST: Dore Mann (Keith), Paul Grimstad (Charles), David Sandholm (Sandy), Carmine Marino (Carmine), Paul Grant (Exam-Man), Mary Wall (Laura)

FIGHTING FOR LIFE (Truly Indie) Producer/Director, Terry Sanders; Executive Producer, Tammay Alvarez; Coproducer, Jennifer Glos; Screenplay, Terry Sanders, Christine Wiser; Photography, Erik Daarstad, Buddy Squires; Music, Scott Michael Ford; Editors, Brian Johnson, Anne Stein; a Sanders & Mock/American Film Foundation production; Color; HD; Not rated; 89 minutes; Release date: March 7, 2008. Documentary on the men and women of the Uniformed Services University of the Health Sciences who have tended to those wounded in combat; with Crystal Davis, David Welling, Daniel Inouye.

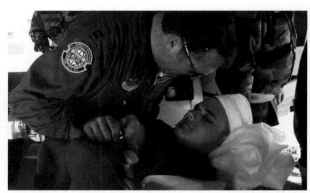

Fighting for Life © *Truly Indie*

GIRLS ROCK! (Shadow Distribution) Producer, Arne Johnson: Directors/Editors, Arne Johnson, Shane King; Photography, Shane King; a Girls Rock production; Dolby; Color; Rated PG; 90 minutes; Release date: March 7, 2008. Documentary on four eight to eighteen-year-olds who are transformed by their stay at the Rock 'n' Roll Camp for Girls.

Amelia in Girls Rock! © *Shadow Distribution*

BODY OF WAR (The Film Sales Company) Producer/Photography, Ellen Spiro; Executive Producer, Phil Donahue; Coproducer, Karen Bernstein; Directors, Ellen Spiro, Phil Donahue; Music, Jeff Layton; Songs, Eddie Vedder; Editor, Bernadine Colish; Color; Not rated; 87 minutes; Release date: March 7, 2008. Documentary on how Tomas Young ended up paralyzed after being sent to fight in Iraq in 2004; with Tomas Young, Robert Byrd, Brad Friedman, Cathy Smith, Nathan Young.

Tomas Young in Body of War © *The Film Sales Company*

MEAT LOAF: IN SEARCH OF PARADISE (Atlas Media Corp.) Producers, Greg Moyer, Sal LoCurto, Jordan Berliant, Bruce David Klein; Director, Bruce David Klein; Photography, David West; Editor, Erik Klein; Produced in association with Voom HD, Tenth Street Management; Color; HD; Not rated; 90 minutes; Release date: March 13, 2008. Documentary on rock performer Meat Loaf; with Meat Loaf, Kasim Sulton, John Miceli, Mark Alexander, Paul Crook, Randy Flowers, Carolyn Coletti, Aspen Miller, David Luther, Dennis Quaid, Roxanne Fairman.

TOWARDS DARKNESS (Peace Arch Entertainment) a.k.a. *Hacia la Oscuridad*; Producers, Craig Anderson, Luiza Ricupero; Executive Producers, America Ferrara, Brett Etre, Justin Goodman, Randy Holleschau, Daniel Negret, Alex Yanev; Coproducers, Anel Moreno, Antonio Negret, Jenny Sandell; Director/Screenplay, Antonio Negret; Photography, John Ealer; Designer, Jason Sweers; Music, Chris Westlake; Editors, Luis Carballar, Paulo Carballar, Evan Schiff; a Negret Films production; Dolby; Color; not rated; 94 minutes; Release date: March 14, 2008. CAST: Roberto Urbina (Jose Gutierrez), America Ferrera (Luiza), David Sutcliffe (Charlie Bain), Tony Plana (Carlos Gutierrez), William Atherton (John), Alejandra Borrero (Marta Gutierrez), Fernando Solózano (Umberto Pompeo), Roberto Cano (Pedro), Juan Carlos Arango (Bucko), Carlos Humberto Camacho (Roberto "El Lobo" Sanchez), Cameron Daddo (Victor), Claudia Degustini (Sheila Mendoza), Omar Diaz (Customs Official), Jose Vicente Gutierrez (Felipe Mendoza), Jorge Monterrosa (Cuate), Rafael Negret (Ramiro), Kate Siegel (Jenn), David Simmons (Juan Martinez), Andres Toro (Jaime), Carlos Valencia (Manuel), Selah Victor (Larissa)

WETLANDS PRESERVED: THE STORY OF AN ACTIVIST ROCK CLUB (First Run Features) Producer, Peter Shapiro; Executive Producers, Robert Difazio; Co-Executive Producers, John Turk, Karol Martesko; Director, Dean Budnick; Photography/Editor, Jonathan Healy; Color; DV; Not rated; 97 minutes; Release date: March 14, 2008. Documentary on Wetlands, a New York eco-saloon that combined music with social advocacy; with Mabili Kregg Ajamu, Rob Barraco, Chris Barron, Tim Barry, Larry Bloch, Steve Bloom, Rob Bookman, Marty Bostoff, Marc Brownstine, Oteil Burbridge, Edward Cisneros, Aaron Comess, Rob Derhak, Carol De Saram, Mike Doughty, Jimmy Drescher, Walter Durkacz, John Dwork, Steve Eichner, Richard Gehr, Mike Gordon, Jon Gutwillig, Issac Hanson, Taylor Hanson, Zac Hanson, Warren Haynes, Vince Herman, Nick Hexum, Brendan Hill, David Hoffman, Kenneth Jackson, Joel Johnson, Chan Kinchla, Eric Krasno, Dave Matthews, Jeff Mattson, John Medeski, Ryan Miller, Michael Musto, Dave Nolan, Danny Owen, Sherri Kohl Owles, John Popper, Robert Randolph, Andrew Rasiej, Cindy Rosin, Darius Rucker, Joe Russo, Joe Sarkis, Eric Schenkman, Al Schnier, Dave Schools, Peter Shapiro, Jim "Soni" Sonefeled, Terry Stewart, Vinnie Stigma, Jake Szufnarowski, Denise Teperino, Ricky Tepperberg, Ahmir-Khalib Thompson, Jon Topper, Derek Trucks, Bob Weir, Adam Weissman, Kirk West, Mark White, Eric Wilson, Chris Zahn

Dave Matthews Band in Wetlands Preserved © *First Run Features*

WAR MADE EASY: HOW PRESIDENTS & PUNDITS KEEP SPINNING US TO DEATH (MED) Producer, Loretta Alper; Coproducer, Andrew Killoy; Executive Producers, Jeremy Earp, Sut Jhally; Directors/Screenplay, Loretta Alper, Jeremy Earp; Photography, David Rabinowitz; Music, John Van Eps, Leigh Philips; Editor/Motion Graphics, Andrew Killoy; Narrator, Sean Penn; Color; Mini-DV-to-DV; Not rated; 73 minutes; Release date: March 14, 2008. Documentary on how the Bush administration has used manipulation and lies to win public support for the war in Iraq; with Norman Solomon.

SLEEPWALKING (Overture Films) Producers, J.J. Harris, Charlize Theron, Beth Kono, A.J. Dix, Rob Merilees, William Shively; Executive Producers, Anthony Rhulen, Michael Sterling, Charles Mason, Justin Moore-Lewy; Coproducer, Stephen Onda; Director, William Maher; Screenplay, Zac Stanford; Photography, Juan Ruiz Anchia; Designer, Paki Smith; Costumes, Cathy McComb; Music, Christopher Young; Editor, Stuart Levy; Casting, Brenda McCormick, Betia Hovedskov; an Icon Entertainment Intl. presentation; American-Canadian; Dolby; Widescreen; Color; Rated R; 101 minutes; Release date: March 14, 2008. CAST: Nick Stahl (James), AnnaSophia Robb (Tara), Charlize Theron (Joleen), Woody Harrelson (Randall), Dennis Hopper (Mr. Reedy), Deborra-Lee Furness (Danni), Milan Aveyard (Girl #1), Simon Chin (Randall's Friend), Mike Ennis (Cop #2), Shannon Jardine (Mom), Lori Ann Kennedy (Foster Care Worker), Amy Matysio (Sharon), Callum Keith Rennie (Will), Peter Scoular (Dad), Troy Skog (Warren), Emily Wees (Nicole)

AnnaSophia Robb, Nick Stahl in Sleepwalking © *Overture Films*

Sputnik Mania © *Balcony Releasing*

SPUTNIK MANIA (Balcony) a.k.a. *The Fever of 57*; Producer, Eric A. Reid; Director, David Hoffman; Screenplay, David Hoffman, Paul Dickson, Lindsey Palatino; Associate Producer, Joseph Ferrera; Editor, John Vincent Barrett; Narrator, Liev Schreiber; a Varied Directions International production; Dolby; Color; Not rated; 92 minutes; Release date: March 14, 2008. Documentary on the effect Russia's Sputnik satellite has had over the past fifty years; with Sergei Khrushchev, Jay Barbree, Paul Dickson, Susan Eisenhower, Daniel Schorr.

THE GRAND (Anchor Bay) Producers, Bret Saxon, Jeff Bowler, Zak Penn, Gary Marcus, Bobby Schwartz, Ross M. Dinerstein; Director, Zak Penn; Screenplay, Zak Penn, Matt Bierman; Photography, Anthony Hardwick; Designer, Shepherd Frankel; Costumes, Valerie Laven-Cooper; Music, Stephen Endelman; Editor, Abby Schwarzwalder; Music Supervisors, G. Marq Roswell, Adam Swart; Casting, Richard Pagano; an Insomnia Media Group/Eleven Eleven Films production; Dolby; Color; Rated R; 104 minutes; Release date: March 21, 2008. CAST: Woody Harrelson (One Eyed Jack Faro), David Cross (Larry Schwartzman), Dennis Farina (LBJ "Deuce" Fairbanks), Cheryl Hines (Lainie Schwartzman), Richard Kind (Andy Andrews), Chris Parnell (Harold Melvin), Werner Herzog (The German), Jason Alexander (Dr. Yakov Achmed), Ray Romano (Fred Marsh), Mike Epps (Reggie Marshall), Judy Greer (Sharon Andrews), Gabe Kaplan (Seth Schwartzman), Michael Karnow (Mike Werbe), Michael McKean (Steve Lavisch), Julie Claire (Dr. Jamie Sellers), Barry Corbin (Jiminy "Lucky" Faro), Shannon Elizabeth (Toni), Estelle Harris (Ruth Melvin), Andrew Hill Newman (Russell Kalenich–The Dealer), Andrea Savage (Renee Jensen), Phil Gordon, Robert Thompson, Richard Brodie, Tilman J. Fertitta, Munchkin the Rabbit (Themselves), Andy Bellin, Doyle Brunson, Antonio Esfandiari, Phil Hellmuth, Jr., Phil Laak, Daniel Negreanu (Poker Pros), Hank Azaria (Mike "The Bike" Heslov), Tom Hodges (Tim "Tiny Wonder" Woolrich), David Pressman (Melville "Murph Murph" Murphy), Brett Ratner ("Sob Story" Barry Blausteen), Avi Arada (Abdul Shavit), K.D. Aubert (Julie the Waitress), Tommy "Tiny" Lister, Lance Stockton (German's Bodyguards), Tim Mikuletky (Bitch Slapped Man), Trula Marcus (Front Desk Clerk), Cynthia Petrello (Waitress at Vic & Anthony's), Linda Button (Jack's Secretary), Rusty Meyers (Long Island Poker Player), Peter O'Meara (Dave Esme), Tara G. Wise (Laine's Daughter Ellen), Catherine Rose Young (Lainie's Daughter Catherine), Alec Holden (Little Larry), Hailey McCann (Little Lainie), Orly Shani, Naomi Fabe (Lavisch's Assistants), Errol Guidry II (Cajun Larry), Jeff Bowler (Poker Player), Sharon Fann (Dealer at TV Tournament), Marc J. Chaiet, Garrett McKechnie (Hotel Guests)

Dennis Farina, Hank Azaria in The Grand © *Anchor Bay*

THE HAMMER (Intl. Film Circuit) Producers, Eden Wurmfeld, Heather Juergensen, Eric Ganz; Executive Producers, Adam Carolla, Steven Firestone, Gregory Firestone; Coproducer, Kevin Hench; Director, Charles Herman-Wurmfeld; Screenplay, Kevin Hench; Story, Adam Carolla; Photography, Marco Fargnoli; Designer, Mickey Siggins; Costumes, Abigail Nicto; Music, John Swihart, Matt Mariano; Editor, Rich Fox; Casting, Michael Hothorn; an Eden Wurmfeld Films, Bentley Film Group production; Dolby; Color; Rated R; 93 minutes; Release date: March 21, 2008. CAST: Adam Carolla (Jerry Ferro), Heather Juergensen (Lindsay Pratt), Oswaldo Castillo (Oswaldo Sanchez), Tom Quinn (Coach Bell), Harold House Moore (Robert Brown), Jonathan Hernandez (Victor Padilla), Paul Alayo (Boxer Opponent), Rian Bishop (Nationals Trainer), Derrick Dean (Gym Member), Keeshan Giles, Lorenzo Eduardo (Posse Members), John Enos III (Steve), Kevin Ferguson (Jeff), Jim FitzGerald (Announcer), Alison Flierl (Boxing Fan), Julia Galasso (Boxing Class Trainee), Stacy Michelle Gold (Tarpits Visitor), Leah Gottfried (Secretary), Andy Hnilo (Knockout Victim), Karen Jefferson (Hardware Store Cashier), Justin Kelly (Construction Worker), Jeff Lacy (Malice Blake), Billy Moses (Boxing Student), Lily Rey (Waitress), Bruce Schroffel (Timekeeper), Shadii (Malice Blake Entourage), Robyn Sheridan (Boxer), Ray Siegle (Final Match Referee), Keith Stanisiewski (Hardware Store Customer), Jimmy Walker, Jr. (The Oldtimer), Constance Zimmer (Nicole)

Oswaldo Castillo, Adam Carolla in The Hammer © Intl. Film Circuit

SHUTTER (20th Century Fox) Producers, Taka Ichise, Roy Lee, Doug Davison; Executive Producers, Arnon Milchan, Sonny Mallhi, Gloria Fan; Coproducers, Paiboon Damrongchaitham, Boosaba Daorueng, Visute Poolvoralaks, Yodphet Sudsawat; Director, Masayuki Ochiai; Screenplay, Luke Dawson; Based on the 2004 Tai motion picture *Sutter kodtid winyan* directed by Banjong Pisanthanakun and Parkpoom Wongpoon, with screenplay by Banjong Pisanthanakun, Parkpoom Wongpoon, and Sopon Sukdapisit; Photography, Katsui Yanagijima; Designer, Norifumi Ataka; Music, Nathan Barr; Editors, Michael N. Knue, Tim Alverson; Visual Effects Supervisors, Hajimie Matsumoto, Raymond McIntyre, Jr.; Stunts, Masanori Saito; Casting, Donna Isaacson, Christian Kaplan; a Regency Enterprises presentation of a New Regency, Vertigo Entertainment, Ozla Pictures production; Dolby; Color; Rated PG-13; 85 minutes; Release date: March 21, 2008. CAST: Joshua Jackson (Benjamin Shaw), Rachael Taylor (Jane Shaw), Megumi Okina (Megumi Tanaka), David Denman (Bruno), John Hensley (Adam), Maya Hazen (Seiko), James Kyson Lee (Ritsuo), Yoshiko Miyazaki (Akiko), Kei Yamamoto (Murase), Daisy Betts (Natasha), Adrienne Pickering (Megan), Pascal Morineau (Wedding Photographer), Masaki Ota, Heideru Tatsuo (Police Officers), Eri Otoguro (Yoko), Rina Matsuki (TGK Receptionist), Tomotaka Kanzaki, Jun Yakushiji (Clients), Emi Tamura (Emi), Polina Kononova, Yulia Ryzhova (Studio Models), Mika Kinose (Office Lady), Masakazu Magakura (Pachinko Parlor Employee), Shinji Furukawa (Pachinko Parlor Customer), Maria Takagi (Waitress at Japanese Restaurant), Alessandra, Katrina B., Tanya (Models), Takao Toji

(Tokyo Doctor), Shizuka Fujimoto (Tokyo Exam Room Nurse), Yutaka Mishima (Ghost Magazine Layout Designer), Maiko Asano (Mother on Train), Rei Sato (Boy on Train), Runa Kozuki (Girl in Park), Natsuki (TGK Staff), Akihio Shimomura (Megumi's Father), Gen Takatsuka (Monk), Natalia Tsvetkova (Brooklyn Nurse)

Rachael Taylor, Joshua Jackson in Shutter © Regency Ent.

PLANET B-BOY (Elephant Eye Films) Producers, Benson Lee, Amy Lo; Executive Producers, Johnny Lee, Christopher C. Kim, Danny Huang; Photography, Vasco Lucas Nunes; Director, Benson Lee; Editors, Benson Lee, Jeff Marcello; Music, Woody Pak; Mondo Paradiso Films NYC, Mental Pictures; Color; Not rated; 101 minutes; Release date: March 21, 2008. Documentary on the international world of "b-boying" or breakdancing; with Knucklehead Zoo, Skwall.

Planet B-Boy © Elephant Eye Film

SHOTGUN STORIES (Intl. Film Circuit) Producers, David Gordon Green, Lisa Muskat, Jeff Nichols; Executive Producers, Todd Williams, Nick Thurlow, John Portnoy; Director/Screenplay, Jeff Nichols; Photography, Adam Stone; Designer, Lindsay Millar; Costumes, Rachel Worthen; Music, Ben Nichols, Lucero; Editor, Steven Gonzales; an Upload Films presentation of a Lucky Old Sun production in association with Muskat Film; Dolby; Color; Rated PG-13; 90 minutes; Release date: March 26, 2008. CAST: Michael Shannon (Son Hayes), Douglas Ligon (Boy Hayes), Barlow Jacobs (Kid Hayes), Michael Abbott, Jr. (Cleaman Hayes), Travis Smith (Mark Hayes), Lynsee Provence (Stephen Hayes), Glenda Pannell (Annie Hayes), G. Alan Wilkins (Shampoo Douglas), Natalie Canerday (Nicole Hayes), Coley Canpany (Cheryl), Cole Hendixson (Carter Hayes), Vivian Morrison Norman (Melissa), Tucker Prentiss (Paul), Wyatt Ashton Prentiss (Kevin), David Rhodes (John Hayes)

Barlow Jacobs, Douglas Ligon in Shotgun Stories © *Vertigo Films*

CHAPTER 27 (Peace Arch Entertainment Group) Producers, Bob Salerno, Naomi Despres, Alexandra Milchan; Executive Producers, Jared Leto, Rick Chad, Gilbert Alloul, John Flock, Gary Hosam, Lewin Webb; Director/Screenplay, Jarrett Schaefer; Photography, Tom Richmond; Designer, Kalina Ivanov; Costumes, Ane Crabtree; Music, Anthony Marnelli; Music Supervisor, Tracy McKnight; Editors, Jim Makiej, Andrwe Hafitz; Inspired by the book *Let Me Take You Down* by Jack Jones; an Artina Films production; Dolby; Color; Rated R; 84 minutes; Release date: March 28, 2008. CAST: Jared Leto (Chapman), Lindsay Lohan (Jude), Judah Friedlander (Paul), Ursula Abbott (Jeri), George Bryant II (Limo Driver), Kevin Cannon (Precision Driver/Street Hood), Mark Lindsay Chapman (John Lennon), Melissa Demyan (Lennon Groupie), Jeane Fournier (European Woman), Molly Griffith (Covergirl/Centerfold), Matthew Humphreys (Frederic Seaman), Redman Maxfield (Maitre D'), Lauren Milberger (Gilda Radner), Matthew Nardozzi (Little Kid), Brian O'Neill (Patrick), Adam Scarimbolo (Clerk Riley), Michael Sirow (Joseph Many), Jeff Skowron (Waiter), Mariko Takai (Yoko Ono), Victor Verhaeghe (Spiro), Erik Wolfe (Lennon Band Member)

HATS OFF (Abramorama) Producers, Jyll Johnstone, Michael Arlen Davis; Director, Jyll Johnstone; Photography, Eddie Marritz, Sophie Constantinou, Jamie McEwen, Richard Numeroff, Alex Rappaport, Paolo Santangelo, Fawn Yacker; Editors, Kate Stilley Steiner, Bill Weber, Frankie Spellman, Stevie Buzzell; a Canobie Films presentation; Color; DV; Not rated; 84 minutes; Release date: March 28, 2008. Documentary on ninety-three-year-old model-actress Mimi Weddell.

Lindsay Lohan, Jared Leto in Chapter 27 © *Peace Arch Entertainment*

Mimi Weddell in Hats Off © *Abramorama*

BACKSEAT (Truly Indie) Producers, Terry Leonard, Josh Alexander; Executive Producers, John Textor, Casey Cummings, Jeff Mooallem, Henry Hardaway; Director, Bruce Van Dusen; Screenplay, Josh Alexander; Photography, Ari J. Issler; Designer/Costumes, Amanda Ford; Music, BC Smith; Music Supervisors, Jonathan Fine, Glen Caplin; Editors, Gavin Cutler, Andy Kier; a Group Effort Films production; Color; Super 16-to-HD; Not rated; 80 minutes; Release date: March 28, 2008. CAST: Josh Alexander (Colton), Rob Bogue (Ben), Aubrey Dollar (Shelle), Will Janowitz (Frankie), Mark Rosenthal (Henry), Helen Coxe (Honey), Sarah Lord (Candi), Danny Mastrogiorio (Andres), Starla Benford (Patty), William Bogert (Dad), Chris Carley, Alan Katz (Guys at Party), Jeffrey Carlson (Jason), Glenn Daniels (Casting Director), Malcolm Goodwin (Ricky)

Jesse Archer in A Four-Letter Word *© Embrem Entertainment*

Aubrey Dollar, Rob Bogue in Backseat *© Truly Indie*

A FOUR LETTER WORD (Embrem Entertainment) Producers, Casper Andreas, Markus Goetze; Executive Producers, Simon Jorna, Mich Lyon; Director, Casper Andreas; Screenplay, Casper Andreas, Jesse Archer; Photography, Jon Fordham; Designer, Urvashi Satghare; Costumes, Martina Melendez; Music, Scott Starrett; Editor, Christina Kelly; Color; Not rated; 87 minutes; Release date: March 28, 2008. CAST: Jesse Archer (Luke), Charlie David (Stephen), Cory Grant (Zeke), Steven M. Goldsmith (Peter), JR Rolley (Derek), Virginia Bryan (Marilyn), Jeremy Gender (Mace), Allison Lane (Trisha), John Kaisner (Bart), William Hernandez (Silvio), Paul Haje (Bouncer at Bar), Aaron Star (Yoga Instructor), Jonathan P. Baird (Disgruntled Customer), Max Rishoj (Long John), Margaret RR Echeverria (Audrey), Paul Jessiman (South African Bar Patron), Michael Ferreira (Tes Ticles), Thomas Whitfield, Shon Middlebrocks (Hot Guys Outside Bar), Carol Carter (Sheila), Mike Stickland, Deirdre Brennan (AA Leaders), Robert Lehrer (Flamboyant Customer), Edison Farrow (Luke's Former Trick), Jamie Greco, Sue Tarlton (Customers), Alexander (Spinning Instructor), Michael Rogers (Guy in Staircase at Gym), Steve Deitsch (Man at AA Meeting), Kevin Kean Murphy (Drunk Man at AA Meeting), Patrick Askin (Sam), Miguel Pinzon (Restaurant Waiter), Andy Zeffer (Tripod), Michael Bamford (Jockhammer), Hal Moskowitz (SCA Leader), Macho Peinado (Nacho), Ginny Hikel (Nicky), Lair Paulsen (Lair), Artem Shcherbakov (Vlad), Darcey Levendis (Sarah), Jamie Bixby (Brandy), Mich Lyon (Michael), Scott Weston (Roger), Clover Honey (Drinking Drag Queen), Daniel Lynott (Military Drag Queen), Christopher Kenney (Edie), Garbeilla Bring (Carol), Shawn Mathis Gooden (Woman at AA Meeting), Emanuele Ancorini (Ryan), Alejandro Garvito (Carlos), Ames Gigounas (Dale), Adam Joseph (Singer at Bar), Austin Head (Uninterested Guy at Bar), Lorenzo Jimenez (Preppy Guy at Bar), Dixie (Jasper)

THE COOL SCHOOL (Arthouse Films) Producers/Screenplay, Kristine McKenna, Morgan Neville; Executive Producer, Cedd Moses; Director, Morgan Neville; Music, Dan Crane, William Ungerman; Editors, Morgan Neville, Dylan Robertson; Narrator, Jeff Bridges; from American Arts Documentary Foundation, CPF, ITVS, Oregon Public Broadcasting, Tremolo Productions; Color/Black and white; Not rated; 86 minutes; Release date: March 28, 2008. Documentary on Los Angeles' Ferus Gallery, which operated between 1957 and 1966; with Ed Ruscha, Dennis Hopper, Frank Gehry, Robert Irwin, Ed Moses, Billy Al Bengston, John Baldessari, Ken Price, Larry Bell, Walter Hopps, Irving Blum, Craig Kaufman, Ivan Karp, Peter Plagens, Dean Stockwell, Vivian Rowan, Harvey Hopps.

Cool School *© Art House Films*

SHELTER (here!/Regent) Producer, J.D. Disalvatore; Executive Produces, Anne Clements, Paul Colichman, Stephen P. Jarchow; Director/Screenplay, Jonah Markowitz; Photography, Joseph White; Designer, Denise Hudson, Gabor Norman; Costumes, Derek Lee; Music, J. Peter Robinson; Editor, Michael Hoface; Casting, Jason L. Wood; a GP Pictures production; Color; Rated R; 97 minutes; Release date: March 28, 2008. CAST: Trevor Wright (Zach), Brad Rowe (Shaun), Tina Holmes (Jeanne), Jackson Wurth (Cody), Ross Thomas (Gabe), Katie Walder (Tori), Albert Reed (Billy), Joy Gohring (Ellen), Matt Bushell (Alan), Don Margolin (John), Alejandro Patino (Moe), Caitlin Crosby (Shari), Alicia Sixtos (Amber), Sarah Peterson (Cashier), Joe Ferran (Surfer Boy #1), Tarek Zohdy (Drunk Partier), Robbi Chong (Receptionist), Tricia Pierce, Christina Blevins (Partiers), C-Sharp, Sybil Martinez (Art Students)

Logan Lerman, Aaron Eckhart in Meet Bill © First Look

Trevor Wright, Brad Rowe in Shelter © Regent Releasing

MEET BILL (First Look International) formerly *Bill*; Producers, John Penotti, Fisher Stevens, Matthew Rowlands; Executive Producers, Tim Williams, Aaron Eckhart; Directors, Melisa Wallack, Bernie Goldmann; Screenplay, Melisa Wallack; Photography, Peter Collister; Designer, Bruce Curtis; Costumes, Mari-An Ceo; Music, Edward Shearmur; Editors, Greg Hayden, Nick Moore; a GreeneStreet Films production; Dolby; Color; Rated R; 92 minutes; Release date: April 4, 2008. CAST: Aaron Eckhart (Bill), Jessica Alba (Lucy), Elizabeth Banks (Jess), Timothy Olyphant (Chip), Logan Lerman (The Kid), Holmes Osbourne (Mr. Jacoby), Craig Bierko (Sargeant), Kristen Wiig (Jane Whitman), Jason Sudeikis (Jim Whitman), Todd Louiso (John, Jr.), Sarah Arend (John, Jr.'s Assistant), Shirly Brener (Nurse), Marisa Coughlan (Laura), Reed Diamond (Paul), Paul Goetz (Tom the Fireworks Cashier), Ken Goth (Donny), Sarah Howard (Becky), Ana Lucasey (Sarah Sheldon), Julia Pace Mitchell (Dana), Joseph Patrick Moynihan (Jim), Ben Nordstrom (The Barista), Brad Schmidt (Jimmy), Elise Thorpe (Kelly), Andy Zou (Donald Choo)

SEX AND DEATH 101 (Anchor Bay) Producers, Cary Brokaw, Lizzie Friedman, Greg Little; Executive Producers, Aaron Craig Geller; Coproducer, Jerry P. Jacobs; Director/ Screenplay, Daniel Waters; Photography, Daryn Okada; Art Director, Helen Harwell; Costumes, Julia Caston; Music, Rolfe Kent; Editor, Trudy Ship; Casting, Andrea Stone; an Arclight Films presentation of an Avenue Pictures Prods., Sandbar Pictures production, in association with S and D Prods.; Dolby; Color; Rated R; 100 minutes; Release date: April 4, 2008. CAST: Simon Baker (Roderick Blank), Winona Ryder (Gilian/Nell), Leslie Bibb (Miranda), Mindy Cohn (Trixie), Julie Bowen (Fiona), Frances Fisher (Hope Hartwell), Tanc Sade (Beta), Patton Oswalt (Fred), Dash Mihok (Lester), Neil Flynn (Zack), Thom Bishop (Malcolm), Corinne Reilly (Lizzie), Sophie Monk (Cynthia Rose), Marshall Bell (Victor Rose III), Robert Patrick Benedict (Bow-Tie Bob), Natassia Malthe

(Bambi), Pollyanna McIntosh (Thumper), Indira Varma (Devon Server), Cindy Pickett (Roderick's Mother), Jessica Kiper (Carlotta Valdes), David Magidoff (Humorless Creep), Candice Coke (Greta Samsa), Amanda Walsh (Kathleen the Stewardess), Winter Ave Zoli (Alexis the Fast Food Beauty), Patrick Holland (Waiter), Siobhan Flynn (Esther Fenchel), Christopher Stapleton (Terry Fenchel), Lauren Michelle Hill (Amberette), Nicole Bilderback (Dr. Mirabella Stoen), David Bortolucci (Agent Baxter), Yara Brighton, Cate Ferguson (Death Nell Wannabes), William Caploe (Barista), Ingrid Coree (Waitress), Aaron Geller (Death Nell's First Victim), Zachary Gordon (Snot Nosed Kid), Marcus Alexander Hart (Comic Store Geek), Keram Malicki-Sánchez (DJ Bitchslap), Ashley McCarthy (Mona Farlow), Marshall McClean (Party Guy), Jonas Neal, Tom Nowicki (Frat Guys), Cean Okada (Homeless Woman), Retta (Ethel Waters), Bryan Ross (Xavier), Skyler James Sandak (Adorable Young Boy), Elisha Skorman (Helena Hartford), Heather Tocquigny (Catholic School Girl), Greg Travis (Magazine Vendor), Vitaliy Versace (Waiter)

Simon Baker (right) in Sex and Death 101 © Anchor Bay

JACK AND JILL VS. THE WORLD (Empera Pictures) Producer/Director, Vanessa Parise; Executive Producers, Scott J. Sloan, Michael Jaffe, Stephen Hays, Peter Graham, Jordan Gertner, Freddie Prinze, Jr., Nicholas Tabarrok; Coproducer, Robin Dunne; Screenplay, Peter Stebbings, Vanessa Parise; Photography, Manfred Guthe; Designer, Peter Cosco; Music, Jeremy Parise; Editors, Matthew Booth, David Ostry, Gareth C. Scales; Casting, Jason L. Wood; an Empera Pictures and Myriad Pictures and Lantern Lane and Urbantone Media Group presentation in association with 120dB Films/Myriad Pictures/Magnet Pictures/Lucky Dog Film Group/One for the Soul/a Darius Films production; American-Canadian; Dolby; Color; Rated PG-13; 89 minutes; Release date: April 4, 2008. CAST: Freddie Prinze, Jr. (Jack), Taryn Manning (Jill), Kelly Rowan (Kate), Vanessa Parise (Lucy), Robert Forster (Norman), Peter Stebbings (George), Hannah Lochner (Holly), Robin Dunne (Gary), Charles Martin Smith (Carlin), Claudia Besso (Melony), Darrin Brown (T-Bone), Lisa Ciara (Amberly), Rosa Laborde (Audition Girl), Sean T. MacDonald (Barry), Josh Milko (Guy in Beer Commercial), Ethan Penner (Wyatt), Julian Richings (Mr. Smith), Krista Sutton (Emily)

Taryn Manning, Freddie Prinze, Jr. in Jack and Jill vs. the World
© Empera Pictures

CHAOS THEORY (Warner Bros.) Producers, Frederic Golchan, Erica Westheimer; Executive Producer, Fred Westheimer; Coproducer, Barbara Kelly; Director, Marcos Siega; Screenplay, Daniel Taplitz; Photography, Ramsey Nickell; Designer, Sandy Cochrane; Costumes, Tish Monaghan; Music, Gilad Benamram; Editor, Nicholas Erasmus; Casting, Rick Montgomery; a Castle Rock Entertainment and Lone Star Film Group presentation of a Frederic Golchan Prods. production; Dolby; Panavision; Technicolor; Rated PG-13; 88 minutes; Release date: April 11, 2008. CAST: Ryan Reynolds (Frank Allen), Emily Mortimer (Susan Allen), Stuart Townsend (Buddy Endrow), Sarah Chalke (Paula Crowe), Mike Erwin (Ed), Constance Zimmer (Peg the Teacher), Matreya Fedor (Jesse Allen at 7 years), Elisabeth Harnois (Jesse Allen), Chris William Martin (Damon), Jovanna Huguet (Maid of Honor), Christopher Jacot (Simon, Best Man), Alessandro Juliani (Ken), Lisa Calder (Sherri), Ty Olsson (Evil Ferryman), Jocelyne Loewen (Pregnant Nancy), Patricia Idlette (Nurse), Denalda Williams (Head Nurse), David Berner (Frank's Doctor), Christine Chatelain (Tracey), Simon Chin (Target of Frank's Attack), Sarah Edmondson (Tequila Girl), Christina Twidale, Cassandra Brianne Hearle (Girls at Bar), Kevin Foley (Flower Delivery Boy), Donavon Stinson (Nevin), Daryl Shuttleworth (Officer Fields), Laurie Murdoch (Judge at Wedding)

Ryan Reynolds, Ty Olsson, Christine Chatelain in Chaos Theory
© Warner Bros.

THE TAKE (Screen Gems) Producers, Braxton Pope, Andrew Weiner; Executive Producers, Alexander Tabrizi, Matthew Hatchette, Stephen Quarles; Coproducer, John Saviano; Director, Brad Furman; Screenplay, Joshua Pate, Jonah Pate; Photography, Lukas Ettlin; Designer, Charissa Cardenas; Costumes, Estee Ochoa; Music, Chris Hajian; Music Supervisors, Eileen Hochberg, Willie Wisely; Editors, Edie Ichioka, Luis Caballar; an Ithaka Films production; Dolby; Panavision; Color; Rated R; 96 minutes; Release date: April 11, 2008. CAST: John Leguizamo (Felix De La Pena), Rosie Perez (Marina De La Pena), Tyrese Gibson (Adell Baldwin), Bobby Canavale (Agent Steve Perelli), Matthew Hatchette (Agent Forest Baxter), Yul Yazquez (Marco Ruiz), Carlos Sanz (Det. Victor Martinez), Jake Muxworthy (Jimmy Grannis), Laurence Mason (Curtis Fellows), Roger Guenveur Smith (Peter Reese), Jessica Steinbaum (Rosey De La Pena), David Castro (Bartender), Taylor Gray (Javy De La Pena), Tina Adams, Mari Haig (Doctors), Nick Rey Angelus (Hospital Homeboy), Curt Bouril (Fireman), Cass Alexander Brown, Greg Siff (Coroners), Victor Buno (Preacher), Cristos (Barry Munoz), Kevin Dunigan (Ellis Hawk), Bryeon Earle (Surgical Nurse), Christian George (Bill White), Pride Grinn (Tony Oppenheimer), Julanne Chidi Hill (Nikki Singletary), Astrelle Johnquest (Nurse), Ray Latulipe (Jim Clark), Joshua LeBar (Officer), Margarita Lugo (Dolores Furcal), Aris Mendoza (Bonnie), James Molina (Antonio Cruz), Juan Pacheco (Manuel Padilla), Jerrod Paige (Cop), Russell Peters (Dr. Sharma), Danielle Sapia (Jimmy's Girlfriend), Sam Upton (Phillip Morrison)

YOUNG & RESTLESS IN CHINA (Intl. Film Circuit) Producers, Sue Williams, Kathryn Dietz; Executive Producers, Judith Vecchione, Michael Sullivan, David Fanning; Director/Screenplay, Sue Williams; Photography, Bestor Cram, Jeremy Leach, Bill Turnley, Scott Anger; Music, Jason Kao Hwang; Editor, Howard Sharp; Narrator, Ming Wen; an Ambrica production; Color; HD; Not rated; 106 minutes; Documentary focusing on four years in the lives of nine Chinese expatriates who returned to their country in order to take advantage of lucrative business opportunities; with Lu Dong, Ben Wu, Wei Zhanyan, Wang Xiaolei, Zhang Jingjing, Xu Weimin, Zhang Yao, Yang Haiyan, Miranda Hong.

THE DHAMMA BROTHERS (Balcony) Producers, Jenny Phillips, Andrew Kukura, Anne Marie Stein; Executive Producers, Nicole Guillemet, Geralyn Dreyfous, Bestor Cram; Coproducer, Peter Broderick; Directors/Screenplay, Jenny Phillips, Andrew Kukura, Anne Marie Stein; a Freedom Behind Bars production, in association with Northern Lights Prods., the Lionheart Foundation; Color; HD; Not rated; 76 minutes; Release date: April 11, 2008. Documentary on 36 hardened criminals, incarcerated in Alabama's Donaldson Correction Facility, who participative in an intensive, 10-day Buddhist meditation course; with Grady Bankhead, Edward Johnson, Ben Oryang, Rick Smith, Jonathan Crowley, Bruce Stewart, Ron Cavanaugh.

The Dhamma Brothers © *Balcony Releasing*

NEVER FOREVER (Arts Alliance America) Producers, Joon Dong Lee, Chang Dong Lee, Andrew Fierberg; Executive Producers, Jong Jin Baek, Sang Han Shin; Co-Executive Producers, Steven Shainberg, Christina Weiss Lurie, Yung Guen Kang, Chul Woo Kim; Coproducers, Kyung Hyun Kim, Brian Bell, Steven Nam; Director/Screenplay, Gina Kim; Photography, Matthew Clark; Designer, Lucio Seixas; Costumes, Tere Duncan; Music, Michael Nyman; Editor, Pete Beaudreau; Casting, Heidi Levitt, Paul Schnee; a Prime Entertainment presentation of a Vox3 Films and Now Films production; American-South Korean; Dolby; Technicolor; Not rated; 101 minutes; Release date: April 11, 2008. CAST: Vera Farmiga (Sophie), Jung-woo Ha (Jihah), David McInnis (Andrew), Eric L. Abrams (Officer #1), Richard Chang (Waiter), Clem Cheung (Plain-clothed Detective), Robert Dahey (Laundromat Owner), Joseph DeBona (Jihah's Co-Worker), Lenny Levi (Cab Driver), Alex Manette (Jesse), Jackson Pace (Adam), Hettienne Park (Ming Ming), Kari Swenson Riely (Miriam), Shirley Roeca (Tania), Asa Somers (Rich)

Jung-woo Ha, Vera Farmiga in Never Forever © *Arts Alliance America*

REMEMBER THE DAZE (First Look/Freestyle) formerly *The Beautiful Ordinary*; Producers, Judd Payne, Matthew Rhodes, Jess Manafort; Executive Producers, Jim Dominello, Amanda Van Sickle; Director/Screenplay, Jess Manafort; Photography, Steve Gainer; Designer, John D. Kretschmer; Costumes, Emmy Taylor; Music, Dustin O'Halloran; Music Supervisor, Karyn Rachtman; Editors, Meg Reticker, Larry Bock; Casting, Mary Vernieu, Venus Kanani; a Persistent Entertainment, Mirror Cube Films presentation; Dolby; Technicolor; 35mm-to-DV; Rated R; 101 minutes; Release date: April 11, 2008. CAST: Amber Heard (Lucy), Alexa Vega (Holly), Leighton Meester (Tori), Melonie Diaz (Brianne), Douglas Smith (Pete), Katrina Begin (Sylvia), Charles Chen (Thomas), Sunny Doench (Mrs. Turner), Caroline Dollar (Kiki), Shahine Ezell (Eddie), Lyndsay Fonseca (Dawn), Eric Santiago, Robert X. Golphin (Boys), Duncan M. Hill (Mod's Classmate), Aaron Himelstein (Riley), Max Hoffman (Zack), Thomas Holmes III (Ponte), Wesley Jonathan (Biz), Belinda Keller (Mrs. Cherry), Brett Kelley (West Po Boy), Taylor Kowalski (Andrew), Bill Ladd (Mr. Shapiro), Brie Larson (Angie), Stella Maeve (Lighty), Chris Marquette (Felix), Sean Marquette (Mod), Marnette Patterson (Stacey Cherry), Elizabeth Roberts (Miss Evelyn), John Robinson (Bailey), Christopher Shand (Clifford), Foster Solomon (Mr. Cooter), David Temple (Mr. Ford), Khleo Thomas (Dylan), Ed Wagenseller (Mr. Turner), Josh Waters (Hanky), Michael Welch (Stephen)

CONSTANTINE'S SWORD (First Run Features/Red Envelope) Producers, Oren Jacoby, James Carroll, Michael Solomon, Betsy West; Executive Producers, James Carroll, Oren Jacoby; Coproducer, Donald Cutler; Director, Oren Jacoby; Screenplay, James Carroll, Oren Jacoby; Based on the book by James Carroll; Photography, Bob Richman; Music, Joel Goodman; Editor, Kate Hirson; a Metropole Film Board presentation, in association with Prologue Prods. of a Storyville Films production; Dolby; Color; HD-to-35mm; Not rated; 93 minutes; Release date: April 18, 2008. Documentary in which author James Carroll journeys to the U.S. Air Force Base in Colorado Springs and to Rome to examine the link between organized religion and military power; with James Carroll, and the voices of Phillip Bosco, Natasha Richardson, Liev Schreiber, and Eli Wallach.

Constantine's Sword © *First Run Features*

EXPELLED: NO INTELLIGENCE ALLOWED (Premise Media Corp.) Producers, Logan Craft, Walt Ruloff, John Sullivan; Director/Photography, Nathan Frankowski; Screenplay, Kevin Miller, Ben Stein; Music, Andy Hunter; Editor, Simon Tondeur; Lead Animator, Joseph Condeelis; Animation, Light Prods., Out of Our Mind Studios; a Premise Media presentation of a Rampant Films production; Dolby; Color/black and white; Rated PG; 97 minutes; Release date: April 18, 2008. Documentary attempting to discredit Darwinism; with Ben Stein, Richard Sternberg, Mark Souder, Guillermo Gonzalez, Caroline Crocker, Richard

Dawkins, P.Z. Myers, Eugenie Scott, Christopher Hitchens, Michael Shermer, John Lennox, David Berlinski, Alister McGrath, Stephen C. Meyer.

Ben Stein in Expelled: No Intelligence Allowed
© *Rocky Mountain Pictures*

PATHOLOGY (MGM) Producers, Gary Lucchesi, Tom Rosenberg, Richard Wright, Gary Gilbert, Mark Neveldine, Brian Taylor, Skip Williamson; Executive Producers, Marc Bienstock, Eric Reid, Barrett Stuart, Yan Fisher-Romanovsky, Phyllis Carlyle; Director, Marc Scholermann; Screenplay, Mark Neveldine, Brian Taylor; Photography, Ekkehart Pollack; Designer, Jerry Fleming; Costumes, Frank Helmer; Music, Johannes Kobilke, Robert Williamson; Editor, Todd E. Miller; Special Effects Makeup, Ken Niederbaumer, Steve E. Anderson; Casting, Nancy Nayor Battino, Kelly Martin Wagner; a Lakeshore Entertainment/Camelot Pictures presentation; Dolby; Super 35 Widescreen; Color; Rated R; 94 minutes; Release date: April 18, 2008. CAST: Milo Ventimiglia (Ted Grey), Michael Weston (Jake Gallo), Alyssa Milano (Gwen Williamson), Lauren Lee Smith (Juliette Bath), Johnny Whitworth (Griffin Cavenaugh), John de Lancie (Dr. Quentin Morris), Mei Melançon (Catherine Ivy), Keir O'Donnell (Ben Stravinsky), Buddy Lewis (Harper Johnson), Dan Callahan (Chip Bentwood), Larry Drake (Fat Bastard), Med Abrous (Young Pathology Resident), Alan Blumenfeld (Mr. Williamson), Gary Buckner (Motherfu—er), Jeb Burris (Worker), Eurydice Davis (Hooker), Jarvis George (ICU Doctor), Anne Girard (Donna, Ben's Date), Eric Kaldor (Homeless Lunatic), Keith Morris (Hitchhiker), Kate Mulligan (Woman on Bus), Don Smith (Man on Bus), Yvonne Mojica-Nelson (Hispanic IC Nurse), Deborah Pollack (Mrs. Williamson), Cheryl Starbuck-Rocca (Panicked Woman), Sam Witwer (Party Boy)

Milo Ventimiglia, Lauren Lee Smith in Pathology © *MGM*

ZOMBIE STRIPPERS (Triumph/Stage 6) Producers, Andrew Golov, Angela Lee, Larry Schapiro; Executive Producer, Michael J. Zampino; Director/Screenplay/ Photography, Jay Lee; Designer, Sara Kugelmass; Costumes, Brendan Cannon; Special Effects, Chris Dawson, Jonathan Kombrinck; Makeup Effects, Patric Magee; Stunts, Bobby C. King; a Scream Headquarters production; Dolby; Color; Rated R; 94 minutes; Release date: April 18, 2008. CAST: Robert Englund (Ian Essko), Jenna Jameson (Kat), Roxy Saint (Lillith), Joey Medina (Paco), Shamron Moore (Jeannie), Penny Drake (Sox), Jennifer Holland (Jessy), John Hawkes (Davis), Jeannette Sousa (Berenge), Whitney Anderson (Gaia), Carmit Levite (Madame Blavatski), Calvin Green (Cole), Zak Kilberg (Brydflough), Catero Colbert (Major Camus), Jen Alex Gonzalez (Lt. Ryker), Laura Bach (Sassy Sue), Jessica Custodio (Kwan), Billy Beck (Rincon), Travis Wood (Oxnard), Brad Milne (Dr. Chushfeld), Shannon Malone (Dr. Genet), Adam Lamas (Victim), Gary Kraus (Burt), Jim Roof (Sleezy Sammy), Adam Smith (Jimmy), Asante Jones (Terrence)

THE FIRST SATURDAY IN MAY (Truly Indie) Producers, Brad Hennegan, John Hennegan, Ellen Dux; Executive Producers, Bruce Carusi, Susan Altamore Carusi; Coproducer, Karen Hennegan; Co-Executive Producers, Steve Bell, Eugene Johns, Aron Schnell; Directors/Photography, Brad Hennegan, John Hennegan; Screenplay, Brad Hennegan, John Hennegan, Mark Krewatch; Editors, Brad Hennegan, John Hennegan, Tamara McDonough; Music, The Ryan Brothers; a Hennegan Brothers production, in association with Churchill Downs; Color; HD; Not rated; 100 minutes; Release date: April 18, 2008. Documentary following six trainers hoping to compete their thoroughbreds in the 2006 Kentucky Derby; with Frank Amonte, Michael Matz, Dan Hendricks, Kiaran McLaughlin, Bob Holthus, Chuck Chambers, Dale Romans.

Scott Speedman, Willem Dafoe in Anamorph © *IFC Films*

ANAMORPH (IFC) Producer, Marissa McMahon; Director, H.S. Miller; Screenplay, H.S. Miller, Tom Phelan; Photography, Fred Murphy; Designer, Jackson De Govia; Costumes, Eric Daman; Music, Reinhold Heil, Johnny Klimek; Editor, Geraud Brisson; Senior Visual Effects Supervisor, Richard Edlund; Casting, Kerry Barden, Suzanne Crowley, Billy Hopkins, Paul Schnee; a Bandito Entertainment presentation of a Kamala films production; Dolby; Panavision; Color; Rated R; 103 minutes; Release date: April 18, 2008. CAST: Willem Dafoe (Stan), Scott Speedman (Carl Uffner), Peter Stormare (Blair Collet), Clea Du Vall (Sandy Stickland), James Rebhorn (Chief Llewellyn Brainard), Amy Carlson (Alexandra Fredericks), Yul Vazquez (Jorge Ruiz), Don Harvey (Killer), Paul Lazar (Medical Examiner), Edward Hibbert (Gallery Owner), Dennis Albanese, Martin Pfefferkorn (AA Members), Amir Arison (Criminal Profiler), Robert McKay, Michael Buscemi (Detectives), Desiree Casado (Teenage Checkout Girl), Jordan Charney (Review Board Chairman), Tandy Cronyn (Moderator), Monique Curnen (Student), Elizabeth West, Stephen Daniels (Reporters), Paz de la Huerta (Young Woman), Mick Foley (Antique Store Owner), Lolita Foster (Drink Waitress), Edwin

Freeman (Police Officer), Robin Goldsmith (Stone-Faced Detective), Malcolm Goodwin (Museum Guard), Deborah Harry (Neighbor), Marcia Haufrecht (Diner Waitress), Allison Hope (Crime Scene Photo Victim), Robert C. Kirk (Heavy-Set Detective), Tim Lamendola (Off-Duty Detective), Samantha MacIvor (Crystal), Lucy Martin (Uptight Woman), David McDaniel, Virginia Wing (Board Members), Sharrieff Pugh (ECT Technician), Nicolas Quilter (Dead Man at Tugboat), Gary Ray (Officer #1), Cassandra Seidenfeld (NYPD Officer), Barbara Sicuranza (Forensic Technician), Ashley Spring (Jeff Sarno), Paul Sutt (Hanged Man), Billy Wheelan (Young Man)

DEAL (MGM/Seven Arts) Producers, Michael Arata, Marc Weinstock, Steven Austin; Executive Producers, Scott Lazar, Nzinga N. Garvey, Richard Gabai, Michael Amato; Coproducers, Albert J. Salzer, John J. Anderson; Director, Gil Cates, Jr.; Screenplay, Gil Cates, Jr., Marc Weinstock; Photography, Thomas M. Harting; Designer, Frank J. Zito III; Costumes, Liz Staub; Music, Peter Rafelson; Editors, Eric Strand, Jonathan Cates; Casting, Barbara Fiorentino, Wendy Weidman, Rebecca Mangieri; a Seven Arts/TAG Entertainment production; Dolby; Technicolor; Rated PG-13; 86 minutes; Release date: April 25, 2008. CAST: Burt Reynolds (Tommy Vinson), Bret Harrison (Alex Stillman), Shannon Elizabeth (Michelle), Charles Durning (Charlie Adler), Jennifer Tilly (Karen "Razor" Jones), Maria Mason (Helen Vinson), Gary Grubbs (Mr. Stillman), Caroline McKinely (Mrs. Stillman), Brandon Olive (Ben Thomas), Jon "JT" Eyes (Mike "Double Diamond" Jackson), J.D. Evermore (Tex Button), Michael Sexton, Vincent Van Patten, Phil Laak, Antonio Esfanfiari, Courtney Friel, Scott Lazar, Isabelle Mercier, Chris Moneymaker, Joe Hachem, Greg Raymer (Themselves), Wallace Merck (Barry), Dustin Evan (Jordan Stillman), Flloyd Lewis, Evelyn Mulilns (Chatter People), Neal Rivet (Jesse), Marcus Stanley (Kevin Small), Preston Lorio (Matt), Kenny Bordes (Wally), Tayana Kanavka, Irina Beskaravaynaya (Russian Girls), Larry Beron (Front Desk Clerk), Tony Bentley (Maitre D'), Rio Hackford (Chasen), Summer Lee (Ann Kim), Tommy Perna, Lyle Brocato (New Players), Ritchie Montgomery (Man at Bar), Sherri Marina (Chaniqua), Michael Arata (Passerby), Amanda Jane Columbus (Girl at Bar), John Lambremont, Jr., Billy Slaughter (Announcers)

Bret Harrison in Deal © *MGM/Seven Arts*

DARE NOT WALK ALONE (Indican) Producers, Stephen Cobb, Jeremy Dean, Richard Mergener; Executive Producers, Stephen Cobb, Chey Cobb; Coproducer, H. James Gilmore; Director/Screenplay, Jeremy Dean; Photography, Russell Brownley, Jeremy Dean, Adrian Phillips; Editors, Russell Brownley, Jeremy Dean; a DNWA production in association with Acadia Pictures; Color; 16mm; DV; Not rated; 78 minutes; Release date: April 25, 2008. Documentary on Dr. Martin Luther King's June 1964 crusade against St. Augustine, Florida's segregation laws; with Andrew Young, Errol Jones, James Brock, Christoff, Corrine Brown, David Nolan.

BOMB IT (Flying Cow) Producers, Tracy Wares, Jon Reiss, Jeffrey Levy-Hinte, Kate Christensen; Coproducers, Lia Garibay, Arnel San Pedro; Director, Jon Reiss; Photography, Tracy Wares; Music, Disco D, Mathematics, Illfonics; Music Supervisor, David Garcia; Animation, Jon Gutman, Matt Clauson, Beau DeSilva, Brian Whip, Samir Arghandiwall, James Jaculina; Produced in association with Antidote Films; Color; DV; Not rated; 93 minutes; Release date: April 25, 2008. Documentary on the world of graffiti artists; with Cornbread, Taki 183, Zephry, T-Kid 170, Pose II, Daim, Scage, Blek le Rat, Sixe, Os Gemeos, DJ Lady Tribe, Shepard Fairey, Chaz Bojorquez, Very One, Ron English, Faith 47.

Bomb It © *Flying Cow*

A PLUMM SUMMER (Freestyle Releasing) Producers, Frank Antonelli, Caroline Zelder; Executive Producers, Scott Erickson, Lisa Guerrero; Coproducer, Doug Metzger; Director, Caroline Zelder; Screenplay, Caroline Zelder, Frank Antonelli, T.J. Lynch; Photography, Mark Vargo; Designer, Alan E. Muraoka; Costumes, Nola Roller; Music, Tom Hiel; Music Supervisor, Frank Antonelli; Editor, Jonathan Lucas; Casting, Jory Weitz; a Home Team, Fairplay Pictures production; Dolby; Technicolor; Rated PG; 101 minutes; Release date: April 25, 2008. CAST: William Baldwin (Mick Plumm), Lisa Guerrero (Roxie Plumm), Owen Pearce (Rocky Plumm), Chris J. Kelly (Elliott Plumm), Henry Winkler (Happy Herb), Brenda Strong (Viv), Peter Scolari (Agent Hardigan), Rick Overton (Agent Brinkman), Morgan Flynn (Haley Dubois), Jeff Daniels (Narrator), Tim Quill (Wayne Dubois), Richard Riehle (Art Bublin), Clint Howard (Binky the Clown), Gavin Black (Wally), Ben Trotter (Orin), John Hosking (Dick Spreen), Gregg Bello (Cookie), Steve Altman (Dirty Pat), Quinn Knox (Dave), Ian Lacy (Billy the Bully), Brian Schweitzer (Sheriff Strunk), Noa Benperlas (Clovie), Rusty Hendrickson (Aldo), Fuschia Sumner (Marsha), Jessica John (Channel 8 Newscaster), Annie Semler (Martie), Benjamin Dawley-Anderson (Ice Cream Man), Devan Leder (Kidnapper #1)

Chris J. Kelly, William Baldwin in A Plumm Summer
© *Freestyle Releasing*

WITHOUT THE KING (First Run Features) Producers, Paolo Mendoza, Michael Skolnik; Executive Producer, Ted Sarandos; Director, Michael Skolnik; Photography, James Adolphus; Music, Mark Kilian; Editor, Martha Skolnik; a Red Envelope Entertainment presentation in association with Soze Prods. of a Red Envelope Entertainment production; Color; DV; Not rated; 84 minutes; Release date: April 25, 2008. Documentary on Swaziland, the only absolute monarchy in the world, ruled by King Mswati III; with King Mswati III, Princess Sikhanyiso.

Princess Sikhanyiso, King Mswati III in Without the King
© *First Run Features*

STANDARD OPERATING PROCEDURE (Sony Classics) Producers, Julie Bilson Ahlberg, Errol Morris; Executive Producers, Jeff Skoll, Diane Weyermann, Martin Levin, Julia Sheehan, Robert Fernandez; Director/Screenplay, Errol Morris; Photography, Robert Chappell, Robert Richardson; Designer, Steve Hardie; Costumes, Marim Draghici; Music, Danny Elfman; Editors, Karen Schmeer, Andy Grieve, Brad Fuller, Daniel Mooney, Steven Hathaway, Charles Silver; Casting, Jeff Rosenman; a Participant Media presentation; Dolby; Panavision; Deluxe color; Rated R; 117 minutes; Release date: April 25, 2008. Documentary examining the abuse of Iraqi prisoners at Abu Ghraib prison; with Javal Davis, Ken Davis, Tony

Diaz, Tim Dugan, Lynndie England, Jeffery Frost, Megan Ambuhl Graner, Sabrina Harman, Janis Karpinski, Roman Krol, Brent Pack, Jeremy Sivitz.

Ken Davis in Standard Operating Procedure © *Sony Classics*

VIVA (Anna Biller Prods.) Producer/Director/Screenplay/Editor/Designer/ Costumes, Anna Biller; Photography, C. Thomas Lewis; Coproducer, Jared Sanford; Color; Not rated; 120 minutes; Release date: May 2, 2008. CAST: Anna Biller (Barbi), Jared Sanford (Mark), Bridget Brno (Sheila), Chad England (Rick), Marcus DeAnda (Clyde), John Klemantaski (Arthur), Barry Morse (Sherman), Paolo Davanza (Elmer), Cole Chipman (Reeves)

Marcus DeAnda, Anna Biller in Viva © *Anna Biller Prods.*

HOLLYWOOD CHINESE (Deep Focus Prods.) Producer/Director/Screenplay/ Editor, Arthur Dong; Photography, Hiroki Miyano, Robert Shepard; Music, Mark Adler; Color/black and white; Not rated; 90 minutes; Release date: May 2, 2008. Documentary on the depiction of the Chinese in Hollywood Films; with Turhan Bey, Joan Chen, Tsai Chin, James Hong, David Henry Hwang, Stephen Gong, Nancy Kwan, Christopher Lee, Ang Lee, James Leong, Jr., Justin Lin, Lisa Lu, Luise Rainer, James Shigeta, Amy Tan, Wayne Wang, B.D. Wong.

Hollywood Chinese © *Deep Focus Prods.*

THE FAVOR (Seventh Art) Producers, Eva Aridjis, Heather Greene; Executive Producers, Elisa Salinas, Ricardo Salinas, Howard Gertler; Director/Screenplay, Eva Aridjis; Photography, Andrij Parekh; Designer, Edwige Geminel; Costumes, Tere Duncan; Music, Danny Hole; Music Supervisor, Linda Cohen; Editor, Mathilde Bonnefoy; Casting, Ali Farrell; a Dark Night Pictures presentation in association with Television Azteca and Process; American-Mexican; Dolby; Color; Not rated; 110 minutes; Release date: May 2, 2008. CAST: Frank Wood (Lawrence), Ryan Donowho (Johnny), Paige Turco (Caroline), Isidra Vega (Mariana), Paul Lazar (Mr. Smith), Michael Higgins (Mr. Ritter), Luke Robertson (Young Lawrence), Laura Breckenridge (Young Caroline), Wally Dunn (Dr. Charles), Sterling K. Brown (Policeman #1), Jesse Kelly (Carter), Aldo Perez (Harris), Marceline Hugot (History Teacher), Aurelia Thierree (Photo Shop Girl), Richard M. Davidson (Principal Foreman), Susan Willis (Old Lady), Corey Flaska (Roger), Jeremiah Clancy (Doctor), Justin Christopher (Family Court Officer), Pete Barker (Priest), Donald Eric Cumming (Boy with Iguana), Mario Mendoza (Mariana's Father), C.C. Loveheart (Woman on Phone), Jayne Haynes (Waitress in Diner), Annette Arnold (Young Woman), Emma Bell (Jenny), Brian Delate (Det. Stewart), Pablo Hernandez (Mauricio), Cassidy Hinkle (Jeannie)

UNSETTLED (Resonance Pictures) Producer/Director/Screenplay/Editor, Adam Hootnick; Coproducers, Mickey Elkeles, Tony Felzen; Photography, Mickey Elkeles, Adam Hootnick; Music, Jon Lee; Color; DigitBeta; Not rated; 81 minutes; Release date: May 9, 2008. Documentary in which six Israelis reflect upon the 2005 withdrawal of settlers from the Gaza Strip.

Unsettled © *Resonance Pictures*

THE MEMORY THIEF (Seventh Art) Producers, Gil Kofman, Marika Van Adelsberg; Executive Producers, Amy Ziering, Marilyn Ziering; Coproducers, Matt Abrams, Christine Sheaks; Director/Screenplay, Gil Kofman; Photography, Richard Rutkowski; Designer, Marika Van Adelsberg; Costumes, Kiki Van Adelsberg; Music, Ted Reichman; Editor, Curtiss Clayton; Casting, Christine Sheaks; a Jane Doe Films presentation in association with Bad Habit Films; Color; DV; Not rated; 95 minutes; Release date: May 9, 2008. CAST: Mark Webber (Lukas), Rachel Miner (Mira), Jerry Adler (Mr. Zweig), Allan Rich (Zvi Birnbaum), Peter Jacobson (Mr. Freeman), Douglas Spain (Dominic), Stella Hudgens (Amanda), Patrick Bauchau (Mr. Fisher), Kevin Breznahan (The Clerk), Farah Afnan (Nurse), June Claman (Zvi's Wife), Blu de Golyer (Skinhead), Chris Ellis (Mr. DeSilva), Brian Patrick Farrell (Mort), Brent David Fraser (Pound Custodian), Jeremy Fultz (Intern #1), Mary Pat Gleason (Hospital Patient), Carlos Gómez (Mr. Celeste), Angie Gregory (Restaurant Patron), Luck Hari (Mrs. Sarkar), Kim Harper (Mrs. Feldman), Ricky Harris (Hearse Driver), Matt Kahn (Dwayne's Friend), Jamie Kaler, Blaine Pate (Cameramen), Pete Kasper (Angry Driver), Valerie Long, Ginger Williams (Receptionists), Bess Meisler (Joanna Kaufman), Kristin Mente (Mom in Park), Ralf Mosig (German Tourist), Amelia Mulkey (Teacher), Elizabeth Mulkey (Kristina), Art Oughton (Moviegoer), Glen Page (Tattoo Artist), Benjamin John Parrillo (Mercedes Driver), Richard Riehle (Judaica Clerk), Paul Schackman (Orthodox Jew), Vikrum Shah (Mr. Sarkar), Jane Silvia (Librarian), Patrick Stack (Senior Resident), Richard Stobie (Mr. Milewicz), Jennie Ventriss (Survivor), Josh Wheeler (Dwayne), Mitchell Whitfield (Tom)

BLOODLINE (Cinema Libre Studio) Producer, René Barnett; Executive Producers, William Billingsley, René Barnett, Bruce Burgess; Director/Screenplay, Bruce Burgess; Photography, Sebastian Rich; Music, Miriam Cutler; Editor, Daniel E. Brown; a 1244 Films production; Dolby; Color; Not rated; 113 minutes; Release date: May 9, 2008. Documentary examining the Prior of Sion, a secret society claiming to hold evidence of the marriage of Mary Magdalene and Jesus Christ; with Ben Hammott.

Ben Hammott in Bloodline © *Cinema Libre Studio*

THE BABYSITTERS (Peace Arch Entertainment) Producers, Cora Olson, Jennifer Dubin, Jason Dubin, John Leguizamo, Kathy DeMarco; Executive Producers, John Portnoy, Nick Thurlow, Todd Williams, Chira Cassel, Laura Lynn Knight, Scott Macaulay, Robin O'Hara; Director/Screenplay, David Ross; Photography, Michael McDonough; Designer, Ray Kluga; Music, Chad Fischer; Editor, Zene Baker; an O.D.D. Entertainment, Upload Films production in association with Rebel Films, Forensic Films; Dolby; Deluxe color; Rated R; 90 minutes; Release date: May 9, 2008. CAST: Katherine Waterston (Shirley Lyner), John Leguizamo (Michael Beltran), Cynthia Nixon (Gail Beltran), Andy Comeau (Jerry Tuchman), Lauren Birkell (Melissa Brown), Louisa Krause (Brenda Woodberg), Denis O'Hare (Stan Lyner), Halley Wegryn Gross (Nadine Woodberg), Ann Dowd (Tammy Lyner), Ethan "Johnnie" Phillips (Mark Wessler), Alexandra Daddario (Barbara

Yates), Spencer Treat Clark (Scott Miral), Jason Dubin (George), Chria Cassel (Health Teacher), Paul Borghese (Joe the Cook)

POULTRYGEIST: NIGHT OF THE CHICKEN DEAD (Troma) Producers, Andy Deemer, Kiel Walker; Executive Producers, Lloyd Kaufman, Michael Herz, Patricia Swinney Kaufman; Director, Lloyd Kaufman; Screenplay, Gabriel Friedman, Dan Bova, Lloyd Kaufman; Photography, Brendan Flynt; Designer, Alyssa Hill, Doug Markuson, Jr.; Costumes, Holly Hojnkoski, Anna Chiaretta Lavatelli; Music, Duggie Banas, Jason "Shack" Kozun; Editor, Gabriel Friedman; Special Effects, Tom Devlin, David Molloy, Scott Fields; Makeup FX, Xochitl Gomez, Chris Bowen; Choreographer, Maria Gismondi; Color; Not rated; 103 minutes; Release date: May 9, 2008. CAST: Jason Yachanin (Arbie), Kate Graham (Wendy), Allyson Sereboff (Micki), Robin L. Watkins (General Lee Roy), Joshua Olatunde (Denny), Caleb Emerson (Carl, Jr.), Rose Ghavami (Humus), Khalid Rivera (Paco Bell), Joe Fleishaker (Jared), Faith Sheehan (Little Katie), Tessa Lew (Katie's Mother), Brian Cheverie (Father O'Houlihan), Ron Jeremy (Crazy Ron), Martin Victor (Chief Whats-His-Face), John Karyus (Graveyard Peeper), Debbie Rochon (Famous Actress Hit by Beer), Glenn Lasky (Colonel Kluck), Jamie Greco (Big Mitch), Kelsey Ruvolo (Humus Undressed), James J. Alfieri (TV News Reporter), Zack Beins (Long John), Jay Best (Lonely Guy), Paul Bradley ("Oy … It's that #%**!@! General" Protestor/Chicken Zombie), Michael Ciesla (Geroni-Larry), Arvid Cristina (Hardee), Tyler Dolph (Puking Guy), D.J. Markuson (Eyes Pecked Out Massacre Victim), Alexander S. McBryde (Chicken Zombie in Wife Beater T-Shirt), Kevin Sean Michaels (Puked-On Zombie), Anna Gabriella Olson (C.L.A.M.), Ruth Phelps (Red Lobster), Louie Podalski (Spine Boy Customer), Simon Savory (Fancy Pants), Joshua Samuel Strauss (Poparrazzi/Neckbrace Chicken Zombie), Karen Tuccio (Protesting Chant Leader)

Joshua Olatunde in Poultrygeist © Troma

SURFWISE (Magnolia) Producers, Graydon Carter, Tommy Means, Matthew Weaver, Jonathan Paskowitz; Executive Producers, Todd Wagner, Mark Cuban, Joana Vicente, Jason Kliot; Coproducers, Tony Lord, Jonathan Pine; Director, Doug Pray; Photography, Dave Homcy; Music, John Dragonetti; Music Supervisor, Janet Billig Rich; Editor, Lasse Jarvi; an HDNet Films production in association with Prospect Pictures, Mekanism and Consolidated Documentaries; Dolby; Color; HD Cam; Rated R; 93 minutes; Release date: May 9, 2008. Documentary on the Paskowitz family's obsession with surfing; with Dorian "Doc" Paskowitz, Juliette Paskowitz, Jonathan Paskowitz, Abraham Paskowitz, Israel Paskowitz, Moses Paskowitz, Adam Paskowitz, Salvador Paskowitz, Navah Paskowitz, Joshua Paskowitz.

The Paskowitz Family in Surfwise © Magnolia Films

REFUSENIK (The Foundation for Documentary Projects) Producer/Director/Screenplay, Laura Bialis; Photography, John Ealer, Sarah Levy; Music, Charles Bernstein; Editors, Allan Holzman, Tchavdar Georgiev; Dolby; Color/black and white; Not rated; 117 minutes; Release date: May 9, 2008. Documentary about the thirty-year international movement to free Soviet Jews.

Refusenik © Foundation for Documentary

VICE (41) Producer, Matthew Robert Kelly; Executive Producers, Michael Madsen, Graham Taylor, Michael Tan, Daryl Hannah; Director/Screenplay, Raul Sanchez Inglis; Photography, Andrzej Sekula; Designer, Michael Nemirsky; Costumes, Sheila Bingham; Music, Cliff Martinez; Editor, Kelly Herron; Casting, Lindsay Chag; an Arcview Entertainment production; Color; Rated R; 98 minutes; Release date: May 9, 2008. CAST: Michael Madsen (Walker), Daryl Hannah (Salt), Mykelti Williamson (Sampson), Mark Boone Junior (Bugsby), Kurupt (TJ Greene), John Cassini (Travalino), Nicholas Lee (Jenkins), Aaron Pearl (Chambers), Matthew Robert Kelly (Zelco), Peter LaCroix (Coburg), Emy Aneke (Darius), Betty Linde (Mom), Justine Warrington (Hooker), Martin Cummins (Agent Arnaud), Frank Cassini (Agent Linder), Darcy Laurie (Spoonie), Brenda Crichlow (Jackie), Anna Galvin (Gwen), Vanessa Tomasino (Paula), Donny Lucas (Milo), Sean Owen Roberts (Junkie), Brenda Matthews (Heather), Lynda Boyd (Madame), Alberta Mayne (Chris), Brandon Jay McLaren (Gangbanger Driver), Matt Ward

(Gangbanger Passenger), Chelah Horsdal (Woman in Elevator), Benjamin Easterday (Thug), Dave Collette (24 Hour Cop), Kyle Cassie (Drunk Guy), Josh Kamau (Cook)

THE TRACEY FRAGMENTS (ThinkFilm) Producer, Sarah Timmins; Executive Producers, Paul Barkin, Phyllis Laing; Director, Bruce McDonald; Screenplay, Maureen Medved, based on her novel; Photography, Steve Cosens; Designer, Ingrid Jurek; Costumes, Lea Carlson; Music, Broken Social Scene; Editors, Jeremiah Munce, Gareth C. Scales; Conceptual Design, Jeremiah Munce; Casting, Sara Kay, Jenny Lewis; a Shadow Shows production in association with Corvid Pictures and Alcina Pictures; Dolby; Color; Not rated; 77 minutes; Release date: May 9, 2008. CAST: Ellen Page (Tracey Berkowitz), Max McCabe-Lokos (Lance), Ari Cohen (Mr. Berkowitz), Erin McMurtry (Mrs. Berkowitz), Zie Souwand (Sonny Berkowitz), SlimTwig (Billy Zero), Julian Richings (Dr. Heker), Stephen Amell (Detective #1), Leonard Dunbar (Laughing Man), Chris Ratz (Donut Shop Cashier), Daniel Fathers (Elegant Pimp Daddy), Ryan Cooley (David Goldberg), Jeffery Bornstein (The Boy with Curious Hair), Jackie Brown (Mrs. Dorchester the Teacher), Kate Todd (That Knockout Bitch Debbi Dodge), Derek Scott (Headstand Johnny), Domenic Cuzzocrea (Waiter in Bar), Enid Rose (Woman in Fur), Curtis Fletcher (Man in Fur), Shawn Ahmed (Satanic Cashier), Norman Yeung (VJ), George Stroumboulopoulos (Himself), Tasha Davidson, Ashley Archer (Bathroom Bullies), Todd Sandomirsky (Angry Man on Bus), Kristina Nicoll (Junkie Woman on Bus), Rufus Crawford (Bus Cop), Gordon Masten (Bus Driver), Libby Adams (Young Tracey), Tara Nicodemo (Nurse on Street), Rebecca Auerbach (Girl on Street), Martin Villafana (The Man)

Ellen Page in The Tracey Fragments © *ThinkFilm*

TURN THE RIVER (Screen Media Films) Producer, Ami Armstrong; Executive Producers, Darby Parker, Catherine Kellner, Chris Eigeman; Richard Fitzgerald, Douglas Schmidt; Director/Screenplay, Chris Eigeman; Photography, Hernan Michael Otano; Designer, Paola Ridolfi; Costumes, Erika Munro; Music, Bryce Dessner, Padma Newsome; Editor, Michael Lahaie; Casting Todd Thaler; a Mr. Nice presentation in association with Bandora, of a Mr. Nice production; Dolby; Widescreen; Color; 16mm-to-HD; Rated R; 92 minutes; Release date: May 9, 2008. CAST: Famke Janssen (Kailey Sullivan), Jaymie Dornan (Gulley), Rip Torn (Teddy Quinette), Matt Ross (David), Lois Smith (Abigail), Marin Hinkle (Ellen), Terry Kinney (Markus), John Juback (Duncan), Tony Robles (Ralphie), Jordan Bridges (Brad), Ari Graynor (Charlotte), Santo D'Asaro (Scott), Zoe Lister Jones (Kat), Elizabeth Atkeson (Sally), Joseph Siravo (Warren), Brennan Brown (Randolph), Jordan Lage (Det. Crippen), Pete MacNamara (Chasm Falls Officer), Henry Leyva (Dale Armstrong), Greg Haas (Darby Jackson), Paul Thode (Eric Muftic), Judith Greentree (Senior Citizen), David Calicchio (Det. Calicchio), Chris Eigeman (Mike Simms), James Avondolio, Kevin Barber, Tom Carney, Theresa Purcell, Rebecca Silberry-Tatafu (Pool Players), Bill Sorice (Charlie)

Famke Janssen in Turn the River © *Screen Media Films*

SANGRE DE MI SANGRE (IFC Films) a.k.a. *Padre Nuestro*; Producers, Benjamin Odell, Per Melita; Executive Producers, Daniel Carey, Gloria Reuben, James Shiffren; Director/ Screenplay, Christopher Zalla; Photography, Igor Martinovic; Designer, Tommaso Ortino; Costumes, Taphat Tawil; Music, Brian Cullman; Editor, Aaron Yanes; Casting, Maria E. Nelson, Ellyn Long Marshall; a Panamax Films presentation of a Benjamin Odell production, in association with Two Lane Pictures/Cinergy Pictures/True True Stories; Color; DV; Not rated; 111 minutes; Release date: May 14, 2008. CAST: Jorge Adrián Espindola (Pedro), Armando Hernández (Juan), Jesús Ochoa (Diego), Paola Mendoza (Magda), Eugenio Derbez (Anibal), Lenny Ligotti, Sean Andrew (Police Officers), Leonardo Anzures (Simon), Luis Antonio Aponte (Foreman), Jean Brassard (Restaurant Owner), Barbara Danicka (Polish Woman), Ricky Garcia (Restaurant Worker), Scott Glascock (John), Lev Gorn (Rough-Shave), Israel Hernández (Ricardo), Yarida Hernandez (Woman), Matthew Kehoe (Art Handler), Jessica Kelly (Pig-Tails), Edward McGinty (US Border Patrol Officer), Randall Newsome (Truck Driver), Don Puglisi (Jimmy), Greta Quispe (Coat Check Girl), Rajiv Rao (Store Clerk), Jaime Santiago Sánchez (Skinny Man), Santos (Cowboy Hat Mexican), Yury Tsykun (Russian Man), Juan Villarreal (Shopkeeper), Teresa Yenque (Senora)

Armando Hernandez in Sangre de Mi Sangre © *IFC Films*

QUANTUM HOOPS (Green Forest Films) Producer/Director/Screenplay/ Photograph/ Editor, Rick Greenwald; Music, Brian Arbuckle; Narrator, David Duchovny; Color/black and white; HD; Not rated; 84 minutes; Release date: May 16, 2008. Documentary on California Institute of Technology's basketball team; with Brett Bush, Jordan Carlson, Scott Davies, Roy Dow, Travis Haussler, Jim Helgren, Day Ivy, Chris Kyriakakis, David Liu, Dean Oliver, Gregg Popovich, Brian Porter, Dean Reich, Huckleberry Seed, Ben Sexson, Ben Turk, Dick Van Kirk, Gene Victor, Chris Yu, Ed Zanelli.

Quantum Hoops © *Green Forest Films*

POSTAL (Freestyle Releasing) Producers, Uwe Boll, Dan Clarke, Shawn Williamson; Executive Producers, Vince Desiderio, Steve Wik; Director, Uwe Boll; Screenplay, Uwe Boll, Bryan C. Knight; Based on the videogame by Running with Scissors; a Boll Kingo (Germany) production in association with Brightlight Pictures (Canada); Photography, Mathias Neumann; Designer, Tink; Costumes, Maria Livingstone; Music, Jessica di Rooij; Editor, Julian Clarke; Casting, Maureen Webb; American-German-Canadian; Dolby; Panavision; Color; Rated R; 106 minutes; Release date: May 23, 2008. CAST: Zack Ward (Postal Dude), Dave Foley (Uncle Dave), Chris Coppola (Richard), Michael Benyaer (Mohammed), Jackie Tohn (Faith), J.K. Simmons (Candidate Wells), Ralf Moeller (Officer John), Verne Troyer (Himself/Voice of Krotchy), Chris Spencer (Officer Greg), Larry Thomas (Osama bin Laden), Brent Mendenhall (George W. Bush), Michael Paré (Panhandler), Erick Avari (Habib), Lindsay Hollister (Recorder), Rick Hoffman (Blither), David Huddleston (Peter), Seymour Cassel (Paul), Uwe Boll, Vince Desiderio (Themselves), Michaela Mann (Jenny), Holly Eglington (Karen), Lucie Guest (Cindy), Jonathan Bruce (Harry the Wheelchair Guy), Carrie Genzel (Reporter Gayle Robinson), Geoff Gostafson (Morning Show Host Bob), Daniel Boileau (Cooter), Samir El Sharkawi (Tariq), Jason Emanuel (Boback), Melanie Papalia (Nassira), Jodie Stewart (Bitch), Derek Anderson (Abdul the Retarded Taliban), Heather Feeney (Bank Teller), Marlaina Stewartt (Old Lady in Audience), Michael Robinson (Speaker), Bill Mondy (Paul the Mob Leader)

A JIHAD FOR LOVE (First Run Features) Producer, Sandi DuBowski; Executive Producers, Michael Huffington, Andrew Herwitz, Linda Saetre, Eileen Opatut, Dave Mac; Director/ Screenplay, Parvez Sharma; Photography, Parvez Sharma, Berke Bas; Music, Sussan Deyhim, Richard Horowitz; Editor, Juliet Weber; a Halal films production in association with ZDF-Arte, Channel 4, Logo, SBS-Australia, Katahdin Foundation and Realise; American-British-French-German-Australian; Color; HD Cam; Not rated; 81 minutes; Release date: May 21, 2008. Documentary on the struggle of gays who are still tied to their Muslim beliefs.

Jihad for Love © *First Run Features*

TWISTED: A BALLOONAMENTARY (Eliot Lives Prods.) Producers/Directors/ Screenplay/Photography/Editors, Sara Taksler, Naomi Greenfield; Executive Producers, Lauren Versel, Nick Rotondo; Music, Mayfair Workshop; Animators, Jonah Elgart, John Higgins, Eric Rosenbaum, Sarah Orenstein; Narrator, Jon Stewart; Presented in association with Lucky Monkey Pictures; Documentary on balloon twisters, with Vera Stalker, John Holmes, David Grist, James Smith, Don Caldwell, Laura Dakin, Sheree Brown-Rosner, Michele Rothstein.

HEAVY METAL IN BAGHDAD (VBS TV/Vice Films) Producers, Eddy Moretti, Suroosh Alvi, Monica Hampton; Executive Producers, Shane Smith, Spike Jonze; Directors, Eddy Moretti, Suroosh Alvi; Screenplay, Bernardo Loyola, Suroosh Alvi; Photography, Eddy Moretti; Music, Acrassicauda; Editor, Bernardo Loyola; Color; HD Cam; Not rated; 92 minutes; Release date: May 23, 2008. Documentary on the heavy metal band Acrassicauda's efforts to find an audience in the Muslim world.

Heavy Metal in Baghdad © *VBS TV/Vice Films*

INSIDIOUS (Romantic Troubadour Entertainment) Producer/Director/Screenplay/Music, Jerry Schram; Line Producer, Randall Ehrmann; Photography, Karl Kim; Designer, Jeanelle Marie; Editor, Katie Best; Casting, Kathy Carpenter; Color; HD; Not rated; 96 minutes; Release date: May 23, 2008. CAST: Peter Claymore (Doc), Brenda Cooney (Arin), Megan Corry (Naomi), Roger Dean (Moonboy), Augustus Diorio (Gigetto), Devonee Duchein (Rosalie), Kelly Dynan (Kelly D.), Brian Lee Elder (Tuddle), Lise Fisher (Gloria), Brian Ish (Ken), Adrienne LaValley (Addy), Michael Lepre (Scanlon), Lou Martini, Jr. (Glock), Meilana McLean Gillard (Meilana), Joe Mento (Bartender), Tommy D. Modesto (Cyclone), Joe Pagnatta (Cook), Tristan Laurence Perez (Nik), Alexa Poller (Maud), James Scharm (Donny), Jerry Schram (Duke), Michelle Sims (Harris), Karen Sours (Paige), Lynn Spencer (Blondie), Elisabeth Steen (Cristina), Zoltan Szalas (Zee), Allison Carter Thomas (Lane), Darby Lynn Totten (Dee), Kelly Wallace (Kelly W.), Katya Zakharova (Gabrielle)

Megan Corry, Brenda Cooney in Insidious © *Romantic Troubadour*

THE FOOT FIST WAY (Paramount Vantage) Producers, Erin Gates, Robert Hill, Jody Hill, Jennifer Chikes; Executive Producer, Paul Hill; Director, Jody Hill; Screenplay, Jody Hill, Danny McBride, Ben Best; Photography, Brian Mandle; Designer, Randy Gambill; Music, Pyramid; Editors, Zene Baker, Jeff Seibenick; a You Know I Can't Kiss You presentation; Color; Rated R; 87 minutes; Release date: May 30, 2008. CAST: Danny R. McBride (Fred Simmons), Ben Best (Chuck "The Truck" Wallce), Mary Jane Bostic (Suzie Simmons), Ken Aguilar (Rick), Tyler Baum (Armand), Sean Baxter (Roy Powers), Bruce Cameron (Bruce), Erin Fisher (Ticket Girl #1), Libertad Green (Drunk Model), Juan-Carlos Guzman (Carlos), Jody Hill (Mike McAlister), Jeff Hoffman (Dr. Love), Danielle Jarchow (Connie), Deborah Loates (Marge), Carlos Lopez IV (Henry Harrison), Spencer Moreno (Julio Chavez), Erica Owens (Mrs. Fisher), Nicholas Stanley (Lil' Stevie Fisher), Chris Walldorf (Shane), Collette Wolfe (Denise)

Danny McBride in The Foot Fist Way © *Paramount Vantage*

KISS THE BRIDE (Regent/here!) Producers, C. Jay Cox, Bob Schuck, Richard Santilena; Executive Producers, Scott Zimmerman, Les Williams, Paul Colichman, Steve P. Jarchow; Director, C. Jay Cox; Screenplay, Ty Lieberman; Photography, Carl Bartels; Designer, Chris Anthony Miller; Costumes, Laura Brody; Music, Ben Holbrook; Editor, John Keitel; Casting, Dan Shaner, Michael Testa; a Shadow Factory, WriteMCowboy production; Color; DV; Rated R; 115 minutes; Release date: May 30, 2008. CAST: Tori Spelling (Alex), Philipp Karner (Matt), James O'Shea (Ryan), Robert Foxworth (Wayne), Tess Harper (Barbara), Joanna Cassidy (Evelyn), Garrett M. Brown (Gerald), E.E. Bell (Dan), Amber Benson (Elly), Steve Sandvoss (Chris), Michael Medico (Sean), Jane Cho (Stephanie), Ralph Cole, Jr. (Barry), Brooke Dillman (Virginia), Dean McDermott (Plumber), Elizabeth Kell (Monica), Dean Nolen (Reverend), Connie Sawyer (Aunt Minnie), Les Williams (Larry), Charlie David (Joey), Paul Meacham (Waiter Worthie)

James O'Shea, Philipp Karner in Kiss the Bride © *Regent Releasing*

BIGGER, STRONGER, FASTER* (Magnolia) Producers, Alex Buono, Tamsin Rawady, Jim Czarnecki; Executive Producers, Terrance J. Aarnio, Robert Weiser, Richard Schiffrin; Director, Christopher Bell; Screenplay, Christopher Bell, Alex Buono, Tamsin Rawady; Photography, Alex Buono; Music, Dave Porter; Music Supervisor, Julianne Jordan; Editor, Brian Singbiel; a BSF Films production; Color; HD; Rated PG-13; 105 minutes; Release date: May 30, 2008. Documentary on the use of steroids among professional athletes; with Chris Bell, Mark Bell, Mike Bell, Rosemary Bell, Sheldon Bell, Christian Boeving, Rick Collins, Wade Exum, Donald Hooton, Ben Johnson, Floyd Landis, Stan Lee, Carl Lewis, John Romano, Giovanni Roselli, Arnold Schwarzenegger, John Sweeney, Jeff Taylor, Gregg Valentino, Dr. Gary Wadler, Diane Watson, Henry Waxman.

Big Will Harris, Christopher Bell in Bigger, Stronger, Faster* © *Magnolia Films*

WONDERS ARE MANY: THE MAKING OF DOCTOR ATOMIC (Actual Films/ITVS) Producers, Bonni Cohen, Jon Else; Director/Screenplay, Jon Else; Photography, Jon Schenk, Michael Chin, Jon Else; Music, John Adams; Editor, Deborah Hoffmann; a Jon Else/Actual Films/Independent Television Service co-production in association with PBS; Color/B&W, HD Video; Not rated; 94 minutes; Release date: May 30, 2008. Documentary about the creation of John Adams and Peter Sellars' opera *Doctor Atomic* for the San Francisco Opera; with John Adams, Peter Sellars.

Wonders Are Many © *Actual Films/ITVS*

DREAMS WITH SHARP TEETH (Creative Differences) Producers, Erik Nelson, Randall M. Boyd; Director/Screenplay, Erik Nelson; Photography, Wes Dorman; Music, Richard Thompson; Editor, Randall M. Boyd; Color; Not rated; 96 minutes; Release date: June 4, 2008. Documentary on science fiction writer Harlan Ellison; with Harlan Ellison, Robin Williams, Neil Gaiman, Peter David, Ronald D. Moore, Josh Olson, Tom Snyder

Harlan Ellison in Dreams with Sharp Teeth © *Creative Differences*

THE GO-GETTER (Peace Arch) Producers, Lucy Barzun, Lori Christopher, Larry Furlong; Executive Producers, Gavin Parfitt, Don Truesdale, Kimberly McKewon, Martin Hynes; Coproducers, Rauy Celya, Miri Yoon; Director/Screenplay, Martin Hynes; Photography, Byron Shah; Designer, Damon Fortier; Costumes, Marie Schley; Music, M. Ward; Music Supervisor, Linda Cohen; Editor, David Birdsell; Casting, Emily Schweber; a Two Roads Entertainment and etc. films presentation; Dolby: CFI color; Rated R; 93 minutes; Release date: June 6, 2008. CAST: Lou Taylor Pucci (Mercer), Zooey Deschanel (Kate), Jena Malone (Joely), William Lee Scott (Rid), Nick Offerman (Nick the Potter/Dutch the Trumpeteer/Joaquin the Motel Clerk), Judy Greer (Better Than Toast), Julio Oscar Mechoso (Sergio Leone), Jsu Garcia (Arlen), Colin Fickes (Cousin Buddy), Maura Tierney (Hal's Pets), Bill Duke (Liquor Supply), Giuseppe Andrews (Stock Boy), Kathleen M. Darcy (J's Mom), Johny Anthony Delgado (Helpful Guy), Saul Huezo (Valet), Marissa Ingrasci (Laurel), Paul Palo (Old Man), Eliska Sursova (Candy Striper), M. Ward (J), Sita Young (Colder)

THE PROMOTION (Dimension Films/Weinstein Co.) Producers, Jessika Borsiczky Goyer, Steven A. Jones; Executive Producers, Bob Weinstein, Harvey Weinstein; Director/Screenplay, Steve Conrad; Photography, Lawrence Sher; Designer, Martin Whist; Costumes, Susan Kaufmann; Music, Alex Wurman; Editor, Tim Streeto; Dolby; Color; Rated R; 86 minutes; Release date: June 6, 2008. CAST: Seann Williams Scott (Doug Stauber), John C. Reilly (Richard Welhner), Fred Armisen (Scott Fargas), Jenna Fischer (Jen Stauber), Chris Conrad (Teddy Grahams), Lili Taylor (Lori Welhner), Gil Bellows (Mitch, Board Executive), Abby Allen (Christine Welhner), Bobby Cannavale (Dr. Mark Timms), Kelli Clevenger (Daycare Worker), Stephanie G. Conti (Toll Booth Lady), David Charles DuBois, Randall Jones (Doctors), Tory O. Davis (Keith), Matt Dworzanczyk (Drug Addict), Anastasia Esper (Sylvia Rojas), Joe Farina (Kevin Conway – Pepsi Rep), Ellen Fliesler, Anita Showalter (Cashiers), Brian Gallivan (Banjo Player), Nathan Geist (Donnie Wahls), Rick Gonzalez (Ernesto), Emerald Gunther (Craft Maker at Party), Richard Henzel (Narrator, *The Good Life*), David Hernandez (Rafael Velazquez), Bob Kolbey (Supermarket Manager), Michael Kuster (Dr. Reid), Mario Larraza (Edgar), Maestro Harrell, Kristopher Lofton, Jarreau Brown, Jamal C. Adams, Edwin M. Walker (Gang Members), Javier Lopez (Little Javier), Adrian Martinez (Octavio), Eddie Martinez (Sylvia's Husband), Betsy McIntyre (Cute Pedestrian), Nikki Taylor Melton (Lizzie), David Moscow (Teddy's Friend), Masi Oka (Loan Officer), David Dino Wells, Jr. (Dodgy Guy), Joy Yascone (2nd Nurse), Peter Grosz (Guy in Windbreaker), Denny Anderson, Kevin Patrick Smith, Paul Thomas, Rich Tanis (Board Members), Jason Bateman (Retreat Leader), Steve Park (David Kim), Tony Fitzpatrick (Police Officer), Angel Guzman (Javier), Chris Gardner, Shaun Gayle (Community Leaders), Ernest Perry, Jr. (Man in Audience), Joshua Eber (Hardy), Rebecca Cox (Dance Studio Employee)

Seann William Scott, John C. Reilly in Promotion © *Weinstein Co.*

OPERATION FILMMAKER (Icarus) Producers, Nina Davenport, David Schisgall; Director/Photography, Nina Davenport; Music, Sheldon Mirowitz; Editors, Nina Davenport, Aaron Kuhn; a Nina Davenport production; Color; Mini-DV-to-HD; Not rated; 92 minutes; Release date: June 6, 2008. Documentary on the troubles faced by Iraqi film student Muthana Mohmed, who, after his film school is bombed, is invited to Prague by actor-director Liev Schreiber to work on his movie *Everything is Illuminated* as an intern; with Muthana Mohmed, Liev Schreiber, Alberto Bonilla, Steven Chinni, Eugene Hutz, Peter Saraf, Dwayne "The Rock" Johnson, Elijah Wood.

Elijah Wood, Muthana Mohmed in Operation Filmmaker
© *Icarus Films*

TAKE OUT (CAVU Pictures) Producers/Directors/Screenplay, Shih-Ching Tsou; Executive Producer, Isil Bagdadi; Photography/Editor, Sean Baker; Color; Not rated; 87 minutes; Release date: June 6, 2008. CAST: Charles Jang (Ming Ding), Jeng-Hua Yu (Young), Wang-Thye Lee (Big Sister), Justin Wan (Wei), Shih-Yun Tsou, Joe Chien (Collectors), Kenny Pang (Door Opener), Waley Liu, Ed Jansen, David Liu (Ming's Roommates), Eva Huang (Ming's Cousin), Jeff Huang (Ma), Wang-Thye Lee (Big Sister), Ethel Brooks (1st Delivery), Victor Sally (Fried Hard), Tanya Perez (2nd Delivery), Maria Greenspan (Portuguese-Speaking Delivery), Sandra McCullogh (Mother with Two Children), Sharinee McCullogh (Running Toddler), Renee McCullogh (Older Sister), Javier Cortes (Nice Tipper), J.P. Partland (Horn Delivery), Theodore Bouloukos II (No Speakee English), Oliver (English Bull Dog), Yessica Amadis (Smoking Phone Woman), Patrice A. Duffy (Nice Woman Delivery), James Price, Carlos Eleutice, Juan Carlos Perdomo (Hardware Store), Eunice Wong (Dark Hallway Delivery), Yaron Prywes (Young Prep Delivery), Kevin Karagulian (Chicken or Beef), Alia Carpenter (Mother with Crying Baby), Kamali Smith (Crying Baby), Tim Hummel, Althia A. Cline (Fighting Couple), Rory Kelly (Dog Hallway Delivery), Michael Fuehrer (Mail Order Faster), Monica Kester (Thank-you Delivery), B.J. Anthony Pass II (Bad Hair Day), Cailin Pitt (Barber Shop Kid), Ronald Garret (Barber), Marie Pitt (Barber Shop Mom), Joe Franza (Not a Word Delivery), Harold Edmondson, Theresa Leak (Fork Couple), John Sloan (Discount Customer), Barbara Levenson (Long Hallway Delivery), Claudia Ganzales (Spanish-Speaking Teen), Baqi Abdush-Shaheed (Clean the Shrimp), Gil Selinger, Preet Pannu (Only Euros), Amy Daniels (845 Westend), Tony Roach (Change Man), Devin Haqq (Elephants and Tigers), Josh Wick (Elephants and Tigers Friend), Luca Bigni (Quiet Teen Delivery), Peter Camacho (Other Half of the Chicken), Angel Feliciano, Juliio Lugo, Edwin Banyar (Ketchup on the Fries Guys), Omar A. Franco, Omar Jennett, Amin Joseph, Jeron Moss, Jake Walker (Hip-Hop Apartment), Chris Espinal (Six Girls, Six Numbers), Sandra Cartagena (Spanish-Speaking Mother), Sylvan Wallach (Side-Door Delivery), Anetra V. Humphries (Last Delivery), Andrew Ko, Leighton Whezler (Muggers), Vickeya Miller, Peter Corrigan, Helen Corrigan, Katrina Sturdivant, Annette Sturdivant, Gary Garcia, Wilson Rodriguez, Fausto Peralta, Alexander Johnson (Take-Out Customers)

Charles Jang (right) in Take Out © *CAVU Pictures*

ENCOUNTERS AT THE END OF THE WORLD (ThinkFilm) Producer, Henry Kaiser; Executive Producers, Erik Nelson, Dave Harding, Phil Fairclough, Julian P. Hobbs; Director/Screenplay, Werner Herzog; Photography, Peter Zeitlinger; Music, Henry Kaiser, David Lindley; Editor, Joe Bini; a Discovery Films presentation of a Creative Differences production in association with Discovery Films and the Discovery Channel; Color; HD; Rated G; 99 minutes; Release date: June 11, 2008. Documentary on the researchers and scientists who inhabit Antarctica. (This film received an Oscar nomination for documentary feature).

Encounters at the End of the World © *ThinkFilm*

QUID PRO QUO (Magnolia) Producers, Sarah Pillsbury, Midge Sanford; Executive Producers, Jason Kliot, Joana Vicente, Todd Wagner, Mark Cuban; Coproducer, Per Melita; Director/Screenplay, Carlos Brooks; Photography, Michael McDonough; Designer, Roshelle Berliner; Costumes, Eric Daman; Music, Mark Mothersbaugh; Editors, Lauren Zuckerman, Charles Ireland; Casting, Randi Hiller, Sarah Halley Finn; an HDNet Films presentation of a Sanford/Pillsbury production; Dolby; Color; Rated R; 82 minutes; Release date: June 13, 2008. CAST: Nick Stahl (Isaac Knott), Vera Farmiga (Fiona), Aimee Mullins (Raine), Leonardo Nam (Engineer), Rachel Black (Janice Musslewhite), Jessica Hecht (Edie), Jacob Pitts (Hugh), Ashlie Atkinson (Candy), Jamie McShane (Man on Sidewalk), Pablo Schreiber (Brooster), Jeane Fournier (Charlene Coke), Carmela Marner (A Female Wannabe), Phil LaMarr (Wannabe Group Leader), Matthew Carey (A Male Wannabe), Ben Siegler (Man with Trachea Tube), Michal Sinnott (Isaac's Mom), Joshua Leonard (Isaac's Dad), For Chan (Asian Restaurant Owner), James Frain (Father Dave), Dulan Bruno (Scott), Kate Burton (Merilee), Ellen Marlow (Young Fiona), Tommy Nelson (Young Isaac)

Forest Whitaker, Minnie Driver in Ripple Effect © *Monterey Media*

Vera Farmiga, Nick Stahl in Quid Pro Quo © *Magnolia Films*

KICKING IT (Liberation Entertainment) Producers, Ted Leonsis, Susan Koch, Jedd Wider, Todd Wider; Executive Producers, Rick Allen, Randy Boe, Kat Byles, Jack Davies, Joe Edelman, Mark Ein, Raul Fernandez, Sheila Johnson, Nigel Morris, Soroush Shedhabi; Director/Screenplay, Susan Koch; Photography, Neil Barrett; Music, Charlie Barnett; Editor/Co-Director, Jeff Werner; Narrator, Colin Farrell; Play-by-Play, Garth Lagerwey; a Ted Leonsis presentation in association with Cabin Films and Wider Film Projects; Color; HD; Not rated; 98 minutes; Release date: June 13, 2008. Documentary on the fifth annual Homeless World cup.

RIPPLE EFFECT (Monterey Media) Producer/Director/Screenplay, Philippe Caland; Executive Producers, Forest Whitaker, Pierre Caland, Virginia Madsen, Minnie Driver; Photography, Daron Keet; Designer, Shirley Leong; Costumes, Asia Ahearn, Amanda Riley; Music, Anthony Marinelli; Editors, Joseph Semense, Yvan Gauthier; Casting, Lindsay Chag; a YBG Prods. production; Color; HD; Rated R; 87 minutes; Release date: June 20, 2008. CAST: Philippe Caland (Amer Atrash), Forest Whitaker (Philip), Virginia Madsen (Sherry), Minnie Driver (Kitty), Kali Rocha (Alex), John Billingsley (Brad), Jerry Katell (Gordon), Orlando Seale (Brian), Kip Pardue (Tyler), Betsy Clark (Amy), Joanna Krupa (Victoria), Ken Sylk (Ronald), Robin Arcuri (Andrea), Denise Crosby (Ronald's Wife), Elena Satine (Sophia), Michael Weiss (Michael), Gwendolyn Bailey (Lara), Kelli Nordhus (Sylvia Myron), Ilona Alexandra (Makeup Artist), Bryan Black (Promoter), Johnny D. Boyd (Attorney), Evans Butterworth (Ad Salesman), Charley Mae Caland (Charley), Stacy Cunningham (Susan), Timothy Donovan (Tim), Emily Johnson (Bar Girl), Don Le (Partygoer), Maisie Pacia (Student), Joe Roach (Tattooed Cowboy), Becca Sweitzer (Jewelry Clerk), Kimberly Van Luin (Second Girl at Party)

EXPIRED (Truly Indie) Producers, Jeffrey Coulter, Fred Roos; Executive Producers, Antoni Stutz, Alexander Shing, Lawrence Wang; Director/Screenplay, Cecilia Miniucchi; Photography, Zoran Popovic; Designer, Natalie Sanfilippo; Costumes, Swinda Reichelt; Music, Jeffrey Coulter; Editors, Anne Goursaud, Fritz Feick; Casting, John Jackson; an Agá Films, FR Productions presentation of a Jeffrey Coulter production; Dolby; Color; Not rated; 112 minutes; Release date: June 20, 2008. CAST: Samantha Morton (Claire Barney), Jason Patric (Jay Caswell), Teri Garr (Mother Barney/Aunt Tilde), Illeana Douglas (Wilma), Anthony John Crane (Blue Car Owner), Gina St. John (Woman with Expired Meter), Ron King (Ex-Boyfriend), Rolando Molina (Meters Money Collector), Joe Camareno (Stephen), Sonia Lozada (Jade), Terrence Bernie Hines (Mark), Carlease Burke (Supervisor at Roll Call), Kyle Hatch (Pedestrian), Kestrin Pantera (Woman with Baby), Adam Gropman (Green Car Owner), James C. Burns (Red SUV Owner), Hans Uder, Michele Maso, J. Mills Pierre, Nancye Ferguson, Phyllis Franklin, Timothy Starks (Drivers), Isaac Bright (Kid Putting Money in Meters), Jonny Mack (Jay's Son), Darci Dixon (Waitress at Coffee Shop), Arnold "Skip" Abelson (Build-it-Yourself Show Host), Del Zamora (Photographer), Roberta E. Bassin (Waitress at Diner), Leticia Peredo (Stephen's Wife), Elizabeth J. Martin (Daughter), Baba Ji (Wilma's Fiance), Charles Hutchins (Charlie), Linda Phillips, Paul Palo (Martha & Stewart Food Show), Dave Adams (Boot Trucker Driver), Joanne Baron (Supervisor), David Garland Pires (Angry Man with Groceries), Tony Rivard (Karaoke Singer), William S. Campos (Karaoke Operator), Alexander Roos (Passerby), Rachel Wittman (Amber), Charles Kim (Man with White Car)

FULL GROWN MEN (Emerging Pictures) Producers, Xandra Castleton, Brian Benson, David Munro; Executive Producers, Sheila Ennis; Paul Zaentz; Coproducers, Alan Cumming, David Ilku; Director, David Munro; Screenplay, David Munro; Xandra Casleton; Photography, Frank G. DeMarco; Designer, Susan Block; Costumes, Alexis Scott; Music, Charlie Campbell; Editors, Alex Blatt, Affonso Goncalves; Casting, Susan Shopmaker; a Grottofilms presentation; Dolby; Color; Not rated; 78 minutes; Release date: June 25, 2008. CAST: Matt McGrath (Alby Cutrera), Judah Friedlander (Elias Guber), Alan Cumming (The Hitchhiker), Deborah Harry (Beauty), Amy Sedaris (Trina), Kaite Kreisler (Suzanne Cutrera), Joie Lee (Annie), Jerry Grayson (Mr. Tinsman), Benjamin Karpf (Rollie), Jim Fyfe (Night Manager), David Ilku (Pool Man), Zully Montero (Teya), Peter Donald Badalamenti II (Bert), Madia da Silva (Mrs. Cutrera), Louis Echavarria (Truck Stop Father), Don Festge (Diner Patron), Bruce Fontaine (Old Man in Laundromat), Monika Gaba (Neighbor), Jadin Gould (Halloween Party Girl), Kathleen LaGue (Operator), Carol LeNeveau (Newspaper Lady), Ace Ligherman (Young Elias), Richard Lozano, Steven Lozano (Josh), Blair McClure (Bus Passenger), Nicholas S. Morrison (Kid in Van), Hunter Ryan (Parking Lot Kid), Vivienne Sendaydiego (Young Mom), Erika Watkins (Truck Stop Patron)

Matt McGrath, Benjamin Karpf in Full Grown Men © *Emerging Pictures*

LOUISE BOURGEOIS: THE SPIDER, THE MISTRESS AND THE TANGERINE (Zeitgeist) Producers/Directors, Marion Cajori, Amei Wallach; Executive Producers, George Griffin, The Art Kaleidoscope Foundation; Photography, Mead Hunt, Ken Kobland; Editor, Ken Kobland; an Art Kaleidoscope Foundation presentation; Color; Not rated; 99 minutes; Release date: June 25, 2008. Documentary on artist Louise Bourgeois; with Louise Bourgeois, Pandora Tabatabai Asbaghi, Jean-Louis Bourgeois, Jerry Gorovoy, Guerilla Girls, Charlotta Kotik, Frances Morris, Robert Storr, Deborah Wye.

Louise Bourgeois in The Spider, the Mistress and the Tangerine © *Zeitgeist Films*

GUNNIN' FOR THAT #1 SPOT (Oscilloscope Laboratories) Producers, Jon Doran, Adam Yauch; Director/Photography, Adam Yauch; Editor, Neal Usatin; Color; HD—to-35mm; Not rated; 90 minutes; Release date: June 27, 2008. Documentary follows eight high school basketball players as they are invited to compete at Harlem's Rucker Park; with Jerryd Bayless, Michael Beasley, Tyreke Evans, Donte Greene, Brandon Jennings, Kevin Love, Kyle Singler, Lance Stephenson.

Michael Beasley in Gunnin' for That #1 Spot © *Oscilloscope*

WICKED LAKE (Fever Dreams) Producers, John Carchietta, Carl Morano, Chris Sivertson; Executive Producer, John Sirabella; Screenplay, Adam Rockoff, Chris Sivertson; Photography, Stephen Osbron; Music, Al Jourgensen; Editor, Kevin Ford; a Fever Dreams Prods. production, in association with Scattershot Prods., ZP Studios; Color; Not rated; 95 minutes; Release date: June 27, 2008. CAST: Carlee Baker (Mary), Frank Birne (Sir Jim), Eve Mauro (Jill), Michael Esparza (Ray), Eryn Joslyn (Helen), Robin Sydney (Ilene), Damien DeKay (Palmer), Marc Senter (Caleb), Tim Thomerson (Jake), Angela Bettis (Mother), J.D. Brown (Runt), Mike McKee (Cyrus), Phoenix Rae (Little Girl), Justin Stone (Fred), Luke Y. Thompson (Half-Idiot)

RED ROSES AND PETROL (World Wide Motion Picture Corp.) Producers, Tamar Simon Hoffs, Gail Wager Stayden, Georganne Aldrich Haller, Alfred Sapse; Executive Producers, Josh Hoffs, Susanna Hoffs; Coproducer, Pierce Boyce; Director/Story, Tamar Simon Hoffs; Screenplay, Tamar Simon Hoffs, Gail Wager Stayden; Based upon the play by Joseph O'Connor; Photography, Nancy Schreiber; Designer, Julieann Getman; Music, Seth Pedowitz; Editor, Dathai Keane; a Rock 'N' Read Prods. presentation of an Alfred Sapse production in association with Abu Media; 2003; Technicolor; Rated R; 97 minutes; Release date: June 27, 2008. CAST: Malcolm McDowell (Enda Doyle), Olivia Tracey (Moya Doyle), Heather Juergensen (Medbh Doyle), Max Beesley (Johnny Doyle), Greg Ellis (Tom Ivres), Susan Lynch (Catherine Doyle), Catherine Farrell (Helen), Sean Lawlor (Prof. Thompson), Robert Easton (Old Geezer), Aubrey Morris (Father Morton), Arie Verveen (Doc), Timothy V. Murphy (Eamoon), Zola Glassman (Young Medbh), Kathryn Joosten (Nurse), Lou Mulford (Neighbor Woman), Christopher Paci (Baby Johnny), Jackson Roach (Young Johnny), Shiva Rose McDermott (Evie), Deidra Sarego (Irish Singer), Georgiana Sirbu (Young Catherine), Shahar Sorek (Bar Patron)

All in This Tea © *Flower Films*

ALL IN THIS TEA (Flower Films) Producers/Directors, Les Blank, Gina Leibrecht; Photography, Les Blank; Editor, Gina Leibrecht; Color; DigiBeta; MiniDV; Not rated; 70 minutes; Release date: June 27, 2008. Documentary follows American tea importer, David Lee Hoffman, as he searches China to find the finest handmade teas in the world; with David Lee Hoffman, James Norwood Pratt, Gaetano Kazuo Maida, Song Diefeng, Winnie W. Yu.

RAZZLE DAZZLE: THE LOST WORLD (Anthology Film Archives) Director, Ken Jacobs; Color/Black and white; Digital Video; Not rated; 93 minutes; Release date: June 27, 2008. Ken Jacobs' experimental narrative exploring the filming techniques of Thomas Edison using his minute-long, 1903 film an amusement park.

GONZO: THE LIFE & WORK OF DR. HUNTER S. THOMPSON (Magnolia) Producers, Alison Ellwood, Eva Orner, Jason Kliot, Joana Vicente, Graydon Carter, Alex Gibney; Executive Producers, Todd Wagner, Mark Cuban; Co-Executive Producers, Roy Ackerman, Nick Fraser; Director/Screen Story, Alex Gibney; Writing, Hunter S. Thompson; Photography, Maryse Alberti; Music, David Schwartz; Music Supervisor, John McCullough; Editor, Alison Ellwood; Associate Producer, Salimah El-Amin; Narrator, Johnny Depp; an HDNet Films presentation; Dolby; Color; Rated R; 119 minutes; Release date: July 4, 2008. Documentary on the life of influential writer Hunter S. Thompson; with Anita Thompson, Bob Braudis, Charles Perry, Douglas Brinkley, Gary Hart, George McGovern, George Stranahan, Jann Wenner, Jimmy Buffett, Jimmy Carter, Juan Thompson, Laila Nablusi, Pat Buchanan, Pat Caddell, Ralph Steadman, Sandy Thompson, Sonny Barger, Timothy Crouse, Tom Wolfe.

Hunter S. Thompson in Gonzo © *Magnolia Films*

VERY YOUNG GIRLS (Showtime) Producers/Photography, David Schisgall, Priya Swaminathan, Nina Alvarez; Executive Producers, John Moser, Diana Barrett, Jack Lechner; Director, David Schisgall; Editor, Jane Jo; Music, Nathan Larson; a Swinging T Prods. production; Color; DV; Not rated; 83 minutes; Release date: July 4, 2008. Documentary on teen age girls pressed into prostitution.

HOLDING TREVOR (Regent/here!) Producer/Director, Rosser Goodman; Executive Producer/ Screenplay, Brent Gorski; Coproducer/Costumes/Designer, Oneita Parker; Photography, Kara Stephens; Editor, Donna Mathewson; a Here! Films presentation of a Stray Films, KGB Films production; Color; HD-to-DigiBeta; Rated R; 87 minutes; Release date: July 4, 2008. CAST: Brent Gorski (Trevor), Jay Brannan (Jake), Melissa Searing (Andie), Eli Kranski (Ephram), Chris Wyllie (Darrell), Isaiah Garnica (BBQ Boy), Yaniv Madmon (Party Guy), Dawn Mondie (Mary C), Mathew Pasillas (Bar Boy), Joseph Roslan (Naked Guy), Megan Sheperd (Co-Worker), Monica Todd (HIV Counselor)

FULL BATTLE RATTLE (Market Road/Mile End/Don't Foam) Producers/Directors, Tony Gerber, Jesse Moss; Executive Producers, Britton Fisher, Pascal Demko; Coproducer, Tamas Bojtor; Photography, Tony Gerber, Jesse Moss, Adam Keker; Music, Paul Brill; Editors, Alex Hall, Pax Wasserman, Youna Kwak; presented in association with Pop's Paper Route, Tapwater Media; Dolby; Color; HD; Not rated; 92 minutes; Release date: July 9, 2008. Documentary following a battalion's training at a fake Iraqi village in the Mojave Desert; with Robert McLaughlin, Cam Kramer, Amber Gates, Nagi Moshi, Azhar Cholagh, Sherine Halim.

Full Battle Rattle © *Market Road*

AUGUST (First Look Intl.) Producers, Charles Corwin, Clara Markowitz, Elisa Pugliese, David Guy Levy; Executive Producer, Patrick Morris; Coproducer, Jonathan Shoemaker; Director, Austin Chick; Screenplay, Howard A. Rodman; Photography, Andrij Parekh; Designer, Roshelle Berliner; Music, Nathan Larson; Music Supervisor, Howard Paar; Editor, Pete Beaudreau; a 57th & Irving presentation of an Original Media production in association with Periscope Entertainment; Dolby; Color; Sony HD Cam; Rated R; 88 minutes; Release date: July 11, 2008. CAST: Josh Harnett (Tom Sterling), Naomie Harris (Sarah), Adam Scott (Joshua Sterling), Robin Tunney (Melanie), Andre Royo (Dylan), Emanuelle Chriqui (Morela), David Bowie (Ogilvie), Rip Torn (David Sterling), Caroline Lagerfelt (Nancy Sterling), Laila Robins (Ottmar Pivo), Ron Insana, Jason Calacanis (Themselves), Marc Klee (Guest Analyst), Athena Currey (Girl in Bathroom), John Lavelle, Sanjit De Silva, Jeremy Bobb (Suits), Carmine DiBenedetto (Tyler), Zoe Kazan (Gal Employee), Robin Lord Taylor (Guy Employee), Francesca Tedeschi (Cheyenne), Jeffrey Evan Thomas (Chad), Mozhan Marnò (Ashley), Martha Millan (Kuniko), Sandriel Frank (Mrs. Gibeau), Alan Cox (Barton)

Josh Hartnett, David Bowie in August © *First Look*

THE REFLECTING POOL (BW FilmWorks) Producers, Jodie Baltazar, Joseph Culp; Director/Screenplay, Jarek Kupsc; Photography, Jodie Baltazar; Art Director, J von K; Music, Dan Radlauer; Color; DV; Not rated; 106 minutes; Release date: July 11, 2008. CAST: Jarek Kupsc (Alex Prokop), Joseph Culp (Paul Cooper), Lisa Black (Georgia McGuire), Alex Hyde-White (Jack Mahoney), Dominick LaRae (Video Joe), Bennett Dunn (Jimmy), Boris Mackovic (Holman), Jason Culp (Mr. Alonzo), Eric De Gama (Mr. Brown), Peter Coca (Boccacio), Jennipher Foster (Archivist), Melanie Mitchell (Ms. Bauer), Philippe Denham (Prof. Ballard), Thomas Wagner (Mr. Mingus), Doug Knott (Mr. Pierce), Elizabeth Morehead (Maggie Cooper), T. Stephen Neave (Corley), Jillian Fisher (Ms. Koenig), Mark Daneri (Agent Abbot), Ryan Fox, Jr. (Agent Hill), Michael Shepperd (Maj. Fredericks), Casey Jones Bastiaans (Agent Bennett), Lee Michael Cohn (Benjamin Katz), Michael Fairman (Berman)

NATIONAL LAMPOON'S HOMO ERECTUS (National Lampoon) Producers, Carolyn Pfeffer, Brad Wyman; Executive Producer, Tom Schatz; Director/Screenplay, Adam Rifkin; Photography, Scott Billups; Designer, Chris Stull; Costumes, Alysia Raycraft; Music, Alex Wurman; Music Supervisor, Roanna Gillespie; Editor, Martin Apelbaum; Casting, Deanna Brigidi, Beth Sepko; a Town Lake Films presentation of a Burnt Orange/Brad Wyman production; Dolby; Color; Rated R; 87 minutes; Release date: July 11, 2008. CAST: Adam Rifkin (Ishbo), Ali Larter (Fardart), Hayes MacArthur (Thudnik), David Carradine (Mookoo), Talia Shire (Ishbo's Mom), Carol Alt (Queen Fallopia), Gary Busey (Krutz), William A. Tyree (Old Fool), Ron Jeremy (Oog), Giuseppe Andrews (Zig), Gregory Robert Dean (Krot), Troy DeWalt (Schlonk), Miles Dougal (Zog), Tom Hodges (Bork), Nick Krause (Young Thudnik), Olivia Lee (Ulwin), Taylor Maddux (Archeologist), Cole McKeel (Ishbo at 12), Matt Potter (Zag), Jilina Scott (Estrogena), Kat Smith (Ovaria)

ROMAN POLANSKI: WANTED AND DESIRED (HBO Documentary Films/Weinstein Co.) Producers, Jeffrey Levy-Hinte, Lila Yacoub, Marina Zenovich; Executive Producers, Steven Soderbergh, Randy Wooten; Coproducer, P.G. Moran; Director, Marina Zenovich; Screenplay, Joe Bini, P.G. Morgan, Marina Zenovich; Photography, Tanja Koop; Music, Mark Deli Antoni; Editor, Joe Bini; Associate Producer, Michelle Sullivan; a Graceful Pictures presentation in association with the BBC of an Antidote Films production; American-British; Color/Black and white; Not rated; 100 minutes; Release date: July 11, 2008. Documentary on how director Roman Polanski fled to France after pleading guilty to unlawful sexual intercourse with a minor in 1978 and remains in exile to this day; with Roman Polanski, Douglas Dalton, Roger Gunson, Samantha Gailey Geimer, Lawrence Silver, Laurence J. Rittenband, David Wells, Jim Grodin, Phillip Vannatter, Richard Brenneman, Claus Preute, Andrew Braunsberg, Gene Gutowski, Daniel Melnick, Hawk Koch, Anthea Sylbert, Mia Farrow, Lorenzo Semple, Jr., Fred Sidewater, Marilyn Beck, Hans Mollinger, Pierre-Andre Boutang, Istvan Bajat, Arnaud D'Hauterives, Michael M. Crain, Steve Barshop, Ronald Markman, Diane Tschekaloff, Elliot Rittenband, Marlene Roden, Madeline Bessmer. (This film had its premiere on HBO on June 9, 2008).

HAROLD (City Lights) Producers, William Sherak, Jason Shuman, Cuba Gooding, Jr., Morris S. Levy; Executive Producers, Danny Fisher, Jack Fisher, Max Sinovoi, Sam Zietz; Coproducer, Jeff Mazzola; Co-Executive Producers, Donald Brodsky, Gregory Seagal, Michael Califra, David Daks; Director, T. Sean Shannon; Screenplay, T. Sean Shannon, Greg Fields; Photography, Christopher Lavasseur; Designer, Jory Adam; Costumes, Mary Margaret O'Neill; Music, Brady Harris; Editors, Colleen Sharp, Harp Pekin; a Mega Films/Blue Star Entertainment production; Dolby; Color; Rated PG-13; 90 minutes; Release date: July 11, 2008. CAST: Cuba Gooding, Jr. (Cromer), Spencer Breslin (Harold Clemens), Ally Sheedy (Maureen Clemens), Nikki Blonsky (Rhonda Baxter), Chris Parnell (Coach Vanderpool), Stella Maeve (Shelly Clemens), Suzanne Shepherd (Maude Sellers), Rachel Dratch (Ms. Norris), Fred Willard (Dr. Pratt), Colin Quinn (Reedy), Robert Gorrie (Patrick), Dan "Dietz" Fracher (Brad), Elizabeth Gillies (Evelyn Taylor), Kate Hodge (Dusty), Angel Sing (Chang), Christina Jackson (Traci), William Wiggins (Vince), Jake Sokoloff (Byron), Alan Aisenberg (Malcolm), Samantha Futerman (Katy), Edward Gelbinovich (Derek), Derek Nelson (Mason), Nohman Sakhi (Jugdish), Evan Daves (Dennis), Lou Wagner (Principal Nelson), Jim Downy (Mr. Pinchot), Nicola Peltz (Becky), Julian Mazzola (Kid), Michelle Fields (Michelle), Lorraine Mazzola (Teacher), Judy Nazemetz (Nurse), Jill Weigand (Waitress), Meredith Ann Bull (Belinda), Nicky Katt, Kid Million (Cops), Pat Shannon (Rhonda's Dad), Sarge Pickman (Alibi Club DJ), Wass Stevens (Prisoner), Dave Attell (Barker), Judith Knight Young (Lunch Lady), Joey Blonsky (Malcolm)

Spencer Breslin, Nikki Blonsky in Harold © *City Lights*

GARDEN PARTY (Roadside Attractions) Producer/Director/Screenplay, Jason Freeland; Photography, Robert Benavides; Designer, Jason Bistarkey; Costumes, Jennifer Levy, Debra Le Claire; Music, John Swihart; Editor, Daniel R. Padgett; Casting, Joseph Middleton; a Lookout Films production; Dolby; Color; Not rated; 88 minutes; Release date: July 11, 2008. CAST: Willa Holland (April), Vinessa Shaw (Sally), Richard Gunn (Todd), Erik Smith (Sammy), Alexander Cendese (Nathan), Christopher Allport (Davey), Ross Patterson (Joey Zane), Patrick Fischler (Anthony), Jeff Newman (Carlos), Tierra Abbott (Lana), Lisa Arturo (April's Mother), Erik Bragg (Dirk), Candice A. Buenrostro (Bartender), Alesha Clarke (Adriana), Lindley Domingue, Jessica Havard, Malea Richardson (Groupies), Fiona Dourif (Becky), Shellye Dowdy (Anna), Robert Ellsworth (Waiter), Carrie Grossman (Super Duper), Aaron Hanson (Party Goer/Pool Guy), Roy Hausmann (Real Estate Agent), Jordan Havard (Wayne), Sonita Henry (Celine), Jim Holmes (Therapist), Travis Huff (Young Hacker), Tadhg Kelly (John), Lora Kojovic (Leni), Griffin Lamers (Harry), Jennifer Lawrence (Tiff), Kevin Makely (Kevin, Bartender), Jason Medwin (Big Man), Kirsten Myburgh (Friend with Money), Jake Richardson (Kevin), Marc Rose (Counter Guy), Reed Rudy (Earl), Lola Sanchez (Clare), Scott Seymour (Neil), Robin Sydney (Sara), Lady Luck (Bridgetta Tomarchio), Shelly Varod (Jasmine), Jim Cody Williams (Dougie)

Roman Polanski in Wanted and Desired © *HBO*

THE DOORMAN (Gigantic Pictures) Producers, Melvut Akkaya, Brian Devine, Jonathan Gray, Wayne Price, Lucas Akoskin; Director/Editor, Wayne Price; Photography, Patriyk Rebisz; Music, Brazilian Girls; a Sad Films production; Color; HD Video; Not rated; 79 minutes; Release date: July 18, 2008. CAST: Lucas Akoskin (Trevor W), Fabrizio Brienza, Brian Devine, Thom Filicia Wayne Price, Jonathan Gray (Themselves), Matthew Mabe (Stanley), Letty Serra (Nonna Robbie Alessi), Sir Bato the Yugo (Francois Daniel), Melvut Akkaya (The Waiter), Brian Blessinger (Trevor's Roommate), Peter Bogdanovich (Peter), Alex Dawson (Yoga Teacher), Jamie Hatchett (Quo), George Lapinsky (Doorman at Claudia's Apartment), Lisette Lee (Baby Sugar Mama), Claudia Mediza (Trevor's Girlfriend), Dereck O'Connor (Bouncer at Trevor's club), Amy Sacco (Amy), Letty Serra ("Nonna" Robbie Alessi)

Lucas Akoskin in The Doorman © Gigantic Pictures

A MAN NAMED PEARL (Shadow Distribution) Producers/Directors, Scott Galloway, Brent Pierson; Photography, J. Steven Anderson; Music, Fred Story; Editor, Greg Grzeszczak; a Tentmakers Entertainment production; Dolby; Color; Rated G; 78 minutes; Release date: July 18, 2008. Documentary on topiary artist Pearl Fryar; with Pearl Fryar, Metra Fryar, Ronnie Williams, Reverend Jerome McCray, Polly Laffittte, Tom Stanley, Jean Grosser, Ennis Bryant, Betty Scott.

Pearl Fryar in A Man Named Pearl © Shadow Distribution

LOU REED'S BERLIN (Third Rail) Producer, Jon Kilik, Tom Sarig; Executive Producers, Stanley Buchthal, Maya Hoffman; Coproducer, Ann Ruark; Director/ Set Designer, Julian Schnabel; Photography, Ellen Kuras; Music, Lou Reed; Editor, Benjamin Flaherty; a Waterboy and Jon Kilik presentation of a Grandview Pictures/ LM Media GMbH production; Concert documentary in which Lou Reed gives the first live performance of his 1973 cult album, Berlin.

Lou Reed in Lou Reed's Berlin
© Third Rail

DISFIGURED (Cinema Libre) Producer, David W. Higgins; Director/Screenplay, Glenn Gers; Photography, Idit Dvir; Designer/Costumes, Tabitha Johnson; Music, Kayla Schmah; Editors, Glenn Gers, Gregory Plotkin; Casting, Valerie McCaffrey; a Dialogue Heavy Pictures production, in association with Launchpad Prods.; Color; Mini-DV; Not rated; 95 minutes; Release date: July 18, 2008. CAST: Deidra Edwards (Lydia), Staci Lawrence (Darcy), Ryan C. Benson (Bob), Elizabeth Sampson (Carol), Sonya Eddy (Pam), Lindsay Hollister (Alice), Heather Brooker (Judy), April M. Walsh (Gwen), Juanita Guzman (Roxanne), Trevor Mitchell (Hilliard), Patrick Gorman (Marcus), Laurie O'Brien (Sheila), Cheyenne Wilbur (Patrick), Lori Ada (Arda), Sarah Bassak (Sarah), Mercedes Castro (Mercy), Bruce Cronander, Elias McCabe (Party Guests), Edward Rodrigo Diaz (Ed), Tricia Dickson (Cordelia), Henry Dittman (Mr. Devreaux), Judith Drake (Sugar), Sasha Harris (Carmen), Catherine Anne Hayes (Catherine), Julie Inmon (Julie), Chenese Lewis (Chenese), John Stewart Muller (Buyer Husband), Donna Pieroni (Sophia), Shant'e Reese (Shant'e), Gene Richards (Plum), Seirah Royin (Thin Woman), Stuart Randy Smith (The Counter Guy), Florence Young (Buyer Wife)

Staci Lawrence, Deidra Edwards in Disfigured © Cinema Libre

FELON (Stage 6) Producers, Tucker Tooley, Dan Keston; Executive Producers, Vincent Newman, Stephen Dorff, David Peters; Coproducers, Chris Wilhem, Ryan Breen; Director/Screenplay, Ric Roman Waugh; Photography, Dana Gonzales; Designer, Vincent Reynaud; Costumes, Meriwether Nichols; Music, Gerhard Daum; Editor, Jonathan Chibnall; Casting, Nancy Naylor Battino; a Tooley prods., Pantry Films production; Dolby; Widescreen; Color; Rated R; 104 minutes; Release date: July 18, 2008. CAST: Stephen Dorff (Wade Porter), Harold Perrineau (Lt. Jackson), Val Kilmer (John Smith), Marisol Nichols (Laura), Anne Archer (Maggie), Sam Shepard (Gordon), Nick Chinlund (Sgt. Roberts), Johnny Lewis (Snowman), Vincent Miller (Michael Porter), Larnell Stovall (Viper), Shawn Prince (Todd Jackson), Chris Browning (Danny Samson), Greg Serano (Officer Diaz), Jake Walker (Warden Harris), Nate Parker (Officer Collins), Mike Seal (Williams), Louie Pescador (Oso), Gabriel "Bam Bam" Merendon (Oso's Lieutenant), Mark Sivertsen (Agent Skiletti), Mara Holguin (Public Defender), Carrie Fleming (Kelly Collins), Roman Mitchiyan (Swamper Deputy), Adam Taylor (Investigator Hammond), Brittany Perrineau (Stacy Jackson), Harry Zimmerman (LA Judge), Kevin Wiggins (SQ Guard), Brian Keith Gamble (Joe), Rosalia De Aragon (IRC Deputy), Jesus Payan, Jr. (Lead Hispanic), Ivan Brutsch (Invited Guard), John Trejo (ADSEG Guard), Cynthia Ruffin (Guard), Christien Tinsley (Belligerent Man), William Allen (Drunk Driver), Esodie Geiger (Judge), Richard Caruso (Gang Investigator), Erik Gomez (Bodie), Elton Walker (Corn Rows), Tait Fletcher (White Inmate), Adrian Ponce, Ben James Roybal (Hispanic Fighters), Joey Villasenor (Loco), Antonio Leyba (Gonzalez), John Koyama (Asian Fighter), Jermaine Washington (Large Black Inmate), Mike Smith (Rooker), Shawn Rosales (CSI Tech), Steve Ulibarri (Intruder)

TAKE (Liberation Entertainment) Producer, Chet Thomas; Executive Producers, Tyler Measom, Brady Whittingham, Ryan Oliver; Director/Screenplay, Charles Oliver; Photography, Tristan Whitman; Designer, Luke Freeborn; Costumes, Jayme Bohn; Music, Roger Neill; Editor, Andrew McAllister; a Crux Entertainment presentation of a Telos production; Dolby; Widescreen; Color; Rated R; 99 minutes; Release date: July 18, 2008. CAST: Minnie Driver (Ana), Jeremy Renner (Saul), Bobby Coleman (Jesse), David Denman (Marty Nichols), Adam Rodriguez (Steven), Bill McKinney (Bengamin Gregor), Emily Harrison (Wendy), Griff Furst (The Mechanic), Patrick Brennan (Incensed Man), Tom Schmid (Boss), Jessica Stier (Mrs. Bachanas), Rocky Marquette (Mark), Paul Schackman (Sam), Allison Miller (Shoe Sales Girl), Patrick Dollaghan (Supervising Officer), Michael Ciulla (Chuck), Shane Woodson (Older Mechanic), Courtenay Taylor (Truck Driver), Louis Mandylor (Terrel), Rob Elk (Senile Man), Lisa Robert (Bartender), Richard Bairos (Customer), Veronica Lauren (Patron), Theo Micholas Pagones (The Pharmacist), Dale Dickey (Truck Woman), Edward James Gage (Older Man), Keith Biondi (Camper Man), Willie C. Carpenter (Aging Man), Todd Waring (Loud Talker), Kendall Clement, Andrew Thacher (Guards), Shane Johnson (Runyan), Katia Louise (Waitress), Connie Wong (Pregnant Lady), Cindy S. Benton (SUV Mom), Tyrone Benton III (SUV Son), Jasmine Benton (SUV Daughter), Bryeon Earle (Bar Patron), Alastair Gilbert (Busboy), Aaron J. Hartnell (Last Meal Prison Guard), Alonzo F. Jones (Arguing Husband), John Kihm (Day Player), Francesca Roberts (Principal), Ryan Layton Simmons (Bank Teller), Frank J. Tsacrios (Homeless Man)

Eddie Aikau in Bustin' Down the Door © *Screen Media*

BUSTIN' DOWN THE DOOR (Screen Media) Producers, Monika Gosch, Robert Traill; Executive Producers, Shaun Tomson, Chris Blair; Director, Jeremy Gosch; Screenplay, Jeremy Gosch, Robert Traill, Monika Gosch, Shaun Tomson; Inspired by Wayne "Rabbit" Bartholomew; Narration Written by Phil Jarratt; Narrator, Edward Norton; Photography, Gary Rohan; Music, Stuart Michael Thomas; Music Supervisor, Ray Espinola, Jr.; Editor, Danny Bresnik; a Fresh & Smoked production; Dolby; Color; Not rated; 95 minutes; Release date: July 25, 2008. Documentary on a group of Australian and South African surfers and their conquest of the waves on Oahu's North Shore in 1974; with Wayne "Rabbit" Bartholomew, Ian Cairns, Mark Richards, Shaun Tomson, Michael Tomson, Peter Townend, Drew Kampion, Eddie Rothman, Fred Hemmings, Barry Kanaiaupuni, Jeff Rakman, Clyde Aikau, Dave Gilovich, Rob Machado, Kelly Slater.

Stephen Stills, Neil Young, Graham Nash, David Crosby in CSNY Déjà vu © *Roadside Attractions*

CSNY DÉJÀ VU (Roadside Attractions) Producer, L.A. Johnson; Director, Bernard Shakey; Screenplay, Neil Young, Mike Cerre; Photography, Mike Elwell; Music, Neil Young; Editor, Mark Faulkner; a Shangri-La Entertainment presentation of a Shakey Pictures production; Dolby; Color; Rated R; 96 minutes; Release date: July 25, 2008. Documentary on Crosby, Stills, Nash & Young's "Freedom of Speech" tour; with David Crosby, Stephen Stills, Graham Nash, Neil Young, Bo Alexander, Stephen Colbert, Eric Von Haessler, Josh Hisle, Rick Rosas, Larry Wachs.

Minnie Driver in Take © *Liberation Entertainment*

The Order of Myths © *The Cinema Guild*

THE ORDER OF MYTHS (The Cinema Guild) Producers, Margaret Brown, Sara Alize Cross; Executive Producer, Christine Mattson; Coproducer, Gabby Stein; Co-Executive Producer, Stephen Bannatyne; Director, Margaret Brown; Photography, Michael Simmonds, Lee Daniels; Music Supervisor, Janice Ginsberg; Editors, Michael Taylor, Geoffrey Richman, Margaret Brown; a NetPoint Prods. presentation in association with Lucky Hat Entertainment; Color; HD Cam; Not rated; 80 minutes; Release date: July 25, 2008. Documentary on Mobile, Alabama's segregated Mardi Gras celebration.

AMERICA THE BEAUTIFUL (First Independent Pictures) Producers, Darryl Roberts, Kurt Engfehr, Stela Georgieva, Michele G. Blumenthal; Executive Producers, Henry N.K. Anderson, Michael Beach, Dennis Damore, Terence Wright; Coproducers, Sherese Locke, Sharon Newport, Kimberly Bennick, Jason Brousseau; Director/ Screenplay, Darryl Roberts; Photography, Michele G. Blumenthal, Terence Wright, Cassie; Music, Various; Supervising Editor, Kurt Engfehr; a Sensory Overload production; Color; DV; Rated R; 100 minutes; Release date: August 1, 2008. Documentary in which filmmaker Darryl Roberts investigates America's obsession with beauty; with Darryl Roberts, Gerren Taylor, Paris Hilton, Eve Ensler, Anthony Kiedis, Martin Short, Ted Casablanca, Chris Keefe, Jessica Simpson.

STEALING AMERICA: VOTE BY VOTE (Direct Cinema Limited) Producer, Dorothy Fadiman; Executive Producers, Mitchell Block, James Fadiman; Coproducers, Bruce O'Dell, Carla Henry; Director, Dorothy Fadiman; Narrator, Peter Coyote; Photography, Matthew Luotto; Music, Laurence Rosenthal; Editors, Katie Larkin, Matthew Luotto, Xuan Vu, Ekta Bansal Bhargava; a Concentric Media production, presented in association with Abramorama & Mitropoulos Films; Color; DV-to-35mm; Not rated; 90 minutes; Release date: August 1, 2008. Documentary on the flaws in America's current electronic voting system.

Steal America: Vote by Vote © *Direct Cinema Ltd.*

PROFIT MOTIVE AND THE WHISPERING WIND (Traveling Light) Producer/ Director/Screenplay/Editor/Animator, John Gianvito; Photography, John Gianvito, Mary-Helena Clark, Lesley Gall, Tatiana McCabe; Music, Various; Color; 16mm-to-DigiBeta; Not rated; 60 minutes; Release date; August 1, 2008. Documentary on the history of American activism.

THE MIDNIGHT MEAT TRAIN (Lionsgate) Producers, Tom Rosenberg, Gary Lucchesi, Clive Barker, Jorge Saralegui, Eric Reid, Richard Wright; Executive Producers, Joe Daley, Anthony DiBlasi, David Scott Rubin, Robert McMinn, Fisher Stevens, John Penotti, Peter Block, Jason Constantine; Coproducers, Beth DePatie, James McQuade; Director, Ryuhei Kitamura; Screenplay, Jeff Buhler; Based on the short story by Clive Barker; Photography, Jonathan Sela; Designer, Clark Hunter; Costumes, Christopher Lawrence; Music, Robb Williamson, Johannes Kobilke; Editor, Toby Yates; Visual Effects Supervisor, James McQuade; Stunts, David Leitch; Casting, Nancy Nayour Battino, Kelly Martin Wagner; Visual Effects and Animation, Furious FX; a Lakeshore Entertainment/Lionsgate production, in association with Midnight Picture Show and GreeneStreet Films; Dolby; Widescreen; Color; Rated R; 98 minutes; Release date: August 1, 2008. CAST: Bradley Cooper (Leon), Leslie Bibb (Maya), Brooke Shields (Susan Hoff), Vinnie Jones (Mahogany), Roger Bart (Jurgis), Tony Curran (Driver), Barbara Eve Harris (Det. Lynn Hadley), Ted Raimi (Randle Cooper), Peter Jacobson (Otto), Stephanie Mace (Leigh Cooper), Nora (Erika Sakaki), Quinton "Rampage" Jackson (Guardian Angel), Dan Callahan (Troy Tavelski), Don Smith (Station Cop), Earl Carroll (Jack Franks), Allen Maldonado (Lead Gangbanger), Michael McCracken, Ryan McDowell, Eddie Vargas (Fathers), Kelvin O'Bryant, Jayson Sanchez (Scrawny Kids), Brian Taylor (Young Man), Geoffrey Gould (Subway Passenger), Kate Mulligan (Newscaster)

Bradley Cooper in The Midnight Meat Train © *Lionsgate*

IN SEARCH OF A MIDNIGHT KISS (IFC Films) Producers, Seth Caplan, Scoot McNairy; Executive Producer, Anne Walker-McBay; Director/Screenplay, Alex Holdridge; Photography, Robert Murphy; Editors, Frank Reynolds, Jacob Vaughn; a Midnight Kiss production; Black and white; HD; Not rated; 97 minutes; Release date: August 1, 2008. CAST: Scoot McNairy (Wilson), Sara Simmonds (Vivian), Brian McGuire (Jacob), Katleen Luong (Min), Twink Caplan (Wilson's Mother), Robert Murphy (Jack), Ann Chatterton (Cindy Drummond (Neighbors), Nic Harcourt (Radio DJ), Justin Huen (Neptune), Sandra Lindqvist (Craig's List Caller), Tony Morgan (Guy on Answering Machine), Via Osgood (Karen), Bret Roberts (Bui)

Scoot McNairy, Sara Simmonds in In Search of the Midnight Kiss
© IFC Films

FIRE UNDER THE SNOW (Imakoko Media) Producer/Director, Makoto Sasa; Coproducers, Jim Browne, Vladan Nikolic; Screenplay, Makoto Sasa, Aaron Mendez; Photography, Vladimir Subotic; Editor, Milica Zec; presented in association with Argot Pictures, Sulra Films; Black and white/color; HD; Not rated; 75 minutes; Release date: August 8, 2008. Documentary on how Tibetan monk Palden Gyatso's thirty-three years of imprisonment and torture became a rallying cry for his country's liberation; with Palden Gyatso, Manfred Nowak, Lawrence Gerstein, Tenzin Tsundue, Ana Adhe, Lobsang Khenrab.

BEER FOR MY HORSES (Roadside Attractions) Producers, Toby Keith, Donald Zuckerman; Executive Producers, T.K. Kimbrell, Jeff Yapp, Leslie Belzberg, Brent Morris; Director, Michael Salomon; Screenplay, Toby Keith, Rodney Carrington; Story, Toby Keith; a Show Dog Movies production, association with CMT Prods. and B4MH Prods.; Rated PG-13; 88 minutes; Release date: August 8, 2008. CAST: Toby Keith (Bill "Rack" Racklin), Rodney Carrington (Lonnie), Tom Skerritt (Sheriff Landry), Ted Nugent (Skunk), Brit Morgan (Harveyetta), Barry Corbin (Buck Baker), Greg Serano (Tito Garza), Claire Forlani (Annie), Willie Nelson (Charlie), Gina Gershon (Cammie), Chris Browning (Deputy Stippins), Myk Watford (Norvel), Carlos Sanz (Manuel), Chad Brummett (Johnny Franks), David Allan Coe (Gypsy Gene), Mark Povinelli (Merriweather), Beth Bailey (Becky), Mike Miller (Peabody), Michael-David Aragon (Henchman #3), Ray Aguayo (Chico), Tish Rayburn-Miller (Mavis), Kate Schroeder (Sandy), Danielle Brown (Two Ton Tina), Charles Dowdy (Bathroom Singer), Brad Romberg, Marc Schaffer (Bad Guys), Trailer Choir (Themselves), Mel Tillis (Plumber)

Toby Keith, Claire Forlani in Beer for My Horses © Roadside Attractions

WHAT WE DO IS SECRET (Vitagraph/Vision Films) Producers, Kevin Mann, Matthew Pernciaro, Rodger Grossman, Todd Traina; Executive Producers, Stephen Nemeth, Shane West, Michael LaFetra, Damon Martin, David Mack; Coproducer, Michelle Ghaffari; Co-Executive Producers, Lisa Romanoff, Andre Relis; Director/ Screenplay, Rodger Gorssman; Story, Rodger Grossman, Michelle Baer Ghaffari; Photography, Andrew Huebscher; Designer, John R. Mott; Costumes, Julia Castor; Music, Anna Waronker; Editors, Ross Albert, Joel Plotch; Casting, Anne McCarthy, Jay Scully; a Rhino Films presentation in association with Picture Machine, Red Rover Films, King Records, Hopeless Romantic, Foundation Films; Deluxe color/Black and white; Super 16; Rated R; 92 minutes; Release date: August 8, 2008. CAST: Shane West (Darby Crash), Bijou Phillips (Lorna Doom), Rick Gonzalez (Pat Smear), Noah Segan (Don Bolles), Ashton Holmes (Rob Henley), Tina Majorino (Michelle), Lauren German (Belinda), Keir O'Donnell (Chris Ashford), Azura Skye (Casey Cola), Ray Park (Brendan Mullen), Sebastian Roché (Claude Kickboy Bessy), Amy Halloran (Becky), Katharine Leonard (Jena), Rachael Santhon (Malissa), Noah Abrams, Chad Liffman (Audience Members), Gary Alcock (Beer Guy), Daniel Alvarado, David Alvarado (Bar Patrons), Ozzy Benn (Captain Sensible), Thom Bishops (Tony the Hustler), Christopher Boyd (Dave Vanian), Missy Doty (Amber), Brian Gleason (Regi Mental), Michele Hicks (Penelope Spheeris), J.P. Manoux (Rodney Bingenheimer), Chandra McWhorter (Farrah-Fawcett Minor), Greg McWhorter (Eddie Subtitle), Lachlan McWhorter (John Morris), Howard S.Miller (Starwood Manager), Jonathan Milliken (Young Darby), Bru Muller (Teacher), Randi Newton (Gerber), Paul Nygro (Bob Biggs), Brian Oerly (Bouncer), Ray Park (Brendan Mullen), Trevor Parsons (Billy Zoom), Chris Pontius (Black Randy), Sara Rivas (Shannon), Scott L. Schwartz (Biker), Anna Waronker (Joan Jett), John Westernoff (Auditioning Drummer), Richard Wharton (Whiskey Manager)

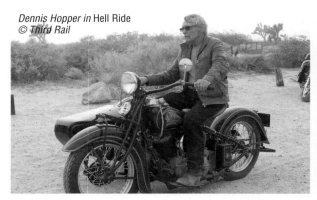

Dennis Hopper in Hell Ride
© Third Rail

HELL RIDE (Third Rail) Producers, Michael Steinberg, Shana Stein, Larry Bishop; Executive Producers, Quentin Tarantino, Bob Weinstein, Harvey Weinstein; Coproducer, Todd King; Director/Screenplay, Larry Bishop; Photography, Scott Kevan; Designer, Tim Grimes; Costumes, Ariyela Wald-Cohain; Music, Daniele Luppi; Music Superivsor, Mary Ramos; Editors, William Yeh, Blake West; Casting, Johanna Ray, Jenny Jue; Stunts, Jimmy N. Roberts, Jeff Dashnaw; a Quentin Tarantino and Dimension Films presentation of a Steinberg & Stein production; Dolby; Color; Rated R; 84 minutes; Release date: August 8, 2008. CAST: Larry Bishop (Pistolero), Michael Madsen (The Gent), Eric Balfour (Comanche/Bix), Vinnie Jones (Billy Wings), Leonor Varela (Nada), David Carradine (The Deuce), Dennis Hopper (Eddie "Scratch" Zero), Michael Beach (Goody Two-Shoes), Laura Cayouette (Dani), Julia Jones (Cherokee Kisum), Francesco Quinn (Machete), Cassandra Hepburn (Maria), David Grieco (Dr. Cement), Dean Delray (Apeshit), Mike Macecsko (Shyster), Tracy Phillips (Yvonne), Austin Galuppo (Sonny Kisum), Pete Randall (St. Louie), Steve McCammon (Bob the Bum), Lee Alfred (Joint), Kanin Howell (Opium), Theresa Alexandria (Carmen), Andrea Fellers (Echo), Terry Fradet (Holy Smoke), Alyson Kiperman (Gigi), Maja Mandzuka (Danka), Bonnie Aarons (Mud Devils Ref), Alison McAtee (The Swede)

WRANGLER: ANATOMY OF AN ICON (Automat Pictures) Producer/Director, Jeffrey Schwarz; Photography, Gary Corrigan, Kevin M. Graves, David Hallinger, Rob Jakubik, Tanja Koop, Doron Schlair, Clay Westervelt; Music, Michael "The Millionaire" Cudahy; Editor, Jaime Myers; Produced in association with Making It Big; Color; BetaSP/DV-to-DigiBeta; Not rated; 85 minutes; Release date: August 8, 2008. Documentary on one of gay porn's leading names of the 1970's, Jack Wrangler; with Jack Wrangler, Margaret Whiting, Bruce Vilanch, Marc Shaiman, Christine Ebersole, Sharon Mitchell, Michael Musto, Chi Chi LaRue, Jamie Gillis, Rod McKuen, Gloria Leonard, Al Goldstein, Gino Colbert, Candida Royalle, Samantha Fox, Joe Gage, Debbie Whiting, Robert Alvarez, Brooks Ashmanskas, Michael Bronski, Durk Dehner, Samuel R. Delany, Michael Denneny, Jerry Douglas, Kevin Duda, Peter Ford, Arnie Kantrowitz, Tim Kincaid, William Ivey Long, William Margold, Alan Oppenheimer, Henri Pachard, Robert Patrick, Robert W. Richards, Mark Sendroff, David J. Skal, Kevin Thomas, Debbi Whiting, Carol Woods

Jack Wrangler in Wrangler: Anatomy of an Icon © *Automat Pictures*

BEAUTIFUL LOSERS (Arthouse Films) Producers, Rich Lim, Jon Barlow, Chris Green, Noah Khoshbin; Executive Producers, Ravi Anne, Jared Moshe; Coproducers, Adam Glickman, Tobin Yelland, Arlo Rosner; Director, Aaron Rose; Co-Director, Joshua Leonard; Photography, Tobin Yelland; Music, Money Mark; Music Supervisor, Randall Poster; Editor, Lenny Mesina; Animation, Geoff McFetridge; a Sidetrack Films presentation of a Manzanita Bros. production in association with Perception Media and Blacklake Prods.; Color/Black and white; HD; 8mm; 16mm; Betamax; Mini-DV; Not rated; 91 minutes; Release date: August 8, 2008. Documentary focusing on eleven New York street artists; with Thomas Campbell, Shepard Fairey, Jo Jackson, Chris Johanson, Margaret Kilgallen, Harmony Korine, Geoff McFetridge, Barry McGee, Mike Mills, Stephen Powers, Aaron Rose, Ed Templeton.

THE FLYBOYS (Voltage Pictures) Producer/Director/Editor, Rocco Devilliers; Executive Producers, Lisle H. Moore, Jr.; Kelley Feldsott Reynolds; Coproducer, Dan Urness; Screenplay, Jason Devilliers, Rocco Devilliers, Richard Dutcher; Story, Rocco Devilliers, Gregory C. Haynes; Photography, Jim Orr; Designer, Chris Davis; Costumes, Debra Box; Music, Lisle Moore; Casting, Jennifer Buster; a Dark Coast Pictures production; Dolby; Color; Rated PG-13; 118 minutes; Release date: August 15, 2008. CAST: Jesse James (Jason McIntyre), Reiley McClendon (Kyle Barrett), Stephen Baldwin (Silvio Esposito), Tom Sizemore (Angelo Esposito), J. Todd Adams (Lenny Drake), Dallen Gettling (Ed Thomas), Jennifer Slimko (Samantha Barret), Robert Costanzo (Carmine), Vince Cecere

(Manny), Frank D'Amico (Sal), Harrison Young (Grandpa Thomas), Blaire Baron (Susan Thomas), Tommy Hinkley (John McIntyre), Joanne Baron (Ms. Poulson), Dylan Kasch (Rick), David Stevens (Jack), Rainbow Borden (Dirk), Garret Sato (Sato), Yoshi Jenkins (Kubota), Yoshio Be (Kuboto), Marvin Payne (Ray), Jossara Jinaro (Felicitas), Laurel Snow (Sara McIntyre), Ashley Thomas (Katie McIntyre), Jesse Plemons, Travis Whitney (Bullies), Malcolm Sonsire (Mechanic), Jude Alley (Reporter), Dan Urness, Joe Sigg (Cops), Don Kenworthy (Mr. Gardner), Dawna Kenworthy (Mrs. Gardner), Natali Wyson (Shelly), Doug Caputo (Car Washer), Jennifer Chadburn (Bikini Girl), James Gaskell (Farmer)

ANITA O'DAY: THE LIFE OF A JAZZ-SINGER (Ugo/Elan) Producers, Robbie Cavolina, Ian McCrudden, Melissa Davis; Executive Producer, Nancy Fields O'Connor; Directors/Editors, Robbie Cavolina, Ian McCrudden; a Ugo Prods., Elan Entertainment production; Color; HDcam; Not rated; 93 minutes; Release date: August 8, 2008. Documentary on jazz singer Anita O'Day; with Buddy Bregman, Charles Britton, David Boska, Ken Druker, Joe Franklin, Will Friedwald, Russel Garcia, Jim Gavin, Freeman Guunther, Bill Holman, Karen Kramer, Eddie Locke, Johnny Mandel, John Cameron Mitchell, Mark Morris, John Pietranowicz, Denny Roche, Annie Ross, Mary "Bunny" Sellers, Dr. Billy Taylor, George Win, Margaret Whiting, Joe Wielding, Gerald Wilson.

HENRY POOLE IS HERE (Overture) Producers, Tom Rosenberg, Gary Lucchesi, Richard Wright, Gary Gilbert, Tom Lassally; Executive Producers, Norman Reiss, Eric Reid, Michael Aguilar, Mark Pellington; Coproducers, Beth DePatie, David Kern; Director, Mark Pellington; Screenplay, Albert Torres; Photography, Eric Schmidt; Designer, Richard Hoover; Costumes, Wendy Chuck; Music, John Frizzell; Editor, Lisa Zeno Churgin; Visual Effects Supervisor, James McQuade; Casting, Tricia Wood, Deborah Aquila; a Lakeshore Entertainment and Camelot Pictures presentation of a Lakeshore Entertainment production; Dolby; Panavision; Deluxe color; Rated PG; 100 minutes; Release date: August 15, 2008. CAST: Luke Wilson (Henry Poole), Radha Mitchell (Dawn), Adriana Barraza (Esperanza), George Lopez (Father Salazar), Cheryl Hines (Meg), Richard Benjamin (Dr. Fancher), Morgan Lily (Millie Stupek), Rachel Seiferth (Patience), Beth Grant (Josie), Earl Carroll (Mr. Lawrence), Noah Dahl (Young Henry), Nick Dash (Security Guard), Gizza Elizondo (Cancer Survivor), Elaine Anne Furst, Don Smith (Supermarket Shoppers), Gloria Garayua (Worshipper), Molly Hagan (Pediatrician), Marcus Maria Jung (Mortician), Michelle Krusiec (Young Nurse), Kate Mulligan (Waitress), Andrew Santino (Orderly)

George Lopez, Adriana Barraza in Henry Poole is Here © *Overture Film*

THE ROCKER (20ᵗʰ Century Fox) Producers, Shawn Levy, Tom McNulty; Coproducer, Lyn Lucibello-Brancatella; Director, Peter Cattaneo; Screenplay, Maya Forbes, Wallace Wolodarsky; Story, Ryan Jaffe; Photography, Anthony B. Richmond; Designer, Brandt Gordon; Costumes, Christopher Hargadon; Music, Chad Fischer; Music Supervisor, Patrick Houlihan; Editor, George Folsey, Jr.; Casting, Julie Ashton; a Fox Atomic presentation of a 21 Laps production, in association with Dune Entertainment III; Dolby; Deluxe color; Rated PG-13; 102 minutes; Release date: August 20, 2008. CAST: Rainn Wilson (Robert "Fish" Fishman), Christina Applegate (Kim), Josh Gad (Matt Gadman), Teddy Geiger (Curtis), Emma Stone (Amelia), Jeff Garlin (Stan), Jane Lynch (Lisa), Jason Sudeikis (David Marshall), Will Arnett (Lex), Howard Hesseman (Gator), Fred Armisen (Kerr), Bradley Cooper (Trash), Lonny Ross (Sticks), Jon Glaser (Billy), Jane Krakowski (Carol), Samantha Weinstein (Violet), Demetri Martin (Kip), Aziz Ansari (Aziz), Ellie Knaus (Erica), Laura DeCarteret (Amelia's Mom), Steve Adams (Amelia's Dad), Mark Forward (Leon), Vik Sahay (Gary), Brittany Allen (I Heart Matt Girl), Jonathan Malen (Jeremy), Rebecca Northan (Jeremy's Mother), Keir Gilchrist (Moby Type Kid), Simon Sinn (Mr. Lee), SuChin Pak, Pete Best (Themselves), Ennis Esmer (Barney), Nicole Arbour (Trashy Groupie), Wesley Morgan (Prom King Josh), Tanya Bevan (Prom Queen Jennifer), Marvin Karon (School Principal), Sandi Ross (Ms. Kopelson), Talia Russo (Amy), Jon Cor (Paul), Darrel Gamotin (Beat Box Kid), Angela Maiorano Thurston (Frazzled Stylist), Nicholas Spencer (Harry), Allan Roberto (Max), Patrick Hagarty (Gund Arena P.A.), Jessica Porter (Desk Sergeant), Dave Kiner (Speedy Rocker Guy), Guy Sanvido (Old Barber), Christian Potenza (Dry Engineer)

Josh Gad, Teddy Geiger, Emma Stone, Rainn Wilson in The Rocker © 20th Century Fox

CTHULHU (Regent) Producers, Alexis Ferris, Daniel Gildark, Anne Rosellini, Jeffrey Brown; Executive Producers, Gar Godfrey, Grant Cogswell, Roxanne Tarn; Coproducer, Laurie Hicks; Director, Daniel Gildark; Screenplay, Grant Cogswell; Based on the works of H.P. Lovecraft; Photography, Sean Kirby; Designer, Etta Lilienthal; Costumes, Doris Black; Music, Willy Greer; Music Supervisor, Van Riker; Editor, World Famous; Visual Effects Supervisor, Deborah Ristic; a Regent Entertainment presentation in association with Cascadia Film Collective, of an Arkham NW production; Color; Rated R; 109 minutes; Release date: August 22, 2008. CAST: Jason Cottle (Russ), Scott Patrick Green (Mike), Cara Buono (Dannie), Tori Spelling (Susan), Robert Padilla (Ancestor), Ethan Atkinson (SUV Driver), Jeffrey Brown (Brown), Lyall Bush (Voice of Allen Combs), Grant Cogswell (NPR Newscaster's Voice), Charles Creasy (Charlie), Casey Curran (Club Kid), Tarame Del Guidici (Asylum Nurse), Eben Eldridge (EBS Announcer's Voice), Richard Garfield (Zadok), Ian Geoghegan (Ralph), Robin Gordon (Auctioneer), Ryan Gorman (Writhing Bag Figure, Tiara Beast), Keifer Grimm (Teen Mike), Rob Hamm (Jake), Dennis Kleinsmith (Rev. Marsh), Nathan Ladd (Boy Russ), Kellan

Larson (Blind Boy), Barbara Lindsay (Evelyn Marsh), Emilie Maslow (Caller's Voice), Liza Maslow (Astrologist's Voice), Patrick McKnight (SUV Passenger), Scott McKnight (Liquor Store Weirdo/Prison Guard/Will O'Really), Jessi Meyer (Jilly Bronstein), Greg Michaels (Sheriff), Amy Minderhout (Julie), Brandon Mitchell (Auctioneer's Assistant), Cary Moon (Pacifica Newscaster's Voice), Sabrina Prada (Soccer Mom), Tom Prince (Gilbert, Bartender), Jonathan Raban (BBC Newscaster's Voice), Megan Rider (Walking Woman), Jan Sewell (Voice of Anne Colder), Joe Shapiro (Barnes), Hilary H.J. Specht (Librarian), Nancy Stark (Aunt Josie), Alex Stroud (Hustler #2), Hunter Stroud (Teen Russ), Dennis Tracy (Deputy Ben), Jasminka Vukcevic (Victorian Woman), Ruby Wood (Girl on Stairs)

Jason Cottle, Scott Green in Cthulhu © *Regent Releasing*

I.O.U.S.A. (Roadside Attractions) Producers, Christine O'Malley, Sarah Gibson, Open Sky Entertainment; Executive Producers, Addison Wiggin; Director, Patrick Creadon; Screenplay, Patrick Creadon, Christine O'Malley, Addison Wiggin; Inspired by the book *Empire of Debt: The Rise of an Epic Financial Crisis* by William Bonner and Addison Wiggin; Story, Addison Wiggin, Kate Incontrera; Photography, Patrick Creadon; Music, Peter Golub; Editor, Doug Blush; an Agora Entertainment presentation, in association with O'Malley Creadon Prods.; Color/Black and white; HD; Rated PG; 87 minutes; Release date: August 22, 2008. Documentary following U.S. Comptroller General David M. Walker and Concord Coalition Executive Director Robert Bixby's efforts to draw attention to America's increasing financial problems by traveling city to city with their Fiscal Wake-Up Tour; with David M. Walker, Robert Bixby, Diana Rehm, Alice Rivlin, William Bonner, Harry Zeeve, Robert Rudin, Ron Paul, David Yepsen, Kay Harms, Warren Buffet, David Chia, James Arredy, Kent Conrad, Paul O'Neill.

Ron Paul in I.O.U.S.A. © *Roadside Attractions*

THE LONGSHOTS (MGM) Producers, Ice Cube, Matt Alvarez, Nick Santora; Executive Producers, Bob Weinstein, Harvey Weinstein, Andy LaMarca; Director, Fred Durst; Screenplay, Nick Santora; Photography, Conrad W. Hall; Designer, Charles Breen; Costumes, Mary McLeod; Music, Teddy Castellucci; Music Supervisor, Spring Aspers; Editor, Jeffrey Wolf; a Dimension Films presentation of a Cube Vision and Blackjack Films production; Dolby; Color; Rated PG; 94 minutes; Release date: August 22, 2008. CAST: Ice Cube (Curtis Plummer), Keke Palmer (Jasmine Plummer), Dash Mihok (Cyrus), Tasha Smith (Claire Plummer), Jill Marie Jones (Ronnie Macer), Matt Craven (Coach Fisher), Miles Chandler (Damon), Glenn Plummer (Winston), Garrett Morris (Rev. Pratt), Malcolm Goodwin (Roy), Michael Colyar (Ennis), Dean Delray (Andrew Kosowski), Earthquake (Karl), Hugo Perez (Edgar Mejavar), Sheran Goodspeed Keyton (Barb), Greg Dorchak (Ernie), Kofi Siriboe (Javy Hall), Alan Aisenberg (Feather), Shane Kaufman (Rodriguez), Malcolm Phillips (Manny), Justin Dale (Browning), Chloe Bridges (Tammy), Debby Ryan (Edith), Gerald Richardson (Defensive End), Wayne Dehart (Mr. Peppers), Zhailon Levingston (Opposing Cornerback), Peyton "Alex" Smith (Opposing Linebacker), George Wilson (Testifier), Vincent Laresca, Jim Flowers (Pop Warner Officials), Athena Hawkins (Young Girl), Zorianna Kit (News Reporter), Calbe Jones (Jonesy), Ed Walsh (Announcer), Maria Anita Howard (Local News Anchor), Sophia Taylor, Katy Peppard (Girls), Jessica Fain (Big Girl), Dale Lee Ward, Jr. (Player)

Ice Cube, Keke Palmer in The Longshots © MGM

COLLEGE (MGM) Producers, Adam Rosenfelt, Marc Schaberg; Executive Producer, Sam Nazarian; Coproducer, John J. Anderson; Director, Deb Hagan; Screenplay, Dan Callahan, Adam Ellison; Photography, Dan Stoloff; Designer, Ethan Tobman; Costumes, Caroline Marx; Music, Transcenders; Music Supervisors, Joel C. High, Rebecca Rienks; Editor, David Codron; an Element Films presentation, in association with Lift Prods.; Dolby; Color; Rated R; 94 minutes; Release date: August 29, 2008. CAST: Drake Bell (Kevin Brewer), Andrew Caldwell (Carter Scott), Andree Moss (Ashley), Carolyn Moss (Riley), Wendy Talley (Kevin's Mom), Kevin Covais (Morris Hooper), Alona Tal (Gina), Ryan Pinkston (Fletcher), Brandi Coleman, Jessica Heap (College Girls), Finch Nissen (Sweaty Guy), Camille Mana (Heather), Haley Bennett (Kendall), Nathalie Walker (Amy), Nick Zano (Teague), Gary Owen (Bearcat), Zach Cregger (Cooper), Reggie Martinez (Goose), Deejay Buras (Assless Chaps Guy), Ethan Tobman (Jean Shorts Guy), Todd Voltz (Nitrous Guy), Melissa Lingafelt (Junior Girl), Brandy Blake, Ava Santana (Girls), Nick Erickson (Mr. Hooper), Wallace Merck (Dean Chandler), Stephanie Honore (Gina's Friend), Marissa D'Onofrio (Tour Guide), Tracy Mulholland (Bitchy Sorority Sister), Romeo Clarke (Bouncer), Valentina Vaughn, Heather Vandeven (Penthouse Pets), Verne Troyer (Himself), Lisa Morrison (Mrs. Chandler), Earl Maddox (Farmer), Amanda Abadie (Sorority Girl), Michael J. Gaeta (Police Sergeant), Michael P. Cahill (Mr. Hays), Armando Leduc (Frat Boy)

Andre Caldwell, Drake Bell, Kevin Covais in College © MGM

ANOTHER GAY SEQUEL: GAYS GONE WILD! (TLA Releasing) Producers, Todd Stephens, Derek Curl; Executive Producers, Eric Eisenbrey, Markus Goetze, Raymond Murray, Richard Wolff, Claire Brown Kohler, Eric Moore, Patrick Murray, Jonah Blechman, Michael Wolfson, Charlie Know, Johnny Behr; Director/Screenplay, Todd Stephens; Story, Todd Stephens, Eric Eisenbrey; Photography, Carl Bartels; Designer, Thom Lussier; Costumes, Peter Lovello; Music, Marty Beller; Music Supervisor, Bill Coleman; Editor, Spencer Schilly; Casting, Eve Battaglia, Collin Daniel, Brett Greenstein; a TLA Releasing production, in association with Luna Pictures and Caveat Films; Dolby; Color; HD-to-35mm; Not rated; 98 minutes; Release date: August 29, 2008. CAST: Jonah Blechman (Nico), Jake Mosser (Andy Wilson), Aaron Michael Davies (Griff), Jimmy Clabots (Jarod), Perez Hilton (Himself), RuPaul (Turell Tyrelle), Scott Thompson (Andy's Dad), Lady Bunny (Sandi Cove), Will Wikle (Jasper), Brandon Lim (Jasper Chan), Isaac Webster (Jasper Pledge/Fake Griff), Brent Corrigan (Stan the Merman), Lypsinka (Andy's Mom), Amanda Lepore (Transamerican Stewardess Debbie Gottakunt), William Belli (Transamerican Stewardess Nancy Needatwat), Colton Ford (Butch Hunk), Jim Verraros (Singing Priest), Michael Lucas (Pizza Boy), Stephanie McVay (Bonnie Hunter – Nico's Mom), Ashlie Atkinson (Muffler), Andersen Gabrych (Rod the Wino Queen), Jeffrey Coon (Surfer Boy), Ellen Jacoby (Crusty Nurse), Eric Eisenbrey (Gay Nerd), Bobbi Mar (Jewish Lady #3), Tony Dee (Persnickety Waiter), Yos Menendez (Random Trick), Jordan Jaric, Aden Jaric (Vana Wintos), Anthon Anselmi (Fake Jarod/Gordon Sea Dancer), Tommy Blade, Neo, Dallas Reeves (Jasper's Paramours)

Jake Mosser, Aaron Michael Davies, Jimmy Clabots, Jonah Blechman in Another Gay Sequel © TLA Releasing

YEAR OF THE FISH (Gigantic Releasing) Producers, David Kaplan, Rocco Caruso; Executive Producer, Janet Yang; Coproducer, Jason Orans; Director/Screenplay, David Kaplan; Designer, Mylene Santos; Costumes, Mattie Ullrich; Music, Paul Cantelon; Editors, David Kaplan, Frank Keraudren; Casting, David Caparelliotis; a Funny Cry Happy presentation in association with Gigantic Pictures; Dolby; Color; HD Cam; Not rated; 96 minutes; Release date: August 29, 2008. CAST: Tsai Chin (Mrs. Su), Ken Leung (Johnny), Randall Duk Kim (Auntie Yaga/Old Man/Foreman), An Nguyen (Ye Xian), Sally Leung Bayer (Grandmother), Henry Russell Bergstein (Hasidic Customer), Lori Tan Chinn (Shuk yee), Andre De Leon (Thug), Philip Levy, Buzz Bovshow (Businessmen), Esther Cheng, Kim Dong, Tina Duong, Lillian Leong, Janet Lau, Susan Li, Eva Liu, Jessica Moon, Masae Taniguchi, Migina Tsai (Salon Workers), Wai Ching Ho, Jane Wu (Seamstresses), David Lee (Fish Narration), Paul J. Q. Lee (Wu), Barry Sacker, Bunny Levine (Tourists), Gine Lui (Fortuneteller), Ken Marks (Ye Xian's Customer), Hettienne Park (Hong Ji), Matthew Saldivar (Gang Leader), Lloyd Suh (Chik), Akira Takayama (Lin), Sophia Tam (Little Girl), Lee Wong (Vinnie), Constance Wu (Lucy), Corrine Hong Wu (Katty), Henry Yuk (Mr. Meng)

Ken Leung in Year of the Fish © *Gigantic Releasing*

DISASTER MOVIE (Lionsgate) Producers, Peter Safran, Jason Friedberg, Aaron Seltzer; Executive Producer, Hal Olofsson; Directors/Screenplay, Jason Friedberg, Aaron Seltzer; Photography, Shawn Maurer; Designer, William Elliott; Costumes, Frank Helmer; Music, Christopher Lennertz; Music Supervisors, Dave Jordan, Jojo Villanueva; a 3 in the Box production, presented with Grosvenor Park; Dolby; Deluxe color; Rated PG-13; 88 minutes; Release date: August 29, 2008. CAST: Matt Lanter (Will), Vanessa Minnillo (Amy), Gary "G Thang" Johnson (Calvin), Nicole Parker (Enchanted Princess/Amy Winehouse Look-a-Like), Crista Flanagan (Juney/Hannah Montana), Kim Kardashian (Lisa), Ike Barinholtz (Wolf/Javier Bardem Look-a-Like/Police Officer/Hellboy/Batman/ Beowulf/Prince Caspian), Tad Hilgenbrink (Prince), Jason Boegh (Male Carrie), Carmen Electra (Beautiful Assassin), Tony Cox (Indiana Jones), Nick Steele (Underwear Model), John Di Domenico (Dr. Phil Look-a-Like/Love Guru), Valerie Wildman (Samantha), Abe Spigner (Flava-Flav Look-a-Like), Noah Harpster (Jonah), Austin Michael Scott (McLover), Devin Crittenden (Michael Cera Look-a-Like), Dana Seltzer (Head On Voice), Robin Atkin Downes (Emergency Broadcaster), Michelle Lang (Hot Girl), Jonas Neal (Justin Timberlake Look-a-Like), Walter Harris (Hancock), Ty Wesley (Kid), Gerard Facchini (Iron Man), Jacob Tolano Wood (Bruce Banner), Roland Kickinger (Hulk), Christopher Johnson (Michael Jackson Look-a-Like), Preston James Hillier (Cowboy Fan), Johnny Rock (Male Enchanted Princess), David Born (Referee), Genevieve Guzchack, Hilary Kennedy (Bikini Girls), Lloyd Arnold II (Jojo), Jared S. Eddo (Speed Racer), Yoshio Iizuka (Kung Fu Panda), Lauren Gottlieb, Katrina Norma, Monica Soot, Audra Griffis, Amaris Davidson, Courtney Young (Cheerleader Dancers), Clinton Huff, Devin Walker, Dominique Kelley, Jeremy Barthel, Billy Jackson, Luke Sexton (Basketball Dancers)

Ike Barinholtz, Gary Johnson, Matt Lanter, Nicole Parker in Disaster Movie © *Lionsgate*

THE POOL (Vitagraph) Producer/Casting, Kate Noble; Director/Photography, Chris Smith; Screenplay, Chris Smith, Randy Russell; Based on the short story by Randy Russell; Music, Didier Leplae, Joe Wong; Editor, Barry Poltemann; a Bluemark production; Dolby; Color; HD Video; Not rated; 104 minutes; Release date: September 3, 2008. CAST: Venkatesh Chavan, Jahangir Badshah, Ayesha Mohna, Nana Parker,

Venkatesh Chavan in The Pool © *Vitagraph*

SAVE ME (First Run Features) Producer, Christopher Raacster, Herb Hamsher, Chad Allen, Judith Light; Executive Producers, James Garbus, Robert Kroupa, Robert Epstein, Jeffrey Friedman; Director, Robert Cary: Screenplay, Craig Chester, Alan Hines, Robert Desiderio; Photography, Rodney Taylor; Designer, Ray Kluga; Costumes, Lahly Poore; Music, Jeff Cardoni; Music Supervisor, Debra Baum; Editor, Phillip Bartell; Casting, Billy Hopkins, Suzanne Crowley, Kerry Barden, Jennifer Richiazzi, Angelique Midthunder; a Mythgarden, Garbus Kroup Entertainment and Tetrahedron production; Dolby; Widescreen; Color; Not rated; 96 minutes; Release date: September 5, 2008. CAST: Chad Allen (Mark), Robert Gant (Scott), Judith Light (Gayle), Stephen Lang (Ted), Robert Baker (Lester), Tone Forrest (Doctor), Jeremy Glazer (Trey), William Dennis Hurley (Bill Prior), Colin Jones (Randall), Ross Kelly (Adam), Hunter Krestan (John), Paul McGowen (Dr. Lowney), Carmela Morales (Lydia), David Petruzzi (Dustin), Luce Rains (Motel Clerk), Paul Scallan (Mark's Older Brother), Cherlyn Schaefer (Church Girl/Shy Girl), Carmen Serano (Anna), Greg Serano (Hector), Arron Shiver (Jude)

Chad Allen, Robert Gant in Save Me © *First Run Features*

THE HOUSE OF ADAM (Hollywood Independents) Producer/Director/Screenplay, Jorge Ameer; Photography, Joseph White; Music, Ilia Eshkenazy; Editor, John Lavin; Technicolor; Not rated; 81 minutes; Release date: September 5 2008. CAST: John Shaw (Anthony Ross), Lexi Karriker (Nina), Tiffany McFarland (Helen), Reeve Howard (Mark), Jared Cadwell (Adam), Jorge Ameer (Real Estate Agent), Joella Brown (Monica), Rex Davison (Brett), Thomas Michael Kappler (Albert Ross), Marcelle Lee (Joanne), Ted Ryan (David), Scott Stepp (Roger), Torie Tyson (Jogger)

EVERYBODY WANTS TO BE ITALIAN (Roadside Attractions) Producers, Jaime Burke, James Huntsman; Director/Screenplay, Jason Todd Ipson; Photography, Michael Fimognari; Designer, Marla Altschuler; Costumes, Nicole Capasso; Music, Michael Cohen; Editor, Mike Saenz; an Asgaard Entertainment presentation of a James Huntsman/Jaime Burke production; Dolby; Color; Rated R; 105 minutes; Release date: September 5, 2008. CAST: Jay Jablonski (Jake Bianski), Cerina Vincent (Marisa Costa), John Kapelos (Steve Bottino), John Enos III (Gianluca Tempesti), Richard Libertini (Papa Aldo Tempesti), Marisa Petroro (Isabella), Perry Anzilotti (Silvano the Tailor), Anthony Russell (Nick the Jeweler), Tammy Pescatelli (Katerina), Dan Cortese (Michael), Judith Scarpone (Mrs. Abignali), P.J. Marino (Mario), Penny Marshall (Teresa the Florist), Ben Livingston (Veterinarian), Gabrielle Sanalitro (Receptionist), Sylvia Panacione (Anna the Seamstress), Courtney Andersen (Engaged Woman), Carla Antonio (Carla), Alberto Brosio (Hotel Clerk), Kevin Cirone, Jennifer Welch (Neighbors), Barbara Conway (Cat Lady), Damien Di Paola (Rocco), Elisa Dyann (Mom in Vet's Office), Carisa Engle (Bartender), Abner Genece (Prof. Genece), Grady Justice (Park Walker), Blake Lee (Engaged Man), Zak Lee (The Waiter), John Leo (Fish Pier Boat Owner), Carole Meyers (Susan), Martin Moakler (Paul Baba), Shelby O'Connell (Little Girl in Vet's Office), Roberta Orlandi (Francesca)

Cerina Vincent, Jay Jablonski in Everybody Wants to Be Italian © *Roadside Attractions*

AUGUST EVENING (Maya Releasing) Producers, Connie Hill, Jason Wehling; Director/Screenplay, Chris Eska; Photography, Yasu Tanida; Designer, Elysia Edwards; Costumes, Sarah Balderas; Music, Windy & Carl, Takagi Masakatsu; Editor, Chris Eska; Casting, Megumi Kano; a Doki-Doki Prods. presentation; Color; HD Video; Rated PG-13; 127 minutes; Release date: September 5, 2008. CAST: Pedro Castaneda (Jaime), Veronica Loren (Lupe), Abel Becerra (Victor), Walter Perez (Luis), Sandra Rios (Alice), Raquel Gavia (Maria), Cesar Flores (Salazar), Grisel Rodriguez (Andrea), Tom Spry (Jason), Jeremy Becerra (Gabe), Ethan Mallen (Matthew), Amelia Castillo (Juana), Richard Moreno (Manuel), Rosalba Aguayo Villegas (Wedding Photographer), Stella Romero (Grocery Cashier), Benito Lara (Diego), Marina Hernandez (Young "Maria" at Cleaners)

Pedro Castaneda, Veronica Loren in August Evening © *Maya Releasing*

SURFER, DUDE (Anchor Bay) Producers, Matthew McConaughey, Gus Gustawes, Mark Gustawes; Executive Producers, Jason Berk, Matt Lane, Dennis Weiss, James W. Skotchdopole; Director, S.R. Bindler; Screenplay, George Mays, Mark Gustawes, S.R. Bindler, Cory Van Dyke; Story, George Mays; Photography, Elliot Davis; Designer, T.K. Kirkpatrick; Costumes, Jonny Pray; Music, Blake Neely, Xavier Rudd; Music Supervisor, Matthew McConaughey; Casting, Anne McCarthy, Don Phillips, Jay Scully; a Berk/Lane Entertainment presentation of a J.K. Livin production; Dolby; Color; Rated R; 85 minutes; Release date: September 5, 2008. CAST: Matthew McConaughey (Steve Addington), Alexie Gilmore (Danni Martin), Jeffrey Nordling (Eddie Zarno), Sarah Mason (Stacey), Zachary Knighton (Brillo Murphy), Cassandra Hepburn (Luanne), Todd Stashwick (Vic), Nathan Phillips (Baker Smith), Ramon Rodriguez (Lupe La Rosa), Travis Fimmel (Jonny Doran), K.D. Aubert (April May), Brooke Allison (Reporter), Nancy Fish (Margaret), Woody Harrelson (Jacko), Brad Ashten, Thomas Kijas, Justin Sandler (Surf Punks), Seth Baird (Drunk Dancer), Stephanie Bartak, Courtney Fleming, Kimberly Mulvey, Laundrea Thomas (Bikini Girls), Brynn Bromley, Byron de Marse, Matt Flanagan, Jessica Felice, Amber Hay, Tanner Alexander Redman (Reality House), Gian Carlo, Mary-Jessica Pitts (Market Kid), Julia Carpenter, Kassie Spielman (Punk Surfer Girl), Hannah Cornett (Sam), Marly Coronel (Adds Pads Girl), AnnaMaria Demara (Dancer, Bikini Girl), Brandon DeShazer (Security), Brie Gabrielle (Baker's Girlfriend), Christina Gabrielle (Fruit Girl), Austin Graves (Bikini Model), Cheryl Francis Harrington (Custom Agent), Krysten Klein (Beach Girl), Paula Lemes (Surfer Friend), Liz Lueders (Party Setup Woman), Mickey Meyer, Thomas Lynch, Bill O'Donnell (Surfers), Chayce Marnell (Surfer Boy with Board), Maya McClean, Nancy McLean (Twins), George A. Miki (Security Guard), Bru Muller (Garage Customer), Willie Nelson (Farmer Bob), Nolan North (Mr. Simons), Kristin Peterson (Brunette #2), Stephanie A. Purdy (K-9 Customs Officer), Mario Quinonez, Jr. (Mexican Boy), Lawrence J. Russo (Cabbie), Kimberly Suida (Lupe's Limo Girl), Channing Swift (Mayweather's Gardener), Kate Tomlinson (Victor's Girlfriend), Katherine VanderLinden (Traveler), Joseph Steven Yang (Korean Translator)

CHRISTMAS ON MARS (Cinemapurgatorio) Producers, Scott Booker, The Flaming Lips; Director/Screenplay, Wayne Coyne; Co-Directors, Bradley Beesley, George Salisbury; Photography, Bradley Beesley; Music, The Flaming Lips; Editor, George Salisbury; a Cinemapurgatorio production; Black and white/color; HD; Not rated; 82 minutes; Release date: September 12, 2008. CAST: Steven Droz (Major Syrtis), Wayne Coyne (The Martian), Steve Burns (Astronaut #1), Fred Armisen (Philosophical and Hymn-Singing Astronaut), Scott Booker (Psychiatrist), Adam Goldberg (Mars Psychiatrist), Michael Ivins (Sunglasses-Wearing Astronaut), Michelle Martin-Coyne (Mother), Jimmy Pike (Faithless Astronaut), Kliph Scurlock (Astronaut Confronting Cosmic Reality)

Wayne Coyne in Christmas on Mars © Cinemapurgatorio

GREETINGS FROM THE SHORE (Newstyle Releasing) Producer, Gabrielle Berberich; Executive Producer, Robert I. Schulman; Coproducer, Gregory C. Schaefer; Director, Greg Chwerchak; Screenplay, Gabrielle Berberich, Greg Chwerchak; Photography, Mike Mickens; Designer, Chia-Yi Renee Chao; Music, Jim Latham; Editors, Kimberly Generous White, Daniel Barone; Casting, Adrienne Stern; a Jenny Jump Pictures presentation of a Hudson Mermaid Prods. production; Color; Rated R; 117 minutes; Release date: September 12, 2008. CAST: Kim Shaw (Jenny Chambers), Paul Sorvino (Catch Turner), David Fumero (Benicio Aceveda), Jay O. Sanders (Commodore Callaghan), Andrew Shaifer (Flip Dooley), Lars Arentz-Hansen (Lars Ramkidestrom), Gideon Emery (Sasha Mientkiewicz), Ron Geren (Christos Zazavich), Alexander Cendese (Owen Callaghan), Angela Pietropinto (Mrs. Salducci), Chuck Ardezzone (Foreman), Cordelia Reynolds (Heather), Jason Etter (Tyler), Cristin Milioti (Didi), Shevy Katan (Allison), Mitchel Adams (Beer Chugger at Party), Katharine Higgins, Tina Ward (Students), Pete Schardien (Guy in Poker Game), John Schuman (Tattooed Guy at Party), Brandon Volk (Keg Boy), Alexandra Wagner (Shot Girl)

FLOW: FOR LOVE OF WATER (Oscilloscope Pictures) Producer, Steven Starr; Executive Producers, Stephen Nemeth, Caroleen Feeney, Lee Jaffe, Augusta Brown Holland, Brent Meikle, Cornalia Meikle, Hadley Meikle; Coproducers, Gill Holland, Yvette Tomlinson; Director, Irena Salina; Photography, Pablo de Selva, Irena Salina; Music, Christophe Julien; Editors, Caitlin Dixon, Madeleine Gavin, Andrew Monshein; a Steven Starr Prods. presentation in association with the Group Entertainment; Color; HD; Not rated; 83 minutes; Release date: September 12, 2008. Documentary on the perilous state of the world's water supply; with Maude Barlow, Shelly Brime, Anthony Burgmans, Dr. Kent Butler, Michel Camdessus, Charles-Louis de Maud'huy, Ashwin Desai, Siddharaj Dhadda, Shripad Dharmadhikary, Ashok Gadgil, Peter H. Gleick, Tyrone Hayes, David Hemson, Penn Jillette and Teller, Ronnie Kasrils, Gigi Kellett, Jean Luc-Touly, Anna Debwese Mape, William E. Marks, Patrick McCully, Fatima Meer, Gerard Mestrallet, Bob Nameng, Sunita Narain, Marcela Olivera, Oscar Olivera, Erik D.

Olson, Jim Olson, Rod Parsley, Medha Patkar, Julian Perez, Boone Pickens, Mary Anne Rennet, Jim Schultz, Paul Schwartz, Vandana Shiva, Rajendra Singh, Holly Wren Spaulding, Achim Steiner, Terry Swier, James Wolfensohn.

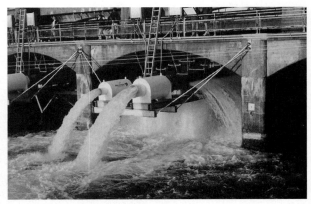

Flow: For Love of Water © Oscilloscope

THE LITTLE RED TRUCK (Tree & Sky Media Arts) Producer, Pam Voth; Executive Producers, Craig Langel, Dirk Visser, Kim Visser; Director/Screenplay/Editor/Music, Rob Whitehair; Photography, Rob Whitehair, Pam Voth; Color; HD-to-35mm; Rated PG; 98 minutes; Release date: September 122008. Documentary following the Missoula Children's Theater as it travels across the country to put on shows; with J.K. Simmons, Jim Caron.

The Little Red Truck © Tree & Sky Media

MOVING MIDWAY (First Run Features) Producers, Godfrey Cheshire, Vincent Farrell, Jay Spain; Executive Producer, R.B. Reeves; Director/Screenplay, Godfrey Cheshire; Photography, Jay Spain; Music, Ahrin Mishan; Editors, Ramsey Fendall, Greg Loser; a CG Film, Iron Films, Wake Drive Prods. presentation and production; Color; HD; Not rated; 98 minutes; Release date: September 12, 2008. Documentary on the moving of the Cheshire family's Midway Plantation to another plot of land; with Godfrey Cheshire, Elizabeth Cheshire, Robert Hinton, Charles Hinton Silver, Dena Williams Silver, Abraham Lincoln Hinton, Al Hinton.

Robert Hinton, Godfrey Cheshire in Moving Midway
© *First Run Features*

PROUD AMERICAN (Slowhand/Lightsource) Producer, Aili Kato; Executive Producer, Fred Ashman; Coproducers, Ron Clark, Carolyn Jogoleff; Director, Fred Ashman; Screenplay, Fred Ashman, Rolland Smith; Photography, Mark Eberle; Editor, Tim Flora; Dolby; Color; IMAX; Rated PG; 105 minutes; Release date: September 12, 2008. CAST: Jonathan Banks (Mr. Moretti), Michael Barreta (Carols Moleda), Kimberlin Brown (Lisa), Edward Gage (Preacher), Grant Goodeve (Naval Doctor), Terrance Hardy (Young Curtis Jackson), Dennis Haskins (Bill), Ken Howard (Dr. Sullivan), Jane Le (Dawn), Mark McClure (Sam), Rob Moran (AJ), Mackenzie Rosman (Bree), Lee Thompson Young (Curtis Jackson), Terry Alexander (Dr. Madison), Ceceila Antionette (Grams), Michelle Ashman (Katie), JonJon Briones (Dawn's Father), Haley Chase (Megan), Chris Emerson (Michael), Monika Gonzalez (Mother), Riely James (Nicole), Richard Garon (Tom), JoNell Kennedy (Lakeesha), Dufflyn Lammers (Julie Rogers), Koda Madison (Annie), A. Lee Massaro (Sarah), Fallon Oskwuosa (Lisa), Laurel Page (Teacher), Julie Skon (Sarah Moleda), Salina Soto (Lucy), Joseph Williamson (Eric)

SECRECY (Louise Rosen Ltd.) Producers/Directors, Peter Galison, Robb Moss; Coproducer, Chyld King; Photography, Austin de Besche, Stephen McCarthy; Designer, Elaine J. McCarthy; Music, John Kusiak; Editor, Chyld King; a Redacted Pictures production; Dolby; Color/Black and white; DV; Not rated; 85 minutes; Release date: September 12, 2008. Documentary exploring the abuses of the government's national security system; with Mike Levin, Tom Blanton, Melissa Boyle Mahle, James B. Bruce, Barton Gellman, Steve Garfinkel, Patricia J. Herring, Wilson Brown, Siegfried Hecker, Steven Aftergood, Neal Kaytal, Charles Swift, Judy Loether.

THE TREE OF LIFE (Ruth Diskin Films) Producer/Director, Hava Volterra; Executive Producer, Andrew Viterbi; Screenplay, Hava Volterra, David N. Donihue; Photography, Eyal Gordin, Oded Plotnitzi, Ram Hani, Giovanni Andreotta; Music, Carlo Silotto, Nico Mansy, Enrico Fink; Editor, Eli Green; an Interim CEO Film production; Color; DV; Not rated; 76 minutes; Release date: September 12, 2008. Documentary in which filmmaker Hava Volterra's journeys to Italy to research her Jewish's family's surprising roots; with Hava Volterra, Viviana Volterra Gerner, Alessandra Veronese, Elia Richette, Mordecai Finley.

WALKING ON DEAD FISH (Variance Films) Producer/Director/Screenplay, Franklin Martin; Coproducers, Sean Presant, Robert Weingard; Executive Producers, Terry Bradshaw, Stan Cassio; Photography, Jason Shane; Music, Scott Gordon, Steffan Fantini, Marc Fantini; Editors, Stephen Goetsch, Sam Citron, Sean Presant; Narrator, Terry Bradshaw; a Dutchmen Films presentation; Rated PG-13; 92 minutes; Release date: September 12, 2008. Documentary on how the tiny town of La Placa, Louisiana was overrun by 20,000 displaced Hurricane Katrina victims; with Debra Schum, Mary Riccard, David Beadle, John Ellis, Mary Tsueno, Scenova Peck, Leon Bailey, Kay Dauterive, Reverend S. Coley, Rich Draeger, Ed Cooke, Harry Bridges, "Scrap" McQuarter, Mr. & Mrs. Stanley Jackson, Sr., Mr. & Mrs. Johnny Owen, Jr., Mr. Johnny Owen, Sr.

VIRTUAL JFK: VIETNAM IF KENNEDY HAD LIVED (Independent) Producers, Peter O. Almond, James G. Blight, Janet M. Lang, Koji Masutani, David A. Welch; Coproducer, Michael Paszt; Director/Editor, Koji Masutani; Screenplay, James G. Blight, Janet M. Lang, Koji Masutani, David A. Welch; Photography, Edward Huff; Music, Joshua Kern; a Sven Kahn Films presentation, in association with the Global Media Project/The Watson Institute for International Studies; Color/Black and white; DV; Not rated; 80 minutes; Release date: September 17, 2008. Documentary on several instances during his administration when President Kennedy resisted engaging the U.S. in conflict despite pressure to do so.

MY BEST FRIEND'S GIRL (Lionsgate) Producers, Adam Herz, Gregory Lessans, Josh Shader, Guymon Casady, Doug Johnson, Barry Katz, Brian Volk-Weiss; Executive Producers, Mike Elliott, Michael Paseornek, John Sacchi; Coproducers, Jerry P. Jacobs, Jordan Cahan; Director, Howard Deutch; Screenplay, Jordan Cahan; Photography, Jack N. Green; Designer, Jane Ann Stewart; Costumes, Marilyn Vance; Music John Debney; Music Supervisor, Jay Faires; Editor, Seth Flaum; Casting, Annie McCarthy, Jay Scully, Freddy Luis; a Lionsgate production, in association with Management 360, Terra Firma Films and Superfinger Entertainment; Dolby; FotoKem color; Rated R; 103 minutes; Release date: September 19, 2008. CAST: Dane Cook (Tank), Kate Hudson (Alexis), Jason Biggs (Dustin), Alec Baldwin (Prof. Turner), Diora Baird (Rachel), Lizzy Caplan (Ami), Riki Lindhome (Hilary), Mini Anden (Lizzy), Hilary Pingle (Claire), Nate Torrence (Craig), Malcolm Barrett (Dwalu), Taran Killam (Josh), Faye Grant (Merrilee), Richard Snee (Brian), Alberto Bonilla (Pedro), Michael O'Toole (Michi Yamana), Sally Pressman (Courtney), Kate Albrecht (Laney the Babysitter), Rakefet Abergel (Heavily Pierced Kid), Amanda Brooks (Carly), Andrew Caldwell (Sad Dork), Maureen Keiller (Seamstress), Tom Kemp (Priest), Tony V. (Chef Slava), Seth Child (Young Kid), Jacqui Holland (Kindly Stripper), Don L. Bagley (Rabbi), Andria Blackman (Ms. Barber), Georgia Lyman (Hot Coed), Melina Lizette (Ms. Reiling), Josh Alexander (Burt), Angel M. Wagner (Mariachi Band Leader), Julio C. Bare, Rafael B. Rodriguez (Mariachi Band), Scott Winters (Annoying Co-Worker), Frank Hsieh (Band Leader), Jenny Mollen (Colleen), Mike Elliott (Man in Bathroom), Eamon Brooks (Random Guy), Nancy Sadsad (Random Guy's Girl), Denise McDonald, Jay Hall, Gretchen Arntz, Micah Sherman, Christopher Nesmith (Office Employees), Rob Rota (Lee), Edna Pangaggio (Grandmother)

Kate Hudson, Jason Biggs in My Best Friend's Girl
© *Lionsgate*

ALL OF US (Pureland Pictures) Producers, Emily Abt, Reva Goldberg; Director/ Photography, Emil Abt; Associate Producers, Valerie Burgher, Sarah Cullen; Music Supervisor, Eric Liebman; Editor, Geeta Gandbhir; Color; Not rated; 82 minutes; release date: September 19, 2008. Documentary in which a doctor sets out to discover why so many black women in the South Bronx are being infected with the AIDS virus.

Dr. Mehret Mandefro, Chevelle Wilson in All of Us © *Pureland Pictures*

AMEXICANO (Brooklyn-Queens) Producers, Carmine Famiglietti, Matthew Bonifacio; Executive Producers, Cesar A. Baez, Stephen Ashkinos; Director, Matthew Bonifacio; Screenplay, Carmine Famiglietti; Photography, William A. Miller; Designer, Sophia Antonini; Music, Kerry Muzzey; Editors, Morty Ashkinos, Ilya Magazanin; Casting, Heather Hurley; a Brooklyn-Queen Project production, in association with Madison Park Pictures; Color; Rated PG-13; 85 minutes; Release date: September 19, 2008. CAST: Carmine Famiglietti (Bruno), Raul Castillo (Ignacio), Jennifer Peña (Gabriela), Manny Perez (Diego), Michael Aronov (Alex), Hugo Aleman (Cesar), Susanna Hari (Station Nurse), Lou Martini, Jr. (Guy), Burton Perez (Willie), Pablo Tufino (Endy)

Carmine Famiglietti, Raul Castillo in Amexicano © *Brooklyn-Queens*

QUILOMBO COUNTRY (Quilombo Films) Producer/Director/Screenplay/ Editor/ Photography, Leonard Abrams; Narrator, Chuck D.; Color; DV; Not rated; 73 minutes; Release date: September 19, 2008. Documentary on the many communities founded by runaway slaves in the forests of Northern Brazil.

Quilombo Country © *Quilombo Films*

BOOGIE MAN: THE LEE ATWATER STORY (InterPositive Media) Producers, Stefan Forbes, Noland Walker; Director/Editor/Photography/Music, Stefan Forbes; Color; DV; Not rated; 87 minutes; Release date: September 26, 2008. Documentary on how Lee Atwater became an influential White House political adviser for the Republican party; with Eric Alterman, Joe Conason, Tom DeLay, Sam Donaldson, Michael Dukakis, Tucker Eskew, Howard Fineman, Chuck Jackson, Mary Matalin, Terry McAuliffe, Jim McCabe, Robert D. Novak, Rich Peterson, Ishmael Reed, Ed Rollins, Joe Sligh, Roger Stone, Tom Turnipseed.

George Bush, Lee Atwater in Boogie Man © *InterPositive Media*

FOREVER STRONG (Crane Movie Co.) Producers, Adam Abel, Ryan Little; Executive Producers, Brad Pelo, David Pliler; Director, Ryan Little; Screenplay, David Pliler; Photography, TC Christensen; Designer, Gary M. Silverstein; Costumes, Anna K. Findley; Music, J Bateman, Bart Hendrickson; Editor, John Lynde; Casting, Sharon Bialy, Sherry Thomas; a Picture Rock Entertainment presentation of a Go Films production in association with BNR Films; Dolby; FotoKem color; Rated PG-13; 112 minutes; Release date: September 26, 2008. CAST: Gary Cole (Coach Larry Gelwix), Sean Faris (Rick Penning), Neal McDonough (Coach Richard Penning), Sean Astin (Marcus), Arielle Kebbell (Emily), Penn Badgley (Lars), Julie Warner (Natalie Penning), Michael J. Pagan (Kurt), Larry Bagby (Coach Cal), Britani Bateman (Renee Tae), Matthew Flynn Bellows (Highland Player #1), Eliot Benjamin (Marty), Ivan Bird (Police Officer), Big Budah (Bingham), Jimmy Chunga (Max Griffin), Jeremy Earl (Sanchez), K. Danor Gerald (Coach JT), Carly Johnston (Reporter), Tyler Kain (Tammy), Max Kasch (Griggs), Carleigh King (Hotel Receptionist), John Kepa Kruse (Tumo), Lauren McKnight (Gina), Maclain Nelson (Scottish Captain), Brian Peck (Colton McDonald), Shareece Pfeiffer (Marty's Girlfriend), Andrew Roach (Joey), William Rubio (Ernesto), Olesya Rulin (Emily's Friend), Junior Salt (Peeta), Irene Santiago (Reporter), Teddi Siddall (Cathy Gelwix), Emily Tyndall (Jamie), Nathan West (Quentin)

SMOTHER (Variance Films) Producers, Bill Johnson, Johnson Chan, Tim Rasmussen, Jay Roach; Executive Producers, Jim Seibel, Vincent Reppert, Diane Keaton, Jeff Abberly, Julia Blackman, Tom Werner, Jennifer Perini, Matt Berenson, Bobby Sheng, Carsten Lorenz; Director, Vince Di Meglio; Screenplay, Vince Di Meglio, Tim Rasmussen; Photography, Julio Macat; Designer, Mark Hutman; Music, Tom Wolfe, Manish Raval; Editor, Kelly Matsumoto; Casting, Rick Montgomery, Chadwick Struck; a Variance Films/Inferno/Germie & Bucky presentation, in association with Double Edge Entertainment, Scion Films, Smother LLC and Grand Army Entertainment; Dolby; Color; Rated PG-13; 92 minutes; Release date: September 26, 2008. CAST: Diane Keaton (Marilyn Cooper), Dax Shepard (Noah Cooper), Liv Tyler (Clare Cooper), Mike White (Myron Stubbs), Ken Howard (Gene Cooper), Selma Stern (Helen Cooper), Jerry Lambert (Donnie Booker), Don Lake (Minister), Sarah Lancaster (Holly), Cameron Bender (Jim), Kimberly Bosso (Baby Shower Guest), Ron Butler (Friendly Man), Rachel Cannon (Waitress), Cindy Clark (Barbara), Jacque Lynn Colton (Cindy), Frank Crim (Bob), Celeste Damron, Sharon Di Meglio, Judy Nishimine, Dawn Rasmussen (Pain Pals), Lucas Gorak (Tommy), Johnny Hagen (Karaoke Singer), Taj Hester (Beagle), Henriette Ivanans (Therapy Receptionist), George Kendall (Tony), James Taku Leung (Hartanto), Carlos McCullers II (Basset Hound), Tara Moore (Pippi), Alexandra Murdy (Annika), Steven Christopher Parker (Dana), Jess Rowland (Karaoke DJ), Jerry Sherman (Art), Matt Steinhauer (Carpet Bazaar Mascot), Cletus Young (Sam)

Diane Keaton, Dax Shepard in Smother © *Variance Films*

OBSCENE (Arthouse Films) Producers, Tanya Ager Meiller, Alexander Meillier; Directors, Neil Ortenberg, Daniel O'Connor; Photography, Alexander Meillier; Music, Askold Buk; Editor, Tanya Ager Meiller; a Double O Film production; Color; HD; Not rated; 97 minutes; Release date: September 26, 2008. Documentary on how publisher Barney Rosset fought to bring controversial works to publication in America; with Amiri Baraka, Jim Carroll, Al Goldstein, Erica Jong, Ray Manzarek, Barney Rosset, John Sayles, Gore Vidal, John Waters.

Barney Rosset in Obscene © *Arthouse Films*

UNSPOOLED (Necessary Nomad) Producers, Michael McKee, Keir Moreano; Director/ Screenplay/Photography, Keir Moreano; Music, Gil Talmi; Editor, Mario Diaz; Narrators, Keir Moreano, Mario Diaz; Color; DV; Not rated; 89 minutes; Release date: September 26, 2008. Documentary on the making of the student film *Bemoana*; with Nicole Vicius, Larry Brustoski, Maurice Singer, Norm Golden, Matthew Santo.

Unspooled © *Necessary Nomad*

RIPPLE EFFECT (Monterey Media) Producer, Philippe Caland; Executive Producers, Forest Whitaker, Pierre Caland, Virginia Madsen, Minnie Driver; Coproducers, Evans Butterworth, Joseph Semense; Director/Screenplay, Philippe Caland; Photography, Daron Keet; Designer, Shirley Leong; Costumes, Asia Ahearn, Amanda Riley; Music, Anthony Marinelli; Editors, Joseph Semense, Yvan Gauthier; Casting, Lindsay Chag; a YBG Prods. production; Color; HD Video; Rated R; 83 minutes; Release date: September 26, 2008. CAST: Philippe Caland (Amer Atrash), Forest Whitaker (Philip), Virginia Madsen (Sherry), Minnie Driver (Kitty), Kali Rocha (Alex), John Billingsley (Brad), Jerry Katell (Gordon), Orlando Seale (Brian), Kip Pardue (Tyler), Betsy Clark (Amy), Joanne Krupa (Victoria), Ken Sylk (Ronald), Robin Arcuri (Andrea), Denise Crosby (Ronald's Wife), Elena Staine (Sophia), Michael Weiss (Michael), Gwendolyn Bailey (Lara), Kelli Nordhus (Sylvia Myron), Ilona Alexandra (Makeup Artist), Bryan Black (Promoter), Johnny D. Boyd (Attorney), Evans Butterworth (Ad Salesman), Charley Mae Caland (Charley), Stacy Cunningham (Susan), Timothy Donovan (Tim), Emily Johnson (Bar Girl), Don Le (Partygoer), Maisie Pacia (Student), Joe Roach (Tatooed Cowboy), Becca Sweitzer (Jewelry Clerk), Kimberly Van Luin (2nd Girl at Party), Michael Weiss (Michael)

WILD COMBINATION: A PORTRAIT OF ARTHUR RUSSELL (Plexifilm) Producers, Kyle Martin, Ben Howe, Matt Wolf; Executive Producers, Mark Lewin, Philip Aarons, Shelley Fox Aarons; Director/Screenplay, Matt Wolf; Photography, Jody Lee Lipes; Costumes, Janicza Bravo; Music, Arthur Russell; Editor, Lane Edmands; a Polari Pictures production; Color; HD; Not rated; 70 minutes; Release date: September 26, 2008. Documentary on musician Arthur Russell; with Bob Blank, Ernie Brooks, Philip Glass, Steven Hall, Steve Knutson, Tom Lee, Jens Lekman, Lola Love, Chuck Russell, Emily Russell, Will Socolov, David Toop, Peter Zummo, Tracey Stewart, Carl Williamson.

Arthur Russell in Wild Combination *© Plexifilm*

AN AMERICAN CAROL (Vivendi Entertainment) Producers, Stephen McEveety, John Shepherd, David Zucker; Executive Producers, Myrna Sokoloff, Kenneth Hendricks, Diane Hendricks, Lisa Maria Falcone; Coproducers, Lewis Friedman, Todd Burns; Director, David Zucker; Screenplay, David Zucker, Myrna Sokoloff, Lewis Friedman; Photography, Brian Baugh; Designer, Patrick Sullivan; Costumes, Rachel Good; Music, James L. Venable; Editor, Vashi Nedomansky; Visual Effects Supervisor, Victor Scalise; Casting, Beverly Holloway; an Mpower Pictures production; Dolby; Technicolor; Rated PG-13; 84 minutes; Release date: October 3, 2008. CAST: Kevin Farley (Michael Malone), Kelsey Grammer (Gen. Patton), Trace Adkins (Angel of Death/Trace Adkins), Robert Davi (Aziz), Geoffrey Arend (Mohammed), Serdar Kalsin (Ahmed), Leslie Nielsen (Osama bin Nielsen/Grandpa), Jon Voight (George Washington), Gail O'Grady (Jane Wagstaffe), Travis

Schuldt (Josh), Kevin Sorbo (George Mulrooney), Nikki Deloach (Lily), David Alan Grier (Rastus Malone), Paris Hilton, Simon Rex, Bill O'Reilly (Themselves), Dennis Hopper (Judge), Chriss Anglin (John F. Kennedy), Jesse Heiman (Young Michael Malone), Gary Coleman (Bacon Stains Malone), Fred Travalena (Jimmy Carter), Zachary Levi (Lab Tech #1), James Woods (Agent Grosslight), Jillian Murray (Heather), Scott Bailey (Celebrity #2), Dana Lyn Baron (Speaker, 1940's), Mark Basil ("Look Out! It's Those Christians"), Morgan Beck ("Free History Term Papers"), Julian Berlin (Woman at Awards Party), Randall Bosley (Mussolini), Joanne Bowland (Intern), Cocoa Brown, Allen Haff (Airport Security Guards), Vicki Browne (Rosie O'Connell), Mary Castro (Hottie), Joe Sikorra, Jeff Corbett (Policemen), Rebekah Crane (Girl Scout), Tony Deale (Security Guard), Nikki Deloach (Lily), Susan Deming ("It's that Michael Malone!"), Alexander DiPersia, Katie Gill (Rehearsal Actors), Chrisanne Eastwood, Lee von Ernst (Hippies), Mell Flynn ("Traitor!"), Lisa Fredrickson (Singer), Carl DeGersdorff (Teddo), Cameron Goodman (Political Aide), Eileen Gonzales (Reporter on TV), Camille Grammer ("I gave up an ass lift for this?"), David Alan Grier (Rastus Malone), Mary Hart (Entertainment Tonight Host), Joe Hartzler ("Marines!"/Sassy Sailor), Mark Henderson (Minister #2), Alaina Kalanj (Celebrity #1), Benton Jennings (Hitler), Jack Kelly ("You're a Disgrace" Protest Yeller), Kaleigh Kennedy (Becca/Kaleigh), Coco Leigh (Nun on Bus), Zachary Levi, Karri Turner (Lab Techs), Simone Lotter (Partygoer #2), Joey Luthman (Boy Scout), Brent Lydic (Wounded Soldier), Christopher McDonald (Lab Supervisor), Rich McDonald ("Thought you hated country music!"), Meghan McEveety (Trophy Girl), Bridget McEveety (Girl at BBQ), Amy Povich, Steve Monroe (Airport Passengers), Tyler Jacob Moore (Marty), Oliver Muirhead (Neville Chamberlain), Joey Naber (Terrorist #2), Durrell Nelson (Chaplain), Gail O'Grady (Jane Wagstaffe), John O'Hurley (Silvano), Anna Osceola (Molly Duncan), David Oved (Afghan Prisoner #2), Norman Panto (Accordion Player), Lu Parker, Jane Park Smith (Reporters), Robert Pierce (Minister #1), Bill Posley (Mose Malone), Oren Rehany (Terrorist on Bike), F. Lee Reynolds (Subway Policeman), Bryant Romo ("Sailors!"), Elizabeth Scott ("I'm starved"), Evan Sayet (Patient in Line), Travis Schuldt (Josh), Atticus Shaffer (Timm/Atticus), Sammy Sheik (Fayed, Subway Terrorist), Abbie Shepherd (Trophy Girl at BBQ), Steve Spiro (Cuban Commander), Richard Tanner (Village Voter), Peter Tegan (Stagehand), Hiroshi Ueha (Tojo), Jenna Vogeler (Tiny Tina/Jenna), Lauren Smith, Josh Zucker, Sarah Zucker (Voices of Reason)

Kevin Farley, Dennis Hopper in An American Carol *© Vivendi Entertainment*

ALLAH MADE ME FUNNY: LIVE IN CONCERT (Truly Indie) Producers, Andrea Kalin, Bryant Moss, Azhar Usman; Executive Producers, Alex Konemer, Michael Wolfe; Director, Andrea Kalin; Photography, John Rhode, Bryan Sarkinen; Designer, Jennifer Spence; Editor, David Grossbach; a Unity Prods. Foundation production in association with Spark Media and Handshake Prods.; Color; HD-to-DV; Not rated; 83 minutes; Release date: October 3, 2008. American-Muslim stand-up comedians in concert; with Mohammed "Mo" Amer, Bryant "Preacher" Moss, and Azhar Usman.

Bryant "Preacher" Moss
in Allah Made Me Funny
© Truly Indie

HUMBOLDT COUNTY (Magnolia) Producer, Jason Weiss; Executive Producer, Todd Senturia; Directors/Screenplay, Darren Grodsky, Danny Jacobs; Photography, Ernest Holtzman; Designer, Freddy Naff; Costumes, Amy Brownson; Music, iZler; Music Supervisor, Peymon Maskan; Editor, Ed Marx; Casting, John Jackson; an Embark Prods. production; Dolby; Technicolor; Rated R; 96 minutes; Release date: October 3, 2008. CAST: Jeremy Strong (Peter), Fairuza Balk (Bogart), Peter Bogdanovich (Prof. Hadley), Brad Dourif (Jack), Frances Controy (Rosie), Madison Davenport (Charity), Chris Messina (Max), Darren Grodsky (Bob), Danny Jacobs (Steve), Elayn Taylor (Zelda), Roy Marin (Harry), Jabari Morgan (Agent Gallant), Julia Oliveira (Agent Weiss), Bethany Therese (Sophie), Nathan Pierce (Deputy Dirksen), Michele Shoshani (Lucy), Rick St. Charles (Tom), Tarek Zohdy (Medical Student), Vicky Monroe (Sondra), Lawrence Bridges (Man in Bathroom), John Murdock (Jazz Club Bassist), Lenny Pettinelli (Jaz Club Pianist), B. Swislo (Jazz Club Drummer), Geoffrey Robinson (Earl), Raylene Rhodes (Store Clerk), Susan Hendry (Store Patron), Toodie Boll, Marny Friedman, Ed Martlett (Townies), Tom Conlon (Frank the Logger), Jerry Droz (Eddie the Logger), Isaac Mosgofian (Mike the Logger), Jonathon Ussery, Robert Wells (Beach Pot Smokers), Brennan Burke-Martin (Teen Beach Pot Smoker), Terry Fleshman (Café Waitress), William Carlson (Bus Driver), Izora Burns (Bus Passenger)

Jeremy Strong, Fairuza Balk in Humboldt County © Magnolia Films

THE PLEASURE OF BEING ROBBED (IFC Films) Producers, Brett Jutkiewicz, Zachary Treitz, Sam Lisenco, Joshua Safdie, Alex Orlovsky; Executive Producers, Andy Spade, Casey Neistat; Director, Joshua Safdie; Screenplay, Joshua Safdie, Eleonore Hendricks; Story, Andy Spade, Anthony Sperduti, Joshua Safdie; Photography, Brett Jutkiewicz, Joshua Safdie; Editors, Brett Jutkiewicz, Joshua Safdie, Benny Safdie; a Red Bucket Films production; Color; 16mm; Not rated; 68 minutes; Release date: October 3, 2008. CAST: Eleonore Hendricks (Eleonore), Joshua Safdie (Josh), Wayne Chin (Wayne), Jordan Zaldez (Jordan the Cop), Jerry Damons (Jerry the Cop), Dawn Glickman (Dawn), Batman (Hello Beautiful/Handsome), Alex Billig (Trumpet Player), John Dwyer (Drinks for Everybody), The Fly (Fly), Alex Greenblatt (Son), Gary Greenblatt (Father), Francesca LaPrelle (Mom), Miranda LaPrelle (Daughter), Astrid Larson (Astrid), Van Neistat (Animal Harraser), Eloy Ortega (Flower), Charlotte Pinson (Girlfriend), Ariel Schulman (Boyfriend), Andy Spade (Andy), Bea Spade (Andy's Daughter), Henry Tejada (Henry the Doorman), Calvin Wilson (TA Cashier)

Eleonore Hendricks in
The Pleasure of Being Robbed
© IFC Films

CHOOSE CONNOR (Strand) Producers, Karuna Eberl, James McLean, Luke Eberl, Andrew McFarlane, Aaron Himelstein; Executive Producers, Chris Lux, Howard Delman, Erik Thomas; Director/Screenplay, Luke Eberl; Photography, Jim Timperman; Designer, Roy Rede; Costumes, Breanna Price; Music, Kaizimir Boyle; Casting, Deborah Maxwell Dion; Surround Sound; Color; Not rated; 109 minutes; Release date: October 10, 2008. CAST: Steven Weber (Lawrence Connor), Alex Linz (Owen Norris), Escher Holloway (Caleb), John Rubinstein (Cary Evor), Chris Marquette (Tony), Eric Avari (Arthur Dennison), Diane Delano (Lara Connor), Richard Riehle (Grant Miller), Don McManus (Daniel Norris), Peter Fox (Henry Andrews), April Grace (Joanne), Aixa Clemente (Christina), Karen Constantine (Samantha), James Horan (James), Charles Hoyes (Richard Wallace), Senta Moses (Stacy), James Runcorn (Howard Neuman), Donna Hardy (Old Woman), Christopher May (Heckler), Don Perry (Old Man), Jeffrey Reeves (Wacky Wayne), Lori Rom (Sally), Lorna Scott (Restaurant Manager), Jeff Holman (Brad), Chuck Kelley (George), Ariel Llinas (Mexican Man)

NIGHTS AND WEEKENDS (IFC Films) Producers, Greta Gerwig, Anish Savjani, Dia Sokol, Joe Swanberg; Directors/Screenplay, Joe Swanberg, Greta Gerwig; Photography, Matthias Grunsky, Benjamin Kasulke; Editor, Joe Swanberg; a Filmscience production; Color; DV; Not rated; 80 minutes; Release date: October 10, 2008. CAST: Greta Gerwig (Mattie), Joe Swanberg (James), Jay Duplass (James' Brother), Elizabeth Donius (James' Brother's Wife), Lynn Shelton (Mattie's Sister), Kent Osborne (Mattie's Sister's Boyfriend), Alison Bagnall (Reporter), Ellen Stagg (Photographer)

CALL + RESPONSE (Fair Trade Pictures) Producer/Director, Justin Dillon; Executive Producers, Kelli Walchek, Jeanie Newman, Greg Newman, Scott Walchek; Screenplay, Justin Dillon, Shadd Williams; Musical Performances Director, Brandon Dickerson; Photography, Matt Uhry, Jordan Valenti, Dave

Cozens, JP Lipa; Editors, Alan Chimenti, Mahoko Kuramasu; Color/black and white; Not rated; 84 minutes; Release date: October 10, 2008. Documentary on filmmaker Justin Dillon's efforts to raise money to fight human trafficking; with Julia Ormond, Ashley Judd, Madeleine Albright, Nicholas Kristof, Moby, Natasha Bedingfield, Talib Kweli, Matisyahu, Cold War Kids, Emmanuel Jal, Imogen Heap, Kevin Bales, David Balstone, Rocco DeLuca, Five for Fighting, Daryl Hannah, Gary Haugen, John Miller, Switchfoot, Cornel West.

GOOD DICK (Abramorama) Producers, Jennifer Dubin, Cora Olson, Marianna Palka, Jason Ritter; Coproducers, Jeremy Glazer, Kevin Lowe; Director/Screenplay, Marianna Palka; Photography, Andre Lascaris; Designer, Andrew Trosmans; Costumes, Daphne Javitch; Music, Jared Nelson Smith; Editor, Christopher Kroll; a Morning Knight and Present Pictures presentation; Color; HD; Rated R; 86 minutes; Release date: October 10, 2008. CAST: Marianna Palk (Woman), Jason Ritter (Man), Eric Edelstein (Eric), Martin Starr (Simon), Mark Webber (Derek), Tom Arnold (Dad), Amanda Barnett (Restaurant Patron), Amberlee Colson (Elle), Charles Durning (Charlie), Jesse Garcia (Jose), Jeremy Glazer (Coffee Shop Patron), Josh Holt (Jared), Dana LaRue (Receptionist), Marge Morgan (Marge), Hunter Stiebel (Skate Clerk), Elisabeth Waterston (Elisabeth), Katherine Waterston (Katherine), Bryce Dallas Howard (Video Store Customer)

Jason Ritter, Marianna Palk in Good Dick *© Abramorama*

LOWER LEARNING (Anchor Bay) Producers, Matthew Leutwyler, Sim Sarna; Executive Producers, Karen Bailey, Miranda Bailey; Director/Screenplay, Mark Lafferty; Story, Shahin Chandrasoma; Photography, David Robert Jones; Designer, Joe Lemmon; Costumes, Julie D. Weiss; Music, Ryan Shore; Editor, Shawna Callahan; a Starz/Anchor Bay Entertainment presentation, in association with Ambush Entertainment; Color; Widescreen; Rated R; 97 minutes; Release date: October 10, 2008. CAST: Jason Biggs (Tom), Eva Longoria Parker (Rebecca), Rob Corddry (Billings), Ryan Newman (Carlotta), Monica Potter (Laura), Will Sasso (Jesse), Zachary Gordon (Frankie Fowler), Nat Faxon (Turner Abernathy/ Grandfather Abernathy), Hayes MacArthur (Digdug O'Shannassy), Jill Latiano (Gretchen), Matt Walsh (Mr. Conroy), Nathan Wesdell (Otis), Allen Alvarado (Miguel), Jarrod Bailey (Dickers), Miranda Bailey (Melody), Patricia Belcher (Colette), Juan Carlos Cantu (Alejandro), Ethynn Tanner Cerney (Asbestos Kid), Michael Cheyovich (Coco), Jack Donner (Old Curt), Johnny Drocco (Flunky), Kyle Gass (Decatur Doublewide), Gigi Goff (Mernay), Brenda Goodbread (Lunch Lady), Geoffrey Gould (Grandfather's Friend), Logan Grove (Nickelby), Maya Harvey (Child Secretary), Maxine Hayden (Teacher), James Howarth (Flunky #2), Nadji Jeter, Patrick Manuel (Sling Shot Kids), Chris Kerner (Homecoming King), Grant Klemann (Zippy), Sandy Martin (Olympia), Miranda May (Sheila), Dannika

Northcott (Adelle), Luca Oriel (Marcos), Erik Palladino (Smooth Bob Willowman), Alejandro Patino (Helado), Andy Pessoa (Walter), Christian Pikes (Bartlett), Jonathan Rackman (Music Teacher), Nicholas Roget-King (Basil), Darius Rose (AJ), Ethan Scheid (Asbestos Kid), Zach Selwyn (Singing Teacher), Uriah Shelton (Prep School Kid), Kiernan Shipka (Sarah), Kaliya Skye (Smelly Alice), Anthony Tavera (Rinaldo), Bryan James Taylor (Tennessee Student Servant), David Weiss (Young Tom)

FALL OF HYPERION (here!/Regent) Producers, Paul Colichman, Stephen P. Jarchow; Coproducer, Charles Berg; Director/Associate Producer, Rex Piano; Screenplay, John Cleland; Photography, Mark Melville; Designer, Travis Zariwny; Music, Eric Allaman; Editor, John Blizek; Casting, Dean E. Fronk, Donald Paul Pemrick; a Mountain Rose Entertainment production; Color; Rated PG; 88 minutes; Release date: October 10, 2008. CAST: Thomas Calabro (John Brighton), Cynthia Gibb (Jenni Hansen), William Gregory Lee (Ken Stone), Johnny Hotel Albergo (EMT), Jon Briddell (Sam Hunter), Traber Burns (Richard Kraft), Jorge Carles (Weeping Fater), Maya Carles (Missing Girl), China Cassel (Dr. Gibbons), Brett Chukerman (Ben Freeman), Randy Crowder (Russ Jackson), Asante Jones (FBI Agent Godfrey), Grant Landry (FBI Agent Morris), Tom Maden (Lucas Hansen), Bunny Manchester (Weeping Mother), Christopher Rocha (Ryan Carter), Bob Rumnock (Mark Hutchinson), J. Karen Thomas (President Graham), Gwen Van Dam (Elderly Woman), Jonna Walsh (Sara Hansen), AJ Wedding (Officer Brimm)

Thomas Calabro in Fall of Hyperion *© Regent Releasing*

BILLY: THE EARLY YEARS (Rocky Mountain Pictures) Producers, William Paul McKay, Lawrence Mortorff, Martin Shiel; Director, Robby Benson; Screenplay, Jana Lyn Rutledge, William Paul McKay; Story, William Paul McKay; Executive Producers, Douglas Edelman, Robert Cooner, Anastasia Brown; Photography, David Rudd; Costumes, Libby Callaway, Jim Alan Cook; Editor, Ryan Folsey; Casting, Kim Petrosky; a Solex productions presentation of a Shiel/Mortorff/McKay production in association with 821 Entertainment Group; Color; Rated PG; 98 minutes; Release date: October 10, 2008. CAST: Armie Hammer (Billy Graham), Stefanie Butler (Ruth Graham), Kristoffer Polaha (Charles Templeton, Young), Cliff Beamis (Dr. Mordecai Ham), Josh Turner (George Beverly Shea), Jennifer O'Neill (Reporter), Lindsay Wagner (Morrow Graham), Martin Landau (Charles Templeton, Older), J. Thomas Bailey (Doctor), Dan Beene (Dr. Minder), Zephyr Benson (Moviegoer), Eric Berner (MC), Abbi Butler (Rosa Bell), Cody Carwile (Grady Wilson), Burton Collins (Torrey Johnson), Bobby Daniels (Custodian), Josh DeVries (T.W. Wilson), Rivkah Edelman (Connie Templeton), Donald Farmer (News Photographer), Jerry Foster (Old Cowboy Song Leader), Neva Howell (Shea Secretary), Tyler Northcott (Melvin), Noel Pittman (Marjorie Bostrom), Lily Taylor-Mortoff (Emily), Jonathan Thomas (Albert), Darius Willis (Darryl)

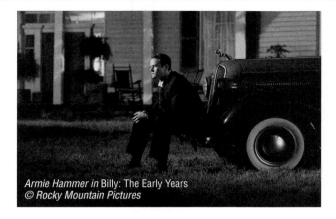

Armie Hammer in Billy: The Early Years
© *Rocky Mountain Pictures*

FRONTRUNNERS (Oscilloscope) Producer, Erika Frankel; Director, Caroline Suh; Photography, Gregory Mitnick; Editor, Jane Rizzo; a Suh Films production; Color; DV; Not rated; 83 minutes; Release date: October 15, 2008. Documentary follows four students at Manhattan's Stuyvesant High School and the campaign to head the student union; with Hannah Freiman, George Zisiadis, Mike Zaytsev, Alex Leonard, Matt Polazzo, Marta Bralic, and Vanessa Charbhumi.

George Zisiadis in Frontrunners © *Oscilloscope*

LOCAL COLOR (Empire) Producers, David Permut, Mark Sennet, Julie Lott Gallo, James W. Evangelatos; Executive Producers, Charlie Arneson, Allen Clauss, John Papadakis, Katherine Angelos Cusenza, Richard Lott, Diana Lott, Tom Adams, Denise Evangelatos Adams; Director/ Screenplay, George Gallo; Photography, Michael Negrin; Designer, Robert Ziembicki; Costumes, Emily Draper; Music, Chris Boardman; Editor, Malcolm Campbell; Casting, Lynn Kressel; an Alla Prima Prods., Permut Presentations presentation of a James W. Evangelatos, Julie Lott Gallo production; Dolby; Panavision; Color; Rated R; 107 minutes; Release date: October 17, 2008. CAST: Armin Mueller-Stahl (Nicoli Seroff), Trevor Morgan (John Talia, Jr.), Ray Liotta (John Talia, Sr.), Charles Durning (Yammi), Samantha Mathis (Carla), Ron Perlman (Curtis Sunday), Diana Scarwid (Edith Talia), Julie Lott (Sandra Sunday), Tom Adams (Grey Artist), Taso Papadakis (Mechanized Artist), David Sosna (Mr. Ross), Nancy Casemore (Mrs. Huntington-Quail), David Sheftell (Girly Voiced Kid), Tim Velasquez (No Good Teenager)

Maye Torres in Who Does She Think She Is? © *Artistic License*

TRU LOVED (here!/Regent) Producers, Antonio Brown, Stewart Wade, David Avallone; Executive Producers, Eric Borsum, Eric Miller, Philip Au, William Mark Bonney, S. Eugene, Marjorie Margolis, Gary Snow, Darren Iverson; Director/ Screenplay, Stewart Wade; Photography, Howard Wexler; Designer, James J. Agazzi; Costumes, Augusta; Music/Music Supervisor, Barry Coffing; a BrownBag production; Color; HD-to-DigiBeta; Rated R; 104 minutes; Release date: October 17, 2008. CAST: Najarra Townsend (Tru), Jake Abel (Trevor), Matthew Thompson (Lodell), Alexandra Paul (Leslie), Cynda Williams (Lisa), Alec Mapa (Mr. Bushnell), Bruce Vilanch (Uncle Daniel), Nichelle Nichols (Grandmother), Jasmine Guy (Cynthia), Jane Lynch (Ms. Maple), Elaine Hendrix (Mrs. Muller), Tye Olson (Walter), Joseph Julian Soria (Manuel), Tony Brown (Principal Velasquez), Vernon Wells (Coach Wesley), Marcia Wallace (Mrs. Lewis), Peter Bedard (Dom), Shani Pride (Tiffany), Jenn Shagrin (Adrienne), Thomas Saunders (Emmet), Ellie Geber (Rhonda), Howard Booth (Joe), Bryan Erickson (Roberto), Jay Costello (Pierced Boy), Morgan Early (Punk Girl), Isabelle Gunning (Voice of High School P.A.), Katta Hules (Goth Girl), Brad Hunter (Student), Cody Kennedy (Cool Cheerleader), Derek Kokinda (Young Man), David Kopay (Himself), Scott Presley (Bell Aire), Jennifer Riker (Nurse Bette)

Najarra Townsend, Jake Abel in Tru Loved © *Regent Releasing*

WHO DOES SHE THINK SHE IS? (Artistic License) Producers, Will Dunning, Michelle Seligson; Executive Producer/Director, Pamela Tanner Boll; Co-Director/ Editor, Nancy Kennedy; Screenplay, Pamela Tanner Boll, Will Dunning; Photography, Gary Henoch; Music, John McDowell; a Mystic Artists Film production; Color; HD; Not rated; 83 minutes; Release date: October 17, 2008. Documentary in which five women try to balance motherhood with their artistic careers; with Maye Torres, Janis Wunderlich, Mayumi Oda, Camille Musser, Angela Williams.

NOT YOUR TYPICAL BIGFOOT MOVIE (Oscilloscope) Producer/Director/Editor, Jay Delaney; Executive Producer, Jeff Montavon; Photography, Shane Allen Davis; Music, Justin Riley, Ben Colburn; Color; Not rated; 62 minutes; Release date: October 17, 2008. Documentary on amateur Appalachian Bigfoot researchers Dallas Gilbert and Wayne Burton.

Dallas Gilbert, Wayne Burton in Not Your Typical Bigfoot Movie © *Oscillscope*

MORNING LIGHT (Walt Disney Pictures) Producers, Roy E. Disney, Leslie DeMeuse; Coproducer, Paul Crowder; Director/Screenplay, Mark Monroe; Based on an original idea by Thomas J. Pollack; Photography, Josef Nalevansky, Richard Deppe; Music, Matter; Editor, Paul Crowder; Visual Effects Supervisor, Scott Ramsey; Narrator, Patrick Warburton; a Roy E. Disney production; Dolby; Deluxe color; Rated PG; 98 minutes; Release date: October 17, 2008. Documentary on the Transpac 16, a 2,500 mile open-sea race from California to Hawaii; with Roy E. Disney, Robbie Haines, Chris Branning, Graham Brant-Zawadzki, Chris Clark, Charlie Enright, Jesse Fielding, Robbie "Turtle" Kane, Steve Manson, Chris Schubert, Kate Theisen, Mark Towill, Genny Tulloch, Piet van Os, Chris Welch, Kit Will, Jeremy Wilmot.

Morning Light © *Walt Disney Pictures*

SEX DRIVE (Summit Entertainment) Producers, Leslie Morgenstein, Bob Levy, John Morris; Executive Producer, Mike Nelson; Director, Sean Anders; Screenplay, Sean Anders, John Morris; Based on the novel *All the Way* by Andy Behrens; Photography, Tim Orr; Designer, Aaron Osborne; Costumes, Kristin M. Burke; Music, Stephen Trask; Editor, George Folsey; Casting, Lisa Beach, Sarah Katzman; an Alloy Entertainment production; Dolby; Deluxe color; Rated R; 109 minutes; Release date: October 17, 2008. CAST: Josh Zuckerman (Ian), Amanda Crew (Felicia), Clark Duke (Lance), James Marsden (Rex), Seth Green (Ezekiel), Alice Greczyn (Mary), Katrina Bowden (Ms. Tasty), Charles McDermott (Andy), Mark L. Young (Randy), Cole Petersen (Dylan), Dave Sheridan (Bobby Jo), Michael Cudlitz (Rick), Allison Weissman (Becca), Andrea Anders (Brandy), Kim Ostrenko (Ian's Stepmom), Brett Rice (Ian's Dad), David Koechner (Hitchhiker), Caley Hayes (Sandy), Michele Feren (Drunk Amish Girl), Shay Roman (Pregnant Kristy), Bella Salinas (Fundraising Girl), John Ross Bowie (Dr. Clark Teddescoe), Keith Hudson (Angry Cop), Marianne Muellerleile (Grandma Prisoner), Jessica Just (Lindsay), Brian Posehn (Carney), Scott Klace (Lance's Dad), Allen Zwolle (Men's Room Predator), Cleo King (Abstinence Host), Josh Duarte (Brandy's Dad), Marcia Koch (Brandy's Mom), Ken Clement (Señor Donut Manager), Susie Abromeit (Cousin Tiffany), Victoria Mallow (Aunt Carol), David Nash (Jail Cop), Giovanni Rodriguez (Thug Prisoner), Alan Lilly (Prisoner in Sports Jacket), Matthew Ramsey (Mall Prankster), Sasha Ramos (Kimberly), Sandra Ives (Seamstress), Olivia Nedza (Little Girl in Mall), Sam Goldberg ("Harsh" Guy), Rebecca Finer (Girl Entering Party), Drake Schirmer (Little Boy in Trailer Park), Massiel Perdomo (Undressed Abstinance Dancer), Brad E. Wilhite (Store Cashier), Dwayne Smith (Dwayne), Santara Sidersky (Angry Prisoner), Natalia Reagan (Pregnant Prisoner), Kiki Harris (Cop), George Steward (Creepy Guy), Chris Charles (Jogger), Jimmy Baron (Church Dad), Kathryn Shasha (Church Mom), Liam Eagan, Gunnar Schneider (Church Boys with Camera), Darryll Scott (Angry Cop's Partner), Shelly Keenan Frasier (Dental Receptionist), Jeremy McGuire (Rex's Boyfriend), Peter Wentz, Joseph Trohman, Patrick Stump, Andrew Hurley (Fall Out Boy)

Clark Duke, Josh Zuckerman in Sex Drive © *Summit Entertainment*

PASSENGERS (TriStar) Producers, Keri Selig, Matthew Rhodes, Judd Payne, Julie Lynn; Executive Producers, Joe Drake, Nathan Kahane; Coproducers, Aubrey Henderson, Kelli Konop, Mary Lee; Director, Rodrigo Garcia; Screenplay, Ronnie Christensen; Photography, Igor Jadue-Lillo; Designer, David Brisbin; Costumes, Katia Stano; Music, Ed Shearmur; Editor, Thom Noble; Visual Effects Supervisors, Doug Oddy, Erik Nordby; Casting, Junie Lowry Johnson, Libby Goldstein; a Mandate Pictures presentation of a Persistent Entertainment/Intuition production; Dolby; Deluxe color; Rated PG-13; 92 minutes; Release date: October 24, 2008. CAST: Anne Hathaway (Claire Summers), Patrick Wilson (Eric), Andre Braugher (Perry), Dianne Wiest (Toni), David Morse (Arkin), William B. Davis (Jack), Ryan Robbins (Dean), Clea DuVall (Shannon), Don Thompson (Norman), Andrew Wheeler (Blonde Man), Clelah Horsdal (Hanice), Karen Austin (Hospital Receptionist), Elzanne Fourie (Young Emma), Stacy Grant (Emma), Conner Dwelly

(Young Claire), Robert Gauvin (Paul), Sammy Fattedad (Building Manager), Balinder Johal (Screaming Woman), Amarjit Johal (Screaming Woman's Husband), Brad Turner (Shannon's Father), Claire Smithies (Shannon's Mother)

Anne Hathaway, Patrick Wilson in Passengers © *TriStar*

NOAH'S ARC: JUMPING THE BROOM (New Open Door Prods.) Producers, Patrik-Ian Polk, Carol Ann Shine, Suzanne L. Berger, Lael McCall; Director, Patrik-Ian Polk; Screenplay, Patrik-Ian Polk, John R. Gordon; Story, Q. Allan Brocka; Photography, Christopher Porter; Designer, William Fleming; Costumes, Kate Rose; Music, Adam S. Goldman, Julian Wass; Editor, Phillip J. Bartell; a co-production of Tally Skinny Black Boy Productions, Logo, Blueprint Entertainment; Dolby; Color; Rated R; 101 minutes; Release date: October 24, 2008. CAST: Darryl Stephens (Noah), Jensen Atwood (Wade), Rodney Chester (Alex), Jennia Fredrique (Brandy), Glen Grant (Arturo), Gary LeRoi Gray (Branon), Jonathan Julian (Eddie), Gregory Kieth (Trey), Tonya Pinkins (Mrs. Robinson), Douglas Spearman (Chance), Trevor Josiah Thomas (Ojemodupe), Christian Vincent (Ricky), Jason Steed (Baby Gat), Phoebe Snow (Herself), John Beale (Flower Truck Guy), Suanne Coy (Noah's Mom), Guy German (Guy in Woods), Rocky Jones (Minister), Danielle Lopresti (Brandon's Mom)

SAVING MARRIAGE (here!/Regent) Producers/Directors, Mike Roth, John Henning; Photography, Mike Roth; Music, Jamie Forsyth; Editor, Paula Gauthier; a Documix production; Color; Video; Rated PG-13; 90 minutes; Release date: October 24, 2008. Documentary about the struggle for gay marriage rights in America; with Sen. Jarrett Barrios, Mary Bonauto, Josh Friedes, Amy Hunt, Sue Hyde, Arline Isaacson, Kris Mineau, Rep. Carl Sciortino.

Saving Marriage © *Regent Releasing*

SAW V (Lionsgate) Producers, Greg Hoffman, Oren Koules, Mark Burg; Executive Producers, Daniel Jason Heffner, James Wan, Leigh Wannell, Stacey Testro; Director, David Hackl; Screenplay, Patrick Melton, Marcus Dunstan; Photography, David A. Armstrong; Designer, Tony Ianni; Music, Charlie Clouser; Editor, Kevin Greutert; Special Effects Supervisor, Jeff Skochko; Casting, Stephanie Gorin; a Twisted Pictures presentation of a Burg/Koules/Hoffman production; Dolby; Deluxe color; Rated R; 92 minutes; Release date: October 24, 2008. CAST:Tobin Bell (Jigsaw/John), Costas Mandylor (Det. Mark Hoffman), Scott Patterson (Agent Strahm), Betsy Russell (Jill), Mark Rolston (Dan Erickson), Julie Benz (Brit), Carlo Rota (Charles), Mike Butters (Paul), Meagan Good (Luba), Greg Bryk (Mallick), Laura Gordon (Ashley), Joris Jarsky (Seth), Al Sapienza (Chief of Police), Mike Realba (Det. Fisk), Lyriq Bent (Rigg), Sheila Shah (Special Agent Corwin), Samantha Lemole (Pamela Jenkins), Jeff Pustil (Bernie), Athena Karkanis (Agent Perez), Justin Louis (Art), Donnie Wahlberg (Eric Mathews), Danny Glover (David Tapp), Dana Sorman (Law Office Receptionist), Shawnee Smith (Amanda Young), Bahar Soomekh (Lynn Denlon), Niamh Wilson (Corbett), Angus Macfadyen (Jeff Reinhart), Lisa Berry (EMT), Bill Vibert (Officer), Tony Nappo (Gus), Brandon McGibbon (Hank), Tim Burd (Obi), Natalie Brown (Heather Miller), Quancetia Hamilton (Person with Dog), Lorraine Foreman (Old Woman), Sarah Power (Angelina), Cory Lee (Jasmine)

Joris Jarsky in Saw V © *Lionsgate*

JOHNNY GOT HIS GUN (Truly Indie) Producers, Rowan Joseph, Shane Partlow, Wesley Horton, Lauri LaBeau; Executive Producers, Robin A. Sateriale, John Meindl; Director, Rowan Joseph; Screenplay, Bradley Rand Smith; Adapted from the novel by Dalton Trumbo; Photography, Andrew K. Sachs; Art Director, Keith Mitchell; Costumes, Denitsa Bliznakova; Editor, Jay Cassidy; Casting, Chadwick Struck; a Greenwood Hill Prods. presentation in association with Tres Hermanos Prods.; Dolby; Color; HD-to-35mm; Not rated; 77 minutes; Release date: October 24, 2008. CAST: Benjamin McKenzie (Joe Boham), Meredith Kendall (Mother's Voice)

THE GAY BED AND BREAKFAST OF TERROR (Ariztical Entertainment) Producers, Jaymes Thompson, Sean Abley; Director/Screenplay, Jaymes Thompson; Photography, Joel Deutsch; Designers, Robert Frye, Noah Naylor; Costumes, Rachel Lynn; Music, Swerve South; Editor, Andrew Van Baal; a MoDean Pictures production; Color; Not rated; 110 minutes; Release date: October 24, 2008. CAST: Mari Marks (Helen), Michael Soldier (Alex), Georgia Jean (Luella), Robert Borzych (Eric), Hilary Schwartz (Starr), Vinny Markus (Dom), Shannon Lee (Deborah), Denis Heller (Gabby), Derek Long (Mike), Allie Rivenbark (Brenda), James Tolins (Todd), Lisa Block-Wieser (Lizette), Jim Polivka (Rodney), Noah Naylor (Manfred), Nora Gaetana (Busty Lesbian), Rachel Lynn, Bob "Bobaloo" Koenig (Sister Mary Marie), Tammy Brynes (Babysitter), Miriel

Rust, Kailee Brynes, Robert Frye, Kelly Herrin (Bingo Players), Timothy Kelley (Bingo Caller), Maria Tomas (Anetta), Andrew Americk (Evangelist), Hudson Gilles (Republican Recruiter), Leo Belladaere (Lead Republican), Kelsey Button, Sara Raftery (Catholic School Girls), Stephen Naugle, Collin Brock, Richard DeGuillo, Corey J. Marshall, Bryan Pisano, Brian Kirschiff, Joan Lee (Republican Convention Delegates)

Michael Soldier, Hilary Schwartz in The Gay Bed and Breakfast of Terror *© Ariztical Entertainment*

THE FIRST BASKET (Laemmle/Zeller) Producer, David Vyorst; Coproducer, Jennifer Crescenzo; Director, David Vyorst; Photography, Gary Griffin; Music, Roberto Juan Rodriguez; Narrator, Peter Riegert; a Zej Media production; Color/Black and white; DV; Not rated; 86 minutes; Release date: October 29, 2008. Documentary on Jews in basketball.

Tamir Goodman in The First Basket *© Laemmle/Zeller*

RUN FOR YOUR LIFE (Screen Media) Producer/Director, Judd Ehrlich; Photography, Ryo Murakami; Music Supervisor, Dawn Sutter Madell; Editor, Alison Shurman; a Flatbush Pictures production; Color; HD; Not rated; 99 minutes; Release date: October 29, 2008. Documentary on Fred Lebow, the man behind the New York City Marathon; with Neil Amdur, Gloria Averbuch, Bob Bright, Vince Chiappetta, Ted Corbitt, Brian Crawford, Gordon Davis, Tom Fleming, Michael P. Frankfurt, George Hirsch, Moshe Katz, Sara Katz, Edward I. Koch, Nina Kuscsik, Mike Lebowitz, Alan Lubell, Charlie McCabe, Gary Muhrcke, Barbara Paddock, Bob Pickett, Anne Roberts, Bill Rodgers, Peter Roth, Howard Rubenstein, Jack Rudin, Alberto Salazar, Norb Sander, Alice Schneider, Frank Shorter, George Spitz, Allan Steinfeld, Henry Stern, Percy Sutton, Kathrine Switzer, Dick Traum George Vecsey, Grete Waitz

Fred Lebow in Run for Your Life *© Screen Media*

THE MATADOR (City Lights) Producers, Stephen Higgins, Nina Gilden Seavey; Executive Producers, Scott Dunklee, Kristie Nova; Directors, Stephen Higgins, Nina Gilden Seavey; Photography, Christopher Jenkins, James Morton-Haworth; Music, John Califra; Editor Ian Rummer; a Lancer Group and Matador Films presentation; Color; HD Video; Not rated; 75 minutes; Release date: October 31, 2008. Documentary on the controversial sport of bullfighting; with David Fandila, Trini Fandila, Santiago Lopez, Juan Alvaro Fandila, Juan Fandila, Sr., Lluis Agusti, Eduardo Lago, Elvira Lindo, Veronica Canete, Jose Antonio del Moral, Antonio Matilla.

David Fandilla in Matador © *City Lights*

MY NAME IS BRUCE (Image Entertainment) Producers, Mike Richardson, Bruce Campbell; Director, Bruce Campbell; Screenplay, Mark Verheiden; Photography, Kurt Rauf; Designer, George Costello; Costumes, Claude Everett; Music, Joseph Lo Duca; Editor, Scott Smith; Associate Producer, Craig "Kif" Sanborn; Line Producer, Gary Kout; Casting, Tia Reagan; a Dark Horse Indie in association with Image Entertainment; Color; Rated R; 86 minutes; Release date: October 31, 2008. CAST: Bruce Campbell (Himself), Grace Thorsen (Kelly Graham), Taylor Sharpe (Jeff), Ted Raimi (Mills Toddner/Wing), Ben McCain (Mayor), Ellen Sandweiss (Cheryl), Tim Quill (Frank), Dan Hicks (Dirt Farmer), Logan Martin (Clayton), Ali Akay (Little Debbie), Ariel Badenhop (Big Debbie), James J. Peck (Guan-Di/Cavealien Monster), Jennifer Brown (Petra), Kurt Rauf (Cinematographer), Mike Kallio (Hack Director/Annoyed Townie), Adam Boyd (Tiny), Stephen A. White, Mike Estes, Michael Meyer (Fans), Vincent Angelini (Wheelchair Fan), Janelle Farber (Kasey), Dana D. Turner (Charlene), Elise Passante (Soccer Mom), Tayves Pelletier (Skippy), Hallie Cameron (Liz), Catherine Rowe (Edna), Robert Faulconer (Split Man), Mike Campbell (Shot in the Chest Guy), Butch McCain (Farmer), Colin Campbell (Shot in the Shoulder Guy), Randy Granstrom (Shot in the Arm Guy), John Bach (Shot in the Leg Guy), Kenny Juttner (Shot in the Ear Guy), Mason Faulconer (Bicycle Kid), Flora R. Albano (Old Lady), Jeff Hunter (Disinterested Townie), Jennifer Diaz (Stripclub Dancer), Mike Richardson (Studio Shemp), Craig "Kif" Sanborn (Bowling Shemp), Loki (Sam 'n Rob), Ronald P. Zwang (The Milkman), Dan Daniella, Brian Tamblin, Nick Vitiello, Tyler Hulsey (Oregon Rain)

DEAR ZACHARY: A LETTER TO A SON ABOUT HIS FATHER (Oscilloscope) Producer/Director/Screenplay/Photography/Music/Editor, Kurt Kuenne; Color; DV; Not rated; 95 minutes; Release date: October 31, 2008. Documentary in which filmmaker Kurt Kuenne documents his friendship with Andrew Bagby, who was murdered by his ex-lover; with Kurt Kuenne, Zachary Andrew, David Bagby, Andrew Bagby, Kathleen Bagby.

Katherine Bagby, Andrew Bagby, David Bagby in Dear Zachary © *Oscilloscope*

REPO! THE GENETIC OPERA (Lionsgate) Producers, Daniel Jason Heffner, Carl Mazzocone, Oren Koules, Mark Burg; Executive Producers, Darren Lynn Bousman, Peter Block, Jason Constantine, Jonathan McHugh, Tim Palen, Sarah Greenberg; Director, Darren Lynn Bousman; Screenplay/Music, Darren Smith, Terrance Zdunich; Photography, Joseph White; Designer, David Hackl; Costumes, Alex Kavanaugh; Editor, Harvey Rosenstock; a Twisted Pictures presentation of a Burg/Koules production; Deluxe color; Rated R; 98 minutes; Release date: November 7, 2008. CAST: Anthony Stewart Head (Nathan Wallace/Repo Man), Alex Vega (Shilo Wallace), Paul Sorvino (Rotti Largo), Sarah Brightman (Blind Mag), Bill Moseley (Luigi Largo), Ogre (Pavi Largo), Terrance Zdunich (Graverobber), Sarah Power (Marni Wallace), Jessica Horn (Jessica Adams), Branko Lebar (Rotti's Chauffeur), Brianna Buckmaster (Sherrie Alviso), Anna Kostan, Brad Austin (Young Mormons), Mary Adams (Big Man), Rebecca Marshall (Woman with Martini Glass), Egidio Tari (Man in Tuxedo), Jake Reardon (Single Mother), J. LaRose (Geneco Spokesperson), John Gallagher, Jr., Howard Glassman (Talking Heads), Darren Smith (Geneco's Band Leader), Dean Armstrong, Athena Karkanis (Victims), Andreja Punkris, Alisa Burket (Rotti's Henchwomen), Martin Samuel, Stephan Dubeau (Amber's Valets), Dena Chiarcossi (Head Sexy Gentern)

Ogre, Anthony Head in Repo the Genetic Opera © *Lionsgate*

HOUSE (Roadside Attractions) Producers, Joe Goodman, Bobby Neutz, Ralph Winter; Executive Producers, Marek Sledziewski, Wotjek Frychowski; Director, Robby Henson; Screenplay, Rob Green; Based on the novel by Ted Dekker, Frank Peretti; Photography, Marcin Koszalka; Music, David E. Russo; Editor, Andrea Bottigliero; a Namesake Entertainment production, in association with Circle Media; Color; Rated R; 118 minutes; Release date: November 7, 2008. CAST: Michael Madsen (Tin Man/Office Lawdale), Reynaldo Rosales (Jack Singleton), Heidi Dippold (Stephanie Singleton), Julie Ann Emery (Leslie Taylor), J.P. Davis (Randy Messarue), Lew Temple (Pete), Leslie Easterbrook (Betty), Bill Moseley (Stewart), Pawel Delag (Officer Lawdale), Weronika Rosati (Mrs. Lawdale), Allan Bale (Susan), Mark Fierer (Randy's Father), Florentyna Synowiecka (Melissa), Andrew Gorzen (Leslie's Uncle), Albert Pietrzal (Young Randy), Bobby Neutz (Sheriff), Jeffrey de Graft-Johnson (Deputy), Holly McClure, Joe Goodman (EMS)

THE GUITAR (Lightning Media) Producers, Bob Jason, Heyward Collins, Amy Redford, Amos Poe, Brad Zions; Executive Producers, Andy Emilio, Robert Lewis, Michael Roban, Damon Martin, Robert Kravitz, Milena Pappas, Rose Ganguzza; Director, Amy Redford; Screenplay, Amos Poe; Photography, Bobby Bukowski; Designer, Marla Weinhoff; Costumes, Eric Daman; Music, David Mansfield; Editor, David Leonard; Casting, Avy Kaufman; an Applecreek Prods. presentation of a Breakout Pictures production, in association with Cold Fusion Media Group, Co-Op.; Dolby; Color; Rated R; 93 minutes; Release date: November 7, 2008. CAST: Saffron Burrows (Melody), Isaach De Bankolé (Roscoe Wasz), Paz de la Huerta (Cookie), Reg Rogers (Brett), Adam Trese (Mr. Laffs), David Wain (Phone

Man), Mia Kucan (Young Mel), Elizabeth Marvel (Ma Wilder), Bill Camp (Pa Wilder), Richard Short (Loser Musician), William Leroy (Billy), Lori Tan Chinn (Mrs. Tzu), Virginia Wing (Ms. Li), Janeane Garofalo (Dr. Murray), Ashlie Atkinson (Receptionist), Lawrence Ballard (Another Doctor), Chris Bauer (Chief of Surgery), Joel Cannon (Everyothers Guitar Player), Mark A. Keeton (Guitar Salesman), Amitesh Manchanda (Punjabi Cab Driver), Sonia Manzano (Lady), Owen McCarthy (Everyothers Singer), John Melville (Everyothers Drummer), Ben Toro (Everyothers Bass Player)

PRAY THE DEVIL BACK TO HELL (Balcony) Producer, Abigail E. Disney; Coproducer, Johanna Hamilton; Director, Gini Reticker; Photography, Kirsten Johnson; Music, Blake Leyh; Editor, Kate Taverna; a Fork Films production; Color; HD; Not rated 72 minutes; Release date: November 7, 2008. Documentary on how the women of Liberia successfully fought to halt decades of fighting in their country; with Leymah Gbowee, Asatu Bah Kenneth, Vaiba Flomo, Janet Johnson-Bryant, Etweda Cooper, Etty Weah.

Pray the Devil Back to Hell © *Balcony Releasing*

THE ALPHABET KILLER (New Films Intl.) Producers, Isen Robbins, Aimee Schoof, Tom Lalloy, Ross Terlecki; Executive Producers, Greg Polisseni, Luzi Filiba, Izak Filiba, Ron Gell, Mark Clark, Nesim Hason, Sezin Sason, Brandon Baker; Director, Rob Schmidt; Screenplay, Tom Malloy; Photography, Joe DeSalvo; Designer, Alicia Keywan; Costumes, Lynn Falconer; Music, Earl Perlmutter; Editor, Frank Reynolds; Casting, Nancy Payer Battino, Kelly Wagner, Natasha Cuba, Nicole Abellera; a New Films Intl./Greg Polisseni presentation of an Intrinsic Value Films/Wideye Films production; Dolby; Color; Rated R; 98 minutes; Release date: November 7, 2008. CAST: Eliza Dushku (Megan Paige), Cary Elwes (Capt. Kenneth Shine), Timothy Hutton (Richard Ledge), Tom Malloy (Stephen Harper), Michael Ironside (Capt. Nathan Norcross), Tom Noonan (Capt. Gullikson), Bill Moseley (Carl Tanner), Martin Donovan (Jim Walsh), Melissa Leo (Kathy Walsh), Meltem Cumbul (Elisa Castillo), Carl Lumbly (Dr. Ellis Parks), Brian Scannell (Jay Castillo), Jack McGee (Hank), Larry Hankin (Perry), Sarah Anderson (Elizabeth Eckers), Glenn Argenti, Michael Ross King (SWAT Team), Renata Batista (Waitress), Liz Cameron (Shopkeeper Wife), Eric Cubitt (Husband), Tony Delgrosso (Webster Police Officer), Nate Dushku (Tim), Farris Ellington, Claire Simpson (Ghost Girls), Tamara Farias (Olga Maestro), Andrew Fiscella (Len Schaefer), Bailey Garno (Carla Castillo), Joseph Giorgione (Paramedic), Kristina Jewell (Wendy Walsh), Ian Kidd (Detective), Cynthia Mace (Rita Schaefer), Eva Mancarella (Melissa Maestro), Peter Mancarella (Jared), Wendy Mancarella (Real Estate Agent), Shawn Michael (Det. Anthony Peters), Frank Rossi (Francis Baker), Rocco Sisto (Father McQuarrie), Nicholas Sprague (Webster Police Officer), Russell Terlecki (Officer Ted)

GARDENS OF THE NIGHT (City Lights) Producers, Ro Robb, Pascal Franchot, Damian Harris, Joseph Dain; Executive Producers, Mark Amin, Todd Olsson; Director/Screenplay, Damian Harris; Photography, Paula Huidobro; Designer, Bradd Fillmann; Costumes, Rhona Meyers; Music, Craig Richey; Music Supervisor, Peymon Maskan; Editor, Michael Shemesh; Casting, Shannon Makhanian; a Sobini Films (U.S.)/La Nuit Americaine (U.K.) presentation of a Fastback Pictures, Station 3, Shoot Prods. (U.S.) production; American-British; Dolby; Color; DV-to-35mm; 8mm-to-35mm; Rated R; 108 minutes; Release date: November 7, 2008. CAST: Gillian Jacobs (Leslie), John Malkovich (Michael), Ryan Simpkins (Young Leslie), Tom Arnold (Alex), Kevin Zegers (Frank), Jermaine Scooter Smith (Young Donnie), Harold Perrineau (Orlando), Jeremy Sisto (Jimmy), Raynold Gideon (Judge Feeney), Cornelia Guest (Mrs. Feeney), Natalie May (Judge's Daughter), Ben Lin (Pa), Alice Lo (Ma), Evan Ross (Donnie), Landall Goolsby (Blackberry John), Shontae Saldana (Baby Loco), Max Van Ville (Surf), Kyle Gallner (Ratboy), Troy Ruptash (Motel John), Shiloh Fernandez (Cooper), Angel Lacy (Waitress), Peta Wilson (Sarah), Evan Peters (Rachel/Brian), Carlie Westerman (Monica), Jeff Swarthout (Gay John), Jeff Feringa (Booster Lady), Jim Cody Williams (Leslie's John), Alexis Jackson (Mia), Raphael Sbarge (Mr. Whitehead), Lisa Akey (Mrs. Whitehead), Gracie Sbarge (Gracie Whitehead), Ty Simpkins (Dylan Whitehead), Michelle Rodriguez (Lucy)

Ryan Simpkins, Jermaine Scooter Smith *in* Gardens of the Night © *City Lights*

THE DUKES (Cavu Pictures) Producers, Don Dunn, James Cypherd, Robert Davi; Executive Producer, Frank A. Visco; Co-Executive Producers, John Paul DeJoria, Herbert F. Boeckmann II, James Hawse, Bob Byers, Jr., R. Rex Parris, Walter Wang; Coproducers, Chazz Palminteri, James Andronica, Eric Weston: Director, Robert Davi; Screenplay, Robert Davi, James Andronica; Photography, Michael Goi; Designer, Derek Hughes; Music, Nic Ten Broek; Music Supervisors, Butch Barbella, Morris I. Diamond; Editor, James Cypherd; Casting, Valerie McCaffrey; a Doo Wop Prods. production in association with Sun Lion Films; Dolby; Deluxe color; Rated PG-13; 96 minutes; Release date: November 14, 2008. CAST: Chazz Palminteri (George Zucco), Robert Davi (Danny DePasquale), Peter Bogdanovich (Lou Fiola), Frank D'Amico (Armond Kaputo), Elya Baskin (Murph), Miriam Margolyes (Aunt Vee), Melora Hardin (Diane), Bruce Weitz (Toulio), Eloise DeJoria (Katherine), Dominic Scott Kay (Brion), Alphonse Mouzon (Ray), Joe Campanella (Giovanni Zorro), James Andronica (Peppe), Elaine Hendrix (Stephanie), Greg London (Greg), Meredith Giangrande (Angela), J.D. Fryberger (Det. Kozlo), Ron Bard (Harry Basil), Joyce Westergaard (Suzette), Roy Abramsohn (Suit #1), Mann Alfonso (Janitor #2), Paul Michael Berman (Duke Candidate #1), Jo Deodato Clark (Old Lady), Patrick Cupo (Phil), Robert Harvey (Contractor), Ben Hermes (ABC Agent), Larry Logsdon (Man Walking Dog), Sean Maguire (Dave), Dan Materdomini (Dr. Phoul), Tonyo Meléndez (Security Guard), Julissa Miro (Mysterious Woman), John Prosky (Brad), Richard Tyson (Ralph), Claudia Villarreal (Plus Size Woman)

BOHICA (Wabi Pictures) Producers, D.J. Paul, Alex Campbell, Inman Young; Director, D.J. Paul; Screenplay, Joseph "Bo" Colen; Story, Joseph "Bo" Colen, D.J. Paul; Photography, Michael Hardwick; Designer, Michael Krantz; Costumes, Carmen Thompson; Music, Isaac Sprintis; Editor, Wes Lipman; a Black and Tan production; Dolby; Color; Not rated; 91 minutes; Release date: November 14, 2008. CAST: Adam Rodriguez (Diz), Nicholas Gonzales (Rivera), Kevin Weisman (Nasty), Brendan Sexton III (Fish), Matthew Del Negro (Nusche), Jaime McAdams (Dean), Tom Wright (Horowitz), Joshua Coleman (Soldier), Joseph "Bo" Colen (Voice of Radio Operator), David Carmichael Greenfield (Gunner), Taylor Gerard Hart (Driver), Brian Unger (Voice of Air Force Pilot)

WE ARE WIZARDS (Brooklyn Underground Films) Producer, Gerald Lewis; Director, Josh Koury; Photography, Josh Koury, Myles Kane, Gerald Lewis, Josh Walinski, Cris Moris; Music, Stan Oh; Editor, Myles Kane; Color; HD; Not rated; 79 minutes; Release date: November 14, 2008. Documentary on the different ways the more extreme fans have responded to the Harry Potter books; with Heather Lawver, Melissa Anelli, Paul De George, Joe De George, Darious Wilkins, Holden Wilkins, Ian Wilkins, Caryl Matriciana, Brad Neely.

We Are Wizards © *Brooklyn Underground Films*

THE BEAUTIFUL TRUTH (Cinema Libre) Producer, Steve Kroschel; Executive Producer, William Bacon III; Director/Screenplay, Steve Kroschel; Photography, William Bacon III, Mario Benassi; Music, Francesca Dego, Francesca Leonardi; Editor, Carey Komadina; a Kroschel Films production; Stereo; Color; Not rated; 91 minutes; Release date: November 14, 2008. Documentary in which teenager Garrett Kroschel sets out to find the reason why a sixty-year-old dietary cure for cancer has been dismissed by the medical establishment; with Garrett Kroschel, Charlotte Gerson, David Kennedy, John Olney, Hal Huggins, Jay Kordich, Russell Blaylock, Wallace Sampson, Howard Straus.

WAR CHILD (Reel U Films) Producers, C. Karim Chrobog, Afshin Molavi; Executive Producers, Dal Lamagna, Jeff Weingarten, Rick Boden, Roshanak Ameli-Tehrani; Director, C. Karim Chrobog; Photography, S.J. Staniski; Music, Charlie Barnett, Emmanuel Jal; Editor, Nels Bangerter; an 18th Street Films production, in association with Interface Media Group, the Global Fund for Children; Color; HD; Rated PG-13; 92 minutes; Release date: November 14, 2008. Documentary on hip-hop performer Emmanuel Jal, who had grown up as a child soldier in a Sudanese children's refugee camp; with Emmanuel Jal, John Prendergast, Ted Dagne, Dan McCarey, Sally Dudmesh.

Harvard Beats Yale 29-29 © *Kino Intl*

HARVARD BEATS YALE 29-29 (Kino) Producer/Director/Photography/Editor, Kevin Rafferty; a Kevin Rafferty Prods. presentation; Color; HD; Not rated; 105 minutes; Release date: November 19, 2008. Documentary on the Nov. 24, 1968 football game between Harvard and Yale; with Tommy Lee Jones, Brian Dowling, Frank Champi, Vic Gatto, J.P. Goldsmith.

SPECIAL (Magnet) Producers, Edward Parks, Frank Mele; Coproducer, Andre Fabrizio; Directors/Screenplay, Hal Haberman, Jeremy Passmore; Photography, Nelson Craig; Designer, Nathan Amondson; Costumes, Dawn Weisberg, Annie Bloom; Music, Tom Wolfe, Manish Raval; Editor, Mike Saenz; a Rival Pictures presentation; Dolby; Fotokem color; Rated R; 81 minutes; Release date: November 21, 2008. CAST: Michael Rapaport (Les), Paul Blackthorne (Jonas Exiler), Josh Peck (Joey), Robert Baker (Everett), Jack Kehler (Dr. Dobson), Alexandra Holden (Maggie), Ian Bohen (Ted Exiler), Christopher Darga (Steve), Eric Anderson (Newscaster), David Bear (Man on Elevator), Karen Bryant (News Co-Host), Amanda Carlin (Mugging Victim), Howard Ferguso-Woitzman (Homeless Man), Andrew Leeds (Bitter Lonely Guy), Ian McConnel (Sweet Lonely Guy), Patricia Ann Nelson (Pregnant Teen), Natalie Richter (Receptionist), Franc Ross (Crackhead), Matthew Troyer (Tall Guy), Michael Shamus Wiles (Police Officer)

Michael Rapaport in Special © *Magnet*

LAKE CITY (Screen Media) Producers, Allison Sarofim, Donna L. Bascom, Mike S. Ryan; Executive Producers, Mark Johnson, Sally Pope, Weiman Seid; Directors/Screenplay, Perry Moore, Hunter Hill; Photography, Robert Gantz; Designer, David Crank; Costumes, Susan Antonelli; Music, Aaron Zigman; Editor, Jeffrey Wolf; Casting, Lisa Mae Fincannon; a Sixty-Six Prods. presentation of a Sixty-Six production; Dolby; Arriflex Widescreen; Color; Super 16mm-to-35mm; Rated R; 93 minutes; Release date: November 21, 2008. CAST: Sissy Spacek (Maggie), Troy Garity (Billy), Rebecca Romijn (Jennifer), David Matthews (Red), Drea de Matteo (Hope), Colin Ford (Clayton), Keith Carradine (Roy), Barry Corbin (George), Allison Sarofim (Beth), Sydney ter Avest (Young Jennifer), Heather Bailey (Loretta the Bartender), Pete Burris (Foreman), Jason Davis (Tom), Justin Dray (Rick), Cheryl Fare (Irma), James Green (Pool Player), Kenny Hinkle (Andy), Jessica Hutson (Lucy), Todd A. Langenfeld (Plain Clothes Street Cop), Joseph T. Lee (AA Member), Alina Phelan (Linda), Dexter Romweber (Frank), Victoria Van Dorn (Young Jennifer Look-Alike), Jack Weber (Young Billy), Jeff Wincott (Leo), Irene Ziegler (Nancy Kaye)

Troy Garity, Sissy Spacek in Lake City © *Screen Media*

THE BETRAYAL – NERAKHOON (Cinema Guild) Producers, Ellen Kuras, Flora Fernandez-Marengo; Executive Producer, Cara Mertes; Director/Photography, Ellen Kuras; Co-Director/Editor/Narrator, Thavisouk Phrasavath; Screenplay, Ellen Kuras, Thavisouk Phrasavath; a Pandinlao Films presentation in co-production with P.O.V./American Documentary; Color; HD Video; Not rated; 96 minutes; Release date: November 21, 2008. Documentary on how Laos refugee Thavisouk Phrasavath and his family attempted to start life anew in America. (This film received an Oscar nomination for documentary feature).

The Betrayal – Nerakhoon © *Cinema Guild*

ROME & JEWEL (Emerging Pictures) Producers/Story, Charles T. Kanganis, Neil Bagg; Executive Producers, Roberta Walski, Greg Walski; Director/Screenplay, Charles T. Kanganis; Photography, John Buckley; Designer, Chris Miller; Costumes, Laura Brody; Music, Eric Monsanty; Lyrics, Neil Bagg; Music Supervisor, Ashley Revell; Editor, Lee Grubin; a 61 Street Films presentation of Walksi/Bagg/Kanganis production; Eastmancolor; Not rated; 91 minutes; Release date: November 28, 2008. CAST: Nate Parker (Rome), Lindsey Haun (Jewel), Allen Maldonado (Mercury), Elijah Kelley (Ben), John Rubinstein (Mayor Capps), Cleavant Derricks (Reverend Q), Greg Siff (Ty), Stephanie Dyann (Kara), Russell Howard (Perry), Cole Griffin (Jay), Ted Lyde (Parishoner), Alison Coster, Joe Palese (Vegas Cops), Les Feltmate (Policeman), Thomas Magazeno (Security Guard), Faith Yascone (Jasmine), Raul G. Perez, Jeran Pascascio (Men in Alley), David Cubero (LA Cop)

PUNISHER: WAR ZONE (Lionsgate) Producers, Gale Ann Hurd; Executive Producers, Oliver Hengst, Ernst-August Schneider, Ari Arad, Ogden Gavanski, Michael Paseornek, John Sacchi; Coproducers, Jack Murray, Gary Ventimiglia; Director, Lexi Alexander; Screenplay, Nick Santora, Art Marcum, Matt Holloway; Based on Marvel's *Punisher* comic book series; Photography, Steve Gainer; Designer, Andrew Neskoromny; Costumes, Odette Gadoury; Music, Michael Wandmacher; Music Supervisor, Dan Hubbert; Editor, William Yeh; Visual Effects Supervisor, Robert Short; Stunts, Pat E. Johnson; Casting, Tricia Wood, Jennifer Smith, Deborah Aquila; a Lionsgate, Valhalla Motion Pictures (U.S.)/MHF Zweite Academy Film (Germany) production, in association with SGF Entertainment; American-German; Dolby; Super 35 Widescreen; Technicolor; Rated R; 101 minutes; Release date: December 5, 2008. CAST: Ray Stevenson (Frank Castle), Dominic West (Billy Russoti/Jigsaw), Doug Hutchison (Loony Bin Jim), Colin Salmon (Paul Budiansky), Wayne Knight (Micro), Dash Mihok (Martin Soap), Julie Benz (Angela Donatelli), Stephanie Janusauskas (Grace), Mark Camacho (Pittsy), Nick Donatelli (Romano Orzari), Keram Malicki-Sánchez (Ink), Larry Day (Agent Miller), Ron Lea (Captain Ross), Tony Calabretta (Saffiotti), T.J. Storm (Maginty), Carlos Gonzalez-vlo (Carlos), David Vadim (Cristu Bulat), John Dunn-Hill (Cesare), Niko Nikovlov (Pompiliu), Aubert Pallascio (Tiberiu), Francis P. Goldberg (Mrs. Gordlock), Pat Fry (Asylum Orderly), Robert Harrop (Priest), Linda Smith (Mrs. Cesare), Lynne De Bel (Micro's Mother), Bill Hall (TV News Reporter), Matt Holland (EMT), Bjanka Murgel (Arm Candy), Brent Skagford (Waiter), James Murray (Bodyguard #2), Cas Anvar (Plastic Surgeon), Ethan Gould (Schoolboy), Michael Paterson (Motel Manager), Kane Chan, Steven P. Park (Bangers), Edward Yankie (Father Mike), Tracy Phillips (Harlem Gangleader), Giovanni Cipolla (Wiseguy), Andrew Farmer (Guard), Jean-Loup Yale (Mugger), Miro Bedard (Frank's Son), Edouard Keller (Thug), Marco Desjean (Alpha Dog), Lise Sita (Nicki's Mom), Nick Sita (Nicki's Dad), Oleg Popkov (Old Man), Eric Dauphin (Cesare Wiseguy), Stéphane Byl (FBI Van Agent), Jon Barton (Ice Team Leader)

Doug Hutchison, Ray Stevenson in Punisher: War Zone © *Lionsgate*

EXTREME MOVIE (Dimension) Producers, Laura Lichstein, Richard Suckle, Warren Zide; Directors, Adam Jay Epstein, Andrew Jacobson; Screenplay, Adam Jay Epstein, Andrew Jacobson, Will Forte, John Solomon, Andy Samberg, Akiva Schaffer, Jorma Taccone, Erica Rivinoja, Phil Lord, Chris Miller; Photography, Eric Haase; Costumes, Dayna Pink; Music, Jim Latham; Editors, Ivan Victor, Bruce Green; Casting, David Rapaport, Lindsey Hayes Kroeger; Dolby; Color; Rated R; 75 minutes; Release date: December 5, 2008. CAST: Ryan Pinkston (Mike), Michael Cera (Fred), Christina DeRosa (Nancy), Frankie Muniz (Chuck), Cherilyn Wilson (Stacy), Jamie Kennedy (Mateus), Rob Pinkston (Griffin), Royal Binion (Basketball Boner Guy), Denise Boutte (New Tabitha), Rich Ceraulo (Angus), Vanessa Lee Chester (Charlotte), Shasa Dabner (Lindsey), Danny Ehrhardt (Biff), John Farley (Sex Ed. Teacher), Ben Feldman (Len), Dan Finnerty (Gigundocock), Adam Frost (Kevin), Joanna Garcia (Sweetie Pie), Brent Gore (Asst. Director), Aaron Haedt, Jon Westernoff (Guys in Underwear), Danneel Harris (Melissa), Hank Harris (Ronnie), Margo Harshman (Ted's Girlfriend), Kevin Hart (Barry), Heather Hogan (Kat), Kyle Howard (Drunk Girl's Boyfriend), Kendra Krull (Judy), Vanessa Lengies (Carla), Matthew Lillard (Himself), Bobbie Sue Luther (Gabriella), Cristin Michele (Jackie), Andy Milonakis (Justin), Shacolby Randell, "Big" LeRoy Mobley (Black Guys), Steven Christopher Parker (Doug), Allison Queal (Cowgirl), Lisa Richman (Jessica's Mom), Sonia Rockwell (Kim), Melvin "Shorty" Rossi (Shorty the Cowboy), Jake Sandvig (Hank), Ashley Schneider (Betty), Jane Silvia (Penny), Anne Son (Friend), Kira Verrastro (Black Chick), Katie Walder (Drunk Girl), Rheagan Wallace (Jessica), Jermaine Williams (Wyatt), Mika Winkler (Cowgirl Lasso)

LET THEM CHIRP AWHILE (Blitstein Film) Producers, Jonathan Blitstein, Anouk Frosch; Director/Screenplay/Editor, Jonathan Blitstein; Photography, Andrew Shulkind; Designer, Michael Bednark; Music, Giulio Carmassi; Casting, Jonathan Blitstein, Heidi Handelsman; Color; Not rated; 92 minutes; Release date: December 5, 2008. CAST: Justin Rice (Bobby), Brendan Sexton III (Scott), Laura Breckenridge (Dara), Pepper Brinkley (Michelle), Zach Galligan (Hart Carlton), Charlotte Af Geijerstam (Charlotte), Anthony Rapp (Himself), Amy Chow (Ariel), Ilana Meredith (Deirdre), Abe Goldfarb (Pigeon #1 – Levene), Peter Parks (Paul the Dog Breeder), Brian Silliman (Pigeon #2 – Roma), Dennis Hurley (Pigeon #3 – Williamson), Robert Aberdeen (NYU Professor), Josh Alexander (Richard Buxton), Ashley N. Anderson (Girl who Kisses Hart), Morgan Baker (Harvard Guy), Allegra Cohen (Jewish Activist), Melina Lizette, Dana Corral, Marisol Sacramento (Students), Lori Fine (Scarsdale Mom), Sam Gustafsson (Kid), Rebecca Hart (Brooklyn Vegan), Carol Neiman, Mary Ann Hay (Upper West Side Ladies), Daryl Lathon (Opera Lover), Will McAdam (Leo), Katey Parker (English Major), Jeff Schaeffer (Book Store Customer), Boomer Tibbs (Real Estate Owner), Lauren Waisbren (Jane), Erik Wolfe (Film Student)

Pepper Brinkley, Brendan Sexton III in Let Them Chirp Awhile
© *Blitstein Films*

CIAO (here!/Regent) Producer, Jim McMahon; Director, Yen Tan; Screenplay, Yen Tan, Alessandro Calza; Photography, Michael Victor Roy; Designer, Clare Floyd DeVries; Music, Stephan Altman; Editor, David Patrick Lowery; an Unauthorized production; Color; HD; Rated R; 87 minutes; Release date: December 5, 2008. CAST: Adam Neal Smith (Jeff), Alessandro Calza (Andrea), Ethel Lung (Lauren), Chuck Blaum (Mark), John S. Boles (Mark's Father), Margaret Lake (Mark's Mother), Tiffany Vollmer (Doctor)

Alessandro Calza, Adam Neal Smith in Ciao © *Regent Releasing*

A GOOD DAY TO BE BLACK & SEXY (Magnolia) Producer, Layla Mashavu; Director/ Screenplay/Music Supervisor, Dennis Dortch; Photography, Brian Harding; Editors, Dennis Dortch, Tangier Clarke; a 1976 Experience presentation in association with Ramcity Pictures; Color; HD; Not rated; 92 minutes; Release date: December 5, 2008. CAST: *Reciprocity*: Kathryn Taylor (Jeanette), Brandon Valley Jones (Tony); *Her Man*: Chonte Harris (Helena), Marcuis Harris (D'Andre), LaKeisha Blackwell (Jade); *Tonight*: Mylika Davis (Tamala), Allen Maldonado (Jabari), Jerome Anthony Hawkins (Julian), Natalia Morris (Meagan), Alisa Sherrod (Jill), Tangier Anil Dortch (Baby), Micah Marie (Tracy); *Reprise*: Nana Hill (Candi), Kareem MJ. Grimes (Russell); *American Boyfriend*: Alphonso Johnson (Jesse), Emily Liu (Jasmine), Chris Yen (Jennie), Raymond Ma (Mr. Li), Dana Pan (Mrs. Li)

Nana Hill in A Good Day to Be Black and Sexy © *Magnolia Films*

DELGO (Freestyle) Executive Producer, Marc F. Adler; Director, Marc F. Adler, Jason F. Maurer; Animation Director, Warren Grubb; Screenplay, Marc F. Adler, Scott Bieear, Patrick Cowan, Carl F. Dream, Jennifer A. Jones, Jason F. MaUruer; Story, Marc F. Adler, Scott Biear, Jason F. Maurer; Photography, Herb Kossover; Art Director, Mark A. W. Jackson; Music, Geoff Zanelli; Editors, Marc F. Adler, Jason F. Maurer; Visual Effects Supervisor, Floyd Casey; an Electric Eye Entertainment presentation of a Fathom Studios production; Dolby; Color; Rated PG; 88 minutes; Release date: December 12, ,2008. VOICE CAST: Freddie Prinze, Jr. (Delgo), Chris Kattan (Filo), Jennifer Love Hewitt (Princess Kyla), Anne Bancroft (Sedessa), Val Kilmer (Bogardus), Malcolm McDowell (Raius), Michael Clarke Duncan (Elder Marley), Louis Gossett, Jr. (King Zahn), Eric Idle (Spig), Burt Reynolds (Delgo's Father), Kelly Ripa (Kurrin), Sally Kellerman (Narrator), Jed Rhein (Ando), Melissa McBride (Miss Sutley/Elder Pearo), Jeff Winter (Giddy/Lockni Man).

SCOTT WALKER: 30 CENTURY MAN (Plexifilm) Producers, Mia Bays, Stephen Kijak, Elizabeth Rose; Executive Producers, David Bowie, Mark Vennis, Gary Phillips, Colin Burch, Julia Short; Director/Screenplay, Stephen Kijak; Photography, Grant Gee; Music Supervisors, Fiona McBlane, Sophie Urquhart, Tanya Sweeney; Editors, Grant Gee, Mat Whitecross; a Missing in Action Films, Plastic Palace production; American-British; Dolby; Color; Not rated; 96 minutes; Release date: December 17, 2008. Documentary on influential musician Scott Walker; with Damon Albarn, Dot Allison, Marc Almond, David Bates, Ed Bicknell, David Bowie, Al Clark, Cathal Coughlan, Rob Ellis, Brian Eno, Gavin Friday, Brian Gascoigne, Alison Goldfrapp, Colin Greenwood, Neil Hannon, Richard Hawley, Ute Lemper, Lulu, Dave MacRae, Angela Morley, Ed O'Brien, Peter Olliff, Evan Parker, Simon Raymonde, Sting, Peter Walsh, and Hector Zazou.

Scott Walker in 30 Century Man © Plexifilm

WHERE GOD LEFT HIS SHOES (IFC Films) Producers, Richard Hutton, Michael Caldwell, Daniel Edelman, Salvatore Stabile; Executive Producers, Petra Hoebel, Rosanne Korenberg, Paul G. Allen, Jody Patton; Director/Screenplay, Salvatore Stabile; Photography, Vanja Cernjul; Designer, Ernesto Solo; Costumes, Kaela Wohl; Music, Jeff Beal; Editor, Chris Monte; Casting, Sig de Miguel; a Vulcan production; Dolby; Color; Super 16mm-to-35mm; Not rated; 110 minutes; Release date: December 12, 2008. CAST: John Leguizamo (Frank Diaz), Leonor Varela (Angela Diaz), David Castro (Justin), Samantha M. Rose (Christina), Jeannie Andresakes, Jennifer Holguin, Adam S. Phillips (Shoppers), Rosa Arredondo (Shelter Assistant), Michael Basile (Waiter), J. King, D.C. Benny (Security Guards), Kimberly Bigsby (Waitress), Paola Cancellieri (Mother of Trick-or-Treaters), Toni D'Antonio (Nurse), Charles Dumas (Morris), Chris Edwards (Pedestrian), Jerry

Ferrara (Vinny), Jason Fiore-Ortiz (Longo Kid), Cheryl Freeman (Shelter Director), Billy Griffith (Eviction Marshall), Sakina Jaffrey (Doctor), Chance Kelly (Police Officer), Elisabeth Kiernan (Hostess), Rock Kohli (News Stand Clerk), Jill Marie Lawrence (Human Resource Woman), Adriane Lenox (Carita), Stephen Payne (Smiddy), Manny Perez (Luis), Frank Rodriguez (Hector), Dave Salerno (Aldo), Christian Shorter (Pianist), Hope Shorter (Singer), Clifton Waddington (Vagrant).

David Castro, John Leguizamo in Where God Left His Shoes
© IFC Films

THEATER OF WAR (White Buffalo Entertainment) Producer, Nina Santisi; Executive Producers, Jack Turner, Dany Garcia Johnson, Antonio Ortega, Emery Sheer, Leslie Jose Zigel; Director/Editor, John Walter; Photography, Felix Andrew Walter; Music, Robert Miller; Color/Black and white; Not rated; 96 minutes; Release date: December 24, 2008. Documentary examining Bertolt Brecht's anti-war play *Mother Courage and Her Children*, notably the 2006 Central Park production; with Meryl Streep, Tony Kushner, George C. Wolfe, Kevin Kline, Jay Cantor, Barbara Brecht-Schall, Oskar Eustis, Jeanine Tesori, Carl Weber.

PAGEANT (Wolfe Releasing) Producers, Ron Davis, Stewart Halpern-Fingerhut; Directors/ Screenplay, Ron Davis, Stewart Halpern-Fingerhut; Photography, Clay Westervelt; Music, Rob Johnson; Editors, William Haugse, James Cude; an Illusion Arts production; Color; Mini-DV/DVD Pro to DigiBeta; Not rated; 95 minutes; Release date: December 28, 2008. Documentary on the 34th Annual Miss Gay America event; with Carl Glorioso, Anthony Brewer, David Lowman, Robert Martin, Victor Parker, Jake Fisher.

Kerri Nichols in Pageant
© Wolfe Releasing

FOREIGN FILMS A

BEAUFORT

(KINO) Producers, David Silber, David Mandil; Executive Producers, Moshe Edry, Leon Edry; Director, Joseph Cedar; Screenplay, Ron Leshem, Joseph Cedar, based on a novel by Joseph Cedar; Photography, Ofer Inov; Designer, Miguel Merkin; Costumes, Maya More; Editor, Zohar M. Sela; Music, Ishai Adar; a United King Films, Metro Communications, Movie Plus production; Israeli, 2007; Dolby; Super Widescreen; Color; Not rated; 125 minutes; American release date: January 18, 2008

Cast

Liraz	**Oshri Cohen**
Koris	**Itay Tiran**
Oshry	**Eli Eltonyo**
Zitlawy	**Itay Turgeman**
Ziv	**Ohad Knoller**
Shpitzer	**Arthur Perzev**
Balis	**Gal Friedman**
Meir	**Danny Zahavi**
Kimchy	**Alon Abutbul**
Pavel	**Daniel Brook**
Avishai	**Nevo Kimchi**
Rubi	**Ygal Resnik**
Emilio	**Itay Schor**
Amox Faran	**Ami Weinberg**
Nadav	**Hanan Yishai**

The true story of Israel's 2000 evacuation of the Beaufort fortress in South Lebanon after eighteen years of occupation.

Ohad Knoller

Oshri Cohen

Ohad Knoller

Sanziana Tarta, Madalina Ghitescu, Anamaria Marinca, Catalina Harabagiu © IFC Films

Anamaria Marinca, Laura Vasiliou

Anamaria Marinca

4 MONTHS, 3 WEEKS & 2 DAYS

(IFC) a.k.a. *4 luni, 3 saptamini si 2 zile*; Producers, Oleg Mutu, Cristian Mungiu; Executive Producer, Florentina Onea; Coproducer, Alex Teodorescu; Director/Screenplay, Cristian Mungiu; Photography, Oleg Mutu; Editor, Dana Bunescu; Designer, Mihaela Poenaru; Costumes, Dana Istrate; Associate Producer, Dan Burlac; Casting, Catalin Dordea; a Mobra Films production, in association with Saga Film; Romanian; Dolby; Super 35 Widescreen; Color; Not rated; 113 minutes; American release date: January 25, 2008

Cast

Otilia	**Anamaria Marinca**
Gabita Dragut	**Laura Vasiliu**
Mr. Bebe	**Vlad Ivanov**
Adi Radu	**Alexandru Potocean**
Dr. Rusu	**Ioan Sapdaru**
Unireal Hotel Receptionist	**Teo Corban**
Night Receptionist	**Tania Popa**
Benzanirul	**Doru Ana**
Bebe's Mother	**Eugenia Bosànceanu**
Adela Racoviceanu	**Marioara Sterian**
Adi's mother Gina	**Luminita Gheorghiu**
Adi's father Grigore	**Adi Carauleanu**
Daniela	**Mihaela Alexandru**

Costica Babu (Tatal Gabitei), Constantin Bojog (Martu), Cirstina Burbuz (Marie-Jeanne Rusu), Georgeta Paduraru Burdujan (Mrs. Aldea), Cristian Ciuzan, Cristina Iosif (Doctors), Alexandru Conovaru (Barbatal din Statie), Emil Coseru (Dr. Racoviceanu), Geo Dobre (Dr. Aldea), Hazim E'Layan (Ahmed), Robert Emmanuel, Daniel Iancu (Military), Madalina Ghitescu (Dora), Ion Grosu (Portar), Catalina Harabagiu (Miahela), Traian Tudorica State (Chelnerul), Simona Stoicescu (Soldier), Sanziana Tarta (Carmen)

In 1987 Romania, pregnant college student Otilia reluctantly subjects herself to the humiliating demands of an illegal abortionist.

Righjt: *Alexandru Potocean, Anamaria Marinca*

Dwain Murphy, Kevin Duhaney

HOW SHE MOVE

(PARAMOUNT VANTAGE) Producers, Jennifer Kawaja, Julia Sereny, Brent Barclay. Coproducer, Claire Prieto; Director, Ian Iqbal Rashid; Screenplay, Annmarie Morais; Photography, Andre Pienaar; Designer, Aidan Leroux; Costumes, Blair Holder; Editor, Susan Maggi; Music, Andrew Lockington; Music Supervisor, Amy Fritz; Choreographer, Hi Hat; Stunts, Alison Reid; Line Producer, Colin Brunton; Casting, Stephanie Gorin; a Celluloid Dreams presentation of a Sienna Films production; Canadian; Dolby; Color; Rated PG-13; 98 minutes; American release date: January 25, 2008

Cast

Raya Green	**Rutina Wesley**
Michelle	**Tré Armstrong**
Quake	**Brennan Gademans**
Garvey	**Clé Bennett**
E.C.	**Kevin Duhaney**
Trey	**Shawn Desman**
Manny	**Tristan D. Lalla**

Daniel Morrison (Wayne), Romina D'Urgo (Selia), Melanie Nicholls-King (Faye Green), Djanet Sears (Vice Principal Wilson), Sarah-Jaiyn Ruglass, Tanisa Scott (Sorority Steppers), Alison Sealy-Smith (Mrs. Davis), Dwain Murphy (Bishop), Boyd Banks (Mike Evans), Ardon Bess (Uncle Cecil), Keyshia Cole, DeRay Davis (Themselves), Eve Crawford (Seaton Teacher), Nina Dobrev (Tall Girl in Bathroom), Ingrid Gaynor (Pam Green), Balford Gordon (Neighborhood Guy), Patrick Hayes (Customer), Malvin Jacobs (Scrawny Guy), Rogue Johnston (DJ), Jai Jai Jones (Lester Johnson), Evelynking Nanatakyi (Bishop Teen Groupie), Merwin Mondesir (Niko Niles), Dwain Murphy (Bishop), Vanessa Oryema (Raya Green, age 12), Brian Paul (Mr. Duncan), Sydney Van Delft (Short Girl in Bathroom)

Her life spiraling out of control into the world of drugs that claimed her sister's life, Raya Green sees a chance to prove her worth when she joins an otherwise all-male group of step dancers.

CARAMEL

(ROADSIDE ATTRACTION) a.k.a. *Sukkar banat*; Producer, Anne-Dominique Toussaint; Director, Nadine Labaki; Screenplay, Nadine Labaki, Jihad Hojeily, Rodney Al Haddad; Photography, Yves Sehnaoui; Editor, Laure Gardette; Music, Khaled Mouzanar; Designer, Cynthia Zahar; Costumes, Caroline Labaki; a Les Films des Tournelles (France)/Les Films de Beyrouth (Lebanon)/Roissy Films (France)/ Sunnyland (Lebanon)/Arte France Cinema (France) production, with the participation of Fonds Sud Cinema, Ministere de la Culture et de la Communication, Centre National de la Cinematographie, Ministere des Affaires Etrangeres (France), Agence de la Francophonie; Lebanese-French; Dolby; Color; Rated PG; 95 minutes; American release date: February 1, 2008

Cast

Layale	**Nadine Labaki**
Nisrine	**Yasmine Al Masri**
Rima	**Joanna Moukarzel**
Jamale Tarabay	**Gisèle Aouad**
Youssef	**Adel Karam**
Rose	**Siham Haddad**
Lili	**Aziza Semaan**

Fatmeh Safa (Siham), Dimitri Stancofski (Charles), Fadia Stella (Christine), Ismaïl Antar (Bassam), Victoria Bader, Yousra Karam (Beauty Salon Customers), Nancy (Woman in Taxi)

At a Beirut beauty salon, Layale and her friends cope with affairs, relationships and other issues facing Lebanese women.

Nadine Labaki, Joanna Moukarzel © Roadside Attractions

THE WITNESSES

(STRAND) a.k.a. *Les témoins*; Producer, Saïd Ben Saïd; Director, André Téchiné; Screenplay, André Téchiné, Laurent Guyot, Viviane Zingg; Photography, Julien Hirsch; Designer, Michèle Abbe; Costumes, Khadija Zeggaï; Music, Philippe Sarde; Editor, Martine Giordano; A SBS Films production, in coproduction with France 2 Cinéma, with the participation of Canal + and TPS Star, with the support of Région Ile de France and the European Community's Media Plus Programme in association with Sofica UGC 1 and Soficinéma 2 and 3; French, 2007; Color; Not rated; 113 minutes; American release date: February 1, 2008

Cast

Adrien	**Michel Blanc**
Sarah	**Emmanuelle Béart**
Mehdi	**Sami Bouajila**
Julie	**Julie Depardieu**
Manu	**Johan Libéreau**
Sandra	**Constance Dollé**
Steve	**Lorenzo Balducci**
Sheriff	**Alain Cauchi**
Julie and Manu's Mother	**Raphaëline Goupilleau**
The Hotel Manager	**Jacques Nolot**
The Publisher	**Xavier Beauvois**
Sarah's Mother	**Maïa Simon**

Manu, Adrien's young pick-up, agrees to become a friend minus any sexual intimacy, instead having an affair with Mehdi, the sexually voracious husband of Adrien's good friend Sarah.

Emmanuelle Béart, Michel Blanc, Johan Libéreau

Johan Libéreau, Sami Bouajila © Strand Releasing

Emmanuelle Béart

Johan Libeéreau

IN BRUGES

(FOCUS) Producers, Graham Broadbent, Pete Czernin; Executive Producers, Tessa Ross, Jeff Abberley, Julia Blackman; Coproducer, Sarah Harvey; Director/Screenplay, Martin McDonagh. Photography, Eigil Bryld; Designer, Michael Carlin; Costumes, Jany Temime; Editor, Jon Gregory; Music, Carter Burwell; Music Supervisor, Karen Elliott; Visual Effects Supervisor, Richard Briscoe; Special Effects Supervisor, Mark Holt; Stunts, Paul Herbert; Line Producer, Ronaldo Vasconcellos; Casting, Jina Jay; a Blueprint Pictures production in association with Scion Films; British; Dolby; Arri Widescreen; Deluxe color; Rated R; 107 minutes; American release date: February 8, 2008

Colin Farrell © Focus Features

Cast

Ray	**Colin Farrell**
Ken	**Brendan Gleeson**
Harry Waters	**Ralph Fiennes**
Chloë	**Clémence Poésy**
Eirik	**Jérémie Renier**
Marie	**Thekla Reuten**
Jimmy	**Jordan Prentice**
Canadian Guy	**Zeljko Ivanek**
Yuri	**Eric Godon**
Natalie	**Elizabeth Berrington**
Ticket Seller	**Rudy Blomme**
Film Director	**Olivier Bonjour**
Overweight Man	**Mark Donovan**
Overweight Women	**Ann Elsley, Emily Thorling**
Policeman	**Jean-Marc Favorin**
Imamoto	**Sachi Kimura**
Denise	**Anna Madeley**
Harry's Children	**Bonnie Witney, Angel Witney, Louis Nummy**
Boy in Church	**Theo Stevenson**
Kelli	**Inez Stinton**

After a botched job, a pair of hit men are reluctantly sent by their boss to bide their time in the city of Bruges, unaware of what is in store for them.

This film received an Oscar nomination for original screenplay.

Brendan Gleeson, Ralph Fiennes

Ralph Fiennes

Thekla Reuten, Brendan Gleeson

Ralph Fiennes, Jérémie Renier

Jordan Prentice, Clémence Poésy, Colin Farrell

Ralph Fiennes, Rudy Blomme, Brendan Gleeson

Brendan Gleeson, Colin Farrell

THE YEAR MY PARENTS WENT ON VACATION

(CITY LIGHTS) a.k.a. *O Ano em Que Meus Pais Saíram de Férias*; Producers, Caio Gullane, Cao Hamburger, Fabiano Gullane; Executive Producers, Caio Gullane, Fabiano Gullane, Sonia Hamburger; Coproducers, Fernando Meirelles, Daniel Filho; Director, Cao Hamburger; Screenplay, Claudio Galperin, Braulio Mantovani, Anna Muylaert, Hamburger; Photography, Adriano Goldman; Editor, Daniel Rezende; Music, Beto Villares; Art Director, Cassio Amarante; Associate Producers, Debora Ivanov, Patrick Siaretta, Paulo Ribeiro; a Gullane Filmes/Caos Producoes/ Miravista/Globo Filmes production; Brazilian; Dolby; Color; Not rated; 103 minutes; American release date: February 15, 2008

Cast

Mauro	**Michel Joelsas**
Shlomo	**Germano Haiut**
Italo	**Caio Blat**
Hanna	**Daniela Piepszyk**
Irene	**Liliana Castro**
Bia, Mother	**Simone Spoladore**
Daniel, Father	**Eduardo Moreira**
Edgar	**Rodrigo dos Santos**
Mótel, Grandfather	**Paulo Autran**

Felipe Hanna Braun (Caco), Gabriel Eric Bursztein (Bóris), Abrahão Farc (Anatol), Kaim Fridman (Duda), Edu Guimarães (Alfredo), Hugueta Sendacz (Dona Eidel)

In 1970 Brazil, young Mauro is obliged to live in a Jewish community outside of Sao Paolo after his parents flee the country.

Daniela Piepszyk

Michel Joelsas © City Lights

Michel Joelsas, Germano Haiut

Right: *Liliana Castro, Michel Joelsas*

THE DUCHESS OF LANGEAIS

(IFC) a.k.a. *Don't Touch the Axe* and *Ne touchez pas la hache*; Producers, Martine Marignac, Maurice Tinchant; Coproducers, Luigi Musini, Roberto Cicutto, Ermanno Olmi; Director, Jacques Rivette; Screenplay, Jacques Rivette, Pascal Bonitzer, Christine Laurent, from the novella *The Duchess of Langeais* by Honore de Balzac; Photography, William Lubtchansky; Designers, Manu de Chauvigny, Giuseppe Pirrotta; Costumes, Maira Ramedhan-Levi; Editor, Nicole Lubtschansky; Music, Pierre Allio; a Pierre Grise Prods. (France), Cinemaundici (Italy), Arte France Cinema (France) production; French-Italian; Dolby; Color; Not rated; 137 minutes; American release date: February 22, 2008

Cast
Antoinette de Langeais	**Jeanne Balibar**
Armand de Montriveau	**Guillaume Depardieu**
Princesse de Blamont-Chauvry	**Bulle Ogier**
Vidame de Pamiers	**Michel Piccoli**
Le Duc de Grandlieu	**Barbet Schroeder**
Clara de Sérizy	**Anne Cantineau**
Julien	**Mathias Jung**
Lisette	**Julie Judd**
Marquis de Ronquerolles	**Marc Barbé**

Nicolas Bouchard (De Trailles), Thomas Durand (De Marsay), Beppe Cierici (L'alcade), Victoria Zinny (Mother Superior), Remo Girone (Convent Confessor), Paul Chevilland (Le duc de Navarreins), Birgit Ludwig (Diane de Maufrigneuse), Denis Freyd (Abbé Gondrand), Claude Delaugerre (Auguste)

A soldier from the Napoleonic wars arrives at a nunnery to seek the former socialite with whom he once had a hopeless affair five years earlier.

Marc Barbé, Guillaume Depardieu © IFC Films

Guillaume Depardieu, Jeanne Balibar

Darlan Cunha, Douglas Silva © Miramax Films

CITY OF MEN

(MIRAMAX) a.k.a. *Cidade dos Homens*; Producers, Andrea Barata Ribeiro, Bel Berlinck, Fernando Meirelles, Paulo Morelli; Director, Paulo Morelli; Screenplay, Elena Soarez; Story, Paulo Morelli, Elena Soarez, inspired by the characters created by Braulio Mantovani; Photography, Adriano Goldman; Editor, Daniel Rezende; Music, Antonio Pinto; Art Director, Rafael Ronconi; Costumes, Ines Salgado; Associate producer, Guel Arraes; an O2 Filmes production, in association with Fox Film, Globo Filmes; Brazilian; Dolby; Color; Rated R; 105 minutes; American release date: February 29, 2008

Cast
Acerola, "Ace"	**Douglas Silva**
Laranjinha, "Wallace"	**Darlan Cunha**
Madrugadão, "Midnight"	**Jonathan Haagensen**
Heraldo	**Rodrigo dos Santos**
Cris	**Camila Monteiro**
Camila	**Naima Silva**
Nefasto, "Fasto"	**Eduardo BR**

Luciano Vidigal (Fiel), Vitor Oliveira, Vinicius Oliveira (Clayton), Rafaela Santos (Beauty of the Dawn), Fabio Lago (Ceara), Claudio Jaborandy (Heraldo's Partner), Babu Santana (Boss of Bald Hill), Maria Francisca (Elvira), Sonia Lino (Esmeralda), Michel Gomes (Fininho), Barbara Borgga (Prison Employee), Airan Pinheriro (Public Notary's Office Employee), Vinicius Messias, Erik Burdon, Alex Borges, Mario Hermeto (Waiters), Robson Luiz (Young Boy), Claudio Cinti (Goiano–Butcher), Murilo Macedo (Patronage's Guard), Jose Mario Farias (Helinho), Brenno Neves (Madrugadão as a Child), Alexandro Brito (Pharmacy Boy), Mauricio Goncalves (Nestor), Robson Santos (Bald Hill Informer), Thogun (Ace's Father), Andrea Bacellar (Cris's Employer), Luisao Seixas (Pedreira), Charles Torres (Preacher), Flavio Borja Officer #1, Juarez), Marcello Barcellos (Officer #2), Luca de Castro (Condominium's Manager), Aldene Abreu, Isaac Borges, Marcio Costa, Robson Rocha (Soldiers), Fagner Santos, Jerisano Vieira (Bald Hill Soldiers), Kamilla Rodrigues (Tina), Michelle Cardoso (Valeria), Carolina Bezerra (Shop Assistant), Eber Inacio (Zeze, Pharmacist)

Having grown up without a father while struggling to survive in the slums of Rio, Wallace, needing the old man's signature to secure an ID card, goes in search of his long absent parent.

Jim Sturgess © Columbia Pictures

Natalie Portman, Eric Bana

Scarlett Johansson, Natalie Portman

THE OTHER BOLEYN GIRL

(COLUMBIA/FOCUS) Producer, Alison Owen; Executive Producers, Scott Rudin, David M. Thompson; Coproducer, Mark Cooper; Director, Justin Chadwick; Screenplay, Peter Morgan, based on the novel by Philippa Gregory; Photography, Kieran McGuigan; Designer, John-Paul Kelly; Costumes, Sandy Powell; Editors, Carol Littleton, Paul Knight; Music, Paul Cantelon; Associate Producer, Faye Ward; Casting, Karen Lindsay-Stewart; a Universal Pictures Intl., Columbia Pictures (U.S.) presentation, in association with BBC Films and Relativity Media, of a Ruby Films (U.K.)/Scott Rudin (U.S.) production; British-American; Dolby; Deluxe; HD-to-35mm; Rated PG-13; 115 minutes; American release date: February 29, 2008

Cast

Anne Boleyn	**Natalie Portman**
Mary Boleyn	**Scarlett Johansson**
Henry VIII	**Eric Bana**
Duke of Norfolk	**David Morrissey**
Lady Elizabeth Boleyn	**Kristin Scott Thomas**
Sir Thomas Boleyn	**Mark Rylance**
George Boleyn	**Jim Sturgess**
William Stafford	**Eddie Redmayne**
William Carey	**Benedict Cumberbatch**
Jane Parker	**Juno Temple**
Catherine of Aragon	**Ana Torrent**
Henry Percy	**Oliver Coleman**
Rider	**Tom Cox**
Physician	**Michael Smiley**
Lady in Waiting	**Montserrat Roig de Puig**
Thomas Cromwell	**Iain Mitchell**
Francis Weston	**Andrew Garfield**

Lewis Jones (Brandon Mark), Corinne Galloway (Jane Seymour), Alfie Allen (King's Messenger), Joseph Moore (Young Henry), Tiffany Freisberg (Mary Talbot), Bill Wallis (Archbishop Cranmer), Joanna Scanlan (Midwife), Brodie Judge (Young Catherine), Oscar Negus (Little Henry), Maisie Smith (Young Elizabeth), Daisy Doidge-Hill (Young Anne), Lizzy Fassett (Young Mary), Finton Reilly (Young George), Emma Noakes (Maid), Poppy Hurst (Little Catherine), Constance Stride (Mary Tudor)

Thomas Boleyn sees his chance to achieve position in the royal court when King Henry VIII takes an interest in both his daughters, Mary and Anne. Previous versions of the story include *Anne of the Thousand Days* (Universal, 1969) with Richard Burton as Henry and Genevieve Bujold as Anne.

MISS PETTIGREW LIVES FOR A DAY

(FOCUS) Producers, Nellie Bellflower, Stephen Garrett; Executive Producer, Paul Webster; Coproducer, Jane Frazer; Director, Bharat Nalluri; Screenplay, David Magee, Simon Beaufoy; Based on the novel by Winifred Watson; Photography, John de Borman; Designer, Sarah Greenwood; Costumes, Michael O'Connor; Music, Paul Englishby; Editor, Barney Pilling; Music Supervisor, Karen Elliott; Associate Producer, Maggi Townley; Casting, Leo Davis; a Kudos Pictures (UK)/Keylight Entertainment (U.S.) production; British-American; Dolby; Panavision; Deluxe color; Rated PG-13; 92 minutes; American release date: March 7, 2008

Amy Adams,
Frances McDormand

Cast

Guinevere Pettigrew	**Frances McDormand**
Delysia Lafosse (Sarah Grubb)	**Amy Adams**
Michael Pardue	**Lee Pace**
Joe Blumfield	**Ciarán Hinds**
Edythe Dubarry	**Shirley Henderson**
Nick Colderelli	**Mark Strong**
Phil Goldman	**Tom Payne**
Charlotte Warren	**Christina Cole**
Chestnut Seller	**David Alexander**
Margery	**Clare Clifford**
Miss Holt	**Stephanie Cole**
Mrs. Brummegan	**Beatie Edney**
Annabel Darlington	**Sarah Kants**
Woman at Train Station	**Sally Leonard**
Mrs. Holt's Assistant	**Katy Murphy**
Nightclub Patron	**Tim Potter**
Gerry	**Matt Ryan**
Lenny	**Mo Zinal**

Frances McDormand, Amy Adams,
Shirley Henderson

Unable to hold on to any of her servant jobs, Guinevere Pettigrew lies her way into a position as social secretary to unstable, romantically overextended actress Delysia Lafosse.

Ciarán Hinds, Frances McDormand

Right: *Lee Pace © Focus Features*

THE BANK JOB

(LIONSGATE) Producers, Charles Roven, Steven Chasman; Executive Producers, George McIndoe, Ryan Kavanaugh, David Alper, Alan Glazer, Gary Hamilton, Alex Gartner, Christopher Mapp, Matthew Street, David Whealy; Coproducer, Mairi Bett; Director, Roger Donaldson; Screenplay, Dick Clement, Ian La Frenais; Photography, Michael Coulter; Designer, Gavin Bocquet; Costumes, Odile Dicks-Mireaux; Music, J. Peter Robinson; Editor, John Gilbert; Stunts, Greg Powell; Casting, Lucinda Syson; a Mosaic Media Group production, in association with Relativity Media, Omnilab Media; British; Dolby; Color; HD-to-35mm; Rated R; 111 minutes; American release date: March 7, 2008

Cast

Terry Leather	**Jason Statham**
Martine Love	**Saffron Burrows**
Kevin Swain	**Stephen Campbell Moore**
Dave Shilling	**Daniel Mays**
Guy Singer	**James Faulkner**
Bambas	**Alki David**
Eddie Burton	**Michael Jibson**
Ingrid Burton	**Georgia Taylor**
Tim Everett	**Richard Lintern**
Miles Urquhart	**Peter Bowles**
Philip Lisle	**Alistair Petrie**
Gale Benson	**Hattie Morahan**
Lew Vogel	**David Suchet**

Julian Lewis Jones (Snow), Andrew Brooke (Quinn), Rupert Frazer (Lord Drysdale), Chris Owens (Mountbatten), Keeley Hawes (Wendy Leather), Taelor Samways (Catherine Leather), Kasey Baterip (Julie Leahter), Don Gallagher (Gerald Pyke), Craig Fairbrass (Nick Barton), Gerard Horan (Roy Given), Robert Whitelock (Alfie Hook), Peter De Jersey (Michael X), Johann Myers (Stanley "The Knife" Abbot), Colin Salmon (Hakim Jamal), Sharon Maughan (Sonia Bern), Ray Nicholas (Vogel's Driver), Les Kenny-Green (Pinky), James Kenna (Perky), Angus Wright (Eric Addey), Mark Phoenix (Mr. Brown), James Hall (Customs Agent), Cameron Anderson (Young Soldier), Julian Firth (Lawyer), Norma Dixit (Customs Matron), Antony Gabriel (Reporter), Rupert Vansittart (Sir Leonard Plugge), Bronson Webb (Chicken Inn Waiter), Omar Mostafa (Chicken Inn Cook), Dylan Charles (Chicken Inn Customer), Michael Haughey (Bank Manager), Ray Trickett (Beat Policeman), Steve Gibbs (Newspaper Hawker), Ursula Mohan (Dave's Mum), Alan Swoffer (John Lennon), Louise Chambers (The Princess), Bonnie Simon (Island Woman), Dimitri Pappadopoullos (Island Man), Dai Smith, Alan Thomas, Brian Thomas, Rob Thompson, Andy Colilns, Steve Balsamo (Wedding Band: The Storys)

Terry Leather rounds up a group of criminals to break into the vault of a London bank, unaware that his accomplice and sometime lover Martine is hoping to retrieve a group of scandalous photos from a safety deposit box incriminating a member of the royal family.

David Suchet (right)

Saffron Burrows © Lionsgate

Daniel Mays, Jason Statham

Jason Statham, Stephen Campbell Moore, James Faulkner, Alki David, Daniel Mays

Jiao Xu, Kitty Zhang

Min Hun Fung, Wen Xue Yao © Sony Classics

CJ7

(SONY CLASSICS) a.k.a. *Cheung Gong 7 hou*; Producers, Stephen Chow, Chui Po-chu, Han Sanping; Coproducers, Vincent Kok, Connie Wong; Director, Stephen Chow; Screenplay, Stephen Chow, Vincent Kok, Tsang Kan-cheong, Lam Fung, Sandy Shaw, Fung Chih-chiang; Photography, Poon Hang-seng; Designer, Oliver Wong; Costumes, Dora Ng; Music, Raymond Wong; Editor, Angie Lam; Action Choreographers, Ku Huen-chi, Yuen Shun-yi; Visual Effects Supervisors, Eddy Wong, Victor Wong; Visual Effects, Menfond Electronic Art & Computer Design Co.; a Columbia Pictures Film Production Zasia Limited, the Star Overseas (Hong Kong)/Beijing Film Studio of China Film Group Corp. (China) presentation of a Star Overseas production; Hong Kong-Chinese; Dolby; Super 35 Widescreen; Technicolor; Rated PG; 88 minutes; American release date: March 7, 2008

Jiao Xu, Yong Hua Han

Cast

Ti	**Stephen Chow**
Dicky	**Jiao Xu**
P.E. Teacher	**Min Hun Fung**
The Boss	**Tze Chung Lam**
Mr. Cao	**Sheung Ching Lee**
Miss Yuen	**Kitty Zhang**
Maggie	**Yong Hua Han**
Johnny	**Lei Huang**
Storm Dragon	**Wen Xue Yao**

A bullied boy discovers an abandoned alien with magical powers.

Jiao Xu, Stephen Chow

UNDER THE SAME MOON

(WEINSTEIN CO/FOX SEARCHLIGHT) a.k.a. *La Misma Luna*; Producers, Patricia Riggen, Gerardo Barrera; Executive Producers, Ram Bergman, Ligiah Villalobos, Norman Dreyfuss; Director, Patricia Riggen; Screenplay, Ligiah Villalobos; Photography, Checco Varese; Designer, Carmen Gimenez Cacho; Music, Carlo Siliotto; Music Supervisor, Lynn Fainchtein; Editor, Aleshka Ferrero; Casting, Manuel Teil; a Potomac Pictures and Creando Films presentation in association with Fidecine; Mexican-American; Dolby FotoKem color; Rated PG-13; 106 minutes; Release date: March 19, 2008

Cast
Rosario	**Kate del Castillo**
Enrique	**Eugenio Derbez**
Carlitos	**Adrian Alonso**
Alicia	**Maya Zapata**
Dona Carmen "La Coyota"	**Carmen Salinas**
Benita Reyes	**Angelina Peláez**
Paco	**Gabriel Porras**
Reyna	**Maria Rojo**
Leonardo	**Ignacio Guadalupe**
Padrino	**Mário Almada**
Oscar	**Ernesto D'Alessio**
Marta	**America Ferrera**
Themselves	**Los Tigres del Norte**

Isaac Bravo (Chito), Julie Dove (Voice of El Paso Bus Station Announcer), J. Teddy Garces (Police Officer Jones), Jesse Garcia (David), Pailo Heitz (Billy), Boris Kievsky (Russian Taxi Driver), Yvette Mercedes (Border Patrol Agent), Maria Moreno (Voice of Border Patrol Announcer), Lil Steve Niel (Police Officer Bacci), Guillermo Ríos (Guero), Jorge Rojas (Mr. Snyder), Bob Saldana (Shifty LA Latino), Gustavo Sánchez Parra (Manuel), Jacqueline Voltaire (Mrs. McKenzie), Maya Zapata (Alicia)

When his grandmother dies, young Carlitos decides to cross the border into the U.S. in hopes of reconnecting with his mother, who has been working as a cleaning lady in Los Angeles for the past four years.

Adrian Alonso, Eugenio Derbez

America Ferrera, Jessie Garcia, Adrian Alonso

Kate del Castillo

Kate del Castillo, Adrian Alonso © Weinstein/Fox Searchlight

Grégoire Leprince-Ringuet, Louis Garrel

Ludivine Sagnier, Clotilde Hesme, Louis Garrel

Ludivine Sagnier, Chiara Mastroianni

LOVE SONGS

(IFC FILMS) a.k.a. *Les Chansons d'amour*; Producer, Paulo Branco; Director/Screenplay, Christophe Honoré; Photography, Remy Chevrin; Designer, Samuel Deshors; Costumes, Pierre Canitrot; Music and Lyrics, Alex Beaupain; Casting, Richard Rousseau; an Alma Films production, in partnership with Flach Film, with the participation of CNC, Canal+, Cinecinema, in partnership with Cofinova 3 &4, Coficup Backup Films; French, 2007; Dolby; Color; Not rated; 95 minutes; American release date: March 21, 2008

Cast

Ismaël Bénoliel	**Louis Garrel**
Julie Pommeraye	**Ludivine Sagnier**
Jeanne	**Chiara Mastroianni**
Alice	**Clotilde Hesme**
Erwann	**Grégoire Leprince-Ringuet**
Julie's Mother	**Brigitte Roüan**
Julie's Father	**Jean-Marie Winling**
Jasmine, Julie's Sister	**Alice Butaud**
Gwendal	**Yannick Renier**
Erwann's Friend	**Esteban Carvajal Alegria**
Barmaid	**Annabelle Hettmann**
Police	**Sylvain Tempier, Guillaume Clérice**
The Singer	**Alex Beaupain**

Ismaël Bénoliel's unconventional arrangement of sharing his girlfriend Julie with her coworker Alice is unexpectedly disrupted by tragedy, forcing Ismaël to confront his life and his future relationships.

Louis Garrel © IFC Films

Dylan Moran © Picturehouse

Hank Azaria, Simon Pegg

RUN FATBOY RUN

(PICTUREHOUSE) Producers, Robert Jones, Sarah Curtis; Executive Producers, Joseph Infantolino, Alexa L. Fogel, Nigel Green, Camela Galano, Rolf Mittweg, Martha Coleman; Director, David Schwimmer; Screenplay, Michael Ian Black, Simon Pegg; Story, Michael Ian Black; Photography, Richard Greatrex; Designer, Sophie Becher; Costumes, Anne Hardinge; Music, Alex Wurman; Music Supervisor, Kle Savidge; Editor, Michale Parker; Casting, Michelle Guish; an Entertainment Films presentation of a Material Entertainment production; British; Dolby; Color; Rated PG-13; 100 minutes; American release date: March 28, 2008

Simon Pegg, Matthew Fenton

Cast

Dennis Doyle	**Simon Pegg**
Libby Odell	**Thandie Newton**
Whit	**Hank Azaria**
Gordon	**Dylan Moran**
Mr. Goshdashtidar	**Harish Patel**
Maya Goshdashtidar	**India de Beaufort**
Jake	**Matthew Fenton**
Vincent	**Simon Day**
Claudine	**Ruth Sheen**
Grover	**Tyrone Huggins**
Mickey	**Nevan Finegan**
News Reporter	**Iddo Goldberg**
Taxi Driver	**Ameet Chana**
Themselves	**Chris Hollins, Denise Lewis**

Lorna Gayle (Nurse), Gabriel Fleary (Dragon Queen), Pandora Colin (Claire), Stephen Merchant (Man with Broken Leg), David Walliams (Man in Bakery), Hazel Douglas (Older Woman), Anna Tolputt (Receptionist), Simon Lenagan (Under Cop/Dad), David Cann (Marathon Official), Trevor Bowen (Doctor), Margaret John (Libby's Grandmother), Floella Benjamin (Libby's Mum), David Milne (Libby's Dad), Henrietta Clemett (Reception Nurse), Peter Serafinowicz (TV Commentator)

Thandie Newton

His life having fallen apart after abandoning his pregnant fiancée Libby at the altar, Dennis Doyle hopes to make amends and prove his worth by running in the same London marthon in which Libby's new boyfriend is participating.

FLAWLESS

(MAGNOLIA) Producers, Mark Williams, Michael Pierce; Executive Producers, Stephen Margolis, Natalia Malkin, Vitaly Malkin, Lisa Wilson; Coproducers, Albert Martinez-Martin, Jimmy de Brabant, Richard Pierce; Director, Michael Radford; Screenplay, Edward A. Anderson; Photography, Richard Greatrez; Designer, Sophie Becher; Costumes, Dinah Collin; Music, Stephen Warbeck; Editor, Peter Boyle; Casting, John Hubbard; a Pierce/Williams Entertainment (U.S.)/Delux Prods. (Luxembourg)/Future Films (U.K.) production; British-American-Luxembourg; Dolby; Color; Rated PG-13; 106 minutes; American release date: March 28, 2008

Cast

Hobbs	**Michael Caine**
Laura Quinn	**Demi Moore**
Finch	**Lambert Wilson**
Ollie	**Nathaniel Parker**
Eaton	**Shaughan Seymour**
Jameson	**Nicholas Jones**
Fenton	**David Barras**
Mika	**Joss Ackland**
Reece	**Silas Carson**
Sinclair	**Derren Nesbitt**
Penelope	**Rosalind March**
Lewis	**Kevan Willis**

Stanley Townsend (Henry), Jonathan Aris (Boyle), Ben Righton (Bryan), Constantine Gregory (Dmitriev), Simon Day (Boland), David Henry (Sir Edmund Gottfried), Yemi Goodman Ajibade (Guinean Negotiator), William Scott-Masson (Henry), Natalie Dormer (Cassie), Kate Maravan (Trudy), Steve Preston (Investigator), Claire Thill (Secretary), Julian Nest (Harold's Friend), Roya Zargar (Trudy's Friend), Violaine Miller, Carole Bruere, Philippe Bruere, Jean Adolphe (Ballroom Quartet), Peter Rnic (Honest Alfred)

Realizing she is about to be fired, high powered London Diamond Corp. executive Laura Quinn agrees to help the company's retiring janitor Hobbs heist some valuable diamonds from the establishment.

Michael Caine, Demi Moore © Magnolia Films

Gad Elmaleh, Audrey Tautou © Samuel Goldwyn

Gad Elmaleh, Audrey Tautou

PRICELESS

(GOLDWYN) a.k.a. *Hors de Prix*; Producer, Philippe Martin; Director, Pierre Salvadori; Screenplay, Pierre Salvadori, Benoit Graffin; Photography, Gilles Henry; Designer, Yves Fournier; Costumes, Virginie Montel; Music, Camille Bazbaz; Editor, Isabelle Devinck; a les Films Pelleas presentation of a Les Films Pelleas, France 2 Cinema, France 3 Cinema, Tovo Films, KS2 Prods. production with the participation of Canal+ and TPS Star, in association with Wild Bunch; Dolby; Panavision; Color; Rated PG-13; 106 minutes; American release date: March 28, 2008

Cast

Jean	**Gad Elmaleh**
Irène	**Audrey Tautou**
Madeleine	**Marie-Christine Adam**
Jacques	**Vernon Dobtcheff**
Gilles	**Jacques Spiesser**
Agnès	**Annelise Hesme**
François	**Didier Brice**
Woman with Chihuaha	**Charlotte Vermeil**
Woman with Mastiff	**Claudine Baschet**
Plastic Surgeon	**Jean-Michel Lahmi**
Pool Waiter	**Guillaume Verdier**
Jean's Colleague at Biarritz	**Bernard Bourdeau**
Monaco Receptionist	**Frédéric Bocquet**
Bartender at Biarritz	**Laurent Claret**
Maid	**Blandine Pélissier**
Waiter at Biarritz Restaurant	**Philippe Vendan-Borin**

A golddigger on the prowl for wealthy men on the French Riviera mistakes a hotel employee for another potential mark.

MY BROTHER IS AN ONLY CHILD

(THINKFILM) a.k.a. *Mio fratello è figlio unico*; Producers, Riccardo Tozzi, Giovanni Stabilini, Marco Chimenz; Executive Producers, Bruno Ridolfi, Matteo De Laurentiis; Director, Daniele Luchetti; Screenplay, Sandro Petraglia, Stefano Rulli, Daniele Luchetti; Based on the novel *Il Fasciocomunista* by Antonio Pennacchi; Photography, Claudio Collepiccolo; Designer, Francesco Frigeri; Costumes, Maria Rita Barbera; Music, Franco Piersanti; Editor, Mirco Garrone; Casting, Gianni Costantino; a Cattleya (Italy)/Babe Films (France) production; Italian-French; Dolby; Color; Not rated; 108 minutes; American release date: March 28, 2008

Cast

Accio Benassi	**Elio Germano**
Manrico Benassi	**Riccardo Scamarcio**
Amelia Benassi	**Angela Finocchiaro**
Ettore Benassi	**Massimo Popolizio**
Violetta Benassi	**Alba Rohrwacher**
Mario Nastri	**Luca Zingaretti**
Bella Nastri	**Anna Bonaiuto**
Francesca	**Diane Fleri**

Ascanio Celestini (Padre Cavalli), Vittorio Emanuele Propizio (Young Accio), Claudio Botosso (Prof. Montagna), Antonio Burschetta (Bombacci)

Rebelling against his family's leftist beliefs, Accio joins a fascist organization, putting him at odds with his brother Manrico's politics.

Elio Germano, Diane Fleri
© ThinkFilm

Elio Germano, Riccardo Scamarcio

ALEXANDRA

(THE CINEMA GUILD) Producer, Andrei Sigle; Coproducer, Laurent Danielou; Executive Producer, Dmitri Gerbachevsky; Director/Screenplay, Alexander Sokurov; Photography, Aleksandr Burov; Designer, Dmitri Malich-Konkov; Costumes, Lidiya Kryukova; Music, Andrei Sigle; Editor, Sergei Ivanov; a Proline Film (Russia) production, with the participation of Rezo Films (France), with the support of the Russian Federal Culture and Film Agency, the Centre National de la Cinematographie; Russian-French; Dolby; Color; Not rated; 95 minutes; American release date: March 26, 2008

Cast

Alexandra Nikolaevna	**Galina Vishnevskaya**
Denis	**Vasily Shevtsov**
Malika	**Raisa Gichaeva**

Andrei Bogdanov, Alexander Kladko, Aleksei Nejmyshev, Rustam Shahgireev, Evgeni Tkachuk

Visiting her grandson's military base, Alexandra Nikolaevna begins to question the conflict in Chechnya and the futility of war in general.

Galina Vishnevskaya
© The Cinema Guild

Juliette Binoche, Fang Song © IFC First Take

Simon Iteanu, Juliette Binoche

Fang Song, Simon Iteanu

FLIGHT OF THE RED BALLOON

(IFC FILMS) a.k.a. *Le voyage du ballon rouge*; Producers, Francois Margolin, Kristina Larsen; Director, Hou Hsiao Hsien; Screenplay, Hou Hsiao Hsien, Francois Margolin; Photography, Mark Lee Ping Bing; Designers, Paul Fayard, Hwarng Wern Ying; Costumes, Jean-Charline Tomlinson; Line Producer, Liao Ching Sung; a 3H Prods. (Taiwan)/Margo Films, Les Films du Lendemain (France) presentation, in coproduction with Arte France Cinema, in partnership with Le Musee d'Orsay, with the support of La Region Ile de France, with the participation fo Canal Plus, CineCinema, La Sofica Poste Image, Soficinema 3; Taiwanese-French; Dolby; Color; Not rated; 114 minutes; American release date: April 4, 2008

Cast

Suzanne	**Juliette Binoche**
Simon	**Simon Iteanu**
Song	**Fang Song**
Marc	**Hippolyte Girardot**
Louise	**Louise Margolin**
Anna	**Anna Sigalevitch**

Overworked and emotionally needy Suzanne leaves her neglected young son Simon in the hands of his Chinese nanny in this drama inspired by the classic 1956 short film *The Red Balloon*.

Jude Law

MY BLUEBERRY NIGHTS

(WEINSTEIN CO.) Producer, Jacky Pang Yee Wah; Executive Producer, Chan Ye Cheng; Director/Story, Wong Kar Wai; Screenplay, Wong Kar Wai, Lawrence Block; Photography, Darius Khondji; Costumes, Sharon Globerson; Music, Ry Cooder; Designer/Editor, William Chang Suk Ping; a Block 2 Pictures/Jet Tone Films/Studio Canal presentation; Hong Kong-French; Dolby; Super 35 Widescreen; Technicolor; Rated PG-13; 90 minutes; American release date: April 4, 2008

Cast
Elizabeth	**Norah Jones**
Jeremy	**Jude Law**
Arnie Copeland	**David Strathairn**
Sue Lynne	**Rachel Weisz**
Leslie	**Natalie Portman**
Elizabeth's Boyfriend	**Chad Davis**

Katya Blumenberg (Girlfriend), John Malloy (Diner Manager), Demetrius Butler (Customer), Frankie Faison (Travis), Adriane Lenox (Sandy), Benjamin Kanes (Randy), Michael Hartnett (Sunglasses), Michael May (Aloha), Jesse Garon (Young Poker Player), Sam Hill (Fat Guy), Tracy Blackwell (Matron), Michael Delano (Cowboy), Audrei Kairen (Poker Player), Bill Hollis (Doctor), Charles Clayton Blackwell (Used Car Salesman), Hector Leguillow (Cook)

Following a breakup with her boyfriend, Elizabeth finds herself working two jobs in Memphis, while keeping up a correspondence with the New York café owner, Jeremy, who has consoled her over her woes.

JELLYFISH

(ZEITGEIST) Producers, Amir Harel, Ayelet Kait, Yael Fogiel, Laetitita Gonzalez; Directors, Etgar Keret, Shira Geffen; Screenplay, Shire Geffen; Photography, Antoine Heberle; Designer, Avi Fahima; Costumes, Li Almebik; Music, Christopher Bowen; Editors, Sasha Franklin, Francois Gedigier; a Lama Films (Israel) & Les Films du Poisson (France) production, supported by the Israel Film Fund in coproduction with Arte France Cinema, with the participation of Canal Plus, TPS Star, Keshet; Israeli-French, 2007; Dolby; Color; Not rated; 78 minutes; American release date: April 4, 2008

Cast
Batia	**Sarah Adler**
Tamar	**Tsipor Aizen**
Relly	**Bruria Albek**
Galia	**Ilanit Ben-Yaakov**
Eldad	**Assi Dayan**
Nili	**Miri Fabian**
Tikva	**Shosha Goren**
Policeman	**Tzahi Grad**
Amir	**Johnathan Gurfinkel**
Doctor	**Amir Harel**
Nurse	**Tami Harel**
Malka	**Zaharira Harifai**
Eytan	**Yitzhak Hizkiya**

Dror Keren (Taxi Driver), Etgar Keret (Manager), Noa Knoller (Keren), Nicole Leidman (Keren), Naama Nisim (Neomi), Gera Sandler (Michael), Shalom Shmuelov (Menachem), Amos Shoov (Eyal), Yali Sobol (Amir), Liron Vaisman (Shiri)

A look at three Tel Aviv women, a recently dumped waitress, a new bride, and a domestic, as they try to find meaning and fulfillment in their seemingly listless lives.

Nicole Leidman, Sarah Adler © Zeitgeist Films

Alexandru Papadopol, Razvan Vasilescu

Alexandru Papadopol, Razvan Vasilescu © Mitropoulos

STUFF AND DOUGH

(MITROPOULOS) a.k.a. *Marfa si banii*; Producer/Director, Cristi Puiu; Screenplay, Razvan Radulescu, Cristi Puiu; Photography, Silviu Stavila; Designer, Andrea Hasnas; Editors, Ines Barbu, Nita Chivulescu; a Rofilm production, with the support of the National Center for Cinematography in Romania; Romanian; Color; Not rated; 91 minutes; American release date: April 23, 2008.

Cast

Ovidiu	**Alexandru Papadopol**
Vali	**Dragos Bucur**
Bety	**Ioana Flora**
Mama	**Luminita Gheorghiu**
Marcel Ivanov	**Razvan Vasilescu**
Doncea	**Doru Ana**
Tata	**Constantin Dragnaescu**
Bodyguard	**Serban Georgevici**

Hoping to establish his own business, Ovidiu agrees to transport a bag of unspecified goods for a local gangster with the promise of a cash reward if he gets the shipment through.

ROMAN DE GARE

(SAMUEL GOLDWYN FILMS) a.k.a. *Crossed Tracks*; Producer/Director/Story, Claude Lelouch; Screenplay, Claude Lelouch, Pierre Uytterhoeven; Executive Producer, Remi Bergman; Photography, Gerard De Battista; Designer, Francois Chauvaud; Costumes, Marite Coutard; Music, Gilbert Becaud, Alex Jaffray; Editors, Stephane Mazalaigue, Jean Gargonne; a Les Films 13 production; French; Dolby; Color; HD-to-35mm; Rated R; 104 minutes; American release date: April 25, 2008.

Cast

Pierre Laclos	**Dominique Pinon**
Judith Ralitzer	**Fanny Ardant**
Huguette	**Audrey Dana**
Captain Leroux	**Zinedine Soualem**
Florence, The Sister	**Michèle Bernier**
Patricia	**Myriam Boyer**
Alain	**Boris Ventura Diaz**

Cyrille Eldin (Paul), Serge Moati (Mr. Moati), Marc Rioufol (The Vineyard Owner), Marine Royer (Huguette's Mother), Shaya Lelouch (Sabrina), Marie-Victoire Debre, Bernard Werber, Arlette Gordon (Novelists).

The police detect a link between crime writer Judith Ralitzer and a serial killer known as the "Magician," who has just escaped from a high-security prison.

Dominique Pinon, Audrey Dana © Samuel Goldwyn

Fanny Ardant

SON OF RAMBOW

(PARAMOUNT VANTAGE) Producer, Nick Goldsmith; Executive Producers, Hengameh Panahi, Bristol Baughan, Benjamin Goldhirsh; Director/Screenplay, Garth Jennings; Photography, Jess Hall; Designer, Joel Collins; Costumes, Harriet Cawley; Music, Joby Talbot; Editor, Dominic Leung; Visual Effects Supervisors, Jon Hollis, Sean Mathiesen; Stunts, Paul Heasman; Casting, Susie Figgs; a Celluloid Dreams/Hammer and Tongs/Reason Pictures/Good production in association with Arte France Cinema/Network Movie/ZDF/Arte/Soficinema 2 & 3; British-French-German; Dolby; Panavision; Technicolor; Rated PG-13; 95 minutes; American release date: May 2, 2008

Ed Westwick, Bill Milner

Cast

Will Proudfoot	**Bill Milner**
Lee Carter	**Will Poulter**
Didier Revol	**Jules Sitruk**
Mary Proudfoot	**Jessica Stevenson**
Joshua	**Neil Dudgeon**
Grandma	**Anna Wing**
Jess Proudfoot	**Tallulah Evans**
French Teacher	**Emile Chesnais**
Geography Teacher	**Paul Ritter**
Gail Graham	**Finola McMahon**
Marie Plante	**Rachel Mureatroyd**
David Smart	**Taylor Richardson**
Lucas Dupont	**Peter Robinson**
Duncan Miller	**Charlie Thrift**

Sam Kubrick-Finney (Danny), James Clarke (Shaun), Zofia Brooks (Tina), Denise Orita (Orderly), Eric Sykes (Frank), Ed Westwick (Lawrence), Lee Long, Adam Paul Harvey (Lawrence's Henchmen), Atila Emirali (Rambo Double), Dave Shaw (Cobbler), Adam Godley (Brethren Leader), Asa Butterfield (Brethren Boy), Adam Buxton (Science Teacher), Edgar Wright (Metal Work Teacher), Imogen Aboud (Young Mary), Louise Jennings (Nurse), Sam Spivack (Policeman), Roebrt Styles (Medic)

Will Poulter, Bill Milner

Two school boys become unlikely friends when they team up to make a home movie inspired by the *Rambo* films.

Bill Milner

Jules Sitruk (center) © Paramount Vantage

Justine Waddell

Lee Pace, Cantica Untaru

Marcus Wesley, Robin Smith, Lee Pace, Julian Bleach, Leo Bill
© Roadside Attractions

THE FALL

(ROADSIDE ATTRACTIONS) Producer/Director, Tarsem; Executive Producers, Arjit Singh, Tommy Turtle; Coproducers, Nico Soutanakis, Lionel Kopp; Screenplay, Dan Gilroy, Nico Soultanakis; Based on the film *Yo Ho Ho*, written by Valeri Petrov, directed by Zako Heskija; Photography, Colin Watkinson; Designer, Ged Clarke; Costumes, Eiko Ishioka; Music, Krishna Levy; Editor, Robert Duffy; Casting, Dan Hubbard; a David Fincher and Spike Jonze presentation of a Googly Films production in association with M.I.A. Films, Kas Movie Maker, Absolute Entertainment, Deep Films, Radical Media and Tree Top Films; Indian-British-American; Dolby; Color; Rated R; 118 minutes; Release date: May 9, 2008

Cast

Alexandria	**Catinca Untaru**
Nurse Evelyn/Sister Evelyn	**Justine Waddell**
Roy Walker	**Lee Pace**
Doctor/Alexander the Great	**Kim Uylenbroek**
Alexander's Messenger	**Aiden Lithgow**
Walt Purdy	**Sean Gilder**
Otto	**Ronald France**
Mr. Sabatini	**Andrew Roussouw**
Dr. Whitaker	**Michael Huff**
Father Augustine	**Grant Swanby**
Alexandria's Father/Bandit	**Emil Hostina**
Luigi/One Legged Actor	**Robin Smith**
Indian Orange Picker	**Jeetu Verma**
Darwin/Orderly	**Leo Bill**

Marcus Wesley (Otta Benga/Ice Delivery Man), Ayesha Verman (Indian's Bride), Julian Bleach (Mystic/Orange Picker), Ketut Rina (Chief Mystic), Camilla Waldman (Crying Woman), Elvira Deatcu (Alexandria's Mother), Emma Johnson (Alexandria's Sister), Daniel Caltagirone (Sinclair/Governor Odious), Nico Soultanakis (Horace), Jon Kamen (Morty), Karen Haacke (Alice), Emma Maria Landberg (Flicker Film Woman), Miguel Hernández, Oscar Moreno, David Parra (Cowboys)

While convalescing in an L.A. hospital, young Alexandria befriends a paralyzed stunt man who spins a fantastical tale of adventure.

Leo Bill

Bérénice Bejo, Jean Dujardin © Music Box

OSS 117: CAIRO, NEST OF SPIES

(MUSIC BOX FILMS) a.ka. *OSS 117: Le Caire nid d'espions*; Producers, Eric Altmayer, Nicolas Altmayer; Executive Producers, Mandarin Films, Sarim Fassi Fihri; Director, Michel Hazanavicius; Screenplay, Jean-François Halin; Based on the *OSS 117* novels by Jean Bruce; Adaptation and Dialogue, Jean-François Halin, Michel Jazanavicius; Photography, Guillaume Schiffman; Designer, Maamar Ech-Cheikh; Costumes, Charlotte David; Music, Ludovic Bource, Kamel Ech-Cheikh; Editor, Reynald Bertrand; Special Effects, David Dansei; a Mandarin Films-Gaumont-M6 Films production; French; Dolby; Color; Not rated; 99 minutes; American release date: May 9, 2008

Cast

Hubert Bonisseur de La Bath (OSS 117)	**Jean Dujardin**
Larmina El Akmar Betouche	**Bérénice Bejo**
Princess Al Tarouk	**Aure Atika**
Jack Jefferson	**Philippe Lefebvre**
Setine	**Constantin Alexandrov**
Eygtian Spokesperson	**Saïd Amadis**
Gardenborough	**Laurent Bateau**
The Boss	**Claude Brosset**

François Damiens (Raymond Pelletier), Youssef Hamid (The Imam), Khalid Maadour (The Follower), Arsène Mosca (Loktar), Abdallah Moundy (Slimane), Eric Prat (Plantieux), Richard Sammel (Moeller), Michael Hofland (Von Umsprung), Jean-François Halin (Rubrecht), Marc Bodnar (Bar Owner), Brenard Nissille (Man at Airport), Alain Khouani (Receptionist), Diego Diengo (Bell Boy), Mouloud Ikhaddelene (Princess' Helper), Hassan Chabaki (Helpful Passerby), Hedi Naili (Muezzin), Choukri Gtari (Man with Whip), Hafid F. Benamar (Friend of Man with Whip), Jean-Pierre Paris (Khalid), Laura Schiffman (Waitress), Roger To-Thanh-Hein (Manadrin)

When a fellow agent is assassinated, OSS 117 is ordered to impersonate the head of a Cairo poultry company in order to solve the murder.

BEFORE THE RAINS

(ROADSIDE ATTRACTIONS) Producers, Doug Mankoff, Andrew Spaulding, Paul Hardart, Tom Hardart, Mark Burton; Executive Producers, Ashok Rao, Jane Villiers, Howard Frumes; Coproducers, Mubina Rattonsey, Jessica Stamen, Amotz Zakai, Pauline Piechota; Director/ Photography, Santosh Sivan; Screenplay, Cathy Rabin; Designer, Sunil Babu; Costumes, S.B. Satheesan; Music, Mark Kilian; Editors, Steven Cohen, A. Sreekar Prasad; an Echo Lake Entertainment production; Indian-British-U.S.; Dolby; Color; Rated PG-13; 98 minutes; American release date: May 9, 2008

Cast

Henry Moores	**Linus Rache**
T.K. Neelan	**Rahul Bose**
Sajani	**Nandita Das**
Laura Moores	**Jennifer Ehle**
Peter Moores	**Leopold Benedict**
Manas	**Indrajit**
Rajat	**Lal Paul**
Charles Humphries	**John Standing**
T.K.'s Father	**Thilakan**
Inspector Sampath	**Ejji K. Umamahesh**

In 1937 India, the illicit romance between British spice baron Henry Moores and his housemaid Sajani leads to tragedy.

Linus Roache, Nandita Das © Roadside Attractions

*Anders Danilesen Lie,
Viktoria Winge
© Miramax Films*

Anders Danielsen Lie, Viktoria Winge

Christian Rubeck, Anders Danielsen Lie, Viktoria Winge

REPRISE

(MIRAMAX) Producer, Karin Julsrud; Director, Joachim Trier; Screenplay, Eskil Vogt, Joachim Trier; Photography, Jackob Ihre; Costumes, Maria Bollin; Music, Ola Flottum, Knut Schreiner; Editor, Olivier Bugge Coutte; a 4 ½ presentation, in association with Shortcut (Norway)/Filmlance (Sweden), with the support of the Norwegian Film Fund, the Swedish Film Insitute, Nordic Film- and TV-Fund; Norwegian-Swedish, 2006; Dolby; Color; Rated R; 105 minutes; American release date: May 16, 2008

Cast

Phillip Reisnes	**Anders Danielsen Lie**
Erik	**Espen Klouman-Høiner**
Kari Brekke	**Viktoria Winge**
Henning	**Henrik Elvestad**
Lars Etterstad	**Christian Rubeck**
Morten	**Odd Magnus Williamson**
Johanne	**Rebekka Karijord**
Jan Eivind	**Henrik Mestad**
Geir	**Pål Stokka**
Sten Egil Dahl	**Sigmund Sæverud**
Inger	**Tone Danielsen**
Hanne	**Elisabeth Sand**
Mathis Wergeland	**Thorbjørn Harr**
Lillian	**Silje Hagen**
TV Host	**Anne Sandvik Lindmo**
Telemarketing Boss	**Ivar Lykke**
Rune	**Andreas Tylden**
Narrator	**Eindride Eidsvold**
Joy Division Jogger	**Anders Brochgrevink**
Sebastian	**Emil Trier**

Fredrik Borgun (Sten, 20 years), John S. Kristensen (Jon), Kristian Warness Wraa (Svein), Oscar Lørås (Svein, 10 years), Frida Aune Froland (Merethe), Hege Golf (Geirs' Girl at Party), Hafrid Hagemoen (Stine), Jonas Thorsdalen Wik (Erik, 14 years), Martin Nicolay Lae (Erik, 10 years), David Avetisian (Fhaisal), Anders Eide (Bjørn), Helene Ruys (French Girl), Arben Bala (Svein's Buddy), Sindre Tveiten, John Sverre Sande, Joakim Hallås (Steinerskolen Young Men), Stine I. Johnsen (Geir's Girlfriend), Hilma Nicolaisen (Morten's Girlfriend), Nicholas J. Marthinsen (Frode), Dagny Holte (Frode's Mom), Thea Bay (Kathinka), Cecilie Bertran de Lis (Nurse Dikemark), Wenche Lindeberg Wang, Geir Bore Roaas (Nurses, Hospital), Henrik Elvestad, Andreas Tylden, Per Vigmostad, Torgny Amdam (Kommune), Hans Petter Heggeli, Anders Nilsen Tjore, Jonas Thire, Andreas Tylden (Mondo Topless)

Two best friends, hoping to make their mark in the literary world, find their lives taking different and unexpected paths when one has his novel accepted for publication.

Baki Davrak, Nursel Köse

Tuncel Kurtiz, Nursel Köse © Strand Releasing

THE EDGE OF HEAVEN

(STRAND) a.ka. *Auf der anderen Seite*; Producers, Andreas Thiel, Klaus Maeck, Faith Akin; Coproducers, Erhan Ozogul, Funda Odemis, Ali Akdeniz; Director/Screenplay, Faith Akin; Photography, Rainer Klausmann; Art Directors, Tamo Kunz, Sirma Bradley; Costumes, Katrin Aschendorf; Music, Shantel; Editor, Andrew Bird; Casting, Monique Akin; a Corazon Intl. (Germany)/Anka Film (Turkey) production in association with NDR, Dorje Film; German-Turkish, 2007; Color; Not rated; 120 minutes; American release date: May 21, 2008

Cast

Nejat Aksu	**Baki Davrak**
Ali Aksu	**Tuncel Kurtiz**
Yeter Ozturk	**Nursel Köse**
Ayten Ozturk	**Nurgül Yesilçay**
Suanne Staub	**Hanna Schygulla**
Lotte Staub	**Patrycia Ziolkowska**
Flute Player	**Yusuf Kaba**
Emine	**Yelda Reynaud**
Markus Obermüller	**Lars Rudolph**
Konsulatsmitarbeiter	**Andreas Thiel**

Realizing the prostitute his father has patronized had been sending her daughter money for college, Nejat Aksu journeys to Istanbul to find the girl after her mother passes away.

Hanna Schygulla, Nurgül Yesilçay

Left: *Nurgül Yesilçay, Patrycia Ziolkowska*

THE CHILDREN OF HUANG SHI

(SONY CLASSICS) Producers, Arthur Cohn, Wieland Schulz-Keil, Peter Loehr, Jonathan Shteinman, Martin Hagemann; Executive Producers, Taylor Thomson, Lillian Birnbaum; Coproducer, Yuan Mei; Director, Roger Spottiswoode; Screenplay, James MacManus, Jane Hawksley; Photography, Zhao Xiaoding; Designer, Steven Jones-Evans; Costumes, Gao Wenyan, Kym Barrett; Music, David Hirschfelder; Editor, Geoffrey Lamb; Casting, Nikki Valko, Shuai "Ruby" Hou; a Film Finance Corp. Australia presentation of an Arthur Cohn/Wieland Schulz-Keil production and a a Ming Prods. (China)/Bluewater Pictures (Australia)/Zero Fiction (Germany)/Cheerland (China) production; Australian-American-Chinese-German; Dolby; Color; Rated R; 125 minutes; American release date: May 23, 2008

Chow Yun-Fat, Jonathan Rhys Meyers

Cast

George Hogg	**Jonathan Rhys Myers**
Lee Pearson	**Radha Mitchell**
Chen Hansheng	**Chow Yun-Fat**
Mrs. Wang	**Michelle Yeoh**
Shi-Kai	**Guang Li**
Barnes	**David Wenham**

Lin Ji (Horse Rider), Matt Walker (Andy Fisher), Anastasia Kolpakova (Duschka), Ping Su (Eddie Wei), Imai Hideaki (Japanese Officer), Schiichiro Hashimoto (Urban Japanese Officer), Shinichi Takashima (Hostile Kempetai Officer), Xing Mang (Young Communist), Ruixiang Zhu (Japanese Officer #2), Yuelong Fang (Rou Ding), Shimin Sun (Yu Lin), Xucheng Shi (Kao Tung), Naihan Yang (Ching), Weijuan Wu (Young Mother), Zhi Zang (Lao Si), Liu Hui (Fallen Soldier), Shunzen Zhao (Colonel Ma), Qing Xuan Alan Li (Wei Ping), Shu Li (Magistrate), Shane Briant (Roger Appsley), Hong Bin Zhang (SSS Officer)

The true story of how British reporter George Hogg helped rescue dozens of orphaned children from the advancing Japanese army in 1937 war torn China.

Guang Li

Michelle Yeoh

Radha Mitchell, Jonathan Rhys Meyers © Sony Classics

SAVAGE GRACE

(IFC FILMS) Producers, Iker Monfort, Katie Roumel, Pamela Koffler, Christine Vachon; Executive Producers, John Wells, Temple Fennell, Johnathan Dorfman, Hengameh Panahi, Stephen Hays, Peter M. Graham II, Howard Morales; Co-Executive Producers, Elvira Morales, Christian Baute; Coproducers, Alberto Aranda, Xavi Granada, Yulene Monfort, Tom Kalin; Director, Tom Kalin; Screenplay, Howard A. Rodman; Based on the book by Natalie Robins and Steven M.L. Aronson; Photography, Juanmi Azpiroz; Designer, Victor Molero; Costumes, Gabriela Salaverri; Music, Fernando Velazquez; Editors, Tom Kalin, John F. Lyons, Enara Goikoetxea; Casting, Laura Rosenthal; a Monfort Producciones (Spain)/Killer Films (U.S.)/Celluloid Dreams (France) production, in association with ATO Pictures, 120 dB Films, A Contraluz Films, Videntia Frames; Spanish-French-American; Dolby; Color; Not rated; 97 minutes; American release date: May 30, 2008

Cast

Barbara Baekeland	**Julianne Moore**
Brooks Baekeland	**Stephen Dillane**
Antony Baekeland	**Eddie Redmayne**
Blanca	**Elena Anaya**
Black Jake Martinez	**Unax Ugalde**
Sam Green	**Hugh Dancy**
Nini Daly	**Anne Reid**
Tony as a Child	**Barney Clark**
Jean Pierre Souvestre	**Simón Andreu**
Joost Van Den Heuvels	**Jim Arnold**
Carlos Durán	**Abel Folk**
Simone Lippe	**Mapi Galán**
Aschwin Lippe	**Martin Huber**
Missy	**Lina Lambert**
Midge Van Den Heuvels	**Minnie Marx**

Xavier Capdet (Gate Man), Peter Vives (Mishka), Brendan Price (PC Roebrts), Belén Rueda (Pilar Durán), Melina Matthews (Lorna Moffat)

The true story of how wealthy socialite Barbara Baekeland's domineering and unhealthy relationship with her homosexual son led to tragedy.

Eddie Redmayne, Hugh Dancy © IFC Films

Eddie Redmayne, Unax Ugalde, Julianne Moore

Julianne Moore, Bélen Rueda

Eddie Redmayne, Unax Ugalde

THE UNKNOWN WOMAN

(OUTSIDER) a.k.a. *La Sconosciuta*; Executive Producer, Laura Fattori; Director/Screenplay, Giuseppe Tornatore; Photography, Fabio Zamarion; Art Director, Tonino Zera; Costumes, Nicoletta Ercole; Music, Ennio Morricone; Editor, Massimo Quaglia; a Medusa Film presentation; Italian; Dolby; Color; Not rated; 118 minutes; American release date: May 30, 2008

Cast
Irena/The Unknown Woman	**Xenia Rappoport**
Muffa	**Michele Placido**
Valeria Adacher	**Claudia Gerini**
Donato Adacher	**Perfrancesco Favino**
Irena's Lawyer	**Margherita Buy**
Porter	**Alessandro Haber**
Gina	**Piera Degli Esposti**
Thea Adacher	**Clara Dossena**
Lucrezia	**Angela Molina**

Nicola Di Pinto (Irena's Lover), Paolo Elmo (Nello), Simona Nobili (Waitress), Giulia Di Quillo (Secretary), Pino Calabrese (Magistrate), Gisella Marengo (Policewoman), Gabriella Barbuti (Nurse)

A mysterious Russian woman insinuates herself into the lives of an affluent Italian family.

Michele Placido, Xenia Rappoport, Claudia Gerini

Clara Dossena, Xenia Rappoport, Claudia Gerini © Outsider Films

Jim Broadbent, Colin Firth

Jim Broadbent, Matthew Beard © Sony Classics

WHEN DID YOU LAST SEE YOUR FATHER?

(SONY CLASSICS) a.k.a. *And When Did You Last See Your Father?*; Producers, Elizabeth Karlsen, Stephen Woolley; Executive Producers, Tessa Ross, Lizzie Francke, Kate Wilson, Paul White, Gary Smith; Coproducer, Laurie Borg; Director, Anand Tucker; Screenplay, David Nicholls; Based on the memoir by Blake Morrison; Photography, Howard Atherton; Designer, Alice Normington; Costumes, Caroline Harris; Music, Barrington Pheloung; Editor, Trevor Waite; Casting, Priscilla John; a Film4, U.K. Film Council, EM Media, Intandem Films presentation of a Number 9 Films production, in association with Audley Films; British; Dolby; Widescreen; Color; Rated PG-13; 92 minutes; American release date: June 6, 2008

Cast
Arthur Morrison	**Jim Broadbent**
Blake Morrison	**Colin Firth**
Kim Morrison	**Juliet Stevenson**
Kathy Morrison	**Gina McKee**
Blake, teenager	**Matthew Beard**
Beaty	**Sarah Lancashire**
Sandra	**Elaine Cassidy**
Gillian Morrison	**Claire Skinner**
Blake, age 8	**Bradley Johnson**

Carey Mulligan (Rachel), Tara Berwin (Gillian, Younger), Tilly Curtis (Josie), Chris Middleton (Racing Steward), Elliot Avery (Peter), Rhiannon Howden (Sophie), Tom Butcher (Dr. Taggart), Alannah Barlow (Gillian, child), Richard Standing (Publican), Olivia Lindsay (Josie, child), Justin McDonald (Steve), Graham Turner (Undertaker), Blake Morrison (Awards Ceremony Attendee)

Blake Morrison looks back on his difficult relationship with his charismatic but overbearing father.

Tadanobu Asano

MONGOL

(PICTUREHOUSE) Producers, Sergey Selyanov, Sergei Bodrov, Anton Melnik; Executive Producers, Bulat Galimgereyev, Alec Schulmann, Bob Berney; Coproducers, Stefan Arndt, Manuela Stehr, Gulnara Sarsenova, Zhang Xia; Director, Sergei Bodrov; Screenplay, Arif Aliyev, Sergei Bodrov; Photography, Sergey Trofimov, Rogier Stoffers; Designer, Dashi Namdakov; Costumes, Karin Lohr; Music, Tuomas Kantelinen; Additional Music, Altan Urag; Editors, Zach Staenberg, Valdis Oskarsdottir; Casting, Guka Omarova; a CTB Films Co., Andreevsky Flag Co., X Filme Creative Pool production; Kazakstan, 2007; Dolby; Super 35 Widescreen; Color; Rated R; 126 minutes; American release date: June 6, 2008

Cast

Temudgin	**Tadanobu Asano**
Jamukha	**Honglei Sun**
Börte	**Khulan Chuluun**
Young Temudgin	**Odnyam Odsuren**
Young Jamukha	**Amarbold Tuvinbayar**
Young Börte	**Bayertsetseg Erdenebat**
Targutai	**Amadu Mamadakov**
Esugei	**Ba Sen**
Taichar	**Bu Ren**
Oelun	**Aliya**
Charkhu	**Tegen Ao**

Ying Bai (Merchant with Golden Ring), Bao Di (Todoen), Deng Ba Te Er (Daritai), Sorgan-Shira (You Er), Sai Xing Ga (Chiledu), Ba Yin Qi Qi Ge (Temulun), Ba De Rong Gui (Young Taichar), Sun Ben Hon (Monk), Zhang Jiong (Tangut Garrison Chief), He Qi (Dai-Sechen), Li Jia Qi (Mungun), Su Ya La Su Rong (Girkhai), Ba Te (Khasar), Ba Ti (Khasar), Ba Ti (Dzhuchi), Ba Tu (Altan), Ji Ri Mu Tu (Boorchu), Tunga (Sochikhel), Amarbold Tuvshinbayar (Young Jamukha)

The true story of how legendary warrior Genghis Khan united the feuding nomadic clans in thirteenth century Central Asia.

This film received an Oscar nomination for foreign language film (2007).

Khulan Chuluun

Odnyam Odsuren © Picturehouse

Clotilde Hesme, Nicolas Cazalé © Film Movement

Nicolas Cazalé, Clotilde Hesme

THE GROCER'S SON

(FILM MOVEMENT) a.k.a. *Le Fils de l'epicier*; Producers, Milena Poylo, Gilles Sacuto; Director/Screenplay, Eric Guirado; Photography, Laurent Brunet; Designer, Valerie Faynot; Costumes, Ann Dunsford; Music, Christophe Boutin; Editor, Pierre Haberer; Casting, Brigitte Moidon; a TS Prods., Rhone Alpes Cinema production, with the participation of Canal Plus; French; 2007; Dolby; Widescreen; Color; Not rated; 96 minutes; American release date: June 6, 2008

Cast

Antoine	Nicolas Cazalé
Claire	Clotilde Hesme
Antoine's Father	Daniel Duval
Antoine's Mother	Jeanne Goupil
Françoise	Stéphan Guérin-Tillié
Luciénne	Liliane Rovére
Father Clément	Paul Crauchet
Hassan	Chad Chenouga
Fernand	Benoît Giros
Sophie	Ludmila Ruoso

When his estranged father suffers a heart attack, Antoine reluctantly returns to the town he left a decade before, taking charge of the family grocery store.

MY WINNIPEG

(IFC FILMS) Producers, Jody Shapiro, Phyllis Lang; Executive Producer, Michael Burns; Director, Guy Maddin; Screenplay, Guy Maddin, George Toles; Photography, Jody Shapiro; Editor, John Gurdebeke; an Everyday Pictures/Buffao Gal production; Canadian; Dolby; Black & white/color; Not rated; 80 minutes; American release date: June 13, 2008.

Cast

Guy Maddin	Darcy Fehr
Mother	Ann Savage
Janet Maddin	Amy Stewart
Mayor Cornish	Louis Negrin
Cameron Maddin	Brendan Cade
Ross Maddin	Wesley Cade

Lou Profeta, Fred Dunsmore (Themselves), Kate Yacula (Citizen Girl), Jacelyn Lobay (Gwenyth Lloyd), Eric Nipp (Viscount Gort), Jennifer Palichuk (Althea Cornish)

Filmmaker Guy Maddin's interpretation of growing up in his hometown of Winnipeg, Canada.

Hollies Snowshoe Club © Zeitgeist Films

Wesley Cade, Ann Savage

Christopher Simpson, Tannishtha Chatterjee

Lalita Ahmed

Lana Rahman, Naeema Begum, Tannishtha Chatterjee, Satish Kaushik
© Sony Classics

BRICK LANE

(SONY CLASSICS) Producers, Alison Owen, Christopher Collins; Executive Producers, Tessa Ross, Paula Jalfon, Duncan Reid, Paul Trijbits; Director, Sarah Gabron; Screenplay, Abi Morgan, Laura Jones; Based on the novel by Monica Ali; Photography, Robbie Ryan; Designer, Simon Elliott; Costumes, Michael O'Connor; Music, Jocelyn Pook; Editor, Melanie Oliver; Casting, Shaheen Baig, Uma Da Cunha; a Film Four, Ingenious Film Partners, U.K. Film Council presentation of a Ruby Films production; British; Dolby; Panavision; Deluxe color; Rated PG-13; 101 minutes; American release date: June 20, 2008

Cast
Nanzeen Ahmed	**Tannishtha Chatterjee**
Chanu Ahmed	**Satish Kaushik**
Karim	**Christopher Simpson**
Shahana Ahmed	**Naeema Begum**
Bibi Ahmed	**Lana Rahman**
Hasina	**Zafreen**
Mrs. Islam	**Lalita Ahmed**
Dr. Azad	**Harsh Nayyar**
Razia	**Harvey Virdi**
News Reporter	**Bernard Holley**

Married off to the older Chanu and sent to live in London's East End, Nazneen hopes to break from the limitations imposed upon her by her Muslim community.

Tannishtha Chatterjee, Satish Kaushik

THE LAST MISTRESS

(IFC FILMS) a.k.a. *Une vieille maîtresse*; Producer, Jean-François Lepetit; Director/Screenplay, Catherine Breillat; Photography, Yorgos Arvanitis; Designer, François-Renaud Labarthe; Costumes, Anaïs Romand; Editor, Pascale Chavance; a Jean-François Lepetit presentation of a Flach Film, CB Films, France 3 Cinema, Studio Canal (France)/Buskin Film (Italy) production, with the participation of Canal Plus, CNC, TPS Star; French-Italian; Dolby; Color; Not rated; 114 minutes; American release date: June 27, 2008

Asia Argento, Fu'ad Aït Aattou

Cast
La Vellini	**Asia Argento**
Ryno de Marigny	**Fu'ad Aït Aattou**
Hermangarde	**Roxane Mesquida**
The Marquise de Flers	**Claude Sarraute**
The Comtesse d'Artelles	**Yolande Moreau**
The Victome de Prony	**Michael Lonsdale**
Madame de Solcy	**Anne Parillaud**
Mademoiselle Marie-Cornélie Falcon	**Amira Casar**
The Singer	**Lio**
The Queen of Diamonds	**Caroline Ducey**
The Arrogant One	**Isabelle Renauld**
The Comte de Mareuil	**Jean-Philippe Tesse**
Sir Reginald	**Nicholas Hawtrey**
Oliva	**Léa Seydoux**
The Cardinal de Flers	**Frédéric Botton**

Aurlien Foubert (The Best Man), Jean-Claude Binoche (The Comte de Cerisy), Jean-Gabriel Mitterand (Ryno's Valet), Marie-Victoire Debré (The Courtesan), Camille Schnebelen (The Abandoned Woman), Ashley Wanninger, Thomas Hardy (Vellini's Suitors), Jean-François Lepetit (The Court Jester), Ezéquiel Spucches (The Pianist), Éric Bouhier (The Surgeon), Patrick Roig (The Castle Doctor), Patrick Tetu (Father Griffon), Suzanne Marty (The Chambermaid), Stéphanie Hausauer (The Castle Valet), Daniel Lemoine (The Butler), Éric Turanzas (Diner Waiter), Josian Taleux (The Kitchen Maid), Alain Connan (The Vicar), Frédéric Laforêt (The English Witness), Malika Kadri (The Old Berber Woman), Azza et Meïssa Souif (Vellini, Young Girl)

Although betrothed to the virginal Hermangarde, artistocratic Ryno de Marigny refuses to give up his passionate relationship with his tempestuous lover La Vellini.

Asia Argento, Fu'ad Aït Aattou

Roxane Mesquida © IFC Films

Asia Argento, Fu'ad Aït Aattou

TELL NO ONE

(MUSIC BOX) a.k.a. *Ne le dis à personne*; Producer, Alain Attal; Director, Guillaume Canet; Screenplay, Guillaume Canet, Philippe Lefebvre; Based on the novel by Harlan Coben; Photography, Christophe Offenstein; Designer, Philippe Chiffre; Costumes, Carine Sarfati; Music, Mathieu Chedid; Editor, Herve De Luze; a Les Prods. du Tresor, EuropaCorp, M6 Films production, with the participation of Canal Plus, CineCinema, M6; French, 2006; Dolby; Color; Not rated; 126 minutes; American release date: July 2, 2008.

Cast

Dr. Alex Beck	**François Cluzet**
Margot Beck	**Marie-Jose Croze**
Jacques Laurentin	**André Dussollier**
Hélène Perkins	**Kristin Scott Thomas**
Eric Levkowitch	**François Berléand**
Elsyabeth Feldman	**Nathalie Baye**
Gilbert Neuville	**Jean Rochefort**
Anne Beck	**Marina Hands**
Bruno	**Gilles Lellouche**
Lt. Philippe Meynard	**Philippe Lefebvre**
Charlotte Bertraud	**Florence Thomassin**

Olivier Marchal (Bernard Valenti), Guillaume Canet (Philippe Neuville), Brigitte Catillon (Capt. Barthas), Samir Guesmi (Lt. Saraoui), Jean-Pierre Lorit (Adjudant-chef Lavelle), Jalil Lespert (Yaël Gonzales), Eric Savin (Prosecutor), Eric Naggar (Maître Pierre Ferrault), Philippe Canet (François Beck), Danielle Ajoret (Madame Beck), Daniel Znyk (Physician), Laurent Lafitte (The Basque), Jean-Christophe Pagnac (Valenti), Dorothée Brière (Airline Hostess), Jean-Noël Brouté (Dr. Dubois), Joël Dupuch (Big Man), Martine Chevallier (Martine Laurentin), Thierry Neuvic (Marc Bertraud), Mikaela Fisher (Zak), François Bredon (Mouss), Christophe Veillon (Customs Officer), Anne Marivin (Alex's Secretary), Maxime Nucci (Assistant to Charlotte), Hugo Sélignac (Studio Model), Ludovic Bergerie (Young Policeman), Robin Marmisse (Young Alex), Marie Martin (Young Margot), Brooklyn Beral (Color Blind Child), Christelle Beral (Mme. Abdibal, Color Blind Child's Mother), Sarah Martins (Bruno's Friend), Alexandra Mercouroff (Lucille's Mother), Lola Lefebvre (Lucille), Christian Carion (Lucille's Father), Brian Lucas (Gunman in City), Mamadou Gary (PlayStation Player), Pierre-Benoît Varcolier, Nicolas Mouchet (Male Nurses), Karim Adda (Impatient Patient), Christopher Rossignon (Police Scientist), Saïd Bjaoui (Man Held by Valenti), Jean-Marc Valenti (Internet Café Server), Pascal Rigot (Flower Deliverer), Marie-Antoinette Canet (Maître Ferrault's Secretary), Françoise Bertin (Antoinette Levkowitch), Andrée Damant (Simone), Jean-Maurice Bonneau (Horse Race Leader), Jérémie Covillaut (Junkie), Arnaud Henriet (SRPJ Technician), Albert Goldberg (Bartola), Eva Saint-Paul (Madme Neuville), Raphaël de Crozals (Child at Airport)

The discovery of two bodies revives interest in a crime from several years earlier, when Dr. Alex Beck's wife was mysteriously murdered.

François Cluzet, Kristin Scott Thomas

François Cluzet

François Cluzet, Marie-Josée Croze © Music Box Films

Marie-Josée Croze

DAYS & CLOUDS

(FILM MOVEMENT) a.k.a. *Giorni e nuvole*; Producer, Lionello Cerri; Director, Silvio Soldini; Story/Screenplay, Doriana Leondeff, Francisco Piccolo, Frederic Pontremoli, Silvio Soldini; Photography, Ramiro Civita; Art Director, Paola Bizzari; Costumes, Silvia Nebiolo, Patrizia Mazzon, Cinzia Castiana; Editor, Carlotta Cristiani; Casting, Jorgelina Depertris; Italian-Swiss, 2007; Dolby; Color; Not rated; 115 minutes; American release date: July 10, 2008

Cast
Elsa	**Margherita Buy**
Michele	**Antonio Albanese**
Vito	**Giuseppe Battiston**
Alice	**Alba Rohrwacher**
Nadia	**Carla Signoris**
Riki	**Fabio Troiano**
Salviati	**Paolo Sassanelli**
Michele's Father	**Arnaldo Ninchi**
Luciano	**Antonio Francini**
Accountant Terzetti	**Teco Celio**

A seemingly well-to-do couple face a financial and emotional crisis when Michele admits that he was fired two months ago from the company he helped found.

Margherita Buy © Film Movement

Antonio Albanese, Margherita Buy

Kevin Zegers, Ellen Burstyn © Vivendi

THE STONE ANGEL

(VIVENDI/ALLIANCE) Producers, Liz Jarvis, Kari Skogland; Executive Producers, Bryan Gliserman, Seaton McLean, Michael MacMillan, Guy Collins, Michael Ryan, Phyllis Laing; Director/Screenplay, Kari Skogland; Based on the novel by Margaret Laurence; Photography, Bobby Bukowski; Designer, Rob Gray; Music, John McCarthy; Editor, Jim Munro; a Handmade Films International presentation of a Buffalo Gal Pictures, Skogland films production; Canadian; Dolby; Color; Rated R; 115 minutes; American release date: July 10, 2008

Cast
Hagar Shipley	**Ellen Burstyn**
Young Hagar	**Christine Horne**
Young Bram	**Cole Hauser**
John	**Kevin Zegers**
Arlene	**Ellen Page**
Marvin	**Dylan Baker**
Older Bram	**Wings Hauser**

Olie Alto (Bus Driver), Evelyne Anderson (Old Cronie at Charity Dance), Aaron Ashmore (Matt), Ted Atherton (Reverend Troy), Sharon Bajer (Emergency Room Nurse), Devon Bostick (Young Marvin), Ardith Boxall (Lottie's Mother), Doreen Brownstone (Silver Elms Bridge Player), Jessica Burleson (Cell Phone Woman on Bus), Hilary Carroll (Bank Teller), Sarah Constible (Young Lottie), Janet-Laine Green (Lottie), Josette Halpert (Young Arlene), Alicia Johnston (Charlotte), Peter Jordan (Henry Pearl), Luke Kirby (Leo), Joyce Krenz (Auntie Doll), Katherine J. Lane (Labor Nurse), Peter MacNeill (Jason), Arne MacPherson (Doctor, Present Day), Judy Marshak (Silver Elms Matron), Sheila McCarthy (Doris), Telford (Ross McMillan), Noah Meade (John, Child), Mackenzie Munro (Young Charlotte), Wayne Nicklas (Mr. Cooper), Landon Norris (Young John), Connor Price (Young Matt), Christopher Read (Currie Store Clerk), Chris Sigurdson (Pasto–Manawaka), Jan Skene (Dialect Coach), R. Morgan Slade (Young Telford), Jason Spevack (Marvin, Child), Ryland Thiessen (Telford, Child), Jordan Todosey (Lottie, age 9), Samanthan Weinstein (Hagar, Child), Nada Yousif (Missy)

Ninety-year-old Hagar Shipley defies her son's efforts to place her in a nursing home, instead journeying north through Manitoba where she thinks back on her life.

Guy Pearce, Catherine Zeta-Jones © Weinstein Co.

DEATH DEFYING ACTS

(WEINSTEIN CO.) Producers, Chris Curling, Marian MacGowan; Executive Producers, Dan Lupovitz, David M. Thompson, Kirk D'Amico, Marcia Nasatir, Lucas Foster; Coproducers, Tony Grisoni, Brian Ward; Director, Gillian Armstrong; Screenplay, Tony Girsoni, Brian Ward; Photography, Haris Zamarloukos; Designer, Gemma Jackson; Costumes, Susannah Buxton; Music, Cezary Skubiszewski; Editor, Nicholas Beauman; Casting, Gail Stevens; a Film Finance Corp. Australia/ BBC Films, U.K. Film Countil/Myriad Pictures (Australia) presentation, in association with the New South Wales Film and Television Officer, of a MacGowan Lupovitz Nasatir Films (Australia)/Zephyr Films (U.K.) production; Australian-British; Dolby; Color; Rated PG; 96 minutes; American release date: July 11, 2008

Cast

Harry Houdini	**Guy Pearce**
Mary McGarvie	**Catherine Zeta-Jones**
Mr. Sugarman	**Timothy Spall**
Benji McGarvie	**Saoirse Ronan**
The Red Haired Pilot	**Jack Bailey**
Sugarman's Assistant	**Aaron Brown**
Younger Reporter	**MacKay Crawford**

James Fiddy (American Assistant), Martin Fisher (Concierge), Tim Frost (Tap Dancer), Campbell Graham, Chris Wilson (Reporters), Emma Humphries (The Chambermaid), Miles Jupp (Ventriloquist), Silvia Lombardo (Usherette), Cloe Mackie, Holly Mackie (Psychic Twins), Frankey Martyn (Rose), Aileen O'Gorman (Effie, Elderly Seamstress), Dodger Phillips (Voice of the Press), Carol Robb (Young Woman)

When magician Harry Houdini offers $10,000 to any psychic who can decipher valuable information about his late mother, con artist Mary McGarvie sets her sites on the prize.

BEFORE I FORGET

(STRAND) a.k.a. *Avant que j'oublie*; Producer, Pauline Duhault; Director/ Screenplay, Jacques Nolot; Photography, Josee Deshaies; Designer, Gaelle Guitard; Costumes, Eleonore O'Byrne, Sophie Lifshitz; Editor, Sophie Reine; Casting, Jacques Grant, Stephane Batut; an Elia Films and ID Distribution presentation of an Elia Films production with the participation of CNC and support from Procirep and Angoa-Agicoa; French; Dolby; Color; Not rated; 108 minutes; American release date: July 18, 2008

Cast

Pierre	**Jacques Nolot**
The Man	**Jean-Pol Dubois**
Paul	**Marc Rioufol**
Marc	**Bastien d'Asnières**
Cute Guy in Chinese Restaurant	**Gaetano Weysen-Volli**
Bruno	**Bruno Mongelia**
Manosky, the Shrink	**David Kessler**

Rémy Le Fur (Auctioneer), Jean Pommier (Georges, the Attorney), Rebia Lyes (Khalid, the Delivery Man), Lionel Goldstein (David), Bernard Herlem (Richard), Claudine Sainderichin (Insurance Lady), Albert Mainella (Toutoune), Jean-Paul Chagniot (Willem), Isabelle Boudot de la Motte (Marie-Odile), Josianne Daussy (Woman in Art Gallery), Florence Bouteau (Captain Laforge), Raphaëline Goupilleau, Isabel Arias (Toutoune's Neighbors), Alimata Camara (Building Manager), David Lefevre (Policeman), Yann Gohiec (Store Manager)

A former gigolo who has been HIV-positive for more than twenty years continues his pursuit of sexual gratification as he faces an uncertain future.

Florence Bouteau, Jacques Nolot

Jacques Nolot, Gaetano Weysen-Volli © Strand Releasing

Ben Kingsley

Emily Mortimer

Kate Mara, Eduardo Noriega

Emily Mortimer, Woody Harrelson
© First Look

TRANSSIBERIAN

(FIRST LOOK) Producer, Julio Fernández; Executive Producers, Antonio Nava, Julio Fernández, Carlos Fernandez; Coproducers, Tania Reichert-Facilides, Alvaro Augustin, Todd Dagress; Director, Brad Anderson; Screenplay, Will Conroy; Photography, Xavier Gimenez; Designer, Alain Bainee; Costumes, Thomas Olah; Music, Alfonso De Vilallonga; Editor, Jaume Marti; Visual Effects, Infinia, Cubica; Casting, John & Ros Hubbard; a Filmax Intl. presentation of a Julio Fernández production for Castelao Prods. in association with Scout Prods., co-produced with Universum Film, GmbH Telecino Cinema, Future Films, and Lithuanian Film Studios; Spanish-German-British-Lithuanian; Dolby; Super 35 Widescreen; Color; Rated R; 111 minutes; American release date: July 18, 2008

Cast
Roy	**Woody Harrelson**
Jessie	**Emily Mortimer**
Abby	**Kate Mara**
Carlos	**Eduardo Noriega**
Kolzak	**Thomas Kretschmann**
Grinko	**Ben Kingsley**
Frenchman	**Etienne Chicot**
Minister	**Mac McDonald**
Embassy Official	**Colin Stinton**
Drunk Pole	**Saulius Bagaliunas**
Provodnik	**Alfredas Butkevicius**
Russian Officer	**Mindaugas Capas**
Perter Tulun Station	**Vidmantas Jasiunevicius**

Visockaite Sonata, Larisa Kalpokaite (Train Attendants), Valentinas Krulikovskis (Young Waiter, Dining Car), Kristina Kulinic, Jin Zhou (School Girls), Sergej Oskin (Engineer), Mindaugas Papinigis (Young Detective), Andrius Paulavicius (Backpacker), Aleksandrs Petukhovs (Russian Cop), Antanas Radinskas (Sullen Clerk), Antanas Surgailis (Young Russian), Perlis Vaisieta (Manager, Hotel Pushkin), Emilis Welyvis (Russian Cop)

Traveling aboard the Transsiberian express, Roy and Jessie encounter a mysterious couple whose motivations for bonding with them leave Jessie increasingly suspicious after Roy fails to reboard the train at one of its designated stops.

BOY A

(WEINSTEIN CO.) Producer, Lynn Horsford; Executive Producers, Nick Marston, Tally Garner, Liza Marshall; Director, John Crowley; Screenplay, Mark O'Rowe; Based on the novel by Jonathan Trigell; Photography, Rob Hardy; Designer, Jon Henson; Music, Paddy Cunningham; Editor, Lucia Zucchetti; Casting, Fiona Weir; a Cuba Pictures production for Channel 4; British, 2007; Dolby; Color; HD; Rated R; 99 minutes; American release date: July 23, 2008

Cast

Jack Burridge	**Andrew Garfield**
Terry	**Peter Mullan**
Eric Wilson	**Alfie Owen**
Michelle	**Katie Lyons**
Philip Craig	**Taylor Doherty**
Chris	**Shaun Evans**
Steve	**Anthony Lewis**
Kelly	**Siobhan Finneran**
Zeb	**James Young**
Angela Milton	**Skye Bennett**
Teacher	**Victoria Brazier**
Schoolgirl	**Madeleine Rakic-Platt**
Bullies	**Josef Altin, Dudley Brewis**
Eric's Dad	**Leigh Symonds**
Eric's Mum	**Maria Gough**

Jeremy Swift (Dave), Carlene Hansom (Waitress), John Catterall (Man in Club), Tilly Vosburgh (Shopkeeper), Phil Rowson, Luke Broughton (Policemen), Paul-Michael Giblin (Photographer), Helen Wilding (Carol), Steve Pacey (Prosecution Barrister), Cyriack Stevenson (Council Officer), Tom Cottle, Nathan Kershaw (Reporters), Josh Moran (Ticket Collector), Iris Sharple (Woman in Train)

Released into the outside world and given a new identity, a young man who had been imprisoned for an unspeakable crime committed as a child tries to find his place in society, all the while hoping his past remains buried from others.

Andrew Garfield

Andrew Garfield, Peter Mullan

Andrew Garfield

Katie Lyons, Andrew Garfield © Weinstein

Ben Whishaw, Michael Gambon, Hayley Atwell

Ben Whishaw, Matthew Goode

Greta Scacchi © Miramax Films

BRIDESHEAD REVISITED

(MIRAMAX) Producers, Robert Bernstein, Douglas Rae, Kevin Loader; Executive Producers, David M. Thompson, Nicole Finnan, Tim Haslam, Hugo Heppell; Coproducer, James Saynor; Director, Julian Jarrold; Screenplay, Andrew Davies, Jeremy Brock; Based on the novel by Evelyn Waugh; Photography, Jess Hall; Designer, Alice Normington; Costumes, Eimer Ni Mhaoldomhnaigh; Music, Adrian Johnston; Editor, Chris Gill; Casting, Priscilla John; a Miramax Films (U.S.)/U.K. Film Council, BBC Films (U.K.) presentation, in association with Hanway Films, 2 Entertain, Screen Yorkshire, of an Ecosse Films (U.K.) production; British-American; Dolby; Panavision; Color; Rated PG-13; 134 minutes; American release date: July 25, 2008

Cast

Charles Ryder	**Matthew Goode**
Sebastian Flyte	**Ben Whishaw**
Julia Flyte	**Hayley Atwell**
Lady Marchmain	**Emma Thompson**
Lord Marchmain	**Michael Gambon**
Cara	**Greta Scacchi**
Rex Mottram	**Jonathan Cake**
Edward Ryder	**Patrick Malahide**
Hooper	**Thomas Morrison**
Celia Ryder	**Anna Madeley**
Cousin Jasper	**Richard Teverson**
Anthony Blanche	**Joseph Beattie**
Lunt	**Roger Walker**
Nanny Hawkins	**Rita Davies**
Lady Cordelia Flyte	**Felicity Jones**

Geoffrey Wilkinson (Wilcox), Ed Stoppard (Bridley Flyte), James Bradshaw (Mr. Samgrass), David Barrass (Ship's Barber), Sarah Crowden (Lady Guest), Stephen Carlile (English Lord), Peter Barnes (American Professor), Tom Wlaschiha (Kurt), Stephane Cornicard (Doctor Henri), Susan Brown (Nurse), Niall Buggy (Father Mackay)

Charles Ryder looks back on how his encounter with ne'er do well Sebastian Flyte brought him into close contact with the latter's wealthy but troubled family.

Emma Thompson

Javier Bardem, Scarlett Johansson © Weinstein Co.

Rebecca Hall, Scarlett Johansson

Javier Bardem, Rebecca Hall

VICKY CRISTINA BARCELONA

(WEINSTEIN CO.) Producers, Letty Aronson, Gareth Wiley, Stephen Tenenbaum; Executive Producer, Jaume Roures; Coproducer, Helen Robin; Co-Executive Producers, Jack Rollins, Charles H. Joffe, Javier Mendez; Director/Screenplay, Woody Allen; Photography, Javier Aguirresarobe; Designer, Alain Bainee; Costumes, Sonia Grande; Editor, Alisa Lepselter; Line Producer, Bernat Elias; Casting, Juliet Taylor, Patricia DiCerto; a Mediapro & Gravier production in association with Anetna 3 Films & Antena 3 TV of a Dumaine production; Spanish-American; Dolby; Deluxe color; Rated PG-13; 96 minutes; American release date: August 15, 2008

Cast

Juan Antonio	**Javier Bardem**
Judy Nash	**Patricia Clarkson**
Maria Elena	**Penélope Cruz**
Mark Nash	**Kevin Dunn**
Vicky	**Rebecca Hall**
Cristina	**Scarlett Johansson**
Doug	**Chris Messina**
Narrator	**Christopher Evan Welch**
Ben	**Pablo Schreiber**
Sally	**Carrie Preston**
Adam	**Zak Orth**
Jay	**Abel Folk**
Charles	**Julio Perillán**

Juan Quesada (Guitarist in Barcelona), Josep Maria Domènech (Julio Josep), Manel Barceló (Doctor), Emilio de Benito (Guitarist in Asturias), Richard Salom, Maurice Sonnenberg (Art Gallery Guests), Jaume Montané, Lloll Bertran, Joel Joan, Silvia Sabaté (Juan Antonio's Friends)

While on vacation in Spain, adventurous Cristina and her more reserved friend Vicky both find themselves falling under the spell of free spirited painter Juan Antonio.

2008 Academy Award winner for Best Supporting Actress (Penélope Cruz).

Penélope Cruz

Ludivine Sagnier © IFC Films

François Berléand, Ludivine Sagnier

Benoît Magimel, Ludivine Sagnier

A GIRL CUT IN TWO

(IFC FILMS) a.k.a. *La fille coupée en deux*; Producer, Patrick Godeau; Executive Producer, Francoise Galfre; Director, Claude Chabrol; Screenplay, Claude Chabrol, Cecile Maistre; Photography, Eduardo Serra; Designer, Francoise Benoit-Fresco; Costumes, Mic Cheminal; Music, Matthieu Chabrol; Editor, Monique Fardoulis; Casting, Cecile Maistre; a Patrick Godeau presentation of an Aliceleo Cinema, Aliceleo, Rhone-Aples Cinema, France 2 Cinema (France)/Ingeral Film (Germany) production, with the participation of Canal Pluse, CineCinema; French-German, 2007; Dolby; Color; Not Rated; 114 minutes; American release date: August 15, 2008

Cast

Gabrielle Aurore Deneige	**Ludivine Sagnier**
Paul André Claude Gaudens	**Benoît Magimel**
Charles Denis	**François Berléand**
Capucine Jamet	**Mathilda May**
Geneviève Gaudens	**Caroline Sihol**
Marie Deneige	**Marie Bunel**
Dona Saint-Denis	**Valeria Cavalli**
Denis Deneige	**Etienne Chicot**
Stéphane Lorbach	**Thomas Chabrol**
Gérard Briançon	**Jean-Marie Winling**
Philippe Le Riou	**Didier Bénureau**

Eduard Baer (Eduard), Clémence Bretécher (Joséphine Gaudens), Charley Fouquet (Eléonore Gaudens), Hubert Saint-Macary (Bernard Violet), Alain Bauguil (Louis Giraudet), Emanuel Booz (Alban), Stéphane Debac (Antoine Volte), Pierre-François Dumeniaud (Monsieur Junot), Cécile Maistre (Cécile)

A television weather girl finds herself desired by a successful veteran writer and a spoiled heir.

Benoît Magimel, Ludivine Sagnier

Ivan Barnev © Sony Classics

Martin Huba, Ivan Barnev

Ivan Barnev, Julia Jentsch

I SERVED THE KING OF ENGLAND

(SONY CLASSICS) a.k.a. *Obsluhoval jsem anglického krále*; Producers, Robert Schaffer, Andrea Metcalfe; Executive Producer, Rudolf Biermann; Director/Screenplay, Jirí Menzel; Based on the novel by Bohumil Hrabal; Photography, Jaromir Sofr; Designer, Milan Bycek; Costumes, Milan Corba; Music, Ales Brezina; Editor, Jiri Brozek; a Bioscop, AQS, TV Nova, Barrandov Studio, UPP (Universal Production Partners) (Czech Republic), Magic Box Slovakia (Slovakia) production; Czech-Slovakian; Dolby; Color; Rated R; 118 minutes; American release date: August 29, 2008

Cast
Jan Díte, younger	**Ivan Barnev**
Jan Díte, older	**Oldrich Kaiser**
Liza	**Julia Jentsch**
Shrivánek	**Martin Huba**
Walden	**Marián Labuda**
Professor	**Milan Lasica**
Hotelier Brandejs	**Josef Abrhám**
Hotel Boss	**Jirí Lábus**
Waiter Karel	**Jaromír Dulava**
General	**Pavel Nový**
Stock Marketeer	**István Szabó**
Abyssinian Emperor	**Tonya Graves**
Tichota	**Rudolf Hrusínský**

Petr Ctvrtnícek (Stockbroker), Jirí Sesták (Waiter), Zdenek Zák (Militiaman), Emília Vásáryová (Mrs. Rajska), Zuzana Fialová (Marcela), Václav Chalupa (Hrdlicka), Petra Hrebícková (Jaruska), Eva Kalvoská (Wanda), Sárka Petruzelová (Julinka)

Ivan Barnev (left, standing)

Jan Díte rises from waiter to the owner of a posh Prague hotel, all the while remaining unware of the changing political situation around him.

Claire Forlani, Ciarán Hinds

Jamie Bell

Jamie Bell, Sophia Myles

Jamie Bell © Magnolia Films

MISTER FOE

(MAGNOLIA) a.k.a. *Hallam Foe*; Producer, Gillian Berrie; Executive Producers, Matthew Justice, David Mackenzie, Peter Carlton, Carole Sheridan, Lenny Crooks, Peter Touche, Duncan Reid; Director, David Mackenzie; Screenplay, Ed Whitmore, David Mackenzie; Based on the novel *Hallam Foe* by Peter Jinks; Photography, Giles Nuttgens; Designer, Tom Sayer; Costumes, Trisha Biggar; Editor, Colin Monie; Casting, Kathleen Crawford, Des Hamilton; a Film 4, Ingenious Film Partners, Scottish Screen and Glasgow Film Finance Ltd. Presentation; British; Dolby; Super 35 Widescreen; Deluxe color; Not rated; 95 minutes; American release date: September 5, 2008

Cast

Hallam Foe	**Jamie Bell**
Kate Breck	**Sophia Myles**
Julius Foe	**Ciarán Hinds**
Alasdair	**Jamie Sives**
Raymond	**Maurice Roëves**
Andy	**Ewen Bremner**
Verity Foe	**Claire Forlani**
Jenny	**Ruthie Milne**
Carl	**John Paul Lawler**
Lucy	**Lucy Holt**
Kilt Man	**Malcolm Shields**
Raincoat Man	**Paul Blair**

John Comerford, Gerry Cleary (Grumpy Glaswegians), Neil McKinven (Police Officer), Stuart Hepburn (Police Inspector), Kirsty Shepheard (Alasdair's Wife)

A trouble young man with a voyeuristic habit runs away from his wealthy family to Edinburgh where he becomes obsessed with a young woman who bears a striking resemblance to his late mother.

A SECRET

(STRAND) a.k.a. *Un Secret*; Producer, Yves Marmion; Coproducer, Alfred Hurmer; Director, Claude Miller; Screenplay, Claude Miller, Natalie Carter; Based on the novel by Philippe Grimbert; Photography, Gerard de Battista; Designer, Jean-Pierre Koht-Svelko; Costumes, Jacqueline Bouchard; Music, Zbigniew Priesner; Editor, Veronique Lange; Casting, Elsa Pharaon; a UCG YM, Integral Film production, in association with France 3 Cinema; French; Dolby; Color/Black and white; Not rated; 105 minutes; American release date: September 5, 2008

Cast

Tania	**Cécile De France**
Maxime Nathan Grinberg	**Patrick Bruel**
Hannah Gold Sirn Grinberg	**Ludivine Sagnier**
Louise	**Julie Depardieu**
François Grimbert	**Mathieu Amalric**
Esther	**Nathalie Boutefeu**
Commander Béraud	**Yves Jacques**
Guillaume	**Yves Verhoeven**
Joseph	**Sam Garbarski**
Simon	**Orlando Nicoletti**
Francois (age 7)	**Valentin Vigourt**
Francois (age 14)	**Quentin Dubuis**

Myriam Fuks (Hannah's Mother), Robert Plagnol (Robert), Michael Israel (Hannah's Father), Eric Gordon (Serge Klarsfeld), Justine Jouxtel (Rebecca), Timothée Laissard (Paul), Annie Savarin (Mathilde), Arthur Mazet (Sly Pupil), Philippe Grimbert (Smuggler)

Young François discovers the truth behind how his parents came together under tragic circumstances during the German occupation of France.

Patrick Bruel, Mathieu Amalric © Strand Releasing

Ludivine Sagnier, Nathalie Boutefeu, Julie Depardieu

Patrick Bruel, Valentin Vigourt

Patrick Bruel, Cécile De France

Keira Knightley, Hayley Atwell

Charlotte Rampling, Ralph Fiennes, Hayley Atwell, Keira Knightley
© *Paramount Vantage*

Ralph Fiennes, Keira Knightley

THE DUCHESS

(PARAMOUNT VANTAGE) Producers, Gabrielle Tana, Michael Kuhn; Executive Producers, Francois Ivernel, Cameron McCracken, Christine Langan, David M. Thompson, Carolyn Marks-Blackwood, Amanda Foremann; Coproducers, Colleen Woodcock, Alexandra Arlango; Director, Saul Dibb; Screenplay, Jeffrey Hatcher, Anders Thomas Jensen, Saul Dibb; Based on the book *Georgianna, Duchess of Devonshire* by Amanda Foreman; a Paramount Vantage/Pathé, BBC Films presentation, in association with Pathé Renn Production and BIM Distribuzione, of a Qwert Films (U.K.)/Magnolia Mae Films (U.S.) production; British-American; Dolby; Panavision; Deluxe color; Rated PG-13; 109 minutes; American release date: September 19, 2008

Cast

Georgianna Spencer (Duchess of Devonshire)	**Keira Knightley**
William Cavendish, Duke of Devonshire	**Ralph Fiennes**
Lady Spencer	**Charlotte Rampling**
Charles Grey	**Dominic Cooper**
Lady Elizabeth "Bess" Foster	**Hayley Atwell**
Charles Fox	**Simon McBurney**
Richard Brinsley Sheridan	**Aidan McArdle**
General Grey	**John Shrapnel**
Heaton	**Alistair Petrie**
Dr. Neville	**Patrick Godfrey**
Speechmaker	**Michael Medwin**
Macaroni	**Justin Edwards**
Sir James Hare	**Richard McCabe**
Devonshire House Servant	**Calvin Dean**
Devonshire House Maid	**Hannah Stokely**

Emily Jewell (Nanny), Sir P Bruce Makinnon (Sir Peter Teazle), Georgia King (Lady Teazle), Luke Norris (Footman), Eva Hrela (Charlotte, age 3), Poppy Wigglesworth (Charlotte, age 10), Emily Cohen (Harriet, Countess of Bessborough), Mercy Fiennes Tiffin (Little G), Sebastian Applewhite (Augustus), Angus McEwan (Lord Robert), Kate Burdette (Lady Harriet), Laura Stevely (Lady Elizabeth), Ben Garlick (Lord Ambrose), Max Bennett (Lord Walter), Camilla Arfwedson (Lady Charlotte), Fiona Sheehan (Young Girl in Theater), Sarah Wyatt (Servant Girl), Thomas Arnold (Dealer), Gilbert Wynne (Althorpe Servant), Richard Curzon (Heaton's Clerk), Sophia Johnston, Katerina Tana (Guests at Lady Melbourne's Bal

After her parents arrange for her to marry the fifth Duke of Devonshire, Georgiana Spencer realizes she is now trapped in a loveless marriage to a cold and unfaithful husband who expects nothing from her other than a male heir.

2008 Academy Award winner for Best Costume Design.

Dominic Cooper, Keira Knightley

Julianne Moore, Mark Ruffalo

Danny Glover

Mark Ruffalo, Julianne Moore © Miramax Films

BLINDNESS

(MIRAMAX) Producers, Niv Fichman, Andrea Barata Ribeiro, Sonoko Sakai; Executive Producers, Gail Egan, Simon Channing Williams, Tom Yoda, Akira Ishii, Victory Loewy; Coproducers, Bel Berlinck, Sari Friedland; Director, Fernando Meirelles; Screenplay, Don McKellar; Based on the novel by José Saramago; Photography, César Charlone; Designer, Tulé Peake; Costumes, Renée April; Music, Marco Antônio Guimarães, Uakti; Editor, Daniel Rezende; Casting, Susie Figgis, Deirdre Bowen; a Rhombus Media (Canada)/02 Filmes (Brazil)/Bee Vine Pictures (Japan) production, presented in association with Alliance Films, Fox Filmes do Brasil, Gaga Communications, Asmik Ace Entertainment, Mikado, IFF/CINV, Telefilm Canada, Ancine Potboiler Productions with the participation of T.Y. Limited, Corus Entertainment, FIAT, BINDES, C&A; Canadian-Brazilian-Japanese; Dolby; Technicolor; Rated R; 120 minutes; American release date: October 3, 2008

Cast

Doctor's Wife	**Julianne Moore**
Doctor	**Mark Ruffalo**
Man with Black Eye Patch	**Danny Glover**
Bartender/King of Ward Three	**Gael Garcia Bernal**
Woman with Dark Glasses	**Alice Braga**
First Blind Man	**Yusuke Iseya**
First Blind Man's Wife	**Yoshino Kimura**
Thief	**Don McKellar**
Accountant	**Maury Chaykin**
Boy	**Mitchell Nye**

Jason Bermingham, Ciça Meirelles (Drivers), Eduardo Semerjian, Antôbui Fragoso, Lilian Blanc (Concerned Pedestrians), Douglas Silva, Daniel Zettel (Onlookers), Joe Pingue (Taxi Driver), Susan Coyne (Receptionist), Fabiana Gugli (Mother of the Boy), Joe Cobden (Policeman), Mpho Koaho (Pharmacist's Assistant), Sari Friedland (Woman in Bar), Tom Melissis (Engineer), Tracy Wright (Thief's Wife), Amanda Hiebert (Maid), Jorge Molina (Hotel Security Guard), Patrick Garrow (Hotel Assistant Manager), Gerry Mendicino (Silver Haired Doctor), Matt Gordon (Minister's Assistant), Sandra Oh (Minister of Health), Anthero Montenegro, Fernando Patau (Cops), Otavio Martins (Police Captain), João Velho (Ambulance Attendant), Marvin Karon (Announcer), Joseph Motiki (Guard), Johnny Goltz (Soldier), Robert Bidaman (Minister's Advisor), Niv Fichman (Israeli Scientist), Oscar Hsu (Prominent Opthamologist), Martha Burns (Woman with Insomnia), Scott Anderson (Meek Inmate), Michael Mahonen (Sergeant), Joris Jarsky (Hooligan), Billy Otis (Hoodlum), Linlyn Lue (Emmisary from Ward Two), Toni Ellwand, Mariah Inger, Nadia Litz (Women of Ward One), Isai Rivera Blas, Rick Demas, Kelly Fiddick, Matt Fitzgerald, Mike G-Yohannes, Norm Owen (Men of Ward Three), Jackie Brown, Victoria Fodor, Agi Gallus, Bathsheba Garnett, Alice Poon (Women of Ward Two), Plínio Soares (Hulking Scavenger), Rodrigo Arijon, Mel Ciocolato, Heraldo Firmino, Carol Hubner, Fernando Macário, Eduardo Parisi, Rodrigo Pessin (Scavengers), Domingos Antonio (Preacher), Barnie & Jim (Dog of Tears)

Panic ensues when the majority of the population inexplicably goes blind and those suffering are promptly incarcerated.

Gael Garcia Bernal

HOW TO LOSE FRIENDS & ALIENATE PEOPLE

(MGM) Producers, Stephen Woolley, Elizabeth Karlsen; Executive Producers, Tessa Ross, Paul White, Simon Fawcett, Gary Smith, Brian Gilmore; Coproducers, Toby Young, Laurie Borg; Director, Robert Weide; Screenplay, Peter Straughan; Based on the book by Toby Young; Photography, Oliver Stapleton; Designer, John Beard; Costumes, Annie Hardinge; Music, David Arnold; Editor, David Freeman; Casting, Jina Jay, Justine Baddeley, Kim Davis-Wagner; a PI Pictures, Intandem Films, Film 4 and the U.K. Film Council presentation in association with Aramid Entertainment and Lipsync Productions presentation of a Stephen Woolley/Elizabeth Karlsen/Number 9 Films production in association with Audley Films; British; Dolby; Deluxe color; Rated R; 109 minutes; American release date: October 3, 2008

Cast

Sidney Young	**Simon Pegg**
Alison Olsen	**Kirsten Dunst**
Clayton Harding	**Jeff Bridges**
Lawrence Maddox	**Danny Huston**
Eleanor Johnson	**Gillian Anderson**
Sophie Maes	**Megan Fox**
Mrs. Kowalski	**Miriam Margolyes**

Bill Paterson (Richard Young), Max Mingella (Vincent Lepak), Diana Kent (Rachel Petkoff), Kelan Pannell (Young Sidney), Janette Scott (Sidney's Mother), Kelly Jo Charge (Apollo Awards Presenter), Christian Smith (Apollo Awards Guest), Katherine Parkinson (PR Woman), Felicity Montagu (Clipboard Nazi), Thandie Newton, Daniel Craig, Kate Winslet (Themselves), John Lightbody (Assistant Hotel Manager), Ian Bonar, James Corden, Fenella Woolgar, Chris O'Dowd, Hugh Thompson, Emily Thorling (Postmodern Review Staff), Miquel Brown (Clayton's Assistant), Nathalie Cox (Woman in Bar), Sam Douglas (Barman), Charlotte Devaney (Bobbie), Gillian King (Sharp's Assistant), Margo Stilley (Ingrid), Isabella Calthorpe (Anna), Hannah Waddingham (Elizabeth Maddox), Emily Denniston (Maddox's Assistant), Ashley Madekew (Vicky), Lisa McAllister (Sophie Maes' Assistant), Brona C. Titley (Nun–Trailer), Charles De Bromhead (Young Priest–Trailer), Jane Perry (Mrs. Harding), Connie Wheeler, Lara Edmunds (Harding Children), Allen Lidkey, Robert B. Weide (July 4th Party Guests), Nathan Nolan (July 4th Party Waiter), Andy Lucas (Wizard/Dentist), Bill Paterson (Richard Young), Alexandra Aitken (Nightclub Girl), Sarah Mennell (Flight Desk Attendant), Liat Baruch, Eivind Karlsen (Couple on Blanket)

A boorish British journalist makes his share of enemies when he joins the staff of a top New York magazine.

Jeff Bridges, Simon Pegg © MGM

Stranded © *Zeitgeist Films*

STRANDED: I'VE COME FROM A PLANE THAT CRASHED IN THE MOUNTAINS

(ZEITGEIST) Producer, Marc Silvera; Coproducer, Helen Coldefy; Director/Screenplay, Gonzalo Arijón; Photography, César Charlone, Pablo Hernán Zubizaretta; Music, Florencia di Concilio-Perrin; Editors, Claudio Hughes, Samuel Lajus, Alice Larry; a coproduction of ARTE France–Ethan Productions–La Realidad–The ITVS International Media Development Fund (IMDF) in association with Alea Doc & Films (Barcelona), Morocha Films (Buenos Aires), Sylicone (Paris); French-Spanish; Color/black and white; Video; 16mm; Not rated; 126 minutes; American release date: October 22, 2008.
Documentary on how sixteen Uruguyan rugby players managed to survive after the plane carrying them crashed in the Andes

With

Jose Pedro Algorta, Roberto Canessa, Alfredo Delgado, Daniel Fernández, Roberto François, Roy Harley, José-Luis Inclarte, Alvaro Mangino, Javier Methol, Carlos Páez, Fernando Parrado, Ramón Sabella, Adolfo Strauch, Eduardo Strauch, Antonin Vinzintín, Gustavo Zerbino (The 16 Survivors); José Gilberto Bravo Castro, Laura Inés Canessa, Antonio Caruso, Juan Catalán, Sergio Catalán, Jorge Massa, Juan Pedro Nicola, Mateo Nicola, Carlos Páez-Vilaró, Madelón Rodríguez, Alejandra Strauch, Gustavo Zerbino Payssé, Lucas Zerbino Payssé, Martin Zerbino Payssé, and Sebastian Zerbino Payssé

ROCKNROLLA

(WARNER BROS.) Producers, Joel Silver, Susan Downey, Steve Clark-Hall, Guy Ritchie; Executive Producers, Steve Richards, Navid McIlhargey; Director/Screenplay, Guy Ritchie; Photography, David Higgs; Designer, Richard Bridgland; Costumes, Suzie Hartman; Music, Steve Isles; Music Supervisor, Ian Neil; Editor, James Herbert; Casting, Reg Poerscout-Edgerton; a Castle Rock Entertainment production, in association with Toff Guy Films; British; Dolby; Technicolor; Rated R; 114 minutes; American release date: October 8, 2008

Jeremy Piven, Chris Bridges © Warner Bros.

Cast

One Two	**Gerard Butler**
Lenny Cole	**Tom Wilkinson**
Stella	**Thandie Newton**
Archy	**Mark Strong**
Mumbles	**Idris Elba**
Handsome Bob	**Tom Hardy**
Uri Obamavich	**Karel Roden**
Johnny Quid	**Toby Kebbell**
Roman	**Jeremy Piven**
Mickey	**Chris Bridges**
Councillor	**Jimi Mistry**
Cookie	**Matt King**
Tank	**Nonso Anozie**

Charlotte Armer (Nurse), Gemma Arterton (June), David Bark-Jones (Bertie), Geoff Bell (Fred the Head), Morne Botes (Jimmy), Jamie Campbell Bower (Rocker), David Leon (Malcolm), Andy Linden (Waster), Roland Manookian (Bandy), Dragan Micanovic (Victor), Tiffany Mulheron (Jackie), Laurence Richardson, James Puddephatt (Policemen), Blake Ritson (Johnny Sloane), Thomas Rooke (Waiter), Michael Ryan (Pete), Anton Saunders (Copper), David Sterne (Barman), Robert Stone (Bouncer), Johan van Vuuren (Sloan 2), Bronson Webb (Paul)

One Two and his gang borrow money from crime boss Lenny Cole in order to purchase some property, only to have Cole snatch the land from under them and still demand the payment.

Jimi Mistry, Tom Wilkinson

Thandie Newton, Gerard Butler

Toby Kebbell

Sally Hawkins

Eddie Marsan, Sally Hawkins

Sally Hawkins, Alexis Zegerman

HAPPY-GO-LUCKY

(MIRAMAX) Producer, Simon Channing Williams; Executive Producers, James Clayton, Gail Egan, David Garrett, Duncan Reid, Tessa Ross; Coproducer, Georgina Lowe; Director/Screenplay, Mike Leigh; Photography, Dick Pope; Designer, Mark Tidesley; Costumes, David Crossman; Music, Gary Yershon; Editor, Jim Clark; Casting, Nina Gold; a Summit Entertainment, Ingenious film Partners, Film 4, U.K. Film Council presentation of a Thin Man Films production; British; Dolby; Widescreen; Color; Rated R; 118 minutes; American release date: October 10, 2008

Cast

Poppy	**Sally Hawkins**
Zoe	**Alexis Zegerman**
Dawn	**Andrea Riseborough**
Alice	**Sinead Matthews**
Suzy	**Kate O'Flynn**
Tash	**Sarah Niles**
Scott	**Eddie Marsan**
Heather	**Sylvestra Le Touzel**
Flamenco Instructor	**Karina Fernandez**
Tim	**Samuel Roukin**
Helen	**Caroline Martin**
Jamie	**Oliver Maltman**
Bookseller	**Elliot Cowan**
Suzy's Boyfriend	**Joseph Kloska**
Ezra	**Nonso Anozie**
Tramp	**Stanley Townsend**

Trevor Cooper (Patient), Philip Arditti, Viss Elliot (Flamenco Students), Jack MacGeachin (Nick), Charlie Duffield (Charlie), Ayotunde Williams (Ayotunde)

Poppy, a relentlessly optimistic school teacher, has a sizable effect on those she comes in contact with, including a short-tempered driving instructor.

This film received an Oscar nomination for original screenplay.

Sally Hawkins © Miramax Films

Elsa Zylberstein, Kristin Scott Thomas

Kristin Scott Thomas, Laurent Grévil

Lise Ségur, Kristin Scott Thomas
© Sony Classics

I'VE LOVED YOU SO LONG

(SONY CLASSICS) a.k.a. *Il y a longtemps que je t'aime*; Producer, Yves Marmion; Executive Producer, Sylvestre Guarino; Coproducer, Alfred Hürmer; Director/Screenplay, Philippe Claudel; Photography, Jérôme Alméras; Art Director, Samuel Deshors; Costumes, Jacqueline Bouchard; Music, Jean-Louis Aubert; Editor, Virginie Bruant; a UCG YM (France)/Integral Film (Germany) production, in association with France 3 Cinema, with the participation of Canal Plus, TPS Star; French-German; Dolby; Color; Rated PG-13; 115 minutes; American release date: October 24, 2008

Cast

Juliette Fontaine	**Kristin Scott Thomas**
Léa	**Elsa Zylberstein**
Luc	**Serge Hazanavicius**
Michel	**Laurent Grévil**
Captain Fauré	**Frédéric Pierrot**
P'tit Lys	**Lise Ségur**
Papy Paul	**Jean-Claude Arnaud**
Samir	**Mouss Zouheyri**
Kaisha	**Souad Mouchrik**
The Teacher	**Catherine Hosmalin**
Juliette and Léa's Mother	**Claire Johnston**
Gérard	**Olivier Cruveiller**
Emélia	**Lily-Rose**

Nicole Dubois (Hospital DRH), Laurent Claret (Hospital Director), Marcel Ouendeno (Bamakalé), Gérard Barbonnet (Monsieur Luien), Jérémie Cuvillault (The Young Inspector), Kevin Lipka (Student), Bruno Raffaelli (Monsieur Dupuis), Pascal Demolon (Man in Bar), Aïcha Mimouni (Waiter in Bar), Catherine Antoine (Bimbo Lucien), Valentin Jalet (Baby Kaisha), Claire Lefevre (Marie-Paule Voice), Pascal Bordes (Patrick), Alain Buron (François), Isabelle Destrez (Muriel), Nathalie Hamel (Nathalie), Dominique Kucharzewski (Anne), Marc Léonian (Yves), Eva Quinto (Florence), Elio Guarino, Alixane Pachot, Laurine Pachot, Hannah Peytavi-Müller, Olga Peytavi-Müller, Théo Urbauer, Alexandre Voisin, Maryse Voisin, Angèle Zidi, Paul Zidi (Children)

Léa agrees to take in the older sister she has never really known, a former doctor who has spent fifteen years in prison for killing her own son.

Kristin Scott Thomas

LET THE RIGHT ONE IN

(MAGNET) a.k.a. *Låt den rätte komma in*; Producers, John Nordling, Carl Molinder; Coproducers, Gunnar Carlsson, Per-Erik Svensson, Lena Rehnberg, Ricard Constantinou; Director, Tomas Alfredson; Screenplay, John Ajvide Lindqvist, based on his novel; Photography, Hoyte van Hoytema; Designer, Eva Noren; Costumes, Maria Strid; Music, Johan Soderqvist; Editors, Dino Jonaster, Tomas Alfredson; Casting, Anna Zakrisson, Maggie Windstrand; an EFTI production, in association with Filmpool Nord, Sandrew Metronome, Distribution Sveirge, SVT, Chimney Pot, Fido Film, Ljudligan, WAG; Swedish; Dolby; Super 35 Widescreen; Color; Rated R; 114 minutes; American release date: October 24, 2008

Ilka Nord

Cast

Oskar	**Kåre Hedebrant**
Eli	**Lina Leandersson**
Håkan	**Per Ragnar**
Erik	**Henrik Dahl**
Yvonne	**Karin Bergquist**
Lacke	**Peter Carlberg**
Virginia	**Ika Nord**
Jocke	**Mikael Rahm**
Gösta	**Karl Robert Lindgren**
Morgan	**Anders Peedu**
Larry	**Paul Olofsson**
Magister Avila	**Cayetano Ruiz**
Conny	**Patrik Rydmark**
Andreas	**Johan Sömnes**
Martin	**Mikael Erhardsson**
Jimmy	**Rasmus Luthander**

Sören Källstigen, Malin Cederbladh, Lena Nilsson, Bernt Östman, Kajsa Linderholm, Adam Stone, Jonas Kruse, Ingemar Raukola, Kent Rishaug, Linus Hannu, Tom Ljungman, Fredrik Ramel, Christoffer Bohlin, Julia Nilsson, Elin Almén, Bengt Bylund

A bullied twelve-year-old boy finds a soul-mate when he befriends a mysterious girl who turns out to be a vampire.

Kåre Hedebrant

Lina Leandersson

Kåre Hedebrant © Magnet

Hippolyte Girardot, Jeanne Moreau © Kino

Hippolyte Girardot, Emmanuelle Devos

Samuel Cohen, Jeanne Moreau

ONE DAY YOU'LL UNDERSTAND

(KINO) a.k.a. *Plus tard*; Producers, Serge Moati, Nicole Collet, Laurent Truchot; Director, Amos Gitai; Screenplay, Jérôme Cléments, Dan Franck, from an adaptation by Amos Gitai and Marie Jose Sanselme of the book by Jérôme Cléments; Photography, Caroline Champetier; Designer, Emmanuel Chauvigny; Costumes, Moira Douguet; Music, Louis Sclavis; Editor, Isabelle Ingold; an Image et Compaigne, France 2 (France)/NDR (Germany)/Agav Films (Israel) production; French-German-Israeli; Dolby; Color; Not rated; 89 minutes; American release date: October 31, 2008

Cast

Victor Bastien	**Hippolyte Girardot**
Rivka	**Jeanne Moreau**
Françoise	**Emmaneulle Devos**
Tania	**Dominique Blanc**
Sipa Gornick	**Denise Aron-Schropfer**
Georges Gornick	**Daniel Duval**
German Officer	**Jan Oliver Schroeder**
Lewis	**Samuel Cohen**
Esther	**Mouana Soualem**
Pharmacist	**Serge Moati**
Superintendent	**Max Denes**
German Officer	**Jan Oliver Schroeder**

French businessman Victor Bastien becomes determined to find out the truth behind his Jewish parents' actions during World War II.

Hippolyte Girardot

Asa Butterfield © Miramax Films

Asa Butterfield, Vera Farmiga

Jack Scanlon, Asa Butterfield

David Thewlis

THE BOY IN THE STRIPED PAJAMAS

(MIRAMAX) Producer, David Heyman; Executive Producers, Mark Herman, Christine Langan; Coproducer, Rosie Alison; Hungarian Coproducers, Gabor Varadi, Peter Miskolczi; Photography, Benoit Delhomme; Designer, Martin Childs; Costumes, Natalie Ward; Music, James Horner; Editor, Michael Ellis; Visual Effects Supervisor, Mike Ellis; Stunts, Gyorgy Kives; Casting, Leo Davis, Pippa Hall; a Miramax Films presentation, in association with BBC Films, of a Heyday Films production; British-American; Dolby; Rated PG-13; 94 minutes; American release date: November 7, 2008

Cast
Mother	Vera Farmiga
Father	David Thewlis
Lt. Kotler	Rupert Friend
Pavel	David Hayman
Bruno	Asa Butterfield
Shmuel	Jack Scanlon
Gretel	Amber Beattie
Grandma	Sheila Hancock
Grandpa	Richard Johnson
Herr Liszt	Jim Norton
Maria	Cara Horgan
Leon	Zac Mattoon O'Brien
Martin	Domonkos Németh
Karl	Henry Kingsmill
Berlin Cook	Zsuzsa Holl
Lars	László Áron
Meinberg	Iván Verebély
Schultz	Béla Fesztbaum
Heinz	Attila Egyed

László Nádasi, László Quitt, Zsolt Sáfár Kovács (Kapos), Gabor Harsay (Elderly Jewish Man)

When his father is placed in charge of a concentration camp, eight-year-old Bruno ends up befriending a prisoner of the same age, unaware of the horrific nature of his new friend's circumstances.

JCVD

(PEACE ARCH ENTERTAINMENT) Producer, Sidonie Dumas; Coproducers, Jani Thiltges, Arlette Zylberberg, Patrick Quinet; Executive Producers, Jean-Claude Van Damme, Marc Fiszman; Director, Mabrouk El Mechri; Screenplay, Mabrouk El Mechri, Frédéric Bénudis, Christophe Turpin; Based on a concept by Frederic Taddei, Vincent Ravalec; Photography, Pierre-Yves Bastard; Art Director, Andre Fonsny; Music, Gast Waltzing; Music Supervising, Varda Kakon; Editor, Kako Kelber; Casting, Francoise Menidrey; a Gaumount (France), Artemis Prods. (Belgium), and Samsa Films (Luxembourg) production; French-Belgian-Luxembourg; Dolby; Panavision; Color; Rated R; 96 minutes; American release date: November 7, 2008

Cast
JCVD	**Jean-Claude Van Damme**
Bruges	**Francçois Damiens**
Man with Bonnet	**Zinedine Soualem**
Vigile	**Karim Belkhadra**
Man in His 30s	**Jean-François Wolff**
Clerk	**Annie Paulicevich**
Budapest Film Widow	**Valerie Bodson**
Lieutenant Smith	**Herve Sogne**

Rock Chen (Asian Director), Huifang Wang (Asian Translator), John Flanders (Ex-Woman Lawyer), Renata Kamara (Judge Tribunal, Los Angeles), Mourade Zeguendi (Client in Video Club), Vincent Lecuyer (Clerk in Video Club), Jenny De Chez "The Oldies" (Taxiwoman JCVD), Patrick Steltzer (Police Officer #1), Bernard Eylenbosch (Telecom Technician), Pascale Lefebvre (Képi 2), Jacky Lambert (Képi 3), Norbert Rutili (Perthier), Olivier Bisback (Doctor GIGN, Eric), Armelle Gysen, Caroline Donnellyl, Eric Boever (Journalists), Michel Bouris (Cigarette Hostage), Raphaelle Lubansu, Claudio Dos Santos (Hostages), Hippolyte Eloy (Son of Clerk), Charles Suberville (Injured Hostage), Alan Rossett (Leon Bernstein), Saskia Flanders (Daughter of JCVD), Jesse Joe Walsh (Agent of JCVD), Bella Wajnberg (Woman at Police Station), Jerome Varanfrain (Képi Police Station), Liliane Becker (Mother of JCVD), Francois Beukelaers (Father of JCVD), François De Brigode (Television Studio Journalist), Gregory Jones (Prisoner), Paul Rockenbrod (Tobey Wood), Dean Gregory (Movie Director), Alice Hubbal (Tobey's Assistant), Steve Preston (JCVD's Prop Manager), Janine Horsburgh (JCVD's Assistant), Isabelle De Hertogh (Toy Store Manager), Ingrid Heiderscheidt (Grandmother of Toy Manager), Fjoralba Cuni (Nightclub Waitress), Yves Girard (Assistant)

His career and personal life already in turmoil, action star Jean-Claude plunges into further trouble when he finds himself in the middle of a post office heist.

Jean-Claude Van Damme © Peace Arch Entertainment

Brenda Fricker, Joss Ackland, Imelda Staunton, Hayley Atwell, Vanessa Redgrave

HOW ABOUT YOU

(STRAND) Producers, Noel Pearson, Sarah Radclyffe; Executive Producers, Bill Godfrey, Paul Brett (Prescience Films), Tim Smith (Prescience Films); Director, Anthony Byrne; Screenplay, Jean Pasley; Photography, Des Whelan; Designer, Tom McCullough; Costumes, Hazel Webb-Crozier; Line Producer, John McDonnell; Casting, Nuala Moiselle, Frnak Moiselle; a Ferndale Films presentation, in association with Bankside Films and Head Gear Films; Irish; Dolby; Panavision; Color; Not rated; 91 minutes; American release date: November 14, 2008

Cast
Ellie Harris	**Hayley Atwell**
Georgia Platts	**Vanessa Redgrave**
Donald Vanston	**Joss Ackland**
Heather Nightingale	**Brenda Fricker**
Hazel Nightingale	**Imelda Staunton**
Kate Harris	**Orla Brady**
Alice Peterson	**Joan O'Hara**
Nuse Healy	**Elizabeth Moynihan**

Doreen Keogh (Mary), Kevin Flood (William), Danielle Ryan (Maria), Tim McDonnell (Man with Battered Hat), Paschal Friel (Minibus Driver), Darragh Kelly (Mr. Evans), Ryan O'Connor (Dan), Kevin Maher, Andrew Canning (Young Boys), Patricia Martin (Vegetable Seller), Fionnuala Murphy (Assistant Vegetable Seller), Mick Nolan (Postman)

During the Christmas holidays, footloose Ellie Harris is left in charge of a home for seniors run by her sister, taking care of its four grumpy residents.

Brenda Fricker, Imelda Staunton © Strand Releasing

A CHRISTMAS TALE

(IFC FILMS) a.k.a. *Une conte de Noël*; Executive Producer, Martine Cassinelli; Director, Arnaud Desplechin; Screenplay, Arnaud Desplechin, Emmanuel Bourdieu; Inspired by the book *La greffe* by Jacques Ascher and Jean-Pierre Jouet; Photography, Eric Gautier; Art Director, Dan Bevan; Costumes, Natalie Raoul; Music, Gregoire Hetzel; Editor, Laurence Briaud; Casting, Stephane Touitou; a Why Not Prods. presentation of a Why Not, Franc 2 Cinema, Wild Bunch, Bac Films production, in association with Canal Plus, CineCinema, CNC; French; Dolby; Super 35 Widescreen; Color; Not rated; 152 minutes; American release date: November 14, 2008

Chiara Mastroianni, Melvil Poupaud

Cast

Junon Vuillard	**Catherine Deneuve**
Abel, Junon's Husband	**Jean-Paul Roussillon**
Elizabeth, their oldest child	**Anne Consigny**
Henri, their middle child	**Mathieu Amalric**
Ivan, their youngest child	**Melvil Poupaud**
Claude, Elizabeth's husband	**Hippolyte Girardot**
Faunia, Henri's lover	**Emmanuelle Devos**
Sylvia, Ivan's wife	**Chiara Mastroianni**
Simon, Junon's nephew, the painter cousin	**Laurent Capelluto**
Paul, Elizabeth and Claude's son	**Emile Berling**
Basile, Ivan and Sylvia's son	**Thomas Obled**
Baptiste, Ivan and Sylvia's son	**Clément Obled**
Rosaimée, Abel's mother's girlfriend	**Françoise Bertin**
Spetafora, the family friend at Roubaix	**Samir Guesmi**
Dr. Zraïdi, the oncologist	**Azize Kabouche**

Coming together for Christmas, Junon Vuillard's extended family must decide who among them who might be the compatible donor for the bone-marrow transplant Junon needs to extend her life by a few years.

Anne Consigny, Hippolyte Girardot, Catherine Deneuve

Mathieu Amalric

Jean-Paul Roussillon, Catherine Deneuve © IFC Films

QUANTUM OF SOLACE

(MGM/COLUMBIA) Producers, Michael G. Wilson, Barbara Broccoli; Executive Producers, Anthony Waye, Calium McDougall; Director, Marc Forster; Screenplay, Paul Haggis, Neal Purvis, Robert Wade; Photography, Roberto Schaefer; Designer, Dennis Gassner; Costumes, Louise Frogley; Music, David Arnold; Editors, Matt Chesse, Richard Pearson; Special Effect Supervisor, Chris Corbould; Stunts, Gary Powell; Casting, Debbie McWilliams; an Albert R. Broccoli's Eon Prods. presentation; British-American; Dolby; Super 35 Widescreen; Color; Rated PG-13; 105 minutes; American release date: November 14, 2008

Joaquin Cosio, Mathieu Amalric, Anatole Taubman, Jesús Ochoa

Cast

James Bond	**Daniel Craig**
Camille	**Olga Kurylenko**
Dominic Greene	**Mathieu Amalric**
M	**Judi Dench**
Rene Mathis	**Giancarlo Giannini**
Agent Fields	**Gemma Arterton**
Felix Leiter	**Jeffrey Wright**
Gregg Beam	**David Harbour**
Mr. White	**Jesper Christensen**
Elvis	**Anatole Taubman**
Tanner	**Rory Kinnear**
Foreign Secretary	**Tim Pigott-Smith**
General Medrano	**Joaquin Cosio**
Colonel of Police	**Fernando Guillén Cuervo**
Lieutenant Orso	**Jesús Ochoa**
Gemma	**Lucrezia Lante della Rovere**
Mitchell	**Glenn Foster**
Guy Haines	**Paul Ritter**
Yusef	**Simon Kassianides**
Corinne	**Stana Katic**
Mr. Slate	**Neil Jackson**

Daniel Craig, Gemma Arterton

Oona Chaplin (Perla de las Dunas Receptionist), Brendan O'Hea (Forensics Tech), Rufus Wright (Treasury Agent), Kari Patrice Coley (Hotel Dessalines Clerk), Sarah Hadland (Ocean Sky Receptionist), Jake Seal (Bartender on Virgin Flight), Peñarandam Felix (Bolivian Taxi Driver), Emiliano Valdés (Andean Grand Hotel Receptionist), Daniel da Silva (Andean Grand Hotel Porter), Elizabeth Arciniega (Mr. White's Girlfriend), Alessio Sossas (Carabinieri on Radio), Mark Wakeling (M16 Agent), Susana Alboronz (Woman with Bucket), Jacques Duckins (Haitian Gang Member), Anthony Hansell (Dockside Valet), Karin Lanz (Gift Bag Girl), Christian Heller (Man with Gift Bag), Dante Concha, Diego Fernández de Córdoba, Edwin Cedeño, Mike Pérez, Juan Carlos Avendaño (Motorcycle Cops), Rachel McDowall (CIA Flight Attendant), Rodrigo Farrugia (Hotel Bolivar Receptionist), Carl von Malaisé (Greene's Driver), Raffaello Degruttola (Alfa 2 Driver), Robert Braithwaite (Speedboat Captain), Santos Varas Ramos (DC-3 Caretaker), Antonio Gil (Marchetti Pilot), Luis Antonio Gotti (Bureaucrat at Party), Jaime Newball (La Paz Bartender), Kamil Krejcí, Gustavo Nanez, Erosi Margiani, Uygar Tamer, Alexandra Prusa, Muhamed Gandura, Shamel El-Salhy, Tsedor Gyalzur, Daniel Stüssi (Quantum Members), Karine Babajanyan (Floria Tosca), Sebastien Soules (Baron Scarpia), Brandon Jovanovich (Mario Cavaradossi), Martin Busen (Sciarrone), Alexandre Krawetz, Dale Albright (Spolettas), Katia Velletaz, Emilia Pountney (Hirtenknabes)

Daniel Craig, Olga Kurylenko

Sent to Port-au-Prince to investigate the existence of a mysterious organization calling itself Quantum, Secret Agent James Bond encounters a shady businessman who is negotiating with a Bolivian general for a precious strip of desert land.

Daniel Craig, Mathieu Amalric © MGM/Columbia

Daniel Craig

Daniel Craig

Daniel Craig, Jeffrey Wright

Daniel Craig, Judi Dench

Olga Kurylenko

Hugh Jackman, Nicole Kidman

Nicole Kidman

Nicole Kidman, Brandon Walters

Hugh Jackman

Brandon Walters , Nicole Kidman

Hugh Jackman, Nicole Kidman

AUSTRALIA

(20TH CENTURY FOX) Producers, Baz Luhrmann, G. Mac Brown, Catherine Knapman; Coproducer/Designer/Costumes, Catherine Martin; Director/Story, Baz Luhrmann; Screenplay, Baz Luhrmann, Stuart Beattie, Ronald Harwood, Richard Flanagan; Photography, Mandy Walker; Music, David Hirschfelder; Executive Music Producer, Anton Monsted; Editors, Dody Dorn, Michael McCusker; Visual Effects Supervisor, Chris Godfrey; Associate Producer, Paul Watters; Stunts, Guy Norris; Casting, Ronna Kress, Nikki Barrett; Presented in association with Dune Entertainment LLC and Ingenious Film Partners; Australian-American; Dolby; Super 35 Widescreen; Color; Rated PG-13; 165 minutes; American release date: November 26, 2008

Brandon Walters

Cast

Lady Sarah Ashley	**Nicole Kidman**
Drove	**Hugh Jackman**
Neil Fletcher	**David Wenham**
King Carney	**Bryan Brown**
Kipling Flynn	**Jack Thompson**
King George	**David Gulpilil**
Nullah	**Brandon Walters**
Magarri	**David Ngoombujarra**
Captain Dutton	**Ben Mendelsohn**
Cath Carney	**Essie Davis**
Administrator Allsop	**Barry Otto**
Myrtle Allsop	**Kerry Walker**
Gloria Carney	**Sandy Gore**
Daisy	**Ursula Yovich**
Bandy Legs	**Lillian Crombie**
Sing Song	**Yuen Wah**
Goolaj	**Angus Pilakui**
Ivan	**Jacek Koman**
Sgt. Callahan	**Tony Barry**
Ramsden	**Ray Barrett**
Old Drunk	**Max Cullen**
Bull	**Eddie Baroo**
Magarri's Niece	**Rebecca Chatfield**
Father Benedict	**Arthur Dignam**
Hairdresser	**Michelle Dyzla**
Lady Sarah's Butler	**Peter Gwynne**

Brandon Walters, Hugh Jackman © Twentieth Century Fox

Nathin Butler, John Walton, Shea Adams, Nigel Harbach (Carney Boys), Jamal Bednarz-Metallah, Terence Gregory, Jarwyn Irvin-Collins, Liam Lannigan, Logan Mattingley, Dylan Minggun, Nyalik Munungurr (Mission Boys), Damian Bradford, Nathan Lawson (Constables), Tara Carpenter, Haidee Gaudry, Joy Hilditch (Essential Services Women), Jamie Gulpilil, Mark Malabirr (Porters, Wharf), Sean Hall (Soldier, Government House), Matthew Hills (Flying Boat Steward), Jimmy Hong (Carney Manservant), Bill Hunter (Skipper, Quantas Sloop), Robert Drago (Military Police), John Jarratt (Sergeant), Eugene Kaug, Charles Leung (Waiters), Crusoe Kurdal (Aboriginal Tracker), Siena Larsson (Flying Boat Passenger Child), Jack Leech, John Martin, Robin Queree, Elaine Walker (Ball Guests), Jacob Linger (Evacuee Child), Adam McMonigal (Darwin Policeman), Philippe Moon (Ball Photographer), Patrick Mylott (Naval Officer), Mark Rathbone (Stockman), Garry Scott (Downtown Pub Patron), John Sheerin (Fireman), Bruce Spence (Dr. Barker), Matthew Whittet (Brother Frank)

Aristocratic Sarah Ashley inherits an Australian cattle ranch which she fights to keep out of the hands of a ruthless land baron.

This film received an Oscar nomination for costume design.

Nicole Kidman

Jason Statham, Robert Knepper © Lionsgate

TRANSPORTER 3

(LIONSGATE) Producers, Luc Besson, Steven Chasman; Director, Olivier Megaton; Screenplay, Luc Besson, Robert Mark Kamen, based on their characters; Photography, Giovanni Fiore Coltellacci; Designer, Patrick Durand; Costumes, Olivier Beriot; Music, Alexandre Azaria; Editors, Camille Delamarre, Carlo Rizzo; Special Effects Supervisor, Philippe Hubin; Martial Arts Choreographer, Cory Yuen; Stunts, Dominique Fouassier; Casting, Swan Pham; a EuropaCorp production, in association with TF1 Films Production, Grive Prods., Apipoulai Production, Current Entertainment, with the participation of Canal Plus; French; Dolby; Super 35 Widescreen; Color; Rated PG-13; 100 minutes; American release date: November 26, 2008

Cast

Frank Martin	**Jason Statham**
Valentina	**Natalya Rudakova**
Tarconi	**François Berléand**
Johnson	**Robert Knepper**
Leonid Vasilev	**Jeroen Krabbé**
Leonid's Aide	**Alex Kobold**
Malcolm Manville	**David Atakchi**

Yann Sundberg (Flag), Eriq Ebouaney (Ice), David Kammenos (Driver Market), Silvio Simac (Mighty Joe), Oscar Relier (Thug/Driver), Timo Dierkes (Otto), Igor Koumpan (Cop Ukraine), Paul Barrett (Captain), Elef Zack (Mate), Katia Tchenko (Leonid's Secretary), Michael Neugarten (Assassin Driver, Serguei), Faird Elouardi (Yuri), Philippe Maymat, Franck Neel (Americans), Jean-Luc Boucherot (Truck Driver), Tonio Descanvelle, Stephen Croce, Martial Bezot (Crewmen), Stephen Shagov (Port Captain), Julien Muller (Cop, Frank's House), Arnaud Gibey (French Cop, Forensic Lab), Guillaume Nail (Ambulance Man), Denis Braccini, Stefo Linard (Custom Officers), Aline Sitinus, Kait Tenison (Custom Officers, Kiev), Favien-Aïssa Busetta, Venugopal Balakrishnan (Asian Clerk, Eletronics Store), Sebastien Vandenberghe (Assassin #2, Mercedes), Semmy Schilt (The Giant)

Mob currier Frank Martin is assigned to look after the kidnapped daughter of the head of Odessa's environmental protection agency. Third in the series starring Jason Statham, following *The Transporter* (20th, 2002) and *Transporter 2* (20th, 2005).

THE BLACK BALLOON

(NEOCLASSICS) Producer, Tristram Miall; Coproducers, Sally Ayre-Smith, Elissa Down, Jimmy the Exploder, Mark Turnbull; Co-Executive Producers, Anita Belgiorno-Nettis, Sally Chesher, Toni Collette, Mark Gooder; Director, Elissa Down; Screenplay, Elissa Down, Jimmy the Exploder; Photography, Denson Baker; Designer, Nick McCullum; Music, Michael Yezerski; Editor, Veronica Jenet; a Film Finance Corp, Australia, Black Balloon Prods. (Australia)/Icon Entertainment Intl. (U.K.) presentation of a Black Balloon production, in association with the New South Wales Film & TV Office, Australian Film Commission, Anita and Luca Belgiorno-Nettis; Australian-British; Dolby; Super 35 Widescreen; Color; Rated PG-13; 97 minutes; American release date: December 5, 2008

Cast

Thomas Mollison	**Rhys Wakefield**
Charlie Mollison	**Luke Ford**
Maggie Mollison	**Toni Collette**
Simon Mollison	**Erik Thomson**
Jackie Masters	**Gemma Ward**
James	**Lloyd Allison-Young**
Chris	**Nathin Butler**
Sally	**Lisa Kowalski**
Russell	**Firass Dirani**

Aaron Glennane (Bucko), Andy Meritakis (Daniel), Henry Nixon (Trevor), Sally Evans (Girl on Bus), Kate Box (Elizabeth), Ryan Clark (Dean), Sofia Fedirchuk (Baby Sophie), Elle-May Patterson (Kylie), Ngoc Phan (Teacher's Aide)

Moving to their new home on the outskirts of Sydney, teenager Thomas Mollison must once again face the ordeal of coping with his autistic brother Charlie while trying to establish his own life outside his home.

Luke Ford © NeoClassics

Rhys Wakefield, Gemma Ward

Michael Fassbender © IFC Films

HUNGER

(IFC FILMS) Producers, Laura Hastings-Smith, Robin Gutch; Executive Producers, Jan Younghusband, Peter Carlton, Linda James, Edmund Coulthard, Iain Canning; Director, Steve McQueen; Screenplay, Enda Walsh, Steve McQueen; Photography, Sean Bobbitt; Designer, Tom McCullagh; Costumes, Anushia Nieradzik; Music, David Holmes, Leo Abrahams; Editor, Joe Walker; a Blast! Films production for Film4/Channel 4, in association with Northern Ireland Screen, the Broadcasting Commission of Northern Ireland, the Wales Creative IP Fund; British-Irish; Dolby; Widescreen; Color; Not rated; 96 minutes; American release date: December 5, 2008

Cast

Bobby Sands	**Michael Fassbender**
Raymond Lohan	**Stuart Graham**
Father Dominic Moran	**Liam Cunningham**
Davey Gillen	**Brian Milligan**
Gerry Campbell	**Liam McMahon**
Raymond's Wife	**Laine Megaw**
Gerry's Girlfriend	**Karen Hassan**

Frank McCusker (The Governor), Lalor Roddy (William), Helen Madden (Mrs. Sands), Des McAleer (Mr. Sands), Geoff Gatt (Bearded Man), Rory Mullen (Priest), Stephen Graves (Riot Prison Officer), Helena Bereen (Raymond's Mother), Paddy Jenkins (Hitman), Billy Clarke (Chief Medical Officer), Ciaran Flynn (Twelve-Year-Old Bobby), B.J. Hogg (Loyalist Orderly)

The true story of how Irish Republican Bobby Sands led a hunger strike as a protest against the British's government's refusal to recognize convicted IRA members as political prisoners.

ADAM RESURRECTED

(BLEIBERG ENTERTAINMENT) Producers, Ehud Bleiberg, Werner Wirsing; Executive Producers, Ulf Israel, Marion Forster Bleiberg; Coproducers, July August Prods., Hildegard Luke; Director, Paul Schrader; Screenplay, Noah Stollman; Based on the novel by Yoram Kaniuk; Photography, Sebastian Edschmid; Designer, Alexander Manasse; Costumes, Inbal Shuki; Music, Gabriel Yared; Editor, Sandy Saffeels; Casting, Esther King, Anja Dihrberg, Floriela Grapini, Joanna Ray, Crowley/Pull; a Bleiberg/3L Filmproduktion presentation of an Ehud Bleiberg & Werner Wirsing production; Israeli-German; Dolby; Super 35 Widescreen; Color/Black and white; Not rated; 107 minutes; American release date: December 12, 2008

Cast

Adam Stein	**Jeff Goldblum**
Commandant Klein	**Willem Dafoe**
Dr. Nathan Gross	**Derek Jacobi**
Gina Grey	**Ayelet Zurer**
Joseph Gracci	**Moritz Bleibtreu**
Arthur	**Idan Alterman**
Gretchen	**Jenya Dodina**
Frau Fogel	**Veronica Ferres**

Benjamin Jagendorf (Rabbi Lichtenstein), Dror Keren (Dr. Slonin), Juliane Köhler (Rutchen Edelson), Joachim Król (Wolfowitz), Hana Laszlo (Nurse Shwester), Cristian Motiu (Volk), Tudor Rapiteanu (Davey), Gabriel Spahiu (Taub), Vasile Albinet (Nazi)

A former German nightclub entertainer ends up in an Isareali sanitarium where he continues to be haunted by his experiences as an inmate at the Stellring concentration camp.

Jeff Goldblum, Jenya Dodina

Willem Dafoe, Jeff Goldblum © Bleiberg Entertainment

CHE

(IFC FILMS) Producers, Laura Bickford, Benicio Del Toro; Executive Producers, Alvaro Augustin, Belen Atienza, Frederic W. Brost, Gregory Jacobs, Alvaro Longoria; Director, Steven Soderbergh; Screenplay, Peter Buchman; Part One inspired by *The Cuban Revolutionary War* by Ernesto Che Guevara, Part Two inspired by *The Bolivian Diary* by Ernest Che Guevara; Photography, Peter Andrews; Designer, Antxon Gomez; Costumes, Bina Daigeler; Music, Alberto Iglesias; Editor, Pablo Zumarraga; Casting, Mary Vernieu; a Wild Bunch and Telecino presentation of a Laura Bickford/Morean Films production; Spanish-French; Dolby; Widescreen; Color/black and white; Not rated; 257 minutes (Part 1: 129 minutes; Part Two: 128 minutes); American release date: December 12, 2008

Cast

Ernesto Che Guevara	**Benicio Del Toro**
Fidel Castro	**Demián Bichir**
Camilo Cienfuegos	**Santiago Cabrera**
Celia Sánchez	**Elvira Mínguez**
Vilo/Joaquin	**Jorge Perugorria**
Ciro Redondo Garcia	**Édgar Ramírez**
Rogelio Acevedo	**Victor Rasuk**
Benigno	**Armando Riesco**
Aleida March	**Catalina Sandino Moreno**
Raúl Castro	**Rodrigo Santoro**
Vaquerito	**Unax Ugalde**
Alejandro Ramirez	**Yul Vazquez**
Moisés Guevara	**Carlos Bardem**
President René Barrientos	**Joaquim de Almeida**
Ciro Algarañaz	**Eduard Fernández**
Régis Debray	**Marc-André Grondin**
Darío	**Óscar Jaenada**
Leonardo Tamayo Nuñez/Urbano	**Kahlil Mendez**
Fr. Schwartz	**Matt Damon**
Capt. Mario Vargas	**Jordi Mollá**
Rolando	**Ruben Ochandiano**
Lisa Howard	**Julia Ormond**
Ciros Bustos	**Gaston Pauls**
Mario Monje	**Lou Diamond Phillips**
Tania	**Franka Potente**
George Roth	**Mark Umbers**

Pablo Guevara, Franklin Díaz, Armando Suárez Cobián (Dinner Guests), María Isabel Díaz (María Antonia), Mateo Gómez, René Lavan (Cuban Diplomats), Jose Caro (Esteban), Pedro Adorno (Epifanío Díaz), Jsu Garcia (Jorge Sotus), Luis Rodriguez Sanchez, Rafael Simón (Rebel Messengers), Roberto Santana (Juan Almeida), Vladimir Cruz (Ramiro Valdés Menéndez), Marisé Alvarez (Vilma Espín), Jorge Perugorría (Vilo), Christian Nieves (Oñante Cantiflás), Andres Munar (Joel Iglesias Leyva), Liddy Paoli Lopez (Quike Escalona), Francisco Cabrera (Rebel Guide), Pedro Telémaco (Eligio Mendoza), Yamil Adorno (Mario Leal), Miguel Ángel Suárez (Army Doctor), Alfredo De Quesada (Israel Pardo), Roberto Urbina (Guile Pardo), Juan Pedro Torriente (Pedro Chape), Io Bottoms (Make-Up Artist), Manuel Cabral, Oscar A. Colon (Cuban Men at Bar), Sam Robards (Tad Szulc), Jay Potter (Richard Hottelet), Stephen Mailer (Paul Niven), Octavio Gómez (Otto), Blanca Lissette Cruz (Maria), Laura Andújar (Laura), Georgina Borri, Victoria Espinosa (Old Women), Euriamis Losada (Carlos), Alejandro Renteria (Umberto), Israel Lugo Graniela (Omar), Bryant Huffman (Cuervo), Xavier Antonio Morales (Esteban's Accomplice), José Luis Gutiérrez (Polo), Jon DeVries (Sen. Eugene McCarthy), Leslie Lyles, Meg Gibson, Alex Manette, Elvis Nolasco, Sheridan Lowell (Partygoers), Eugenio Monclova (Emilio Cabrera), Luis Gonzaga Hernandez (Lalo Sardiñas), Jose A. Nieves (Dr. Julio Martínez Páez), Joksan Ramos (Raúl Chibás), Javier Ortiz (Felipe Pazos), Luis Rosario (Rebel Luis), Santa Fe Osmin Hernandez (Jesús), Leonardo Castro (Army Medic), Oscar De La Fe Colon, Xaiex Arriaga (Bazooka Guys), Monique Curnen (Secretary), P.J. Benjamin (Capt. Stanton), Al Espinosa, Ana Maria Andricain (Angry Demonstrators), Michael Countryman (U.S. Ambassador Stevenson), Jorge Armando (Enrique Acevedo), Aris Mejias (Carmen), Carlitos Ruiz Ruiz (Ventriloquist), Othello Resnoli (Pombo), Joe Urla (Nicaragua Ambassador), Diego Arria (Venezuela Ambassador), Oscar Chagall (Panama Ambassador), Eduardo Cortés (Sánchez Mosquera), Joaquín Méndez (Faustino Pérez), Pablo Venegas Colón (René Ramos Latour), Jerry Nelson Soto (Nico Torres), Jose Brocco (Ovidio Díaz Rodríguez), Norman Santiago (Tuma), Juan Carlos Arvelo (Rolando Cubela), Roy Sánchez-Vahamondes (Faure Chomón), Yamil Collazo (Enrique Oltuski), Alejandro Carpio (Eloy Gutiérrez Menoyo), Andres Santiago Bravo (Hermes Peña Torres), Aurelio Lima (Victor Bordón Machado), Alba Caraballo (Aleida's Friend), Doel Alicea (Oltuski's Messenger), Rafa Alvarez (Lt. Pérez Valencia), Jose Cottte (Dr. Fernandez Mell), Naya Rivera (Woman in Crowd), Néstor Rodulfo (Miguel), Luis Alberto Garcia (Col. Joaquín Casillas Lumpuy), Teofilo Torres (Col. Hernández), Ernesto Flaxas (Fernández Suero), Ricardo Alvarez (Antonio Jiménez Calderón), Victor Angulo Villacis (Red Cross Worler), Fernando Gutiérrez Vargas (Aide to Hernández), Ramiro Garza Balboa (Man Greeting Che), Carmen Mahiques (Cook at Cuban Embassy), Oscar Isaac (Interpreter), Maria D. Sosa (Aledita), Raúl Beltrán, Raúl 'Pitin' Gómez (Bolivian Customs Agents), Paty M. Bellott (Woman at Airport), Pablo Durán (Pacho), Ezequiel Diaz (Loro), Juan Salinas (Polo), Luis Muñoz (Camba), Antonio Peredo (Coco), Aaron Vega (Ricardo), Rubén Ochandiano (Rolando), Cristian Mercado (Inti), Roberto Guilhon (Ernesto), Carlos Acosta (Antonio Domínquez Flores), Edgardo Rodríguez (Arturo), José Juan Rodrígez (Moro), Daniel Larrzábal (Ñato), Wilder Salinas (Julio), Jimmy A. Céspedes (Eustaquio), Eitán Vázquez (Salustio Choque Choque), Óscar Avilés (Pedro), Rúben Salinas (Paco), Daniel Aguirre (Aniceto Reinaga), Miguel Villarroel (Carlos), Diego Ortiz (Willy), Jorge Arturo Lora (Chapaco), Marisé Alvarez (Vilma Espín), Eduardo Espinosa (El Vallegrandino), Antonio de la Torre (Lt. Carlos Fernández), Marco Antonio (Plainclothes Policeman), Luis Bedrow (Honorato Roojas), María Cristina Calá (Honorato's Wife), Edison Narváez (Pablito), Bart Santana (Daniel), Raúl Núñez (Eusbeio Tapia Arune), Jesús Carrillo (Vicente Roaebado Terrazas), Gastón Pauls (Ciros Bustos), José Julio Park Shin (Chino), Juan Carlos Vellido (Major Hernán Plata), Raúl Arévalo, Daniel Holguín, Sergio Deustua (Captured Soldiers), Tom Minder, Andrew Petrotta, Frederic W. Brost (Americans), Geischglin Rojas (Padilla), Stephen Casmier (Capt. Mitchell), James D. Dever (Maj. Ralph "Pappy" Shelton), Roberto Sanmartín (Capt. Gary Prado), Luis Callejo (Bolivian Interrogator), Eduardo Sanjines, Diego Salazar, René Aragón (Reporters), Pedro Casablanc (Col. Joaquín Zenteno), Tomás del Estal (Gen. Alfredo Ovando Candía), David Zambrana (Chingolo), Flavio Morales (Soldier Playing Possum), José María Piñeda (Hiding Soldier), Mónica Montoya (Store Owner), Saúl Avila (Coco Vendor), Miguel Antelo (Prado's Radio Operator), David Selvas (Lt. Col. Andés Selich), Jesús Carroza (Eduardo), César Salgado (Guard at Door), Martín Bello (Bolivian Soldier), Vismark Tito Rojas (Lt. Eduardo Huerta), Enrique Arce (Lt. Carlos Pérez), Christian Esquivel (Sgt. Mario Terán), Benjamin Benítez (Rudolfo)

A two part examination of the life of revolutionary Che Guevara and how he helped overthrow the corrupt Cuban president and establish a communist government. This was shown both as a single film with an intermission as well as two separate films for separate admissions.

Benicio Del Toro

Benicio Del Toro (right)

Catalina Sandino Moreno, Benicio Del Toro © IFC Films

Demián Bichir, Benicio Del Toro

Franka Potente

Juan Carlos Vellido, Jorge Peruggoría, Franka Potente

Dalla Doucoure, Damien Gomes

Esmarelda Quertani, Rachel Régulier

Wei Huang, Esmeralda Quertani, Rachel Regulier

François Bégaudeau

Below: *Samantha Soupirot, Henriette Kasaruhanda, Boubacar Touré*

Jean-Michel Simonet, François Bégaudeau

François Bégaudeau, Franck Keita, Boubacar Touré

Laura Baquela © Sony Classics

THE CLASS

(SONY CLASSICS) a.k.a. *Entre les murs*; Producers, Carole Scotta, Caroline Benjo, Barbara Letellier, Simon Arnal; Director, Laurent Cantet; Screenplay, Laurent Cantet, François Bégaudeau, Robin Campillo; Based on the novel *Entre les murs* by François Bégaudeau; Photography, Pierre Milon, Catherine Pujol, Georgi Lazarevski; Set Decorators, Sabine Barthélémy, Héléne Bellanger; Costumes, Marie Le Garrec; a Haut et Court, France 2 Cinema co-production, with the participation of Canal Plus, France 2, Cinecinema, in association with Soficas Cofinova 4, Soficinema 3, with the participation of Centre National de la Cinematographie and the support of Fonds Images de la Diversite, with the support of the Region Ile de France, with the participation of Acse—Fonds Images de la Diversite; French; Dolby; Widescreen; Color; HD; Rated PG-13; 129 minutes; American release date: December 19, 2008

Cast

François	**François Bégaudeau**

The Students:

Nassim	**Massim Amrabt**
Laura	**Laura Baquela**
Cherif	**Cherif Bounaïdja Rachedi**
Juliette	**Juliette Demaille**
Dalla	**Dalla Doucoure**
Arthur	**Arthur Fogel**
Damien	**Damien Gomes**
Louise	**Louise Grinberg**
Qifei	**Qifei Huang**
Wei	**Wei Huang**
Souleymane	**Franck Keïta**
Henriette	**Henriette Kasaruhanda**
Lucie	**Lucie Landrevie**
Agame	**Agame Malembo-Emene**
Rabal	**Rabal Naït Oufella**
Carl	**Carl Nanor**
Sandra	**Esméralda Ouertani**
Burak	**Burak Özyilmaz**
Eva	**Eva Paradiso**
Khoumba	**Rachel Régulier**
Angélica	**Angélica Sanico**
Samantha	**Samantha Soupirot**
Boubacar	**Boubacar Touré**

Atouma Dioumassy, Nitany Gueyes (Student Representatives); *The Teachers*: Vincent Caire (Vincent), Olivier Dupeyron (Olivier), Patrick Dureuil (Patrick), Frédéric Faujas (Fred), Dorothée Guilbot (Rachel), Cécile Lagarde (Cécile), Anne Langlois (Sophie), Yvette Mournetas (Yvette), Vincent Robert (Hervé), Anne Wallimann-Charpentier (Anne); *The Administration and Personnel*: Julie Athenol (The Counselor), Jean-Michel Simonet (The Principal), Olivier Pasquier (Financial Administrator), Stéphane Longour, Abdoul Drahamane Sissoko (Supervisors), Aline Zimierski (Kitchen Staff), Silma Aktar, Marie-Antoinette Sorrente (Cleaning Women); *The Parents*: Fatoumata Kanté (Souleymane's Mother), Cheick Baba Doumbia (Souleymane's Brother), Khalid Amrabt (Nassim's Father), Adeline Fogel (Arthur's Mother), Lingfen Huang (Wei's Mother), Wenlong Huang (Wei's Father), Sezer Özyilmaz (Burak's Mother), Marie-Laure Bulliard, Robert Demaille, Céline Spang (The Parents' Delegate)

Teacher and writer François Bégaudeau enacts his own life story of teaching a group of racially mixed students in a lower class Parisian neighborhood.

This film received an Oscar nomination for foreign language film.

THE SECRET OF THE GRAIN

(IFC FILMS) a.k.a. *La graine et le mulet*; Producer, Claude Berri; Executive Producer, Pierre Grunstein; Director/Screenplay, Abdellatif Kechiche; Photography, Lubomir Bakchev; Designer, Benoit Barouh; Costumes, Maria Beloso Hall; Editors, Ghalya Lacroix, Camille Toubkis; Casting, Monya Galby; a Hirsch, Pathe Renn production, in association with France 2 Cinema; French, 2007; Dolby; Color; Not rated; 151 minutes; American release date: December 24, 2008

Cast

Slimane Beiji	**Habib Boufares**
Rym	**Hafsia Herzi**
Karima	**Farida Benkhetache**
Hamid	**Abdelhamid Aktouche**
Souad	**Bouraouïa Marzouk**
Julia	**Alice Houri**
Sergueï	**Cyril Favre**
Favre Lilia	**Leila D'Issernio**
Kader	**Abelkader Djeloulli**
José	**Olivier Loustau**
Majid	**Sami Zitouni**
Olfa	**Sabrina Ouzani**
Riadh	**Mohamed Benabdeslem**
Latifa	**Hatika Karoui**
Henri	**Henri Rodriguez**
Sarah	**Nadia Taouil**

Fired from his shipyard job where he has worked for thirty-five years, Slimane decides to open his own restaurant.

Alice Houri, Bouraouïa Marzouk © IFC Films

Hafsia Herzi

Hafsia Herzi , Habib Boufares

Ari Folman, Boaz Rein Buskila

Ari Foman, Carmi Cna'an

Waltz with Bashir © *Sony Classics*

WALTZ WITH BASHIR

(SONY CLASSICS) a.k.a. *Vals im Bashir*; Producers, Ari Folman, Yael Nahlieli, Serge Lalou, Gerhard Meixner, Roman Paul; Coproducers, Thierry Garrel, Pierrette Ominetti; Director /Screenplay, Ari Folman; Animation, Bridgit Folman Film Gang; Animation Director, Yoni Goodman; Art Director and Illustrator, David Polonsky; Visual Effects Supervisor, Roiy Nitzan; a Bridgit Folman Film Gang (Israel)/Les Films d'Ici (France)/Razor Gilm (Germany) production, in association with Arte France (France), ITVS Intl. (U.S.) in collaboration with Noga Communications-Channel 8, the New Israeli Foundation for Cinema & TV, Medienboard Berlin-Brandenburg, Israel Film Fund, HOT Telecommunication System, RTBF, TSR, YLE, SBS; Israeli-French-German; Dolby; Color/black and white; Rated R; 90 minutes; American release date: December 26, 2008

Voice cast
Ron Ben-Yishai, Ronny Dayag, Ari Folman, Dror Harazi, Ori Sivan, Zahava Solomon (Themselves), Yehezkel Lazarov (Carmi Cna'an), and Mickey Leon (Boaz Rein-Buskila)

Documentary about the 1982 massacres at the Sabra and Shantila refugee camps in Lebanon.

This film received an Oscar nomination for foreign language film.

Jason Isaacs, Viggo Mortensen

Viggo Mortensen

Viggo Mortensen, Jodie Whittaker © ThinkFilm

GOOD

(THINKFILM) Producers, Miriam Segal, Sarah Boote, Kevin Loader, Dan Lupovitz, Billy Dietrich; Coproducers, Michael Morales, Kornel Sipos; Executive Producers, Danielle Dajani, Simon Fawcett, Peter Hampden, Stephen Hays; Director, Vicente Amorim; Screenplay, John Wrathall; Based on the stage by play C.P. Taylor; Photography, Andrew Dunn; Designer, Andrew Laws; Costumes, Gyorgi Szakacs; Music, Simon Lacey; Editor, John Wilson; Casting, Jeanne McCarthy, Laura Scott; an Aramid Entertainment presentation of a Good Films production, in association with Miromar Entertainment, 120dB Films, Lipsync Prods., BBC Films; British-German; Dolby; Panavision; Color; Not rated; 96 minutes; American release date: December 31, 2008

Cast

John Halder	**Viggo Mortensen**
Maurice	**Jason Isaacs**
Anne	**Jodie Whittaker**
Freddie	**Steven Mackintosh**
Bouhler	**Mark Strong**
Mother	**Gemma Jones**
Helen	**Anastasia Hille**
Elizabeth	**Ruth Gemmell**
Brunau	**Ralph Riach**
Eichmann	**Steve Elder**
Commandant	**Kevin Doyle**
Mandelstam	**David de Keyser**
Doctor	**Guy Henry**
Goebbels	**Adrian Schiller**
Brownshirt	**Rick Warden**
Bekemeier	**Charlie Condou**
Lotte	**Tallulah Boote-Bond**
Erich	**Benedict Segal**

Kelly Wenham (Pretty Secretary), Declan Hannigan (Handsome Doctor, Movie Studio), Anna Mária Cseh (Beautiful Woman, Movie Studio), Paul Brennan (Clerk), Matt Devere (SS Motorcycle Courier), Mike Kelly (Party Guest), Attila Szatmari (Policeman), Peter Linka (SS Officer), László Görög (Neighbor)

Literature professor John Halder is asked by a member of Hitler's Chancellary to write a scholarly paper on euthanasia, little realizing the hidden agenda behind the proposal.

Jason Isaacs

FOREIGN FILMS B

2008 Releases / January 1–December 31

THE KILLING OF JOHN LENNON (IFC First Take) Producer, Rakha Singh; Executive Producer, Rod Pearson; Director/Screenplay, Andrew Piddington; Photography, Roger Eaton; Designer, Tora Peterson; Art Directors, Anu Schwartz, Skeeter Stanback; Costumes, Michael Bevins; Editor, Tony Palmer; Music, Makana; a Redstone Pictures presentation of a Picture Players production; British, 2007; Dolby; Super 35 Widescreen; Color; Not rated; 114 minutes; American release date: January 2, 2008. CAST: Jonas Ball (Chapman), Joe Abbate (Taxi Driver), Sofia Dubrawsky (Jude), Krisha Fairchild (Chapman's Mom), James Hadde (Scientologist), Robert C. Kirk (Det. John Sullivan), Thomas A. McMahon (Spiro), Mie Omori (Gloria Chapman), Tom Zolandz (Goresh), Anthony Solis (Gun Salesman), Vera Felice (Prostitute), J. Francis Curley (Security Guard), Nicole Delorey (Record Shop Girl)

Jonas Ball in The Killing of John Lennon © *IFC First Take*

WOMAN ON THE BEACH (New Yorker Films) a.k.a. *Haebyonui yoni*; Producer, Oh Jung-wan; Executive Producer, Photography, Kim Hyung-koo; Music, Jeong Yong-jin; Editor, Hahm Sung-won; a Mirovision presentation in association with Max Venture Capital, C&S Intl.of a b.o.m. film production coproduced by Jeonwonsa; South Korean, 2006; Color; Not rated; 100 minutes; American release date: January 9, 2008. CAST: Kim Seung-woo (Kim Jonog-rae), Kim Tae-woo (Won Chang-wook), Go Hyun-jung (Kim Mun-suk), Song Seon-mi (Choi Sun-hee), Choi Ban-ya (Sun-hee's Friend), Chan Jung (Guy Driving Mun-suk Home), Lee Ki-woo (Beach Resort Caretaker), Oh Tae-keying (Waiter at Empty Sushi Restaurant)

Go Hyun-jung, Kim Seung-woo, Kim Tae-woo in Woman on the Beach © *New Yorker Films*

THE BET COLLECTOR (Global Film Initiative) a.k.a. *Kubrador*; Producer, Joji Alonso; Director, Jeffrey Jeturian; Screenplay, Ralston G. Jover; Photography, Roberto Yniguez; Designer, Leo Abaya; Music, Jerrold Tarog; Editor, Jay Halil; an MLR Films production. Filipino, 2006; Color; Not rated; 100 minutes; American release date: January 10, 2008. CAST: Gina Pareño (Amy Basmayor), Soliman Cruz (Police Chief), Nanding Josef (Priest), Johnny Manahan (Treasurer), Jhong Del Rosario (Eric), Nico Antonio (Baste, The Bet Collector), Fonz Deza (Amy's Husband), Elmo Redrico (Kabo)

IN THE NAME OF THE KING: A DUNGEON SIEGE TALE (Freestyle) Producers, Shawn Williamson, Dan Clarke; Executive Producers, Uwe Boll, Chet Holmes, Wolfgang Herold; Director, Uwe Boll; Screenplay, Doug Taylor, from a story by Joseph Rappaport, Dan Stroncak, Doug Taylor, inspired by the videogame *Dungeon Siege* developed by Chris Taylor; Photography, Mathias Neumann; Designer, James Steuart; Costumes, Toni Burroughs-Rutter, Carla Hetland; Editors, Paul Klassen, David M. Richardson; Music, Jessica de Rooij, Henning Lohner; Fight Choreographer, Tony Ching; Casting, Maureen Webb; a Boll KG Prods. (Germany) production, in association with Herold Prods. (Germany)/ Brightlight Pictures (Canada); German-Canadian; Dolby; Super 35 Widescreen; Color; Rated PG-13; 126 minutes; American release date: January 11, 2008. CAST: Jason Statham (Farmer), John Rhys-Davies (Merick), Ray Liotta (Gallian), Matthew Lillard (Duke Fallow), Leelee Sobieski (Muriella), Burt Reynolds (King Konreid), Ron Perlman (Norick), Claire Forlani (Solana), Kristanna Loken (Elora), Will Sanderson (Bastian), Brian White (Cmdr. Tarish), Mike Dopud (Gen. Backler), Tania Saulnier (Tawlyn), Gabrielle Rose (Delinda), Terence Kelly (Trumaine), Colin Ford (Zeph), Michelle Harrison (Hysterical Woman), Eva Padberg (Handmaiden), Darren Shahlavi (Gatekeeper), Aaron Pearl (Gen. Aziel), Michael Eklund (Scout), Ron Selmour (Gen. Hallette), Paul Wu (Lt. Rawden), Stephen Park (Armed Slave), Marcel Maillard (Merchant), Daniel Boileau (Slave), Christopher Rosamond, Sage Brocklebank (Soldiers), Carrie Ann Fleming (Crying Woman), Jacqueline Ann Steuart, Travis MacDonald (Caravan Slaves), Alana Kagan, Naomi Lazarus (Concubines), Duncan Fraser (Old Man), Aidan Williamson (Town Boy)

Jason Statham, Kristianna Loken in In the Name of the King © *Freestyle Releasing*

TIMES AND WINDS (Kino) a.k.a. *Best Vakit*; Producer, Omer Atay; Director/ Screenplay/Editor, Reha Erdem; Photography, Florent Herry; Art Director, Omer Atay; Costumes, Mehtap Tunay; Music, Arvo Part; Casting, Ozlem Sungur; an Atlantik Film production; Turkish; Dolby; Super 35 Widescreen; Color; Not rated; 107 minutes; American release date: January 11, 2008. CAST: Taner Birsel (Zekeriya), Nihan Asli Elmas (Yildiz's Mother), Köksal Engür (Halil Dayi), Sevniç Erbulka (Yakup's Mother), Selma Ergeç (The Teacher), Elit Iscan (Yildiz), Ali Bey Kayali (Yakup), Yigit Özsener (Yusuf), Tilbe Saran (Omer's Mother), Tarik Sönmez (Shepherd Davut), Cüneyt Türel (Grandfather), Bülent Emin Yarar (Imam)

OPERA JAWA (Independent) Producer, Garin Nugroho; Executive Producers, Simon Field, Keith Griffiths; Director/Screenplay, Garin Nugroho; Photography, Teoh Gay Hian; Art Director, Nanang Rakhmat Hidayat; Costumes, Samuel Watimena; Editor, Andhy Pulung; Music, Rahayu Supanggah; a SET Film Workshop (Indonesia)/New Crowned Hope (Austria) production; Indonesian-Austrian, 2006; Dolby; Color; Not rated; 119 minutes; American release date: January 16, 2008. CAST: Artiak Sara Devi (Siti), Martinus Miroto (Setyo), Eko Supriyanto (Ludiro), Retno Maruti (Sukesi), Nyoman Sure (Sure)

SUMMER PALACE (Palm Pictures) a.k.a. *Yihe yuan*; Producers Fang Li, Nai An, Sylvain Bursztejn; Executive Producers, Fang Li, Nai An; Coproducers, Lin Fan, Helge Alebrs, Lou Ye; Director, Lou Ye; Screenplay, Lou Ye, Mei Feng, Ma Yingli; Photography, Hua Qing; Editors, Lou Ye, Zeng Jian; Music, Peyman Yazdanian; Art Director, Liu Weixin; Costumes, Lu Yue; a Laurel Films, Dream Factory, Fantasy Pictures (China)/Rosem Films (France) production, with participation of Ministere de la Culture & de la Communication, CNC, Ministere des Affaires Etrangeres; Chinese-French, 2007; Dolby; Color; Not rated; 140 minutes; American release date: January 18, 2008. CAST: Hao Lei (Hong Yu), Bai Xueyun (Bo Wang), Cui Lin (Jun Xiao), Duan Long (Caoshi Tang), Guo Xiadong (Wei Zhou), Hu Ling (Ti Li), Le Chi (Woman), Zhang Xianmin (Gu Ruo)

Hao Lei, Guo Xiadong in Summer Palace © *Palm Pictures*

BLONDE AND BLONDER (Hannover House) Producers, Dean Hamiton, Kirk Shaw; Executive Producers, Pamela Anderson, Alexander Tabrizi, Frederico Lapenda, Alain Siritzky; Director, Dean Hamilton; Screenplay, Rolfe Kanefsky, Dean Hamilton, Gerry Anderson; Story, Rolfe Kanefsky; Additional Comedy Material, Eric Parkinson; Photography, C. Kim Miles; Designer, Rick Whitfield; Costumes, Allisa Swanson Music, William Goodrum; Casting, Candice Elzinga; a Rigel Entertainment and First Look Studios Inc. presentation in association with Pneumatic Pictures and Canadian Global Media, Inc. of an Insight Studios production; Canadian; Color; Rated PG-13; 95 minutes; Release date: January 18, 2008. CAST: Pamela Anderson (Dee), Denise Richards (Dawn), Emmanuelle Vaugier (The Cat), Byron Mann (Mr. Wong), Meghan Ory (The Kit), John Farley (Swan), Kevin P. Farley (Leo), Alistair Abell (Mr. Laine), Julia Anderson (Last Dancer in Line), Joey Aresco (Agent Campbell), Kevin Blatch (Maitre D'), Gary Chalk (Agent Gardenia), Sandra-Jessica Couturier (Stripper), Tosha Doiron (Auditioning Dancer), Nathalie Fay (Roulette Girl), Teach Grant, Drew McCreadie (Canadian Guys), Dean Hamilton (Hotel Business Man), Woody Jeffreys (Ken), Keith Lewis (Thug #2), Phoenix Ly (One Eye), Patrick Pon (Hugo), Alfonso Quijada (Info Man), Michael Roberds (Movie Director), John Tench (Ed Gates), Reg Tupper (Middle Aged Man)

STILL LIFE (New Yorker) a.k.a. *Sanxia haroen*; Producers, Xu Pengle, Wang Tianyun, Zhu Jiong; Executive Producers, Chow Keung, Dan Bo, Ren Zhonglun; Director, Jia Zhangke; Screenplay, Jia Zhangke, Sun Jianmin, Guan Na; Photography, Yu Lik-wai; Art Directors, Laing Jingdong, Liu Qiang; Music, Lim Giong; Editor, Kong Jinlei; an Xstream Pictures presentation of an Xstream (Hong Kong)/Shanghai Film Group (China) production; Hong Kong-Chinese, 2007; Color; HD; Not rated; 107 minutes; American release date: January 18, 2008. CAST: Han Sanming (Sanming), Zhao Tao (Shen Hong), Liz Zhu Bing (Guo Bing), Wang Hongwei (Wang Dong Ming), Ma Lizhen (Missy Ma), Lan Zhou (Huang Mao), Li Zhubin (Guo Bin), Xiang Haiyu (Mr. he), Zhou Lin (Brother Pony), Huang Yong (Little Yong), Luo Mingwang (Old Ma)

Zhao Tao, Wang Hongwei in Still Life © *New Yorker Films*

ALICE'S HOUSE (Vitagraph) a.k.a. *A Casa De Alice*; Producers, Leblanc Carvalhosa, Zita Carvalhosa; Director, Chico Teixeira; Screenplay, Chico Teixeira, Julio Pessoa, Sabina Anzuategui, Marcelo Gomes; Photography, Mauro Pinheiro, Jr.; Editor, Vania Debs; Designer, Marcos Pedroso; Costumes, Andre Simonetti; a Superfilmes production. Brazilian; Dolby; Color; Not rated; 94 minutes; American release date: January 25, 2008. CAST: Carla Ribas (Alice), Berta Zemel (Dona Jacira), Zecarlos Machado (Lindomar), Luciano Quirino (Nilson), Renata Zhaneta (Carmen), Vinicius Zinn (Lucas), Ricardo Vilaga (Edinho), Felipe Mazzula (Junior), Mariana Leighton (Thaïs), Dirce Couto (Neide), Jorge Cerruti (Toninho), Cicero Augusto (Carlinhos Abranches), Elias Andreato (Gabriel), Claudio Jaborandy (Ivanildo), Talita Craveiro (Vanessinha), Roberto Leite (Taxi Passenger), Marcos Pedroso (Client in the Car), Thiago de Mello (Opthamologist), Francisco Gaspar, Monicah Duarte (Beauty Salon Employees)

LOST IN BEIJING (New Yorker) a.k.a. *Ping guo*; Producer, Fang Li; Director, Li Yu. Screenplay/Story, Li Yu, Fang Li; Photography, Costumes, Xu Zhen; a Laurel Films production; Chinese; Dolby: Color; Not rated; 113 minutes; American release date: January 25, 2008. CAST: Tony Leung Ka-fai (Dong Lin), Fan Bingbing (Ping Guo Liu), Tong Dawei (Kun An), Elaine Jin (Mei Wang)

Right: Fan Bingbing, Tong Dawei in Lost in Beijing © *New Yorker Films*

TRAILER PARK BOYS: THE MOVIE (Screen Media/CAVU) Producers, Mike Clattenburg, Barrie Dunn, Michael Volpe; Executive Producers, Ivan Reitman, Tom Pollock, Joe Medjuck, Jackie Marcus; Director, Mike Clattenburg; Screenplay, Mike Clattenburg, Robb Wells; Photography, Miroslaw Baszak; Designer, Hardkhrome; Music, Blain Morris; Music Supervisor, Velma Barkwell; a Screen Media Films/Ivan Reitman presentation of a Trailer Park Prods./Topsail Prods./Showcase Original production; Canadian; Dolby; Color; 16mm-to-35mm; Rated R; 95 minutes; American release date: January 25, 2008. CAST: Robb Wells (Ricky), John Paul Tremblay (Julian), Mike Smith (Bubbles), Lucy Decoutere (Lucy), Lydia Lawson-Baird (Trinity), Cory Bowles (Cory), Michael Jackson (Trevor), Gord Downie, Alex Lifeson (Cops), Gerry Dee (Donny), Glen Grant (Darren), Eugene Clark (Cadillac), Barrie Dunn (Ray), John Dunsworth (Mr. Lahey), Patrick Roach (Randy), Sarah E. Dunsworth (Sarah), Hugh Dillon (Sonny), Nichole Hiltz (Wanda), Sherry Davis, Valerie Fougere, Stephanie Godin, Thea Harvey, Cadence MacMichael, Tammy Mills (Dancers at Aristocrat), Nicole Nikerson (Bartender), Christina Parker (Waitress), Blain Morris (Drive Through Voice), Shelley Thompson (Barb Lahey), Jacob Rolfe (Jacob), Paul LeBlanc (Postal Worker), Jonathan Torrens (J-Roc), Tyron Parsons (T), Veronica Reynolds (Dazzle), Natasha Noriega (Galaxy), Richard Collins (Phil Collins), Hampton Kelly (Pizza-Eating Dog), James Swansburg (Office Ted Johnson), Shawn Duggan (Theatre Man), Tara Doyle (Theatre Woman), Justin Blackburn (Theatre Boy), Linda J. Brooks (Donny's Wife), Liam Cyr (Donny's Older Son), Wyn Crowson (Donny's Younger Son), George Green (Officer Geoge Green), Paul MacLeod (Minister), Jeremy Akerman (Judge), Gary Levert (Mr. Stevenson), Jennifer Overton (Mrs. Brown), Shaun Clarke (Bailiff), Alvena Poole, Bill Parsons, Cecil Wright (Park Residents), Annemarie Cassidy-Clatte (Sarah's Bike Friend), Nicole Frost (Woman Getting Haircut)

John Paul Tremblay, Mike Smith, Robb Wells in Trailer Park Boys
© *CAVU Pictures*

THE SILENCE BEFORE BACH (Films 59) Director, Pere Portabella; Screenplay, Pere Portabella, Carles Santos, Xavier Alberti; Photography, Alberta Manera; Art Director, Quim Roy; Spanish-German; Dolby; Color; Not rated; 102 minutes; American release date: January 30, 2008. A visual celebration of the music of Johan Sebastian Bach; with Christian Atanasiu, Féodor Atkine, George-Christoph Biller, Christian Brembeck; Alex Brendemühl.

LIVE AND BECOME (Menemsha) a.k.a. *Va, Vis et deviens;* Producers, Denis Carot, Marie Masmonteil, Radu Mihaileanu; Director, Radu Mihaileanu; Screenplay, Radu Mihaileanu, Alain-Michel Blanc; Photography, Remy Chevrin; Designer, Eytan Levy; Costumes, Rona Doron; Editor, Ludo Troch; Music, Armand Amar; an Elzevir Films, Oi Oi Oi Prods. production, in association with Cattleya, K2, Transfax, France 3 Cinema, TRL-TVI, Scope Invest, with the support of Eurimages, CNC and the participation of Canal Plus, Cinecinema, Kiosque; French-Israeli, 2005; Dolby; Super 35 Widescreen; Color; Not rated; 148 minutes;

American release date: February 1, 2008. CAST: Yaël Abecassis (Yaël Harrari), Roschdy Zem (Yoram Harrari), Moshe Agazai (Schlomo, as a child), Sirak M. Sabahat (Scholomo, as an adult), Roni Hadar (Sarah), Yitzak Edgar (Qès Amrah), Rami Danon (Papy), Meskie Shibru Sivan (Schlomo's Mother), Mimi Abonesh Kebede (Hana), Raymonde Abecassis (Suzy)

BUILD A SHIP, SAIL TO SADNESS (National Film and Television School) Producer/Director, Laurin Federlein; Screenplay, Laurin Federlein, Magnus Aronson; Photography, Sadik Ahmed; Editor, Bert Hunger; Music, Magnus Aronson; British; Color, Hi-8-to-16mm-to-HD; Not rated; 69 minutes; Release date: February 1, 2008. Mockumentary about one man's efforts to build a mobile disco service in the Scottish Highlands.

SHROOMS (Magnolia) Producers, Robert Walpole, Paddy McDonald; Executive Producers, Gail Egan, Simon Channing-Williams; Coproducers, Nina Lyng, Eva Juel Hammerich; Director, Paddy Breathnach; Screenplay, Pearse Elliott; Photography, Nanu Segal; Editor, Dermot Diskin; Music, Dario Marianelli; Designer, Mark Geraghty; Costumes, Rosie Hackett; Special Effects Supervisor, Kevin Byrne; Visual Effects Supervisor, Alexander Marthin; Special Makeup Effects, Simon Rose; Stunts, Joe Condron; an Ingenious Film Partners presentation, in association with Irish Film Board, Nordisk Film, Northern Ireland Film & TV Commission, of a Treasure Entertainment (Ireland)/Potboiler Prods. (U.K.)/Nepenthe Film (Denmark) production; Irish-British-Danish; Dolby; Super 35 Widescreen; Color; Rated R; 82 minutes; American release date: February 8, 2008. CAST: Lindsey Haun (Tara), Jack Huston (Jake), Max Kasch (Troy), Maya Hazen (Lisa), Alice Greczyn (Holly), Don Wycherley (Ernie), Sean McGinley (Bernie), Robert Hoffman (Bluto), Toby Sedgwick (Black Brother)

Robert Hoffman, Toby Sedgwick in Shrooms © *Magnolia Films*

LONDON TO BRIGHTON (Outsider Pictures) Producers, Alastair Clark, Rachel Robey, Ken Marshall, Paul Andrew Williams; Executive Producers, Tony Bolton, Gisela Evert, Paul Trijbits; Director/Screenplay, Paul Andrew Williams; Photography, Christopher Ross; Photography, Christopher Ross; Editor, Tom Hemmings; Music, Laura Rossi; Music Supervisor, Lol Hammond; Designer/Costumes, Jane Levick; Casting, Tania Polentarutti; a U.K. Film Council presentation of a Steel Mill Pictures, Wellington Films production; British; Dolby; Panavision; Color; Not rated; 83 minutes; American release date: February 8, 2008. CAST: Lorraine Stanley (Kelly), Johnny Harris (Derek), Georgia Groome (Joanne), Sam Spruell (Stuart Allen), Alexander Morton (Duncan Allen), Nathan Constance (Chum), Claudie Blakely (Tracey), Jamie Kenna (Tony), Davis Keeling (Charlie), Jack Deam (Paul), Chloe Bale (Karen), Tim Matthews (Shane)

Lorraine Stanley, Georgia Groome in London to Brighton
© *Outsider Pictures*

BAB'AZIZ: THE PRINCE CONTEMPLATING HIS SOUL (Typecasting Releasing) Producers, Cyriac Auriol, Ali-Reza Shoojanoori; Coproducers, Mehran Haghighi, Nacer Khemir, Karl Baumgartner, Ernest Szebedits, Chris Curling, Phil Robertson, Andras Muhi; Director, Nacer Khemir; Screenplay, Nacer Khemir, Tonino Guerra; Photography, Mahmoud Kalari; Editor, Isabelle Rathery; Music, Armand Amar; Designer, Nacer Khemir; Costumes, Maud Perl; a Les Films du Requin (Paris)/Behnegar (Teheran) /Pegasos (Frankfurt)/Hannibal /Zephyr Films Ltd (London)/Inforg Studio(Hungary) coproduction; French-Tunisian-German-British-Hungarian; Color; Not rated; 96 minutes; American release date: February 8, 2008. CAST: Parviz Shahinkhou (Bab'Aziz), Maryam Hamid (Ishtar), Nessim Khaloul (Zaid), Mohamed Graïaa (Osman), Golshifteth Farahani (Nour), Soren Mehrabiar (Dervish)

EZRA (California Newsreel) Producers, Michel Loro, Girune Aprikian; Executive Producers, Newton I. Aduaka, Lamia Guellati, Jean-Michel Dissard; Director, Newton I. Aduaka; Screenplay, Newton I. Aduaka, Alain-Michel Blanc; Photography, Carlos Arango de Montis; Editor, Sebastien Touta; Music, Nicolas Baby; Designers, Malek Hamzaoui, Pierrick Lepochat; Costumes, Sophie Campana; an ARTE-France presentation of a Cinefacto/ARTE-France production, in association with Amou Fou FilmProduktion (Austria)/Sunday Morning, Pierre Javaux Prods. (France)/Granite Filmworks (U.K.)/Fat City (U.S.), with the participation of the Centre National de la Cinematographie and RTR Fernsehfonds (Austria); French-Austrian-British-American; Dolby; Color; Not rated; 110 minutes; American release date: February 13, 2008. CAST: Mamoudu Turay Kamara (Ezra), Mariame N'Diaye (Onitcha), Mamusu Kallon (Mariam), Merveille Lukeba (Moses), Richard Gant (Mac Mondale), Mercy Ojelade (Cynthia), Wale Ojo (Blackjesus)

Mamoudu Turay Kamara in Ezra
© *California Newsreel*

JODHAA AKBAR (UTV Motion Pictures) Producers, Ronnie Screwvala, Ashutosh Gowariker; Executive Producer, Sunita A. Gowariker; Director, Ashutosh Gowariker; Screenplay, Haider Ali, Sunita A. Gowariker, K.P. Saxema; Story, Haider Ali; Photography, Kiiraan Deohans; Editor, Ballu Saluja; Music, A.R. Rahman; Lyrics, Javed Akhtar; Art Director, Nitn Chandrakant Desai; Costumes, Neeta Lulla; Visual Effects, Pankaj Khandpur; Choreographers, Raju Khan, Rekha Chinni Prakash, Ash Kumar; Action Director, Ravi Dewan; a UTV Motion Pictures, Ashutosh Gowariker Prods. Production; Indian; Dolby; Widescreen; Color; Not rated; 205 minutes (I: 118 mins.; II: 87 mins.); American release date: February 15, 2008. CAST: Hrithik Roshan (Jalaluddin Mohammad Akbar), Aishwarya Rai Bachchan (Jodhaa Bai), Ila Arun (Maham Anga), Kulbhushan Kharbanda (Raja Bharmal), Suhasini Mulay (Padmavati), Digvijay Purohit (Bhagwan Das), Mrs. Punam S. Sinha (Hamida Banu), Sonu Sood (Sujamal), Rucha Vaidya (Rucha), Rajesh Vivek (Chughtai Khan), Yui (Bairam Khan) Ambitabh Bachcah (Narrator)

VIVERE (Regent) Producer, Anita Elsani; Coproducers, Raymond Van Der Kaaij, Susanne Kusche; Director/Screenplay, Angelina Maccarone; Photography, Judith Kaufmann; Designer, Peter Menne; Costumes, Ute Paffendorf; Music, Jakob Hansonis, Hartmut Ewert; an Elsani Film, Media Luna Entertainment production in association with Revolver, Screenart Filmprudktion; German-Netherlands; Dolby; Widescreen; Color; Not rated; 97 minutes; American release date: February 29, 2008. CAST: Hannelore Elsner (Gerlinde von Habermann), Esther Zimmering (Francesca Conchiglia), Kim Schnitzer (Antoinetta Conchiglia), Egbert Jan Weeber (Snickers), Aykut Kayacik (Enrico Conchiglia), Friederike Wagner (Inge Grewe), Nina Vorbrodt (Frau Polder), Inger Hansen, Evert Aalten, Maarten Hemmen (Bandmembers)

Egbert Jan Weeber, Kim Schnitzer in Vivere © *Regent Releasing*

ROMULUS, MY FATHER (Magnolia) Producers, Robert Connolly, John Maynard; Executive Producers, Andrew Myer, Gary Hamilton, Victor Syrmis; Director, Richard Roxburgh; Screenplay, Nick Drake; Based on the book by Raimond Gaita; Photography, Geoffrey Simpson; Designer, Robert Cousins; Music, Basil Hogios; Editor, Suresh Ayyar; a Film Finance Corp. Australia presentation of an ArenaFilm production, in association with the New South Wales Film and Television Office, Pick Up Truck Pictures; Australian; Dolby; Color; Rated R; 103 minutes; American release date: February 29, 2008. CAST: Eric Bana (Romulus), Franka Potente (Christina), Marton Csokas (Hora), Kodi Smit-McPhee (Rai), Russell Dykstra (Mitru), Jacek Koman (Vacek), Alethea McGrath (Mrs. Lillie), Esme Melville (Miss Collard), Terry Norris (Tom Lillie), Veronica Sywak (Lidia Vukovic)

Eric Bana, Kodi Smit-McPhee in Romulus, My Father © Magnolia Films

BLINDSIGHT (Abramorama) Producer, Sybill Robson Orr; Executive Producer, Steven Haft; Director, Lucy Walker; Photography, Petr Cikhart, Keith Partridge, Michael Brown; Editor, Sebastian Duthy; Music, Nitin Sawhney; a Robson Entertainment presentation; British; Dolby; Color; Mini-DV-and HD-to-35mm; Not rated; 104 minutes; American release date: March 5, 2008. Documentary on how visually impaired mountain-climber Erik Weinhenmayer climbed Mt. Everest with six bllind pupils from Lhasa, Tibet; With: Sabriye Tenberken, Erik Weinhenmayer, Sonam Bhumtso, Gyenshen, Dachung, Kyila, Tenzin, Tashi Pasang, Gavin Attwood, Sally Berg, Jeff Evans, Paul Kronenberg.

Erik Weihenmayer, Tashi Pasang in Blindsight © Abramorama

J'ENTENDS PLUS LA GUITARE (The Film Disk) a.k.a. *I Can No Longer Hear the Guitar*; Producers, Bernard Palacios, Gérard Vaugeois; Director/ Screenplay, Philippe Garrel; Dialogue, Marc Cholodenko; Adaptation, Jean-François Goyet; Photography, Caroline Champetier; Music, Faton Cahen; Editors, Sophie Coussein, Yann Dedet; a coproduction of Procirep, Centre National de la Cinématographie, Les Films de l'Atalante; French, 1991; Color; Not rated; 98 minutes; American release date: March 7, 2008. CAST: Benoît Régent (Gerard), Johanna ter Steege (Marianne), Yann Collette (Martin), Mireille Perrier (Lola), Brigitte Sy (Aline), Anouk Grinberg (Adrienne), Adélaïde Blasquez (Linda), Philippe Morier-Genoud (The Stepbrother), Edith Boulogne (The Grandmother), Thomas Salsmann (Marianne's Son), Alexis Piccolo (Ben), Chantal Trichet (Aline's Friend)

BLIND MOUNTAIN (Kino) a.k.a. *Mang shan*; Producer/Director/Screenplay, Li Yang; Executive Producers, Li Shan, Li Jua, Alexandra Sun; Photography, Jong Lin; Art Director, Shu Yang; Costumes, Liu Yi; Editors, Li Yang, Mary Stephen; Hong Kong-Chinese; Dolby; Color; Not rated; 95 minutes; American release date: March 12, 2008. CAST: Huang Lu (Bai Xuemei), Yang Youan (Huang Degui),

Zhang Yuli (Ding Xiuying, The Mother), He Yunie (Huang Decheng), Jia Yinqqao (Huang Changui, The Father), Zhang Youping (Li Qingshan)

Huang Lu in Blind Mountain © Kino Intl.

FLASH POINT (Genius Products) a.k.a. *Dao Huo Xian*; Producers, Nansun Shi, Donnie Yen, Shan Dong Bing, Zhang Zhao; Executive Producers, Raymond Wong, Yu Dong, Wang Chang Tian; Director, Wilson Yip; Action Director, Donnie Yen; Screenplay, Szeto Kam-Yuen; Photography, Cheung Man-po; Designer, Kenneth Mak; Costumes, Lee Pik-kwan; Music, Chan Kwon-wing; Editor, Cheung Ka-fai; Visual Effects, Menfond Electronic Art & Computer Design Co.; Action Choreographers, Kenji Tanigaki, Yan Hua; a Mandarin Films Distribution Co. production; Hong Kong, 2007; Dolby; Super 35 Widescreen; Color; Rated R; 88 minutes; American release date: March 14, 2008. CAST: Donnie Yen (Det. Sgt. Ma Jun), Louis Koo (Wilson), Collin Chou (Tony), Lui Leung Wai (Archer Sin), Fan Bing Bing (Julie), Kent Cheng (Inspector Wong), Xing Yu (Tiger), Xu Qing (Madam Lau), Ben Lam (Sam), Law Lan (Madam Ma), Ha Ping (Tony's Mum), Irene Wang (Cindy), Austin Wai (Four Eyes), Al Wai (Hero), Wong Chi Wai (Baldy), Aaron Leung (Deco), Kenji Tanigaki, Yu Kang (Tony's Underlings), Damian Green, Damon Howe, Min Yoo, Drafus Chow, Dus Luu (Boxers)

HEARTBEAT DETECTOR (Film Distribution) a.k.a. *La Question humaine*; Producers, Sophie Dulac, Michel Zana; Director, Nicolas Klotz; Screenplay, Elisabeth Perceval; Based on the book by Francois Emmanuel; Photography, Josee Deshaies; Designer, Antoine Platteau; Costumes, Dorothee Guiraud; Music, Syd Matters; Editor, Rose Marie Lausson; a Sophie Dulac Prods. production, in association with CNC and CineCinema, with the participation of Region Ile-de-France, Region des Pays de la Loire, Conseil General du Val de Marne, Conseil General de la Sarthe; French; Dolby; Color; Not rated; 140 minutes; American release date: March 14, 2008. CAST: Mathieu Amalric (Simon), Michael Lonsdale (Mathias Jüst), Edith Scob (Lucy Jüst), Lou Castel (Arie Neumann), Jean-Pierre Kalfon (Karl Rose), Valérie Dréville (Lynn Sanderson), Laetitia Spigarelli (Louisa), Delphine Chuillot (Isabelle), Nicolas Maury (Tavera), Rémy Carpentier (Jacques Paolini), Miguel Poveda (Flamenco Singer), Erwan Ribard (Miguel), Patrick Zocco (Cop)

Laetitia Spigarelli, Mathieu Amalric in Heartbeat Detector © Film Distribution

MALDEAMORES (Maya Releasing) Producer, Luillo Ruiz; Executive Producers, Benicio Del Toro, Robert Bevan, Cyril Megret, Donald Ranvaud; Director, Carlos Ruíz Ruíz; Screenplay, Carlos Ruíz Ruíz, Jorge Gonzales; Photography, P.J. López; Costumes, Suzanne Krim; Music, Omar Silva; Editor, Mariem Pérez Riera; Casting, Patricia Alonso; a Buena Onda, Puerto Rico Film Commission production; Puerto Rican-U.S.; Dolby; Color; Rated R; 83 minutes; American release date: March 14, 2008. CAST: Luis Guzmán (Ismael), Miguel Ángel Álvarez (Pellín), Silvia Brito (Flora), Yaraní del Valle (Luisa), Ednali Figueroa (Tati), Luis Gonzaga (Miguel), Teresa Hernández (Lourdes), Chavito Marrero (Cirilo), Dolores Pedro (Marta), Norman Santiago (Macho), Fernando Tarrazo (Ismaelito)

DOOMSDAY (Rogue) Producers, Steven Paul, Benedict Carver; Executive Producers, Peter McAleese, Trevor Macy, Marc D. Evans, Jeff Abberley, Julia Blackman; Director/Screenplay, Neil Marshall; Photography, Sam McCurdy; Designer, Simon Bowles; Costumes, John Norster; Music, Tyler Bates; Editor, Andrew MacRitchie; Visual Effects Supervisor, Hal Couzens; Visual Effects, Double Negative, The Senate Visual Effects; Special Makeup Effects Designer, Paul Hyett; Stunts, Cordell McQueen; Casting, Jeremy Zimmermann; a Crystal Sky Pictures production, in association with Scion Films, presented with Intrepid Pictures; British; Dolby; Color; Rated R; 109 minutes; American release date: March 14, 2008. CAST: Rhona Mitra (Eden Sinclair), Bob Hoskins (Bill Nelson), Adrian Lester (Norton), Alexander Siddig (John Hatcher), David O'Hara (Michael Canaris), Malcolm McDowell (Kane), Craig Conway (Sol), MyAnna Buring (Cally), Lee-Anne Liebenberg (Viper), Sean Pertwee (Dr. Talbot), Darren Morfitt (Dr. Ben Stirling), Les Simpson (Carpenter), Nora-Jane Noone (Read), Rick Warden (Chandler), John Carson (George Dutton), Jon Falkow (Capt. Hendrix), Nathalie Boltt (Jane Harris), Caryn Peterson (Vagrant Girl), Adeola Ariyo (Nurse), Emma Cleasby (Katherine Sinclair), Christine Tomlinson (Young Eden), Vernon Willemse (David/Gimp), Paul Hyett (Hot Dog Victim), Daniel Read (Sergeant #1), Karl Thaning (Pilot), Stephen Hughes (Johnson, Soldier #1), Jason Cope (Wall Guard), Ryan Kruger (Soldier), Nathan Wheatley (Patient "X"), Cecil Carter (DDS Assault Trooper), Jeremy Crutchley (Richter), Tom Fairfoot (John Michaelson), Eloise Cupido (Afro Girl), Lily Anderson (Bathtub Blonde), Az Abrahams (Pin Stripe), Susan Danford (Command Center Official), Chris Robson (Stevie Miller), Alessia Ramazzotti (Starved Girl), Shaamilla Noordien (Carpenter's Bat Attacker), Craig Conway (Sol), Nicholas Pauling (Cellar Jailer), Riaz Solker (Cellar Guard), Porteus Xandau Steenkamp (DJ), Axelle Carolyn (Drop Dead Girl), Benedict Carver (Podium Marauder #2), Martin Compston (Joshua), Henie Bosman (Telamon), Cal Macaninch (Chancellor Falco), Martin Ball (DDS Guard), Tyrell Kemlo (Pit Audience Member), Garry George, George Bailey (Pin Stripe's Security), Dermot Brogan (Command Center Guard)

Craig Conway, Rhona Mitra in Doomsday © Rogue Pictures

POISONED BY POLONIUM (Kino) formerly *Rebellion: The Litvinenko Case*; Producer, Olga Konskaya; Director, Andrei Nekrasov; Screenplay/Editors, Andrei Nekrasov, Olga Konskaya; Photography, Sergei Tsikhanovich, Marcus Winterbauer; Music/Vocals, Irina Bogushevskaya; Russian; Color; Not rated; 105 minutes; American release date: March 21, 2008. Documentary on the truth surrounding the death by poisoning of former Russian spy Alexander Litvinenko; with Alexander Litvinenko, Boris Berezovsky, Andr Glucksmann, Marina Litvinenko, Andrei Lugovoi, Anna Politkovskaya, Vladimir Putin

Boris Berezovsky in Poisoned by Polonium © Kino Intl.

BOARDING GATE (Magnolia) Producer, François Margolin; Director/Screenplay, Olivier Assayas; Photography, Yorick Le Saux; Designer, Francois-Renaud Labarthe; Music, Brian Eno; Editor, Luc Barnier; French-Luxembourg; Dolby; Color; Rated R; 106 minutes; American release date: March 21, 2008. CAST: Asia Argento (Sandra), Michael Madsen (Miles Rennberg), Carl Ng (Lester Wang), Kelly Lin (Sue), Joana Preiss (Lisa), Alex Descas (André), Kim Gordon (Kay)

Michael Madsen, Asia Argento in Boarding Gate © Magnolia Films

IRINA PALM (Strand) Producer, Sebastien Delloye; Coproducers, Diana Elbaum, Thanassis Karathanos, Karl Baumgartner, Jani Thiltges, Claude Waringo, Christine Alderson; Director, Sam Garbarski; Screenplay, Martin Herron, Philippe Blasband; Story, Philippe Blasband; Photography, Christophe Beaucarne; Designer, Veronique Sacrez; Costumes, Anushia Nieradzik; Music, Ghinzu; Editor, Ludo Troch; an Entre Chien et Loup (Belgium), Pallas Film (Germany), Samsa Film (Luxembourg), Ipso Facto Films (UK) production, in association with Liaison Cinematographique (France), Ateliers de Baere, RTBF Television (Belgium), with the support of MDM Foederung, Communaute Francaise de Blegique, Eurimages, Filmfoerderungsanstalt, FONSPA, Wallimage, Idi Media development, in association with Future Films, and the participation of Canal Plus; Belgian-German-Luxembourg-British-French; Dolby; Color; Rated R; 103 minutes; American release date: March 21, 2008. CAST: Marianne Faithful (Maggie, a.k.a. Irina Palm), Miki Manojlovic (Miki), Kevin Bishop (Tom), Siobhan Hewlett (Sarah), Dorka Gryllus (Luisa), Jenny Agutter (Jane), Corey Burke (Ollie), Meg Wynn Owen (Julia), Susan Hitch (Beth), Flip Webster (Edith), Tony O'Brien (Shopkeeper), Jules Werner (Doctor), Ann Queensberry, June Bailey (Old Ladies), Jonathan Coyne (Dave), Tim Plester (Frank), Malina Ebert (Dunia), Peter Sproule (Physio), Hassani Shapi (Consultant), Liam Reilly (Agency Man), Doraly Rosen (Bank Clerk), Ibrahima Sano (Ibrahim), Simon Anderson (Lad), Steve Kingett (A Pimp)

Kevin Bishop, Siobhan Hewlett, Marianne Faithful in Irina Palm
© *Strand Releasing*

WATER LILIES (Koch Lorber) a.k.a. *Naissance des pieuvres*; Producers, Jérome Dopffer, Benedicte Couvreur; Director/Screenplay, Celine Sciamma; Photography, Crystel Fournier; Designer, Gwendal Bescond; Costumes, Marine Chauveau; Music, Para One; Editor, Julien Lacheray; Casting, Christel Baras, Laure Cochener; a Balthazar production, in association with CNC, with participation of Canal Plus, and support of Region Ile-de-France, with the participation of Arte/Cofinova3; French; Dolby; Color; Not rated; 85 minutes; American release date: April 4, 2008. CAST: Pauline Acquart (Marie), Louise Blachère (Anne), Adele Haenel (Floriane), Warren Jacquin (François), Christelle Baras (Inspector), Marie Gili-Pierre (Cashier), Alice de Lencquesaing, Claire Pierrat (Cloakroom Girls), Esther Sironneau (Saleswoman), Jeremi Steib (Masseur), Yvonne Villemaire (Neighbor), Christophe Van de Velde (Box Type)

NANA (Viz Pictures) Producers, Toshiaki Nakazawa, Osamu Kubota; Executive Producers, Kunikatsu Kondo, Kazuya Hamana; Director, Kentaro Otani; Screenplay, Kentaro Otani, Taeko Asano; Based on the manga series by Ai Yazawa; Photography, Kazuhiro Suzuki; Art Director, Norihiro Isoda; Music, Tadashi Ueda; Song: "Glamorous Sky" by Ai Yazawa and Hyde; Editor, Hidekazu Kakesu; a Tokyo Broadcasting System presentation of a Tokyo Broadcasting System, Toho Co., Sedic Intl., Shueisha, True Project, IMJ Entertainment Corp., Mainichi Broadcasting System, Aniplex coproduction; Japanese; Color; Not rated; 113 minutes; American release date: April 4, 2008. CAST: Mika Nakashima (Nan Osaki), Aoi Miyazaki (Nana Komatsu), Hiroki Narimiya (Nobuo Terashima), Ken'ichi Matsuyama (Shin), Saeko (Sachiko), Yuna Ito (Reira Serizawa), Momosuke Mizutani (Naoki), Anna Nose (Jyunko), Takehisa Takayama (Kyosuke), Tomoki Maruyama (Yasu), Tetsuiji Tamayama (Takumi), Ryuhei Matsuda (Ren Honjou)

TUYA'S MARRIAGE (Music Box Films) a.k.a. *Tuya de hun shi*; Producer, Yan Jugang; Executive Producers, Yuan Hanyuan, Wang Le, Zhang Dehang; Director/Editor, Wang Quanan; Screenplay, Lu Wei; Photography, Lutz Reitemeier; Art Director, Wei Tao; Costumes, Lu Yi; a Maxyee Culture Industry Co. production, in association with Xi'an Motion Picture Co.; Chinese; Dolby; Color; Not rated; 86 minutes; American release date: April 4, 2008. CAST: Yu Nan (Tuya), Bater, Sen'ge, Zhaya.

Yu Nan in Tuya's Marriage
© *Music Box Films*

STALAGS (Yes, New Israeli Foundation on Cinema & TV) Producer, Barak Heymann; Coproducer/Director/Screenplay, Ari Libsker; Photography, Uri Levi, Dror Lebendiger; Editor, Morris Ben-Mayor; a Heymann Brothers film; Israeli; Black and white/color; DV; Not rated; 63 minutes; American release date: April 9, 2008. Documentary on Stalags, Israel's pulp fiction paperbacks, that were popular until outlawed for being pornographic; with Edi Keider, Ezra Narkis, Na'ama Shik, Sidra Ezxrahi, Hanna Yablonska.

BRA BOYS (Hopscotch/Berekela Films) Producers, Sunny Abberton, Mark Lawrence; Executive Producers, Nicholas Cook, Mark Lawrence, John Mossop; Director/Screenplay, Sunny Abberton; Codirector/Photography/Editor, Macaraio De Souza; Music, Jamie Holt; Narrator, Russell Crowe; a Bradahood Prods., Garage Industries production; Australian; Color; DV-to-35mm; Rated R; 86 minutes; American release date: April 11, 2008. Documentary on a band of surfers who dwell at Sydney's Maroubra beach; with Kelly Slater, Cheyne Horan, Jack Kingsley, Sean Doherty, Koby Abberton, Sunny Abberton, Jai Abberton, Wayne Cleveland, Maurice Cole, John Gannon, Mark Matthews, Wayne "Rabbit" Bartholomew, Nick Carroll, Derek Hynd, Inferno Man, Mark Occhilupo, Evan Faulks, Richie "Vas" Vaculik, Debbie Polock, Lynn Errington, Joel Errington, Prof. Paul Chandler, Rev. Steve Bligh, Laird Hamilton, Bruce Irons, William Brewer, Paul Hardin, Barry Waterson, Frog, Ommy-Tay, Billy Olsen, Ronnie "The Grouse" Reardon, John Sutton, Reni Maitua, Damon Alley-Tovio, Luke Kingsley, Nate Ford, Nick Nassar, Pete Abordi, Danny Birdran, Macario De Souza, James "Rooster" Adams, Paulo Brito, Chris Enaharo, Jess Chonga, Troy McDonald, Jimmy Olsen.

Bra Boys © *Hopscotch/Berekela*

GLASS: A PORTRAIT OF PHILIP IN TWELVE PARTS (Kino) Producers, Scott Hicks, Susanne Preissler; Executive Producers, Keerry Heysen, Roger Sexton; Coproducer, Lindsay Skutch; Director/Photography, Scott Hicks; Music, Philip Glass; Editor, Stephen Jess; an Independent Media presentation of a Mandalay Motion Pictures Pty Ltd. production, in association with Kojo Pictures; Australian; Color; DV; Not rated; 115 minutes; American release date: April 18, 2008. Documentary on minimalist composer Philip Glass; with Philip Glass, Holly Glass, Dennis Russell Davies, JoAnne Akalaitis, Chuck Close, Woody Allen.

Philip Glass in Glass © *Kino Intl*

YOUNG YAKUZA (Cinema Epoch) Producers, Hengameh Pahani, Christian Baute; Executive Producer, Sally Jo Fifer; Director, Jean-Pierre Limosin; Photography, Julien Hirsch, Celine Bozon; Music, RGM, Xavier Jamaux; Editor, Tina Baz; a Celluloid Dreams production, in coproduction with Arte France, ITVS in associaiton with COFICUP with the participation of the Centre National de la Cinematographie; French; Color; Not rated; 99 minutes; American release date: April 18, 2008. Documentary follows young Naoki Watanabe's indoctrination into a life of crime in the Japanese underworld; with Naoki Watanabe, Chiyozo Ishii, Hideyuki Ishii.

Right: Up the Yangtse © *Zeitgeist Films*

Naoki Watanabe in Young Yakuza © *Cinema Epoch*

FOUR MINUTES (Wolfe Releasing) a.k.a. *Vier Minuten*; Producers, Meike Kordes, Alexandra Kordes; Executive Producer, Meike Kordes; Director/Screenplay, Chris Kraus; Photography, Judith Kaufmann; Designer, Silke Buhr; Costumes, Gioia Raspe; Music, Annette Focks; Editor, Uta Schmidt; a Kordes & Kordes Film production; German; Color; 16mm-to-35mm Not rated; 114 minutes; American release date: April 18, 2008. CAST: Monica Bleibtreu (Traude Krüger), Hannah Herzsprung (Jenny von Loeben), Sven Pippig (Mütze), Richy Müller (Kowalski), Jasmin Tabatabai (Ayse), Amber Bongard (Clara Mütze), Stefan Kurt (Director Meyerbeer), Vadim Glowna (Gerhard von Loeben), Nadja Uhl (Nadine Hoffmann), Peter Davor (Journalist Wahrig), Edita Malovcic (Young Traude), Kathrin Kestler (Hannah), Christian Koerner (SS Head Storm Trooper), Dietrich Hollinderbaumer (Father Vincens), Dieter Moor (TV Moderator), Maria Hartmann (TV Contestant), Isolde Fischer (Usherette), Torsten Ranft (Entrepreneur)

TASHAN (Yash Raj Films) a.k.a. *Style*; Producers, Aditya Chopra, Yash Chopra; Executive Producers, Aashish Singh, Sanjay Shivalkar; Director/Screenplay, Vijay Krishna Acharya; Photography, Ayananka Bose; Art Director, Sukant Panigrahy; Editor, Ritesh Soni; Indian; Color; Not rated; 148 minutes; American release date: April 25, 2008. CAST: Akshay Kumar (Bachchan Pandey), Saif Ali Khan (Jeetnender "Jimmy Cliff" Kumar Makhwana), Kareena Kapoor (Pooja Singh), Anil Kapoor (Lakhan Singh urf Bhaiyyaji)

UP THE YANGTSE (Zeitgeist) Producers, Mila Aung-Thwin, Germaine Ying Gee Wong, John Christou; Executive Producers, Daniel Cross, Mila Aung-Thwin, Ravida Din, Sally Bochner; Director/Screenplay, Yung Chang; Photography, Wang Shi Qing; Associate Producers, Lixin Fan, Li Li; Music, Olivier Alary; Editor, Hannele Halm; an Eyesteelfilm presentation in coproduction with the National Film Board of Canada; Canadian; Dolby; Color; Not rated; 93 minutes; American release date: April 25, 2008. Documentary follows Cindy Yu Shui as she takes a job aboard a luxury cruise boat on the Yangtse River; with Cindy Yu Shui, Jerry Chen Bo Yu.

XXY (Film Movement) Producers, Luis Puenzo, Jose Maria Morales; Executive Producer, Fernando Sirianni; Director/Screenplay, Lucia Puenzo; Photography, Natasha Braier; Art Director, Roberto Samuelle; Editor, Alex Zito; a Wanda Vision (Spain)/Pyramide Prods. (France)/Historias Cinematograficas (Argentina) production; Spanish-French-Argentine; Color; Not rated; 86 minutes; American release date: May 2, 2008. CAST: Ricardo Darin (Kraken), Valeria Bertuccelli (Suli), Germán Palacios (Ramiro), Carolina Pelleritti (Erika), Martín Piroyansky (Alvaro), Inés Efron (Alex), Guillermo Angelelli (Juan), César Troncoso (Washington), Jean Pierre Reguerraz (Esteban), Ailín Salas (Roberta), Luciano Nóbile (Vando), Lucas Escariz (Saul)

Martin Piroyansky, Inés Efron in XXY © *Film Movement*

MISTER LONELY (IFC Films) Producer, Nadja Watson; Executive Producer, Peter Watson; Director, Harmony Korine; Screenplay, Harmony Korine, Avi Korine; Photography, Marcel Zyskind; Designer, Richard Campling; Costumes, Judy Shrewsbury; Music, Jason Spaceman, The Sun City Girls; Editors, Paul Zucker, Valdis Oskarsdottir; Coproducers, Adam Bohling, David Reid; an O'Salvation production, presented by Agnes B and Jeremy Thomas in association with Dreamachine, Gaga and Film4; British-French-Irish-American; Dolby; Color; Not rated; 112 minutes; American release date: May 2, 2008. CAST: Diego Luna (Michael Jackson), Samantha Morton (Marilyn Monroe), Denis Lavant (Charlie Chaplin), James Fox (The Pope), Melita Morgan (Madonna), Anita Pallenberg (The Queen), Rachel Korine (Little Red Riding Hood), Jason Pennycooke (Sammy Davis, Jr.), Richard Strange (Abe Lincoln), Michael-Joel Stuart (Buckwheat), Esme Creed-Miles (Shirley Temple), Mal Whiteley (Larry), Daniel Rovai (Moe), Nigel Cooper (Curly), Joseph Morgan (James Dean), Walid Afkir (Habib), Camillede Pazzis, Britta Gartner (Nuns), Werner Herzog (Father Umbrillo), David Blaine (Priest #2), Leos Carax (Renard), Alisa Grace Greaves (Autograph), Quentin Grosset (Le Petit Garçon)

Diego Luna in Mister Lonely
© *IFC Films*

Rade Sherbedgia, Robbie Kay in Fugitive Pieces © *Samuel Goldwyn*

FUGITIVE PIECES (Goldwyn) Producer, Robert Lantos; Executive Producers, Anras Hamori, Takis Veremis, Christina Ford, Mark Musselman; Director/Screenplay, Jeremy Podeswa; Based on the novel by Anne Michaels; Photography, Gregory Middleton; Designer, Matthew Davies; Costumes, Anne Dixon; Music, Nikos Kypourgos; Editor, Wiebke von Carolsfeld; Casting, John Buchan, Nina Gold, Laura Rosenthal, Makis Gazis; a Serendipity Point Films (Canada) presentation of a Robert Lantos production, in association with StraDa Prods. (Canada)/Cinegram S.A. (Greece); Canadian-Greek; Dolby; Deluxe color; Rated R; 108 minutes; American release date: May 2, 2008. CAST: Stephen Dillane (Jakob), Rade Sherbedgia (Athos), Rosamund Pike (Alex), Ayelet Zurer (Michaela), Robbie Kay (Young Jakob), Ed Stoppard (Ben), Rachelle Lefevre (Naomi), Nina Dobrev (Bella), Themis Bazaka (Mrs. Serenou), Diego Matamoros (Jozef), Sarah Orenstein (Sara), Larissa Laskin (Irena), Giorgos Karamihos (Ioannis), Danai Skiadi (Young Allegra), Memos Begnis (Makis), Marcia Bennett (Mrs. Taylor), Devon Bostick (Ben-Teen), Hakan Coskuner, Stefen Rollpiller, Jonathan Soja (German Soldiers), Elli Fotiou (Allegra–'50's), Daniel Kash (Maurice), Jennifer Podemski (Marylin), Gray Powell (Allen), Monika Schurmann (Jakob's Mother), Birgitte Solem (Ellen), Michael Stevens (Book Publisher)

BATTLE FOR HADITHA (Hanway) Producer/Director, Nick Broomfield; Executive Producers, Peter Dale, Charles Finch; Coproducer, Anna Telford; Screenplay, Nick Broomfield, Marc Hoeferlin, Anna Telford; Photography, Mark Wolf; Designer, David Bryan; Music, Nick Laird-Clowes; Editors, Ash Jenkins, Stuart Gazzard; a Film Four/Lafayette Film Ltd. presentation; British; Dolby; Super 35 Widescreen; Color; HD Video; Not rated; 93 minutes; American release date: May 7, 2008. CAST: Elliot Ruiz (Cpl. Ramirez), Yasmine Hanani (Hiba), Andrew McLaren (Capt. Sampson), Matthew Knoll (Cpl. Matthews), Thomas Hennessy (Doc), Vernon Gaines (Lcpl. Sosa), Danny Martinez (Lcpl. Santos), Joe Chacon (Lcpl. Lopez), Eric Mehalacopoulos (Sgt. Ross), Jase Willette (Pfc. Cuthbert), Antonio Tostado (Lcpl. Jimenez), Tony Spencer (Pfc. Roberts), Nick Shakoour (Pfc. Hanoon), Alysha Westlake (CNN News Anchor), Oliver Bytrus (Jafar), Nathan DelaCruz (Cpl. Marcus), Ali Adill Al-kaanan Desher (Shrek), Falah Abrahemm Flayeh (Ahmade – Gunman), Duraid A. Ghaieb (Rashied)

FRONTIER(S) (Lionsgate/After Dark) Producer, Laurent Tolleron; Director/Screenplay, Xavier Gens; Photography, Laurent Bares; Designer, Jeremy Streliski; Music, Jean-Pierre Taieb; Editor, Carlo Rizzo; a EuropaCorp. presentation in association with Cartel Prods., Chemin Vert Prods., Pacific Films, BR Films, Canal Plus and Cinecinema; French-Swiss; Dolby; Color; Rated NC-17; 108

minutes; American release date: May 9, 2008. CAST: Karina Testa (Yasmine), Aurélien Wiik (Alex), Patrick Ligardes (Karl), David Saracino (Tom), Maud Forget (Eva), Samuel Le Bihan (Goetz), Chems Dahmani (Farid), Amélie Daure (Klaudia), Estelle Lefébure (Gilberte), Rosine Favey (The Old Windpipe), Adel Bencherif (Sami), Joël Lefrançois (Hans), Jean-Pierre Jorris (Le Von Geisler)

Estelle Lefébure, Amélie Daure in Frontier(s) © *Lionsgate*

A PREVIOUS ENGAGEMENT (Palisades Pictures) Producer, David Gordian; Executive Producers, Antony Blakey, Toby Mathews, Damita Nikaporta; Coproducer, Savitri Gordian; Co-Executive Producer, Mark Paladini; Director/Screenplay, Joan Carr-Wiggin; Photography, Bruce Worrall; Art Director, Ino Bonello; Costumes, Charlotte Walter; Editors, Pamela Benwick, Richard Benwick, Joan Carr-Wiggin; Casting, Simone Reynolds, Mark Paladini; a Paragraph Pictures presentation with UFKS Films, of an Ashdale Films (Malta)/Buccaneer Films production; Canadian-Maltese-British; Color; Not rated; 118 minutes; Release date: May 9, 2008. CAST: Juliet Stevenson (Julia Reynolds), Tchéky Karyo (Alex Belmont), Daniel Stern (Jack Reynolds), Valerie Mahaffey (Grace), Claire Brosseau (Jenny Reynolds), Hendrik Jansen (Hendrik), Kate Miles (Samantha), Derek Riddell (Hotel Desk Clerk), Daniela Saioni (Woman in Café), Pierre Stafrace (Store Clerk), Elizabeth Whitmere (Jill Reynolds), Simon Woods (Tyler)

Tchéky Karyo, Juliet Stevenson, Daniel Stern in A Previous Engagement © *Palisades Pictures*

MY FATHER MY LORD (Kino) a.k.a. *Hofshat Kaits*; Producer, Eyal Shiray; Director/Screenplay, David Volach; Photography, Boaz Yehonatan Yaacov; Editor, Haim Tabacmen; Israeli; Color; Not rated; 72 minutes; American release date: May 16, 2008. CAST: Assi Dayan (Reb Abraham Eidelman), Ilan Griff (Menahem Eidelman), Sharon Hacohen (Esther)

Ilan Griff in My Father My Lord © *Kino Intl.*

YELLA (Cinema Guild) Producers, Florian Koerner von Gustorf, Michael Weber; Director/Screenplay, Chrsitian Petzold; Photography, Hans Fromm; Art Director, Kade Gruber; Costumes, Anette Guther, Lotte Sawatzki; Casting, Simon Baer; a Schramm Film, ZDF, Arte production; German, 2007; Dolby; Color; Not rated; 89 minutes; American release date: May 16, 2008. CAST: Nina Hoss (Yella), Devid Striesow (Philipp), Hinnerk Schönemann (Ben), Burghart Klaußner (Dr. Gunthen), Barbara Auer (Barbara Gunthen), Christian Redl (Yellas Vater), Selin Barbara Petzold (Dr. Gunthens Tochter), Wanja Mues (Sprenger), Michael Wittenborn (Schmidt-Otto), Martin Brambach (Dr. Fritz), Joachim Nimtz (Prietzel), Peter Benedict (Friedrichs Anwalt), Ian Norval (Receptionist)

Nina Hoss in Yella © *Cinema Guild*

THE MACHINE GIRL (Media Blasters) a.k.a. *Kataude mashin gâru*; Producers, Yoko Hayama, Yoshinori Chiba, Satoshi Nakamura; Executive Producer, John Sirabella; Director/Screenplay, Noboru Iguchi; Photography, Yasutaka Magano; Designer, Yasuo Kuroso; Music, Koh Nakagawa; Editor, Kenji Tanabe; Special Effects & Gore Effects, Yoshihiro Nishimura; a Fever Dreams presentation of a Tokyo Shock Original, Nikkatsu, Fever Dreams production; Japanese; Color; Not rated; 96 minutes; American release date: May 23, 2008. CAST: Asami, Honoka, Yûya Ishikawa, Ryôsuke Kawamura, Noriko Kijima, Kentarô Kishi, Nobuhiro

Nishihara, Ryôji Okamoto, Kentarô, Tarô Suwa, Demo Tanaka, Erika Terajima, Hiroko Yashiki, Minase Yashiro.

RFK MUST DIE: THE ASSASSINATION OF BOBBY KENNEDY (3DD Entertainment) Producer/Director/Screenplay/Editor, Shane O'Sullivan; Photography, George Dougherty; Music, Pyratek; Associate Producer, Anita Lewton; an E2 Films production; British; Color; Not rated; 139 minutes; American release date: June 6, 2008. Documentary on the June 1968 assassination of Senator Robert Kennedy during his campaign for the presidency; with Bradley Ayers, Frank Burns, Ruben Carbajal, Evan Freed, Haynes Johnson, Robert Blair Kaiser, Ed Lopez, Michael McCowan, David Rabern, Paul Schrade, Munir Sirhan, Wayne Smith, Herbert Spiegel, Lawrence Teeter, Robert Walton.

Martin Luther King Jr., Robert Kennedy in RFK Must Die
© 3DD Entertainment

MOTHER OF TEARS (Mitropolous) a.k.a. *La Tezra Madre*; Producers, Dario Argento, Claudio Argento; Executive Producers, Claudio Argento, Kirk D'Amico, Giulia Marletta; Director/Story, Dario Argento; Screenplay, Dario Argento, Jace Anderson, Adam Gierasch; Photography, Frederic Fasano; Designers, Francesca Bocca, Valentina Ferroni; Costumes, Ludovica Amati; Music, Claudio Simonetti; Editor, Walter Fasano; Special Makeup F/X, Sergio Stivaletti; Visual Effects, Lee Wilson, Lisa-Sepp Wilson, Anthem Visual Effects; Casting, Helena Palmer; a Medusa Film production in association with Myriad Pictures; Italian-U.S.; Dolby; Color; Not rated; 98 minutes; American release date: June 6, 2008. CAST: Asia Argento (Sarah Mandy), Cristian Solimento (Det. Enzo Marchi), Adam James (Michael Pierce), Moran Atias (Mater Lachrymarum), Valeria Cavalli (Marta Colussi), Philippe Leroy (Guglielmo De Witt), Daria Nicolodi (Elisa Mandy), Coralina Cataldi-Tassoni (Giselle Mares), Udo Kier (Father Johannes), Robert Madison (Agent Lissoni), Jun Ichikawa (Katerina), Tommaso Banfi (Father Milesi), Paolo Stella (Julian), Clive Riche (Man in Overcoat), Massimo Sarchielli (Vagabond), Barbara Mautino (Valeria), Gisella Margeno, Marcia Coco (Witches in Catacombs), Diego Bottigelieri (Indian), Franco Leo (Monsignor Brusca), Silvia Rubino (Elga), Claudio Fadda, Roberto Donati, Gianni Gatta (Demons), Luca Pescatore (Paul Pierce), Alessandro Zeme (Luigi), Antonio Pescatore (Agent), Stefano Fregni (Cab Driver), Simonetta Solder (Giovane Mother), James Kelly Caldwell (TV Announcer), Simone Sitta (Guide)

Mother of Tears © *Mitropolous*

ON THE RUMBA RIVER (First Run Features) a.k.a. *Le Batelier de la Rumba*; Producer/Director, Jacques Sarasin; Photography, Remon Fromont; Music, Wendo Kolosoy; Editor, Bernard Josse; French-Congolese, 2007; Dolby; Color; Not rated; 83 minutes; American release date: June 6, 2008. Documentary on Congolese singer Wendo "Papa Wendo" Kolosoy; with Wendo Kolosoy, Mbinga Kabata, Antoine Moudanda, Joseph Munange, Mukubuele Nzoku, Aminata Panda, Alphonse Biolo Batilangandi, and Michel Vula Makonzo.

Wendo Kolosoy, Antoine Moudanda in On the Rumba River
© First Run Features

MISS CONCEPTION (First Look Studios) Producer, Doris Kirch; Coproducer, Michel Morales; Director, Eric Styles; Screenplay, Camilla Leslie; Photography, Ed Mash; Designer, Humphrey Jaeger; Music, Christian Henson; Editor, Danny Tull; a Blue Angel Films production, in coproduction with Miromar Entertainment, in association with Northern Ireland Screen and Intl. Film Finance; British-Irish; Dolby; Widescreen; Color; Rated R; 103 minutes; American release date: June 6, 2008. CAST: Heather Graham (Georgina), Mia Kirshner (Clem), Tom Ellis (Zak), Will Mellor (Brian), Orlando Seale (Justin), Laurence Doherty (Funeral Director), Ruta Gedmintas (Alexandra), Laura Goulding (Aunt Harriet), Nathan Hughes (Tease), Laure James (Model), Debbie Javor (Dalia), Robert Kane (Nerdy Guy), Charlie Kranz (Bob Tushy), Nicholas Le Prevost (Dr. Dupompe), Edward MacLiam (Ben), Mary Ellen McCartan, Bronagh Waugh (Receptionists), Anthony McKenna

(Gay Wake Guest), Vivienne Moore (Mrs. Salt), Olivia Nash (Cash Till Lady), Davina ONCall (Drag Queen), Richard Parkin (Hotel Manager), Cathal Sheahan (Malcolm), Jeremy Sheffield (James), Paul Telfer (Luca), Maria Watton-Graham (Rebecca)

Heather Graham, Maria Watton-Graham in Miss Conception
© *First Look*

LOVE COMES LATELY (Kino Intl.) Producers, Martin Hagemann, Kai Kunnemann; Executive Producers, W. Wilder Knight II, Alex Gibney; Coproducers, Danny Krausz, Heidi Levitt, Friedemann Schuchardt, Jan Schutt, Matt Salinger; Director/Screenplay, Jan Schuette; Based on the short stories "The Briefcase," "Alone," and "Old Love" by Isaac Bashevis Singer; Photography, Edward Klosinski, Chris Squires; Designer, Amanda Ford; Music, Henning Lohner; Editors, Katja Dringenberg, Renate Merck; a Zero West production in coproduction with Zero Fiction, Dor Film; German-American; Dolby; Color; Not rated; 86 minutes; Release date: June 13, 2008. CAST: Otto Tausig (Max Kohn), Tovah Feldshuh (Ethel), Rhea Perlman (Reisel), Barbara Hershey (Rosalie), Elisabeth Pena (Esperanza), Caroline Aaron (Rachel Meyerowitz), Olivia Thirlby (Sylvia), Lee Wilkof (Alfred Meyer), Leander Suleiman (Chambermaid), Brad Lee Wind (Window Repairman), Michael Edward Brooks (Window Repairman's Helper), Jason Hedges (Waiter), Elizabeth Marley (Caterer), Christina Szápáry (Hotelier's Wife)

Otto Tausig, Caroline Aaron in Love Comes Lately © *Kino Intl.*

TO THE LIMIT (First Run Features) a.k.a. *Am Limit*; Producers, Kirsten Hager, Erich Lackner, Mirjam Quinte; Director/Screenplay, Pepe Danquart; Photography, Wolfgang Thaler; Music, Christoph Israel, Dorian Cheah; Editor, Mona Brauer; a Hager Moss Film, Quinte Film (Germany)/Lotus Film (Vienna) production; German-Austrian; Dolby; Color; Not rated; 95 minutes; American release date: June 13, 2008. Documentary on speed rock climbing; with Thomas Huber, Alexander Huber, Dean S. Potter, Chongo.

Alexander Huber, Thomas Huber in To the Limit © *First Run Features*

WARSAW BRIDGE (Films 59) a.k.a. *El Puente de Varsovia*; Producer, J.A. Gonzalez Serret; Director, Pere Portabella; Screenplay, Pere Portabella, Octavi Pellissa, Carles Santos; Photography, Tomas Pladevall; Music, Carles Santos; Color; Not rated; 85 minutes; American release date: June 13, 2008. CAST: Paco Guijar (Musician), Jordi Dauder (Writer), Carmen Elias, Francesc Orella (Professors), Ona Planas (Fille), Jose Maria Pou (Editor), Jaume Comas (Maire), Pep Ferrer (Doctor), Ricard Borras, Ferran Rane, Joan Lluis Bozzo, Quim Llobet, Joan Miralles (Jury Members)

BEAUTY IN TROUBLE (Menemsha) a.k.a. *Kráska v nesnázích*; Producer, Ondrej Trojan; Coproducer, Jaroslav Kucera; Director, Jan Hrebejk; Screenplay, Petr Jarchovsky; Story, Petr Jarchovsky, Jan Hrebejk; Photography, Jan Malir; Art Director, Milan Bycek; Costumes, Katarina Bielkova; Music, Ales Brezina; Editor, Vladimir Barak; a Total HelpArt production, in association with Czech TV, HBO; Czech, 2006; Dolby; Color; Not rated; 110 minutes; American release date: June 13, 2008. CAST: Ana Geislerová (Marcela Cmolikova), Roman Luknár (Jarda Smolik), Emília Vásáryová (Liba Cmolikova), Jana Brejchová (Zdena Hrstkova), Jirí Schmitzer (Richard Hrstka), Josef Abrhám (Evzen Benes), Jan Hrusinksy (Havlik), Jirí Machácek (Patocka), Andrei Toader (Mirek), Nikolai Penev (Picus), Jaromíra Mílová (Havliková), Adam Misík (Kuba Cmolik), Michaela Mrvíková (Lucina Cmolikova), Raduza (Herself)

Ana Geislerova in Beauty in Trouble © *Menemsha*

HAIR EXTENSIONS (Media Blasters) a.k.a. *Ekusuke*; Producers, Makoto Okada, Thuguo Hattori; Executive Producers, Mitsuru Kurosaw, Shigeyuki Endo; Director, Sion Sono; Screenplay, Sion Sono, Masanori Adachi, Makoto Sanda; Photography, Hiroo Yanagida; Designer, Katsuhiro Fukuzawa; Music, Tomoki Hasegawa; Editor, Junichi Ito; a Toei Co. presentation of a Toei Picture production; Japanese; Dolby; Color; Not rated; 108 minutes; American release date: June 20, 2008. CAST: Chiaki Kuriyama (Yuko Mizushima), Ren Osugi (Gunji Yamazaki), Megumi Sato (Yuki Morita), Tsugumi (Kiyomi Mizumshima), Eri Machimoto (Sachi Koda), Miku Sato (Mami Mizushima)

Hair Extensions © *Media Blaster*

ELSA & FRED (DistriMax) Producer, Jose Antonio Felez; Director, Marcos Carnevale; Screenplay, Marcos Carnevale, Lily Ann Martin, Marcela Guerty, Jose Antonio Felez; Photography, Juan Carlos Gomez; Music, Lito Vitale; Editor, Nacho Ruiz Capillas; a Tesela (Spain)/Shazam (Argentina) production, with the participation of TVE, Canal Plus; Spanish-Argentine; Dolby; Widescreen; Color; Not rated; 106 minutes; American release date: June 27, 2008. CAST: Manuel Alexandre (Fred), China Zorrilla (Elsa), Blanca Portillo (Cuca), Jose Ángel Egido (Paco), Omar Muñoz (Javi), Roberto Carnaghi (Gabriel), Carlos Álvarez-Nóvoa (Juan), Gonzalo Urtizberéa (Alejo), Fanny Gautier (laura), Federico Luppi (Pablo), Tomás Sáez (Goyo), Manolo Solo, Julián Villagrán (Doctors), Roberto Mosca (Conserje), Fabrizio Meschini (Botones), Claudia Álvarez (Carla), Pilar Valero (Mujer Bar)

WE ARE TOGETHER (THINA SIMUNYE) (Palm Pictures) Producers, Teddy Leifer, Paul Taylor; Executive Produces, Leigh Blake, Sheila Nevins, Jess Search; Director, Paul Taylor; Screenplay, Slindile Moya, Paul Taylor; Photography, Pauline von Moltke; Designer, Pixeco.com; Music, Dario Marianelli; Editors, Masahiro Hirakubo, Ollie Huddleston; a Rise Films production in association with the Channel 4 British Documentary Film Foundation/ HBO Documentary Films; British-South African; Dolby; Color; Rated PG; 83 minutes; American release date: July 4, 2008. Documentary on the importance of music at the "Grandma" Zodwa Mqadi's Agape orphanage in South Africa; with Slindile Moya, Sifiso Moya, "Grandma" Zodwa Mqadi, Mbali, Mthobisi Moya, Nonkululeko Moya, Swaphiwe Moya, Lorraine Bracco, Alicia Keys, Paul Simon, Kanye West.

EIGHT MILES HIGH (Dokument Films) a.k.a. *Das wilde leben*; Producers, Eberhard Junkersdorf, Dietmar Guntsche; Executive Producers, Moritz Eckes, Wolfgang Behr; Director, Achim Bornhak; Screenplay, Olaf Kraemer, Achim Bornhak; Based on the autobiography by Uschi Obermaier; Photography, Benjamin Dernbecher; Designer, Eduard Karjewski; Costumes, Petra Kay; Music, Alexander Hacke; Editor, Peter Pryzgodda; a Neue Bioskop Germany production, in coproduction with Studio Babelsberg film, Hofmann & Voges Entertainment, Senator film Produktion, TV60 Filmproduktion, Kinowelt Filmproduktion, Munich animation Fil, Neue Bioskop Film; German, 2007; Dolby; Widescreen; Color; Not rated; 114 minutes; American release date: July 11, 2008. CAST: Natalia Avelon (Uschi Obermaier), David Scheller (Dieter Bockhorn), Matthias Schweighöfer

(Rainer Langhans), Friederike Kempter (Sabine), Alexander Scheer (Keith Richards), Victor Norén (Mick Jagger), Milan Peschel (Freiberg), Georg Friedrich (Lurchi), Valerie Lasserre (Angel), Stefan Sieweke (Charlie Watts), Sebastian Stielke (Journalist), Christian Quander (Stones Groupie)

Natalia Avelon, Alexander Scheer in Eight Miles High
© *Dokument Films*

LA FRANCE (Independent) Producer, David Thion; Director, Serge Bozon; Screenplay, Axelle Ropert; Photography, Celine Bozon; Designer, Brigitte Brassart; Costumes, Renaud Legrand; Music, Medhi Zannad, Benjamin Esdraffo; Lyrics, Serge Bozon; Editor, Francois Quiquere; a Les Films Pelleas presentation, with the participation of Centre National de la Cinematographie and Cinecinema; French, 2007; Dolby; Color; Not rated; 102 minutes; American release date: July 11, 2008. CAST: Sylvie Tustud (Camille), Pascal Greggory (The Lieutenant), Guillaume Verdier (Le Cadet), Bob Boisadan (Guitarist), Jean-Christophe Bouvet (Elias), Didier Brice (Jean), Philippe Chemin (Liaison Officer), Guillaume Depardieu (François), Benjamin Esdraffo (Pierre), Michel Fossiez (The Oboist), Laurent Lacotte (Frédéric), Pierre Léon (Alfred), Emmanuel Levaufre (Elias's Son), François Négret (Jacques), Cécile Reigher (Camille's Sister), Laurent Talon (Antoine), Lionel Turchi (The Violinist)

A VERY BRITISH GANGSTER (Anywhere Road Entertainment) Producer/ Director, Donal MacIntyre; Executive Producer, Chris Shaw; Photography, Nick Manly, Mike Turnbull; Editor, Sally Hilton; a Dare Films presentation in association with the Irish Film Board, Extreme Prods., and Belfast TV3 Dublin; British-Irish, 2007; Release date: July 18, 2008. Documentary on British mobster Dominic Noonan.

Dominic Noonan in A Very British Gangster © Anywhere Road

MAD DETECTIVE (IFC Films) a.k.a. *San Taam*; Producers, Johnnie To, Wai Ka-fai; Executive Producer, Charles Heung; Directors, Johnny To, Wai Ka-Fai; Screenplay, Wai Ka-fai, Au Kin-yee; Photography, Cheng Siu-keung; Designer, Raymond Chan; Costumes, Stanley Cheung; Music, Xavier Jamaux; Editor, Tina Baz; a One Hundred Years of Cinema presentation of a Milkyway Image (H.K.) production; Hong Kong, 2007; Dolby; Widescreen; Color; Not rated; 89 minutes; American release date: July 18, 2008. CAST: Lau Ching Wan (Inspector Chan Kwai Bun), Andy On (Inspector Ho Ka On), Lam Ka Tung (Ko Chi Wai), Kelly Lin (May Cheung), Lee Kwok Lun (Wong Kwok Chu), Karen Lee (Gigi), Flora Chan (May Cheung), Cheung Siu Fai (Violent Man, Ko's Inner Personality), Lam Suet (Fatso–Ko's Inner Personality), Lau Kam Ling (Calculating Woman–Ko's Inner Personality), Eddy Ko (The Chief), Jo Koo (Cunning Woman–Ko's Inner Personality), Yuen Ling To (Policeman), Jonathan Lee (Weak Boy–Ko's Inner Personality), Ronald Yan (Chi-Wai's Boss)

WONDERFUL TOWN (Kino) Producers, Soros Sukhum, Jetnipith Teerakulchanyut; Director/Screenplay, Aditya Assarat; Photography, Umpornpol Yugala; Designer, Karanyapas Khamsin; Costumes, Thanon Songsil; Music, Zai Kuning, Koichi Shimizu; Editor, Lee Chatametikool; a Pop Pictures production; Thai, 2007; Color; HD-to-35mm; Not rated; 92 minutes; American release date: July 18, 2008. Documentary on how the Thai town of Pakua Park struggles to rebuild itself following the devastating 2004 tsunami.

Wonderful Town © Kino Intl.

NO REGRET (here!/Regent) a.k.a. *Huhwaehaji Anah*; Producer, Peter Kim; Executive Producer, Shin Hye-yeun; Director/Screenplay, Leesong Hee-il; Photography, Yun Ji-un; Designer, Park Hye-sung; Costumes, Lee Yoon-shin; Music, Lee Byung-hoon; Editors, Leesong Hee-il, Lee Jeong-min; a DCG Plus presentation of a Generation Blue Films production; South Korean, 2006; Dolby; Color; HD Cam; Not rated; 114 minutes; American release date: July 25, 2008. CAST: Lee Young-hoon (Sumin), Lee Han (Jaemin), Cho Hyun-chul, Kim Dong-wook, Jung Seung-gil

Lee Young-hoon, Lee Han in No Regret © Regent Releasing

BACK TO NORMANDY (Kino) a.k.a. *Retour en Normandie*; Producers, Serge Lalou, Gilles Sandoz, Michel Reilhac, Thierry Garrel, Remi Burah; Director/ Screenplay/ Photography/Narrator, Nicolas Philibert; Editors, Nicolas Philibert, Thaddee Bertrand; a Les Films d'Ici, Maia Films, Arte France Cinema production, with backing from Canal Plus, TPS Star, CNC and France Televisions Distribution; French, 2007; Color; Not rated; 113 minutes; American release date: July 25, 2008. Documentary in which filmmaker Nicolas Philibert speaks with the villagers who had participated in the 1975 film *I, Pierre Riviere, Having Slaughtered My Mother, My Sister and My Brother …* on which Philibert was the assistant director; with Joseph Leportier, Marie-Louise Leportier, Nicole Picard, Gilbert Peschet, Blandine Peschet, Annick Bisson, Michel Bisson, Jacqueline Milliere, Anne Borel, Catherine Borel, Christopher Borel, Olivier Borel, Pierre Borel, Yvonne Borel, Norbert Delozier, Charles Lihou, Annie Lihou, Roger Peschet, Caroline Itasse, Janine Callu, Nicole Cornue, Bruno Gahery, Claude Hebert.

LATE BLOOMER (Tidepoint) a.k.a. *Osoi hito*; Producer, Toshiki Sima; Director, Gô Shibata; Screenplay, Go Shibata, Satoshi Naka, Masakiyo Sumida, Narihito Terauchi; Photography, Masaaki Takakura, Atsushi Takeuchi; Music, World's End Girlfriend; Editors, Keita Ichikawa, Keisuke Suzuki; a Shima Films production; Japanese, 2004; Black and white/color; DV; Not rated; 83 minutes; American release date: July 25, 2008. CAST: Ariko Arita (Oba-chan), Toshihisa Fukunaga (Fukunaga), Naozô Hotta (Take), Sumiko Shirai (Aya), Masakiyo Sumida (Sumida), Mari Torii (Nobuko)

CANARY (Bandai Visual/ImaginAsian Pictures) a.k.a. *Kanaria*; Producer, Hiroko Matsuda; Executive Producers, Shiro Sasaki, Shigehiro Nakagaawa, Kazumi Kawashiro; Director/Screenplay, Akihito Shiota; Photography, Yutaka Yamazaki; Music, Yoishihide Otomo; Editor, Toshihide Fukano; an ImaginAsian Pictures, Bandai Visual presentation of an Office Shirious, Bandai Visual, Canary Film Partners production; Japanese, 2005; Color; Not rated; 132 minutes; American release date: July 25, 2008. CAST: Hoshi Ishida (Koichi Iwase), Mitsuki Tanimura (Yuki Niina), Hidetoshi Nishijima (Akira Izawa), Miyako Koda (Michiko Iwase), Noriko Eguchi (Kimura), Yukiko Inoue (Old Woman), Kenji Mizuhasi (Juana), Ryô (Saki), Tôru Shinagawa (Koichi's Grandfather), Masahiro Toda (Yoshioka), Tsugumi (Kozue)

SIXTY SIX (First Independent) Producers, Tim Bevan, Eric Fellner, Elizabeth Karlsen; Executive Producers, Richard Curtis, Natascha Wharton; Director/Story, Paul Weiland; Screenplay, Peter Straughan, Bridget O'Connor; Photography, Daniel Landin; Designer, Michael Howells; Costumes, Rebecca Hale; Music, Joby Talbot; Music Supervisor, Nick Angel; Editor, Paul Tothill; a Universal Pictures, Working Title Films presentation, in association with Studiocanal, of a WT2 production, in association with Ingenious Film Partners 2 LLP; British, 2006; Dolby; Technicolor; Super 8-to-35mm; Rated PG-13; 94 minutes; American release date: August 1, 2008. CAST: Helena Bonham Carter (Esther Reubens), Eddie Marsan (Manny Reubens), Gregg Sulkin (Bernie Reubens), Ben Newton (Alvie Reubens), Stephen Rea (Dr. Barrie), Catherine Tate (Aunt Lila), Peter Serafinowicz (Uncle Jimmy/Mr. Reubens, Sr./Football Commentator), Geraldine Somerville (Alice Barrie), Richard Katz (Rabbi Linov), Thomas Drewson (Terry Shivers), Matt Bardock (Mr. Grieg), Alex Black (Linton), Cameron Crighton (Captain), Charlie Clark (Boy with Caliper), Nick Shrim (Michael Hempel), Francine Simmons (Lady at Door), Martin Savage (Senior Doctor), Ony Uhiara (Nurse), Charles Ferber (Student Doctor), Vincenzo Nicoli (Leo), Jason Watkins (Mr. Spender), Stephen Grief (Uncle Henry), Joseph Weiland, Hannah Weiland, Bella Weiland (Children at Table), Daniel Dresner, Lawrence Lambert (Bar Mitzvah Fathers), Daniel Marks (Raymond), Sam Marzell (Stephen), David Verrey (Mr. Kimmel), Adam Nikel (Kimmel, Jr.), Maria Charles (Mrs. Gliztman), Mali Harries (Mrs. Shivers), Angus Barnett (Stan Shivers), Romolo Bruni (Shoe Shop Owner), Sean McGinley (Mr. O'Connor), Peter Stern (Shoe Shop Customer), David Bark-Jones (Alice's Young Man), Robert Horwell, Carston Hayes (Firemen), Esther Coles (Cousin Sarah), Rosella Emanuell (Woman Sewing), Moya Brady (Fiji Woman), James Puddephatt (Onlooker at Shoe Shop), Stephen Robins (Cantor), Esther Weiland (Bar Mitzvah Guest), Daniel Cerqueira (Mr. Levine), Gareth Marks (Mr. Wall), Dave Cohen (Bar Mitzvah Garden Husband), Frankey Martyn (Bar Mitzvah Garden Wife), Rory McCann (Policeman), Alfie Allen (Younger Trout), Gawn Grainger (Guest)

Gregg Sulkin, Helena Bonham Carter in Sixty Six © *First Independent*

JACK BROOKS: MONSTER SLAYER (Anchor Bay) Producers, Patrick White, Trevor Matthews, Neil Bregman; Executive Producers, Terry & Ann Matthews, Wesley Clover International; Director, Jon Knautz; Screenplay, Jon Knautz, John Ainslie; Story, Jon Knautz, Trevor Matthews, Patrick White, John Ainslie; Photography, Joshua Allen; Designer, Jason MacIsaac; Music, Ryan Shore; Editor, Matthew Brulotte; Special Effects & Creature Design, David Scott, Form and Dynamics; Casting, Jenny Lewis, Sara Kay; Brookstreet Pictures Corp.; Canadian; Dolby; Color; Rated R; 85 minutes; American release date: August 15, 2008. CAST: Trevor Matthews (Jack Brooks), Robert Englund (Prof. Gordon Crowley), Rachel Skarsten (Eve), Daniel Kash (Guidance Counselor Silverstein), David Fox (Old Howard), Stefanie Drummond (Janice), James A. Woods (John), Ashley Bryant (Kristy), Meghanne Kessels (Suzy), Meg Charette (Erica), Kristyn

Butcher (Celia), Andrew Butcher (Raymond), Simon Rainville (Slim), Matthew Stefiuj (Omar), Austin Macdonald (Young Howard), Evan Gilchrist (Young Jack), Dean Hawes (Emmet), John Ross (Charles Brooks), Victoria Fodor (Gene Brooks), Ariel Waller (Cindy Brooks), Brennan Delaney, Valerie Casault (Students), Rick Bramucci (Mr. Burns), Chad Harber (Pat), Patrick Henry (Trevor), Derrick Damon Reeve (Cyclops), Pascal Petardi (Janitor), Norman Mikeal Berketa (Man in Nuts and Bolts), Steve Stransman (Tall Student), Christina Sauvé (Student), Melinda Gilhen (Yogalates Teacher)

Robert Englund in Jack Brooks: Monster Slayer © *Anchor Bay*

RICHARD SERRA: THINKING ON YOUR FEET (Independent) Director/Screenplay, Maria Anna Tappeiner; Photography, Jürgen Behrens; Editor, Brigitte Warken-Königs; a Westdeutscher Rundfunk (WDR), Zweites Deutsches Fernsehen (ZDF) production; German, 2005; Color; Not rated; 93 minutes; American release date: August 20, 2008. Documentary on artist Richard Serra and his *The Matter of Time* creation for the Guggenheim Museum Bilbao; with Richard Serra, Ernst Fuchs, Philip Glass, Alexander von Berswordt.

Richard Serra in Thinking on Your Feet © *WDR/ZDF*

CROSSING BORDERS (Morocco Exchange) Producer/Director/Screenplay, Arnd Wächter; Photography, Jorge Sousa, Paul Pryor; Music, Rhett Brewer; Editors, Jorge Sousa, Jose Iglesias, Arnd Wächter; German; Color; Not rated; 97 minutes; American release date: August 22, 2008. Documentary on four young Americans who join four Moroccans of similar ages for a tour of the latter's country.

MARIA BETHANIA: MUSIC IS PERFUME (Art Mattan) Producer/Director/Screenplay, Georges Gachot; Coproducer, Pierre-Olivier Bardet; Photography, Mathias Kalin; Editors, Anja Bombelli, Ruth Schlapfer; a Georges Gachot production, in association with Ideale Audience with support from SF DRS, TSI, France 5, SVT; French-Swiss, 2005; Color; Not rated; 82 minutes; American release date: August 29, 2008. Documentary on performer Maria Bethânia and the tropicalia music movement; with Maria Bethânia, Caetano Veloso, Gilberto Gil, Miúcha, Chico Buarque, Jaime Alem.

YOUNG PEOPLE FUCKING (Blowtorch Entertainment) Producers, Steven Hoban, Tracey Boulton; Executive Producers, Aaron Abrams, Martin Gero, Michael Baker, Jeff Sackman, Lorne Abrams, Glenn Cockburn; Director, Martin Gero; Screenplay, Aaron Abrams, Martin Gero; Photography, Arthur E. Cooper; Designer, Diana Abbatangelo; Costumes, Alex Kavanagh; Music, Todor Kobakov; Music Supervisor, Vapor; Editor, Michael Banas; a ThinkFilm presentation, in association with the Movie Network; Canadian; Dolby; Deluxe color; Rated R; 90 minutes; American release date: August 29, 2008. CAST: Aaron Abrams (Matt), Carly Pope (Kris), Kristin Booth (Abby), Josh Dean (Andrew), Sonja Bennett (Mia), Josh Cooke (Eric), Diora Baird (Jamie), Callum Blue (Ken), Ennis Esmer (Gord), Peter Oldring (Dave), Natalie Lisinska (Inez)

Josh Dean in Young People Fucking © *Blowtorch*

MY MEXICAN SHIVAH (Emerging Pictures) a.k.a. *Morirse está en Hebreo*; Producers, Alejandro Springall, Maite Arguelles; Executive Producers, Maggie Renzi, Lemore Syvan, Tenoch Ochoa; Director, Alejandro Springall; Screenplay, Jorge Goldenberg, Alejandro Sprignall; Story, Ilan Stavans; Photography, Celiana Cardenas; Art Director, Luisa Guala; Costumes, Monica Neumaier; Music, Jacobo Lieberman; Editor, Madeleine Gavin; an Instituto Mexicano de Cinematografia/Foprocine/Emilio & Jose Achar/Daniel Andreu-Von Euw/Meir & Roy Raphael/Zury Levy/Goliat Films/Maggie Renzi & John Sayles presentation of a Springall Pictures production; Mexican, 2007; Dolby; Widescreen; Color; Not rated; 98 minutes; American release date: August 29, 2008. CAST: Raquel Pankowsky (Esther), David Ostrosky (Ricardo), Sharon Zundel (Galia), Emilio Savinni (Nicolás), Lenny Zundel (Jevreman), Sergio Klainer (Moishe), Enrique Cimet (Zalmen), Max Kerlow (Rubinstein), Blanca Guerra (Julia Palafox), Martha Roth (Rosita), Guillermo Murray (Dr. Berman), Martin LaSalle (Isaac Fischer), Gustavo Sánchez Parra (Antúnez), Margot Wagner (Eva Wolf), Jacqueline Volataire (Martha),

Ricardo Kleinbaum (Ari), Paloma Woolrich (Ruth), Esther Cimet (Noemí), Anna Gilbert (Sara), Hugo Macías Macotela (Rabino), Julio Richter (Rubén), Ilan Arditti (Abie), Roberto D'Amico (Wolkowisky), Vicky de Fuentas (Trini), Miguel Ángel Ferriz (Comisario), Sophie Gómez (Tamara), Rosa María Hernández (Nati), Fernando Sarfatti (Beto Brenner), Abraham Stavans (Balkoff)

Sharon Zundel, Emilio Savinni in My Mexican Shivah
© *Emerging Pictures*

GOAL II: LIVING THE DREAM (Arenas Entertainment) Producers, Mike Jefferies, Mark Huffam, Matt Barrell; Screenplay, Mike Jefferies, Adrian Butchart, Terry Loane; Photography, Flavio Martinez Labiano; Designer, Joel Collins; Costumes, Lindsay Pugh; Music, Stephen Warbeck; Editor, Niven Howie; a Milkeshake Films production; CAST: Kuno Becker (Santiago Munez), Alessandro Nivola (Gavin Harris), Anna Friel (Roz Harmison), Stephen Dillane (Glen Foy), Ruger Hauer (Rudi Van Der Merwe), Nick Cannon (TJ Harper), Frances Barber (Carol Harmison), Miriam Colón (Mercedes), Sean Pertwee (Barry), Elizabeth Peña (Rosa Maria), Leonor Varela (Jordana Garcia), Mike Jefferies (Mad Director), Alejandro Tapia (Julio), Danny Stepper (American Tourist), William Beck (Steve Parr), Emma Field-Rayner (Lorraine), Kevin Knapman (Jamie Drew), Carmelo Gómez (Burruchaga), Kieran O'Brien (Hughie McGowan), Rhydian Jones (Wedding Planner), Nitin Kundra (Indian Waiter), Michael Novack (Leo Vegaz), Leslie Randall (Mr. Ives), Shammi Aulakh (Newcastle Doctor), Karen Asemper (Roz's Friend), Matt Sutton, Charlie Richmond (News Reporters), Adam Robertson (Small Boy), Danni Brook (Newcastle Nurse), Daniele Lydon (Duty Nurse), Carlos Kaniowsky (Niguel), Felix Casales Noriega (Jose), Jorge Garcia Jurado (Enrique), Maria Palacios Valhondo (Scrawny Girl), Andreas Munoz Blazquez (Tito), Ricardo de Burgos (Bodega Owner), Elena De Jose (Tanned Model), Aurora Novato, Laura Lamzouri Edagdaqui (Hookers), Andy Ansah (Tofu Commercial Producer), Craig Heaney (Phil), Jack McBride (Walter), Sara Rico Solera, Zay Nuba (Girls with Gavin), Ronald Wood (Mistletoe Patient), Javier Gonzalez Traba (Pedro), Alfredo Rodriguez (Julio), Santiago Cabrera (Diego Rivera), David Beckham, Julio Baptista, Emilio Butragueño, Iker Casillas, Thomas Gravesen, Guti, Steve McManaman, Alfredo di Stéfano, Pablo Gabriel Garcia, Iván Helguera, Francisco Pavón, Florentiono Pérez, Sergio Ramos, Raúl, Robinho, Predgrag Djordjevic, Ronaldo, Michel Salgado, Jonathan Woodgate, Zinedine Zidane, Thierry Henry, Cesc Fàbregas, Jose Antonio Reyes, Freddie Ljungberg, Jens Lehmann, Alexander Hleb, Cicinho, Shay Given, Ronaldhinho, Samuel Eto'o, Victor Valdés, Santiago Cañizares, Vicente, Juninho Pernambucano, Gregory Coupet, Rivaldo, Stefano Farina (Themselves)

SUKIYAKI WESTERN DJANGO (First Look) Producers, Hirotsugu Yoshida, Toshinori Yamaguchi; Executive Producers, Toshiaki Nakazawa, Nobuyuki Tohya; Co-Executive Producer, Dick N. Sano; Director, Takashi Miike; Screenplay, Masaru Nakamura, Takashi Miike; Photography, Toyomichi Kurita; Designer, Takashi Sasaki; Costumes, Michiko Kitamura; Music, Koji Endo; Editor, Taiji Shimamura; CGI Supervisor, Misako Saka; a Sukiyaki Western Django Partners, Sedic Intl. Geneon Entertainment, Sony Pictuers Entertainment, Dentsu, TV Asahi, Shogakukan, A Team, Nagoya Broadcasting Network, Tokyu Recreation production; Japanese, 2007; Dolby; Super 35 Widescreen; Color; Rated R; 120 minutes; American release date: August 29, 2008. CAST: Hideaki Ito (Gunman), Koichi Sato (Kiyomori), Yusuke Iseya (Yoshitsune), Masanobu Ando (Yoichi), Takaaki Ishibashi (Benkei),Yoshino (Kimura Shizuka), Teruyuki Kagawa (The Sheriff), Masato Sakai (Shigemori), Shun Oguri (Akira), Quentin Tarantino (Ringo), Kaori Momoi (Ruriko)

YOUSSOU N'DOUR: RETURN TO GOREE (Independent) Producers, Jean-Louis Porchet, Gérard Ruey; Director, Pierre-Yves Borgeaud; Screenplay/Musical Conception, Emmanuel Getaz, Pierre-Yves Borgeaud; based on an idea by Youssou N'dour, Emmanuel Getaz; Photography, Camille Cootagnoud; Swiss-Luxemburg; Dolby; Color; Not rated; 108 minutes; American release date: August 29, 2008. Documentary on Muslim performer Youssou N'dour; with Youssou N'dour, Moncef Genoud, Boubacar Joseph Ndiaye, Harmony Harmoneers, Idris Muhammad, James Cammack, Pyeng Threadgill, Grégoire Maret, Leroi Jones, Ernie Hammes, Wolfgang Muthspiel.

BABYLON A.D. (20th Century Fox) Producer, Ilan Goldman; Director, Mathieu Kassovitz; Screenplay, Mathieu Kassovitz, Eric Besnard; Based on the novel *Babylon Babies* by Maurice G. Dantec; Photography, Thierry Arbogast; Designers, Sonja Klaus, Paul Cross; Costumes, Chattoune, Fab; Music, Atli Orvarsson; Editor, Benjamin Weill; Visual Effects Supervisor, Stephane Ceretti; Fight Choreographer, Alain Figlarz; Casting, Jina Jay; a Babylon A.D. SAS, Babylon Films, StudioCanal, M6 Films production, with the participation of M6, Canal Plus CineCinema; French; Dolby; Panavision; Color; Rated PG-13; 100 minutes; American release date: August 29, 2008. CAST: Vin Diesel (Toorop), Melanie Thierry (Aurora), Michelle Yeoh (Sister Rebeka), Lambert Wilson (Darquandier), Mark Strong (Finn), Jérôme Le Banner (Killa), Charlotte Rampling (High Priestess), Gérard Depardieu (Gorsky), Joel Kirby (Dr. Newton), Souleymane Dicko (Jamal), David Belle (Kid with Tattoos), Radek Bruna (Karl), Jan Unger (Fight Promoter), Abraham Belaga (Assistant to High Priestess), Gary Cowan (Neolite Executive), Lemmy Constantine (Neolite Marketing Executive), David Gasman (Neolite Researcher), Kirstyna Kingsley, Lou Jenny (Twin Girls), Filip Matejka (Young Boy on Toorop's Stairs), Curtis Matthew (Submarine Captain), Robert Polo, Drew Harding Smith, Jeff Smith (Border Guards), Pete Thias (Neolite MIB), Magda Vavrusova (Woman in Toorop's Corridor)

Gerard Depardieu, Vin Diesel in Babylon A.D. © *Twentieth Century Fox*

LOINS OF PUNJAB PRESENTS (Emerging Pictures) Producer/Director, Manish Acharya; Screenplay, Anuvab Pal, Manish Acharya; Photography, Arvind Kannabiran; Designers, Rohit Shinkre, Ayesha Punvani; Costumes, Rabiah Troncelliti; Music, Michael Cohen; Editor, Christopher Dillon; Casting, Pravin; a Horn OK Please Entertainment production; Indian; Dolby; Color; Not rated; 88 minutes; Release date: September 12, 2008. CAST: Shabana Azmi (Rrita Kapoor), Ajay Naidu (Turbanotorious B.D.G.), Ayesha Dharker (Opama Menon), Michael Raimondi (Josh Cohen), Seema Rahmani (Sania Rehman), Jameel Khan (Mr. Bokade), Darshan Jariwala (Sanjeev Patel), Ishitta Sharma (Preeti Patel), Manish Acharya (Vikram Tejwani), Kunaal Roy Kapur (Mr. White), Loveleen Mishra (Alpa Patel), Kory Bassett (Otto), Samrat Chakrabarti (Trance Sen), Sanjiv Jhaveri (Chris G.), Avantika Akerkar (Ashwini)

Ajay Naidu, Kory Bassett in Loins of Punjab Presents
© *Emerging Pictures*

FORGIVENESS (Intl. Film Circuit) Producers, David Silber, Lemore Syvan, Udi Aloni; Executive Producers, Moshe Edery, Leon Edery, Micky Rabinovitz, Andre Malignac, Sigal Primor; Director, Udi Aloni; Screenplay, Udi Aloni, Paul Hond; Based on the book by Udi Aloni; Photography, Ammon Zalait; Designers, Kuly Sander, Tommaso Ortino; Costumes, Danny Bar Shay, Amanda Ford; Music, Tamir Muskat; Editor, Galia Gill Moors; a Metro Communications (Tel Aviv)/Elevation Filmworks (New York) production; Israeli-America, 2006; Color; HD-to-35mm; Not rated; 97 minutes; American release date: September 12, 2008. CAST: Itay Tiran (David), Clara Khoury (Lila), Moni Moshonov (Muselmann), Makram J. Khoury (Dr. Isaac Shemesh), Michael Sarne (Henry Adler), Tamara Mansour (Little Girl/Ghost/Amal), Ruba Blal (Nawal), Idit Teperson (Col. Daniel), Omar Barnea (Yoni), Gregory J. Lucas (Johnny), Eli Eltanany Eltonyo (Dror), Yaffit Hallely (Fortune Teller), Katie Quarrier (Margaret), Ryan P. Shrime (Tarek), Eric Silver (James), Paul Zakrzewski (Lou), Tricia Norris (Dowager), Tamer Nafar, Suhell Nafar, Mahmud Jreri (Palestinian Rappers)

Clara Khoury, Itay Tiran in Forgiveness © *Intl. Film Circuit*

ELITE SQUAD (IFC Films) a.k.a. *Elite da Tropa*; Producers, Marcos Prado, Jose Padilha; Executive Producers, Maria Clara Ferreira, Bia Castro, Genna Terranova, Scott Martin, Eduardo Costantini; Director, José Padilha; Screenplay, José Padilha, Rodrigo Pimentel, Bráulio Mantovani; Based on the book *Elite da Tropa* by André Batista, Rodrigo Pimentel, Luiz Eduardo Soares; Photography, Lula Carvalho; Designer, Tule Peake; Costumes, Claudia Kopke; Music, Poedro Bromfman; Editor, Daniel Rezende; Casting, Fatima Toledo; a Weinstein Co./ Zazen Producoes, Posto 9, Feijao Filmes production; Brazilian; Dolby; Color; Rated R; 114 minutes; American release date: September 19, 2008. CAST: Wagner Moura (Captain Nascimento), Caio Junqueira (Neto), André Ramiro (André Matias), Maria Ribeiro (Rosane), Fernanda Machado (Maria), Fernanda de Freitas (Roberta), Paulo Vilela (Edu), Milhem Cortaz (Captain Fábio), Marcelo Valle (Captain Oliveira), Fábio Lago (Claudio Mendes de Lima "Baiano"), Bruno Delia (Captain Azevedo), Marcelo Escorel (Colonel Otávio), André Mauro (Rodrigues), Thelmo Fernandes (Sgt. Alves), Emerson Gomes (Xaveco), Paulo Hamilton (Paulo), Bernardo Jablonski (Law Teacher), Alexandre Mofatti (Sub-Commandante Carvalho), Erick Oliveira (Marcinho)

Wagner Moura in Elite Squad © *IFC Films*

TAKING FATHER HOME (Tidepoint) a.k.a. *Bei yazi de nanhai*; Producer, Peng Shan; Director/Screenplay, Ying Liang; Screenplay/Designers, Ying Liang, Peng Shan; Photography, Li Rongsheng, Ying Liang; Music, Zhang Xiao; a 90 Minutes Film Studio production; Chinese, 2006; Color/black and white; Video: Not rated; 100 minutes; American release date: September, 19, 2008. CAST: Xun Yun, Liu Xiaopei, Wang Jie, Song Cijun, Chen Xikun, Liu Ying, Deng Siwei, Chen Xiyang, Chen Jianxun, Zhang Honglang, Peng Shan, Zeng Yigang, Zhang Yuan.

Taking Father Home © *Tidepoint*

FRAULEIN (Film Movement) Producers, Susann Rüdlinger, Samir Mirjam Quinte, Davor Pušić; Executive Producer, Sascha Schwill; Director, Andrea Štaka; Screenplay, Andrea Štaka, Barbara Albert, Marie Kreutzer; Photography, Igor Martinović; Designer, Sue Erdt; Costumes, Bettina Marx; Music, Peter von Siebenthal, Till Wyler, Daniel Jakob; Editor, Gion-Reto Killias; Casting, Corinna Glaus; a Dschoint Ventschr Filmproduktion (Switzerland) in coproduction with Quinte Film (Germany); Swiss-German, 2006; Dolby; Color; Not rated; 77 minutes; American release date: September 19, 2008. CAST: Mirjana Karanović (Ruza), Marija Škaričić (Ana), Ljubica Jovic (Mila), Andrea Zogg (Franz), Zdenko Jelcic (Ante), Pablo Aguilar (Fredi), David Imhoof (Stefan), Sebastian Krähenbühl (Young Man), Oliver Zgorelec (Violinist), Annette Wunsch, Kenneth Huber (Doctors), Aniko Donath (Pharmacist), Hans Suter (Old Man), Stefan Suske (Car Driver), Vera Bommer (Sheila), Robin Rehmann (Momo), Tiziana Jelmini (Artist), Sanja Ristic (Vera)

Ljubica Jovic, Marija Skaricic in Fraulein © *Film Movement*

THE AMAZING TRUTH ABOUT QUEEN RAQUELA (here!/Regent) Producers, Arlen Cuevas, Olaf de Fleur Johannesson, Stefan Schaefer, Helgi Sverrisson; Executive Producer, Baltasar Kormakur; Director/Screenplay, Olaf de Fleur Johannesson; Photography, Butch Maddul; Music, Pavel E. Smid; Editors, Dagur Kari, Olaf de Fleur Johannesson; a Poppoli Pictures production; Icelandic-Filipino-French-Thai; Color/Black and white; Widescreen; HD; Rated R; 79 minutes; American release date: September 26, 2008. CAST: Raquela Rios (Herself), Stefan Schaefer (Ardilo, Michael), Via Galudo (Olivia), Brax Villa (Aubrey), Valerie Grand Einarsson (Vala), Amor Alingasa (Amor), Raniel Dave Balasabas (Young Raquela Friend), Ren Christian Balasabas (Young Raquela), Margret Eggertsdottir (Horse Shepherd), Edith Galudo (Via's Mom), Marcus Kalberer (Johnny K), Hronn Kristinsdottir (Woman in Fish Factory), Luis Labandero (Pimp), Archie Modequillo (Clerk), Reynald Palatulon (Taxi Driver), Ingibjorg Sigurdardottir (Lonely Older Woman), Eggert Horgdal Snorrason (Driver Fish Factory), Alexsis Yap (Joselito)

SHOOT ON SIGHT (Aron Govil Prods.) Producer, Aron Govil; Executive Producers, Vandana Govil, Aron Govil; Director, Jag Mundhra; Screenplay, Carl Austin; Photography, Madhu Ambat; Designer, Roger Harris; Costumes, Sarah Tapscott; Music, John Altman, Craig Pruess; Editors, Jag Mundhra, Sanjeev Mirajkar; a Cine Boutique Entertainment (U.K.)/Aron Govil Prods. (U.S.); British-American; Color; Rated R; 112 minutes; American release date: September 26, 2008. CAST: Clemency Burton-Hill (Pamala Davies), Brian Cox (Daniel Tennant), Taru Devani (Farzana), Jamie Doyle (Sean), Sadie Frost (Fiona Monroe), Stephen Greif (Cmdr. John Shepherd), Gulshan Grover (Yunus), Arrun Harker (Imran Ali), Ralph Inesno (Marber), Avtar Kaul (Baqir Hassan), Robert Lowe (Sean's Mate), Alex McSweeney (PC Brian Andrews), Faye Peters (Hannah Marber), Om Puri (Ruby Kaur), Tolga Safer (Aziz), Clifford Samuel (Elijah), Greta Scacchi (Susan), Naseeruddin Shah (Police Cmdr. Tariq Ali), Claudia Swann (PC Justine Miller),

India Wadsworth (Zara Ali), John Warman (Armed Response), Jayson Whiteley (Police Officer), Chris Wilson (Police CO19 Officer), Mikaal Zulfikar (Zaheer Khan)

WHALEDREAMERS (Monterey Media) Producers, Julian Lennon, Kim Kindersley; Executive Producers, Wayne Young, David Jowsey, Napier Marten; Director/Screenplay, Kim Kindersley; Photography, Paul Dalowitz, Jeff Pantukhoff, Kurt E. Soderling, David Warth; Editors, Chris Liddell, Mark Law, Michael Balson, Constantine Dumba; a Julian Lennon production; Australian; Color; Not rated; 90 minutes; American release date: September 26, 2008. Documentary on the Mirning, an Aboriginal tribe who sing and pray to whales in an effort to find unity and peace; with Pierce Brosnan, John Hurt, Julian Lennon, Geoffrey Rush, Jack Thompson.

Whaledreamers © *Monterey Media*

TOKYO GORE POLICE (Media Blasters) Producers, Yoko Hayama, Yoshinori Chiba, Satoshi Nakamura; Executive Producer, John Sirabella; Director, Yoshihiro Nishimura; Screenplay, Yoshihiro Nishimura, Kengo Kaji, Sayako Nakoshi; Photography, Shu G. Momose; Music, Koh Nakagawa; a Nikkatsu Tokyo Shock Original presentation of a Fever Dreams production; Japanese; Color; DigitBeta; Not rated; 109 minutes; American release date: October 3, 2008. CAST: Eihi Shiina (Ruka), Itsuji Itao (Keyman/His Father), Yukihide Benii (Tokyo Police Chief), Jiji-bu (Barbara-Man), Kesisuke Horibe (Ruka's Father), Ikuko Sawada (Bar Independent Diner), Shun Sugata (Tokyo Police Commissioner), Taku Sakaguchi, Shoko Nakahara, Sayoko Nakoshi.

JUST BURIED (Liberation Entertainment) Producers, Pen Densham, Bill Niven, Chaz Thorne, John Watson; Executive Producers, Devesh Chetty, Neil Kaplan; Director/ Screenplay, Chaz Thorne; Photography, Christopher Porter; Designer, Bill Fleming; Costumes, Kate Rose; Music, Darren Fung; Editor, Christopher Cooper; a Trilogy Entertainment North and Standing 8 production, in association with Telefilm Canada and RGM Entertainment; Canadian; Color; Not rated; 94 minutes; American release date: October 4, 2008. CAST: Jay Baruchel (Oliver Zinck), Rose Byrne (Roberta Knickel), Graham Greene (Henry Sanipass), Nigel Bennett (Chief Knickle), Thomas Gibson (Charlie Richmond), Sergio Di Zio (Jackie Whynacht), Reagan Pasternak (Luanne), Slavko Negulic (Armin Imholz), Jeremy Akerman (Rollie Whynacht), Brian Downey (Pickles), Christopher Shore (Wayne Shorr), Craig Wood (Lawyer), Martha Irving (Mrs. Imholz), Michael Pellerin (Sam the Wrecker), Bill Wood (Crispin Imholz), Gay Hauser (Waitress), Loretta Yu (Patricia), Leah Randell (Cindy)

Jay Baruchel, Rose Byrne, Graham Greene in Just Buried © *Liberation*

BREAKFAST WITH SCOT (Regent/here!) Producer, Paul Brown; Executive Producers, Bob Rousseau, Howard Rosenman, Nadine Schiff; Director, Laurie Lynd; Screenplay, Sean Reycraft; based on the novel by Michael Downing; Photography, David Makin; Designer, Tamara Deverell; Costumes, Alexander Reda; Music, Robert Carli; Editor, Susan Shipton; Casting, Forrest and Forrest Casting, Karen Margiotta; a Miracle Pictures production; Canadian; Color; Rated PG-13; 93 minutes; American release date: October 10, 2008. CAST: Tom Cavanagh (Eric McNally), Ben Shenkman (Sam Miller), Noah Bernett (Scot), Graham Greene (Bud Wilson), Fiona Reid (Mildred Monterossos), Jeananne Goossen (Nula), Colin Cunningham (Billy), Benz Antoine (Greg Graham), Dylan Everett (Ryan Burlington), Alexander Franks (Joey Morita), Vanessa Thompson (Carla), Anna Silk (Mia), Megan Follows (Barbara Warren), Travis Ferris (George, Jr.), Kathryn Haggis (Andrea Burlington), Sheila McCarthy (Ms. Patterson), Robin Brûlé (Ms. Paul), Shauna MacDonald (Joan), Benjamin Morehead (Hank), Cameron Ansell (Finn O'Brien), Mark Forward (Snickering Businessman), Adam Korson (Referee), Billy Parrott (Security Guard #2), Alex Popovic (Walter Wodlowski), Edwina Renout (Mrs. Morita)

Ben Shenkman, Noah Bernett, Tom Cavanaugh in Breakfast with Scot © *Regent Releasing*

ASHES OF TIME: REDUX (Sony Classics) a.k.a. *Dung che sai duk redux*; Producers, Wong Kar Wai, Jeff Lau, Jacky Pang, Yee Wah; Executive Producers, Tsai Mu Ho, Chan Ye Cheng; Director/Screenplay, Wong Kar Wai; Based on the story by Louis Cha; Photography, Christopher Doyle; Designer, William Chang Suk Ping; Music, Frankie Chan, Roel A. Garcia; Editors, William Chang Suk Ping, Patrick Tam; Action Choreographer, Sammo Hung; a Block 2 Pictures, Scholar Film Co. presentation of a Jet Tone Prods. Production, in association with Beijing Film Studio; Hong Kong; Dolby; Color; Rated R; 93 minutes; American release date: October 10, 2008. CAST: Leslie Cheung (Ouyang Feng), Brigitte Lin (Murong Yin/Murong Yang), Tony Leung Chiu Wai (Blind Swordsman), Carina Lau (Peach Blossom), Tony Leung Ka Fai (Huang Yaoshi), Charlie Young (Girl), Jacky Cheung (Hong Qi), Bai Li (Hong Qi's Wife), Collin Chou (Swordsman), Maggie Cheung (The Woman)

Carina Lau in Ashes of Time: Redux © *Sony Classics*

LA LEÓN (Music Box) Producers, Juan Solanas, Pablo Salomon, Alexis Vonarb, Aton Soumache, Pierre Rambaldi, Catherine Barra; Executive Producer, Pablo Salomon; Director/ Screenplay, Santiago Otheguy; Photography, Paula Grandio; Designer, Sergio Rud; Costumes, Betina Andreose; Music, Vincent Artaud; Editors, Sebastian Sepulveda, Valeria Otheguy; a Polar Films (Argentina)/Onyx Films, Big World (France)/Morocha Films (Argentina) production, in association with Mandragola Prods.; Argentine-French, 2007; Dolby; Widescreen; Black & white; HD; Not rated; 80 minutes; American release date: October 10, 2008. CAST: Jorge Román (Alvaro), Daniel Valenzuela (El Turu), José Muñoz (Iribarren), Juan Carlos Rivas, Mirta Duran Rivas (Missionaries), Esteban Gonzalez, Alfredo Rivas, Alberto Rivas (Missionary Brothers), Lorena Rivas (Nina Missionary), Aida Merel (Librarian), Diego Quiroz (Marinaro Julio), Mariano González (Youth on Yacht), Marcos Woinsky (El Alemán), Jimena Cavaco (Laura), Elba Estela Vargas (Laura's Mother), José Aguilar (Day Laborer), Ignacio Jiménez (Chico Lopez), Pedro Rossi (Shipyard Seller), Daniel Sosa (Gadea Father), Ana Maria Montalyo (Gadea Mother), Hernan Sosa (El Muerto), Leonardo Rodriguez (Laura's Brother)

Jorge Román in La León © Music Box Films

TALENTO DE BARRIO (Maya Releasing) a.k.a. *Straight from the Barrio*; Producers, George Rivera; Executive Producers, Daddy Yankee, Edwin Prado, George Rivera; Coproducer, Angel Sanjuro; Directors, José Iván Santiago, George Rivera; Screenplay, George Rivera, Angel Sanjuro; Photography, Leslie J. Colombani, Jr.; Designer, Pascual Febus; Music, Samuel Lopez; Editor, Mariem Perez; Puerto Rican; Color; Rated R; 106 minutes; American release date: October 10, 2008. CAST: Daddy Yankee (Edgar), Maestro (Jeico), Katiria Soto (Soribel), César Farrait (Wichy), Angélica Alcaide (Natasha), Norma Colón (Edgar's Mother), Norman Santiago (Matías), Welmor (Leo), Rey Pirín (Javier), Pepe Fuentes (Don Joaquín), Moncho Conde (Popó), Gringo (Angelo), Eric Rodriguez (Wito), Glory (Tata), Zojaira Martínez (Ana), Ángel Centeno (Cuso), D.N.T. (Aníbal), Eric Meléndez (Natasha's Boyfriend), Christian Rivera (Little Raper), Neysha Vega (Leo's Daughter), Nahielis López (Javier's Daughter), Llandel Veguilla (Milton), Victor Roque (El Domi), Tania Román (Julia), Osvaldo Lasalle (Don Pedro), Alondra Cruz López (Tata's Daughter), Gregoria Febus (Doña Nicolasa), Juan Oyola (Don Jacinto), Michelle Concepción (Ana's Girlfriend), Jorge Antares (Drug Buyer with Kids)

Daddy Yankee in Talento de Bario © *May Releasing*

AZUR & ASMAR (Genius) Producer, Christophe Rossignon; Director/Story/ Screenplay/Storyboards/Characters/Drawings, Michel Ocelot; English Language Version Written and Directed by Michel Ocelot & George Roubicek; a Nord-Ouest Production, Mac Guff Ligne Studio 0, France 3 Cinema, Rhone-Alpes Cinema (France)/Artemis Prods. (Belgium)/Lucky Red (Italy)/Zahorimedia, Intuitions Films (Spain) production; French-Belgian-Italian-Spanish, 2006; Rated PG; 95 minutes; American release date: October 17, 2008. VOICE CAST: Steven Kyman (Azur), Nigel Pilkington (Asmar), Suzanna Nour (Jenane), Nigel Lambert (Crapoux), Leopold Benedict (Azur as a Child), Frederick Benedict (Asmar as a Child), Imogen Bailey (Princess Chamsous Sabah), Emma Tate (The Djinn Fairy), Suzanne David (The Elf Fairy), Sean Barrett (Wise Man Yadoa), Keith Wickham (The Father)

Azur & Asmar © *Genius*

FLASHBACKS OF A FOOL (Left Turn Films/Sherezade) Producers, Lene Bausager, Damon Bryant, Genevieve Hofmeyr, Claus Clausen; Executive Producers, Steffan Aumueller, Glenn M. Stewart, Said Boudarga, Marina Grasic, Jan Korbelin, Sean Ellis, Susanne Bohnet, Brian Avery, Jay Jopling, Daniel Craig, Robert Mitchell; Director/Screenplay, Baillie Walsh; Photography, John Mathieson; Designer, Laurence Dorman; Costumes, Stevie Stewart; Music, Richard Hartley; Editor, Struan Clay; Casting, Des Hamilton, Gaby Kester; a Mrs. Rogers (U.K.) production, presented in association with DRS Entertainment, Lipsync Prods. (U.K.)/Visitor Pictures (U.S.); British-American-South African; Dolby; Panavision; Technicolor; Rated R; 113 minutes; American release date: October 17, 2008. CAST: Daniel Craig (Joe Scott), Eve (Ophelia Franklin), Harry Eden (Teenage Joe), Olivia Williams (Grace Scot), Helen McCrory (Peggy Tickell), Evelyn Adams (Jodhi May), Miriam Karlin (Mrs. Rogers), Kelley Hawes (Adult Jesse Scot), Emilia Fox (Sister Jean), Mark Strong (Manny Miesel), James D'Arcy (Jack Adams), Claire Forlani (Adult Ruth Davies), Max Deacon (Boots McKay), Jodie Tomlinson (Jane Adams), Mia Clifford (Young Jesse), Felicity Jones (Young Ruth), Sid Mitchell (Chillo), Alfie Allen (Kevin Hubble), Annabel Linder (Dawn), Angie Ruiz (Priscilla), Gina Athans (Apple), Julie Ordon (Carrie Ann), Mia Clifford (Jessie), Darron Meyer (Valet)

MARY (IFC Films) Producers, Roberto De Nigris, Fernando Sulichin; Executive Producers, Massimo Cortesi, Andrea Groppiero, Jean Cazes, Angelo Arena; Director, Abel Ferrara; Screenplay, Simone Lageoles, Abel Ferrara, Mario Isabella; Photography, Stefano Falivene; Designer, Frank DeCurtis; Costumes, Frank DeCurtis, Silvia Nebiolo; Music, Francis Kuipers; Editors, Fabio Nunziata, Langdon F. Page; Casting, Stefania De Santis; a Fernando Sulichin presentation of a De Nigris Prods., SRL (Italy)/Central Films (France)/Associated Filmmakers Inc. (U.S.) production, in association with Wild Bunch; Italian-French-American, 2005; Dolby; Kodak Color; Not rated; 86 minutes; American release date: October 17, 2008. CAST: Juliette Binoche (Marie Palesi/Mary Magdalene), Forest Whitaker (Ted Younger), Matthew Modine (Tony Childress/Jesus), Heather Graham (Elizabeth Younger), Marion Cotillard (Gretchen Mol), Stefania Rocca (Brenda Sax), Marco Leonardi (Apostle Peter), Luca Lionello (Apostle Thomas), Mario Opinato (Apostle James), Elio Germano (Matteo), Emanuela Iovannitti (Johanna, Mary's Follower), Chiara Picchi (Salome), Angelica Di Majo (Martha), Ettore D'Alessandro (Apostle Andrew), Alex Grazioli (Apostle Matthew), Roy-Oronzo Casalini (John), Frank De Curtis (Joseph of Arimathea), Gabriella Wright (TV Studio Manager), Aza Benyatov (TV Studio Ad), Gisella Marengo (Nurse Nicu), Francine Berting (Nurse #2), Cherif (Super), Massimo Cortesi (Priest), Dominot, Dennis Kuipers (Angels), Jamil Hammoudi (Gang Leader), Giampiero Judica (Police Captain), Joe Capalbo (Policeman), Ada Perotti (Reporter Bam), Shanyn Leigh (Jerusalemite), Francesco Serina (Doctor), Maximo Velasquez (Baby Younger), Jean Yves Leloup, Ph.D; Ivan Nicoletto; Dr. Amos Luzzatto; Elaine Paigels Ph.D. (Religious Experts, Themselves)

FILTH AND WISDOM (IFC Films) Producer, Nicola Doring; Executive Producer/Director, Madonna; Screenplay, Madonna, Dan Cadan; Photography, Tim Maurice Jones; Designer, Gideon Ponte; Costumes, B; Editor, Russell Icke; Casting, Dan Hubbard; a Semtex Films production, in associatgion with HIS London; British; Dolby; Color; Not rated; 80 minutes; American release date: October 17, 2008. CAST: Eugene Hutz (A.K.), Holly Weston (Holly), Vicky McLure (Juliette), Richard E. Grant (Prof. Flynn), Inder Manocha (Sardeep), Elliot Levey (Benjamin Goldfarb), Francesca Kingdon (Francine), Clare Wilkie (Chole), Stephen Graham (Harry Beechman), Shobu Kapoor (Sardeep's Wife), Olegar Fedorov (A.K.S. Father), Ade (DJ), George Keeler (Frail Man), Tim Wallers (Mr. Frisk), Hannah Walters (Mrs. Goldfarb)

Holly Weston in Filth and Wisdom © *IFC Films*

FEAR(S) OF THE DARK (IFC) a.k.a. *Peur(s) do Noir*; Producers, Valerie Schermann, Christophe Jankovic; Executive Producers, Valerie Schermann, Christophe Jankovic, Denis Friedman, Vincent Tavier, Philippe Kauffmann; Directors, Blutch, Charles Burns, Marie Caillou, Pierre di Sciullo, Lorenzo Mattotti, Richard McGuire; Screenplay, Blutch, Charles Burns, Romain Slocombe, Pierre di Sciullo, Jerry Kramsky, Richard McGuire, Michel Pirus; Music, Rene Aubry, Boris Gronemberger, Laurent Perez del Mar, George Van Dam; Editor, Celine Kelepikis; a Prima Linea production, in association with La Parti Production, Def2shoot, Denis Friedman Prods.; French; Dolby; Black and white; Not rated; 82 minutes; American release date: October 22, 2008. Six animated stories; with the voices of Aure Atika, Arthur H, Guillaume Depardieu, Nicole Garcia, Luisa Pili, Gil Alma, Francois Creton, Sarah-Laure Estragnat, Nicolas Feroumont, Christian Hecq, Christian Hincker, Lino Hincker, Melaura Honnay, Amelie Lerma, Florence Maury, Adriana Piasek-Wanski, Amaury Smets, Brigitte Sy, Laurent Van Der Rest, Charlotte Vermeil, and Andreas Vuillet.

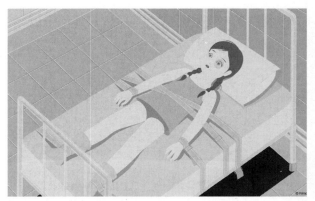

Fear(s) of the Dark © *IFC Films*

ZIDANE, A 21ˢᵗ CENTURY PORTRAIT (Katapult) Producers, Sigurjon Sigvatsson, Anna Vaney, Victorien Vaney; Directors, Douglas Gordon, Philippe Parreno; Photography, Darius Khondji; Music, Mogwai; Editor, Herve Schneid; French-Icelandic; Dolby; Super 35 Widescreen; Color; HD-to-35mm; Not rated; 91 minutes; American release date: October 24, 2008. Documentary on Real Madrid's French soccer star Zinédine Zidane.

THE SOVIET STORY (Perry Street Advisors) Producer, Kristaps Valdnieks; Director/Screenplay/Editor, Edvins Snore; Photography, Edgars Daugavvnags; a SIA, Labvakar, Riga, Latvia production; Latvian; Stereo; DV; Not rated; 86 minutes; American release date: October 24, 2008. Documentary on how the Soviet regime helped the Nazis instigate the Holocaust; with Andre Brie, Vladimir Bukovsky, Norman Davies, Aleksandr Guryanov, Vladimir Karpov, Emma Korpa, Girts Valdis Kristovskis, Rita Papina, Pierre Rigoulo, Boris Sokolov, Viktor Sokolov, Viktor Suvorov, Inese Vaidere, Ari Vatanen, and George Watson.

THE UNIVERSE OF KEITH HARING (Arthouse Films) Producers, Paolo Bruno, Eric Ellena, Marco Genone; Director/Photography, Christina Clausen; Screenplay, Christina Clausen, Gianni Mercurio; Music, Angelo Talocci; Editor, Silvia Giuletti; an OverCom (Italy)/French Connection Film (France)/Absolute Film (Italy) production; Italian-French; Color/Black and white; HD; Not rated; 90 minutes; American release date: October 24, 2008. Documentary on artist Keith Haring; with Joan Haring, Allen Haring, Jeffrey Deitch, Kermit Oswald, Karen DeLong, Kay Haring, Kristen Haring, Kenny Scharf, Samantha McEwen, Bruno Schmidt, Tony Shafrazi, Fred Brathwaite, Carlo McCormick, Kim Hastreiter, David LaChapelle, Junior Vasquez, Bill T. Jones, Julia Gruen, Yoko Ono, Hans Mayer, Roger Nellens, and Gil Vazquez.

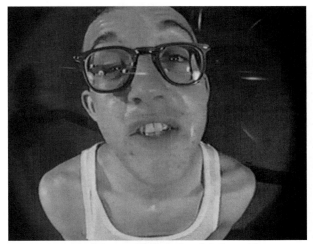

Keith Haring in The Universe of Keith Haring © Arthouse Films

BEN X (Film Movement) Producers, Peter Bouckaert, Erwin Provoost; Director/Screenplay, Nic Balthazar; Based on his novel *Niets was Alles Wat Hij Zei* and his play *Niets*; Photography, Lou Berghmans; Designer, Kurt Loynes; Costumes, Heleen Heintjes; Music, Praga Khan; Editor, Philippe Ravoet; Casting, Gunter Schmid; an MMG Film production; Belgian-Dutch, 2007; Dolby; Color; HD-to-35mm; Not rated; 93 minutes; American release: October 24, 2008. CAST: Greg Timmermans (Ben), Marijke Pinoy (Mother), Laura Verlinden (Scarlite), Pol Goossen (Father), Titus De Voogdt (Bogaert), Maarten Claeyssens (Desmet), Cesar De Sutter (Jonas), Gilles De Dchryver (Coppola), Bavo Smets (Ben–6 years), Katrien Pierlet (Kleuterjuf), Rebecca Lenaerts (Opvoedster), Michael Bauwens (Oorarts), Koen De Sutter (Oogarts), Peter De Graef (Psychiater), An Van Gijsegem (Maaike), Jakob Berks (Metal Teacher), Johan Heldenbergh (Religion Teacher), Matthieu Sys, Jonas Dumon, Ilya Van Autreve (Classmates), Ron Cornet (School Principal), Wim De Vilder (Journal Anker), Tania Van der Sanden (Sabine)

Greg Timmermans in Ben X © Film Movement

ROADSIDE ROMEO (Yash Raj Films) Producer, Aditya Chopra; Executive Producer, Swaratmika Mishra; Director/Screenplay, Jugal Hansraj; Animation Directors, Shrirang Sathaye, Suhail Merchant; Photography, Anshul Chobey; Visual Design and Animation, Tata Elxsi/Visual Computing Labs; Editor, Arif Ahmed; Song and Background Music, Salim-Sulaiman; Lyrics, Jaideep Sahni; a Yash Raj Films (India)/Walt Disney Pictures (U.S.) presentation; Indian-American; Dolby; Widescreen; Color; Not rated; 91 minutes; American release date: October 24, 2008. VOICE CAST: Saif Ali Khan (Romeo), Kareena Kapoor (Laila), Jaaved Jaaferi (Charlie Anna), Vrajesh Hirjee (Guru), Tannaz Irani (Mini), Suresh N. Menon (Interval), Kiku Sharda (Hero English), Sanjay Mishra (Chhainu)

NEWS FROM HOME/NEWS FROM HOUSE (New Yorker) Producers, Amos Gitai, Michael Tapuach, Laurent Truchot, Patrick Quinet; Director/Screenplay, Amos Gitai; Photography, Haim Assias, Nurith Aviv, Vladimir Truchovski, Emanuel Aldema; Editors, Isabelle Ingold, Nili Richter, Rina Ben Melech; an Agav Films (Tel Aviv)/Hamon Hafakot (Tel Aviv)/Agat Films (Paris)/Artemis Prods. (Brussels) coproduction; Israeli-French-Belgian; Color; HD; Not rated; 96 minutes; American release date: October 24, 2008. Documentary focuses on a house in West Jerusalem as it changes hands with each new government. This third part of the trilogy is a continuation of the films *House* (1980) and *A House in Jerusalem* (1997).

Abu Muhamad in News from Home/News from House
© New Yorker Films

MONKS–THE TRANSATLANTIC FEEDBACK (Play Loud! Prods.) Producers/Directors/ Photography, Dietmar Post, Lucia Palacios; Music, The Monks; Editor, Dieter Jaufmann; Produced in association with 3sat and ZDF; German-Spanish-American; Color/Black and white; DigiBeta; Not rated; 100 minutes; Documentary on '60s cult rock group The Monks; with Jimmy Bowien, Gary Burger, Larry Clark, Dave Day, Wolfgang Gluszczewski, Gerd Henjes, Hans Joachim Irmler, Genesis P-Orridge, Eddie Shaw, Jon Spencer, Charles Wilp

Monks – The Transatlantic Feedback © PlayLoud! Prods.

STAGES (Lemming) a.k.a. *Tussenstand*; Producers, Joost de Vries, Leontine Petit; Director, Mijke de Jon; Screenplay, Jolein Laarman, Mijke de Jong; Photography, Ton Peters; Art Director, Jolein Laarman; Costumes, Monica Petit; Music, Paul M. Brugge; Editor, Dorith Vinken; a Lemming Film, VPRO presentation; Widescreen; Color; Not rated; 80 minutes; American release date: November 5, 2008. CAST: Elsie de Brauw (Roos), Jennifer Jago (Ineke), Marcel Musters (Martin), Stijn Koomen (Isaac), Joan Nederlof (Carolien), Shireen Strooker (Jawa), Jeroen Willems (Joris)

OTTO, OR UP WITH DEAD PEOPLE (Strand) Producers, Bruce La Bruce, Jürgen Brüning, Jörn Hartmann, Michael Huber, Jennifer Jonas; Director/Screenplay, Bruce La Bruce; Photography, James Carman; Designer, Stefan Dickfeld; Music, Mikael Karlsson; Editors, Bruce La Bruce, Jörn Hartmann; Makeup, Pascal Herr; German-Canadian; Not rated; 95 minutes; American release date: November 7, 2008. CAST: Jey Crisfar (Otto), Katharina Klewinghaus (Medea Yarn), Susanne Sachße (Hella Bent), Marcel Schlutt (Fritz Fritze), Guido Sommer (Adolf), Christophe Chemin (Maximilian), Gio Black Peter (Rudolf), Mo (Zombie Boy), Fabrice, Scott Sechs (Gay Men), Nicholas Fox Ricciardi (Young Man in Hooded Sweatshirt), Keith Böhm (Man in Suit & Hat), Olivia Barth (Woman in Black Burqa), John Edward Heys (Old Man), Stefanie Heinrich (Old Woman), Stefan Kuschner (Butcher/Otto's Father), Max Di Costanzo, Orion Zombie (Zombie-Like Young Men), John Wloch (Headstone Shop Owner), Nils Jacobson, Josh Ford, Stan Steel, Michael Shade, Marcel Broch (Zombies), Nicolas Koenigsknecht (Man on Subway)

Jey Crisfar in Otto, or Up with Dead People © Strand Releasing

THE WORLD UNSEEN (Regent) Producer, Hanan Kattan; Executive Producers, Katherine Priestley, Lisa Tchenguiz-Imerman; Director/Screenplay, Shamim Sarif, based on her novel; Photography, Mike Downie; Designer, Tanya van Tonder; Costumes, Danielle Knox; Music, Shigeru Umebayashi; Editor, Ronelle; Casting, Hanan Kattan, Mito Skellern, Christa Schamberger; an Enlightenment Prods. (U.K.)/DO Prods. (South Africa); British-South African; Color; 35-to-HD; Rated PG-13; 94 minutes; American release date: November 7, 2008. CAST: Lisa Ray (Miriam), Sheetal Sheth (Amina Harjan), Parvin Dabas (Omar), Nandana Sen (Rehmat), David Dennis (Jacob), Grethe Fox (Madeleine), Colin Moss (De Witt), Natalie Becker (Farah), Rajesh Gopie (Sadru), Bernard White (Mr. Harjan), Avantika Akerkar (Mrs. Harjan), Amber Rose Revah (Begum), Leonie Casanova (Doris), Roderick Priestley (Stewart), Ethan Sarif-Kattan (Sam), Keziah Robinson (Yasmin), Usha Khan (Grandmother), Scott Cooper (James Winston), Sibusiso Menziwa (Robert)

Lisa Ray, Sheetal Sheth in The World Unseen © Regent Releasing

HOUSE OF THE SLEEPING BEAUTIES (First Run Features) a.k.a. *Das Haus der schlafenden Schönen*; Producers, Vadim Glowna, Raymond Tarabay; Director/Screenplay, Vadim Glowna; Based on the novel by Yasunari Kawabata; Photography, Ciro Cappellari; Designer, Peter Weber; Costumes, Lucie Bates; Music, Nikolaus Glowna; Editor, Charlie Lazin; an Atossa Film Produktion presentation of an Atossa Film/Impact Films production; German; Dolby; Widescreen; Color; Not rated; 99 minutes; American release date: November 14, 2008. CAST: Vadim Glowna (Edmond), Angela Winkler (Madame), Maximilian Schell (Kogi), Birol Ünel (Mister Gold), Mona Glass (Secretary), Marina Weis (Maid), Benjamin Cabuk (Balladeer), Peter Luppa (Preacher), Jacqueline Le Saunier, Maria Burghard, Babet Mader, Linda Elsner, Sarah Swenshon, Isabelle Wackers (Sleeping Beauties), Benjamin Seidel (Benni), Raymond Tarabay (Pall Bearer)

House of the Sleeping Beauties © First Run Features

EDEN (Liberation Entertainment) Producer, David Collins; Coproducer, Brian Willis; Director, Declan Recks; Screenplay, Eugene O'Brien, based on his play; Photography, Owen McPolin; Designer, John Hand; Costumes, Louise Stanton; Music, Stephen Rennicks, Hugh Drumm; Editor, Gareth Young; a Samson Films production, in association with Radio Telefis Eireann, Broadcasting Commission of Ireland, with the participation of the Irish Film Board; Irish; Dolby; Widescreen; Color; Not rated; 83 minutes; American release date: November 14, 2008. CAST: Aidan Kelly (Billy Farrell), Eileen Walsh (Breda Farrell), Padraic Delaney (Eoghan), Karl Shiels (Breffni Grehan), Lesley Conroy (Eilish Moore), Sarah Greene (Imelda Egan), Carolyn Murray (Edel Farrell), Brendan Kelleher (James Farrell), Enda Oates (Tony Tyrell), Kate O'Toole (Yvonne Egan), Gary Lilburn (Ernie Egan), Noel O'Donovan (Feggy Fennelly), Michelle Beamish (Naomi), Richie Recks (Quenchers Quinn), Gavin O'Connor (Dessie), Katie McGrath (Dessie's Girlfriend), Leonna Duff (Amanda), Ali Chabanov (Night Watchman), Paul Norton (Flynn's Barman), Pat Ennis, Bernard Coyle, Joe Rabbitte, Alan Recks (Golf Club Band), David Peyton, Harry Shiels (Egan Party Singers)

Aidan Kelly in Eden © *Liberation Entertainment*

ANTARCTICA (here!/Regent) Producer, Eitan Reuven; Executive Producers, Eitan Reuven, Shlomi Aviner; Director/Screenplay, Yair Hochner; Photography, Ziv Berkovich; Designers, Astar Elkayam, Gili Cohen; Music, Eli Soorani; Editor, Anat Saloon; a Sokolov 24/70 production; Israeli; Color; DV-to-DigiBeta; Rated R; 110 minutes; American release date: November 14, 2008. CAST: Tomer Ilan (Omer), Lucy Dubinchik (Shirley), Guy Zo-Artez (Ronen), Liat Akta (Michal), Wiftach Mizrahi (Danny), Ofer Regirer (Boaz), Rikva Neuman (Matilda Rose), Yuval Raz (Miki), Liaila Carry (Shoshana), Dvir Benedek (Tzachy), Yael Deckelbaum (Yael), Hana Coller (Mrs. Caspi), Adi Fain (Shopgirl), Ofer Ein Gal (Young Lover), Alon Harai, Yosefa Kimhy, Korin, Danni Lachman (Group Meeting), Noa Lazar (Tempting Lady), Dina Limon (Mrs. Abramovich), Yoel Noy (Studio Dancer), Dana Ruttenberg (Choreographer), Oshri Sahar (Eitan), Shirli Salomon (Shirli), Tamar Yerushalmi (Suzi the Hairdresser)

Wiftach Mizrahi, Ofer Regirer in Antarctica © *Regent Releasing*

I CAN'T THINK STRAIGHT (Regent/here!) Producer, Hanan Kattan; Executive Producers, Kelly Moss, Lisa Tchenguiz-Imerman, Mervyn Wilson; Director, Shamim Sarif; Screenplay, Shamim Sarif, Kelly Moss; Based on the novel by Shamim Sarif; Photography, Aseem Bajaj; Designer, Katie Lee Carter; Costumes, Charlie Knight; Music, Raiomondo Mirza; Editor, David Martin; an Enlightenment production; British; Dolby; Color; Rated PG-13; 80 minutes; American release date: November 21, 2008. CAST: Lisa Ray (Tala), Sheetal Sheth (Leyla), Antonia Frering (Reema), Dalip Tahil (Omar), Nina Wadia (Housekeeper), Siddiqua Akhtar (Maya), Jessica Allsop (Jennifer), Gabrielle Amies (Aunty Ramzi), Cuba, Daniel Balcaban (Handsome Waiters), Leonie Casanova, Sandra Watfa (Polo Spectators), Antoinette Claessens (Polo Player), Karen Frank, Shamim Sarif (Book Signing Fans), Ari Gill (Indian Servant), Nina Hautumm (Secretary), Alastair Hepher (Ramzi's Companion in Bar), Ernest Ignatius (Sam), Jess Imerman (Zina's Boyfriend in Picture), Rebecca Jameson (Diner), Kimberly Jaraj (Zina), Orly Jaraj (Catty Woman), Jay Karik, Dipti Patel (Beauticians), Hanan Kattan (Jordan Lecturer), Rez Kempton (Ali), Anya Lahiri (Lamia), Ishwar Maharaj (Sami), Ian Mann (Jeff), Steve Motion (Restaurant Host), Brij Patel (Ravi), Amber Rose Revah (Yasmin), Ethan Sarif-Kattan (Child in Park #1), Daud Shah (Hani), George Tardios (Uncle Ramzi), Sam Vincenti (Karim)

Lisa Ray, Sheetal Sheth in I Can't Think Straight © *Regent Releasing*

THE SECRETS (Monterey Media) a.k.a. *Ha-Sodot*; Producers, Avi Nesher, David Silber; Executive Producers, Moshe Edery, Leon Edery, Sharon Harel, Edgard Tenembaum, Andre Malignac; Director, Avi Nesher; Screenplay, Avi Nesher, Hadar Galron; Photography, Michel Abramowicz; Designer, Yoram Shayer; Costumes, Inbal Shuki; Music, Daniel Salomon, Eyal Sela; Editor, Isaac Sehayek; an Artomas Communications, Metro Communications, Tu Vas Voir, United King Films production; Israeli-French, 2007; Dolby; Color; Not rated; 125 minutes; American release date: November 26, 2008. CAST: Fanny Ardant (Anouk), Ania Bukstein (Noemi), Michal Shtamler (Michel), Adir Miller (Yanki), Guri Alfi (Michael), Alma Zack (Racheli), Tiki Dayan (Rabbinit), Dana Ivgy (Sigi), Talli Oren (Sheine), Seffy Rivlin (Rabbi Hess), Rivka Michaeli (Ms. Meizlish)

Michal Shtamler, Ania Bukstein in The Secrets © *Regent Releasing*

OYE LUCKY! LUCKY OYE! (UTV Motion Pictures) Producer, Ronnie Screwvala; Executive Producer, Priya Sreedharan; Director, Dibakar Banerjee; Screenplay, Dibakar Banerjee, Urmi Juvekar; Photography, Kartik Vijay; Music, Sneha Khanwalkar; Editors, Shyamal Karmakar, Namrata Rao; a Freshwater Films production; Indian; Dolby; Color; Not rated; 140 minutes; American release date: November 28, 2008. CAST: Abhay Deol (Lucky), Paresh Rawal (Lucky's Father/Gogi Bhai/Dr. Handa), Neetu Chandra (Sonal), Anurag Arora (Devender Singh, Cop), Richa Chadda (Dolly), Manu Rishi (Bangali), Rajinder Sethi (Criminal), Archana Puran Singh (Mrs. Handa), Manjot Singh (Young Lucky)

TIMECRIMES (Magnet) a.k.a. *Los Cronocrimenes*; Producers, Esteban Ibarretxe, Javier Ibarretxe, Eduardo Carneros, Santi Camunas, Jorge Gomez, Jordi Rediu, Norbert Llaras; Director/Screenplay, Nacho Vigalondo; Photography, Flavio Labiano; Art Directors, Jose Luis Arrizabalaga, Arturo Garcia "Biaffra"; Music, Chucky Namanera; Editor, Jose Luis Romeu; a KV Entertainment, ZIP, Fine, Arsenico production, with the participation of ETB, TVC; Spanish; Dolby; Color; Rated R; 88 minutes; American release date: December 5, 2008. CAST: Karra Elejalde (Hector), Nacho Vigalondo (Chico/Boy), Candela Fernandez (Clara), Barbara Goenaga (Chica/Girl)

Nacho Vigalondo in Timecrimes © Magnet

IN THE CITY OF SYLVIA (Independent) a.k.a. *En la ciudad de Sylvia*; Executive Producers, Luis Minarro, Gaelle Jones; Director/Screenplay, Jose Luis Guerin; Photography, Natasha Braier; Art Director, Maite Sanchez Balcells; Editor, Nuria Esquerra; an Eddie Saeta (Spain)/Chateau Rogue (France) production; Spanish-French; Dolby; Color; Not rated; 90 minutes; American release date: December 12, 2008. CAST: Pilar López de Ayala (Ella), Xavier (Él), Michaël Balerdi, Laurence Cordier, Tanja Czichy, Gladys Deussner, Eric Dietrich, Charlotte Dupont, Philippe Ohrel.

WHILE SHE WAS OUT (Anchor Bay) Producer, Don Murphy; Executive Producer, Guillermo del Toro; Director/Screenplay, Susan Montford; Story, Edward Bryant; Photography, Steve Gainer; Designer, Patrick Banister; Costumes, Cynthia Summers; Music, Paul Haslinger; Editor, William A. Anderson; German-Canadian-American; Color; Rated R; 88 minutes; American release date: December 12, 2008. CAST: Kim Basinger (Della), Lukas Haas (Chuckie), Craig Sheffer (Kenneth), Jamie Starr (Huey), Leonard Wu (Vingh), Luis Chávez (Tomás), Luke Gair (Terri), Erika-Shaye Gair (Tammi), Wayne Bernard (Angry Driver), Ari Solomon (Rent a Cop), Sadie Lawrence (Perfume Sales Lady), Alana Husband (Lingerie Sales Assistant), Katie Messina (Coffee Sales Person), Rachel Hayward (Lynn), Lossen Chambers (Pharmacy Sales Assistant), Steve Archer (Tired Man), Michael Strusievici (Kid)

Lukas Haas in While She Was Out © Anchor Bay

MOSCOW, BELGIUM (NeoClassics, Inc.) a.k.a. *Aanrijding in Moscou*; Producer, Jean-Claude van Rijckeghem; Director, Christophe van Rompaey; Screenplay, Jean-Claude van Rijckeghem, Pat van Beirs; Photography, Ruben Impens; Designer, Steven Liegeois; Costumes, Tina Verbeurgt; Editor, Alain Dessauvage; a Private View production; Belgian; Dolby; Color; Not rated; 102 minutes; American release date: December 19, 2008. CAST: Barbara Sarafian (Matty), Jurgen Delnaet (Johnny), Johan Heldenbergh (Werner), Anemone Valcke (Vera), Sofia Ferri (Fien), Julian Borsani (Peter), Bob De Moor (Jacques), Jits Van Belle (Nicky), Griet van Damme (Nathalie), Thomas Dhanens (Bediende), Camille Friant (Iris), Frederik Imbo (Maxime), Suzy Van Herbergen (Daisy), Robrecht Vanden Thoren (DJ)

Barbara Sarafian, Jurgen Delnaet in Moscow, Belgium © NeoClassics

PROMISING NEW ACTORS

2008

SUMMER BISHIL *(Towelhead)*

CAM GIGANDET *(Never Back Down, Twilight)*

DAVID KROSS *(The Reader)*

MADELINE CARROLL *(Swing Vote)*

KAT DENNINGS *(Charlie Bartlett, The House Bunny, Nick and Nora's Infinite Playlist)*

BILL MILNER *(Son of Rambow)*

DEV PATEL *(Slumdog Millionaire)*

ROSEMARIE DEWITT *(Rachel Getting Married)*

CHRIS PINE *(Bottle Shock)*

MELONIE DIAZ *(Be Kind Rewind, Hamlet 2, Nothing Like the Holidays)*

REBECCA HALL *(Vicky Cristina Barcelona, Frost/Nixon)*

BEE VANG *(Gran Torino)*

ACADEMY AWARD

Winners and Nominees 2008

BEST PICTURE

SLUMDOG MILLIONAIRE

(FOX SEARCHLIGHT) Producer, Christian Colson; Executive Producers, Paul Smith, Tess Ross; Coproducer, Paul Ritchie; Co-Executive Producers, Francois Ivernel, Cameron McCracken; Director, Danny Boyle; Codirector (India), Loveleen Tandan; Screenplay, Simon Beaufoy; Based on the novel *Q&A* by Vikas Swarup; Photography, Anthony Do Mantle; Designer, Mark Digby; Costumes, Suttirat Anne Larlarb; Music, A.R. Rahman; Editor, Chris Dickens; Casting, Loveleen Tandan, Gail Stevens Cog; a Fox Searchlight, Warner Bros. (U.S.)./Celador Films, Film 4 (U.K.) presentation; British-American; Dolby; Super 35 Widescreen; Color; DV- and-35mm; Rated R; 116 minutes; American release date: November 12, 2008

Cast

Jamal Malik	**Dev Patel**
Prem Kumar	**Anil Kapoor**
Sgt. Srinivas	**Saurabh Shukla**
Director	**Raj Zutshi**
Vision Mixer	**Jeneva Talwar**
Latika	**Freida Pinto**
Police Inspector	**Irrfan Khan**
Youngest Salim	**Azharuddin Mohammed Ismail**
Youngest Jamal	**Ayush Mahesh Khedekar**
Mr. Chi	**Sunil Aggarwal**
Airport Security Guards	**Jira Banjara, Sheikh Wali**
Javed	**Mahesh Manjrekar**
Jamal's Mother	**Sanchita Choudhary**
Mr. Nanda	**Himanshu Tyagi**
Prakash	**Sharib Hashmi**
Slum Man	**Virendra Chatterjee**
Amitabh Bachchan	**Feroz Abbas Khan**
Man on Fire	**Virender Kumar Gharu**
Blue Boy	**Devesh Rawal**
Youngest Latika	**Rubiana Ali**
Maman	**Ankur Vikal**
Punnoose	**Tiger**
Young Arvind	**Chirag Parmar**
Baby	**Nazneen Shaikh**
Latika's Friend	**Farzana Ansari**

Old Villager	**Anupam Shyam**
Ticket Collector	**Salim Chaus**
Family in Train	**Singh Shera, Harvinder Kaur, Narendra Singh**
Middle Jamal	**Tanay Hemant Chheda**
Middle Salim	**Ashutosh Lobo Gajiwala**
Taj Mahal Guide	**Satya Mudgal**
Ada	**Janet de Vigne**
Peter	**William Relton**
Clark	**David Gilliam**
Adele	**Mia Inderbitzin**
Driver	**Kinder Singh**
Opera Singers	**Christine Matovich Singh, Thomas Lehmkuhl**
Older Arvind	**Siddesh Patil**

Najma Shaikh, Saeeda Shaikh, Alka Satpute, Tabassum Khan (Women in Brothel), Tanvi Ganesh Lonkar (Middle Latika), Sitaram Panchal (Dance Teacher), Nigel Caesar (Hotel Security Guard), Ajit Pandey, Kedar Thapar, Amit Leonard, Rajesh Kumar, Sagar Ghopalkar, Pradeep Solanki, Hamid Sheikh, Dheeraj Waghela (Javed Goons), Arfi Lamba (Bardi), Taira Colah (Nasreen), Varun Bagri (Call Center Trainee), Ankur Tewari (Dave), Anjum Sharma (Operator), Madhur Mittal (Older Salim), Sarfaraz Khan, Syed Hussain, Umar Khan (Autorickshaw Drivers), Imran Hasnee (Javed's House Doorkeeper), Homai Billimoria (KBC Contestant), Udayan Baijal (Cricket Commentator), Sandeep Kaul (Floor Manager), Rhea Lawyer (TV Reporter), Deepali Dalvi, Anisha Nagar, Farrah Skaikh, Mamta Sharma, Neha M. Khatarawalla (Dancers at Javed's Safehouse), Tanya Singh, Anand Tiwari, Faezeh Jalai, Meghana Jhalani, Rupali Mehra, Anju Singh (Newsreaders), Saurabh Agarwal (Call Center Manager)

As Jamal Malik astounds everyone by winning one category after another on *Who Wants to Be a Millionaire*, the authorities begin to question how someone from the slums of Indian could be so well versed in so many subjects.

2008 Academy Award winner for Best Picture, Best Director, Best Adapted Screenplay, Best Cinematography, Best Film Editing, Best Sound Mixing, Best Original Score, and Best Original Song ("Jai Ho").

This film received additional Oscar nominations for sound editing and original song ("O … Saya").

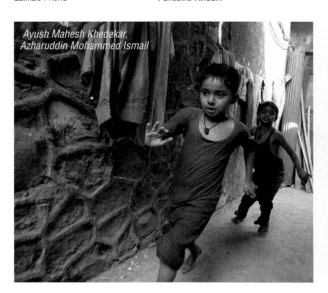

Ayush Mahesh Khedekar, Azharuddin Mohammed Ismail

Ayush Mahesh Khedekar, Azharuddin Mohammed Ismail

Dev Patel, Freida Pinto

Dev Patel, Anil Kapoor

Dev Patel, Anil Kapoor © Fox Searchlight

EVE

WALL•E, EVE © Pixar Animation Studio

Mo, WALL•E

EVE,WALL•E

WALL•E

EVE, WALL•E

WALL•E

Hal, WALL•E

BEST ANIMATED FEATURE

WALL·E

(WALT DISNEY PICTURES) Producer, Jim Morris; Executive Producer, John Lasseter; Co-Producer, Lindsey Collins; Director, Andrew Stanton; Screenplay, Andrew Stanton, Jim Reardon; Original Story, Andrew Stanton, Pete Docter; Photography, Jeremy Lasky; Designer, Ralph Eggleston; Character Art Director, Jason Deamer; Music, Thomas Newman; Song: "Down to Earth" by Thomas Newman and Peter Gabriel; Editor, Stephen Schaffer; Supervising Technical Director, Nigel Hardwidge; Supervising Animators, Alan Barillaro, Steven Clay Hunter; Casting, Kevin Reher, Natalie Lyone; a Pixar Animation Studio production; Dolby; Widescreen; Technicolor; Rated G; 97 minutes; Release date: June 27, 2008

Voice Cast

WALL·E/M·O	**Ben Burtt**
EVE	**Elissa Knight**
Captain McCrea	**Jeff Garlin**
Shelby Forthright	**Fred Willard**
AUTO	**MacInTalk**
John	**John Ratzenberger**
Mary	**Kathy Najimy**
Ship's Computer	**Sigourney Weaver**
Hoverchair Mother	**Kim Kopf**

WALL·E, a robot whose task it is to collect and compact the endless amount of waste left behind on a vacated Earth, finds his loneliness abated when he is unexpectedly visited by a higher grade of robot sent to the planet on a mission.

2009 Academy Award winner for Best Animated Feature.

WALL•E

BEST FEATURE DOCUMENTARY

MAN ON WIRE

(MAGNOLIA) Producer, Simon Chinn; Executive Producers, Jonathan Hewes, Andrea Meditch, Nick Fraser, Lenny Crooks; Coproducers, Victoria Gregory, Maureen A. Ryan; Director, James Marsh; Based on the book *To Reach the Clouds* by Philippe Petit; Photography, Igor Martinovic; Designer, Sharon Lomofsky Walthall; Costumes, Kathryn Nixon; Music, Michael Nyman; Music Consultant, John Boughtwood; Editor, Jinx Godfrey; Casting, Adine Duron; a Discovery Films/BBC/UK Film Council presentation of a Wall to Wall production in association with Red Box Films; British-American; Dolby; DuArt/Deluxe color/black and white; Rated PG-13; 102 minutes; American release date: July 25, 2008. Documentary on how aerialist Philippe Petit managed to tightwalk between the towers of the World Trade Center in 1974

With

Philippe Petit, Jean-Louis Blondeau, Annie Allix, Jim Moore, Mark Lewis, Jean-François Heckel, Barry Greenhouse, David Forman, Alan Welner (Themselves); Reinactments: Ardis Campbell (Annie), David Demato (Jean Louis), David Frank (Alan), Aaron Haskell (Jean-François), Paul McGill (Philippe Petit)

2008 Academy Award winner for Best Feature Documentary.

Philippe Petit

Philippe Petit

Philippe Petit

Philippe Petit © Magnolia Films

ACADEMY AWARD FOR BEST ACTOR: Sean Penn in *Milk*

ACADEMY AWARD FOR BEST ACTRESS: Kate Winslet in *The Reader*

ACADEMY AWARD FOR BEST SUPPORTING ACTOR : Heath Ledger in *The Dark Knight*

ACADEMY AWARD FOR BEST SUPPORTING ACTRESS: *Penélope Cruz in Vicky Cristina Barcelona*

ACADEMY AWARD NOMINEES FOR BEST ACTOR

Richard Jenkins in The Visitor

Frank Langella in Frost/Nixon

Brad Pitt in The Curious Case of Benjamin Button

Mickey Rourke in The Wrestler

ACADEMY AWARD NOMINEES FOR BEST ACTRESS

Anne Hathaway in Rachel Getting Married

Angelina Jolie in Changeling

Melissa Leo in Frozen River

Meryl Streep in Doubt

ACADEMY AWARD NOMINEES FOR BEST SUPPORTING ACTOR

Josh Brolin in Milk

Robert Downey, Jr. in Tropic Thunder

Philip Seymour Hoffman in Doubt

Michael Shannon in Revolutionary Road

ACADEMY AWARD NOMINEES FOR BEST SUPPORTING ACTRESS

Amy Adams in Doubt

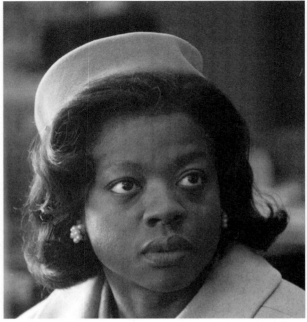

Viola Davis in Doubt

Taraji P. Henson in The Curious Case of Benjamin Button

Marisa Tomei in The Wrestler

TOP BOX OFFICE

Stars and Films 2008

TOP BOX OFFICE STARS OF 2008

1. Will Smith
2. Robert Downey, Jr.
3. Christian Bale
4. Shia LaBeouf
5. Harrison Ford
6. Adam Sandler
7. Reese Witherspoon
8. George Clooney
9. Angelina Jolie
10. Daniel Craig

TOP 100 BOX OFFICE FILMS OF 2008

1. The Dark Knight (WB)	$532,360,000
2. Iron Man (Paramount)	$318,140,000
3. Indiana Jones and the Kingdom of the Crystal Skull (Par)	$317,100,000
4. Hancock (Columbia)	$226,550,000
5. WALL*E (BV)	$223,750,000
6. Kung Fu Panda (DW/Paramount)	$214,950,000
7. Twilight (Summit Entertainment)	$191,470,000
8. Madagascar Escape 2 Africa (DW)	$178,870,000
9. Quantum of Solace (MGM/Columbia)	$168,370,000
10. Dr. Seuss' Horton Hears a Who (20th)	$154,530,000
11. Sex and the City (New Line Cinema)	$152,640,000
12. Gran Torino (WB)	$147,800,000
13. Mamma Mia! (Universal)	$143,710,000
14. Marley & Me (20th)	$143,160,000
15. The Chronicles of Narnia: Prince Caspian (BV)	$141,560,000
16. Slumdog Millionaire (Fox Searchlight)	$141,320,000
17. The Incredible Hulk (Universal)	$134,530,000
18. Wanted (Universal)	$134,400,000
19. Get Smart (WB)	$130,170,000
20. The Curious Case of Benjamin Button (Par/WB)	$127,510,000
21. Four Christmases (New Line)	$120,150,000
22. Bolt (BV)	$112,980,000
23. Tropic Thunder (DW/Paramount)	$110,260,000
24. Bedtime Stories (BV)	$110,000,000
25. Journey to the Center of the Earth 3D (New Line)	$101,710,000

Freddie Highmore in The Spiderwick Chronicles © *Paramount Pictures*

Director Christopher Nolan and Christian Bale on the set of
The Dark Knight © *Warner Bros.*

26. The Mummy: Tomb of the Dragon Emperor (Universal)	$101,600,000
27. Eagle Eye (DW/Par)	$101,150,000
28. Step Brothers (Columbia)	$100,470,000
29. You Don't Mess with the Zohan (Columbia)	$99,690,000
30. Yes Man (WB)	$97,640,000
31. 10,000 B.C. (WB)	$94,780,000
32. Beverly Hills Chihuahua (BV)	$94,500,000
33. High School Musical 3: Senior Year (BV)	$89,560,000
34. Pineapple Express (Columbia)	$87,170,000
35. Valkyrie (MGM/UA)	$83,100,000
36. 21 (Columbia)	$81,160,000
37. What Happens in Vegas (20th)	$80,280,000
38. Jumper (20th)	$79,910,000
39. Cloverfield (Paramount)	$79,810,000
40. The Day the Earth Stood Still (20th)	$79,370,000
41. 27 Dresses (20th)	$76,800,000
42. Hellboy 2: What's It (Universal)	$74,760,000
43. Vantage Point (Columbia)	$71,100,000
44. The Spiderwick Chronicles (Par)	$71,190,000
45. Fool's Gold (WB)	$70,160,000
46. Seven Pounds (Columbia)	$69,960,000
47. Role Models (Universal)	$67,300,000
48. Hannah Montana and Miley Cyrus (BV)	$64,550,000
49. The Happening (20th)	$64,510,000
50. Forgetting Sarah Marshall (Universal)	$62,890,000
51. Burn after Reading (Focus)	$60,310,000
52. Baby Mama (Universal)	$60,270,000
53. Step Up 2 the Streets (BV)	$57,100,000
54. Saw V (Lionsgate)	$55,730,000

55. The Forbidden Kingdom (Lionsgate/Weinstein Co.)	$52,100,000
56. The Strangers (Rogue)	$52,540,000
57. The Tale of Despereaux (Universal)	$50,880,000
58. Australia (20th)	$49,560,000
59. The House Bunny (Columbia)	$48,240,000
60. Nim's Island (20th)	$46,700,000
61. Made of Honor (Columbia)	$45,410,000
62. College Road Trip (BV)	$44,910,000
63. Prom Night (Screen Gems)	$43,480,000
64. Sisterhood of the Traveling Pants 2 (WB)	$42,940,000
65. Rambo (Lionsgate)	$42,730,000
66. Speed Racer (WB)	$42,510,000
67. Welcome Home Roscoe Jenkins (Univ)	$42,180,000
68. Meet the Browns (Lionsgate)	$41,930,000
69. Nights in Rodanthe (WB)	$41,730,000
70. Max Payne (20th)	$40,590,000
71. Righteous Kill (Overture)	$40,100,000
72. Body of Lies (WB)	$39,180,000
73. Lakeview Terrace (Screen Gems)	$39,100,000
74. Meet the Spartans (20th)	$38,000,000
75. First Sunday (Screen Gems)	$37,940,000
76. The Secret Life of Bees (Fox Searchlight)	$37,730,000
77. Harold & Kumar Escape from Guantanamo (New Line)	$37,560,000
78. The Family That Preys (Lionsgate)	$37,110,000
79. Death Race (Universal)	$36,100,000
80. Changeling (Universal)	$35,700,000
81. Star Wars: The Clone Wars (WB)	$34,900,000
82. The Reader (Miramax)	$34,160,000
82. Doubt (Miramax)	$33,450,000
82. Fireproof (Goldwyn)	$32,940,000
83. Drillbit Taylor (Paramount)	$32,860,000
85. Semi-Pro (New Line)	$32,280,000
86. Definitely, Maybe (Universal)	$31,990,000
87. Milk (Focus)	$31,850,000
88. The Love Guru (Paramount)	$31,800,000
89. Zack and Miri Make a Porno (Weinstein)	$31,470,000
90. Quarantine (Screen Gems)	$31,460,000
91. The Eye (Lionsgate)	$31,400,000

Gattlin Griffith, Angelina Jolie in Changeling © *Universal Pictures*

92. Leatherheads (Universal)	$31,200,000
93. Nick and Norah's Infinite Playlist (Col)	$30,840,000
94. Mirrors (20th)	$30,510,000
95. Space Chimps (20th)	$30,110,000
96. Transporter 3 (Lionsgate)	$30,110,000
97. The Bank Job (Lionsgate)	$30,100,000
99. Untraceable (Screen Gems)	$28,690,000
100. Defiance (Paramount Vantage)	$28,630,000

Emile Hirsch in Speed Racer © *Warner Bros.*

Top: *Marley in*
Marley & Me
© *20th Century Fox*

Left: *Jay Baruchel in*
Tropic Thunder
© *DreamWorks*

BIOGRAPHICAL DATA

2008

Aames, Willie (William Upton) Los Angeles, CA, July 15, 1960.
Aaron, Caroline Richmond, VA, Aug. 7, 1954. Catholic U.
Abbott, Diahnne New York, NY, 1945.
Abraham, F. Murray Pittsburgh, PA, Oct. 24, 1939. U Texas.
Ackland, Joss London, England, Feb. 29, 1928.
Adams, Amy Vicenza, Italy, Aug. 20, 1975.
Adams, Brooke New York, NY, Feb. 8, 1949. Dalton.
Adams, Catlin Los Angeles, CA, Oct. 11, 1950.
Adams, Jane Washington, DC, Apr. 1, 1965.
Adams, Joey Lauren Little Rock, AR, Jan. 6, 1971.
Adams, Julie (Betty May) Waterloo, IA, Oct. 17, 1926. Little Rock, Jr. College.
Adams, Maud (Maud Wikstrom) Lulea, Sweden, Feb. 12, 1945.
Adjani, Isabelle Paris, France, June 27, 1955.
Affleck, Ben Berkeley, CA, Aug. 15, 1972.
Affleck, Casey Falmouth, MA, Aug. 12, 1975.
Aghdashloo, Shohreh Tehran, Iran, May 11, 1952.
Agutter, Jenny Taunton, England, Dec. 20, 1952.
Aiello, Danny New York, NY, June 20, 1933.
Aiken, Liam New York, NY, Jan. 7, 1990.
Aimee, Anouk (Dreyfus) Paris, France, Apr. 27, 1934. Bauer Therond.
Akers, Karen New York, NY, Oct. 13, 1945, Hunter College.
Alba, Jessica Pomona, CA, Apr. 28, 1981.
Alberghetti, Anna Maria Pesaro, Italy, May 15, 1936.
Albright, Lola Akron, OH, July 20, 1925.
Alda, Alan New York, NY, Jan. 28, 1936. Fordham.
Aleandro, Norma Buenos Aires, Argentina, Dec. 6, 1936.
Alejandro, Miguel New York, NY, Feb. 21, 1958.
Alexander, Jane (Quigley) Boston, MA, Oct. 28, 1939. Sarah Lawrence.
Alexander, Jason (Jay Greenspan) Newark, NJ, Sept. 23, 1959. Boston U.
Alice, Mary Indianola, MS, Dec. 3, 1941.
Allen, Debbie (Deborah) Houston, TX, Jan. 16, 1950. Howard U.
Allen, Joan Rochelle, IL, Aug. 20, 1956. East Illinois U.
Allen, Karen Carrollton, IL, Oct. 5, 1951. U Maryland.
Allen, Nancy New York, NY, June 24, 1950.
Allen, Tim Denver, CO, June 13, 1953. Western Michigan U.
Allen, Woody (Allan Stewart Konigsberg) Brooklyn, NY, Dec. 1, 1935.
Alley, Kirstie Wichita, KS, Jan. 12, 1955.
Alonso, Maria Conchita Cuba, June 29, 1957.
Alt, Carol Queens, NY, Dec. 1, 1960. Hofstra U.
Alvarado, Trini New York, NY, Jan. 10, 1967.
Amalric, Mathieu Neuilly-sur-Seine, France, Oct. 25, 1965.
Ambrose, Lauren New Haven, CT, Feb. 20, 1978.
Amis, Suzy Oklahoma City, OK, Jan. 5, 1958. Actors Studio.
Amos, John Newark, NJ, Dec. 27, 1940. Colorado U.
Anderson, Anthony Los Angeles, CA, Aug. 15, 1970.
Anderson, Gillian Chicago, IL, Aug. 9, 1968. DePaul U.
Anderson, Kevin Waukeegan, IL, Jan. 13, 1960.
Anderson, Loni St. Paul, MN, Aug. 5, 1946.
Anderson, Melissa Sue Berkeley, CA, Sept. 26, 1962.
Anderson, Melody Edmonton, Canada, Dec. 3, 1955. Carlton U.
Anderson, Michael, Jr. London, England, Aug. 6, 1943.
Anderson, Richard Dean Minneapolis, MN, Jan. 23, 1950.
Andersson, Bibi Stockholm, Sweden, Nov. 11, 1935. Royal Dramatic School.
Andress, Ursula Bern, Switzerland, Mar. 19, 1936.
Andrews, Anthony London, England, Dec. 1, 1948.
Andrews, Julie (Julia Elizabeth Wells) Surrey, England, Oct. 1, 1935.
Andrews, Naveen London, England, Jan. 17, 1969.
Angarano, Michael Brooklyn, NY, Dec. 3, 1987.
Anglim, Philip San Francisco, CA, Feb. 11, 1953.
Aniston, Jennifer Sherman Oaks, CA, Feb. 11, 1969.

Ann-Margret (Olsson) Valsjobyn, Sweden, Apr. 28, 1941. Northwestern.
Ansara, Michael Lowell, MA, Apr. 15, 1922. Pasadena Playhouse.
Anspach, Susan New York, NY, Nov. 23, 1945.
Anthony, Lysette London, England, Sept. 26, 1963.
Anthony, Marc New York, NY, Sept. 16, 1968.
Anthony, Tony Clarksburg, WV, Oct. 16, 1937. Carnegie Tech.
Anton, Susan Yucaipa, CA, Oct. 12, 1950. Bernardino College.
Antonelli, Laura Pola, Italy, Nov. 28, 1941.
Anwar, Gabrielle Lalehaam, England, Feb. 4, 1970.
Applegate, Christina Hollywood, CA, Nov. 25, 1972.
Archer, Anne Los Angeles, CA, Aug. 25, 1947.
Ardant, Fanny Monte Carlo, Monaco, Mar 22, 1949.
Arkin, Adam Brooklyn, NY, Aug. 19, 1956.
Arkin, Alan New York, NY, Mar. 26, 1934. LACC.
Armstrong, Bess Baltimore, MD, Dec. 11, 1953.
Arnaz, Desi, Jr. Los Angeles, CA, Jan. 19, 1953.
Arnaz, Lucie Hollywood, CA, July 17, 1951.
Arness, James (Aurness) Minneapolis, MN, May 26, 1923. Beloit College.
Arnett, Will Toronto, ON, Canada, May 5, 1970.
Arquette, David Winchester, VA, Sept. 8, 1971.
Arquette, Patricia New York, NY, Apr. 8, 1968.
Arquette, Rosanna New York, NY, Aug. 10, 1959.
Arthur, Beatrice (Frankel) New York, NY, May 13, 1924. New School.
Asher, Jane London, England, Apr. 5, 1946.
Ashley, Elizabeth (Elizabeth Ann Cole) Ocala, FL, Aug. 30, 1939.
Ashton, John Springfield, MA, Feb. 22, 1948. USC.
Asner, Edward Kansas City, KS, Nov. 15, 1929.
Assante, Armand New York, NY, Oct. 4, 1949. AADA.
Astin, John Baltimore, MD, Mar. 30, 1930. U Minnesota.
Astin, MacKenzie Los Angeles, CA, May 12, 1973.
Astin, Sean Santa Monica, CA, Feb. 25, 1971.
Atherton, William Orange, CT, July 30, 1947. Carnegie Tech.
Atkins, Christopher Rye, NY, Feb. 21, 1961.
Atkins, Eileen London, England, June 16, 1934.
Atkinson, Rowan Consett, England, Jan. 6, 1955. Oxford.
Attenborough, Richard Cambridge, England, Aug. 29, 1923. RADA.
Auberjonois, Rene New York, NY, June 1, 1940. Carnegie Tech.
Audran, Stephane Versailles, France, Nov. 8, 1932.
Auger, Claudine Paris, France, Apr. 26, 1942. Dramatic Cons.
Aulin, Ewa Stockholm, Sweden, Feb. 14, 1950.
Auteuil, Daniel Alger, Algeria, Jan. 24, 1950.
Avalon, Frankie (Francis Thomas Avallone) Philadelphia, PA, Sept. 18, 1939.
Aykroyd, Dan Ottawa, Canada, July 1, 1952.
Azaria, Hank Forest Hills, NY, Apr. 25, 1964. AADA, Tufts U.
Aznavour, Charles (Varenagh Aznourian) Paris, France, May 22, 1924.
Azzara, Candice Brooklyn, NY, May 18, 1947.

Bacall, Lauren (Betty Perske) New York, NY, Sept. 16, 1924. AADA.
Bach, Barbara Queens, NY, Aug. 27, 1946.
Bach, Catherine Warren, OH, Mar. 1, 1954.
Backer, Brian New York, NY, Dec. 5, 1956. Neighborhood Playhouse.
Bacon, Kevin Philadelphia, PA, July 8, 1958.
Bain, Barbara Chicago, IL, Sept. 13, 1934. U Illinois.
Baio, Scott Brooklyn, NY, Sept. 22, 1961.
Baker, Blanche New York, NY, Dec. 20, 1956.
Baker, Carroll Johnstown, PA, May 28, 1931. St. Petersburg, Jr. College.
Baker, Diane Hollywood, CA, Feb. 25, 1938. USC.
Baker, Dylan Syracuse, NY, Oct. 7, 1959.
Baker, Joe Don Groesbeck, TX, Feb. 12, 1936.
Baker, Kathy Midland, TX, June 8, 1950. UC Berkley.

Baker, Simon Launceston, Tasmania, July 30, 1969.
Bakula, Scott St. Louis, MO, Oct. 9, 1955. Kansas U.
Balaban, Bob Chicago, IL, Aug. 16, 1945. Colgate.
Baldwin, Adam Chicago, IL, Feb. 27, 1962.
Baldwin, Alec Massapequa, NY, Apr. 3, 1958. NYU.
Baldwin, Daniel Massapequa, NY, Oct. 5, 1960.
Baldwin, Stephen Massapequa, NY, May 12, 1966.
Baldwin, William Massapequa, NY, Feb. 21, 1963.
Bale, Christian Pembrokeshire, West Wales, Jan. 30, 1974.
Balk, Fairuza Point Reyes, CA, May 21, 1974.
Ballard, Kaye Cleveland, OH, Nov. 20, 1926.
Bana, Eric Melbourne, Australia, Aug. 9, 1968.
Banderas, Antonio Malaga, Spain, Aug. 10, 1960.
Banerjee, Victor Calcutta, India, Oct. 15, 1946.
Banes, Lisa Chagrin Falls, OH, July 9, 1955. Juilliard.
Banks, Elizabeth Pittsfield, MA, Feb. 19, 1974. U of PA.
Baranski, Christine Buffalo, NY, May 2, 1952. Juilliard.
Barbeau, Adrienne Sacramento, CA, June 11, 1945. Foothill College.
Bardem, Javier Gran Canaria, Spain, May 1, 1969.
Bardot, Brigitte Paris, France, Sept. 28, 1934.
Barkin, Ellen Bronx, NY, Apr. 16, 1954. Hunter College.
Barnes, Christopher Daniel Portland, ME, Nov. 7, 1972.
Barnett, Samuel Whitby, No. Yorkshire, England, Apr. 25, 1980.
Baron Cohen, Sacha London, England, Oct. 13, 1971.
Barr, Jean-Marc Bitburg, Germany, Sept. 27, 1960.
Barr, Roseanne Salt Lake City, UT, Nov. 3, 1952.
Barrault, Marie-Christine Paris, France, Mar. 21, 1944.
Barraza, Adriana Toluca, Mexico, March 5, 1956.
Barrie, Barbara Chicago, IL, May 23, 1931.
Barry, Gene (Eugene Klass) New York, NY, June 14, 1919.
Barry, Neill New York, NY, Nov. 29, 1965.
Barrymore, Drew Los Angeles, CA, Feb. 22, 1975.
Bart, Roger Norwalk, CT, Sept. 29, 1962.
Bartha, Justin West Bloomfield, MI, July 21, 1978.
Baruchel, Jay Ottawa, Canada, Apr. 9, 1982.
Baryshnikov, Mikhail Riga, Latvia, Jan. 27, 1948.
Basinger, Kim Athens, GA, Dec. 8, 1953. Neighborhood Playhouse.
Bassett, Angela New York, NY, Aug. 16, 1958.
Bateman, Jason Rye, NY, Jan. 14, 1969.
Bateman, Justine Rye, NY, Feb. 19, 1966.
Bates, Jeanne San Francisco, CA, May 21, 1918. RADA.
Bates, Kathy Memphis, TN, June 28, 1948. S. Methodist U.
Bauer, Steven (Steven Rocky Echevarria) Havana, Cuba, Dec. 2, 1956.
    U Miami.
Baxter, Keith South Wales, England, Apr. 29, 1933. RADA.
Baxter, Meredith Los Angeles, CA, June 21, 1947. Interlochen Academy.
Baye, Nathalie Maineville, France, July 6, 1948.
Beach, Adam Winnipeg, Manitoba, Canada, Nov. 11, 1972.
Beacham, Stephanie Casablanca, Morocco, Feb. 28, 1947.
Beals, Jennifer Chicago, IL, Dec. 19, 1963.
Bean, Orson (Dallas Burrows) Burlington, VT, July 22, 1928.
Bean, Sean Sheffield, Yorkshire, England, Apr. 17, 1958.
Béart, Emmanuelle Gassin, France, Aug. 14, 1965.
Beatty, Ned Louisville, KY, July 6, 1937.
Beatty, Warren Richmond, VA, Mar. 30, 1937.
Beck, John Chicago, IL, Jan. 28, 1943.
Beck, Michael Memphis, TN, Feb. 4, 1949. Millsap College.
Beckinsale, Kate London, England, July 26, 1974.
Bedelia, Bonnie New York, NY, Mar. 25, 1946. Hunter College.
Begley, Ed, Jr. New York, NY, Sept. 16, 1949.

Belafonte, Harry New York, NY, Mar. 1, 1927.
Bell, Jamie Billingham, England, Mar. 14, 1988.
Bell, Kristen Huntington Woods, WI, July 18, 1980.
Bell, Tobin Queens, NY, Aug. 7, 1942.
Beller, Kathleen New York, NY, Feb. 10, 1957.
Bello, Maria Norristown, PA, Apr. 18, 1967.
Bellucci, Monica Citta di Castello, Italy, Sept. 30, 1964.
Bellwood, Pamela (King) Scarsdale, NY, June 26, 1951.
Belmondo, Jean Paul Paris, France, Apr. 9, 1933.
Belushi, James Chicago, IL, June 15, 1954.
Belzer, Richard Bridgeport, CT, Aug. 4, 1944.
Benedict, Dirk (Niewoehner) White Sulphur Springs, MT, March 1, 1945.
    Whitman College.
Benigni, Roberto Tuscany, Italy, Oct. 27, 1952.
Bening, Annette Topeka, KS, May 29, 1958. San Francisco State U.
Benjamin, Richard New York, NY, May 22, 1938. Northwestern.
Bennent, David Lausanne, Switzerland, Sept. 9, 1966.
Bennett, Alan Leeds, England, May 9, 1934. Oxford.
Bennett, Hywel Garnant, South Wales, Apr. 8, 1944.
Benson, Robby Dallas, TX, Jan. 21, 1957.
Bentley, Wes Jonesboro, AR, Sept. 4, 1978.
Berenger, Tom Chicago, IL, May 31, 1950, U Missouri.
Berenson, Marisa New York, NY, Feb. 15, 1947.
Berg, Peter New York, NY, March 11, 1964. Malcalester College.
Bergen, Candice Los Angeles, CA, May 9, 1946. U Pennsylvania.
Bergen, Polly Knoxville, TN, July 14, 1930. Compton, Jr. College.
Berger, Helmut Salzburg, Austria, May 29, 1942.
Berger, Senta Vienna, Austria, May 13, 1941. Vienna School of Acting.
Berger, William Austria, Jan. 20, 1928. Columbia.
Bergerac, Jacques Biarritz, France, May 26, 1927. Paris U.
Bergin, Patrick Dublin, Ireland, Feb. 4, 1951.
Berkley, Elizabeth Detroit, MI, July 28, 1972.
Berkoff, Steven London, England, Aug. 3, 1937.
Berlin, Jeannie Los Angeles, CA, Nov. 1, 1949.
Berlinger, Warren Brooklyn, NY, Aug. 31, 1937. Columbia U.
Bernal, Gael García Guadalajara, Mexico, Oct. 30, 1978.
Bernhard, Sandra Flint, MI, June 6, 1955.
Bernsen, Corbin Los Angeles, CA, Sept. 7, 1954. UCLA.
Berri, Claude (Langmann) Paris, France, July 1, 1934.
Berridge, Elizabeth Westchester, NY, May 2, 1962. Strasberg Institute.
Berry, Halle Cleveland, OH, Aug. 14, 1968.
Berry, Ken Moline, IL, Nov. 3, 1933.
Bertinelli, Valerie Wilmington, DE, Apr. 23, 1960.
Best, James Corydon, IN, July 26, 1926.
Bettany, Paul London, England, May 27, 1971.
Bey, Turhan Vienna, Austria, Mar. 30, 1921.
Beymer, Richard Avoca, IA, Feb. 21, 1939.
Bialik, Mayim San Diego, CA, Dec. 12, 1975.
Biehn, Michael Anniston, AL, July 31, 1956.
Biel, Jessica Ely, MN, Mar. 3, 1982.
Biggerstaff, Sean Glasgow, Scotland, Mar. 15, 1983.
Biggs, Jason Pompton Plains, NJ, May 12, 1978.
Bikel, Theodore Vienna, Austria, May 2, 1924. RADA.
Billingsley, Peter New York, NY, Apr. 16, 1972.
Binoche, Juliette Paris, France, Mar. 9, 1964.
Birch, Thora Los Angeles, CA, Mar. 11, 1982.
Birkin, Jane London, England, Dec. 14, 1947.
Birney, David Washington, DC, Apr. 23, 1939. Dartmouth, UCLA.
Birney, Reed Alexandria, VA, Sept. 11, 1954. Boston U.
Bishop, Kevin Kent, England, June 18, 1980.

Bisset, Jacqueline Waybridge, England, Sept. 13, 1944.
Black, Jack (Thomas Black) Edmonton, Alberta, Canada, Apr. 7, 1969.
Black, Karen (Ziegler) Park Ridge, IL, July 1, 1942. Northwestern.
Black, Lewis Silver Spring, MD, Aug. 30, 1948.
Black, Lucas Speake, AL, Nov. 29, 1982.
Blackman, Honor London, England, Aug. 22, 1926.
Blades, Ruben Panama City, FL, July 16, 1948. Harvard.
Blair, Betsy (Betsy Boger) New York, NY, Dec. 11, 1923.
Blair, Linda Westport, CT, Jan. 22, 1959.
Blair, Selma Southfield, MI, June 23, 1972.
Blake, Robert (Michael Gubitosi) Nutley, NJ, Sept. 18, 1933.
Blakely, Susan Frankfurt, Germany, Sept. 7, 1950. U Texas.
Blakley, Ronee Stanley, ID, 1946. Stanford U.
Blanchett, Cate Melbourne, Australia, May 14, 1969.
Bledel, Alexis Houston, TX, Sept. 16, 1981.
Blethyn, Brenda Ramsgate, Kent, England, Feb. 20, 1946.
Blonsky, Nikki Great Neck, NY, Nov. 9, 1988.
Bloom, Claire London, England, Feb. 15, 1931. Badminton School.
Bloom, Orlando Canterbury, England, Jan. 13, 1977.
Bloom, Verna Lynn, MA, Aug. 7, 1939. Boston U.
Blount, Lisa Fayettville, AK, July 1, 1957. U Arkansas.
Blum, Mark Newark, NJ, May 14, 1950. U Minnesota.
Blunt, Emily London, England, Feb. 23, 1983.
Blyth, Ann Mt. Kisco, NY, Aug. 16, 1928. New Waybum Dramatic School.
Bochner, Hart Toronto, ON, Canada, Oct. 3, 1956. U San Diego.
Bogosian, Eric Woburn, MA, Apr. 24, 1953. Oberlin College.
Bohringer, Richard Paris, France, Jan. 16, 1941.
Bolkan, Florinda (Florinda Soares Bulcao) Ceara, Brazil, Feb. 15, 1941.
Bologna, Joseph Brooklyn, NY, Dec. 30, 1938. Brown U.
Bonet, Lisa San Francisco, CA, Nov. 16, 1967.
Bonham-Carter, Helena London, England, May 26, 1966.
Boone, Pat Jacksonville, FL, June 1, 1934. Columbia U.
Boothe, Powers Snyder, TX, June 1, 1949. Southern Methodist U.
Borgnine, Ernest (Borgnino) Hamden, CT, Jan. 24, 1917. Randall School.
Bosco, Philip Jersey City, NJ, Sept. 26, 1930. Catholic U.
Bosley, Tom Chicago, IL, Oct. 1, 1927. DePaul U.
Bostwick, Barry San Mateo, CA, Feb. 24, 1945. NYU.
Bosworth, Kate Los Angeles, CA, Jan. 2, 1983.
Bottoms, Joseph Santa Barbara, CA, Aug. 30, 1954.
Bottoms, Timothy Santa Barbara, CA, Aug. 30, 1951.
Boulting, Ingrid Transvaal, South Africa, 1947.
Boutsikaris, Dennis Newark, NJ, Dec. 21, 1952. Catholic U.
Bowie, David (David Robert Jones) Brixton, South London, England, Jan. 8, 1947.
Bowker, Judi Shawford, England, Apr. 6, 1954.
Boxleitner, Bruce Elgin, IL, May 12, 1950.
Boyd, Billy Glasgow, Scotland, Aug. 28, 1968.
Boyle, Lara Flynn Davenport, IA, Mar. 24, 1970.
Bracco, Lorraine Brooklyn, NY, Oct. 2, 1949.
Bradford, Jesse Norwalk, CT, May 27, 1979.
Braeden, Eric (Hans Gudegast) Kiel, Germany, Apr. 3, 1942.
Braff, Zach South Orange, NJ, Apr. 6, 1975.
Braga, Alice São Paolo, Brazil, Apr. 15, 1983.
Braga, Sonia Maringa, Brazil, June 8, 1950.
Branagh, Kenneth Belfast, Northern Ireland, Dec. 10, 1960.
Brandauer, Klaus Maria Altaussee, Austria, June 22, 1944.
Brandon, Clark New York, NY, Dec. 13, 1958.
Brandon, Michael (Feldman) Brooklyn, NY, Apr. 20, 1945.
Brantley, Betsy Rutherfordton, NC, Sept. 20, 1955. London Central School of Drama.

Bratt, Benjamin San Francisco, CA, Dec. 16, 1963.
Brennan, Eileen Los Angeles, CA, Sept. 3, 1935. AADA.
Brenneman, Amy Glastonbury, CT, June 22, 1964.
Breslin, Abigail New York, NY, Apr. 14, 1996.
Brialy, Jean-Claude Aumale, Algeria, 1933. Strasbourg Cons.
Bridges, Beau Los Angeles, CA, Dec. 9, 1941. UCLA.
Bridges, Chris "Ludacris" Champagne, IL, Sept. 11, 1977.
Bridges, Jeff Los Angeles, CA, Dec. 4, 1949.
Bright, Cameron Victoria, BC, Canada, Jan. 26, 1993.
Brimley, Wilford Salt Lake City, UT, Sept. 27, 1934.
Brinkley, Christie Malibu, CA, Feb. 2, 1954.
Britt, May (Maybritt Wilkins) Stockholm, Sweden, Mar. 22, 1936.
Brittany, Morgan (Suzanne Cupito) Los Angeles, CA, Dec. 5, 1950.
Britton, Tony Birmingham, England, June 9, 1924.
Broadbent, Jim Lincoln, England, May 24, 1959.
Broderick, Matthew New York, NY, Mar. 21, 1962.
Brody, Adrien New York, NY, Dec. 23, 1976.
Brolin, James Los Angeles, CA, July 18, 1940. UCLA.
Brolin, Josh Los Angeles, CA, Feb. 12, 1968.
Bron, Eleanor Stanmore, England, Mar. 14, 1934.
Brookes, Jacqueline Montclair, NJ, July 24, 1930. RADA.
Brooks, Albert (Einstein) Los Angeles, CA, July 22, 1947.
Brooks, Mel (Melvyn Kaminski) Brooklyn, NY, June 28, 1926.
Brosnan, Pierce County Meath, Ireland. May 16, 1952.
Brown, Blair Washington, DC, Apr. 23, 1947. Pine Manor.
Brown, Bryan Panania, Australia, June 23, 1947.
Brown, Georg Stanford Havana, Cuba, June 24, 1943. AMDA.
Brown, James Desdemona, TX, Mar. 22, 1920. Baylor U.
Brown, Jim St. Simons Island, NY, Feb. 17, 1935. Syracuse U.
Browne, Leslie New York, NY, 1958.
Bruckner, Agnes Hollywood, CA, Aug. 16, 1985.
Brühl, Daniel (Daniel Domingo) Barcelona, Spain, June 16, 1978.
Buckley, Betty Big Spring, TX, July 3, 1947. Texas Christian U.
Bujold, Genevieve Montreal, Quebec, Canada, July 1, 1942.
Bullock, Sandra Arlington, VA, July 26, 1964.
Burghoff, Gary Bristol, CT, May 24, 1943.
Burgi, Richard Montclair, NJ, July 30, 1958.
Burke, Paul New Orleans, LA, July 21, 1926. Pasadena Playhouse.
Burnett, Carol San Antonio, TX, Apr. 26, 1933. UCLA.
Burns, Catherine New York, NY, Sept. 25, 1945. AADA.
Burns, Edward Valley Stream, NY, Jan. 28, 1969.
Burrows, Darren E. Winfield, KS, Sept. 12, 1966.
Burrows, Saffron London, England, Jan. 1, 1973.
Burstyn, Ellen (Edna Rae Gillhooly) Detroit, MI, Dec. 7, 1932.
Burton, Kate Geneva, Switzerland, Sept. 10, 1957.
Burton, LeVar Los Angeles, CA, Feb. 16, 1958. UCLA.
Buscemi, Steve Brooklyn, NY, Dec. 13, 1957.
Busey, Gary Goose Creek, TX, June 29, 1944.
Busfield, Timothy Lansing, MI, June 12, 1957. East Tennessee State U.
Butler, Gerard Glasgow, Scotland, Nov. 13, 1969.
Buzzi, Ruth Westerly, RI, July 24, 1936. Pasadena Playhouse.
Bygraves, Max London, England, Oct. 16, 1922. St. Joseph's School.
Bynes, Amanda Thousand Oaks, CA, Apr. 3, 1986.
Byrne, David Dumbarton, Scotland, May 14, 1952.
Byrne, Gabriel Dublin, Ireland, May 12, 1950.
Byrnes, Edd New York, NY, July 30, 1933.

Caan, James Bronx, NY, Mar. 26,1939.
Caesar, Sid Yonkers, NY, Sept. 8, 1922.
Cage, Nicolas (Coppola) Long Beach, CA, Jan. 7, 1964.

Cain, Dean (Dean Tanaka) Mt. Clemens, MI, July 31, 1966.
Caine, Michael (Maurice Micklewhite) London, England, Mar. 14, 1933.
Caine, Shakira (Baksh) Guyana, Feb. 23, 1947. Indian Trust College.
Callan, Michael (Martin Calinieff) Philadelphia, PA, Nov. 22, 1935.
Callow, Simon London, England, June 15, 1949. Queens U.
Cameron, Kirk Panorama City, CA, Oct. 12, 1970.
Camp, Colleen San Francisco, CA, June 7, 1953.
Campbell, Bill Chicago, IL, July 7, 1959.
Campbell, Glen Delight, AR, Apr. 22, 1935.
Campbell, Neve Guelph, ON, Canada, Oct. 3, 1973.
Campbell, Tisha Oklahoma City, OK, Oct. 13, 1968.
Canale, Gianna Maria Reggio Calabria, Italy, Sept. 12, 1927.
Cannon, Dyan (Samille Diane Friesen) Tacoma, WA, Jan. 4, 1937.
Capshaw, Kate Ft. Worth, TX, Nov. 3, 1953. U Misourri.
Cara, Irene New York, NY, Mar. 18, 1958.
Cardellini, Linda Redwood City, CA, June 25, 1975.
Cardinale, Claudia Tunis, North Africa. Apr. 15, 1939. College Paul Cambon.
Carell, Steve Concord, MA, Aug. 16, 1962.
Carey, Harry, Jr. Saugus, CA, May 16, 1921. Black Fox Military Academy.
Carey, Philip Hackensack, NJ, July 15, 1925. U Miami.
Cariou, Len Winnipeg, Manitoba, Canada, Sept. 30, 1939.
Carlyle, Robert Glasgow, Scotland, Apr. 14, 1961.
Carmen, Julie Mt. Vernon, NY, Apr. 4, 1954.
Carmichael, Ian Hull, England, June 18, 1920. Scarborough College.
Carne, Judy (Joyce Botterill) Northampton, England, 1939.
    Bush-Davis Theatre School.
Caron, Leslie Paris, France, July 1, 1931. Nationall Conservatory, Paris.
Carpenter, Carleton Bennington, VT, July 10, 1926. Northwestern.
Carradine, David Hollywood, CA, Dec. 8, 1936. San Francisco State.
Carradine, Keith San Mateo, CA, Aug. 8, 1950. Colo. State U.
Carradine, Robert San Mateo, CA, Mar. 24, 1954.
Carrel, Dany Tourane, Indochina, Sept. 20, 1932. Marseilles Cons.
Carrera, Barbara Managua, Nicaragua, Dec. 31, 1945.
Carrere, Tia (Althea Janairo) Honolulu, HI, Jan. 2, 1965.
Carrey, Jim Jacksons Point, ON, Canada, Jan. 17, 1962.
Carriere, Mathieu Hannover, West Germany, Aug. 2, 1950.
Carroll, Diahann (Johnson) New York, NY, July 17, 1935. NYU.
Carroll, Pat Shreveport, LA, May 5, 1927. Catholic U.
Carson, John David Los Angeles, CA, Mar. 6, 1952. Valley College.
Carsten, Peter (Ransenthaler) Weissenberg, Bavaria, Apr. 30, 1929.
    Munich Akademie.
Cartwright, Veronica Bristol, England, Apr 20, 1949.
Caruso, David Forest Hills, NY, Jan. 7, 1956.
Carvey, Dana Missoula, MT, Apr. 2, 1955. San Francisco State U.
Casella, Max Washington D.C, June 6, 1967.
Casey, Bernie Wyco, WV, June 8, 1939.
Cassavetes, Nick New York, NY, 1959, Syracuse U, AADA.
Cassel, Seymour Detroit, MI, Jan. 22, 1935.
Cassel, Vincent Paris, France, Nov. 23, 1966.
Cassidy, David New York, NY, Apr. 12, 1950.
Cassidy, Joanna Camden, NJ, Aug. 2, 1944. Syracuse U.
Cassidy, Patrick Los Angeles, CA, Jan. 4, 1961.
Castellaneta, Dan Chicago, IL, Oct. 29, 1957.
Cates, Phoebe New York, NY, July 16, 1962.
Cattrall, Kim Liverpool, England, Aug. 21, 1956. AADA.
Caulfield, Maxwell Glasgow, Scotland, Nov. 23, 1959.
Cavani, Liliana Bologna, Italy, Jan. 12, 1933. U Bologna.
Cavett, Dick Gibbon, NE, Nov. 19, 1936.
Caviezel, Jim Mt. Vernon, WA, Sept. 26, 1968.
Cedric the Entertainer (Cedric Kyles) Jefferson City, MO, Apr. 24, 1964.

Cera, Michael Brampton, ON, Canada, June 7, 1988.
Chakiris, George Norwood, OH, Sept. 16, 1933.
Chamberlain, Richard Beverly Hills, CA, March 31, 1935. Pomona.
Champion, Marge (Marjorie Belcher) Los Angeles, CA, Sept. 2, 1923.
Chan, Jackie Hong Kong, Apr. 7, 1954.
Chandler, Kyle Buffalo, NY, Sept. 17, 1965
Channing, Carol Seattle, WA, Jan. 31, 1921. Bennington.
Channing, Stockard (Susan Stockard) New York, NY, Feb. 13, 1944.
    Radcliffe.
Chapin, Miles New York, NY, Dec. 6, 1954. HB Studio.
Chaplin, Ben London, England, July 31, 1970.
Chaplin, Geraldine Santa Monica, CA, July 31, 1944. Royal Ballet.
Chaplin, Sydney Los Angeles, CA, Mar. 31, 1926. Lawrenceville.
Charles, Josh Baltimore, MD, Sept. 15, 1971.
Charles, Walter East Strousburg, PA, Apr. 4, 1945. Boston U.
Chase, Chevy (Cornelius Crane Chase) New York, NY, Oct. 8, 1943.
Chatwin, Justin Nanaimo, BC, Canada, Oct. 31, 1982.
Chaves, Richard Jacksonville, FL, Oct. 9, 1951. Occidental College.
Chaykin, Maury Brooklyn, NY, July 27, 1949.
Cheadle, Don Kansas City, MO, Nov. 29, 1964.
Chen, Joan (Chen Chung) Shanghai, China, Apr. 26, 1961. Cal State.
Chenoweth, Kristin Broken Arrow, OK, July 24, 1968.
Cher (Cherilyn Sarkisian) El Centro, CA, May 20, 1946.
Chiklis, Michael Lowell, MA, Aug. 30, 1963.
Chiles, Lois Alice, TX, Apr. 15, 1947.
Cho, John Seoul, Korea, June 16, 1972.
Cho, Margaret San Francisco, CA, Dec. 5, 1968.
Chong, Rae Dawn Vancouver, BC, Canada, Feb. 28, 1962.
Chong, Thomas Edmonton, Alberta, Canada, May 24, 1938.
Christensen, Erika Seattle, WA, Aug. 19, 1982.
Christensen, Hayden Vancouver, BC, Canada, Apr. 19, 1981.
Christian, Linda (Blanca Rosa Welter) Tampico, Mexico, Nov. 13, 1923.
Christie, Julie Chukua, Assam, India, Apr. 14, 1941.
Christopher, Dennis (Carrelli) Philadelphia, PA, Dec. 2, 1955. Temple U.
Christopher, Jordan Youngstown, OH, Oct. 23, 1940. Kent State.
Church, Thomas Hayden El Paso, TX, June 17, 1961.
Cilento, Diane Queensland, Australia, Oct. 5, 1933. AADA.
Clark, Candy Norman, OK, June 20, 1947.
Clark, Dick Mt. Vernon, NY, Nov. 30, 1929. Syracuse U.
Clark, Matt Washington, DC, Nov. 25, 1936.
Clark, Petula Epsom, England, Nov. 15, 1932.
Clark, Susan Sarnid, ON, Canada, Mar. 8, 1943. RADA.
Clarkson, Patricia New Orleans, LA, Dec. 29, 1959.
Clay, Andrew Dice (Andrew Silverstein) Brooklyn, NY, Sept. 29, 1957,
    Kingsborough College.
Clayburgh, Jill New York, NY, Apr. 30, 1944. Sarah Lawrence.
Cleese, John Weston-Super-Mare, England, Oct. 27, 1939, Cambridge.
Clooney, George Lexington, KY, May 6, 1961.
Close, Glenn Greenwich, CT, Mar. 19, 1947. William & Mary College.
Cochrane, Rory Syracuse, NY, Feb. 28, 1972.
Cody, Kathleen Bronx, NY, Oct. 30, 1953.
Coffey, Scott Honolulu, HI, May 1, 1967.
Cole, George London, England, Apr. 22, 1925.
Coleman, Dabney Austin, TX, Jan. 3, 1932.
Coleman, Gary Zion, IL, Feb. 8, 1968.
Coleman, Jack Easton, PA, Feb. 21, 1958. Duke U.
Colin, Margaret New York, NY, May 26, 1957.
Collet, Christopher New York, NY, Mar. 13, 1968. Strasberg Institute.
Collette, Toni Sydney, Australia, Nov. 1, 1972.
Collins, Clifton, Jr. Los Angeles, CA, June 16, 1970.

Collins, Joan London, England, May 21, 1933. Francis Holland School.
Collins, Pauline Devon, England, Sept. 3, 1940.
Collins, Stephen Des Moines, IA, Oct. 1, 1947. Amherst.
Colon, Miriam Ponce, PR., Aug. 20, 1936. UPR.
Coltrane, Robbie Ruthergien, Scotland, Mar. 30, 1950.
Combs, Sean "Puffy" New York, NY, Nov. 4, 1969.
Comer, Anjanette Dawson, TX, Aug. 7, 1942. Baylor, Texas U.
Conant, Oliver New York, NY, Nov. 15, 1955. Dalton.
Conaway, Jeff New York, NY, Oct. 5, 1950. NYU.
Connelly, Jennifer New York, NY, Dec. 12, 1970.
Connery, Jason London, England, Jan. 11, 1963.
Connery, Sean Edinburgh, Scotland, Aug. 25, 1930.
Connick, Harry, Jr. New Orleans, LA, Sept. 11, 1967.
Connolly, Billy Glasgow, Scotland, Nov. 24, 1942.
Connors, Mike (Krekor Ohanian) Fresno, CA, Aug. 15, 1925. UCLA.
Conrad, Robert (Conrad Robert Falk) Chicago, IL, Mar. 1, 1935. Northwestern.
Considine, Paddy Burton-on-Trent, England, Sept. 5, 1974.
Constantine, Michael Reading, PA, May 22, 1927.
Conti, Tom Paisley, Scotland, Nov. 22, 1941.
Converse, Frank St. Louis, MO, May 22, 1938. Carnegie Tech.
Conway, Gary Boston, MA, Feb. 4, 1936.
Conway, Kevin New York, NY, May 29, 1942.
Conway, Tim (Thomas Daniel) Willoughby, OH, Dec. 15, 1933. Bowling Green State.
Coogan, Keith (Keith Mitchell Franklin) Palm Springs, CA, Jan. 13, 1970.
Coogan, Steve Manchester, England, Oct. 14, 1965.
Cook, Dane Boston, MA, March 18, 1972.
Cook, Rachael Leigh Minneapolis, MN, Oct. 4, 1979.
Coolidge, Jennifer Boston, MA, Aug. 28, 1963.
Cooper, Ben Hartford, CT, Sept. 30, 1930. Columbia U.
Cooper, Chris Kansas City, MO, July 9, 1951. U Misouri.
Cooper, Dominic London, England, June 2, 1978.
Cooper, Jackie Los Angeles, CA, Sept. 15, 1921.
Copeland, Joan New York, NY, June 1, 1922. Brooklyn, NY College, RADA.
Corbett, Gretchen Portland, OR, Aug. 13, 1947. Carnegie Tech.
Corbett, John Wheeling, WV, May 9, 1961.
Corbin, Barry Dawson County, TX, Oct. 16, 1940. Texas Tech. U.
Corcoran, Donna Quincy, MA, Sept. 29, 1942.
Cord, Alex (Viespi) Floral Park, NY, Aug. 3, 1931. NYU, Actors Studio.
Corday, Mara (Marilyn Watts) Santa Monica, CA, Jan. 3, 1932.
Cornthwaite, Robert St. Helens, OR, Apr. 28, 1917. USC.
Corri, Adrienne Glasgow, Scotland, Nov. 13, 1933. RADA.
Cort, Bud (Walter Edward Cox) New Rochelle, NY, Mar. 29, 1950. NYU.
Cortesa, Valentina Milan, Italy, Jan. 1, 1924.
Cosby, Bill Philadelphia, PA, July 12, 1937. Temple U.
Coster, Nicolas London, England, Dec. 3, 1934. Neighborhood Playhouse.
Costner, Kevin Lynwood, CA, Jan. 18, 1955. California State U.
Cotillard, Marion Paris, France, Sept. 30, 1975.
Courtenay, Tom Hull, England, Feb. 25, 1937. RADA.
Courtland, Jerome Knoxville, TN, Dec. 27, 1926.
Cox, Brian Dundee, Scotland, June 1, 1946. LAMDA.
Cox, Charlie London, England, Dec. 21, 1982.
Cox, Courteney Birmingham, AL, June 15, 1964.
Cox, Ronny Cloudcroft, NM, Aug. 23, 1938.
Coyote, Peter (Cohon) New York, NY, Oct. 10, 1941.
Craig, Daniel Chester, England, Mar. 2, 1968. Guildhall.
Craig, Michael Poona, India, Jan. 27, 1929.
Craven, Gemma Dublin, Ireland, June 1, 1950.
Crawford, Michael (Dumbel-Smith) Salisbury, England, Jan. 19, 1942.

Cremer, Bruno Saint-Mande, Val-de-Varne, France, Oct. 6, 1929.
Cristal, Linda (Victoria Moya) Buenos Aires, Argentina, Feb. 25, 1934.
Cromwell, James Los Angeles, CA, Jan. 27, 1940.
Crosby, Denise Hollywood, CA, Nov. 24, 1957.
Crosby, Harry Los Angeles, CA, Aug. 8, 1958.
Crosby, Mary Frances Los Angeles, CA, Sept. 14, 1959.
Cross, Ben London, England, Dec. 16, 1947. RADA.
Cross, Joseph New Brunswick, NJ, May 28, 1986.
Crouse, Lindsay New York, NY, May 12, 1948. Radcliffe.
Crowe, Russell New Zealand, Apr. 7, 1964.
Crowley, Pat Olyphant, PA, Sept. 17, 1932.
Crudup, Billy Manhasset, NY, July 8, 1968. UNC, Chapel Hill.
Cruise, Tom (T. C. Mapother, IV) July 3, 1962, Syracuse, NY.
Cruz, Penélope (P.C. Sanchez) Madrid, Spain, Apr. 28, 1974.
Cruz, Wilson Brooklyn, NY, Dec. 27, 1973.
Cryer, Jon New York, NY, Apr. 16, 1965, RADA.
Crystal, Billy Long Beach, NY, Mar. 14, 1947. Marshall U.
Culkin, Kieran New York, NY, Sept. 30, 1982.
Culkin, Macaulay New York, NY, Aug. 26, 1980.
Culkin, Rory New York, NY, July 21, 1989.
Cullum, John Knoxville, TN, Mar. 2, 1930. U Tennessee.
Cullum, John David New York, NY, Mar. 1, 1966.
Culp, Robert Oakland, CA, Aug. 16, 1930. U Washington.
Cumming, Alan Perthshire, Scotland, Jan. 27, 1965.
Cummings, Quinn Hollywood, CA, Aug. 13, 1967.
Cummins, Peggy Prestatyn, North Wales, Dec. 18, 1926. Alexandra School.
Curry, Tim Cheshire, England, Apr. 19, 1946. Birmingham U.
Curtin, Jane Cambridge, MA, Sept. 6, 1947.
Curtis, Jamie Lee Los Angeles, CA, Nov. 22, 1958.
Curtis, Tony (Bernard Schwartz) New York, NY, June 3, 1924.
Curtis-Hall, Vondie Detroit, MI, Sept. 30, 1956.
Cusack, Joan Evanston, IL, Oct. 11, 1962.
Cusack, John Chicago, IL, June 28, 1966.
Cusack, Sinead Dalkey, Ireland, Feb. 18, 1948.
Cyrus, Miley Franklin, TN, nov. 23, 1992.

Dafoe, Willem Appleton, WI, July 22, 1955.
Dahl, Arlene Minneapolis, MN, Aug. 11, 1928. U Minnesota.
Dale, Jim Rothwell, England, Aug. 15, 1935.
Dallesandro, Joe Pensacola, FL, Dec. 31, 1948.
Dalton, Timothy Colwyn Bay, Wales, Mar. 21, 1946. RADA.
Daltrey, Roger London, England, Mar. 1, 1944.
Daly, Tim New York, NY, Mar. 1, 1956. Bennington College.
Daly, Tyne Madison, WI, Feb. 21, 1947. AMDA.
Damon, Matt Cambridge, MA, Oct. 8, 1970.
Damone, Vic (Vito Farinola) Brooklyn, NY, June 12, 1928.
Dance, Charles Plymouth, England, Oct. 10, 1946.
Dancy, Hugh Stoke-on-Trent, England, June 19, 1975.
Danes, Claire New York, NY, Apr. 12, 1979.
D'Angelo, Beverly Columbus, OH, Nov. 15, 1953.
Daniels, Jeff Athens, GA, Feb. 19, 1955. Central Michigan U.
Daniels, William Brooklyn, NY, Mar. 31, 1927. Northwestern.
Danner, Blythe Philadelphia, PA, Feb. 3, 1944. Bard College.
Danning, Sybil (Sybille Johanna Danninger) Vienna, Austria, May 4, 1949.
Dano, Paul Wilton, CT, June 19, 1983.
Danson, Ted San Diego, CA, Dec. 29, 1947. Stanford, Carnegie Tech.
Dante, Michael (Ralph Vitti) Stamford, CT, 1935. U Miami.
Danza, Tony Brooklyn, NY, Apr. 21, 1951. U Dubuque.
D'arbanville-Quinn, Patti New York, NY, May 25, 1951.
Darby, Kim (Deborah Zerby) North Hollywood, CA, July 8, 1948.

Darcel, Denise (Denise Billecard) Paris, France, Sept. 8, 1925. U Dijon.
Darren, James Philadelphia, PA, June 8, 1936. Stella Adler School.
Darrieux, Danielle Bordeaux, France, May 1, 1917. Lycee LaTour.
Davenport, Jack Suffolk, England, March 1, 1973.
Davenport, Nigel Cambridge, England, May 23, 1928. Trinity College.
David, Keith New York, NY, June 4, 1954. Juilliard.
Davidovich, Lolita Toronto, ON, Canada, July 15, 1961.
Davidson, Jaye Riverside, CA, Mar. 21, 1968.
Davidson, John Pittsburgh, PA, Dec. 13, 1941. Denison U.
Davidtz, Embeth Lafayette, IN, Jan. 1, 1966.
Davies, Jeremy (Boring) Rockford, IA, Oct. 28, 1969.
Davis, Clifton Chicago, IL, Oct. 4, 1945. Oakwood College.
Davis, Geena Wareham, MA, Jan. 21, 1957.
Davis, Hope Tenafly, NJ, Mar. 23, 1964.
Davis, Judy Perth, Australia, Apr. 23, 1955.
Davis, Mac Lubbock, TX, Jan. 21,1942.
Davis, Nancy (Anne Frances Robbins) New York, NY, July 6, 1921.
   Smith College.
Davis, Sammi Kidderminster, Worcestershire, England, June 21, 1964.
Davis, Viola Saint Matthews, SC, Aug. 11, 1965.
Davison, Bruce Philadelphia, PA, June 28, 1946.
Dawber, Pam Detroit, MI, Oct. 18, 1954.
Dawson, Rosario New York, NY, May 9, 1979.
Day, Doris (Doris Kappelhoff) Cincinatti, OH, Apr. 3, 1924.
Day-Lewis, Daniel London, England, Apr. 29, 1957. Bristol Old Vic.
Dayan, Assi Israel, Nov. 23, 1945. U Jerusalem.
Deakins, Lucy New York, NY, 1971.
Dean, Jimmy Plainview, TX, Aug. 10, 1928.
Dean, Loren Las Vegas, NV, July 31, 1969.
De Bankole, Isaach Abidjan, Ivory Coast, Aug. 12, 1957.
Dee, Joey (Joseph Di Nicola) Passaic, NJ, June 11, 1940.
   Patterson State College.
Dee, Ruby Cleveland, OH, Oct. 27, 1924. Hunter College.
DeGeneres, Ellen New Orleans, LA, Jan. 26, 1958.
DeHaven, Gloria Los Angeles, CA, July 23, 1923.
DeHavilland, Olivia Tokyo, Japan, July 1, 1916. Notre Dame
   Convent School.
Delair, Suzy (Suzanne Delaire) Paris, France, Dec. 31, 1917.
Delany, Dana New York, NY, March 13, 1956. Wesleyan U.
Delon, Alain Sceaux, France, Nov. 8, 1935.
Delorme, Daniele Paris, France, Oct. 9, 1926. Sorbonne.
Delpy, Julie Paris, France, Dec, 21, 1969.
Del Toro, Benicio Santurce, Puerto Rico, Feb. 19, 1967.
DeLuise, Dom Brooklyn, NY, Aug. 1, 1933. Tufts College.
DeLuise, Peter New York, NY, Nov. 6, 1966.
Demongeot, Mylene Nice, France, Sept. 29, 1938.
DeMornay, Rebecca Los Angeles, CA, Aug. 29, 1962. Strasberg Institute.
Dempsey, Patrick Lewiston, ME, Jan. 13, 1966.
DeMunn, Jeffrey Buffalo, NY, Apr. 25, 1947. Union College.
Dench, Judi York, England, Dec. 9, 1934.
Deneuve, Catherine Paris, France, Oct. 22, 1943.
De Niro, Robert New York, NY, Aug. 17, 1943. Stella Adler.
Dennehy, Brian Bridgeport, CT, July 9, 1938. Columbia U.
Depardieu, Gérard Chateauroux, France, Dec. 27, 1948.
Depp, Johnny Owensboro, KY, June 9, 1963.
Derek, Bo (Mary Cathleen Collins) Long Beach, CA, Nov. 20, 1956.
Dern, Bruce Chicago, IL, June 4, 1936. UPA.
Dern, Laura Los Angeles, CA, Feb. 10, 1967.
DeSalvo, Anne Philadelphia, PA, Apr. 3, 1949.
Deschanel, Zooey Los Angeles, CA, Jan. 17, 1980.
Devane, William Albany, NY, Sept. 5, 1939.

Devine, Loretta Houston, TX, Aug. 21, 1949.
DeVito, Danny Asbury Park, NJ, Nov. 17, 1944.
Dey, Susan Pekin, IL, Dec. 10, 1953.
DeYoung, Cliff Los Angeles, CA, Feb. 12, 1945. California State U.
Diamond, Neil New York, NY, Jan. 24, 1941. NYU.
Diaz, Cameron Long Beach, CA, Aug. 30, 1972.
DiCaprio, Leonardo Hollywood, CA, Nov. 11, 1974.
Dickinson, Angie (Angeline Brown) Kulm, ND, Sept. 30, 1932.
   Glendale College.
Diesel, Vin (Mark Vincent) New York, NY, July 18, 1967.
Diggs, Taye (Scott Diggs) Rochester, NY, Jan. 2, 1972.
Dillahunt, Garrett Castro Valley, CA Nov. 24, 1964.
Diller, Phyllis (Driver) Lima, OH, July 17, 1917. Bluffton College.
Dillman, Bradford San Francisco, CA, Apr. 14, 1930. Yale.
Dillon, Kevin Mamaroneck, NY, Aug. 19, 1965.
Dillon, Matt Larchmont, NY, Feb. 18, 1964. AADA.
Dillon, Melinda Hope, AR, Oct. 13, 1939. Goodman Theatre School.
Dinklage, Peter Morristown, NJ, June 11, 1969.
Dixon, Donna Alexandria, VA, July 20, 1957.
Dobson, Kevin New York, NY, Mar. 18, 1944.
Doherty, Shannen Memphis, TN, Apr. 12, 1971.
Dolan, Michael Oklahoma City, OK, June 21, 1965.
Donat, Peter Nova Scotia, Canada, Jan. 20, 1928. Yale.
Donnelly, Donal Bradford, England, July 6, 1931.
D'Onofrio, Vincent Brooklyn, NY, June 30, 1959.
Donohoe, Amanda London, England, June 29 1962.
Donovan, Martin Reseda, CA, Aug. 19, 1957.
Donovan, Tate New York, NY, Sept. 25, 1963.
Dooley, Paul Parkersburg WV, Feb. 22, 1928. U West Virginia.
Dorff, Stephen Atlanta, GA, July 29, 1973.
Doug, Doug E. (Douglas Bourne) Brooklyn, NY, Jan. 7, 1970.
Douglas, Donna (Dorothy Bourgeois) Baywood, LA, Sept. 26, 1935.
Douglas, Illeana Quincy, MA, July 25, 1965.
Douglas, Kirk (Issur Danielovitch) Amsterdam, NY, Dec. 9, 1916.
   St. Lawrence U.
Douglas, Michael New Brunswick, NJ, Sept. 25, 1944. U California.
Douglass, Robyn Sendai, Japan, June 21, 1953. UC Davis.
Dourif, Brad Huntington, WV, Mar. 18, 1950. Marshall U.
Down, Lesley-Anne London, England, Mar. 17, 1954.
Downey, Robert, Jr. New York, NY, Apr. 4, 1965.
Drake, Betsy Paris, France, Sept. 11, 1923.
Drescher, Fran Queens, NY, Sept. 30, 1957.
Dreyfuss, Richard Brooklyn, NY, Oct. 19, 1947.
Drillinger, Brian Brooklyn, NY, June 27, 1960. SUNY/Purchase.
Driver, Minnie (Amelia Driver) London, England, Jan. 31, 1971.
Duchovny, David New York, NY, Aug. 7, 1960. Yale.
Dudikoff, Michael Torrance, CA, Oct. 8, 1954.
Duff, Hilary Houston, TX, Sept. 28, 1987.
Dugan, Dennis Wheaton, IL, Sept. 5, 1946.
Duhamel, Josh Minot, ND, Nov. 14, 1972.
Dukakis, Olympia Lowell, MA, June 20, 1931.
Duke, Bill Poughkeepsie, NY, Feb. 26, 1943. NYU.
Duke, Patty (Anna Marie) New York, NY, Dec. 14, 1946.
Dullea, Keir Cleveland, OH, May 30, 1936. San Francisco State College.
Dunaway, Faye Bascom, FL, Jan. 14, 1941. Florida U.
Duncan, Lindsay Edinburgh, Scotland, Nov. 7, 1950.
Duncan, Sandy Henderson, TX, Feb. 20, 1946. Len Morris College.
Dunne, Griffin New York, NY, June 8, 1955. Neighborhood Playhouse.
Dunst, Kirsten Point Pleasant, NJ, Apr. 30, 1982.
Duperey, Anny Paris, France, June 28, 1947.

Durbin, Deanna (Edna) Winnipeg, Manitoba, Canada, Dec. 4, 1921.
Duris, Romain Paris, France, May 28, 1974.
Durning, Charles Highland Falls, NY, Feb. 28, 1923. NYU.
Dushku, Eliza Boston, MA, Dec. 30, 1980.
Dussollier, André Annecy, France, Feb. 17, 1946.
Dutton, Charles Baltimore, MD, Jan. 30, 1951. Yale.
DuVall, Clea Los Angeles, CA, Sept. 25, 1977.
Duvall, Robert San Diego, CA, Jan. 5, 1931. Principia College.
Duvall, Shelley Houston, TX, July 7, 1949.
Dysart, Richard Brighton, ME, Mar. 30, 1929.
Dzundza, George Rosenheim, Germany, July 19, 1945.

Easton, Robert Milwaukee, WI, Nov. 23, 1930. U Texas.
Eastwood, Clint San Francisco, CA, May 31, 1930. LACC.
Eaton, Shirley London, England, Jan. 12, 1937. Aida Foster School.
Eckemyr, Agneta Karlsborg, Sweden, July 2, 1950 Actors Studio.
Eckhart, Aaron Santa Clara, CA, Mar. 12, 1968.
Edelman, Gregg Chicago, IL, Sept. 12, 1958. Northwestern.
Eden, Barbara (Huffman) Tucson, AZ, Aug. 23, 1934.
Edwards, Anthony Santa Barbara, CA, July 19, 1962. RADA.
Edwards, Luke Nevada City, CA, Mar. 24, 1980.
Efron, Zac San Luis Obispo, CA, Oct. 18, 1987.
Eggar, Samantha London, England, Mar. 5, 1939.
Eichhorn, Lisa Reading, PA, Feb. 4, 1952. Queens Ont. U RADA.
Eikenberry, Jill New Haven, CT, Jan. 21, 1947.
Eilber, Janet Detroit, MI, July 27, 1951. Juilliard.
Eisenberg, Jesse New York, NY, Oct. 5, 1983.
Ejiofor, Chiwitel London, England, July 10, 1974.
Ekberg, Anita Malmo, Sweden, Sept. 29, 1931.
Ekland, Britt Stockholm, Sweden, Oct. 6, 1942.
Eldard, Ron Long Island, NY, Feb. 20, 1965.
Elfman, Jenna (Jennifer Mary Batula) Los Angeles, CA, Sept. 30, 1971.
Elise, Kimberly Minneapolis, MN, Apr. 17, 1967.
Elizondo, Hector New York, NY, Dec. 22, 1936.
Elliott, Alison San Francisco, CA, May 19, 1970.
Elliott, Chris New York, NY, May 31, 1960.
Elliott, Patricia Gunnison, CO, July 21, 1942. U Colorado.
Elliott, Sam Sacramento, CA, Aug. 9, 1944. U Oregon.
Elwes, Cary London, England, Oct. 26, 1962.
Ely, Ron (Ronald Pierce) Hereford, TX, June 21, 1938.
Embry, Ethan (Ethan Randall) Huntington Beach, CA, June 13, 1978.
Englund, Robert Glendale, CA, June 6, 1949.
Epps, Mike Indianapolis, IN, Nov. 18, 1970.
Epps, Omar Brooklyn, NY, July 23, 1973.
Erbe, Kathryn Newton, MA, July 2, 1966.
Erdman, Richard Enid, OK, June 1, 1925.
Ericson, John Dusseldorf, Germany, Sept. 25, 1926. AADA.
Ermey, R. Lee (Ronald) Emporia, KS, Mar. 24, 1944.
Esposito, Giancarlo Copenhagen, Denmark, Apr. 26, 1958.
Estevez, Emilio New York, NY, May 12, 1962.
Estrada, Erik New York, NY, Mar. 16, 1949.
Etel, Alex Manchester, England, Sept. 19, 1994.
Evans, Chris Sudbury, MA, June 13, 1981.
Evans, Josh New York, NY, Jan. 16, 1971.
Evans, Linda (Evanstad) Hartford, CT, Nov. 18, 1942.
Everett, Chad (Ray Cramton) South Bend, IN, June 11, 1936.
Everett, Rupert Norfolk, England, May 29, 1959.
Evigan, Greg South Amboy, NJ, Oct. 14, 1953.

Fabares, Shelley Los Angeles, CA, Jan. 19, 1944.

Fabian (Fabian Forte) Philadelphia, PA, Feb. 6, 1943.
Fabray, Nanette (Ruby Nanette Fabares) San Diego, Oct. 27, 1920.
Fahey, Jeff Olean, NY, Nov. 29, 1956.
Fairchild, Morgan (Patsy McClenny) Dallas, TX, Feb. 3, 1950. UCLA.
Falco, Edie Brooklyn, NY, July 5, 1963.
Falk, Peter New York, NY, Sept. 16, 1927. New School.
Fallon, Jimmy Brooklyn, NY, Sept. 19, 1974.
Fanning, Dakota Conyers, GA, Feb. 23, 1994.
Farentino, James Brooklyn, NY, Feb. 24, 1938. AADA.
Fargas, Antonio Bronx, NY, Aug. 14, 1946.
Farina, Dennis Chicago, IL, Feb. 29, 1944.
Faris, Anna Baltimore, MD, Nov. 29, 1976. Univ of Washington.
Farmiga, Vera Passaic, NJ, Aug. 6, 1973.
Farr, Felicia Westchester, NY, Oct. 4. 1932. Penn State College.
Farrell, Colin Castleknock, Ireland, Mar. 31, 1976.
Farrow, Mia (Maria) Los Angeles, CA, Feb. 9, 1945.
Faulkner, Graham London, England, Sept. 26, 1947. Webber-Douglas.
Favreau, Jon Queens, NY, Oct. 16, 1966.
Fawcett, Farrah Corpus Christie, TX, Feb. 2, 1947. Texas U.
Feinstein, Alan New York, NY, Sept. 8, 1941.
Feldman, Corey Encino, CA, July 16, 1971.
Feldon, Barbara (Hall) Pittsburgh, PA, Mar. 12, 1941. Carnegie Tech.
Feldshuh, Tovah New York, NY, Dec. 27, 1953, Sarah Lawrence College.
Fellows, Edith Boston, MA, May 20, 1923.
Fenn, Sherilyn Detroit, MI, Feb. 1, 1965.
Ferrell, Conchata Charleston, WV, Mar. 28, 1943. Marshall U.
Ferrell, Will Irvine, CA, July 16, 1968.
Ferrer, Miguel Santa Monica, CA, Feb. 7, 1954.
Ferrera, America Los Angeles, CA, Apr. 18, 1984.
Ferris, Barbara London, England, July 27, 1942.
Fey, Tina (Elizabeth Stamatina Fey) Upper Darby, PA, May 18, 1970.
Field, Sally Pasadena, CA, Nov. 6, 1946.
Field, Shirley-Anne London, England, June 27, 1938.
Field, Todd (William Todd Field) Pomona, CA, Feb. 24, 1964.
Fiennes, Joseph Salisbury, Wiltshire, England, May 27, 1970.
Fiennes, Ralph Suffolk, England, Dec. 22, 1962. RADA.
Fierstein, Harvey Brooklyn, NY, June 6, 1954. Pratt Institute.
Finch, Jon Caterham, England, Mar. 2, 1941.
Finlay, Frank Farnworth, England, Aug. 6, 1926.
Finney, Albert Salford, Lancashire, England, May 9, 1936. RADA.
Fiorentino, Linda Philadelphia, PA, Mar. 9, 1960.
Firth, Colin Grayshott, Hampshire, England, Sept. 10, 1960.
Firth, Peter Bradford, England, Oct. 27, 1953.
Fishburne, Laurence Augusta, GA, July 30, 1961.
Fischer, Jenna Ft. Wayne, IN, Mar. 7, 1974.
Fisher, Carrie Los Angeles, CA, Oct. 21, 1956.
     London Central School of Drama.
Fisher, Eddie Philadelphia, PA, Aug. 10, 1928.
Fisher, Frances Milford-on-the-Sea, England, May 11, 1952.
Fisher, Isla Muscat, Oman, Feb. 3, 1976.
Fitzgerald, Tara London, England, Sept. 17, 1968.
Flagg, Fannie Birmingham, AL, Sept. 21, 1944. U Alabama.
Flanagan, Fionnula Dublin, Ireland, Dec. 10, 1941.
Flannery, Susan Jersey City, NJ, July 31, 1943.
Fleming, Rhonda (Marilyn Louis) Los Angeles, CA, Aug. 10, 1922.
Fletcher, Louise Birmingham, AL, July 22 1934.
Flockhart, Calista Stockton, IL, Nov. 11, Rutgers U.
Fogler, Dan Brooklyn, NY, Oct. 20, 1976.
Foley, Dave Toronto, ON, Canada, Jan. 4, 1963.
Follows, Megan Toronto, ON, Canada, Mar. 14, 1968.

Fonda, Bridget Los Angeles, CA, Jan. 27, 1964.
Fonda, Jane New York, NY, Dec. 21, 1937. Vassar.
Fonda, Peter New York, NY, Feb. 23, 1939. U Omaha.
Fontaine, Joan Tokyo, Japan, Oct. 22, 1917.
Foote, Hallie New York, NY, 1953. U New Hampshire.
Ford, Harrison Chicago, IL, July 13, 1942. Ripon College.
Forlani, Claire London, England, July 1, 1972.
Forrest, Frederic Waxahachie, TX, Dec. 23, 1936.
Forrest, Steve Huntsville, TX, Sept. 29, 1924. UCLA.
Forslund, Connie San Diego, CA, June 19, 1950. NYU.
Forster, Robert (Foster, Jr.) Rochester, NY, July 13, 1941. Rochester U.
Forsythe, John (Freund) Penns Grove, NJ, Jan. 29, 1918.
Forsythe, William Brooklyn, NY, June 7, 1955.
Fossey, Brigitte Tourcoing, France, Mar. 11, 1947.
Foster, Ben Boston, MA, Oct. 29, 1980.
Foster, Jodie (Alicia Christian Foster) Los Angeles, CA, Nov. 19, 1962. Yale.
Foster, Meg Reading, PA, May 14, 1948.
Fox, Edward London, England, Apr. 13, 1937. RADA.
Fox, James London, England, May 19, 1939.
Fox, Megan Rockwood, TN, May 16, 1986.
Fox, Michael J. Vancouver, BC, Canada, June 9, 1961.
Fox, Vivica A. Indianapolis, July 30, 1964.
Foxworth, Robert Houston, TX, Nov. 1, 1941. Carnegie Tech.
Foxx, Jamie Terrell, TX, Dec. 13, 1967.
Frain, James Leeds, England, Mar. 14, 1969.
Frakes, Jonathan Bethlehem, PA, Aug. 19, 1952. Harvard.
Francis, Anne Ossining, NY, Sept. 16, 1932.
Francis, Arlene (Arlene Kazanjian) Boston, MA, Oct. 20, 1908. Finch School.
Francis, Connie (Constance Franconero) Newark, NJ, Dec. 12, 1938.
Francks, Don Vancouver, BC, Canada, Feb. 28, 1932.
Franco, James Palo Alto, CA, Apr. 19, 1978.
Franklin, Pamela Tokyo, Japan, Feb. 4, 1950.
Franz, Dennis Chicago, IL, Oct. 28, 1944.
Fraser, Brendan Indianapolis, IN, Dec. 3, 1968.
Frazier, Sheila New York, NY, Nov. 13, 1948.
Frechette, Peter Warwick, RI, Oct. 1956. U Rhoad Island.
Freeman, Al, Jr. San Antonio, TX, Mar. 21, 1934. CCLA.
Freeman, Martin Aldershot, England, Sept. 8, 1971.
Freeman, Mona Baltimore, MD, June 9, 1926.
Freeman, Morgan Memphis, TN, June 1, 1937. LACC.
Frewer, Matt Washington, DC, Jan. 4, 1958, Old Vic.
Fricker, Brenda Dublin, Ireland, Feb. 17, 1945.
Friel, Anna Rochdale, England, July 12, 1976.
Friels, Colin Glasgow, Scotland, Sept. 25, 1952.
Frost, Nick Essex, England, Mar. 28, 1972.
Fry, Stephen Hampstead, London, England, Aug. 24, 1957.
Fuller, Penny Durham, NC, July 21, 1940. Northwestern.
Funicello, Annette Utica, NY, Oct. 22, 1942.
Furlong, Edward Glendale, CA, Aug. 2, 1977.
Furneaux, Yvonne Lille, France, May 11, 1928. Oxford U.
Futterman, Dan Silver Spring, MD, June 8, 1967.

Gable, John Clark Los Angeles, CA, Mar. 20, 1961. Santa Monica College.
Gabor, Zsa Zsa (Sari Gabor) Budapest, Hungary, Feb. 6, 1917.
Gail, Max Derfoil, MI, Apr. 5, 1943.
Gaines, Boyd Atlanta, GA, May 11, 1953. Juilliard.
Gainsbourg, Charlotte London, England, July 21, 1971.
Galecki, Johnny Bree, Belgium, Apr. 30, 1975.
Gallagher, Peter New York, NY, Aug. 19, 1955. Tufts U.
Galligan, Zach New York, NY, Feb. 14, 1963. Columbia U.

Gallo, Vincent Buffalo, NY, Apr. 11, 1961.
Gam, Rita Pittsburgh, PA, Apr. 2, 1928.
Gamble, Mason Chicago, IL, Jan. 16, 1986.
Gambon, Michael Dublin, Ireland, Oct. 19, 1940.
Gandolfini, James Westwood, NJ, Sept. 18, 1961.
Ganz, Bruno Zurich, Switzerland, Mar. 22, 1941.
Garai, Romola Hong Kong, Aug. 6, 1982.
Garber, Victor Montreal, Quebec, Canada, Mar. 16, 1949.
Garcia, Adam Wahroonga, New So. Wales, Australia, June 1, 1973.
Garcia, Andy Havana, Cuba, Apr. 12, 1956. Flalnt.
Garfield, Allen (Allen Goorwitz) Newark, NJ, Nov. 22, 1939. Actors Studio.
Garfunkel, Art New York, NY, Nov. 5, 1941.
Garlin, Jeff Chicago, IL, June 5, 1962.
Garner, James (James Baumgarner) Norman, OK, Apr. 7, 1928. Oklahoma U.
Garner, Jennifer Houston, TX, Apr. 17, 1972.
Garner, Kelli Bakersfield, CA, April. 11, 1984.
Garofalo, Janeane Newton, NJ, Sept. 28, 1964.
Garr, Teri Lakewood, OH, Dec. 11, 1949.
Garrel, Louis Paris, June 14, 1983.
Garrett, Betty St. Joseph, MO, May 23, 1919. Annie Wright Seminary.
Garrison, Sean New York, NY, Oct. 19, 1937.
Gary, Lorraine New York, NY, Aug. 16, 1937.
Gavin, John Los Angeles, CA, Apr. 8, 1935. Stanford U.
Gaylord, Mitch Van Nuys, CA, Mar. 10, 1961. UCLA.
Gaynor, Mitzi (Francesca Marlene Von Gerber) Chicago, IL, Sept. 4, 1930.
Gazzara, Ben New York, NY, Aug. 28, 1930. Actors Studio.
Geary, Anthony Coalsville, UT, May 29, 1947. U Utah.
Gedrick, Jason Chicago, IL, Feb. 7, 1965. Drake U.
Geeson, Judy Arundel, England, Sept. 10, 1948. Corona.
Gellar, Sarah Michelle New York, NY, Apr. 14, 1977.
Geoffreys, Stephen (Miller) Cincinnati, OH, Nov. 22, 1959. NYU.
George, Susan West London, England, July 26, 1950.
Gerard, Gil Little Rock, AR, Jan. 23, 1940.
Gere, Richard Philadelphia, PA, Aug. 29, 1949. U Mass.
Gerroll, Daniel London, England, Oct. 16, 1951. Central.
Gershon, Gina Los Angeles, CA, June 10, 1962.
Gertz, Jami Chicago, IL, Oct. 28, 1965.
Gervais, Ricky Reading, England, June 25, 1961.
Getty, Balthazar Los Angeles, CA, Jan. 22, 1975.
Gholson, Julie Birmingham, AL, June 4, 1958.
Giamatti, Paul New York, NY, June 6, 1967. Yale.
Giannini, Giancarlo Spezia, Italy, Aug. 1, 1942. Rome Academy of Drama.
Gibb, Cynthia Bennington, VT, Dec. 14, 1963.
Gibson, Henry Germantown, PA, Sept. 21, 1935.
Gibson, Mel Peekskill, NY, Jan. 3, 1956. NIDA.
Gibson, Thomas Charleston, SC, July 3, 1962.
Gibson, Tyrese Los Angeles, CA, Dec. 30, 1978.
Gift, Roland Birmingham, England, May 28 1962.
Gilbert, Melissa Los Angeles, CA, May 8, 1964.
Giles, Nancy New York, NY, July 17, 1960, Oberlin College.
Gillette, Anita Baltimore, MD, Aug. 16, 1938.
Gilliam, Terry Minneapolis, MN, Nov. 22, 1940.
Gillis, Ann (Alma O'Connor) Little Rock, AR, Feb. 12, 1927.
Ginty, Robert New York, NY, Nov. 14, 1948. Yale.
Girardot, Annie Paris, France, Oct. 25, 1931.
Gish, Annabeth Albuquerque, NM, Mar. 13, 1971. Duke U.
Givens, Robin New York, NY, Nov. 27, 1964.
Glaser, Paul Michael Boston, MA, Mar. 25, 1943. Boston U.
Glass, Ron Evansville, IN, July 10, 1945.
Gleason, Joanna Winnipeg, Manitoba, Canada, June 2, 1950. UCLA.

Gleeson, Brendan Belfast, Northern Ireland, Nov. 9, 1955.
Glenn, Scott Pittsburgh, PA, Jan. 26, 1942. William and Mary College.
Glover, Crispin New York, NY, Sept 20, 1964.
Glover, Danny San Francisco, CA, July 22, 1947. San Francisco State U.
Glover, John Kingston, NY, Aug. 7, 1944.
Glynn, Carlin Cleveland, OH, Feb. 19, 1940. Actors Studio.
Goldberg, Adam Santa Monica, CA, Oct. 25, 1970.
Goldberg, Whoopi (Caryn Johnson) New York, NY, Nov. 13, 1949.
Goldblum, Jeff Pittsburgh, PA, Oct. 22, 1952. Neighborhood Playhouse.
Golden, Annie Brooklyn, NY, Oct. 19, 1951.
Goldstein, Jenette Beverly Hills, CA, Feb. 4, 1960.
Goldthwait, Bob Syracuse, NY, May 1, 1962.
Goldwyn, Tony Los Angeles, CA, May 20, 1960. LAMDA.
Golino, Valeria Naples, Italy, Oct. 22, 1966.
Gonzalez, Cordelia San Juan, PR Aug. 11, 1957,. UPR.
Good, Meagan Panorama City, CA, Aug. 8, 1981.
Goodall, Caroline London, England, Nov. 13, 1959. Bristol U.
Goode, Matthew Exeter, England, Apr. 3, 1978.
Gooding, Cuba, Jr. Bronx, NY, Jan. 2, 1968.
Goodman, John St. Louis, MO, June 20, 1952.
Gordon, Keith New York, NY, Feb. 3, 1961.
Gordon-Levitt, Joseph Los Angeles, CA, Feb. 17, 1981.
Gortner, Marjoe Long Beach, CA, Jan. 14, 1944.
Gosling, Ryan London, ON, Canada, Nov. 12, 1980.
Goss, Luke London, England, Sept. 28, 1968.
Gossett, Louis, Jr. Brooklyn, NY, May 27, 1936. NYU.
Gould, Elliott (Goldstein) Brooklyn, NY, Aug. 29, 1938. Columbia U.
Gould, Harold Schenectady, NY, Dec. 10, 1923. Cornell.
Gould, Jason New York, NY, Dec. 29, 1966.
Grace, Topher New York, NY, July 12, 1978.
Graf, David Lancaster, OH, Apr. 16, 1950. Ohio State U.
Graff, Todd New York, NY, Oct. 22, 1959. SUNY/Purchase.
Graham, Heather Milwauke, WI, Jan. 29, 1970.
Grammer, Kelsey St. Thomas, Virgin Islands, Feb. 21, 1955.
Granger, Farley San Jose, CA, July 1, 1925.
Grant, David Marshall Westport, CT, June 21, 1955. Yale.
Grant, Hugh London, England, Sept. 9, 1960. Oxford.
Grant, Kathryn (Olive Grandstaff) Houston, TX, Nov. 25, 1933. UCLA.
Grant, Lee New York, NY, Oct. 31, 1927. Juilliard.
Grant, Richard E. Mbabane, Swaziland, May 5, 1957. Cape Town U.
Graves, Peter (Aurness) Minneapolis, MN, Mar. 18, 1926. U Minnesota.
Graves, Rupert Weston-Super-Mare, England, June 30, 1963.
Gray, Coleen (Doris Jensen) Staplehurst, NB, Oct. 23, 1922. Hamline.
Gray, Linda Santa Monica, CA, Sept. 12, 1940.
Grayson, Kathryn (Zelma Hedrick) Winston-Salem, NC, Feb. 9, 1922.
Green, Eva Paris, France, July 5, 1980.
Green, Kerri Fort Lee, NJ, Jan. 14, 1967. Vassar.
Green, Seth Philadelphia, PA, Feb. 8, 1974.
Greene, Ellen New York, NY, Feb. 22, 1950. Ryder College.
Greene, Graham Six Nations Reserve, ON, Canada, June 22, 1952.
Greenwood, Bruce Quebec, Canada, Aug. 12, 1956.
Greer, Michael Galesburg, IL, Apr. 20, 1943.
Greist, Kim Stamford, CT, May 12, 1958.
Grenier, Adrian Brooklyn, NY, July 10, 1976.
Grey, Jennifer New York, NY, Mar. 26, 1960.
Grey, Joel (Katz) Cleveland, OH, Apr. 11, 1932.
Grieco, Richard Watertown, NY, Mar. 23, 1965.
Grier, David Alan Detroit, MI, June 30, 1955. Yale.
Grier, Pam Winston-Salem, NC, May 26, 1949.
Griffin, Eddie Kansas City, MO, July 15, 1968.

Griffith, Andy Mt. Airy, NC, June 1, 1926. U North Carolina.
Griffith, Melanie New York, NY, Aug. 9, 1957. Pierce Collge.
Griffith, Thomas Ian Hartford, CT, Mar. 18, 1962.
Griffiths, Rachel Melbourne, Australia, June 4, 1968.
Griffiths, Richard Tornaby-on-Tees, England, July 31, 1947.
Grimes, Gary San Francisco, CA, June 2, 1955.
Grimes, Scott Lowell, MA, July 9, 1971.
Grimes, Tammy Lynn, MA, Jan. 30, 1934. Stephens College.
Grint, Rupert Watton-at-Stone, England, Aug. 24, 1988.
Grodin, Charles Pittsburgh, PA, Apr. 21, 1935.
Groh, David New York, NY, May 21, 1939. Brown U, LAMDA.
Gross, Mary Chicago, IL, Mar. 25, 1953.
Gross, Michael Chicago, IL, June 21, 1947.
Gruffud, Ioan Cardiff, Wales, Oct. 6, 1973.
Guest, Christopher New York, NY, Feb. 5, 1948.
Guest, Lance Saratoga, CA, July 21, 1960. UCLA.
Guillaume, Robert (Williams) St. Louis, MO, Nov. 30, 1937.
Guiry, Thomas Trenton, NJ, Oct. 12, 1981.
Gulager, Clu Holdenville, OK, Nov. 16 1928.
Guttenberg, Steve Massapequa, NY, Aug. 24, 1958. UCLA.
Guy, Jasmine Boston, MA, Mar. 10, 1964.
Guzman, Luis Cayey, Puerto Rico, Jan. 1, 1957.
Gyllenhaal, Jake Los Angeles, CA, Dec. 19, 1980.
Gyllenhaal, Maggie Los Angeles, CA, Nov. 16, 1977.

Haas, Lukas West Hollywood, CA, Apr. 16, 1976.
Hack, Shelley Greenwich, CT, July 6, 1952.
Hackman, Gene San Bernardino, CA, Jan. 30, 1930.
Hagerty, Julie Cincinnati, OH, June 15, 1955. Juilliard.
Hagman, Larry (Hageman) Weatherford, TX, Sept. 21, 1931. Bard.
Haid, Charles San Francisco, CA, June 2, 1943. Carnegie Tech.
Haim, Corey Toronto, ON, Canada, Dec. 23, 1972.
Hale, Barbara DeKalb, IL, Apr. 18, 1922. Chicago Academy of Fine Arts.
Haley, Jackie Earle Northridge, CA, July 14, 1961.
Hall, Albert Boothton, AL, Nov. 10, 1937. Columbia U.
Hall, Anthony Michael Boston, MA, Apr. 14, 1968.
Hall, Arsenio Cleveland, OH, Feb. 12, 1959.
Hall, Philip Baker Toledo, OH, Sept. 10, 1931.
Hamel, Veronica Philadelphia, PA, Nov. 20, 1943.
Hamill, Mark Oakland, CA, Sept. 25, 1952. LACC.
Hamilton, George Memphis, TN, Aug. 12, 1939. Hackley.
Hamilton, Josh New York, NY, June 9, 1969.
Hamilton, Linda Salisbury, MD, Sept. 26, 1956.
Hamlin, Harry Pasadena, CA, Oct. 30, 1951.
Hampshire, Susan London, England, May 12, 1941.
Hampton, James Oklahoma City, OK, July 9, 1936. Northern Texas State U.
Han, Maggie Providence, RI, 1959.
Handler, Evan New York, NY, Jan. 10, 1961. Juilliard.
Hanks, Colin Sacramento, CA, Nov. 24, 1977.
Hanks, Tom Concord, CA, July 9, 1956. California State U.
Hannah, Daryl Chicago, IL, Dec. 3, 1960. UCLA.
Hannah, Page Chicago, IL, Apr. 13, 1964.
Harden, Marcia Gay La Jolla, CA, Aug. 14, 1959.
Hardin, Ty (Orison Whipple Hungerford, II) New York, NY, June 1, 1930.
Harewood, Dorian Dayton, OH, Aug. 6, 1950. U Cinncinatti.
Harmon, Mark Los Angeles, CA, Sept. 2, 1951. UCLA.
Harper, Jessica Chicago, IL, Oct. 10, 1949.
Harper, Tess Mammoth Spring, AK, 1952. South Western Missourri State.
Harper, Valerie Suffern, NY, Aug. 22, 1940.
Harrelson, Woody Midland, TX, July 23, 1961. Hanover College.

Harrington, Pat New York, NY, Aug. 13, 1929. Fordham U.
Harris, Barbara (Sandra Markowitz) Evanston, IL, July 25, 1935.
Harris, Ed Tenafly, NJ, Nov. 28, 1950. Columbia U.
Harris, Jared London, England, Aug. 24, 1961.
Harris, Julie Grosse Point, MI, Dec. 2, 1925. Yale Drama School.
Harris, Mel (Mary Ellen) Bethlehem, PA, 1957. Columbia U.
Harris, Neil Patrick Albuquerque, NM, June 15, 1973.
Harris, Rosemary Ashby, England, Sept. 19, 1930. RADA.
Harrison, Gregory Catalina Island, CA, May 31, 1950. Actors Studio.
Harrison, Noel London, England, Jan. 29, 1936.
Harrold, Kathryn Tazewell, VA, Aug. 2, 1950. Mills College.
Harry, Deborah Miami, IL, July 1, 1945.
Hart, Ian Liverpool, England, Oct. 8, 1964.
Hart, Roxanne Trenton, NJ, July 27, 1952. Princeton.
Hartley, Mariette New York, NY, June 21, 1941.
Hartman, David Pawtucket, RI, May 19, 1935. Duke U.
Hartnett, Josh San Francisco, CA, July 21, 1978.
Hassett, Marilyn Los Angeles, CA, Dec. 17, 1947.
Hatcher, Teri Sunnyvale, CA, Dec. 8, 1964.
Hathaway, Anne Brooklyn, NY, Nov. 12, 1982.
Hatosy, Shawn Fredrick, MD, Dec. 29, 1975.
Hauer, Rutger Amsterdam, Holland, Jan. 23, 1944.
Hauser, Cole Santa Barbara, CA, Mar. 22, 1975.
Hasuer, Wings (Gerald Dwight Hauser) Hollywood, CA, Dec. 12, 1947.

Havoc, June (Hovick) Seattle, WA, Nov. 8, 1916.
Hawke, Ethan Austin, TX, Nov. 6, 1970.
Hawn, Goldie Washington, DC, Nov. 21, 1945.
Hayek, Salma Coatzacoalcos, Veracruz, Mexico, Sept. 2, 1968.
Hayes, Sean Chicago, IL, June 26, 1970.
Hays, Robert Bethesda, MD, July 24, 1947. South Dakota State College.
Haysbert, Dennis San Mateo, CA, June 2, 1954.
Headey, Lena Bermuda, Oct. 3, 1973.
Headly, Glenne New London, CT, Mar. 13, 1955. AmCollege.
Heald, Anthony New Rochelle, NY, Aug. 25, 1944. Michigan State U.
Heard, John Washington, DC, Mar. 7, 1946. Clark U.
Heatherton, Joey New York, NY, Sept. 14, 1944.
Heche, Anne Aurora, OH, May 25, 1969.
Hedaya, Dan Brooklyn, NY, July 24, 1940.
Heder, Jon Fort Collins, CO, Oct. 26, 1977.
Hedison, David Providence, RI, May 20, 1929. Brown U.
Hedren, Tippi (Natalie) Lafayette, MN, Jan. 19, 1931.
Hegyes, Robert Metuchen, NJ, May 7, 1951.
Heigl, Katherine Washington, DC, Nov. 24, 1978.
Helmond, Katherine Galveston, TX, July 5, 1934.
Hemingway, Mariel Ketchum, ID, Nov. 22, 1961.
Hemsley, Sherman Philadelphia, PA, Feb. 1, 1938.
Henderson, Florence Dale, IN, Feb. 14, 1934.
Hendry, Gloria Winter Haven, FL, Mar. 3, 1949.
Henley, Georgie Ikley, England, July 9, 1995.
Henner, Marilu Chicago, IL, Apr. 6, 1952.
Henriksen, Lance New York, NY, May 5, 1940.
Henry, Buck (Henry Zuckerman) New York, NY, Dec. 9, 1930. Dartmouth.
Henry, Justin Rye, NY, May 25, 1971.
Henson, Taraji P. Washington, DC, Sept. 11, 1970. Howard Univ.
Henstridge, Natasha Springdale, Newfoundland, Canada, Aug. 15, 1974.
Hernandez, Jay (Javier Hernandez, Jr.) Montebello, CA, Feb. 20, 1978.
Herrmann, Edward Washington, DC, July 21, 1943. Bucknell, LAMDA.
Hershey, Barbara (Herzstein) Hollywood, CA, Feb. 5, 1948.
Hesseman, Howard Lebanon, OR, Feb. 27, 1940.

Hewitt, Jennifer Love Waco, TX, Feb. 21, 1979.
Hewitt, Martin Claremont, CA, Feb. 19, 1958. AADA.
Heywood, Anne (Violet Pretty) Birmingham, England, Dec. 11, 1932.
Hickey, John Benjamin Plano, TX, June 25, 1963.
Hickman, Darryl Hollywood, CA, July 28, 1933. Loyola U.
Hickman, Dwayne Los Angeles, CA, May 18, 1934. Loyola U.
Hicks, Catherine New York, NY, Aug. 6, 1951. Notre Dame.
Higgins, Anthony (Corlan) Cork City, Ireland, May 9, 1947. Birmingham Dramatic Arts.
Higgins, John Michael Boston, MA, Feb. 12, 1963.
Higgins, Michael Brooklyn, NY, Jan. 20, 1921. AmThWing.
Highmore, Freddie London, England, Feb. 14, 1992.
Hill, Bernard Manchester, England, Dec. 17, 1944.
Hill, Jonah Los Angeles, CA, Dec. 20, 1983.
Hill, Steven Seattle, WA, Feb. 24, 1922. U Wash.
Hill, Terrence (Mario Girotti) Venice, Italy, Mar. 29, 1941. U Rome.
Hillerman, John Denison, TX, Dec. 20, 1932.
Hinds, Ciaran Belfast, Northern Ireland, Feb. 9, 1953.
Hingle, Pat Denver, CO, July 19, 1923. Texas U.
Hirsch, Emile Topanga Canyon, CA, Mar. 13, 1985.
Hirsch, Judd New York, NY, Mar. 15, 1935. AADA.
Hobel, Mara New York, NY, June 18, 1971.
Hodge, Patricia Lincolnshire, England, Sept. 29, 1946. LAMDA.
Hoffman, Dustin Los Angeles, CA, Aug. 8, 1937. Pasadena Playhouse.
Hoffman, Philip Seymour Fairport, NY, July 23, 1967. NYU.
Hogan, Jonathan Chicago, IL, June 13, 1951.
Hogan, Paul Lightning Ridge, Australia, Oct. 8, 1939.
Holbrook, Hal (Harold) Cleveland, OH, Feb. 17, 1925. Denison.
Hollander, Tom Oxford, England, Aug. 25, 1967.
Holliman, Earl Tennesas Swamp, Delhi, LA, Sept. 11, 1928. UCLA.
Holm, Celeste New York, NY, Apr. 29, 1919.
Holm, Ian Ilford, Essex, England, Sept. 12, 1931. RADA.
Holmes, Katie Toledo, OH, Dec. 18, 1978.
Homeier, Skip (George Vincent Homeier) Chicago, IL, Oct. 5, 1930. UCLA.
Hooks, Robert Washington, DC, Apr. 18, 1937. Temple.
Hopkins, Anthony Port Talbot, So. Wales, Dec. 31, 1937. RADA.
Hopper, Dennis Dodge City, KS, May 17, 1936.
Horne, Lena Brooklyn, NY, June 30, 1917.
Horrocks, Jane Rossendale Valley, England, Jan. 18, 1964.
Horsley, Lee Muleshoe, TX, May 15, 1955.
Horton, Robert Los Angeles, CA, July 29, 1924. UCLA.
Hoskins, Bob Bury St. Edmunds, England, Oct. 26, 1942.
Houghton, Katharine Hartford, CT, Mar. 10, 1945. Sarah Lawrence.
Hoult, Nicholas Wokingham, England, Dec. 7, 1989.
Hounsou, Djimon Benin, West Africa, Apr. 24, 1964.
Houser, Jerry Los Angeles, CA, July 14, 1952. Valley, Jr. College.
Howard, Arliss Independence, MO, 1955. Columbia College.
Howard, Bryce Dallas Los Angeles, CA, March 2, 1981.
Howard, Ken El Centro, CA, Mar. 28, 1944. Yale.
Howard, Ron Duncan, OK, Mar. 1, 1954. USC.
Howard, Terrence Chicago, IL, Mar. 11, 1969. Pratt Inst.
Howell, C. Thomas Los Angeles, CA, Dec. 7, 1966.
Howes, Sally Ann London, England, July 20, 1930.
Howland, Beth Boston, MA, May 28, 1941.
Hubley, Season New York, NY, May 14, 1951.
Huddleston, David Vinton, VA, Sept. 17, 1930.
Hudson, Ernie Benton Harbor, MI, Dec. 17, 1945.
Hudson, Jennifer Chicago, IL, Sept. 12, 1981.
Hudson, Kate Los Angeles, CA, Apr. 19, 1979.
Huffman, Felicity Bedford, NY, Dec. 9, 1962. NYU.

Hughes, Kathleen (Betty von Gerkan) Hollywood, CA, Nov. 14, 1928. UCLA.
Hulce, Tom Plymouth, MI, Dec. 6, 1953. North Carolina School of Arts.
Hunnicut, Gayle Ft. Worth, TX, Feb. 6, 1943. UCLA.
Hunt, Helen Los Angeles, CA, June 15, 1963.
Hunt, Linda Morristown, NJ, Apr. 1945. Goodman Theatre.
Hunt, Marsha Chicago, IL, Oct. 17, 1917.
Hunter, Holly Atlanta, GA, Mar. 20, 1958. Carnegie-Mellon.
Hunter, Tab (Arthur Gelien) New York, NY, July 11, 1931.
Huntington, Sam Peterborough, NH, Apr. 1, 1982.
Huppert, Isabelle Paris, France, Mar. 16, 1955.
Hurley, Elizabeth Hampshire, England, June 10, 1965.
Hurt, John Lincolnshire, England, Jan. 22, 1940.
Hurt, Mary Beth (Supinger) Marshalltown, IA, Sept. 26, 1948. NYU.
Hurt, William Washington, DC, Mar. 20, 1950. Tufts, Juilliard.
Huston, Anjelica Santa Monica, CA, July 9, 1951.
Huston, Danny Rome, Italy, May 14, 1962.
Hutcherson, Josh Union, KY, Oct. 12, 1992.
Hutton, Lauren (Mary) Charleston, SC, Nov. 17, 1943. Newcomb College.
Hutton, Timothy Malibu, CA, Aug. 16, 1960.
Hyer, Martha Fort Worth, TX, Aug. 10, 1924. Northwestern.

Ice Cube (O'Shea Jackson) Los Angeles, CA, June 15, 1969.
Idle, Eric South Shields, Durham, England, Mar. 29, 1943. Cambridge.
Ifans, Rhys Ruthin, Wales, July 22, 1968.
Ingels, Marty Brooklyn, NY, Mar. 9, 1936.
Ireland, Kathy Santa Barbara, CA, Mar. 8, 1963.
Irons, Jeremy Cowes, England, Sept. 19, 1948. Old Vic.
Ironside, Michael Toronto, ON, Canada, Feb. 12, 1950.
Irving, Amy Palo Alto, CA, Sept. 10, 1953. LADA.
Irwin, Bill Santa Monica, CA, Apr. 11, 1950.
Isaak, Chris Stockton, CA, June 26, 1956. U of Pacific.
Ivanek, Zeljko Lujubljana, Yugoslavia, Aug. 15, 1957. Yale, LAMDA.
Ivey, Judith El Paso, TX, Sept. 4, 1951.
Izzard, Eddie Aden, Yemen, Feb. 7, 1962.

Jackson, Anne Allegheny, PA, Sept. 3, 1926. Neighborhood Playhouse.
Jackson, Glenda Hoylake, Cheshire, England, May 9, 1936. RADA.
Jackson, Janet Gary, IN, May 16, 1966.
Jackson, Joshua Vancouver, BC, Canada, June 11, 1978.
Jackson, Kate Birmingham, AL, Oct. 29, 1948. AADA.
Jackson, Michael Gary, IN, Aug. 29, 1958.
Jackson, Samuel L. Atlanta, GA, Dec. 21, 1948.
Jackson, Victoria Miami, FL, Aug. 2, 1958.
Jacobi, Derek London, England, Oct. 22, 1938. Cambridge.
Jacobi, Lou Toronto, ON, Canada, Dec. 28, 1913.
Jacobs, Lawrence-Hilton Virgin Islands, Sept. 14, 1953.
Jacoby, Scott Chicago, IL, Nov. 19, 1956.
Jagger, Mick Dartford, Kent, England, July 26, 1943.
James, Clifton New York, NY, May 29, 1921. Oregon U.
James, Kevin Stony Brook, NY, Apr. 26, 1965.
Jane, Thomas Baltimore, MD, Jan. 29, 1969.
Janney, Allison Dayton, OH, Nov. 20, 1960. RADA.
Janssen, Famke Amsterdam, Holland, Nov. 5, 1965.
Jarman, Claude, Jr. Nashville, TN, Sept. 27, 1934.
Jean, Gloria (Gloria Jean Schoonover) Buffalo, NY, Apr. 14, 1927.
Jeffreys, Anne (Carmichael) Goldsboro, NC, Jan. 26, 1923.
   Anderson College.
Jeffries, Lionel London, England, June 10, 1926. RADA.
Jenkins, Richard Dekalb, IL, May 4, 1947. Wesleyan Univ.
Jillian, Ann (Nauseda) Cambridge, MA, Jan. 29, 1951.

Johansen, David Staten Island, NY, Jan. 9, 1950.
Johansson, Scarlett New York, NY, Nov. 22, 1984.
John, Elton (Reginald Dwight) Middlesex, England, Mar. 25, 1947. RAM.
Johns, Glynis Durban, S. Africa, Oct. 5, 1923.
Johnson, Don Galena, MO, Dec. 15, 1950. U Kansas.
Johnson, Dwayne (a.k.a. The Rock) Hayward, CA, May 2, 1972.
Johnson, Page Welch, WV, Aug. 25, 1930. Ithaca.
Johnson, Rafer Hillsboro, TX, Aug. 18, 1935. UCLA.
Johnson, Richard Essex, England, July 30, 1927. RADA.
Johnson, Robin Brooklyn, NY, May 29, 1964.
Jolie, Angelina (Angelina Jolie Voight) Los Angeles, CA, June 4, 1975.
Jones, Cherry Paris, France, TN, Nov. 21, 1956.
Jones, Christopher Jackson, TN, Aug. 18, 1941. Actors Studio.
Jones, Dean Decatur, AL, Jan. 25, 1931. Actors Studio.
Jones, Grace Spanishtown, Jamaica, May 19, 1952.
Jones, Jack Bel Air, CA, Jan. 14, 1938.
Jones, James Earl Arkabutla, MS, Jan. 17, 1931. U Michigan
Jones, Jeffrey Buffalo, NY, Sept. 28, 1947. LAMDA.
Jones, Jennifer (Phyllis Isley) Tulsa, OK, Mar. 2, 1919. AADA.
Jones, L.Q. (Justice Ellis McQueen) Beaumont, TX, Aug 19, 1927.
Jones, Orlando Mobile, AL, Apr. 10, 1968.
Jones, Sam J. Chicago, IL, Aug. 12, 1954.
Jones, Shirley Smithton, PA, March 31, 1934.
Jones, Terry Colwyn Bay, Wales, Feb. 1, 1942.
Jones, Toby Oxford, England, Sept. 7, 1967.
Jones, Tommy Lee San Saba, TX, Sept. 15, 1946. Harvard.
Jourdan, Louis Marseilles, France, June 19, 1920.
Jovovich, Milla Kiev, Ukraine, Dec. 17, 1975.
Joy, Robert Montreal, Quebec, Canada, Aug. 17, 1951. Oxford.
Judd, Ashley Los Angeles, CA, Apr. 19, 1968.

Kaczmarek, Jane Milwaukee, WI, Dec. 21, 1955.
Kane, Carol Cleveland, OH, June 18, 1952.
Kaplan, Marvin Brooklyn, NY, Jan. 24, 1924.
Kapoor, Shashi Calcutta, India, Mar. 18, 1938.
Kaprisky, Valerie (Cheres) Paris, France, Aug. 19, 1962.
Karras, Alex Gary, IN, July 15, 1935.
Kartheiser, Vincent Minneapolis, MN, May 5, 1979.
Karyo, Tcheky Istanbul, Oct. 4, 1953.
Kassovitz, Mathieu Paris, France, Aug. 3, 1967.
Katt, Nicky South Dakota, May 11, 1970.
Katt, William Los Angeles, CA, Feb. 16, 1955.
Kattan, Chris Mt. Baldy, CA, Oct. 19, 1970.
Kaufmann, Christine Lansdorf, Graz, Austria, Jan. 11, 1945.
Kavner, Julie Burbank, CA, Sept. 7, 1951. UCLA.
Kazan, Lainie (Levine) Brooklyn, NY, May 15, 1942.
Kazurinsky, Tim Johnstown, PA, March 3, 1950.
Keach, Stacy Savannah, GA, June 2, 1941. U California, Yale.
Keaton, Diane (Hall) Los Angeles, CA, Jan. 5, 1946.
   Neighborhood Playhouse.
Keaton, Michael Coraopolis, PA, Sept. 9, 1951. Kent State U.
Keegan, Andrew Los Angeles, CA, Jan. 29, 1979.
Keener, Catherine Miami, FL, Mar. 26, 1960. Wheaton College.
Keeslar, Matt Grand Rapids, MI, Oct. 15, 1972.
Keitel, Harvey Brooklyn, NY, May 13, 1939.
Keith, David Knoxville, TN, May 8, 1954. U Tennessee.
Keller, Marthe Basel, Switzerland, 1945. Munich Stanislavsky School.
Kellerman, Sally Long Beach, CA, June 2, 1936. Actors Studio West.
Kelley, Elijah LaGrange, GA, Aug. 1, 1986.
Kelly, Moira Queens, NY, Mar. 6, 1968.

Kemp, Jeremy (Wacker) Chesterfield, England, Feb. 3, 1935. Central School.
Kennedy, George New York, NY, Feb. 18, 1925.
Kennedy, Jamie Upper Darby, PA, May 25, 1970.
Kennedy, Leon Isaac Cleveland, OH, Jan. 1, 1949.
Kensit, Patsy London, England, Mar. 4, 1968.
Kerr, John New York, NY, Nov. 15, 1931. Harvard, Columbia.
Kerwin, Brian Chicago, IL, Oct. 25, 1949.
Keynes, Skandar London, Sept. 5, 1991.
Kidder, Margot Yellow Knife, Canada, Oct. 17, 1948. U British Columbia.
Kidman, Nicole Honolulu, HI June 20, 1967.
Kiel, Richard Detroit, MI, Sept. 13, 1939.
Kier, Udo Koeln, Germany, Oct. 14, 1944.
Kikuchi, Rinko Kanagawa, Japan, Jan. 6, 1981.
Kilmer, Val Los Angeles, CA, Dec. 31, 1959. Juilliard.
Kincaid, Aron (Norman Neale Williams, III) Los Angeles, CA, June 15, 1943. UCLA.
Kind, Richard Trenton, NJ, Nov. 22, 1956.
King, Perry Alliance, OH, Apr. 30, 1948. Yale.
Kingsley, Ben (Krishna Bhanji) Snaiton, Yorkshire, England, Dec. 31, 1943.
Kinnear, Greg Logansport, IN, June 17, 1963.
Kinski, Nastassja Berlin, Germany, Jan. 24, 1960.
Kirk, Justin Salem, OR, May 28, 1969.
Kirk, Tommy Louisville, KY, Dec. 10 1941.
Kirkland, Sally New York, NY, Oct. 31, 1944. Actors Studio.
Klein, Chris Hinsdale, IL, March 14, 1979.
Klein, Robert New York, NY, Feb. 8, 1942. Alfred U.
Kline, Kevin St. Louis, MO, Oct. 24, 1947. Juilliard.
Klugman, Jack Philadelphia, PA, Apr. 27, 1922. Carnegie Tech.
Knight, Michael E. Princeton, NJ, May 7, 1959.
Knight, Shirley Goessel, KS, July 5, 1937. Wichita U.
Knightley, Keira Teddington, England, Mar. 26, 1985.
Knox, Elyse Hartford, CT, Dec. 14, 1917. Traphagen School.
Knoxville, Johnny (Phillip John Clapp) Knoxville, TN, March 11, 1971.
Koechner, David Tipton, MO, Aug. 24, 1962.
Koenig, Walter Chicago, IL, Sept. 14, 1936. UCLA.
Kohner, Susan Los Angeles, CA, Nov. 11, 1936. U California.
Korsmo, Charlie Minneapolis, MN, July, 20, 1978.
Koteas, Elias Montreal, Quebec, Canada, 1961. AADA.
Kotto, Yaphet New York, NY, Nov. 15, 1937.
Kozak, Harley Jane Wilkes-Barre, PA, Jan. 28, 1957. NYU.
Krabbe, Jeroen Amsterdam, The Netherlands, Dec. 5, 1944.
Krasinski, John Newton, MA, Oct. 20, 1979.
Krause, Peter Alexandria, MN, Aug. 12, 1965.
Kretschmann, Thomas Dessau, East Germany, Sept. 8, 1962.
Kreuger, Kurt St. Moritz, Switzerland, July 23, 1917. U London.
Krige, Alice Upington, South Africa, June 28, 1955.
Kristel, Sylvia Amsterdam, The Netherlands, Sept. 28, 1952.
Kristofferson, Kris Brownsville, TX, June 22, 1936. Pomona College.
Kruger, Diane Algermissen, Germany, July 15, 1976.
Kruger, Hardy Berlin, Germany, April 12, 1928.
Krumholtz, David New York, NY, May 15, 1978.
Kunis, Mila Kiev, Ukraine, Aug. 14, 1983.
Kudrow, Lisa Encino, CA, July 30, 1963.
Kurtz, Swoosie Omaha, NE, Sept. 6, 1944.
Kutcher, Ashton (Christopher Ashton Kutcher) Cedar Rapids, IA, Feb. 7, 1978.
Kwan, Nancy Hong Kong, May 19, 1939. Royal Ballet.

LaBelle, Patti Philadelphia, PA, May 24, 1944.
LaBeouf, Shia Los Angeles, CA, June 11, 1986.

Lacy, Jerry Sioux City, IA, Mar. 27, 1936. LACC.
Ladd, Cheryl (Stoppelmoor) Huron, SD. July 12, 1951.
Ladd, Diane (Ladner) Meridian, MS, Nov. 29, 1932. Tulane U.
Lahti, Christine Detroit, MI, Apr. 4, 1950. U Michigan.
Lake, Ricki New York, NY, Sept. 21, 1968.
Lamas, Lorenzo Los Angeles, CA, Jan. 28, 1958.
Lambert, Christopher New York, NY, Mar. 29, 1958.
Landau, Martin Brooklyn, NY, June 20, 1931. Actors Studio.
Lane, Abbe Brooklyn, NY, Dec. 14, 1935.
Lane, Diane New York, NY, Jan. 22, 1963.
Lane, Nathan Jersey City, NJ, Feb. 3, 1956.
Lang, Stephen New York, NY, July 11, 1952. Swarthmore College.
Lange, Jessica Cloquet, MN, Apr. 20, 1949. U Minnesota
Langella, Frank Bayonne, NJ, Jan. 1, 1940. Syracuse U.
Lansbury, Angela London, England, Oct. 16, 1925. London Academy of Music.
LaPaglia, Anthony Adelaide, Australia. Jan 31, 1959.
Larroquette, John New Orleans, LA, Nov. 25, 1947.
Lasser, Louise New York, NY, Apr. 11, 1939. Brandeis U.
Lathan, Sanaa New York, NY, Sept. 19, 1971.
Latifah, Queen (Dana Owens) East Orange, NJ, Mar. 18, 1970.
Laughlin, John Memphis, TN, Apr. 3.
Laughlin, Tom Minneapolis, MN, 1938.
Lauper, Cyndi Astoria, Queens, New York, NY, June 20, 1953.
Laure, Carole Montreal, Quebec, Canada, Aug. 5, 1951.
Laurie, Hugh Oxford, England, June 11, 1959.
Laurie, Piper (Rosetta Jacobs) Detroit, MI, Jan. 22, 1932.
Lauter, Ed Long Beach, NY, Oct. 30, 1940.
Lavin, Linda Portland, ME, Oct. 15 1939.
Law, Jude Lewisham, England, Dec. 29, 1972.
Lawrence, Barbara Carnegie, OK, Feb. 24, 1928. UCLA.
Lawrence, Carol (Laraia) Melrose Park, IL, Sept. 5, 1935.
Lawrence, Martin Frankfurt, Germany, Apr. 16, 1965.
Lawrence, Vicki Inglewood, CA, Mar. 26, 1949.
Lawson, Leigh Atherston, England, July 21, 1945. RADA.
Leachman, Cloris Des Moines, IA, Apr. 30, 1926. Northwestern.
Leal, Sharon Tuscon, AZ, Oct. 17, 1972.
Leary, Denis Boston, MA, Aug. 18, 1957.
Léaud, Jean-Pierre Paris, France, May 5, 1944.
LeBlanc, Matt Newton, MA, July 25, 1967.
Lee, Christopher London, England, May 27, 1922. Wellington Col.
Lee, Jason Huntington Beach, CA, Apr. 25, 1970.
Lee, Mark Sydney, Australia, 1958.
Lee, Michele (Dusiak) Los Angeles, CA, June 24, 1942. LACC.
Lee, Sheryl Augsburg, Germany, Arp. 22, 1967.
Lee, Spike (Shelton Lee) Atlanta, GA, Mar. 20, 1957.
Legge, Michael Newry, Northern Ireland, Dec. 11, 1978.
Legros, James Minneapolis, MN, Apr. 27, 1962.
Leguizamo, John Colombia, July 22, 1965. NYU.
Leibman, Ron New York, NY, Oct. 11, 1937. Ohio Wesleyan.
Leigh, Jennifer Jason Los Angeles, CA, Feb. 5, 1962.
Le Mat, Paul Rahway, NJ, Sept. 22, 1945.
Lemmon, Chris Los Angeles, CA, Jan. 22, 1954.
Leno, Jay New Rochelle, NY, Apr. 28, 1950. Emerson Col.
Lenz, Kay Los Angeles, CA, Mar. 4, 1953.
Lenz, Rick Springfield, IL, Nov. 21, 1939. U Michigan.
Leo, Melissa NYC, Sept. 14, 1960. SUNY Purchase
Leonard, Robert Sean Westwood, NJ, Feb. 28, 1969.
Leoni, Téa (Elizabeth Téa Pantaleoni) New York, NY, Feb. 25, 1966.
Lerman, Logan Beverly Hills, Jan. 19, 1992.

Lerner, Michael Brooklyn, NY, June 22, 1941.
Leslie, Joan (Joan Brodell) Detroit, MI, Jan. 26, 1925. St. Benedict's.
Lester, Mark Oxford, England, July 11, 1958.
Leto, Jared Bossier City, LA, Dec. 26, 1971.
Leung, Tony Hong Kong, June 27, 1962.
Levels, Calvin Cleveland. OH, Sept. 30, 1954. CCC.
Levin, Rachel (Rachel Chagall) New York, NY, Nov. 24, 1954. Goddard College.
Levine, Jerry New Brunswick, NJ, Mar. 12, 1957, Boston U.
Levy, Eugene Hamilton, Canada, Dec. 17, 1946. McMaster U.
Lewis, Charlotte London, England, Aug. 7, 1967.
Lewis, Damian London, England, Feb. 11, 1971. Guildhall.
Lewis, Geoffrey San Diego, CA, Jan. 1, 1935.
Lewis, Jerry (Joseph Levitch) Newark, NJ, Mar. 16, 1926.
Lewis, Juliette Los Angeles, CA, June 21, 1973.
Li, Jet Beijing, China, Apr. 26, 1963.
Ligon, Tom New Orleans, LA, Sept. 10, 1945.
Lillard, Matthew Lansing, MI, Jan. 24, 1970.
Lincoln, Abbey (Anna Marie Woolridge) Chicago, IL, Aug. 6, 1930.
Linden, Hal Bronx, NY, Mar. 20, 1931. City College of NY.
Lindo, Delroy London, England, Nov. 18, 1952.
Lindsay, Robert Ilketson, Derbyshire, England, Dec. 13, 1951, RADA.
Linn-Baker, Mark St. Louis, MO, June 17, 1954, Yale.
Linney, Laura New York, NY, Feb. 5, 1964.
Liotta, Ray Newark, NJ, Dec. 18, 1955. U Miami.
Lisi, Virna Rome, Italy, Nov. 8, 1937.
Lithgow, John Rochester, NY, Oct. 19, 1945. Harvard.
Liu, Lucy Queens, NY, Dec. 2, 1967.
Livingston, Ron Cedar Rapids, IA, June 5, 1968.
LL Cool J (James Todd Smith) Queens, NY, Jan. 14, 1968.
Lloyd, Christopher Stamford, CT, Oct. 22, 1938.
Lloyd, Emily London, England, Sept. 29, 1970.
Locke, Sondra Shelbyville, TN, May, 28, 1947.
Lockhart, June New York, NY, June 25, 1925. Westlake School.
Lockwood, Gary Van Nuys, CA, Feb. 21, 1937.
Loggia, Robert Staten Island, NY, Jan. 3, 1930. U Missouri.
Lohan, Lindsay New York, NY, July 2, 1986.
Lohman, Alison Palm Springs, CA, Sept. 18, 1979.
Lollobrigida, Gina Subiaco, Italy, July 4, 1927. Rome Academy of Fine Arts.
Lom, Herbert Prague, Czech Republic, Jan. 9, 1917. Prague U.
Lomez, Celine Montreal, Quebec, Canada, May 11, 1953.
Lone, John Hong Kong, Oct 13, 1952. AADA.
Long, Justin Fairfield, CT, June 2, 1978.
Long, Nia Brooklyn, NY, Oct. 30, 1970.
Long, Shelley Ft. Wayne, IN, Aug. 23, 1949. Northwestern.
Lopez, Jennifer Bronx, NY, July 24, 1970.
Lords, Tracy (Nora Louise Kuzma) Steubenville, OH, May 7, 1968.
Loren, Sophia (Sophia Scicolone) Rome, Italy, Sept. 20, 1934.
Louis-Dreyfus, Julia New York, NY, Jan. 13, 1961.
Louise, Tina (Blacker) New York, NY, Feb. 11, 1934, Miami U.
Love, Courtney (Love Michelle Harrison) San Francisco, CA, July 9, 1965.
Lovett, Lyle Klein, TX, Nov. 1, 1957.
Lovitz, Jon Tarzana, CA, July 21, 1957.
Lowe, Chad Dayton, OH, Jan. 15, 1968.
Lowe, Rob Charlottesville, VA, Mar. 17, 1964.
Lucas, Josh Little Rock, AR, June 20, 1971.
Luckinbill, Laurence Fort Smith, AK, Nov. 21, 1934.
Luft, Lorna Los Angeles, CA, Nov. 21, 1952.
Luke, Derek Jersey City, NJ, Apr. 24, 1974.
Lulu (Marie Lawrie) Glasgow, Scotland, Nov. 3, 1948.

Luna, Barbara New York, NY, Mar. 2, 1939.
Luna, Diego Mexico City, Mexico, Dec. 29, 1979.
Lundgren, Dolph Stockolm, Sweden, Nov. 3, 1959. Royal Institute.
LuPone, Patti Northport, NY, Apr. 21, 1949, Juilliard.
Lydon, James Harrington Park, NJ, May 30, 1923.
Lynch, Jane Dolton, IL, July 14, 1960.
Lynch, Kelly Minneapolis, MN, Jan. 31, 1959.
Lynley, Carol (Jones) New York, NY, Feb. 13, 1942.
Lyon, Sue Davenport, IA, July 10, 1946.
Lyonne, Natasha (Braunstein) New York, NY, Apr. 4, 1979.

MacArthur, James Los Angeles, CA, Dec. 8, 1937. Harvard.
Macchio, Ralph Huntington, NY, Nov. 4, 1961.
MacCorkindale, Simon Cambridge, England, Feb. 12, 1953.
Macdonald, Kelly Glasgow, Scotland, Feb. 23, 1976.
MacDowell, Andie (Rose Anderson MacDowell) Gaffney, SC, Apr. 21, 1958.
MacFadyen, Angus Glasgow, Scotland, Oct. 21, 1963.
MacGinnis, Niall Dublin, Ireland, Mar. 29, 1913. Dublin U.
MacGraw, Ali New York, NY, Apr. 1, 1938. Wellesley.
MacLachlan, Kyle Yakima, WA, Feb. 22, 1959. U Washington.
MacLaine, Shirley (Beaty) Richmond, VA, Apr. 24, 1934.
MacLeod, Gavin Mt. Kisco, NY, Feb. 28, 1931.
MacNaughton, Robert New York, NY, Dec. 19, 1966.
Macnee, Patrick London, England, Feb. 6, 1922.
MacNicol, Peter Dallas, TX, Apr. 10, 1954. U Minnesota.
MacPherson, Elle Sydney, Australia, Mar. 29, 1963.
MacVittie, Bruce Providence, RI, Oct. 14, 1956. Boston U.
Macy, William H. Miami, FL, Mar. 13, 1950. Goddard College.
Madigan, Amy Chicago, IL, Sept. 11, 1950. Marquette U.
Madonna (Madonna Louise Veronica Cicone) Bay City, MI, Aug. 16, 1958. U Michigan.
Madsen, Michael Chicago, IL, Sept. 25, 1958.
Madsen, Virginia Winnetka, IL, Sept. 11, 1963.
Magnuson, Ann Charleston, WV, Jan. 4, 1956.
Maguire, Tobey Santa Monica, CA, June 27, 1975.
Maharis, George Astoria, NY, Sept. 1, 1928. Actors Studio.
Mahoney, John Manchester, England, June 20, 1940. Western Illinois U.
Mailer, Stephen New York, NY, Mar. 10, 1966. NYU.
Majors, Lee Wyandotte, MI, Apr. 23, 1940. Eastern Kentucky State College.
Makepeace, Chris Toronto, ON, Canada, Apr. 22, 1964.
Malden, Karl (Mladen Sekulovich) Gary, IN, Mar. 22, 1914.
Malkovich, John Christopher, IL, Dec. 9, 1953, Illinois State U.
Malone, Dorothy Chicago, IL, Jan. 30, 1925.
Malone, Jena Lake Tahoe, NV, Nov. 21, 1984.
Mann, Leslie San Francisco, CA, Mar. 26, 1972.
Mann, Terrence Kentucky, July 1, 1951. NC School Arts.
Manoff, Dinah New York, NY, Jan. 25, 1958. Cal Arts.
Mantegna, Joe Chicago, IL, Nov. 13, 1947. Goodman Theatre.
Manz, Linda New York, NY, 1961.
Marceau, Sophie (Maupu) Paris, France, Nov. 17, 1966.
Marcovicci, Andrea New York, NY, Nov. 18, 1948.
Margulies, Julianna Spring Valley, NY, June 8, 1966.
Marin, Cheech (Richard) Los Angeles, CA, July 13, 1946.
Marinaro, Ed New York, NY, Mar. 31, 1950. Cornell.
Mars, Kenneth Chicago, IL, Apr. 14, 1936.
Marsden, James Stillwater, OK, Sept. 18, 1973.
Marsh, Jean London, England, July 1, 1934.
Marshall, Ken New York, NY, June 27, 1950. Juilliard.
Marshall, Penny Bronx, NY, Oct. 15, 1942. UN. Mex.
Martin, Andrea Portland, ME, Jan. 15, 1947.

Martin, George N. New York, NY, Aug. 15, 1929.
Martin, Millicent Romford, England, June 8, 1934.
Martin, Pamela Sue Westport, CT, Jan. 15, 1953.
Martin, Steve Waco, TX, Aug. 14, 1945. UCLA.
Martin, Tony (Alfred Norris) Oakland, CA, Dec. 25, 1913. St. Mary's College.
Martindale, Margo Jacksonsville, TX, July 18, 1951.
Martinez, Olivier Paris, France, Jan. 12, 1966.
Mason, Marsha St. Louis, MO, Apr. 3, 1942. Webster College.
Masters, Ben Corvallis, OR, May 6, 1947. U Oregon.
Masterson, Mary Stuart Los Angeles, CA, June 28, 1966, NYU.
Masterson, Peter Angleton, TX, June 1, 1934. Rice U.
Mastrantonio, Mary Elizabeth Chicago, IL, Nov. 17, 1958. U Illinois.
Masur, Richard New York, NY, Nov. 20, 1948.
Matheson, Tim Glendale, CA, Dec. 31, 1947. Cal State.
Mathis, Samantha New York, NY, May 12, 1970.
Matlin, Marlee Morton Grove, IL, Aug. 24, 1965.
Matthews, Brian Philadelphia, PA, Jan. 24. 1953. St. Olaf.
Maura, Carmen Madrid, Spain, Sept. 15, 1945.
May, Elaine (Berlin) Philadelphia, PA, Apr. 21, 1932.
Mayron, Melanie Philadelphia, PA, Oct. 20, 1952. AADA.
Mazursky, Paul Brooklyn, NY, Apr. 25, 1930. Brooklyn, NY College.
Mazzello, Joseph Rhinebeck, NY, Sept. 21, 1983.
McAdams, Rachel London, ON, Canada, Oct. 7, 1976.
McAvoy, James Glasgow, Scotland, Jan. 1, 1979.
McBride, Chi Chicago, IL, Sept. 23, 1961.
McBride, Danny Statesboro, GA, Dec. 29, 1976.
McCallum, David Scotland, Sept. 19, 1933. Chapman College.
McCarthy, Andrew New York, NY, Nov. 29, 1962, NYU.
McCarthy, Kevin Seattle, WA, Feb. 15, 1914. Minnesota U.
McCartney, Paul Liverpool, England, June 18, 1942.
McClanahan, Rue Healdton, OK, Feb. 21, 1934.
McClure, Marc San Mateo, CA, Mar. 31, 1957.
McClurg, Edie Kansas City, MO, July 23, 1950.
McCormack, Catherine Alton, Hampshire, England, Jan. 1, 1972.
McCowen, Alec Tunbridge Wells, England, May 26, 1925. RADA.
McCrane, Paul Philadelphia, PA, Jan. 19. 1961.
McCrary, Darius Walnut, CA, May 1, 1976.
McDermott, Dylan Waterbury, CT, Oct. 26, 1962. Neighborhood Playhouse.
McDonald, Christopher New York, NY, Feb. 15, 1955.
McDonnell, Mary Wilkes Barre, PA, Apr. 28, 1952.
McDonough, Neal Dorchester, MA, Feb. 13, 1966.
McDormand, Frances Illinois, June 23, 1957. Yale.
McDowell, Malcolm (Taylor) Leeds, England, June 19, 1943. LAMDA.
McElhone, Natascha (Natasha Taylor) London, England, Mar. 23, 1971.
McEnery, Peter Walsall, England, Feb. 21, 1940.
McEntire, Reba McAlester, OK, Mar. 28, 1955. Southeastern St. U.
McGill, Everett Miami Beach, FL, Oct. 21, 1945.
McGillis, Kelly Newport Beach, CA, July 9, 1957. Juilliard.
McGinley, John C. New York, NY, Aug. 3, 1959. NYU.
McGoohan, Patrick New York, NY, Mar. 19, 1928.
McGovern, Elizabeth Evanston, IL, July 18, 1961. Juilliard.
McGovern, Maureen Youngstown, OH, July 27, 1949.
McGowan, Rose Florence, Italy, Sept. 5, 1973.
McGregor, Ewan Perth, Scotland, March 31, 1971.
McGuire, Biff New Haven, CT, Oct. 25. 1926. Mass. State College.
McHattie, Stephen Antigonish, Nova Scotia, Feb. 3, 1947. Acadia U AADA.
McKean, Michael New York, NY, Oct. 17, 1947.
McKee, Lonette Detroit, MI, July 22, 1955.
McKellen, Ian Burnley, England, May 25, 1939.
McKenna, Virginia London, England, June 7, 1931.

McKenzie, Ben (Benjamin Schenkkan) Austin, TX, Sept. 12, 1978. U Virginia.
McKeon, Doug Pompton Plains, NJ, June 10, 1966.
McLerie, Allyn Ann Grand Mere, Canada, Dec. 1, 1926.
McMahon, Ed Detroit, MI, Mar. 6, 1923.
McMahon, Julian Sydney, Australia, July 27, 1968.
McNamara, William Dallas, TX, Mar. 31, 1965.
McNichol, Kristy Los Angeles, CA, Sept. 11, 1962.
McQueen, Armelia North Carolina, Jan. 6, 1952. Bklyn Consv.
McQueen, Chad Los Angeles, CA, Dec. 28, 1960. Actors Studio.
McRaney, Gerald Collins, MS, Aug. 19, 1948.
McShane, Ian Blackburn, England, Sept. 29, 1942. RADA.
McTeer, Janet York, England, May 8, 1961.
Meadows, Jayne (Jayne Cotter) Wuchang, China, Sept. 27, 1924. St. Margaret's.
Meaney, Colm Dublin, Ireland, May 30, 1953.
Meara, Anne Brooklyn, NY, Sept. 20, 1929.
Meat Loaf (Marvin Lee Aday) Dallas, TX, Sept. 27, 1947.
Mechlowicz, Scott New York, NY, Jan. 17, 1981.
Medwin, Michael London, England, July 18, 1923. Instut Fischer.
Mekka, Eddie Worcester, MA, June 14, 1952. Boston Cons.
Melato, Mariangela Milan, Italy, Sept. 18, 1941. Milan Theatre Acad.
Mendes, Eva Los Angeles, CA, Mar. 5, 1974.
Menzel, Idina Syosset, NY, May 30, 1971. NYU.
Meredith, Lee (Judi Lee Sauls) River Edge, NJ, Oct. 22, 1947. AADA.
Merkerson, S. Epatha Saganaw, MI, Nov. 28, 1952. Wayne St. Univ.
Merrill, Dina (Nedinia Hutton) New York, NY, Dec. 29, 1925. AADA.
Messing, Debra Brooklyn, NY, Aug. 15, 1968.
Metcalf, Laurie Edwardsville, IL, June 16, 1955. Illinois State U.
Metzler, Jim Oneonta, NY, June 23, 1955. Dartmouth.
Meyer, Breckin Minneapolis, MN, May 7, 1974.
Michell, Keith Adelaide, Australia, Dec. 1, 1926.
Midler, Bette Honolulu, HI, Dec. 1, 1945.
Mihok, Dash New York, NY, May 24, 1974.
Mikkelsen, Mads Copenhagen, Denmark, Nov. 22, 1965.
Milano, Alyssa Brooklyn, NY, Dec. 19, 1972.
Miles, Joanna Nice, France, Mar. 6, 1940.
Miles, Sarah Ingatestone, England, Dec. 31, 1941. RADA.
Miles, Sylvia New York, NY, Sept. 9, 1934. Actors Studio.
Miles, Vera (Ralston) Boise City, OK, Aug. 23, 1929. UCLA.
Miller, Barry Los Angeles, CA, Feb. 6, 1958.
Miller, Dick New York, NY, Dec. 25, 1928.
Miller, Jonny Lee Surrey, England, Nov. 15, 1972.
Miller, Linda New York, NY, Sept. 16, 1942. Catholic U.
Miller, Penelope Ann Santa Monica, CA, Jan. 13, 1964.
Miller, Rebecca Roxbury, CT, Sept. 15, 1962. Yale.
Miller, Sienna New York, NY, Dec. 28, 1981.
Mills, Donna Chicago, IL, Dec. 11, 1945. U Illinois.
Mills, Hayley London, England, Apr. 18, 1946. Elmhurst School.
Mills, Juliet London, England, Nov. 21, 1941.
Milner, Martin Detroit, MI, Dec. 28, 1931.
Mimieux, Yvette Los Angeles, CA, Jan. 8, 1941. Hollywood High.
Minnelli, Liza Los Angeles, CA, Mar. 19, 1946.
Miou-Miou (Sylvette Henry) Paris, France, Feb. 22, 1950.
Mirren, Helen (Ilynea Mironoff) London, England, July 26, 1946.
Mistry, Jimi Scarborough, England, 1973.
Mitchell, James Sacramento, CA, Feb. 29, 1920. LACC.
Mitchell, John Cameron El Paso, TX, Apr. 21, 1963. Northwestern.
Mitchell, Rhada Melbourne, Australia, Nov. 12, 1973.
Mitchum, James Los Angeles, CA, May 8, 1941.
Modine, Matthew Loma Linda, CA, Mar. 22, 1959.

Moffat, Donald Plymouth, England, Dec. 26, 1930. RADA.
Moffett, D. W. Highland Park, IL, Oct. 26, 1954. Stanford U.
Mohr, Jay Verona, NJ, Aug. 23, 1971.
Mokae, Zakes Johannesburg, South Africa, Aug. 5, 1935. RADA.
Mol, Gretchen Deep River, CT, Nov. 8, 1972.
Molina, Alfred London, England, May 24, 1953. Guildhall.
Moll, Richard Pasadena, CA, Jan. 13, 1943.
Monaghan, Dominic Berlin, Germany, Dec. 8, 1976.
Monaghan, Michelle Winthrop, IA, March 23, 1976.
Mo'Nique (Monique Imes) Woodland, MD, Dec. 11, 1967.
Monk, Debra Middletown, OH, Feb. 27, 1949.
Montalban, Ricardo Mexico City, Mexico, Nov. 25, 1920.
Montenegro, Fernanda (Arlete Pinheiro) Rio de Janiero, Brazil, 1929.
Montgomery, Belinda Winnipeg, Manitoba, Canada, July 23, 1950.
Moody, Ron London, England, Jan. 8, 1924. London U.
Moore, Demi (Guines) Roswell, NM, Nov. 11, 1962.
Moore, Dick Los Angeles, CA, Sept. 12, 1925.
Moore, Julianne (Julie Anne Smith) Fayetteville, NC, Dec. 30, 1960.
Moore, Mandy Nashua, NH, Apr. 10, 1984.
Moore, Mary Tyler Brooklyn, NY, Dec. 29, 1936.
Moore, Roger London, England, Oct. 14, 1927. RADA.
Moore, Stephen Campbell (Stephen Thorpe) London, England, 1979.
Moore, Terry (Helen Koford) Los Angeles, CA, Jan. 7, 1929.
Morales, Esai Brooklyn, NY, Oct. 1, 1962.
Moranis, Rick Toronto, ON, Canada, Apr. 18, 1954.
Moreau, Jeanne Paris, France, Jan. 23, 1928.
Moreno, Catalina Sandino Bogota, Colombia, Apr. 19, 1981.
Moreno, Rita (Rosita Alverio) Humacao, P.R., Dec. 11, 1931.
Morgan, Harry (Henry) (Harry Bratsburg) Detroit, MI, Apr. 10, 1915. U Chicago.
Morgan, Michele (Simone Roussel) Paris, France, Feb. 29, 1920. Paris Dramatic School.
Moriarty, Cathy Bronx, NY, Nov. 29, 1960.
Moriarty, Michael Detroit, MI, Apr. 5, 1941. Dartmouth.
Morison, Patricia New York, NY, Mar. 19, 1915.
Morris, Garrett New Orleans, LA, Feb. 1, 1937.
Morrow, Rob New Rochelle, NY, Sept. 21, 1962.
Morse, David Hamilton, MA, Oct. 11, 1953.
Morse, Robert Newton, MA, May 18, 1931.
Mortensen, Viggo New York, NY, Oct. 20, 1958.
Mortimer, Emily London, England, Dec. 1, 1971.
Morton, Joe New York, NY, Oct. 18, 1947. Hofstra U.
Morton, Samantha Nottingham, England, May 13, 1977.
Mos Def (Dante Beze) Brooklyn, NY, Dec. 11, 1973.
Moseley, William Sheepscombe, England, Apr. 27, 1987.
Moses, William Los Angeles, CA, Nov. 17, 1959.
Moss, Carrie-Anne Vancouver, BC, Canada, Aug. 21, 1967.
Mostel, Josh New York, NY, Dec. 21, 1946. Brandeis U.
Mouchet, Catherine Paris, France, 1959. Ntl. Consv.
Moynahan, Bridget Binghamton, NY, Sept. 21, 1972.
Mueller-Stahl, Armin Tilsit, East Prussia, Dec. 17, 1930.
Muldaur, Diana New York, NY, Aug. 19, 1938. Sweet Briar College.
Mulgrew, Kate Dubuque, IA, Apr. 29, 1955. NYU.
Mulhern, Matt Philadelphia, PA, July 21, 1960. Rutgers U.
Mull, Martin N. Ridgefield, OH, Aug. 18, 1941. RI School of Design.
Mulroney, Dermot Alexandria, VA, Oct. 31, 1963. Northwestern.
Mumy, Bill (Charles William Mumy, Jr.) San Gabriel, CA, Feb. 1, 1954.
Muniz, Frankie Ridgewood, NJ, Dec. 5, 1985.
Murphy, Brittany Atlanta, GA, Nov. 10, 1977.
Murphy, Cillian Douglas, Ireland, March 13, 1974.

Murphy, Donna Queens, NY, March 7, 1958.
Murphy, Eddie Brooklyn, NY, Apr. 3, 1961.
Murphy, Michael Los Angeles, CA, May 5, 1938. U Arizona.
Murray, Bill Wilmette, IL, Sept. 21, 1950. Regis College.
Murray, Don Hollywood, CA, July 31, 1929.
Musante, Tony Bridgeport, CT, June 30, 1936. Oberlin College.
Myers, Mike Scarborough, Canada, May 25, 1963.

Nabors, Jim Sylacauga, GA, June 12, 1932.
Nader, Michael Los Angeles, CA, Feb. 19, 1945.
Namath, Joe Beaver Falls, PA, May 31, 1943. U Alabama.
Naughton, David Hartford, CT, Feb. 13, 1951.
Naughton, James Middletown, CT, Dec. 6, 1945.
Neal, Patricia Packard, KY, Jan. 20, 1926. Northwestern.
Neeson, Liam Ballymena, Northern Ireland, June 7, 1952.
Neill, Sam Northern Ireland, Sept. 14, 1947. U Canterbury.
Nelligan, Kate London, ON, Canada, Mar. 16, 1951. U Toronto.
Nelson, Craig T. Spokane, WA, Apr. 4, 1946.
Nelson, David New York, NY, Oct. 24, 1936. USC.
Nelson, Judd Portland, ME, Nov. 28, 1959, Haverford College.
Nelson, Lori (Dixie Kay Nelson) Santa Fe, NM, Aug. 15, 1933.
Nelson, Tim Blake Tulsa, OK, Nov. 5, 1964.
Nelson, Tracy Santa Monica, CA, Oct. 25, 1963.
Nelson, Willie Abbott, TX, Apr. 30, 1933.
Nemec, Corin Little Rock, AK, Nov. 5, 1971.
Nero, Franco (Francisco Spartanero) Parma, Italy, Nov. 23, 1941.
Nesmith, Michael Houston, TX, Dec. 30, 1942.
Neuwirth, Bebe Princeton, NJ, Dec. 31, 1958.
Newhart, Bob Chicago, IL, Sept. 5, 1929. Loyola U.
Newman, Barry Boston, MA, Nov. 7, 1938. Brandeis U.
Newman, Laraine Los Angeles, CA, Mar. 2, 1952.
Newman, Nanette Northampton, England, May 29, 1934.
Newmar, Julie (Newmeyer) Los Angeles, CA, Aug. 16, 1933.
Newton, Thandie Zambia, Nov. 16, 1972.
Newton-John, Olivia Cambridge, England, Sept. 26, 1948.
Nguyen, Dustin Saigon, Vietnam, Sept. 17, 1962.
Nicholas, Denise Detroit, MI, July 12, 1945.
Nicholas, Paul Peterborough, Cambridge, England, Dec. 3, 1945.
Nichols, Nichelle Robbins, IL, Dec. 28, 1933.
Nicholson, Jack Neptune, NJ, Apr. 22, 1937.
Nicholson, Julianne Medford, MA, July 1, 1971.
Nickerson, Denise New York, NY, Apr. 1, 1959.
Nielsen, Brigitte Denmark, July 15, 1963.
Nielsen, Connie Elling, Denmark, July 3, 1965.
Nielsen, Leslie Regina, Saskatchewan, Canada, Feb. 11, 1926. Neighborhood Playhouse.
Nighy, Bill Caterham, England, Dec. 12, 1949. Guildford.
Nimoy, Leonard Boston, MA, Mar. 26, 1931. Boston College, Antioch College.
Nivola, Alessandro Boston, MA, June 28, 1972. Yale.
Nixon, Cynthia New York, NY, Apr. 9, 1966. Columbia U.
Noble, James Dallas, TX, Mar. 5, 1922. SMU.
Nolan, Kathleen St. Louis, MO, Sept. 27, 1933. Neighborhood Playhouse.
Nolte, Nick Omaha, NE, Feb. 8, 1940. Pasadena City College.
Norris, Bruce Houston, TX, May 16, 1960. Northwestern.
Norris, Christopher New York, NY, Oct. 7, 1943. Lincoln Square Acad.
Norris, Chuck (Carlos Ray) Ryan, OK, Mar. 10, 1940.
North, Heather Pasadena, CA, Dec. 13, 1950. Actors Workshop.
Northam, Jeremy Cambridge, England, Dec. 1, 1961.
Norton, Edward Boston, MA, Aug. 18, 1969.

Norton, Ken Jacksonville, IL, Aug. 9, 1945.
Noseworthy, Jack Lynn, MA, Dec. 21, 1969.
Nouri, Michael Washington, DC, Dec. 9, 1945.
Novak, Kim (Marilyn Novak) Chicago, IL, Feb. 13, 1933. LACC.
Novello, Don Ashtabula, OH, Jan. 1, 1943. U Dayton.
Nuyen, France (Vannga) Marseilles, France, July 31, 1939.
Beaux Arts School.

O'Brian, Hugh (Hugh J. Krampe) Rochester, NY. Apr. 19, 1928. Cincinnati U.
O'Brien, Clay Ray, AZ, May 6, 1961.
O'Brien, Margaret (Angela Maxine O'Brien) Los Angeles, CA, Jan. 15, 1937.
O'Connell, Jerry (Jeremiah O'Connell) New York, NY, Feb. 17, 1974.
O'Connor, Glynnis New York, NY, Nov. 19, 1955. NYSU.
O'Donnell, Chris Winetka, IL, June 27, 1970.
O'Donnell, Rosie Commack, NY, March 21, 1961.
Oh, Sandra Nepean, ON, Canada, Nov. 30, 1970.
O'Halloran, Brian Old Bridge, NJ, Sept. 1, 1965.
O'Hara, Catherine Toronto, ON, Canada, Mar. 4, 1954.
O'Hara, Maureen (Maureen Fitzsimons) Dublin, Ireland, Aug. 17, 1920.
O'Hare, Dennis Kansas City, MO, Jan. 17, 1962.
O'Keefe, Michael Larchmont, NY, Apr. 24, 1955. NYU, AADA.
Okonedo, Sophie London, England, Jan. 1, 1969.
Oldman, Gary New Cross, South London, England, Mar. 21, 1958.
O'Leary, Matt Chicago, IL, July 6, 1987.
Olin, Ken Chicago, IL, July 30, 1954. U Pa.
Olin, Lena Stockholm, Sweden, Mar. 22, 1955.
Olmos, Edward James Los Angeles, CA, Feb. 24, 1947. CSLA.
O'Loughlin, Gerald S. New York, NY, Dec. 23, 1921. U Rochester.
Olson, James Evanston, IL, Oct. 8, 1930.
Olson, Nancy Milwaukee, WI, July 14, 1928. UCLA.
Olyphant, Timothy Honolulu, HI, May 20, 1968.
O'Neal, Griffin Los Angeles, CA, Oct. 28, 1964.
O'Neal, Ryan Los Angeles, CA, Apr. 20, 1941.
O'Neal, Tatum Los Angeles, CA, Nov. 5, 1963.
O'Neil, Tricia Shreveport, LA, Mar. 11, 1945. Baylor U.
O'Neill, Ed Youngstown, OH, Apr. 12, 1946.
O'Neill, Jennifer Rio de Janeiro, Brazil, Feb. 20, 1949.
Neighborhood Playhouse.
Ontkean, Michael Vancouver, BC, Canada, Jan. 24, 1946.
O'Quinn, Terry Newbury, MI, July 15, 1952.
Ormond, Julia Epsom, England, Jan. 4, 1965.
O'Shea, Milo Dublin, Ireland, June 2, 1926.
Osment, Haley Joel Los Angeles, CA, Apr. 10, 1988.
O'Toole, Annette (Toole) Houston, TX, Apr. 1, 1953. UCLA.
O'Toole, Peter Connemara, Ireland, Aug. 2, 1932. RADA.
Otto, Miranda Brisbane, Australia, Dec. 16, 1967.
Overall, Park Nashville, TN, Mar. 15, 1957. Tusculum College.
Owen, Clive Keresley, England, Oct. 3, 1964.
Oz, Frank (Oznowicz) Hereford, England, May 25, 1944.

Pace, Lee Chickasha, OK, Mar. 25, 1979.
Pacino, Al New York, NY, Apr. 25, 1940.
Pacula, Joanna Tamaszow Lubelski, Poland, Jan. 2, 1957.
Polish Natl. Theatre Sch.
Page, Ellen Hallifax, Nova Scotia, Feb. 21, 1987.
Paget, Debra (Debralee Griffin) Denver, CO, Aug. 19, 1933.
Paige, Janis (Donna Mae Jaden) Tacoma, WA, Sept. 16, 1922.
Palin, Michael Sheffield, England, May 5, 1943, Oxford.
Palmer, Betsy East Chicago, IN, Nov. 1, 1926. DePaul U.
Palmer, Gregg (Palmer Lee) San Francisco, CA, Jan. 25, 1927. U Utah.

Palminteri, Chazz (Calogero Lorenzo Palminteri) New York, NY,
May 15, 1952.
Paltrow, Gwyneth Los Angeles, CA, Sept. 28, 1973.
Pampanini, Silvana Rome, Italy, Sept. 25, 1925.
Panebianco, Richard New York, NY, 1971.
Pankin, Stuart Philadelphia, PA, Apr. 8, 1946.
Pantoliano, Joe Jersey City, NJ, Sept. 12, 1954.
Papas, Irene Chiliomodion, Greece, Mar. 9, 1929.
Paquin, Anna Winnipeg, Manitoba, Canada, July, 24, 1982.
Pardue, Kip (Kevin Ian Pardue) Atlanta, GA, Sept. 23, 1976. Yale.
Pare, Michael Brooklyn, NY, Oct. 9, 1959.
Parker, Corey New York, NY, July 8, 1965. NYU.
Parker, Eleanor Cedarville, OH, June 26, 1922. Pasadena Playhouse.
Parker, Fess Fort Worth, TX, Aug. 16, 1925. USC.
Parker, Jameson Baltimore, MD, Nov. 18, 1947. Beloit College.
Parker, Mary-Louise Ft. Jackson, SC, Aug. 2, 1964. Bard College.
Parke, Nate Norfolk, VA, Nov. 18, 1979.
Parker, Nathaniel London, England, May 18, 1962.
Parker, Sarah Jessica Nelsonville, OH, Mar. 25, 1965.
Parker, Trey Auburn, AL, May 30, 1972.
Parkins, Barbara Vancouver, BC, Canada, May 22, 1943.
Parks, Michael Corona, CA, Apr. 4, 1938.
Parsons, Estelle Lynn, MA, Nov. 20, 1927. Boston U.
Parton, Dolly Sevierville, TN, Jan. 19, 1946.
Pascal, Adam Bronx, NY, Oct. 25, 1970.
Patel, Dev London, Apr. 23, 1990.
Patinkin, Mandy Chicago, IL, Nov. 30, 1952. Juilliard.
Patric, Jason New York, NY, June 17, 1966.
Patrick, Robert Marietta, GA, Nov. 5, 1958.
Patterson, Lee Vancouver, BC, Canada, Mar. 31, 1929. Ontario College.
Pattinson, Robert London, May 13, 1986.
Patton, Will Charleston, SC, June 14, 1954.
Paulik, Johan Prague, Czech Republic, Mar. 14, 1975.
Paulson, Sarah Tampa, FL, Dec. 17, 1975.
Pavan, Marisa (Marisa Pierangeli) Cagliari, Sardinia, June 19, 1932.
Torquado Tasso College.
Paxton, Bill Fort Worth, TX, May. 17, 1955.
Paymer, David Oceanside, Long Island, NY, Aug. 30, 1954.
Pays, Amanda Berkshire, England, June 6, 1959.
Peach, Mary Durban, South Africa, Oct. 20, 1934.
Pearce, Guy Ely, England, Oct. 5, 1967.
Pearson, Beatrice Dennison, TX, July 27, 1920.
Peet, Amanda New York, NY, Jan. 11, 1972.
Pegg, Simon Gloucester, England, Feb. 14, 1970.
Peña, Elizabeth Elizabeth, NJ, Sept. 23, 1961.
Peña, Michael Chicago, IL, Jan. 13, 1976.
Pendleton, Austin Warren, OH, Mar. 27, 1940. Yale.
Penhall, Bruce Balboa, CA, Aug. 17, 1960.
Penn, Kal Montclair, NJ, Apr. 23, 1977.
Penn, Sean Burbank, CA, Aug. 17, 1960.
Pepper, Barry Campbell River, BC, Canada, Apr. 4, 1970.
Perabo, Piper Toms River, NJ, Oct. 31, 1976.
Perez, Jose New York, NY, 1940.
Perez, Rosie Brooklyn, NY, Sept. 6, 1964.
Perkins, Elizabeth Queens, NY, Nov. 18, 1960. Goodman School.
Perkins, Millie Passaic, NJ, May 12, 1938.
Perlman, Rhea Brooklyn, NY, Mar. 31, 1948.
Perlman, Ron New York, NY, Apr. 13, 1950. U Mn.
Perreau, Gigi (Ghislaine) Los Angeles, CA, Feb. 6, 1941.
Perrine, Valerie Galveston, TX, Sept. 3, 1943. U Ariz.

Perry, Luke (Coy Luther Perry, III) Fredricktown, OH, Oct. 11, 1966.
Perry, Tyler New Orleans, LA, Sept. 13, 1969.
Pesci, Joe Newark, NJ. Feb. 9, 1943.
Pescow, Donna Brooklyn, NY, Mar. 24, 1954.
Peters, Bernadette (Lazzara) Jamaica, NY, Feb. 28, 1948.
Petersen, Paul Glendale, CA, Sept. 23, 1945. Valley College.
Petersen, William Chicago, IL, Feb. 21, 1953.
Peterson, Cassandra Colorado Springs, CO, Sept. 17, 1951.
Pettet, Joanna London, England, Nov. 16, 1944. Neighborhood Playhouse.
Petty, Lori Chattanooga, TN, Mar. 23, 1963.
Pfeiffer, Michelle Santa Ana, CA, Apr. 29, 1958.
Phifer, Mekhi New York, NY, Dec. 12, 1975.
Phillippe, Ryan (Matthew Phillippe) New Castle, DE, Sept. 10, 1975.
Phillips, Lou Diamond Phillipines, Feb. 17, 1962, U Tx.
Phillips, MacKenzie Alexandria, VA, Nov. 10, 1959.
Phillips, Michelle (Holly Gilliam) Long Beach, CA, June 4, 1944.
Phillips, Sian Bettws, Wales, May 14, 1934. U Wales.
Phoenix, Joaquin San Juan, Puerto Rico, Oct. 28, 1974.
Picardo, Robert Philadelphia, PA, Oct. 27, 1953. Yale.
Picerni, Paul New York, NY, Dec. 1, 1922. Loyola U.
Pidgeon, Rebecca Cambridge, MA, Oct. 10, 1965.
Pierce, David Hyde Saratoga Springs, NY, Apr. 3, 1959.
Pigott-Smith, Tim Rugby, England, May 13, 1946.
Pinchot, Bronson New York, NY, May 20, 1959. Yale.
Pine, Chris Los Angeles, Aug. 26, 1980.
Pine, Phillip Hanford, CA, July 16, 1920. Actors' Lab.
Pinsent, Gordon Grand Falls, Newfoundland, July 12, 1930.
Piscopo, Joe Passaic, NJ, June 17, 1951.
Pisier, Marie-France Dalat, Vietnam, May 10, 1944. U Paris.
Pitillo, Maria Elmira, NY, Jan. 8, 1965.
Pitt, Brad (William Bradley Pitt) Shawnee, OK, Dec. 18, 1963.
Pitt, Michael West Orange, NJ, Apr. 10, 1981.
Piven, Jeremy New York, NY, July 26, 1965.
Place, Mary Kay Tulsa OK, Sept. 23, 1947. U Tulsa.
Platt, Oliver Windsor, ON, Canada, Oct. 10, 1960.
Playten, Alice New York, NY, Aug. 28, 1947. NYU.
Plimpton, Martha New York, NY, Nov. 16, 1970.
Plowright, Joan Scunthorpe, England, Oct. 28, 1929. Old Vic.
Plumb, Eve Burbank, CA, Apr. 29, 1958.
Plummer, Amanda New York, NY, Mar. 23, 1957. Middlebury College.
Plummer, Christopher Toronto, ON, Canada, Dec. 13, 1927.
Podesta, Rossana Tripoli, Libya, June 20, 1934.
Poehler, Amy Burlington, MA, Sept. 16, 1971.
Poitier, Sidney Miami, FL, Feb. 27, 1927.
Polanski, Roman Paris, France, Aug. 18, 1933.
Polito, Jon Philadelphia, PA, Dec. 29, 1950. Villanova U.
Polito, Lina Naples, Italy, Aug. 11, 1954.
Pollak, Kevin San Francisco, CA, Oct. 30, 1958.
Pollan, Tracy New York, NY, June 22, 1960.
Pollard, Michael J. Passaic, NJ, May 30, 1939.
Polley, Sarah Toronto, ON, Canada, Jan. 8, 1979.
Popplewell, Anna London, Dec. 16, 1988.
Portman, Natalie Jerusalem, Israel, June 9, 1981.
Posey, Parker Baltimore, MD, Nov. 8, 1968.
Postlethwaite, Pete London, England, Feb. 7, 1945.
Potente, Franka Dulmen, Germany, July 22, 1974.
Potter, Monica Cleveland, OH, June 30, 1971.
Potts, Annie Nashville, TN, Oct. 28, 1952. Stephens College.
Powell, Jane (Suzanne Burce) Portland, OR, Apr. 1, 1928.
Powell, Robert Salford, England, June 1, 1944. Manchester U.

Power, Taryn Los Angeles, CA, Sept. 13, 1953.
Power, Tyrone, IV Los Angeles, CA, Jan. 22, 1959.
Powers, Stefanie (Federkiewicz) Hollywood, CA, Oct. 12, 1942.
Prentiss, Paula (Paula Ragusa) San Antonio, TX, Mar. 4, 1939. Northwestern.
Presle, Micheline (Micheline Chassagne) Paris, France, Aug. 22, 1922. Rouleau Drama School.
Presley, Priscilla Brooklyn, NY, May 24, 1945.
Presnell, Harve Modesto, CA, Sept. 14, 1933. USC.
Preston, Kelly Honolulu, HI, Oct. 13, 1962. USC.
Preston, William Columbia, PA, Aug. 26, 1921. Pennsylvania State U.
Price, Lonny New York, NY, Mar. 9, 1959. Juilliard.
Priestley, Jason Vancouver, BC, Canada, Aug, 28, 1969.
Primus, Barry New York, NY, Feb. 16, 1938. CCNY.
Prince (P. Rogers Nelson) Minneapolis, MN, June 7, 1958.
Principal, Victoria Fukuoka, Japan, Jan. 3, 1945. Dade, Jr. College.
Prinze, Freddie, Jr., Los Angeles, CA, March 8, 1976.
Prochnow, Jurgen Berlin, Germany, June 10, 1941.
Proval, David Brooklyn, NY, May 20, 1942.
Provine, Dorothy Deadwood, SD, Jan. 20, 1937. U Washington.
Pryce, Jonathan Wales, June 1, 1947, RADA.
Pucci, Lou Taylor Seaside Heights, NJ, July 27, 1985.
Pullman, Bill Delphi, NY, Dec. 17, 1954. SUNY/Oneonta, U Mass.
Purcell, Lee Cherry Point, NC, June 15, 1947. Stephens.
Purdom, Edmund Welwyn Garden City, England, Dec. 19, 1924. St. Ignatius College.
Pyle, Missi Houston, TX, Nov. 16, 1972.

Quaid, Dennis Houston, TX, Apr. 9, 1954.
Quaid, Randy Houston, TX, Oct. 1, 1950. U Houston.
Qualls, DJ (Donald Joseph) Nashville, TN, June 12, 1978.
Quinlan, Kathleen Mill Valley, CA, Nov. 19, 1954.
Quinn, Aidan Chicago, IL, Mar. 8, 1959.

Radcliffe, Daniel London, England, July 23, 1989.
Raffin, Deborah Los Angeles, CA, Mar. 13, 1953. Valley Col.
Ragsdale, William El Dorado, AK, Jan. 19, 1961. Hendrix Col.
Railsback, Steve Dallas, TX, Nov. 16, 1948.
Rainer, Luise Vienna, Austria, Jan. 12, 1910.
Ramis, Harold Chicago, IL, Nov. 21, 1944. Washington U.
Rampling, Charlotte Surmer, England, Feb. 5, 1946. U Madrid.
Rapaport, Michael New York, NY, March 20, 1970.
Rapp, Anthony Chicago, IL, Oct. 26, 1971.
Rasche, David St. Louis, MO, Aug. 7, 1944.
Rea, Stephen Belfast, Northern Ireland, Oct. 31, 1949.
Reason, Rex Berlin, Germany, Nov. 30, 1928. Pasadena Playhouse.
Reddy, Helen Melbourne, Australia, Oct. 25, 1942.
Redford, Robert Santa Monica, CA, Aug. 18, 1937. AADA.
Redgrave, Corin London, England, July 16, 1939.
Redgrave, Lynn London, England, Mar. 8, 1943.
Redgrave, Vanessa London, England, Jan. 30, 1937.
Redman, Joyce County Mayo, Ireland, Dec. 9, 1918. RADA.
Redmayne, Eddie London, Jan. 6, 1982.
Reed, Nikki W. Los Angeles, CA, May 17, 1988.
Reed, Pamela Tacoma, WA, Apr. 2, 1949.
Rees, Roger Aberystwyth, Wales, May 5, 1944.
Reese, Della Detroit, MI, July 6, 1932.
Reeves, Keanu Beiruit, Lebanon, Sept. 2, 1964.
Regehr, Duncan Lethbridge, Canada, Oct. 5, 1952.
Reid, Elliott New York, NY, Jan. 16, 1920.
Reid, Tara Wyckoff, NJ, Nov. 8, 1975.

Reid, Tim Norfolk, VA, Dec, 19, 1944.
Reilly, John C. Chicago, IL, May 24, 1965.
Reiner, Carl New York, NY, Mar. 20, 1922. Georgetown.
Reiner, Rob New York, NY, Mar. 6, 1947. UCLA.
Reinhold, Judge (Edward Ernest, Jr.) Wilmington, DE, May 21, 1957. NC
Reinking, Ann Seattle, WA, Nov. 10, 1949.
Reiser, Paul New York, NY, Mar. 30, 1957.
Remar, James Boston, MA, Dec. 31, 1953. Neighborhood Playhouse.
Reno, Jean (Juan Moreno) Casablanca, Morocco, July 30, 1948.
Reubens, Paul (Paul Reubenfeld) Peekskill, NY, Aug. 27, 1952.
Revill, Clive Wellington, NZ, Apr. 18, 1930.
Rey, Antonia Havana, Cuba, Oct. 12, 1927.
Reynolds, Burt Waycross, GA, Feb. 11, 1935. Florida State U.
Reynolds, Debbie (Mary Frances Reynolds) El Paso, TX, Apr. 1, 1932.
Reynolds, Ryan Vancouver, BC, Can, Oct. 23, 1976.
Rhames, Ving (Irving Rhames) New York, NY, May 12, 1959.
Rhoades, Barbara Poughkeepsie, NY, Mar. 23, 1947.
Rhodes, Cynthia Nashville, TN, Nov. 21, 1956.
Rhys, Paul Neath, Wales, Dec. 19, 1963.
Rhys-Davies, John Salisbury, England, May 5, 1944.
Rhys Meyers, Jonathan Cork, Ireland, July 27, 1977.
Ribisi, Giovanni Los Angeles, CA, Dec. 17, 1974.
Ricci, Christina Santa Monica, CA, Feb. 12, 1980.
Richard, Cliff (Harry Webb) India, Oct. 14, 1940.
Richards, Denise Downers Grove, IL, Feb. 17, 1972.
Richards, Michael Culver City, CA, July 14, 1949.
Richardson, Joely London, England, Jan. 9, 1965.
Richardson, Miranda Southport, England, Mar. 3, 1958.
Richardson, Natasha London, England, May 11, 1963.
Rickles, Don New York, NY, May 8, 1926. AADA.
Rickman, Alan Hammersmith, England, Feb. 21, 1946.
Riegert, Peter New York, NY, Apr. 11, 1947. U Buffalo.
Rifkin, Ron New York, NY, Oct. 31, 1939.
Rigg, Diana Doncaster, England, July 20, 1938. RADA.
Ringwald, Molly Rosewood, CA, Feb. 16, 1968.
Rivers, Joan (Molinsky) Brooklyn, NY, June 8, 1933.
Roache, Linus Manchester, England, Feb. 1, 1964.
Robards, Sam New York, NY, Dec. 16, 1963.
Robb, AnnaSophia Denver, CO, Dec. 8, 1993.
Robbins, Tim New York, NY, Oct. 16, 1958. UCLA.
Roberts, Dallas Houston, TX, May 10, 1970.
Roberts, Eric Biloxi, MS, Apr. 18, 1956. RADA.
Roberts, Julia Atlanta, GA, Oct. 28, 1967.
Roberts, Tanya (Leigh) Bronx, NY, Oct. 15, 1954.
Roberts, Tony New York, NY, Oct. 22, 1939. Northwestern.
Robertson, Cliff La Jolla, CA, Sept. 9, 1925. Antioch College.
Robertson, Dale Oklahoma City, OK, July 14, 1923.
Robinson, Chris West Palm Beach, FL, Nov. 5, 1938. LACC.
Robinson, Jay New York, NY, Apr. 14, 1930.
Robinson, Roger Seattle, WA, May 2, 1940. USC.
Rochefort, Jean Paris, France, Apr. 29, 1930.
Rochon, Lela Los Angeles, CA, Apr. 17, 1964.
Rock, Chris Brooklyn, NY, Feb. 7, 1966.
Rockwell, Sam Daly City, CA, Nov. 5, 1968.
Rodriguez, Freddy Chicago, IL, Jan. 17, 1975.
Rodriguez, Michelle Bexar County, TX, July 12, 1978.
Rogen, Seth Vancouver, BC, Canada, Apr. 14, 1982.
Rogers, Mimi Coral Gables, FL, Jan. 27, 1956.
Rogers, Wayne Birmingham, AL, Apr. 7, 1933. Princeton.
Romano, Ray Queens, NY, Dec. 21, 1957.

Romijn, Rebecca Berkeley, CA, Nov. 6, 1972.
Ronan, Saoirse New York, NY, Apr. 12, 1994.
Ronstadt, Linda Tucson, AZ, July 15, 1946.
Rooker, Michael Jasper, AL, Apr. 6, 1955.
Rooney, Mickey (Joe Yule, Jr.) Brooklyn, NY, Sept. 23, 1920.
Rose, Reva Chicago, IL, July 30, 1940. Goodman.
Ross, Diana Detroit, MI, Mar. 26, 1944.
Ross, Justin Brooklyn, NY, Dec. 15, 1954.
Ross, Katharine Hollywood, CA, Jan. 29, 1943. Santa Rosa College.
Rossellini, Isabella Rome, Italy, June 18, 1952.
Rossovich, Rick Palo Alto, CA, Aug. 28, 1957.
Rossum, Emmy New York, NY, Sept. 12, 1986.
Roth, Tim London, England, May 14, 1961.
Roundtree, Richard New Rochelle, NY, Sept. 7, 1942. Southern Il.
Rourke, Mickey (Philip Andre Rourke, Jr.) Schenectady, NY, Sept. 16, 1956.
Routh, Brandon Des Moines, IA, Oct. 9, 1979.
Rowe, Nicholas London, England, Nov. 22, 1966, Eton.
Rowlands, Gena Cambria, WI, June 19, 1934.
Rubin, Andrew New Bedford, MA, June 22, 1946. AADA.
Rubinek, Saul Fohrenwold, Germany, July 2, 1948.
Rubinstein, John Los Angeles, CA, Dec. 8, 1946. UCLA.
Ruck, Alan Cleveland, OH, July 1, 1960.
Rucker, Bo Tampa, FL, Aug. 17, 1948.
Rudd, Paul Boston, MA, May 15, 1940.
Rudd, Paul Passaic, NJ, Apr. 6, 1969.
Rudner, Rita Miami, FL, Sept. 17, 1955.
Ruehl, Mercedes Queens, NY, Feb. 28, 1948.
Ruffalo, Mark Kenosha, WI, Nov. 22, 1967.
Rule, Janice Cincinnati, OH, Aug. 15, 1931.
Rupert, Michael Denver, CO, Oct. 23, 1951. Pasadena Playhouse.
Rush, Barbara Denver, CO, Jan. 4, 1927. U California.
Rush, Geoffrey Toowoomba, Australia, July 6, 1951. U Queensland.
Russell, Jane Bemidji, MI, June 21, 1921. Max Reinhardt School.
Russell, Keri Fountain Valley, CA, Mar. 23, 1976.
Russell, Kurt Springfield, MA, Mar. 17, 1951.
Russell, Theresa (Paup) San Diego, CA, Mar. 20, 1957.
Russo, James New York, NY, Apr. 23, 1953.
Russo, Rene Burbank, CA, Feb. 17, 1954.
Rutherford, Ann Toronto, ON, Canada, Nov. 2, 1920.
Ryan, Amy Queens, NY, Nov. 30, 1969.
Ryan, Meg Fairfield, CT, Nov. 19, 1961. NYU.
Ryder, Winona (Horowitz) Winona, MN, Oct. 29, 1971.

Sacchi, Robert Bronx, NY, 1941. NYU.
Sägebrecht, Marianne Starnberg, Bavaria, Aug. 27, 1945.
Saint, Eva Marie Newark, NJ, July 4, 1924. Bowling Green State U.
Saint James, Susan (Suzie Jane Miller) Los Angeles, CA, Aug. 14, 1946. Conn. College.
St. John, Betta Hawthorne, CA, Nov. 26, 1929.
St. John, Jill (Jill Oppenheim) Los Angeles, CA, Aug. 19, 1940.
Sala, John Los Angeles, CA, Oct. 5, 1962.
Saldana, Theresa Brooklyn, NY, Aug. 20, 1954.
Salinger, Matt Windsor, VT, Feb. 13, 1960. Princeton, Columbia.
Salt, Jennifer Los Angeles, CA, Sept. 4, 1944. Sarah Lawrence College.
Samms, Emma London, England, Aug. 28, 1960.
San Giacomo, Laura Orange, NJ, Nov. 14, 1961.
Sanders, Jay O. Austin, TX, Apr. 16, 1953.
Sandler, Adam Bronx, NY, Sept. 9, 1966. NYU.
Sands, Julian Yorkshire, England, Jan 15, 1958.
Sands, Tommy Chicago, IL, Aug. 27, 1937.

San Juan, Olga New York, NY, Mar. 16, 1927.
Sara, Mia (Sarapocciello) Brooklyn, NY, June 19, 1967.
Sarandon, Chris Beckley, WV, July 24, 1942. U West Virginia., Catholic U.
Sarandon, Susan (Tomalin) New York, NY, Oct. 4, 1946. Catholic U.
Sarrazin, Michael Quebec City, Canada, May 22, 1940.
Sarsgaard, Peter Scott Air Force Base, Illinois, Mar. 7, 1971. Washington U St. Louis
Savage, Fred Highland Park, IL, July 9, 1976.
Savage, John (Youngs) Long Island, NY, Aug. 25, 1949. AADA.
Saviola, Camille Bronx, NY, July 16, 1950.
Savoy, Teresa Ann London, England, July 18, 1955.
Sawa, Devon Vancouver, BC, Canada, Sept. 7, 1978.
Saxon, John (Carmen Orrico) Brooklyn, NY, Aug. 5, 1935.
Sbarge, Raphael New York, NY, Feb. 12, 1964.
Scacchi, Greta Milan, Italy, Feb. 18, 1960.
Scalia, Jack Brooklyn, NY, Nov. 10, 1951.
Scarwid, Diana Savannah, GA, Aug. 27, 1955, AADA. Pace U.
Schell, Maximilian Vienna, Austria, Dec. 8, 1930.
Schlatter, Charlie Englewood, NJ, May 1, 1966. Ithaca College.
Schneider, John Mt. Kisco, NY, Apr. 8, 1960.
Schneider, Maria Paris, France, Mar. 27, 1952.
Schneider, Paul Asheville, NC, Mar. 16, 1976.
Schreiber, Liev San Francisco, CA, Oct. 4, 1967.
Schroder, Rick Staten Island, NY, Apr. 13, 1970.
Schuck, John Boston, MA, Feb. 4, 1940.
Schultz, Dwight Baltimore, MD, Nov. 24, 1947.
Schwartzman, Jason Los Angeles, CA, June 26, 1980.
Schwarzenegger, Arnold Austria, July 30, 1947.
Schwimmer, David Queens, NY, Nov. 12, 1966.
Schygulla, Hanna Katlowitz, Germany, Dec. 25, 1943.
Sciorra, Annabella New York, NY, Mar. 24, 1964.
Scoggins, Tracy Galveston, TX, Nov. 13, 1959.
Scolari, Peter Scarsdale, NY, Sept. 12, 1956. New York, NYC.
Scott, Campbell South Salem, NY, July 19, 1962. Lawrence.
Scott, Debralee Elizabeth, NJ, Apr. 2, 1953.
Scott, Lizabeth (Emma Matso) Scranton, PA, Sept. 29, 1922.
Scott, Seann William Cottage Grove, MN, Oct. 3, 1976.
Scott Thomas, Kristin Redruth, Cornwall, England, May 24, 1960.
Seagal, Steven Detroit, MI, Apr. 10, 1951.
Sears, Heather London, England, Sept. 28, 1935.
Sedgwick, Kyra New York, NY, Aug. 19, 1965. USC.
Segal, George New York, NY, Feb. 13, 1934. Columbia U.
Segel, Jason Los Angeles, Jan. 18, 1980.
Seinfeld, Jerry Brooklyn, NY, Apr. 29, 1954.
Selby, David Morganstown, WV, Feb. 5, 1941. U West Virginia.
Sellars, Elizabeth Glasgow, Scotland, May 6, 1923.
Selleck, Tom Detroit, MI, Jan. 29, 1945. USC.
Sernas, Jacques Lithuania, July 30, 1925.
Seth, Roshan New Delhi, India, Aug. 17, 1942.
Sevigny, Chloë Springfield, MA, Nov. 18, 1974.
Sewell, Rufus Twickenham, England, Oct. 29, 1967.
Seyfried, Amanda Allentown, PA, Dec. 3, 1985.
Seymour, Jane (Joyce Frankenberg) Hillingdon, England, Feb. 15, 1952.
Shalhoub, Tony Green Bay, WI, Oct. 9, 1953.
Shandling, Garry Chicago, IL, Nov. 29, 1949.
Shannon, Michael Lexington, KY, Aug. 7, 1974.
Shannon, Molly Shaker Heights, OH, Sept. 16, 1964.
Sharif, Omar (Michel Shalhoub) Alexandria, Egypt, Apr. 10, 1932. Victoria College.
Shatner, William Montreal, Quebec, Canada, Mar. 22, 1931. McGill U.

Shaver, Helen St. Thomas, ON, Canada, Feb. 24, 1951.
Shaw, Fiona Cork, Ireland, July 10, 1955. RADA.
Shaw, Stan Chicago, IL, July 14, 1952.
Shawn, Wallace New York, NY, Nov. 12, 1943. Harvard.
Shea, John North Conway, NH, Apr. 14, 1949. Bates, Yale.
Shearer, Harry Los Angeles, CA, Dec. 23, 1943. UCLA.
Sheedy, Ally New York, NY, June 13, 1962. USC.
Sheen, Charlie (Carlos Irwin Estevez) Santa Monica, CA, Sept. 3, 1965.
Sheen, Martin (Ramon Estevez) Dayton, OH, Aug. 3, 1940.
Sheen, Michael Newport, Wales, Feb. 5, 1969.
Sheffer, Craig York, PA, Apr. 23, 1960. E. Stroudsberg U.
Sheffield, John Pasadena, CA, Apr. 11, 1931. UCLA.
Shelley, Carol London, England, Aug. 16, 1939.
Shelton, Marley Los Angeles, CA, Apr. 12, 1974.
Shepard, Dax Milford, MI, Jan. 2, 1975.
Shepard, Sam (Rogers) Ft. Sheridan, IL, Nov. 5, 1943.
Shepherd, Cybill Memphis, TN, Feb. 18, 1950. Hunter, NYU.
Sher, Antony Cape Town, South Africa, June 14, 1949.
Sherbedgia, Rade Korenica, Croatia, July 27, 1946.
Sheridan, Jamey Pasadena, CA, July 12, 1951.
Shields, Brooke New York, NY, May 31, 1965.
Shire, Talia Lake Success, NY, Apr. 25, 1946. Yale.
Short, Martin Toronto, ON, Canada, Mar. 26, 1950. McMaster U.
Shue, Elisabeth S. Orange, NJ, Oct. 6, 1963. Harvard.
Siemaszko, Casey Chicago, IL, March 17, 1961.
Sikking, James B. Los Angeles, CA, Mar. 5, 1934.
Silva, Henry Brooklyn, NY, Sept. 15, 1928.
Silver, Ron New York, NY, July 2, 1946. SUNY.
Silverman, Jonathan Los Angeles, CA, Aug. 5, 1966. USC.
Silverman, Sarah Bedford, NH, Dec. 1, 1970.
Silverstone, Alicia San Francisco, CA, Oct. 4, 1976.
Silverstone, Ben London, England, Apr. 9, 1979.
Simmons, J.K. (Jonathan Kimble) Detroit, MI, Jan. 9, 1955. Univ MT.
Simmons, Jean London, England, Jan. 31, 1929. Aida Foster School.
Simon, Paul Newark, NJ, Nov. 5, 1942.
Simpson, O.J. (Orenthal James) San Francisco, CA, July 9, 1947. UCLA.
Sinbad (David Adkins) Benton Harbor, MI, Nov. 10, 1956.
Sinden, Donald Plymouth, England, Oct. 9, 1923. Webber-Douglas.
Singer, Lori Corpus Christi, TX, May 6, 1962. Juilliard.
Sinise, Gary Chicago, IL, Mar. 17, 1955.
Sizemore, Tom Detroit, MI, Sept. 29, 1964.
Skarsgård, Stellan Gothenburg, Sweden, June 13, 1951.
Skerritt, Tom Detroit, MI, Aug. 25, 1933. Wayne State U.
Skye, Ione (Leitch) London, England, Sept. 4, 1971.
Slater, Christian New York, NY, Aug. 18, 1969.
Slater, Helen New York, NY, Dec. 15, 1965.
Slattery, John Boston, MA, Aug. 13, 1963.
Smart, Amy Topanga Canyon, CA, Mar. 26, 1976.
Smith, Charles Martin Los Angeles, CA, Oct. 30, 1953. Cal State U.
Smith, Jaclyn Houston, TX, Oct. 26, 1947.
Smith, Jada Pinkett Baltimore, MD, Sept. 18, 1971.
Smith, Kerr Exton, PA, Mar. 9, 1972.
Smith, Kevin Red Bank, NJ, Aug. 2, 1970.
Smith, Kurtwood New Lisbon, WI, July 3, 1942.
Smith, Lewis Chattanooga, TN, 1958. Actors Studio.
Smith, Lois Topeka, KS, Nov. 3, 1930. U Washington.
Smith, Maggie Ilford, England, Dec. 28, 1934.
Smith, Roger South Gate, CA, Dec. 18, 1932. U Arizona.
Smith, Will Philadelphia, PA, Sept. 25, 1968.
Smithers, William Richmond, VA, July 10, 1927. Catholic U.

Smits, Jimmy Brooklyn, NY, July 9, 1955. Cornell U.
Smollett, Jurnee New York, NY, Oct. 1, 1986.
Snipes, Wesley New York, NY, July 31, 1963. SUNY/Purchase.
Snoop Dogg (Calvin Broadus) Long Beach, CA, Oct. 20, 1971.
Snow, Brittany Tampa, FL, Mar. 9, 1986.
Sobieksi, Leelee (Liliane Sobieski) New York, NY, June 10, 1982.
Solomon, Bruce New York, NY, Aug. 12, 1944. U Miami, Wayne State U.
Somerhalder, Ian Covington, LA, Dec. 8, 1978.
Somers, Suzanne (Mahoney) San Bruno, CA, Oct. 16, 1946.
   Lone Mt. College.
Sommer, Elke (Schletz) Berlin, Germany, Nov. 5, 1940.
Sommer, Josef Greifswald, Germany, June 26, 1934.
Sorvino, Mira Tenafly, NJ, Sept. 28, 1967.
Sorvino, Paul New York, NY, Apr. 13, 1939. AMDA.
Soto, Talisa (Miriam Soto) Brooklyn, NY, Mar. 27, 1967.
Soul, David Chicago, IL, Aug. 28, 1943.
Spacek, Sissy Quitman, TX, Dec. 25, 1949. Actors Studio.
Spacey, Kevin So. Orange, NJ, July 26, 1959. Juilliard.
Spade, David Birmingham, MS, July 22, 1964.
Spader, James Buzzards Bay, MA, Feb. 7, 1960.
Spall, Timothy London, England, Feb. 27, 1957.
Spano, Vincent Brooklyn, NY, Oct. 18, 1962.
Spenser, Jeremy London, England, July 16, 1937.
Spinella, Stephen Naples, Italy, Oct. 11, 1956. NYU.
Springfield, Rick (Richard Spring Thorpe) Sydney, Australia, Aug. 23, 1949.
Stadlen, Lewis J. Brooklyn, NY, Mar. 7, 1947. Neighborhood Playhouse.
Stahl, Nick Dallas, TX, Dec. 5, 1979.
Stallone, Frank New York, NY, July 30, 1950.
Stallone, Sylvester New York, NY, July 6, 1946. U Miami.
Stamp, Terence London, England, July 23, 1939.
Stanford, Aaron Westford, MA, Dec. 18, 1977.
Stang, Arnold Chelsea, MA, Sept. 28, 1925.
Stanton, Harry Dean Lexington, KY, July 14, 1926.
Stapleton, Jean New York, NY, Jan. 19, 1923.
Starr, Ringo (Richard Starkey) Liverpool, England, July 7, 1940.
Statham, Jason London, England, Sept. 12, 1972.
Staunton, Imelda London, England, Jan. 9, 1956.
Steele, Barbara England, Dec. 29, 1937.
Steele, Tommy London, England, Dec. 17, 1936.
Steenburgen, Mary Newport, AR, Feb. 8, 1953. Neighborhood Playhouse.
Stern, Daniel Bethesda, MD, Aug. 28, 1957.
Sternhagen, Frances Washington, DC, Jan. 13, 1932.
Stevens, Andrew Memphis, TN, June 10, 1955.
Stevens, Connie (Concetta Ann Ingolia) Brooklyn, NY, Aug. 8, 1938.
   Hollywood Professional School.
Stevens, Fisher Chicago, IL, Nov. 27, 1963. NYU.
Stevens, Stella (Estelle Eggleston) Hot Coffee, MS, Oct. 1, 1936.
Stevenson, Juliet Essex, England, Oct. 30, 1956.
Stevenson, Parker Philadelphia, PA, June 4, 1953. Princeton.
Stewart, Alexandra Montreal, Quebec, Canada, June 10, 1939. Louvre.
Stewart, Elaine (Elsy Steinberg) Montclair, NJ, May 31, 1929.
Stewart, French (Milton French Stewart) Albuquerque, NM, Feb. 20, 1964.
Stewart, Jon (Jonathan Stewart Liebowitz) Trenton, NJ, Nov. 28, 1962.
Stewart, Kristen Los Angeles, CA, Apr. 9, 1990.
Stewart, Martha (Martha Haworth) Bardwell, KY, Oct. 7, 1922.
Stewart, Patrick Mirfield, England, July 13, 1940.
Stiers, David Ogden Peoria, IL, Oct. 31, 1942.
Stiles, Julia New York, NY, Mar. 28, 1981.
Stiller, Ben New York, NY, Nov. 30, 1965.
Stiller, Jerry New York, NY, June 8, 1931.

Sting (Gordon Matthew Sumner) Wallsend, England, Oct. 2, 1951.
Stockwell, Dean Hollywood, CA, Mar. 5, 1935.
Stockwell, John (John Samuels, IV) Galveston, TX, Mar. 25, 1961. Harvard.
Stoltz, Eric Whittier, CA, Sept. 30, 1961. USC.
Stone, Dee Wallace (Deanna Bowers) Kansas City, MO, Dec. 14, 1948. UKS.
Storm, Gale (Josephine Cottle) Bloomington, TX, Apr. 5, 1922.
Stowe, Madeleine Eagle Rock, CA, Aug. 18, 1958.
Strassman, Marcia New York, NY, Apr. 28, 1948.
Strathairn, David San Francisco, CA, Jan. 26, 1949.Williams Col.
Strauss, Peter New York, NY, Feb. 20, 1947.
Streep, Meryl (Mary Louise) Summit, NJ, June 22, 1949 Vassar, Yale.
Streisand, Barbra Brooklyn, NY, Apr. 24, 1942.
Stritch, Elaine Detroit, MI, Feb. 2, 1925. Drama Workshop.
Stroud, Don Honolulu, HI, Sept. 1, 1937.
Struthers, Sally Portland, OR, July 28, 1948. Pasadena Playhouse.
Studi, Wes (Wesley Studie) Nofire Hollow, OK, Dec. 17, 1947.
Summer, Donna (LaDonna Gaines) Boston, MA, Dec. 31, 1948.
Sumpter, Jeremy Monterey, CA, Feb. 5, 1989.
Sutherland, Donald St. John, New Brunswick, Canada, July 17, 1935.
   U Toronto.
Sutherland, Kiefer Los Angeles, CA, Dec. 18, 1966.
Suvari, Mena Newport, RI, Feb. 9, 1979.
Svenson, Bo Goreborg, Sweden, Feb. 13, 1941. UCLA.
Swank, Hilary Bellingham, WA, July 30, 1974.
Swayze, Patrick Houston, TX, Aug. 18, 1952.
Sweeney, D. B. (Daniel Bernard Sweeney) Shoreham, NY, Nov. 14, 1961.
Swinton, Tilda London, England, Nov. 5, 1960.
Swit, Loretta Passaic, NJ, Nov. 4, 1937, AADA.
Sykes, Wanda Portsmouth, VA, Mar. 7, 1964.
Symonds, Robert Bistow, AK, Dec. 1, 1926. Texas U.
Syms, Sylvia London, England, June 1, 1934. Convent School.
Szarabajka, Keith Oak Park, IL, Dec. 2, 1952. U Chicago.

T, Mr. (Lawrence Tero) Chicago, IL, May 21, 1952.
Tabori, Kristoffer (Siegel) Los Angeles, CA, Aug. 4, 1952.
Takei, George Los Angeles, CA, Apr. 20, 1939. UCLA.
Talbot, Nita New York, NY, Aug. 8, 1930. Irvine Studio School.
Tamblyn, Amber Santa Monica, CA, May 14, 1983.
Tamblyn, Russ Los Angeles, CA, Dec. 30, 1934.
Tambor, Jeffrey San Francisco, CA, July 8, 1944.
Tarantino, Quentin Knoxville, TN, Mar. 27, 1963.
Tate, Larenz Chicago, IL, Sept. 8, 1975.
Tautou, Audrey Beaumont, France, Aug. 9, 1978.
Taylor, Elizabeth London, England, Feb. 27, 1932. Byron House School.
Taylor, Lili Glencoe, IL, Feb. 20, 1967.
Taylor, Noah London, England, Sept. 4, 1969.
Taylor, Renée New York, NY, Mar. 19, 1935.
Taylor, Rod (Robert) Sydney, Australia, Jan. 11, 1929.
Taylor-Young, Leigh Washington, DC, Jan. 25, 1945. Northwestern.
Teefy, Maureen Minneapolis, MN, Oct. 26, 1953, Juilliard.
Temple, Shirley Santa Monica, CA, Apr. 23, 1927.
Tennant, Victoria London, England, Sept. 30, 1950.
Tenney, Jon Princeton, NJ, Dec. 16, 1961.
Terzieff, Laurent Paris, France, June 25, 1935.
Tewes, Lauren Braddock, PA, Oct. 26, 1954.
Thacker, Russ Washington, DC, June 23, 1946. Montgomery College.
Thaxter, Phyllis Portland, ME, Nov. 20, 1921. St. Genevieve.
Thelen, Jodi St. Cloud, MN, June 12, 1962.
Theron, Charlize Benoni, South Africa, Aug. 7, 1975.
Thewlis, David Blackpool, England, Mar. 20, 1963.

Thierot, Max Los Altos Hills, CA, Oct. 14, 1988.
Thomas, Henry San Antonio, TX, Sept. 8, 1971.
Thomas, Jay New Orleans, LA, July 12, 1948.
Thomas, Jonathan Taylor (Weiss) Bethlehem, PA, Sept. 8, 1981.
Thomas, Marlo (Margaret) Detroit, MI, Nov. 21, 1937. USC.
Thomas, Philip Michael Columbus, OH, May 26, 1949. Oakwood College.
Thomas, Richard New York, NY, June 13, 1951. Columbia.
Thompson, Emma London, England, Apr. 15, 1959. Cambridge.
Thompson, Fred Dalton Sheffield, AL, Aug. 19, 1942.
Thompson, Jack (John Payne) Sydney, Australia, Aug. 31, 1940.
Thompson, Lea Rochester, MN, May 31, 1961.
Thompson, Rex New York, NY, Dec. 14, 1942.
Thompson, Sada Des Moines, IA, Sept. 27, 1929. Carnegie Tech.
Thornton, Billy Bob Hot Spring, AR, Aug. 4, 1955.
Thorson, Linda Toronto, ON, Canada, June 18, 1947. RADA.
Thurman, Uma Boston, MA, Apr. 29, 1970.
Ticotin, Rachel Bronx, NY, Nov. 1, 1958.
Tierney, Maura Boston, MA, Feb. 3, 1965.
Tiffin, Pamela (Wonso) Oklahoma City, OK, Oct. 13, 1942.
Tighe, Kevin Los Angeles, CA, Aug. 13, 1944.
Tilly, Jennifer Los Angeles, CA, Sept. 16, 1958.
Tilly, Meg Texada, Canada, Feb. 14, 1960.
Timberlake, Justin Memphis, TN, Jan. 31, 1981.
Tobolowsky, Stephen Dallas, TX, May 30, 1951. Southern Methodist U.
Todd, Beverly Chicago, IL, July 1, 1946.
Todd, Richard Dublin, Ireland, June 11, 1919. Shrewsbury School.
Todd, Tony Washington, DC, Dec. 4, 1954.
Tolkan, James Calumet, MI, June 20, 1931.
Tomei, Marisa Brooklyn, NY, Dec. 4, 1964. NYU.
Tomlin, Lily Detroit, MI, Sept. 1, 1939. Wayne State U.
Topol (Chaim Topol) Tel Aviv, Israel, Sept. 9, 1935.
Torn, Rip Temple, TX, Feb. 6, 1931. U Texas.
Torres, Liz New York, NY, Sept. 27, 1947. NYU.
Totter, Audrey Joliet, IL, Dec. 20, 1918.
Towsend, Robert Chicago, IL, Feb. 6, 1957.
Townsend, Stuart Dublin, Ireland, Dec. 15, 1972.
Trachtenberg, Michelle New York, NY, Oct. 11, 1985.
Travanti, Daniel J. Kenosha, WI, Mar. 7, 1940.
Travis, Nancy Astoria, NY, Sept. 21, 1961.
Travolta, Joey Englewood, NJ, Oct. 14, 1950.
Travolta, John Englewood, NJ, Feb. 18, 1954.
Trejo, Danny Los Angeles, CA, May 16, 1944.
Trintignant, Jean-Louis Pont-St. Esprit, France, Dec. 11, 1930. DullinBalachova Drama School.
Tripplehorn, Jeanne Tulsa, OK, June 10, 1963.
Tsopei, Corinna Athens, Greece, June 21, 1944.
Tubb, Barry Snyder, TX, 1963. Am Consv Th.
Tucci, Stanley Katonah, NY, Jan. 11, 1960.
Tucker, Chris Decatur, GA, Aug. 31, 1972.
Tucker, Jonathan Boston, MA, May 31, 1982.
Tucker, Michael Baltimore, MD, Feb. 6, 1944.
Tudyk, Alan El Paso, TX, March 16, 1971.
Tune, Tommy Wichita Falls, TX, Feb. 28, 1939.
Tunney, Robin Chicago, IL, June 19, 1972.
Turner, Janine (Gauntt) Lincoln, NE, Dec. 6, 1963.
Turner, Kathleen Springfield, MO, June 19, 1954. U Maryland.
Turner, Tina (Anna Mae Bullock) Nutbush, TN, Nov. 26, 1938.
Turturro, John Brooklyn, NY, Feb. 28, 1957. Yale.
Tushingham, Rita Liverpool, England, Mar. 14, 1940.
Twiggy (Lesley Hornby) London, England, Sept. 19, 1949.

Twomey, Anne Boston, MA, June 7, 1951. Temple U.
Tyler, Liv Portland, ME, July 1, 1977.
Tyrrell, Susan San Francisco, CA, Mar. 18, 1945.
Tyson, Cathy Liverpool, England, June 12, 1965. Royal Shake. Co.
Tyson, Cicely New York, NY, Dec. 19, 1933. NYU.

Uggams, Leslie New York, NY, May 25, 1943. Juilliard.
Ulliel, Gaspard Boulogne-Billancourt, France, Nov. 25, 1984.
Ullman, Tracey Slough, England, Dec. 30, 1959.
Ullmann, Liv Tokyo, Japan, Dec. 10, 1938. Webber-Douglas Acad.
Ulrich, Skeet (Bryan Ray Ulrich) North Carolina, Jan. 20, 1969.
Underwood, Blair Tacoma, WA, Aug. 25, 1964. Carnegie-Mellon U.
Unger, Deborah Kara Victoria, BC, Canada, May 12, 1966.
Union, Gabrielle Omaha, NE, Oct. 29, 1973.

Vaccaro, Brenda Brooklyn, NY, Nov. 18, 1939. Neighborhood Playhouse.
Van Ark, Joan New York, NY, June 16, 1943. Yale.
Van Damme, Jean-Claude (J-C Vorenberg) Brussels, Belgium, Apr. 1, 1960.
Van De Ven, Monique Zeeland, Netherlands, July 28, 1952.
Van Der Beek, James Chesire, CT, March 8, 1977.
Van Devere, Trish (Patricia Dressel) Englewood Cliffs, NJ, Mar. 9, 1945. Ohio Wesleyan.
Van Dien, Casper Ridgefield, NJ, Dec. 18, 1968.
Van Doren, Mamie (Joan Lucile Olander) Rowena, SD, Feb. 6, 1933.
Van Dyke, Dick West Plains, MO, Dec. 13, 1925.
Van Houten, Clarice Leiderdorp, Netherlands, Sept. 5, 1976.
Vanity (Denise Katrina Smith) Niagara, ON, Can, Jan. 4, 1959.
Van Pallandt, Nina Copenhagen, Denmark, July 15, 1932.
Van Patten, Dick New York, NY, Dec. 9, 1928.
Van Patten, Joyce New York, NY, Mar. 9, 1934.
Van Peebles, Mario New York, NY, Jan. 15, 1958. Columbia U.
Van Peebles, Melvin Chicago, IL, Aug. 21, 1932.
Vance, Courtney B. Detroit, MI, Mar. 12, 1960.
Vardalos, Nia Winnipeg, Manitoba, Canada, Sept. 24, 1962.
Vartan, Michael Boulogne-Billancourt, France, Nov. 27, 1968.
Vaughn, Robert New York, NY, Nov. 22, 1932. USC.
Vaughn, Vince Minneapolis, MN, Mar. 28, 1970.
Vega, Isela Hermosillo, Mexico, Nov. 5, 1940.
Veljohnson, Reginald New York, NY, Aug. 16, 1952.
Vennera, Chick Herkimer, NY, Mar. 27, 1952. Pasadena Playhouse.
Venora, Diane Hartford, CT, Aug. 10, 1952. Juilliard.
Vereen, Ben Miami, FL, Oct. 10, 1946.
Victor, James (Lincoln Rafael Peralta Diaz) Santiago, D.R., July 27, 1939. Haaren HS/New York, NY.
Vincent, Jan-Michael Denver, CO, July 15, 1944. Ventura.
Violet, Ultra (Isabelle Collin-Dufresne) Grenoble, France, Sept. 6, 1935.
Visnjic, Goran Sibenik, Yugoslavia, Sept. 9, 1972. .
Voight, Jon Yonkers, NY, Dec. 29, 1938. Catholic U.
Von Bargen, Daniel Cincinnati, OH, June 5, 1950. Purdue.
Von Dohlen, Lenny Augusta, GA, Dec. 22, 1958. U Texas.
Von Sydow, Max Lund, Sweden, July 10, 1929. Royal Drama Theatre.

Wagner, Lindsay Los Angeles, CA, June 22. 1949.
Wagner, Natasha Gregson Los Angeles, CA, Sept. 29, 1970.
Wagner, Robert Detroit, MI, Feb. 10, 1930.
Wahl, Ken Chicago, IL, Feb. 14, 1953.
Waite, Genevieve Cape Town, South Africa, Feb. 19, 1948.
Waite, Ralph White Plains, NY, June 22, 1929. Yale.
Waits, Tom Pomona, CA, Dec. 7, 1949.

Walken, Christopher Astoria, NY, Mar. 31, 1943. Hofstra.
Walker, Clint Hartfold, IL, May 30, 1927. USC.
Walker, Paul Glendale, CA, Sept. 12, 1973.
Wallach, Eli Brooklyn, NY, Dec. 7, 1915. CCNY, U Texas.
Wallach, Roberta New York, NY, Aug. 2, 1955.
Wallis, Shani London, England, Apr. 5, 1941.
Walsh, Dylan Los Angeles, CA, Nov. 17, 1963.
Walsh, M. Emmet Ogdensburg, NY, Mar. 22, 1935. Clarkson College, AADA.
Walter, Jessica Brooklyn, NY, Jan. 31, 1944 Neighborhood Playhouse.
Walter, Tracey Jersey City, NJ, Nov. 25, 1942.
Walters, Julie London, England, Feb. 22, 1950.
Walton, Emma London, England, Nov. 1962. Brown U.
Wanamaker, Zoë New York, NY, May 13, 1949.
Ward, Burt (Gervis) Los Angeles, CA, July 6, 1945.
Ward, Fred San Diego, CA, Dec. 30, 1942.
Ward, Rachel London, England, Sept. 12, 1957.
Ward, Sela Meridian, MS, July 11, 1956.
Ward, Simon London, England, Oct. 19, 1941.
Warner, David Manchester, England, July 29, 1941. RADA.
Warner, Malcolm-Jamal Jersey City, NJ, Aug. 18, 1970.
Warren, Jennifer New York, NY, Aug. 12, 1941. U Wisc.
Warren, Lesley Ann New York, NY, Aug. 16, 1946.
Warren, Michael South Bend, IN, Mar. 5, 1946. UCLA.
Washington, Denzel Mt. Vernon, NY, Dec. 28, 1954. Fordham.
Washington, Kerry Bronx, NY, Jan. 31, 1977.
Wasson, Craig Ontario, OR, Mar. 15, 1954. U Oregon.
Watanabe, Ken Koide, Japan, Oct. 21, 1959.
Waterston, Sam Cambridge, MA, Nov. 15, 1940. Yale.
Watson, Emily London, England, Jan. 14, 1967.
Watson, Emma Oxford, England, Apr. 15, 1990.
Watts, Naomi Shoreham, England, Sept. 28, 1968.
Wayans, Damon New York, NY, Sept. 4, 1960.
Wayans, Keenen Ivory New York, NY, June 8, 1958. Tuskegee Inst.
Wayans, Marlon New York, NY, July 23, 1972.
Wayans, Shawn New York, NY, Jan. 19, 1971.
Wayne, Patrick Los Angeles, CA, July 15, 1939. Loyola.
Weathers, Carl New Orleans, LA, Jan. 14, 1948. Long Beach CC.
Weaver, Fritz Pittsburgh, PA, Jan. 19, 1926.
Weaver, Sigourney (Susan) New York, NY, Oct. 8, 1949. Stanford, Yale.
Weaving, Hugo Austin, Nigeria, Apr. 4, 1960. NIDA.
Webber, Mark Minneapolis, MN, July 19, 1980.
Weber, Steven Queens, NY, March 4, 1961.
Wedgeworth, Ann Abilene, TX, Jan. 21, 1935. U Texas.
Weisz, Rachel London, England, Mar. 7, 1971. Cambridge.
Welch, Raquel (Tejada) Chicago, IL, Sept. 5, 1940.
Weld, Tuesday (Susan) New York, NY, Aug. 27, 1943.
    Hollywood Professional School.
Weldon, Joan San Francisco, CA, Aug. 5, 1933. San Francisco Conservatory.
Weller, Peter Stevens Point, WI, June 24, 1947. Am. Th. Wing.
Welling, Tom New York, NY, Apr. 26, 1977.
Wendt, George Chicago, IL, Oct. 17, 1948.
West, Adam (William Anderson) Walla Walla, WA, Sept. 19, 1929.
West, Dominic Sheffield, England, Oct. 15, 1969.
West, Shane Baton Rouge, LA, June 10, 1978.
Westfeldt, Jennifer Guilford, CT, Feb. 2, 1971.
Wettig, Patricia Cincinatti, OH, Dec. 4, 1951. Temple U.
Whaley, Frank Syracuse, NY, July 20, 1963. SUNY/Albany.
Whalley-Kilmer, Joanne Manchester, England, Aug. 25, 1964.
Wheaton, Wil Burbank, CA, July 29, 1972.
Whishaw, Ben Clifton, England, Oct. 14, 1980.

Whitaker, Denzel Torrance, CA, June 15, 1990.
Whitaker, Forest Longview, TX, July 15, 1961.
Whitaker, Johnny Van Nuys, CA, Dec. 13, 1959.
White, Betty Oak Park, IL, Jan. 17, 1922.
White, Charles Perth Amboy, NJ, Aug. 29, 1920. Rutgers U.
White, Julie San Diego, CA, June 4, 1961.
Whitelaw, Billie Coventry, England, June 6, 1932.
Whitman, Stuart San Francisco, CA, Feb. 1, 1929. CCLA.
Whitmore, James White Plains, NY, Oct. 1, 1921. Yale.
Whitney, Grace Lee Detroit, MI, Apr. 1, 1930.
Whitton, Margaret Philadelphia, PA, Nov. 30, 1950.
Widdoes, Kathleen Wilmington, DE, Mar. 21, 1939.
Wiest, Dianne Kansas City, MO, Mar. 28, 1948. U Maryland.
Wilby, James Burma, Feb. 20, 1958.
Wilcox, Colin Highlands, NC, Feb. 4, 1937. U Tennessee.
Wilder, Gene (Jerome Silberman) Milwaukee, WI, June 11, 1935. U Iowa.
Wilkinson, Tom Leeds, England, Dec. 12, 1948. U Kentucky.
Willard, Fred Shaker Heights, OH, Sept. 18, 1939.
Williams, Billy Dee New York, NY, Apr. 6, 1937.
Williams, Cara (Bernice Kamiat) Brooklyn, NY, June 29, 1925.
Williams, Cindy Van Nuys, CA, Aug. 22, 1947. KACC.
Williams, Clarence, III New York, NY, Aug. 21, 1939.
Williams, Esther Los Angeles, CA, Aug. 8, 1921.
Williams, Jobeth Houston, TX, Dec 6, 1948. Brown U.
Williams, Michelle Kalispell, MT, Sept. 9, 1980.
Williams, Olivia London, England, Jan. 1, 1968.
Williams, Paul Omaha, NE, Sept. 19, 1940.
Williams, Robin Chicago, IL, July 21, 1951. Juilliard.
Williams, Treat (Richard) Rowayton, CT, Dec. 1, 1951.
Williams, Vanessa Tarrytown, NY, Mar. 18, 1963.
Williamson, Fred Gary, IN, Mar. 5, 1938. Northwestern.
Williamson, Nicol Hamilton, Scotland, Sept. 14, 1938.
Willis, Bruce Penns Grove, NJ, Mar. 19, 1955.
Willison, Walter Monterey Park, CA, June 24, 1947.
Wilson, Demond New York, NY, Oct. 13, 1946. Hunter College.
Wilson, Elizabeth Grand Rapids, MI, Apr. 4, 1925.
Wilson, Lambert Neuilly-sur-Seine, France, Aug. 3, 1958.
Wilson, Luke Dallas, TX, Sept. 21, 1971.
Wilson, Owen Dallas, TX, Nov. 18, 1968.
Wilson, Patrick Norfolk, VA, July 3, 1973.
Wilson, Rainn Seattle, WA, Jan. 20, 1966.
Wilson, Scott Atlanta, GA, Mar. 29, 1942.
Wilson, Stuart Guildford, England, Dec. 25, 1946.
Wincott, Jeff Toronto, ON, Canada, May 8, 1957.
Wincott, Michael Toronto, ON, Canada, Jan. 6, 1959. Juilliard.
Windom, William New York, NY, Sept. 28, 1923. Williams College.
Winfrey, Oprah Kosciusko, MS, Jan. 29, 1954. Tennessee State U.
Winger, Debra Cleveland, OH, May 17, 1955. Cal State.
Winkler, Henry New York, NY, Oct. 30, 1945. Yale.
Winn, Kitty Washington, DC, Feb, 21, 1944. Boston U.
Winningham, Mare Phoenix, AZ, May 6, 1959.
Winslet, Kate Reading, England, Oct. 5, 1975.
Winslow, Michael Spokane, WA, Sept. 6, 1960.
Winstone, Ray London, England, Feb. 19, 1957.
Winter, Alex London, England, July 17, 1965. NYU.
Winters, Jonathan Dayton, OH, Nov. 11, 1925. Kenyon College.
Withers, Googie Karachi, India, Mar. 12, 1917. Italia Conti.
Withers, Jane Atlanta, GA, Apr. 12, 1926.
Witherspoon, Reese (Laura Jean Reese Witherspoon) Nashville, TN,
    Mar. 22, 1976.

Wolf, Scott Newton, MA, June 4, 1968.
Wong, B.D. San Francisco, CA, Oct. 24,1962.
Wong, Russell Troy, NY, Mar. 1, 1963. Santa Monica College.
Wood, Elijah Cedar Rapids, IA, Jan 28, 1981.
Wood, Evan Rachel Raleigh, NC, Sept. 7, 1987.
Woodard, Alfre Tulsa, OK, Nov. 2, 1953. Boston U.
Woodlawn, Holly (Harold Ajzenberg) Juana Diaz, PR, 1947.
Woods, James Vernal, UT, Apr. 18, 1947. MIT.
Woodward, Edward Croyden, Surrey, England, June 1, 1930.
Woodward, Joanne Thomasville, GA, Feb. 27, 1930.
  Neighborhood Playhouse.
Woronov, Mary Brooklyn, NY, Dec. 8, 1946. Cornell.
Wright, Amy Chicago, IL, Apr. 15, 1950.
Wright, Jeffrey Washington, DC, Dec. 7, 1965. Amherst Col.
Wright, Max Detroit, MI, Aug. 2, 1943. Wayne State U.
Wright, Robin Dallas, TX, Apr. 8, 1966.
Wuhl, Robert Union City, NJ, Oct. 9, 1951. U Houston.
Wyle, Noah Los Angeles, CA, June 2, 1971.
Wymore, Patrice Miltonvale, KS, Dec. 17, 1926.
Wynn, May (Donna Lee Hickey) New York, NY, Jan. 8, 1930.
Wynter, Dana (Dagmar) London, England, June 8. 1927. Rhodes U.

Yelchin, Anton St. Petersburg, Russia, March 11, 1989.
Yoba, Malik Bronx, NY, Sept. 17, 1967.
York, Michael Fulmer, England, Mar. 27, 1942. Oxford.
York, Susannah London, England, Jan. 9, 1941. RADA.
Young, Alan (Angus) North Shield, England, Nov. 19, 1919.
Young, Burt Queens, NY, Apr. 30, 1940.
Young, Chris Chambersburg, PA, Apr. 28, 1971.
Young, Sean Louisville, KY, Nov. 20, 1959. Interlochen.
Yulin, Harris Los Angeles, CA, Nov. 5, 1937.
Yun-Fat, Chow Lamma Island, Hong Kong, May 18, 1955.

Zacharias, Ann Stockholm, Sweden, Sept. 19, 1956.
Zadora, Pia Hoboken, NJ, May 4, 1954.
Zahn, Steve Marshall, MN, Nov. 13, 1968.
Zegers, Kevin Woodstock, ON, Canada, Sept. 19, 1984.
Zellweger, Renée Katy, TX, Apr. 25, 1969.
Zerbe, Anthony Long Beach, CA, May 20, 1939.
Zeta-Jones, Catherine Swansea, Wales, Sept. 25, 1969.
Zimbalist, Efrem, Jr. New York, NY, Nov. 30, 1918. Yale.
Zuniga, Daphne Berkeley, CA, Oct. 28, 1963. UCLA

OBITUARIES
2008

Edie Adams

Cyd Charisse

Mel Ferrer

Nina Foch

Beverly Garland

Van Johnson

Eartha Kitt

Harvey Korman

John Phillip Law

Heath Ledger

Bernie Mac and Isaac Hayes

Robert Mulligan

Paul Newman

Sidney Pollack

Robert Prosky

Brad Renfro

Roy Scheider

Paul Scofield

FORREST J. ACKERMAN, 92, Los Angeles, California-born writer/historian, who brought attention to the sci-fi and horror genres for an entire generation of fans with his magazine *Famous Monsters of Filmland*, died of heart failure at his Los Angeles, California, home on Dec. 4, 2008. Because of his fame he was invited to do bit parts in several genre films including *Queen of Blood, Dracula vs. Frankenstein, The Kentucky Fried Movie, The Howling, Amazon Women on the Moon,* and *Innocent Blood.* There are no immediate survivors.

EDIE ADAMS (Elizabeth Edith Enke), 81, Pennsylvania-born screen, stage, and television actress-singer, died in Los Angeles, California, of pneumonia and cancer on Oct. 15, 2008. Following her debut in the 1960 Academy Award winner *The Apartment*, she was seen in such films as *Lover Come Back, Under the Yum Yum Tree, It's a Mad Mad Mad Mad World, Love with the Proper Stranger, The Best Man, Made in Paris, The Oscar, The Honey Pot,* and *Up in Smoke.* On Broadway she won a Tony Award for *Li'l Abner.* Her first husband was comedian Ernie Kovacs, who left her widowed in 1962. She is survived by her son from her second marriage.

JOHN ALVIN, 59, Massachusetts-born designer/illustrator, died of a heart attack in Rhineback, New York, on Feb. 6, 2008. He was responsible for the memorable movie posters of such films as *Blazing Saddles, "10," E.T. The Extra-Terrestrial, My Favorite Year, Cocoon, The Color Purple, The Princess Bride,* and *City Slickers.* He is survived by his wife, a daughter, and his sister.

ROBERT ARTHUR, 83, screen actor, who portrayed Kirk Douglas' journalist sidekick in the Billy Wilder drama *Ace in the Hole* (*The Big Carnival*), died of congestive heart failure on Oct. 1, 2008, in his birthplace of Aberdeen, Washington. His other films include *Nora Prentiss, Mother Wore Tights, Green Grass of Wyoming, Yellow Sky, Mother is a Freshman, Twelve O'clock High, September Affair, Belles on Their Toes, Just for You, Young Bess, Hellcats of the Navy,* and *Wild Youth.* He retired from acting in the 1960s and later became an activist for the rights of gay senior citizens. No reported survivors.

MAJEL BARRETT, 76, Ohio-born actress, best known for portraying Nurse Chapel on the sci-fi series *Star Trek*, died of leukemia at her home in Bel Air, California, on Dec. 18, 2008. Her films include *The Black Orchid, Love in a Goldfish Bowl, A Guide for the Married Man, Track of Thunder, Westworld, The Domino Principle,* and *Star Trek–The Motion Picture.* She is survived by her son from her marriage to *Star Trek* creator Gene Roddenberry (who died in 1991).

HENRY BECKMAN, 86, Nova Scotia-born character actor died on June 17, 2008, in Barcelona, Spain. His films include *The Wrong Man, Breakfast at Tiffany's, Marnie, Kiss Me Stupid, The Satan Bug, Madigan,* and *Silver Streak.*

PAUL BENEDICT, 70, New Mexico-born screen, stage, and television actor/director, perhaps best known for playing neighbor Harry Bentley on the long-running sitcom *The Jeffersons*, was found dead at his Martha's Vineyard, Massachusetts, home on Dec. 1, 2008. He could also be seen in such films as *Cold Turkey, Taking Off, They Might Be Giants, Jeremiah Johnson, Up the Sandbox, The Front Page* (1974), *Mandingo, Smile, The Goodbye Girl, The Man with Two Brains, Cocktail, The Chair, The Freshman* (1990), *The Addams Family, Waiting for Guffman, A Mighty Wind,* and *After the Sunset.* Survivors include his brother and three sisters.

SAM BOTTOMS, 53, Santa Barbara, California-born actor, who made his debut opposite his older brother Timothy in the 1971 classic *The Last Picture Show*, died of brain cancer at his home in Los Angeles, California, on Dec. 16, 2008. His other films include *Zandy's Bride, The Outlaw Josey Wales, Apocalypse Now, Bronco Billy, Gardens of Stone, Seabiscuit, Shopgirl,* and *SherryBaby.* His three brothers, his parents, and his wife survive him.

IRVING BRECHER, 94, Bronx, New York-born writer, died in Los Angeles, California, on Nov. 17, 2008, following a series of heart attacks. His movie credits include *At the Circus, Go West* (1940), *Shadow of the Thin Man, Du Barry was a Lady, Best Foot Forward, Meet Me in St. Louis, Yolanda and the Thief, Ziegfeld Follies, Somebody Loves Me,* and *Bye Bye Birdie.* He also created the long-running radio show *The Life of Riley.* Survived by his second wife and three stepchildren.

BERNIE BRILLSTEIN, 77, New York, New York-born producer, who was partnered with Brad Grey on most of his productions, died on Aug. 7, 2008, in Los Angeles, California, of chronic obstructive pulmonary disease. In addition to his television credits on such programs as *Politically Incorrect* and *The Larry Sanders Show*, he executive produced such motion pictures as *The Blues Brothers, Continental Divide, Ghostbusters, Summer Rental, Spies Like Us, Dragnet* (1987), *Happy Gilmore,* and *The Cable Guy.*

GEORGE CARLIN, 71, New York, New York-born counterculture comedian/actor, best known for his outspoken stand-up routines, chief among them the controversial "Seven Words You Can Never Say on Television," died of heart failure on June 22, 2008, in Los Angeles, California. In addition to his many television appearances and Grammy Award-winning comedy albums, he acted in such films as *With Six You Get Eggroll, Car Wash, Outrageous Fortune, Bill & Ted's Excellent Adventure, The Prince of Tides, Dogma, Jay and Silent Bob Strike Back,* and *Jersey Girl.* His second wife, his daughter, and his brother survive him.

CYD CHARISSE (Tulea Ellice Finklea), 86, Texas-born actress/dancer, best known for her terpsichorean skills in such classic MGM musicals as *Singin' in the Rain* and *The Band Wagon*, died on June 17, 2008, in Los Angeles, California, after suffering an apparent heart attack. Following her 1943 debut (under the name Lily Norwood) as a dancer in the film *Something to Shout About*, she was seen in such films as *Ziegfeld Follies, The Harvey Girls, Till the Clouds Roll By, Fiesta, The Unfinished Dance, The Kissing Bandit, Words and Music, On an Island with You, East Side West Side, Sombrero, Brigadoon, Deep in My Heart, It's Always Fair Weather, Meet Me in Las Vegas, Silk Stockings, Twilight of the Gods, Party Girl, Black Tights, Two Weeks in Another Town, The Silencers, Maroc 7, Won Ton Ton the Dog Who Saved Hollywood,* and *That's Entertainment III.* She is survived by her husband of sixty years, singer-actor Tony Martin, their son, and a son from her first marriage.

ALEXANDER COURAGE, 88, Philadelphia, Pennsylvania-born composer, orchestrator, and music arranger, best known for penning the theme for the sci-fi series *Star Trek*, died in Pacific Palisades, California, on May 15, 2008. He received Oscar nominations for adapting the scores for *The Pleasure Seekers* and *Doctor Dolittle*, while his many other credits include *Show Boat, The Band Wagon, Guys and Dolls, Gigi, My Fair Lady,* and *Fiddler on the Roof.* Survivors include four stepchildren and six grandchildren.

HAZEL COURT, 82, British actress, died on Apr. 15, 2008, in Lake Tahoe, California. Her films include *Undercover Agent* (*Counterspy*), *The Curse of Frankenstein, The Shakedown, The Man Who Could Cheat Death, Doctor Blood's Coffin, Premature Burial, The Raven* (1963), *The Masque of the Red Death,* and *The Final Conflict.*

FRED CRANE, 90, New Orleans, Louisiana-born actor who made his debut playing Stuart Tarleton in the opening scene of *Gone with the Wind*, died in Georgia on Aug. 21, 2008. His only other film was *The Gay Amigo.* Survived by four children, eight grandchildren, and one great-grandchild.

MICHAEL CRICHTON, 66, Chicago, Illinois-born novelist, screenwriter, director, and producer, died of cancer on Nov. 4, 2008, in Los Angeles, California. While such books of his as *The Andromeda Strain* and *Disclosure* were adapted to the screen by others, he himself wrote the adaptations of *Jurassic Park* and *Rising Sun;* directed *Physical Evidence;* both directed and wrote *Westworld, Coma, The Great Train Robbery* (1979), *Looker,* and *Runaway;* and produced *Disclosure, Twister* (also cowriter), and *Sphere.* His fifth wife and a daughter survive him.

EVA DAHLBECK, 87, Swedish actress, best known for her starring role in Ingmar Bergman's *Smiles of a Summer Night*, died in Stockholm, Sweden, on Feb. 8, 2008, of Alzheimer's disease. Her other films include *Brink of Life, The Counterfeit Traitor, All These Women,* and *The Cats*. She abandoned acting to become a writer.

IRENE DAILEY, 88, New York, New York-born actress, who won an Emmy for her role as Liz Matthews on the daytime serial *Another World*, died of colon cancer on Sept. 24, 2008, in Guerneville, California. In addition to appearing on Broadway in the original production of *The Subject Was Roses*, she was seen in the films *No Way to Treat a Lady, Daring Game, Five Easy Pieces, The Grissom Gang, The Amityville Horror* (1979), and *Stacking*. Her brother, actor/dancer, Dan Dailey, died in 1978. There are no reported survivors.

JULES DASSIN, 96, Connecticut-born filmmaker, best known for his 1960 film *Never on Sunday*, which brought him Oscar nominations as director and writer, died on Mar. 31, 2008 in Athens, Greece. His Hollywood career included such films as *Reunion in France, The Canterville Ghost, Brute Force, The Naked City, Thieves' Highway,* and *Night and the City* (1950). Because of blacklisting he moved to Europe in the early 1950s where he made the majority of his subsequent credits (most of which he also wrote) including *Rififi, He Who Must Die* (the first of many collaborations with Melina Mercouri whom he would marry in 1966), *Where the Hot Wind Blows!, Phaedra, Topkapi, 10:30PM Summer, Promise at Dawn, A Dream of Passion,* and *Circle of Two*. He also appeared as an actor in several of these credits. Mercouri died in 1994. Survivors include two children from his first marriage and his grandchildren.

IVAN DIXON, 76, New York, New York-born actor, who starred in the acclaimed 1964 independent film *Nothing but a Man*, died in Charlotte, North Carolina, on Mar. 16, 2008, of complications from kidney failure. His other movies include *Something of Value, Porgy and Bess, A Raisin in the Sun, A Patch of Blue, Suppose They Gave a War and Nobody Came,* and *Car Wash*, while he was best known to television audiences for his role on the sitcom *Hogan's Heroes*. In later years he turned to directing. His wife of fifty-three years, his daughter, and two sons survives him.

ROBERT DoQUI, 73, Oklahoma-born character actor died on Feb. 9, 2008, in Los Angeles, California. Among his films are *The Fortune Cookie, The Man, Coffy, Nashville, Buffalo Bill and the Indians, I'm Dancing as Fast as I Can, Cloak & Dagger* (1984), *RoboCop, Miracle Mile,* and *Short Cuts*. His partner, four sons, a daughter, his mother, and ten grandchildren survive him.

JULIE EGE, 64, Norwegian actress, died of cancer on Apr. 29, 2008, in Oslo, Norway. Her film credits include *On Her Majesty's Secret Service, Every Home Should Have One* (*Think Dirty*), *Rentadick, Craze, It's Not the Size That Counts* (*Percy's Progress*), and *The Mutations*.

MEL FERRER, 90, New Jersey-born screen, stage, and television actor, who starred in such notable films as *Lili* and *War and Peace* (1956; opposite his then-wife Audrey Hepburn), died at his home near Santa Barbara, California, on June 2, 2008. His other acting credits include *Lost Boundaries, Born to Be Bad, The Brave Bulls, Scaramouche* (1952), *Rancho Notorious, Knights of the Round Table, The Sun Also Rises, The World the Flesh and the Devil, Blood and Roses, The Longest Day, The Fall of the Roman Empire, Sex and the Single Girl, El Greco* (also producer), *Brannigan, The Norsemen,* and *Lili Marleen*. He directed Hepburn in *Green Mansions* and produced her film *Wait Until Dark*, among other behind-the-scenes credits. His fourth wife, his children, and several grandchildren survive him.

NINA FOCH (Nina Consuela Maud Fock), 84, Dutch-born American actress, who earned an Oscar nomination for the film *Executive Suite*, died on Dec. 7, 2008, in Los Angeles, California, of complications from the blood disorder myelodysplasia. Following her 1944 feature debut in *The Return of the Vampire*, she was seen in such films as *She's a Soldier Too, Cry of the Werewolf, A Song to Remember, Escape in the Fog, My Name is Julia Ross, Johnny O'Clock, The Dark

Past, Johnny Allegro, An American in Paris, Young Man with Ideas, Scaramouche (1952), *Sombrero, You're Never Too Young, The Ten Commandments* (1956), *Three Brave Men, Cash McCall, Spartacus, Such Good Friends, Mahogany, Skin Deep, Sliver, It's My Party, Hush, Pumpkin,* and *How to Deal*. Her son from her second marriage and three grandchildren survive her.

GEORGE FURTH (George Schweinfurth), 75, Chicago-born actor-writer, who won a Tony Award for his book of the Stephen Sondheim musical *Company*, died on Aug. 11, 2008, in Santa Monica, California. He had been hospitalized for a lung infection. His films include *The Best Man, A Very Special Favor, The Boston Strangler, Butch Cassidy and the Sundance Kid, Myra Breckinridge, Blazing Saddles, Shampoo, Norman … is That You?, Oh, God!, Hooper, The Man with Two Brains,* and *Bulworth*. There are no reported survivors.

BEVERLY GARLAND (Beverly Fessenden), 82, Santa Cruz, California-born actress, who starred in such cult "B" films as *Not of This Earth* and *It Conquered the World*, died at her home in the Hollywood Hills on Dec. 5, 2008, following a long illness. After debuting in 1949 in the noir *D.O.A.* (billed as Beverly Campbell), she was seen in such movies as *Problem Girls, The Neanderthal Man, The Rocket Man, The Miami Story, Killer Leopard, Swamp Women, New Orleans Uncensored, Sudden Danger, The Steel Jungle, Curucu—Beast of the Amazon, Chicago Confidential, The Joker is Wild, The Alligator People, Pretty Poison, Where the Red Fern Grows,* and *Roller Boogie*. She also ran the Beverly Garland Holiday Inn in North Hollywood and was a regular on *The Bing Crosby Show* and *My Three Sons*. Four children, eight grandchildren, and seven great-grandchildren survive her.

ESTELLE GETTY (Estelle Scher), 84, New York, New York-born actress, best known for her Emmy Award-winning role of Sophia Petrillo on the sitcom *The Golden Girls*, died on July 22, 2008, in Hollywood, California, following a long battle with Lewy Body dementia. She was also seen in such films as *Tootsie, Mask, Mannequin, Stop! Or My Mom Will Shoot,* and *Stuart Little*. She is survived by her two sons, a brother, and a sister.

WILLIAM GIBSON, 94, Bronx, New York-born writer, who earned an Oscar nomination for adapting his play *The Miracle Worker* to the screen, died on Nov. 25, 2008, in Stockbridge, Massachusetts. He also helped adapt his novel *The Cobweb* and his play *Golda's Balcony* for the movies as well. He is survived by his two sons.

DODY GOODMAN, 93, Ohio-born performer, perhaps best known for her many comedic appearances on *The Jack Paar Show*, died of natural causes on June 22, 2008, in Englewood, New Jersey. She was seen in such motion pictures as *Bedtime Story* (1964), *Grease, Max Duggan Returns, Splash,* and *Cool as Ice*. Never married, seven nieces and nephews survive her.

JOHNNY GRANT, 84, Hollywood's "honorary mayor" for twenty-eight years, died of natural causes at the Hollywood Roosevelt Hotel on Jan. 9, 2008. A former reporter and host best known for emceeing the unveiling of celebrity stars on the Hollywood Walk of Fame, he was also seen in such films as *White Christmas, The Girl Can't Help It, The Great Man, Beau James,* and *Hollywood Homicide*. There are no survivors.

BERNIE HAMILTON, 80, Los Angeles, California-born actor, who starred in the acclaimed 1964 interracial drama *One Potato, Two Potato*, died on Dec. 30, 2008, of cardiac arrest. He could also be seen in such films as *Carmen Jones, Kismet* (1955), *Up Periscope, Take a Giant Step, Let No Man Write My Epitaph, The Devil at 4 O'Clock, 13 West Street, Synanon, The Lost Man, The Organization,* and *Bucktown*. On television he was best known for playing Capt. Dobey on *Starsky and Hutch*. Retiring from acting in the late 1980s, he then worked as a music producer. His son, his daughter, his brother, and two grandchildren survive him.

ISAAC HAYES, 65, Tennessee-born musician-singer-actor, who won the Academy Award as composer of "Theme from 'Shaft'," died on Aug. 10, 2008, at his home in Memphis, Tennessee. In addition to his career as a prominent soul music artist he acted in such movies as *Truck Turner, Escape from New York, I'm Gonna Git You Sucka, Guilty as Charged, Posse* (1993), *Robin Hood: Men in Tights, It Could Happen to You, Flipper* (1996), *South Park: Bigger, Longer & Uncut* (as the voice of Chef, repeating his role from the series), *Reindeer Games*, and *Hustle & Flow*. His wife and twelve children survive him.

JOHN MICHAEL HAYES, 89, Massachusetts-born screenwriter, who earned Oscar nominations for *Rear Window* and *Peyton Place*, died of natural causes on Nov. 19, 2008, in Hanover, New Hampshire. His other credits include *Torch Song* (1953), *To Catch a Thief, The Trouble with Harry, The Man Who Knew Too Much* (1956), *Separate Tables, But Not for Me, The Rat Race, Butterfield 8, The Children's Hour, The Carpetbaggers, Nevada Smith,* and *Iron Will*. He is survived by two daughters, two sons, and four grandchildren.

NEAL HEFTI, 85, Nebraska-born composer-arranger-conductor, best known for writing the theme for the TV series *Batman* and the movie *The Odd Couple*, died of unspecified causes on Oct. 11, 2008, in Toluca Lake, California. His other motion picture scores include *Sex and the Single Girl, How to Murder Your Wife, Lord Love a Duck, Duel at Diablo, Barefoot in the Park, A New Leaf,* and *Won Ton Ton the Dog Who Saved Hollywood*. His son, a brother, a sister, and three grandchildren survive him.

EILEEN HERLIE, 90, Glasgow, Scotland-born screen, stage, and television actress, who played Gertrude opposite Laurence Olivier in the 1948 Oscar-winning *Hamlet*, died of pneumonia on Oct. 8, 2008, in New York, New York. Her other films include *The Great Gilbert and Sullivan, Freud,* and *The Seagull* (1968). She was best known to daytime television audiences for playing Myrtle Fargate on *All My Children* for over thirty years. Survivors include her brother.

CHARLTON HESTON (John Charles Carter), 84, Illinois-born screen, stage and television actor, best known for his Oscar-winning performance in the title role of the classic epic *Ben-Hur*, died on Apr. 5, 2008, at his home in Beverly Hills, California. Following his Hollywood debut in 1950's *Dark City*, he was seen in such pictures as *The Greatest Show on Earth, The Savage, Ruby Gentry, The President's Lady, Pony Express, The Naked Jungle, The Far Horizons, The Private War of Major Benson, The Ten Commandments* (his other signature role, as Moses), *Three Violent People, The Big Country, Touch of Evil, The Wreck of the Mary Deare, El Cid, The Pigeon That Took Rome, Diamond Head, 55 Days at Peking, The Greatest Story Ever Told, Major Dundee, The Agony and the Ecstasy* (as Michelangelo), *The War Lord, Khartoum, Will Penny, Planet of the Apes* (1968, as well as the 2001 remake), *Julius Caesar* (1971), *The Omega Man, Skyjacked, Antony and Cleopatra* (which he also directed), *Soylent Green, The Three Musketeers* (1974), *Airport 1975, Earthquake, Midway, Two Minute Warning, Crossed Swords, The Mountain Men, Mother Lode* (also director), *Tombstone, True Lies, In the Mouth of Madness, Alaska, Hamlet* (1996; as the Player King), *Any Given Sunday, Town & Country,* and *Bowling for Columbine*. In 1997 he was a recipient of the Kennedy Center Honors. His wife of sixty-four years; his son, director Fraser Heston; his daughter; and three grandchildren survive him.

CHARLES H. JOFFE, 78, Brooklyn, New York-born film producer, who worked with Woody Allen for nearly forty years, died of lung cancer on July 9, 2008, in Los Angeles, California. In addition to receiving the Best Picture Oscar for *Annie Hall*, his name appeared as producer or executive producer on such Allen films as *Take the Money and Run, Bananas, Sleeper, Love and Death, Manhattan, Zelig, Hannah and Her Sisters, Crimes and Misdemeanors, Bullets Over Broadway,* and *Match Point*. He is survived by his wife, a son, and two stepdaughters.

VAN JOHNSON, 92, Rhode Island-born actor, who starred in such 1940s hits as *A Guy Named Joe* and *Thirty Seconds Over Tokyo*, died of natural causes in Nyack, New York, on Dec. 12, 2008. Following his 1940 debut in *Too Many Girls*, he was seen in such motion pictures as *Dr. Gillespie's Assistant, The Human Comedy, Two Girls and a Sailor, The White Cliffs of Dover, Thrill of a Romance, Week-End at the Waldorf, Easy to Wed, No Leave No Love, Till the Clouds Roll By, The Romance of Rosy Ridge, State of the Union, Command Decision, Mother is a Freshman, In the Good Old Summertime, Battleground, The Big Hangover, Duchess of Idaho, Three Guys Named Mike, Go for Broke!, It's a Big Country, When in Rome, Plymouth Adventure, Easy to Love, Siege at Red River, The Caine Mutiny, Brigadoon, The Last Time I Saw Paris, The End of the Affair* (1955), *The Bottom of the Bottle, Miracle in the Rain, Kelly and Me, Wives and Lovers, Divorce American Style, Where Angels Go Trouble Follows!, Yours Mine and Ours, The Kidnapping of the President,* and *The Purple Rose of Cairo*. He is survived by his daughter.

PETER KASTNER, 64, Canadian actor, best known for his starring role in the 1966 comedy *You're a Big Boy Now*, died of a heart attack in his native Toronto, Canada, on Sept. 18, 2008. His other films include *Nobody Waved Goodbye, Footsteps in the Snow, B.S. I Love You,* and *Unfinished Business*. His survivors include his second wife and his three siblings.

MILTON KATSELAS, 75, Pittsburgh, Pennsylvania-born director and acting teacher, died of heart failure on Oct. 24, 2008, in Los Angeles, California. His film credits as director are *Butterflies are Free, 40 Carats, Report to the Commissioner,* and *When You Comin' Back Red Ryder?* He also founded the Beverly Hills Playhouse acting school. His two brothers and a sister survive him.

EVELYN KEYES, 91, Texas-born actress, who appeared in such notable movies as *Gone with the Wind* (as Scarlett's sister Suellen), *Here Comes Mr. Jordan,* and *The Jolson Story*, died of uterine cancer at her home in Montecito, California, on July 4, 2008. Her other films include *The Buccaneer* (1938), *Union Pacific, The Lady in Question, Before I Hang, The Face Behind the Mask, The Adventures of Martin Eden, There's Something about a Soldier, Nine Girls, A Thousand and One Nights, The Thrill of Brazil, Johnny O'clock, The Mating of Millie, Mr. Soft Touch, Mrs. Mike, The Killer That Stalked New York, 99 River Street, Hell's Half Acre, The Seven Year Itch, Around the World in Eighty Days,* and *Wicked Stepmother*. Her husbands included directors Charles Vidor and John Huston, as well as bandleader Artie Shaw. There are no reported survivors.

EARTHA KITT, 81, South Carolina-born singer-actress, known for her sensual way of performing songs like "C'est Si Bon" and "Santa Baby," died of colon cancer in New York, New York, on Dec. 25, 2008. She was seen in such movies as *The Mark of the Hawk, St. Louis Blues, Anna Lucasta* (1959), *Uncle Tom's Cabin, Friday Foster, Erik the Viking, Ernest Scared Stupid, Boomerang* (1992), *Fatal Instinct, Harriet the Spy, Holes,* and *And then Came Love*. Her daughter survives her.

HARVEY KORMAN, 81, Chicago, Illinois-born actor, best known for his Emmy-winning work as second banana on TV's *The Carol Burnett Show*, died on May 29, 2008, in Los Angeles, California, of complications from the rupture of an abdominal aortic aneurysm. In addition to his television roles, he was seen in such films as *Gypsy, Son of Flubber, Last of the Secret Agents?, Lord Love a Duck, The April Fools, Blazing Saddles* (as Hedley Lamar), *Huckleberry Finn* (1974), *High Anxiety, Americathon, History of the World Part 1, Trail of the Pink Panther,* and *Dracula: Dead and Loving It*. Survivors include his second wife and four children.

JOHN PHILLIP LAW, 70, Los Angeles, California-born actor, who played Russian sailor Alexei Kolchin in the 1966 Oscar-nominated comedy hit *The Russians are Coming The Russians are Coming*, died on May 13, 2008, at his home in Los Angeles, California. His other films include *Hurry Sundown, Barbarella, The Sergeant, Skidoo, Danger: Diabolik, The Hawaiians, The Love Machine, The Last Movie, Open Season* (1974), *The Golden Voyage of Sinbad, The Cassandra Crossing,* and *Tarzan the Ape Man* (1981). His daughter, his brother, and his grandson survive him.

HEATH LEDGER, 28, Australia-born actor, best known for his Oscar-nominated role as gay rancher Ennis Del Mar in the 1995 film *Brokeback Mountain*, was found dead in his Manhattan apartment on Jan. 22, 2008, from an accidental prescription drug overdose. Following his 1999 U.S. debut in *10 Things I Hate About You*, he was seen in such pictures as *The Patriot* (2000), *A Knight's Tale*, *Monsters Ball*, *The Four Feathers* (2002), *Lords of Dogtown*, *The Brothers Grimm*, *Casanova* (2005), *Candy* (2006), and *I'm Not There*. His final films, *The Dark Knight* (in which he played The Joker and for which he received a posthumous Academy Award) and *The Imaginarium of Dr. Parnassus*, were released posthumously. He is survived by his daughter Matilda, his parents, and his sister.

KAY LINAKER, 94, Arkansas-born actress/writer died on Apr. 18, 2008, in Keene, New Hampshire. She acted in such pictures as *Road Gang*, *The Girl from Mandalay*, *Charlie Chan at Monte Carlo*, *I Am a Criminal*, *Young Mr. Lincoln*, *Drums Along the Mohawk*, *Buck Benny Rides Again*, *Kitty Foyle*, *Blossoms in the Dust*, *The More the Merrier*, and *Lady in the Dark*. As Kate Phillips she cowrote the 1958 sci-fi cult film *The Blob*. She is survived by her son and daughter.

PERRY LOPEZ, 78, New York, New York-born screen and television actor, perhaps best known to filmgoers for his role as Lt. Escobar in the 1974 classic *Chinatown*, died of lung cancer on Feb. 14, 2008, in Los Angeles, California. Among his other films are *Battle Cry*, *Mister Roberts*, *I Died a Thousand Times*, *Omar Khayyam*, *Taras Bulba*, *McLintock!*, *The Rare Breed*, *Bandolero*, and *The Two Jakes*. He is survived by several nieces and nephews.

BERNIE MAC (Bernard Jeffrey McCullough), 50, Chicago, Illinois-born comedian/actor, best known for his sitcom *The Bernie Mac Show*, died on Aug. 9, 2008, in Chicago, Illinois, of complications from pneumonia. He could be seen in such films as *Who's the Man?*, *Friday*, *Get on the Bus*, *Booty Call*, *Life*, *What's the Worst That Could Happen?*, *Ocean's Eleven* (and two sequels), *Head of State*, *Bad Santa*, *Mister 3000*, *Guess Who*, *Transformers*, *Soul Men*, and *Old Dogs*. His wife, a daughter, and a granddaughter survive him.

ABBY MANN (Abraham Goodman), 80, Philadelphia, Pennsylvania-born writer, who won the Academy Award for adapting his television drama *Judgment at Nuremberg* to the screen, died of heart failure on Mar. 25, 2008, in Beverly Hills, California. His other motion picture credits were *The Condemned of Altona*, *A Child is Waiting*, *Ship of Fools* (Oscar nomination), *The Detective*, *Report to the Commissioner*, and *War and Love*. He is survived by his wife and son.

DICK MARTIN, 86, Michigan-born comedian/actor/director, who became a part of television history when he and partner Dan Rowan hosted the Sixties series *Rowan & Martin's Laugh-In*, died on May 24, 2008. He appeared in the motion pictures *Once Upon a Horse*, *The Glass Bottom Boat*, *The Maltese Bippy*, *Carbon Copy*, *Air Bud: Golden Receiver*, and *Bartleby*. He is survived by his wife and two sons from his first marriage.

BILL MELENDEZ (José Cuauhtémoc Melendez), 91, Mexican animator/producer, who brought Charles M. Schulz's *Peanuts* characters to life on both television and in movies, died on Sept. 2, 2008, in Santa Monica, California. He had been in declining health since suffering a fall the previous year. In addition to winning six Emmys for such specials as *A Charlie Brown Christmas*, he worked on all four of the *Peanuts* feature films: *A Boy Named Charlie Brown*; *Snoopy Come Home*; *Race for Your Life, Charlie Brown*; *Bon Voyage, Charlie Brown*; and provided the vocal sounds of Snoopy. He is survived by his wife of sixty-eight years, two sons, six grandchildren, and ten great-grandchildren.

ANTHONY MINGHELLA, 54, British filmmaker, who won an Academy Award for directing the 1996 Oscar winner for Best Picture, *The English Patient* (for which he also earned a nomination for his script), died in London, England, on Mar. 18, 2008, of a hemorrhage following surgery on his neck. He also directed-wrote *Truly, Madly, Deeply*; *Mr. Wonderful* (director only); *The Talented Mr. Ripley* (Oscar nomination for screenplay); *Cold Mountain*; and *Breaking and Entering*.

His credits as executive producer include *Michael Clayton* and *The Reader*. His wife; his son, actor Max Minghella; and his daughter survive him.

BARRY MORSE, 89, British-born Canadian actor, best known for playing Lt. Philip Gerard on the 1960s series *The Fugitive*, died on Feb. 2, 2008. His films include *Thunder Rock*, *Kings of the Sun*, *Justine*, *Puzzle of a Downfall Child*, *The Changeling*, and *Murder by Phone*. His wife of sixty years, actress Sydney Sturgess, died in 1999. Four grandchildren and several great-grandchildren survive him.

ROBERT MULLIGAN, 83, Bronx, New York-born director, who earned an Oscar nomination for his work on *To Kill a Mockingbird*, died of heart disease on Dec. 20, 2008, at his home in Lyme, Connecticut. Among his other credits are *Fear Strikes Out*, *The Rat Race*, *The Great Impostor*, *Come September*, *Love with the Proper Stranger*, *Inside Daisy Clover*, *Up the Down Staircase*, *Summer of '42*, *The Other*, *Bloodbrothers*, *Same Time Next Year*, *Kiss Me Goodbye*, *Clara's Heart*, and *The Man in the Moon*. He is survived by his wife, three children, two grandchildren, and a brother.

LOIS NETTLETON, 80, Illinois-born screen, stage, and television actress died on Jan. 18, 2008, in Woodland Hills, California, after a long bout with lung cancer. Her films include *A Face in the Crowd*, *Period of Adjustment*, *Mail Order Bride*, *The Good Guys and the Bad Guys*, *Dirty Dingus Magee*, *The Honkers*, *The Man in the Glass Booth*, *Butterfly*, and *The Best Little Whorehouse in Texas*. On television she received Daytime Emmy Awards for *The America Woman: Portraits of Courage* and *Insight*. There are no reported survivors.

PAUL NEWMAN, 83, Cleveland, Ohio-born actor, who became one of the most enduring and admired of all film stars, earning nine Oscar nominations for his work, winning the award in 1986 for his performance in *The Color of Money*, died at his home in Westport, Connecticut, on Sept. 26, 2008, after a long bout with cancer. Following his 1954 debut in *The Silver Chalice*, he appeared in *Somebody Up There Likes Me*, *The Rack*, *Until They Sail*, *The Helen Morgan Story*, *The Left-Handed Gun*, *The Long Hot Summer*, *Cat on a Hot Tin Roof* (his first Oscar nomination), *Rally 'Round the Flag Boys!*, *The Young Philadelphians*, *From the Terrace*, *Exodus*, *The Hustler* (Oscar nomination), *Paris Blues*, *Sweet Bird of Youth* (repeating his stage role), *Adventures of a Young Man*, *Hud* (Oscar nomination), *A New Kind of Love*, *The Prize*, *What a Way to Go!*, *The Outrage*, *Lady L*, *Harper*, *Torn Curtain*, *Hombre*, *Cool Hand Luke* (Oscar nomination), *The Secret War of Harry Frigg*, *Winning*, *Butch Cassidy and the Sundance Kid*, *King: A Filmed Record … Montgomery to Memphis*, *WUSA* (also coproducer), *Sometimes a Great Notion* (which he also directed and co-executive produced), *Pocket Money*, *The Life and Times of Judge Roy Bean*, *The Mackintosh Man*, *The Sting*, *The Towering Inferno*, *The Drowning Pool*, *Buffalo Bill and the Indians*, *Silent Movie*, *Slap Shot*, *Quintet*, *When Time Ran Out …*, *Fort Apache–The Bronx*, *Absence of Malice*, *The Verdict*, *Harry and Son* (which he also directed, produced, and wrote), *Hello Actors Studio*, *Fat Man and Little Boy*, *Blaze*, *Mr. & Mrs. Bridge*, *The Hudsucker Proxy*, *Nobody's Fool* (Oscar nomination), *Twilight*, *Message in a Bottle*, *Where the Money Is*, *Road to Perdition* (Oscar nomination), *Cars* (voice), and *The Price of Sugar* (narrator). He also directed-produced *Rachel Rachel* (earning an Oscar nomination for producer), *The Effect of Gamma Rays on Man-in-the-Moon Marigolds*, and *The Glass Menagerie* (1987). On television he was given an Emmy for his performance in *Empire Falls*, which he also executive produced. He received a special Academy Award in1986, honoring his career, and a Jean Hersholt Humanitarian Award, for his many charitable contributions, in 1994. His wife of fifty years, actress and frequent costar Joanne Woodward; two daughters from his first marriage; his three daughters with Woodward; two grandchildren; and his brother survive him.

MANUEL PADILLA, 51, Los Angeles, California-born screen and television actor died of unspecified causes on Jan. 29, 2008. Among his films are *Robin and the 7 Hoods*, *Black Spurs*, *Tarzan and the Great River*, *A Man Called Horse*, *The Great White Hope*, *American Graffiti*, and *Scarface* (1983).

ANITA PAGE, 98, New York, New York-born actress, who starred in the 1929 Academy Award-winner *The Broadway Melody*, died in Van Nuys, California, on Sept. 8, 2008. Her other films include *While the City Sleeps* (1928), *Our Dancing Daughters, Our Modern Maidens, Navy Blue, Free and Easy, Our Blushing Brides, Little Accident, Reducing, Sidewalks of New York* (1931), *Skyscraper Souls,* and *Hitchhike to Heaven*, made in 1936. At that point she retired from the business for sixty years before returning for some direct-to-video credits. Her survivors include her two daughters.

JOY PAGE, 83, Los Angeles, California-born actress, best known for playing the newlywed helped by Humphrey Bogart in the Oscar-winning classic *Casablanca*, died of complications from a stroke and pneumonia on Apr. 25, 2008, in Los Angeles, California. Her other credits include *Kismet* (1944), *Bullfighter and the Lady, Conquest of Cochise, The Shrike,* and *Tonka*. Her survivors include her son.

JOSEPH PEVNEY, 96, New York, New York-born actor-turned-director, died on May 18, 2008, at his home in Palm Desert, California. After acting in *Body and Soul* (1947) and *The Street with No Name*, among others, he later directed such films as *Shakedown* (1950; also as an actor), *Undercover Girl, The Lady from Texas, Meet Danny Wilson, It Happens Every Thursday, 3 Ring Circus, Six Bridges to Cross, Female on the Beach, Away All Boats, Tammy and the Bachelor, Man of a Thousand Faces, Cash McCall,* and *The Night of the Grizzly*. His wife, two sons, a daughter, two grandchildren, and three great-grandchildren survive him.

HAROLD PINTER, 78, London, England-born writer, who became one of the most influential playwrights of the twentieth century with such cryptic works as *The Caretaker* and *The Birthday Party*, died on Dec. 24, 2008, following a long battle with cancer. His screenplays include *The Servant, The Pumpkin Eater, The Quiller Memorandum, Accident, The Go-Between, The Last Tycoon, The French Lieutenant's Woman, Betrayal* (from his play), *Turtle Diary, The Handmaid's Tale, The Comfort of Strangers,* and *Sleuth* (2007). As an actor he could be seen in such movies as *Mansfield Park* and *The Tailor of Panama*. A son survives him.

SUZANNE PLESHETTE, 70, New York, New York-born actress, perhaps best known for costarring on the long-running sitcom *The Bob Newhart Show*, died of respiratory failure on Jan. 19, 2008, at her home in Los Angeles, California. She had undergone chemotherapy for lung cancer in 2006. Following her 1958 debut in *The Geisha Boy*, she was seen in such films as *Rome Adventure* (opposite Troy Donahue to whom she was married briefly in 1964), *40 Pounds of Trouble, The Birds, A Distant Trumpet, Fate is the Hunter, Nevada Smith, A Rage to Live, Mister Buddwing, The Ugly Dachshund, Blackbeard's Ghost, The Adventures of Bullwhip Griffin, If It's Tuesday This Must Be Belgium, The Shaggy D.A.* and *Hot Stuff*. Her third husband, actor Tom Poston, died in 2007. There are no survivors.

SYDNEY POLLACK, 73, Indiana-born director/producer/actor, who won two Academy Awards for directing and producing *Out of Africa*, died of cancer at his home in Pacific Palisades, California, on May 26, 2008. He received additional Oscar nominations for directing *They Shoot Horses Don't They?*, for directing and producing *Tootsie*, and for producing *Michael Clayton*. His other credits as director include *The Scalphunters, Jeremiah Johnson, The Way We Were, The Yakuza, Three Days of the Condor, The Electric Horseman, Absence of Malice, Havana, The Firm, Sabrina* (1995), and *The Interpreter*. As an actor he was seen in such films as *War Hunt, The Player, Death Becomes Her, Husbands & Wives, A Civil Action, Eyes Wide Shut,* and *Changing Lanes*. His wife of fifty years, two daughters, his brother, and six grandchildren survive him.

ROBERT PROSKY, 77, Philadelphia, Pennsylvania-born screen, stage, and television character actor died on Dec. 8, 2008, in Washington, DC, of complications from a heart procedure. He was seen in such movies as *Hanky Panky, The Lords of Discipline, Christine, The Natural, Outrageous Fortune, Broadcast News, Things Change, Green Card, Rudy, Mrs. Doubtfire, Dead Man Walking,* and *Dudley Do-Right*. On television he was best known for his role as Sgt. Jablonski on *Hill Street Blues*. His wife and three sons survive him.

JERRY REED, 71, Atlanta, Georgia-born singer/songwriter/actor, best known for his hits "Amos Moses" and "When You're Hot, You're Hot," died of complications from emphysema on Sept. 1, 2008 in Nashville, Tennessee. He was seen in such films as *Gator, Smokey and the Bandit, Hot Stuff, The Survivors, Bat*21,* and *The Waterboy*. He is survived by his wife, two daughters, and two grandchildren.

BRAD RENFRO, 25, Tennessee-born actor, best known for his debut performance in the title role of the 1994 legal thriller *The Client*, was found dead at his Los Angeles, California, home on Jan. 14, 2008, of a drug overdose. His other films include *The Cure, Tom and Huck, Sleepers, Telling Lies in America, Apt Pupil, Bully, Ghost World, The Jacket,* and *10th and Wolf*. His parents and son survive him.

ALAIN ROBBE-GRILLET, 85, French writer, who earned an Oscar nomination for his screenplay for the cryptic Alain Resnais film *Last Year at Marienbad*, died of a heart ailment on Feb. 18, 2008, in Caen, France. He also wrote and directed such other films as *L'Immortale, The Man Who Lies,* and *The Beautiful Prisoner*.

LEONARD ROSENMAN, 83, Brooklyn, New York-born composer, who won Academy Awards for his scoring adaptations for *Barry Lyndon* and *Bound for Glory*, died of a heart attack on Mar. 4, 2008, in Woodland Hills, California. His other movie credits include *East of Eden, Rebel without a Cause, The Chapman Report, Fantastic Voyage, Race with the Devil, Making Love, Cross Creek* (Oscar nomination), and *Star Trek IV: The Voyage Home* (Oscar nomination). He is survived by his wife, three children, and four grandchildren.

ANN SAVAGE (Bernice Maxine Lyon), 87, South Carolina-born actress, who starred in the cult "B" noir *Detour*, died on Dec. 25, 2008, from complications following a series of strokes. Her other credits include *Dangerous Blondes, Klondike Kate, The Unwritten Code, Midnight Manhunt, The Spider, The Last Crooked Mile, Woman They Almost Lynched,* and *My Winnipeg*. There are no reported survivors.

ROY SCHEIDER, 75, New Jersey-born actor, best known for portraying heroic police chief Martin Brody in the 1975 blockbuster hit *Jaws*, died of a staph infection in Little Rock, Arkansas, on Feb. 10, 2008. In addition to *The French Connection* and *All That Jazz*, both of which earned him Oscar nominations, he appeared in such films as *The Curse of the Living Corpse* (debut, 1964), *Star!, Loving, Klute, The Seven-Ups, Sheila Levine is Dead and Living in New York, Marathon Man, Sorcerer, Last Embrace, Still of the Night, Blue Thunder, 2010, The Men's Club, 52 Pick-Up, Listen to Me, The Russia House, Naked Lunch, Romeo is Bleeding, The Myth of Fingerprints, John Grisham's The Rainmaker, The Punisher,* and *If I Didn't Care*. His second wife, three children, a brother, and three grandchildren survive him.

PAUL SCOFIELD (David Paul Scofield), 86, British actor, who won the Academy Award for his memorable portrayal of Sir Thomas More in the 1966 Oscar winner for Best Picture, *A Man for All Seasons* (repeating his Tony-winning stage performance), died of leukemia on Mar. 19, 2008, near his home in West Sussex, England. His other films include *That Lady* (his debut in 1955), *Carve Her Name with Pride, The Train, King Lear, Scorpio, A Delicate Balance, Henry V* (1989), *Hamlet* (1990), *Quiz Show* (Oscar nomination), and *The Crucible*. His wife of sixty-five years, former actress Joy Parker, and two children survive him.

JO STAFFORD, 90, California-born singer, one of the most prolific and notable voices to be heard during World War II, died of congestive heart failure on July 16, 2008. As a vocalist with the Tommy Dorsey Orchestra she was seen in such features as *Honolulu, Las Vegas Nights, Ship Ahoy,* and *Du Barry Was a Lady*. She is survived by her son, her daughter, and four grandchildren.

GIL STRATTON, 86, Brooklyn, New York-born actor/announcer, who played William Holden's sidekick, Cookie, in the classic POW drama *Stalag 17*, died of congestive heart failure at his San Fernando Valley, California, home on Oct. 11, 2008. His other motion picture credits include *Best Foot Forward, Girl Crazy,*

Tucson, Dangerous Years, Here Come the Marines, The Wild One, Bundle of Joy, The Cat from Outer Space, and *Inside Moves.* In later years he became a well-known sports anchor on local Los Angeles, California, radio stations. His wife of forty-seven years, five children, and several grandchildren survive him.

BRAD SULLIVAN, 77, Chicago, Illinois-born screen and television character actor, died in New York on Dec. 31, 2008. He could be seen in such movies as *The Sting, Slap Shot, The Island* (1980), *Ghost Story, Tin Men, The Untouchables, The Dream Team, The Abyss, True Colors, Guilty by Suspicion, The Prince of Tides, The Fantasticks,* and *Canadian Bacon.*

VAMPIRA (Maila Syrjäniemi, later Maila Nurmi), 86, Finland-born late night TV hostess and occasional actress, died of a heart attack on Jan. 10, 2008, at her home in Los Angeles, California. She was seen in such movies as *Plan 9 from Outer Space, The Beat Generation, The Big Operator,* and *Sex Kittens Go to College.* There are no reported survivors.

MALVIN WALD, 90, screenwriter, who earned an Oscar nomination for the original story for the 1948 noir *The Naked City,* died in Sherman Oaks, California, on Mar. 6, 2008, of natural causes. Among his other movie credits are *The Dark Past, Battle Taxi, Man on Fire* (1957), *Al Capone,* and *The Steel Claw.* He is survived by his son and his daughter. His brother, producer Jerry Wald, died in 1962.

DALE WASSERMAN, 94, Wisconsin-born writer, best known for writing the book of the classic musical *Man of La Mancha* (which he also adapted into a film), died of congestive heart failure at his home in Paradise Valley, Arizona, on Dec. 21, 2008. His other film credits are *The Vikings, Quick Before it Melts, Mister Buddwing,* and *A Walk with Love and Death.* He is survived by his wife.

DAVID WATKIN, 82, British cinematographer, who won an Academy Award for his work on the 1985 film *Out of Africa,* died of prostate cancer in Brighton, England, on Feb. 19, 2008. His other credits include *The Knack ... and How to Get It, Help!, How I Won the War, Catch-22, The Devils, The Boy Friend, The Three Musketeers* (1974), *Robin and Marian, Chariots of Fire, Yentl, The Hotel New Hampshire, Moonstruck, Memphis Belle,* and *Tea with Mussolini.* His partner survives him.

DELMAR WATSON, 82, Los Angeles, California-born child actor died of complications from prostate cancer on Oct. 26, 2008 in Glendale, California. He could be seen in such films as *Among the Missing, Annie Oakley, Old Butch, Heidi* (1937), *A Christmas Carol* (1938), *Kentucky, You Can't Cheat an Honest Man, Young Mr. Lincoln, Mr. Smith Goes to Washington,* and *Legion of the Lawless.* Survivors include several of his siblings who had also acted as children.

DONALD E. WESTLAKE, 75, prolific mystery writer, who earned an Oscar nomination for writing *The Grifters,* died of a heart attack on Dec. 31, 2008, while on vacation in Mexico. He also wrote the scripts for such films as *Cops and Robbers* (from his novel), *Hot Stuff, The Stepfather,* and *Why Me?* (from his book). His wife, four sons, two stepdaughters, a stepson, a sister, and four grandchildren survive him.

RICHARD WIDMARK, 93, Minnesota-born actor, who earned an Oscar nomination and became a star with his debut film, *Kiss of Death,* portraying psychotic mobster Tommy Udo, died on Mar. 24, 2008, at his home in Roxbury, Connecticut. After fracturing his vertebrae months prior, his condition had worsened. His many other films include *The Street with No Name, Road House* (1948), *Yellow Sky, Down to the Sea in Ships* (1949), *Slattery's Hurricane, Night and the City* (1950), *Panic in the Streets, No Way Out* (1950), *Halls of Montezuma, Don't Bother to Knock, O. Henry's Full House, Pickup on South Street, Take the High Ground, Garden of Evil, Broken Lance, The Cobweb, The Last Wagon, Saint Joan, Time Limit* (which he also produced), *The Law and Jake Wade, Warlock* (1959), *The Alamo* (1960), *The Secret Ways* (also producer), *Two Rode Together, Judgment at Nuremberg, How the West Was Won, The Long Ships, Cheyenne Autumn, The Bedford Incident, The Way West, Madigan, When the Legends Die, Murder on the Orient Express, Twilight's Last Gleaming, Rollercoaster, Coma, Hanky Panky, Against All Odds,* and *True Colors.* His second wife and his daughter survive him.

STAN WINSTON, 62, Virginia-born special effects and makeup artist, died at his home in Malibu, California, of multiple myeloma on June 15, 2008. He won Academy Awards for his work on *Aliens, Terminator II: Judgment Day* (two Oscars, for effects and makeup), and *Jurassic Park.* His other credits include *The Terminator, Predator, Edward Scissorhands, Iron Man,* and *Indiana Jones and the Kingdom of the Crystal Skull.* His wife, a son, a daughter, and four grandchildren survive him.

Index